The **Rough Guide** to

Brittany and Normandy

written and researched by

Greg Ward

with additional contributions from

Ross Velton

NEW YORK • LONDON • DELHI

www.roughguides.com

Contents

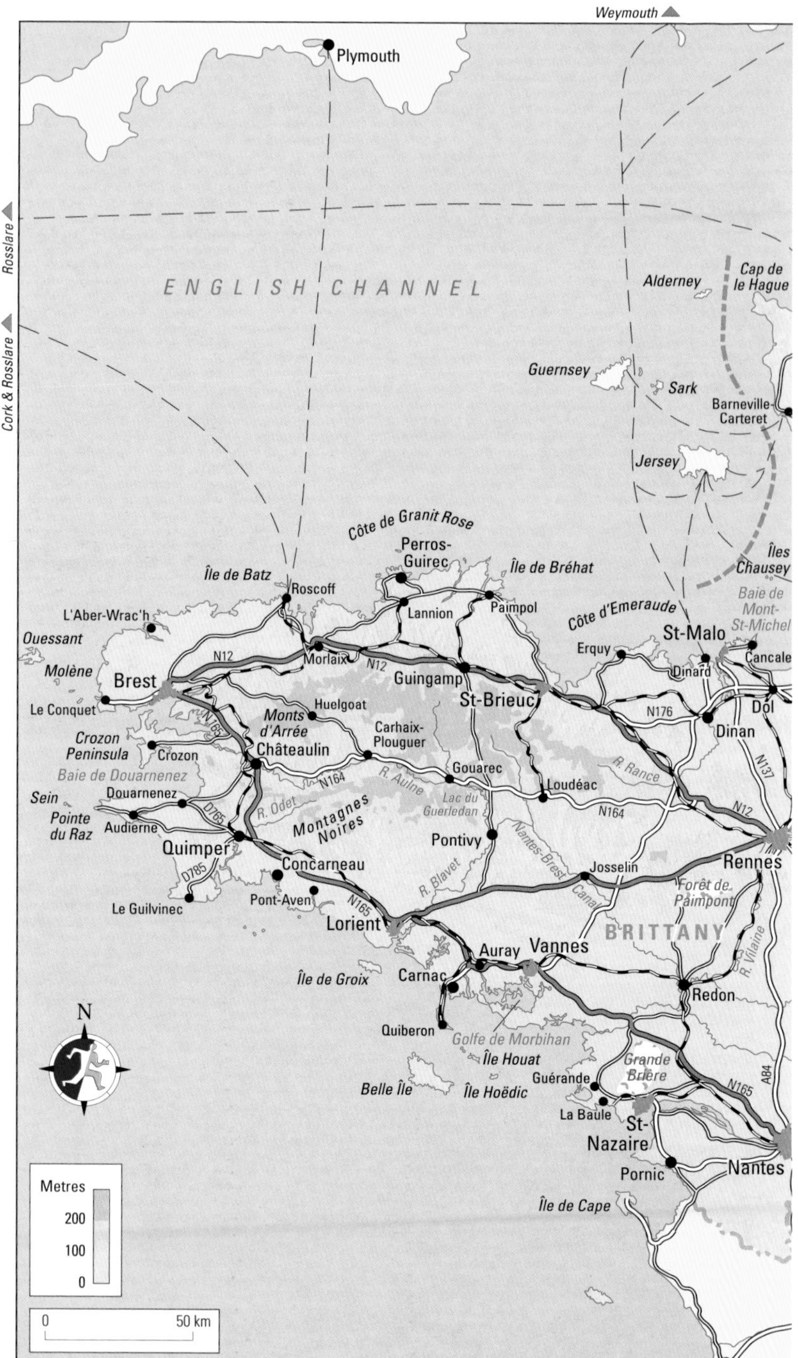

Weymouth
Plymouth
Rosslare
Cork & Rosslare
ENGLISH CHANNEL
Alderney
Cap de le Hague
Guernsey
Sark
Barneville-Carteret
Jersey
Côte de Granit Rose
Perros-Guirec
Île de Bréhat
Îles Chausey
Île de Batz
Roscoff
Lannion
Paimpol
Côte d'Emeraude
Baie de Mont-St-Michel
L'Aber-Wrac'h
Ouessant
St-Malo
Erquy
Cancale
Molène
Brest
N12
Morlaix
Guingamp
Dinard
Le Conquet
Huelgoat
St-Brieuc
N176
Dol
Monts d'Arrée
Dinan
Crozon Peninsula
Carhaix-Plouguer
Crozon
Châteaulin
Baie de Douarnenez
N164
R. Aulne
Gouarec
R. Rance
N137
Sein
Douarnenez
Lac du Guerledan
Loudéac
Pointe du Raz
Audierne
D765
R. Odet
Montagnes Noires
N164
N12
Quimper
Pontivy
Nantes-Brest Canal
Rennes
Concarneau
Josselin
Forêt de Paimpont
D785
R. Blavet
Le Guilvinec
Pont-Aven
N165
Lorient
BRITTANY
Auray
Vannes
R. Vilaine
Île de Groix
Carnac
Redon
N
Quiberon
Golfe de Morbihan
Île Houat
Grande Brière
Belle Île
Île Hoëdic
Guérande
A84
N165
La Baule
St-Nazaire
Metres
200
100
0
Pornic
Nantes
Île de Cape
0
50 km

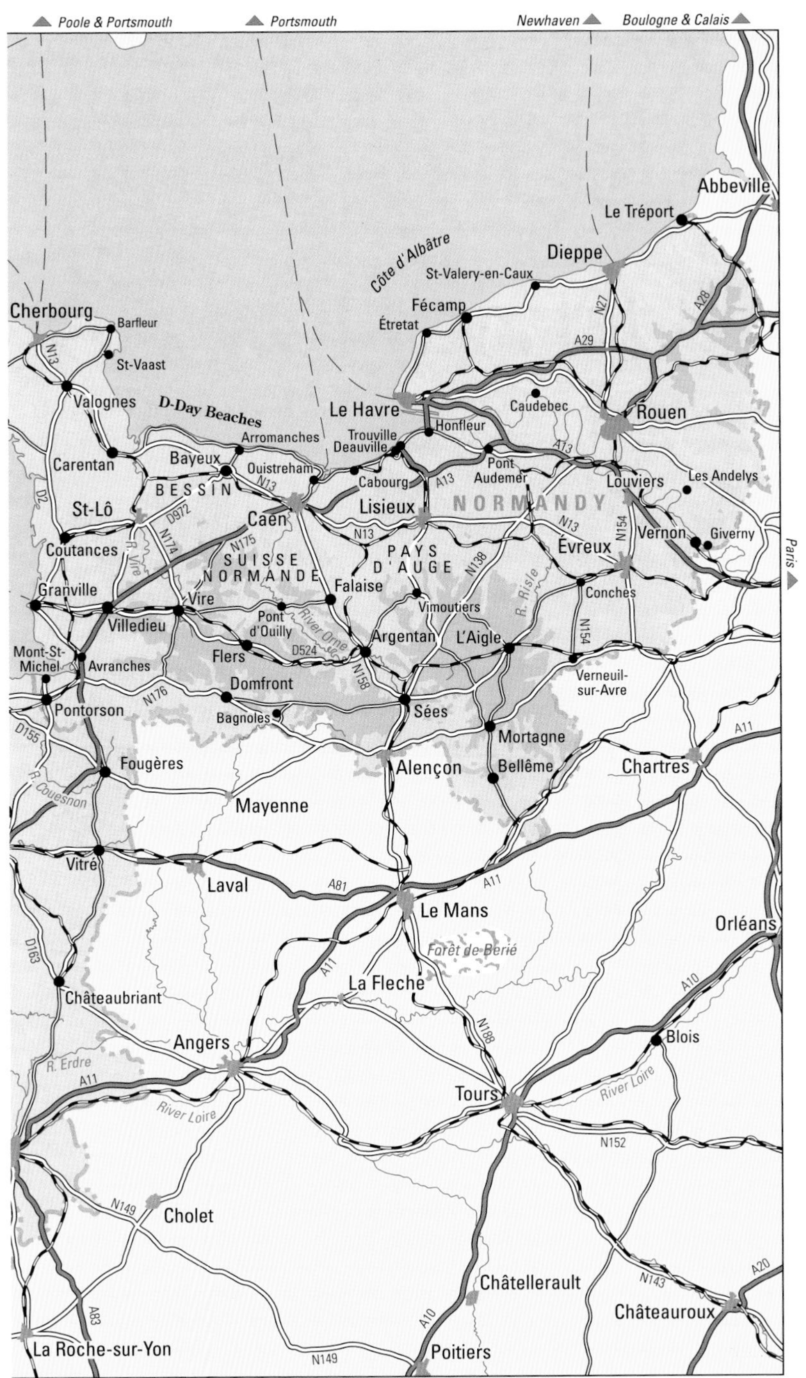

Poole & Portsmouth
Portsmouth
Newhaven
Boulogne & Calais
Abbeville
Le Tréport
Côte d'Albâtre
Dieppe
St-Valery-en-Caux
Fécamp
Étretat
Cherbourg
Barfleur
St-Vaast
N13
A28
N27
A29
Valognes
D-Day Beaches
Le Havre
Caudebec
Rouen
Honfleur
Arromanches
Trouville
Deauville
Pont Audemer
A13
Carentan
Bayeux
Ouistreham
Cabourg
Louviers
Les Andelys
BESSIN
NORMANDY
St-Lô
Caen
Lisieux
D972
N174
N175
N154
Vernon
Giverny
Paris
Coutances
R. Vire
SUISSE NORMANDE
PAYS D'AUGE
N138
Évreux
Conches
R. Risle
Granville
Vire
Falaise
Vimoutiers
Villedieu
Pont d'Ouilly
River Orne
Argentan
L'Aigle
Mont-St-Michel
Avranches
Flers
D524
N158
Verneuil-sur-Avre
Domfront
N176
Sées
Pontorson
Bagnoles
Mortagne
D155
A11
Fougères
Alençon
Bellême
Chartres
R. Couesnon
Mayenne
Vitré
Laval
A81
Le Mans
Orléans
Forêt de Berié
D163
La Fleche
A10
Châteaubriant
N188
Blois
Angers
R. Erdre
Tours
River Loire
N152
N149
Cholet
Châtellerault
N143
A20
A83
Châteauroux
La Roche-sur-Yon
Poitiers
La Rochelle

Introduction to

Brittany and Normandy

Of the many strongly individual regions of France, Brittany and Normandy rank among the most distinct. Each sustains its own proud identity, in terms of culture, peoples, landscape and history. A journey through the two regions enables you to experience much of the best that France has to offer: wild coast and sheltered white-sand beaches; sparse heathland and dense forests; medieval ports and relics of the prehistoric past; fine cities and museums; and, every bit as important, abundant seafood and (especially in Normandy) a compelling and exuberant cuisine.

Highlights in every area are detailed in the chapter introductions throughout this book. While step-by-step itineraries are not specified – much of the fun of exploring consists in rambling off on side roads – the text is structured as far as possible in continuous routes. If you read this before you decide how to travel, consider **cycling**; both provinces are ideal for cycle touring, with short distances between each town and the next. Otherwise, a **car** is probably the best alternative; public transport options tend to be very limited.

Where to go

Brittany is the more popular of the two regions, with both French and foreign tourists. Its most obvious attractions lie along the **coast**, speckled with offshore islands and islets, which makes up over a third of the seaboard of France. In parts of the north, and in the western region of Finistère, the shoreline can be nothing but rocks and

Thanks to the sheer extent of the Breton coastline, it's always possible to find a spot where you can walk alone with the elements.

cliffs, its exposed headlands buffeted by the full force of the Atlantic and swept by dangerous currents. But elsewhere, especially in the sheltered southern resorts around the Morbihan and La Baule, it is caressed by the gentlest of seas, with the sands rambling for kilometres or nestling into coves between steep cliffs.

Thanks to the sheer extent of the Breton coastline, it's always possible to find a spot where you can walk alone with the elements. Although in high season solitude can be scarce on the sandy beaches or in the small bays with their sun-struck swimmers, there could never be enough visitors to cover every twist of the Finistère coast. As well as exploring the mainland resorts and seaside villages – each of which, from ports the size of **St-Malo** or **Vannes** down to little-known harbour communities such as Erquy, Le Pouldu, L'Aber-W'rach or Piriac-sur-mer, can be relied upon to offer at least one welcoming, characterful little hotel or restaurant – it's worth making the time to take in at least one of **the islands**. Boat trips out to these sea-encircled microcosms can be among the most enjoyable highlights of a trip to Brittany. The magical Île de Bréhat is just a ten-minute crossing from the north coast near Paimpol, while historic Belle-Île, to the south, is under an hour from Quiberon. Certain other islands are set aside as bird sanctuaries, while, off Finistère, the Îles d'Ouessant and Molène in the north, and Sein to the south, are as remote and strange as Orkney or the Shetland Isles.

A vast wealth of **megalithic remains** scattered across Brittany evoke the region's prehistoric past. The single most famous site is **Carnac**, whose spectacular alignments of menhirs may have been erected as part of an ancient observatory. Lesser known but equally compelling remains include the pyramid-like burial tumuli on the island of **Gavrinis**, in the gulf of Morbihan, and at **Barnenez** outside Morlaix in the north. Not all such relics are found near the sea; the moors and woodlands of **inland Brittany**, too, conceal unexpected ancient treasures. This is the realm of legend, with the **forests** of Huelgoat and Paimpont in particular – left-overs from Brittany's mythic dark ages – being identified with the tales of Merlin, the Fisher King and the Holy Grail. In the "Little Britain" of King

▲ Cornfields, Norman farm

Fact file

• The historic terms "**Normandy**" and "**Brittany**" remain in constant use, although for centuries the original boundaries of the regions have not been recognized in French law.

• Normandy is split between **Haute Normandie** (Upper Normandy), which consists of the *départements* of Seine Maritime and Eure, and **Basse Normandie** (Lower Normandy), made up of the *départements* of Calvados, Orne and Manche. Taken together, these two regions cover just under 30,000 square kilometres, and are home to 3.2 million people.

• Brittany is officially a single region – **Bretagne** – that combines the *départements* of Ille-et-Vilaine, Côtes d'Armor, Finistère and Morbihan. However, the fact that it has since 1973 excluded the *département* of Loire-Atlantique, and thus also its historical capital of Nantes, is generally ignored by Bretons themselves, who continue to regard Brittany as comprising all five *départements*. By that reckoning, Brittany occupies 34,000 square kilometres, with a population of 4 million.

• Upper Normandy, dominated by industrialized Rouen, leans leftwards **politically**, while agricultural Lower Normandy is more conservative. Brittany, where fishing and agriculture have increasingly been supplanted by tourism as the basis of the economy, splits fairly evenly in elections. Despite pride in Breton (and Celtic) cultural traditions, separatist parties attract few votes.

• **French** is used everywhere; tourists are unlikely to encounter spoken Breton.

Arthur's domain – Petite Bretagne, as opposed to Grande Bretagne – an other-worldly element still seems entrenched in the land and people.

Normandy, on the other hand, has a less harsh appearance and a more mainstream – and more prosperous – history. It too is a seaboard province, first colonized by Norsemen from Scandinavia, and then colonizing in turn; the ruthless Norman formula for success was exported in the eleventh and twelfth centuries to England, Sicily and parts of the Near East, and later on to Canada. Normandy has always boasted large-scale **ports**: Rouen, on the Seine, is as near as ships can get to Paris, while Dieppe, Cherbourg and Le Havre have important transatlantic trade. **Inland**, it is overwhelmingly agricultural – a wonderfully fertile belt of tranquil pastureland, where most visitors head straight for the restaurants of towns such as Vire and Conches.

The pleasures of Normandy are perhaps less intense and unique than those of Brittany. Many of the region's better-known stretches of **seaside** are a little overdeveloped.

Medieval street, Dinan

▲ Carnac megaliths

Towards the end of the nineteenth century, the last of the Napoleons created a "Norman Riviera" around Trouville and Deaville, and a somewhat pretentious air still hangs about their elegant promenades. However, the ancient ports – **Honfleur** and **Barfleur** especially – are visual delights, and numerous coastal villages remain unspoiled by crowds or affectations. Even if you just plan to visit for a weekend break from England, lovely little towns are tucked away within 20km of each of the major Channel ports – the Cotentin peninsula around Cherbourg is one of the best, and least explored, areas – while the banks of the Seine, too, hold several idyllic resorts.

Normandy also boasts extraordinary **architectural** treasures, although only its much-restored traditional capital, **Rouen**, has preserved a complete medieval centre. The attractions are more often single buildings than entire towns. Most famous of all is the spectacular *merveille* on the island of **Mont-St-Michel**, but there are also the monasteries at Jumièges and Caen, and Richard the Lionheart's castle

Lovely little towns are tucked away within 20km of each of the major Channel ports.

From cathedrals to chapels

Thanks in great part to the wealth accrued by its warriors, Normandy has some of France's most imposing and resplendent church architecture. Prime examples include the Gothic cathedrals of Coutances, Bayeux and Rouen, and the monasteries of Mont-St-Michel and Jumièges. In Brittany, by contrast, it's often the tiny rural chapels and roadside crosses that are the most intriguing. Breton Catholicism has always had a distinctive, idiosyncratic character, incorporating Celtic, Druidic, and quite possibly prehistoric elements. Though hundreds of its saints have never been approved by the Vatican, their brightly painted wooden figures adorn every church in the province, along with skeletal statues of death's workmate, Ankou, and their stories merge imperceptibly with tales of moving menhirs, ghosts and sorcery. Noteworthy village churches include those of Kermaria-an-Isquit and Kernascléden, both of which hold painted frescoes of the Dance of Death, and the *enclos paroissiaux* or "parish closes" of Finistère, where the proximity of the dead to the living seems to echo the attitudes of the megalith-builders.

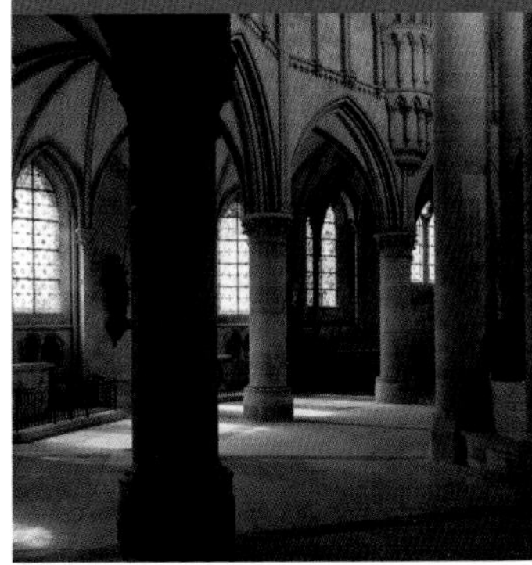

Food

If, like so many visitors, you consider the food to be one of the prime attractions of a trip to France, you're unlikely to be disappointed in either Brittany or Normandy. Ports and resorts all along the coast abound with wonderful restaurants, and fresh seafood dominates almost every menu. Some towns have their own specialities, such as Cancale with its fabulous oysters, or Erquy with its scallops; others simply serve whatever the boats bring back, which in the cases of Dieppe, Étretat and Honfleur in Normandy, or Camaret, Concarneau and Quiberon in Brittany, is enough to keep rows of top-class seafront restaurants in business.

Away from the sea, almost every village in inland Normandy can pride itself on holding at least one gourmet restaurant. Here the emphasis tends to be on the rich dairy produce of the region, with locally reared meat, especially veal, prepared in thick creamy sauces, and wide arrays of trademark Norman cheeses such as Camembert, Livarot, and Pont l'Eveque.

above the Seine at Les Andelys, while **Bayeux**, in addition to its vivid and astonishing **Tapestry**, holds a majestic cathedral. Many other great Norman buildings survived into the twentieth century, only to be destroyed during the Allied landings in 1944 and the subsequent **Battle of Normandy**, which has its own legacy in a series of war museums, memorials and cemeteries. While hardly conventional tourist attractions, as part of the fabric of the province these are moving and enlightening.

When to go

Every French town or district seems to promote its own *"micro-climat"*, maintaining that some meteorological freak makes it milder or drier or balmier than its neighbours. On the whole, however, the bulk of Normandy and Brittany follows a fairly set pattern. A genuine **summer**, more reliable than in Britain, begins around mid-June and lasts, in a good year, through to mid-October. **Spring** and **autumn** are mild but sporadically wet. If you come for a week in April or November, it could be spoilt by rain; the rainy spells seldom last more than a couple of days, however, so a fortnight should yield

▼ Lighthouse, Brittany

▲ Herding cows, Brittany

better luck. **Winter** is not too severe, though in western Brittany especially it can be damp and very misty on the coast.

Sea temperatures are not Mediterranean, and any greater warmth felt in the Channel waters off the Norman coast as opposed to the south of England is probably more psychological than real. The south coast of Brittany is a different matter – consistently warm through the summer months, with no need for you to brace yourself before going into the sea.

The other factor that may affect planning is the **tourist season**. On the coast, this gets going properly around July, reaches a peak during the first two weeks of August and then fades quite swiftly – though you should try to avoid the great *rentrée* at the end of the month, when the roads are jammed with cars returning to Paris. Inland, the season is less defined; highlights such as Monet's gardens at Giverny and parts of the Nantes–Brest canal can be crowded out in midsummer but, in August at any rate, some smaller hotels close to enable their owners to take their own holidays by the sea. Conversely, those seaside resorts that have grown up without being attached to a genuine town take on a distinctly ghostlike appearance during the winter months, when they can often be entirely devoid of facilities.

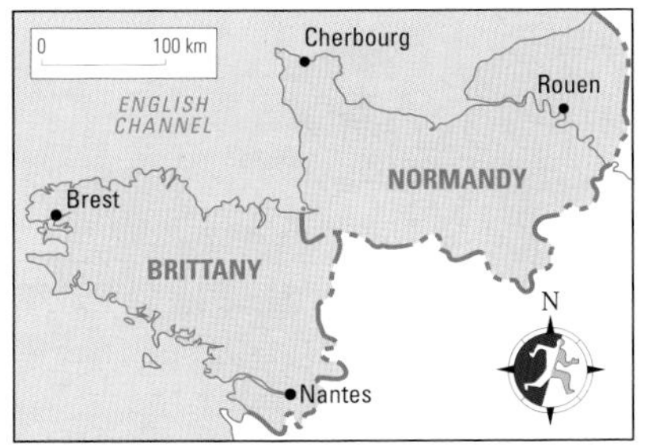

Average daily temperatures (°C) and monthly rainfall (mm)

	Jan	Feb	Mar	Apr	May	June	July	Aug	Sept	Oct	Nov	Dec
BRITTANY												
Brest												
Av Temp °C	6	6	7	9	12	14	15	16	15	12	9	7
Rainfall mm	132	106	101	73	72	58	49	68	85	110	127	148
Nantes												
Av Temp °C	5	6	8	10	13	17	19	19	16	12	8	6
Rainfall mm	78	60	60	53	60	53	50	53	68	88	91	86
NORMANDY												
Cherbourg												
Av Temp °C	5	5	6	7	11	13	15	16	14	12	8	6
Rainfall mm	90	79	78	56	65	48	44	47	80	99	110	103
Rouen												
Av Temp °C	3	3	6	8	12	14	17	17	15	11	6	4
Rainfall mm	59	47	46	47	52	54	58	61	57	65	66	64

things not to miss

It's not possible to sample everything that Brittany and Normandy have to offer in one trip – but you can have a great time trying. What follows is a selective taste of the region's highlights: outstanding scenery, picturesque villages, remarkable history and fabulous fresh produce. They are arranged in five colour-coded categories to help you find the very best things to see, do and experience. Each entry has a page reference which takes you straight into the guide, where you can learn more.

01 **Monet's Garden at Giverny** Page **121** • Despite the summer crowds, the waterlily pond at Claude Monet's Normandy home remains as spellbinding as ever.

02 Moules frîtes Page **47** • If Brittany ever wins its independence, there's not much question what the national dish will be – succulent orange mussels and crisp chips.

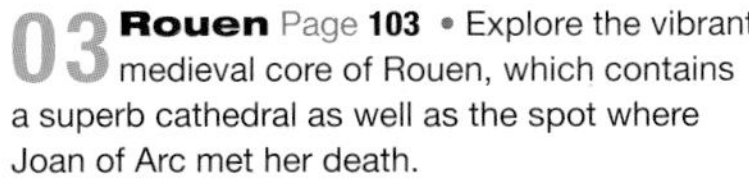

03 Rouen Page **103** • Explore the vibrant medieval core of Rouen, which contains a superb cathedral as well as the spot where Joan of Arc met her death.

04 Memories of D-Day Page **146** • Every June, veterans and their families return to the beaches of Normandy to remember the events of June 6, 1944.

05 The Cairn du Barnenez Page **282** • Brittany's ancient megalith builders didn't restrict themselves to standing stones – they even constructed pyramids, as in this magnificent double edifice crowning an eminence on the northern coast.

06 Fougères Page **256** • Wander the ramparts of the mighty château of Fougères.

07 The Seine Page **98** • Broadening as it approaches the Channel, the premier river of northern France becomes languidly rural, lined by lovely little-known villages such as Villequier.

08 The Seabirds of Sept-Îles Page **278** • Marine bird species have these seven rocky islets all to themselves, but boat trips from Perros-Guirec enable visitors to get close-up views.

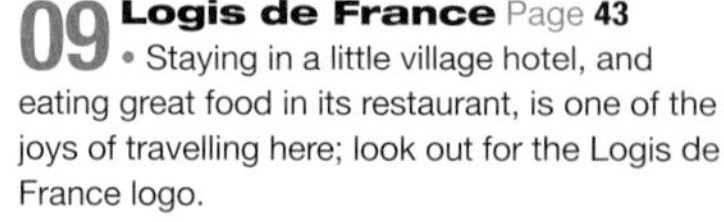

09 Logis de France Page **43** • Staying in a little village hotel, and eating great food in its restaurant, is one of the joys of travelling here; look out for the Logis de France logo.

10 The Bayeux Tapestry Page **157** • Now almost a thousand years old, this colourful embroidery still celebrates the Norman Conquest of England in every tiny detail.

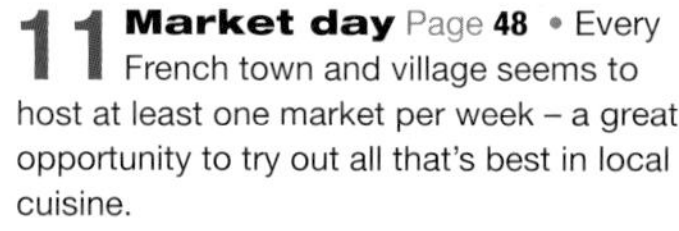

11 Market day Page **48** • Every French town and village seems to host at least one market per week – a great opportunity to try out all that's best in local cuisine.

12 Cycling Page **40** • Slow your pace and cycle through quiet country lanes, undulating hills and enchanted forests.

13 The Forests of Brittany Pages **350 & 357** • In legend, the great woodlands of Brittany witnessed the stirring deeds of King Arthur's knights; even today, ancient forests like Huelgoat seem like refuges from the modern world.

14 A Boat Trip to the Île de Sein Page **325** • Of the many beautiful and remote islands that lie off the coast of Brittany, none is more hauntingly atmospheric than Finistère's tiny Île de Sein.

15 Camembert Page **201** • You might not go to Normandy for the cheese alone, but you'll fall in love with it all over again once you're there.

16 The Cliffs at Étretat Page **90** • Wind and tide have sculpted the chalky cliffs to either side of the delightful Norman resort of Étretat into extraordinary shapes.

17 The Nantes-Brest Canal Page **343** • Meander along Brittany's inland waterways and soak up the stunning scenery.

18 The megaliths of Carnac Page **395** • Europe's oldest town remains surrounded by enigmatic reminders of its prehistoric inhabitants.

19 Mont-St-Michel Page **177** • The glorious medieval abbey that tops this tiny Norman island ranks among the most recognizable silhouettes in the world.

20 Hiking the Côte de Granit Rose Page **274** • The bizarre rock formations that line this stretch of the northern Breton seashore make for some dramatic coastal hikes.

21 Honfleur Page **130** • Normandy's most charming little port has long attracted artists and photographers.

Basics

Basics

Getting there

For British holiday-makers, Brittany and Normandy are extremely easy to visit. Although competition from the Channel Tunnel has forced P&O Ferries to abandon their sailings to Cherbourg and Caen, Brittany Ferries continues to thrive, and now offers several extra-fast (summer only) services. High-speed vessels also cross between Newhaven and Dieppe, while the Channel Tunnel itself provides rapid access to Normandy.

On the down side, **fares** for both the ferries and the Channel Tunnel have risen considerably in the last few years, and the only real bargains to be found these days tend to be off-season – though it is possible to **fly** cheaply to Brittany, using Ryanair's service to Dinard from London Stansted. **Irish** visitors can choose between a small selection of direct ferry services between Ireland and France, most active in summer; one or two summer charter-flight options; or travel via England and/or Paris.

If you're coming to Brittany and Normandy from anywhere outside Europe, then you'll almost certainly have to start by flying to Paris, and travel onwards by train, rental car, or, if money's no object, an internal flight.

From the UK

There are six commercial **ferry ports** arranged along the coastline of Brittany and Normandy, and another half-dozen **airports**, one of which is served by a budget airline. Your choice of route will depend on where you're starting from and where you're heading to. Thus, for example, for anyone living in southwestern England or Wales, taking a ferry from Plymouth or Portsmouth is liable to prove the most convenient option. If price is the only factor, then the **cheapest ferry crossings** of all tend to be those from Dover to Calais, but then again air fares can be so cheap these days that it may cost less to fly and rent a car at the other end.

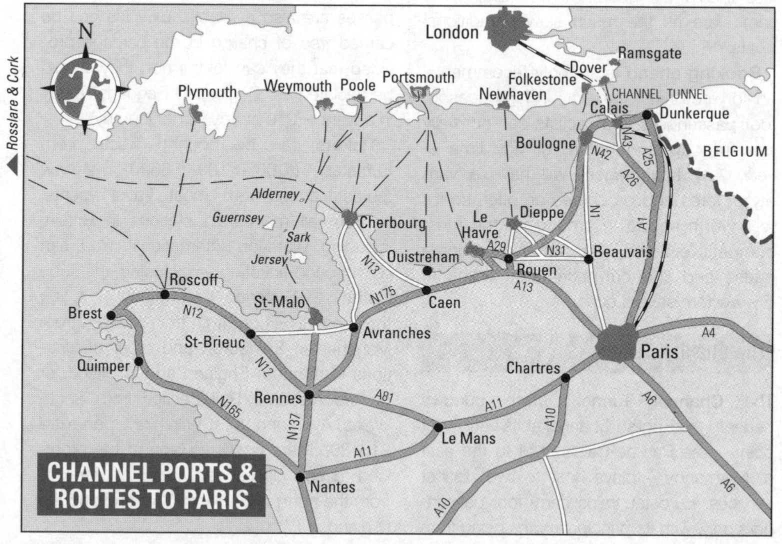

Ferries

The most direct route to Normandy or Brittany, for motorists, cyclists and pedestrians, is still to take the cross-Channel ferry to any of four Norman and two Breton ports. However, it's slightly cheaper to cross the Channel further east, and travel via Calais or Dunkerque. All these services are detailed in the box opposite.

Ferry fares vary so enormously with the season – most operators divide the year into as many as five distinct payment periods, and each individual sailing has its own price code – that it's all but impossible to predict what you will actually pay. Broad ranges are given in the box opposite; as a rule, children under 4 travel free, while those aged up to 15 are charged half the adult fare. Note, in addition, that **cabin accommodation** on overnight crossings tends to cost £20 or more per person, and may be obligatory in high season or on night sailings. Bicycles are typically carried free in low season or for around £5 in summer.

Currently the best deals of all are the **high-speed catamaran services** between Poole and Cherbourg (confusingly, operated by Condor Ferries on behalf of Brittany Ferries), and Newhaven and Dieppe (with Hoverspeed), which cross the Channel in less than three hours, while charging the same fare as the much slower traditional boats.

Booking ahead is strongly recommended for motorists, certainly in high season; foot passengers and cyclists can normally just turn up and board, at any time of year. Any travel agent will have a variety of fares and brochures on offer, so it's well worth shopping around for the most competitive deals. You can also compare prices and find cut-price fares online at Ⓦwww.ferrysavers.com.

The Channel Tunnel

The **Channel Tunnel**, which burrows beneath the English Channel at its narrowest point – the Pas-de-Calais, well to the east of Normandy – plays host to two distinct services. Eurostar trains carry foot passengers only, with its principal routes being from London to Paris or Brussels, while Eurotunnel simply conveys cars and other vehicles between Folkestone and Calais, in direct competition with the ferries.

Eurostar

The **Eurostar** rail service takes a mere two hours forty minutes to get from London Waterloo International to Paris Gare du Nord. More than twenty trains make the journey each day. By catching either the 8.39am (Mon–Sat) or the 8.34am (Sun) departure from London, and changing at Lille, one hour forty minutes out, travellers heading for Brittany and Normandy can use connecting TGV services to bring the total journey time to Rennes or Nantes down to around six or seven hours. **Standard-class return fares** from London to Lille start at £55 for the "Leisure Apex 14", which must be bought at least fourteen days before departure and must include a Saturday night, with fixed outward and return dates and no refunds. The £115 "Leisure Flexi" can be bought on the day if there are still seats available and allows one change of each part of the round-trip journey. However, for a high-season ticket with changeable departure and return times, bought close to your departure date, you're looking at £250. Concessions for young people (under 26), over-60s, and holders of international rail passes are also available. Bicycles can be carried free of charge in the carriage provided that they can fold; if not, they should be declared as "Registered Baggage" a day in advance (£20 per cycle per journey).

Tickets can be bought directly from Eurostar (Ⓣ0870/160 6600, Ⓦwww.eurostar.com), from most travel agents, or from all main train stations in Britain, including Waterloo International. You can get through-ticketing – including the tube journey to Waterloo International – if you travel on GNER or Virgin train services from Manchester, Edinburgh and other destinations in northern England and Scotland, or on the Alphaline Rail Service from South Wales, Avon and West Wiltshire for an extra £10–30. There is still no sign of the promised direct high-speed Eurostar services from the north of England, Scotland and the Midlands.

Sea crossings and fares from the UK

Route	Operator	Crossing Time	Frequency	One-way Fares	
				Small car + 2 adults	Foot Passenger
Brittany					
Portsmouth–St-Malo	Brittany Ferries	8–11hr	1–2 daily	£175– 272	£43–67
Poole–St-Malo (via Jersey or Guernsey)	Condor Ferries	4hr 30min	1 daily late May to Sept	£121–243	£33–35
Plymouth–Roscoff	Brittany Ferries	5hr 30min–8hr	1–3 Jan–mid-Nov	£159–285	£36–64
Weymouth–St-Malo (via Jersey or Guernsey)	Condor Ferries	5hr 15min –7hr 45min 8hr 30min	1 daily Feb–Oct & 2 weekly Nov–Dec	£121–243	£33–35
Normandy					
Newhaven–Dieppe	Hoverspeed	2hr 15min*	2–3 daily June–Sept	£149–162	£30
Newhaven–Dieppe	Transmanche Ferries	4hr	1–3 daily all year	£119–169	£27–28
Portsmouth–Cherbourg	Brittany Ferries	3hr*–4hr 45min	1–3 daily all year	£144–267	£32–56
Portsmouth–Cherbourg	Condor Ferries	5hr	Sun, June to mid–Sept	£251	£19–63
Poole–Cherbourg	Brittany Ferries	2hr 15min* –4hr 30min	1–3 daily Feb to mid-Dec all year	£144–267	£32–56
Portsmouth–Caen	Brittany Ferries	5hr 45min –7hr 15min	2–3 daily June to mid-Nov	£162–307	£36–74
Portsmouth–Le Havre	P&O Ferries	5hr 30min	3 daily all year	£140–250	£19–63
Pas-de-Calais					
Dover–Calais	Hoverspeed*	50min	9–15 daily all year	£119–151	£14
Dover–Calais	P&O Ferries	1hr 15min –1hr 30min	30 daily all year	£71–76	£14–28
Dover–Calais	Sea France	1hr 15min –1hr 30min	15 daily all year	£45–75	£17
Dover–Dunkerque	NorfolkLine	2hr	8–10 daily all year	£99–129	£15–20

*These services use high-speed catamarans

Ferry operators

Brittany Ferries ⓣ08703/665 333, ⓦwww.brittanyferries.co.uk
Condor Ferries ⓣ0845/345 2000, ⓦwww.condorferries.co.uk
Hoverspeed ⓣ0870/240 8070, ⓦwww.hoverspeed.co.uk
NorfolkLine ⓣ08700/870 1020, ⓦwww.norfolkline.com.
P&O Ferries ⓣ0870/600 0600 or 01304/864 003, ⓦwww.poferries.com
Sea France ⓣ08705/711 711, ⓦwww.seafrance.com
Transmanche Ferries ⓣ0800/917 1201, ⓦwww.transmancheferries.com

Eurotunnel

The Channel Tunnel also provides the fastest and most convenient way to take your **car** to France. For motorists, the tunnel entrance is less than two hours' drive from London, off the M20 at Junction 11A, just outside Folkestone. Once there, you drive your car onto a two-tier railway carriage; you're then free to get out and stretch your legs during the 35 minutes (45min for some night trains) before you emerge from the darkness at Coquelles, just outside Calais. The sole operator, **Eurotunnel**, offers a continuous service with up to four departures per hour (only 1 per hour midnight–6am). Because of the frequency of the service, it's not compulsory to buy a ticket in advance, but it's highly advisable in midsummer or during school holidays. You must arrive at least thirty minutes before departure.

Tickets are available through Eurotunnel's Customer Service Centre (information and bookings ⓣ0870/535 3535, ⓦwww.eurotunnel.com) or from your local travel agent. **Fares** are calculated per car, regardless of the number of passengers. Rates depend on the time of year, time of day and length of stay (the cheapest ticket is for a day-trip, followed by a five-day return). It's cheaper to travel between 10pm and 6am, when, outside of the summer months, a round-trip ticket could cost just £200. The highest fares, meanwhile, are reserved for weekend departures and returns in July and August and can be as much as £415. **Bikes** are carried on a specially adapted carriage that makes the crossing twice a day – it costs £61 for bike and person if you are staying more than five days, £32 if it's just a short break.

While the speed and efficiency of the tunnel journey itself is superb, drivers heading for Brittany or Normandy should not underestimate the length of time it takes to drive across northern France from the tunnel exit. Just to reach Le Tréport, the eastern extremity of Normandy, takes a good two hours, while western Brittany would take more like eight hours.

Combined train/ferry routes

You can buy **connecting tickets** from any British station to any French station, via any of the ferry routes. Details and prices (again with various special and seasonal offers) are obtainable from any British Rail travel centre. Students and anyone under 26 can buy heavily discounted tickets from Eurotrain outlets such as STA Travel (see opposite) and most student travel agents.

Rail travellers catching ferries from **Portsmouth** should be warned that "Portsmouth Harbour" station is nowhere near the cross-Channel ferry terminals; there is a connecting bus service operated by Bailey's Transport (ⓣ07721 877722) available from outside the station, but allow plenty of time.

By air

The only **budget airline** to operate flights from England to Brittany (there are no flights to Normandy) is Ryanair (ⓣ0871/246 0000, ⓦwww.ryanair.com), which flies once or twice daily from London Stansted or once daily from London Luton to the Breton town of Dinard. Typical **fares** have been around £60–80 return in low season, £100–330 in summer. If you're **booking online**, keep trying alternative dates; each leg of each trip is priced individually, fares change day by day, and they're only quoted for each specific day you request. Travelling midweek is generally cheaper than weekend flights.

By coach

Eurolines coach services (ⓣ08705/808 808, ⓦwww.eurolines.co.uk) connect London with only the main towns in Brittany and Normandy. Typical adult single **fares** in summer from London are £75 to Rennes and Nantes, £45 to Rouen and £25 to Calais, from where you can make train connections to Normandy and Brittany. Schedules, tickets and further information are available from the Eurolines number and website, National Express (ⓣ0870/580 8080, ⓦwww.nationalexpress.com) and from Eurolines agents nationwide.

Package tours

Any travel agent will be able to provide details of the many operators running

package tours to Brittany and Normandy (see below), which can be a competitively priced way to travel. Some deals are straightforward travel-plus-hotel affairs, while others offer tandem touring, air-and-rail packages and stays in country cottages. If your trip is geared around specific interests – such as cycling or self-catering in the countryside – packages can work out much cheaper than the same arrangements made on arrival.

In addition to the addresses below, bear in mind that most of the **ferry companies** (see p.21) also offer their own travel and accommodation deals. Lists of operators can also be obtained from Maison de la France, the French government tourist office (see p.29), which also handles reservations, and from the Holiday France website (ⓦwww.holidayfrance.org.uk), run by the Association of British Tour Operators to France.

Travel agents

Ebookers ⓣ0870/010 7000, ⓦwww.ebookers.com.
North South Travel ⓣ & ⓕ01245/608 291, ⓦwww.northsouthtravel.co.uk.
STA Travel ⓣ0870/1600 599, ⓦwww.statravel.co.uk.
Trailfinders ⓣ020/7938 3939, ⓦwww.trailfinders.com.

Tours and packages

Blakes Holidays ⓣ0870/220 2498, ⓦwww.blakes.co.uk. Self-catering canal trips in Brittany, starting from either Dinan or Guipry, south of Rennes. High-season rental rates range from around £1000 per week for a two-berth boat to around £2100 for a twelve-berth vessel.
Brittany Travel ⓣ01920/412013, ⓦwww.brittany.co.uk. Self-catering holidays throughout southern Brittany, and especially the Morbihan; weekly rental rates for four-person cottages during peak periods range from £350 to £850.
French Connections ⓦwww.frenchconnections.co.uk. Online advertising portal offering holiday rentals throughout Brittany and Normandy, arranged direct with the owners at advantageous rates.
Gîtes de France ⓦwww.gites-de-france.fr. Comprehensive list of houses, cottages and chalets throughout France which can be booked online, or through Brittany Ferries (ⓣ0870/5360 360) in the UK.
Holt's Battlefield Tours ⓣ01293/455300, ⓦwww.battletours.co.uk. Definitive guided tours to famous battlefields, including five-day tours to Normandy covering either the D-Day landings themselves or other aspects of the invasion, for between £450 and £650.
Matthews Holidays ⓣ01483/284044, ⓦwww.matthewsfrance.co.uk. Inexpensive self-drive mobile-home holidays on good-quality campsites in southern Brittany; a week for a family with four children, staying in La Forêt-Fouesant and including ferry travel and a car, ranges from £300 up to £920 depending on the season.
VFB Holidays ⓣ01242/240340, ⓦwww.vfbholidays.co.uk. Cottages all over Brittany and Normandy, especially southern Finistère, and also self-drive hotel holidays. Prices, including ferry travel, for a two-week cottage stay for two range from around £400 per person in the low season up to as much as £800 in summer.

Camping operators

Canvas Holidays ⓣ01383/629000, ⓦwww.canvasholidays.com.
Eurocamp ⓣ08703/667 558, ⓦwww.eurocamp.co.uk.
Keycamp ⓣ0870/700 0123, ⓦwww.keycamp.com.
Sandpiper ⓣ01746/785123, ⓦwww.sandpiperhols.co.uk.
Select France ⓣ01865/331 350, ⓦwww.selectfrance.co.uk.

From Ireland

Three different operators run **ferries** direct to Brittany or Normandy from Ireland. The year-round routes are between Rosslare and Cherbourg, with Irish Ferries or P&O Irish Sea Ferries and Dublin and Cherbourg with P&O Irish Sea Ferries, but throughout the summer it's also possible to sail from Cork or Rosslare to Roscoff. All routes and operators are detailed on p.24.

All three companies offer reduced rates on fixed-period return tickets, as well as **all-in packages**, with a choice of accommodation in hotels, campsites, or self-catering *gîtes*. You can either contact the companies direct to reserve space in advance (essential at peak season if you're driving), or any competent travel agent at home or in France can do it for you.

Sea crossings and fares from Ireland

Route	Operator	Crossing Time	Frequency	One-way Fares	
				Small car + 2 adults	Foot Passenger
Cork–Roscoff	Brittany Ferries	11hr 30min –12hr 30min	1 weekly April–Nov	€234–466	€60–83
Dublin–Cherbourg	P&O Irish Sea Ferries	19hr	1 weekly all year	€297–634	not allowed
Rosslare–Cherbourg	Irish Ferries	19hr 30min	2–3 weekly all year	€239–579	€50–120
Rosslare–Cherbourg	P&O Irish Sea Ferries	19hr	3 weekly all year	€294–634	not allowed
Rosslare–Roscoff	Irish Ferries	17hr	1–3 weekly April–Sept	€239–579	€50–120

Ferry operators

Brittany Ferries ⓣ08705/561 600, ⓦwww.brittanyferries.ie
Irish Ferries ⓣ0818/300 400, ⓦwww.irishferries.com
P&O Irish Sea Ferries ⓣ1800/409049, ⓦwww.poirishsea.com

By air

Aer Lingus (ⓣ0818/365 000, ⓦwww.aerlingus.ie) fly direct from Dublin, Shannon and Cork to Paris CDG for around €100–370 return, while **Ryanair** (ⓣ0818/303030, ⓦwww.ryanair.com) fly from Dublin and Shannon to London Stansted, from where you can pick up the flight to the Breton town of Dinard.

In addition, Go Holidays (ⓣ01/874 4126, ⓦwww.goholidays.ie) offer **charter flights** in high season between Shannon and Rennes (Saturdays early July to end Aug, €304 return) and Shannon and Nantes (Thursdays mid-May to mid-Sept, €264 return).

Flight and travel agents in Ireland

CIE Tours International ⓣ01/703 1888, ⓦwww.cietours.ie.
First Choice ⓣ091/562 595, ⓦwww.firstchoicetravel.ie.
Go Holidays ⓣ01/874 4126, ⓦwww.goholidays.ie.
Joe Walsh Tours ⓣ01/676 0991, ⓦwww.joewalshtours.ie.
Lee Travel ⓣ021/427 7111, ⓦwww.leetravel.ie.
McCarthy's Travel ⓣ021/427 0127, ⓦwww.mccarthystravel.ie.
Neenan Travel ⓣ01/607 9900, ⓦwww.neenantrav.ie.
Student & Group Travel ⓣ01/677 7834.
Trailfinders ⓣ01/677 7888, ⓦwww.trailfinders.ie.
Usit ⓣ01/602 1600, ⓦwww.usit.ie.

From the US and Canada

Getting to France from the US or Canada is straightforward; there are **direct flights** from over thirty major North American cities to Paris, with connections from all over the continent. From there, it's simple to continue to Brittany or Normandy by rail – Rouen is just over an hour away, while super-fast TGV trains get to either Rennes or Nantes in around two hours – or by air. A connecting flight on Air Inter, Air France's domestic arm, to Brest, the remotest Breton city, costs approximately US$150 extra.

Although **flying to London** is usually the cheapest way to reach Europe, price differences are so minimal that there's no point travelling to France via London unless you've specifically chosen to visit the UK as well.

Transatlantic **fares** to France are very reasonable. Air fares always depend on the season, with the highest being from around early June to the end of August; fares drop during the "shoulder" seasons – roughly September through October and April to May – and are at their lowest during low season, November to March (excluding Christmas and New Year). Flying at weekends is generally more expensive. A typical scheduled return fare for a midweek flight to Paris costs around US$600/1200 in low/high season from Houston, US$540/1050 from Los Angeles and US$350/850 from New York. From Canada, prices to Paris will be upwards of Can$900/1200 from Montreal and Toronto, and Can$1200/1600 from Vancouver.

You can often cut costs by going through a **specialist flight agent** – either a consolidator, who buys up blocks of tickets from the airlines and sells them at a discount, or a discount agent, who in addition to dealing with discounted flights may also offer special student and youth fares and a range of other travel-related services such as travel insurance, rail passes, car rentals, tours and the like. Many airlines and discount travel websites offer the opportunity to book inexpensive **tickets online**; useful addresses include general agents such as ⓦwww.cheaptickets.com, ⓦwww.expedia.com, and ⓦwww.travelocity.com, and auction sites like ⓦwww.hotwire.com and ⓦwww.priceline.com.

Airlines

Air Canada ⓣ1-888/247-2262, ⓦwww.aircanada.ca.
Air France US ⓣ1-800/237-2747, ⓦwww.airfrance.com, Canada ⓣ1-800/667-2747, ⓦwww.airfrance.ca.
American Airlines ⓣ1-800/433-7300, ⓦwww.aa.com.
British Airways ⓣ1-800/AIRWAYS, ⓦwww.ba.com.
Continental Airlines ⓣ1-800/231-0856, ⓦwww.continental.com.
Delta ⓣ1-800/241-4141, ⓦwww.delta.com.
Iberia ⓣ1-800/772-4642, ⓦwww.iberia.com.
Lufthansa US ⓣ1-800/645-3880, Canada ⓣ1-800/563-5954, ⓦwww.lufthansa-usa.com.
Northwest/KLM ⓣ1-800/447-4747, ⓦwww.nwa.com, ⓦwww.klm.com.
United Airlines ⓣ1-800/538-2929, ⓦwww.united.com.
US Airways ⓣ1-800/622-1015, ⓦwww.usair.com.

Discount travel companies

Airtech ⓣ212/219-7000, ⓦwww.airtech.com. Standby seat broker; also deals in consolidator fares and courier flights.
Educational Travel Center ⓣ1-800/747-5551 or 608/256-5551, ⓦwww.edtrav.com. Student/youth discount agent; also sells Eurail passes.
New Frontiers ⓣ1-800/677-0720, ⓦwww.newfrontiers.com. Discount firm, specializing in travel from the US to Europe, with hotels, package deals and especially good offers to France.
Skylink US ⓣ1-800/247-6659 or 212/573-8980, Canada ⓣ1-800/759-5465, ⓦwww.skylinkus.com. Consolidator.
STA Travel US ⓣ1-800/329-9537, Canada ⓣ1-888/427-5639, ⓦwww.statravel.com. Worldwide specialists in independent travel; also student IDs, travel insurance, car rental, rail passes, and more.
Student Flights ⓣ1-800/255-8000 or 480/951-1177, ⓦwww.isecard.com/studentflights. Student /youth fares, student IDs.
Travel Avenue ⓣ1-800/333-3335, ⓦwww.travelavenue.com. Full-service travel agent that offers discounts in the form of rebates.
Travel Cuts US ⓣ1-800/592-CUTS, Canada ⓣ1-888/246-9762, ⓦwww.travelcuts.com. Popular, long-established student-travel organization.
Travelers Advantage ⓣ1-877/259-2691, ⓦwww.travelersadvantage.com. Discount travel club; annual membership fee required (currently $1 for 3 months' trial).
Worldtek Travel ⓣ1-800/243-1723, ⓦwww.worldtek.com. Discount travel agency.

Tour operators

Dozens of tour operators specialize in travel to France. Many can put together very **flexible deals**, sometimes amounting to no more than a flight and accommodation. If you're planning to travel in moderate or luxury style, or if your trip is geared around special interests, such packages can work out cheaper than the same arrangements made on arrival. In addition, while a tour is almost certainly more confining than independent travel, it can help you make the most of your time if you're on a tight schedule.

Abercrombie & Kent ⓣ1-800/554-7016 or 630/954-2944, ⓦwww.abercrombiekent.com. Deluxe hiking, biking, rail and canal journeys, including an 11-day "Signature France" tour for around $10,000 excluding air fare, which includes Paris, the Loire Valley and Normandy.

Backroads ⓣ1-800/GO-ACTIVE or 510/527-1555, ⓦwww.backroads.com. Cycling and hiking tours for families and singles, with the emphasis on going at your own pace. Accommodation ranges from campsites to luxury hotels.

BCT Scenic Walking ⓣ1-800/473-1210 or 760/944-4599, ⓦwww.bctwalk.com. Walking holidays in both Normandy and Brittany.

Classic Journeys ⓣ1-800/200-3887 or 858/454-5004, ⓦwww.classicjourneys.com. Seven-day walking holidays along the northern coast of Normandy and Brittany, incorporating 3–4 hours of walking a day and costing $2795.

EC Tours ⓣ1-800/388-0877, ⓦwww.ectours.com. City tours and individually planned regional tours.

Euro-Bike & Walking Tours ⓣ1-800/321-6060, ⓦwww.eurobike.com. Good range of bike and walking tours all over France for family groups or solo travellers.

France Vacations ⓣ1-800/332 5332, ⓦwww.francevacations.net. Air/hotel and fly-drive packages to Normandy.

The French Experience ⓣ1-800/283-7262 or 212/986-3800, ⓦwww.frenchexperience.com. Flexible escorted and self-drive tours, châteaux, apartment and cottage rentals, air-fare arrangements, plus day-trips from Paris to Norman destinations.

Globus ⓣ1-866/755-8581, ⓦwww.globusjourneys.com. Planned vacation packages.

Infohub ⓦwww.infohub.com. Online operator with a wide range of escorted and self-guided cultural, gastronomy and activity French holidays such as a 7-day Brittany and Normandy cycling tour for $1795.

Viking River Cruises ⓣ1-877/668-4546 or 818/227-1234, ⓦwww.vikingrivercruises.com. French river cruises, including the Seine from Paris to Honfleur in Normandy in seven nights for $1359.

World Expeditions Montreal ⓣ514/844-6364, Ottawa ⓣ613/241-2700, ⓦwww.worldexpeditions.com. Self-guided and escorted cycling and trekking holidays.

From Australia & New Zealand

Although **scheduled services** fly to Paris from Sydney, Melbourne, Brisbane, Cairns, Perth and Auckland, many people travelling to France from Australia and New Zealand choose to travel via London. Most airlines can add on a Paris leg to any Australia/New Zealand–Europe ticket. Travelling time is around 22 hours via Asia and 30 hours via the USA – not counting time spent on stopovers.

Fares to France vary according to the season and the carrier. In general, low season lasts from mid-January to the end of February, and from the beginning of October to mid-November; high season is from mid-May to the end of August, and from the beginning of December to mid-January. Regular return economy fares from Sydney, Perth and Melbourne should cost from around Aus$2000 in low season and Aus$2600 in high season. Low-season scheduled fares from Auckland start at around NZ$2500, rising to NZ$3000 upwards in high season.

Alternatively, the **discount agents** listed below offer much better deals, and have the latest information on limited special offers. Some of them can also help with visas, travel insurance and tours.

If you're planning to visit France as part of a longer trip, then **Round-the-World** tickets offer greater flexibility and better value than a standard return flight. The most comprehensive and flexible routes are offered by One World and Star Alliance, allowing you to take in a huge number of destinations around the globe. Prices, which are either mileage-based or calculated according to how many continents you cover, start at around Aus$2300/NZ$3500, excluding taxes.

If you intend to do a fair amount of travelling within Europe, consider buying an **air pass**. These vary with the airlines, but must be pre-booked with the main ticket. Both One World and Star Alliance offer a European pass priced according to the distance travelled. With One World's "Visit Europe" pass, for example, you have to buy a minimum of two flights within Europe, costing between Aus$100/NZ$110 and Aus$395/NZ$440 depending on the distance; taxes and other surcharges are extra.

Finally, if you wish to travel in style, and especially if your visit is going to be geared around special interests, such as walking, cycling, art or wine, you may want to consider one of the **package tours** offered by the operators below. Though organized tours are inevitably more restrictive than independent travel, they may work out cheaper than making the same arrangements on arrival in France and can help you make the most of time if you're on a tight schedule.

Airlines

Air Canada Australia ⓣ1300/655 747 or 02/8248 5757, New Zealand ⓣ09/379 3371, ⓦwww.aircanada.com.
Air France Australia ⓣ1300/361 400, New Zealand ⓣ09/308 3352, ⓦwww.airfrance.com.
Air New Zealand Australia ⓣ13 24 76, New Zealand ⓣ0800/737 000, ⓦwww.airnz.com.
American Airlines Australia ⓣ1300/130 757, New Zealand ⓣ0800/887 997, ⓦwww.aa.com.
Austrian Airlines ⓣ1800/642 438 or 02/9251 6155, New Zealand ⓣ09/522 5948, ⓦwww.aua.com.
British Airways Australia ⓣ1300/767 177, New Zealand ⓣ0800/274 847 or 09/356 8690, ⓦwww.britishairways.com.
Cathay Pacific Australia ⓣ13 17 47, New Zealand ⓣ09/379 0861 or 0508/800 454, ⓦwww.cathaypacific.com.
Garuda Indonesia Australia ⓣ02/9334 9944 or 1300/365 330, New Zealand ⓣ09/366 1862, ⓦwww.garuda-indonesia.com. No direct flights.
Japan Airlines Australia ⓣ02/9272 1111, New Zealand ⓣ09/379 9906, ⓦwww.jal.com.
KLM/Northwest Airlines Australia ⓣ1300/303 747, New Zealand ⓣ09/309 1782, ⓦwww.klm.com, ⓦwww.nwa.com.
Malaysia Airlines Australia ⓣ13 26 27, New Zealand ⓣ0800/777 747, ⓦwww.malaysia-airlines.com.
Philippine Airlines Australia ⓣ02/9279 2020, New Zealand ⓣ09/379 8522, ⓦwww.philippineairlines.com.
Olympic Airways Australia ⓣ02/9251 2044, ⓦwww.olympic-airways.com.au.
Qantas Australia ⓣ13 13 13, ⓦwww.qantas.com.au, New Zealand ⓣ0800/808 767 or 09/357 8900.
Singapore Airlines Australia ⓣ13 10 11, New Zealand ⓣ0800/808 909, ⓦwww .singaporeair.com.
Swiss Australia ⓣ1800/883 199, New Zealand ⓣ09/977 2238, ⓦwww.swiss.com.
Thai Airways Australia ⓣ1300/651 960, New Zealand ⓣ09/377 3886, ⓦwww.thaiair.com.
United Airlines Australia ⓣ13 17 77, ⓦwww.unitedairlines.com.au, New Zealand ⓣ09/379 3800 or 0800/508 648.

Travel agents

Flight Centre Australia ⓣ13 31 33, ⓦwww.flightcentre.com.au, New Zealand ⓣ0800 243 544, ⓦwww.flightcentre.co.nz.
Holiday Shoppe New Zealand ⓣ0800/808 480, ⓦwww.holidayshoppe.co.nz.
STA Travel Australia ⓣ1300/733 035, ⓦwww.statravel.com.au, New Zealand ⓣ0508/782 872, ⓦwww.statravel.co.nz.
Student Uni Travel Australia ⓣ02/9232 8444, ⓦwww.sut.com.au, New Zealand ⓣ09/379 4224, ⓦwww.sut.com.nz.
Trailfinders Australia ⓣ02/9247 7666, ⓦwww.trailfinders.com.au.

Specialist agents

France Unlimited Australia ⓣ03/9531 8787. All French travel arrangements, including individually tailored châteaux stays and cycling tours.
French Travel Connection Australia ⓣ02/9966 1177, ⓦwww.frenchtravel.com.au. Everything to do with travel to and around France: accommodation, car hire, tours and even cooking classes.
Silke's Travel Australia ⓣ1800 807 860, or 02/8347 2000, ⓦwww.silkes.com.au. Gay and lesbian specialist travel agent.
Travel.com Australia ⓣ1300/130 482 or 02/9249 5444, ⓦwww.travel.com.au, New Zealand ⓣ0800/468 332, ⓦwww.travel.com.nz. Comprehensive online travel company.
Viatour Australia ⓣ02/8219 5400, ⓦwww.viator.com. Bookings for hundreds of travel suppliers worldwide, covering all regions of France.

Red tape and visas

Citizens of European Union (EU) countries can travel freely in France, while those from Australia, Canada, the United States and New Zealand do not need any sort of visa to enter the country, and can stay for up to ninety days. However, as the situation can change, it's advisable to check with your nearest French embassy or consulate before departure.

EU citizens (or other non-visa citizens) who stay **longer than three months** are officially supposed to apply for a *Carte de Séjour*, for which you'll have to show proof of – among other things – a regular income or sufficient funds to support yourself during your stay. However, EU passports are rarely stamped on entry, so there is no evidence of how long you've been in the country. If your passport does get stamped, you can cross the border – to Belgium, for example – and re-enter for another ninety days legitimately.

French embassies and consulates

Australia Embassy: 6 Perth Ave, Yarralumla ACT 2600 ⓣ02/6216 0100, ⓦwww.ambafrance-au.org/index.en.htm. Consulate: Level 26, St Martins Tower, 31 Market St, Sydney, NSW 2000 ⓣ02/9261 5779, ⓦwww.consulfrance-sydney.org.

Canada Embassy: 42 Promenade Sussex, Ottawa, ON K1M 2C9 ⓣ613/789 1795, ⓦwww.ambafrance-ca.org. Consulates: 777 Main St, Suite 800, Moncton, NB E1C 1E9 ⓣ506/857 4191, ⓦwww.consulfrance-moncton.org; 1 place Ville-Marie, Bureau 2601, Montréal, QC H3B 4S3 ⓣ514/878 4385, ⓦwww.consulfrance-montreal.org; 25 rue St-Louis, Québec, QC G1R 3Y8 ⓣ418/694 2294, ⓦwww.consulfrance-quebec.org; 130 Bloor St West, Suite 400, Toronto, ON M5S 1N5 ⓣ416/925 8041, ⓦwww.consulfrance-toronto.org; 1130 West Pender St, Suite 1100, Vancouver, BC V6E 4A4 ⓣ604/681 4345, ⓦwww.consulfrance-vancouver.org.

Ireland 36 Ailesbury Rd, Ballsbridge, Dublin 4 ⓣ01/277 5000, ⓦwww.ambafrance.ie.

New Zealand 34–42 Manners St, 12th Floor, PO Box 11–343, Wellington ⓣ04/384 2555, ⓦwww.ambafrance-nz.org.

UK Embassy: 58 Knightsbridge, London SW1X 7JT ⓣ020/7073 1000, ⓦwww.ambafrance-uk.org. Consulates: 21 Cromwell Road, London SW7 2EN ⓣ020/7073 1200, ⓦwww.consulfrance-londres.org; 21 Randolph Crescent, Edinburgh, EH3 7TT ⓣ0131/225 7954, ⓦwww.consulfrance-edimbourg.org.

USA Embassy: 4101 Reservoir Rd NW, Washington DC 20007 ⓣ202/944 6000, ⓦwww.ambafrance-us.org. Consulates: 3475 Piedmont Rd NE, Suite 1840, Atlanta, GA 30305 ⓣ404/495 1660, ⓦwww.consulfrance-atlanta.org; Park Square Building, Suite 750, 31 St James Ave, Boston, MA 02116 ⓣ617/542 7374, ⓦwww.consulfrance-boston.org; 205 North Michigan Ave, Suite 3700, Chicago, IL 60601 ⓣ312/327-5200, ⓦwww.consulfrance-chicago.org; 777 Post Oak Blvd, Suite 600, Houston, TX 77056 ⓣ713/572 2799, ⓦwww.consulfrance-houston.org; 10990 Wilshire Blvd, Suite 300, Los Angeles, CA 90024 ⓣ310/235 3200, ⓦwww.consulfrance-losangeles.org; Espirito Santo Plaza, Suite 1050, 1395 Brickell Ave, Miami, FL 33131 ⓣ305/372 9799, ⓦwww.consulfrance-miami.org; 1340 Poydras St, Amoco Building, Suite 1710, New Orleans, LA 70112 ⓣ504/523 5772, ⓦwww.consulfrance-nouvelleorleans.org; 934 Fifth Ave, New York, NY 10021 ⓣ212/606 3600, ⓦwww.consulfrance-newyork.org; 540 Bush St, San Francisco, CA 94108 ⓣ415/397 4330, ⓦwww.consulfrance-sanfrancisco.org.

Information, websites and maps

The French Government Tourist Office (Maison de la France, ⓦwww.franceguide.com) gives away large quantities of maps and glossy brochures covering Brittany and Normandy, including lists of hotels and campsites. Some of these, such as the maps of the inland waterways, and lists of festivals and campsites, can be quite useful; others use a lot of space to say very little.

In France itself you'll find a **tourist office** – known as the *Office du Tourisme* (OT) or *Syndicat d'Initiative* (SI) – in practically every town or even village (addresses and opening hours are detailed throughout this book). These supply free or inexpensive town plans, and local information such as listings of hotels, restaurants, leisure activities, bike rental and laundries. Many SIs also publish car and walking itineraries for their areas, while some conduct free town tours, and in addition most have their own websites, again listed wherever applicable throughout this book.

Websites

Information about practically every aspect of French culture and travel can now be picked up online, though many sites do not offer English translations. Many government agencies, including local tourist offices, have their own websites, and individual hotels too have come to realize the importance of an online presence. As anywhere on the Internet, persistent combing of links pages and use of **search engines** such as ⓦwww.google.com should help you find what you're looking for. Web or email addresses are given where available throughout this Guide, while a few of the more useful and well-established general sites are detailed here.

Travel advice

For the latest advice on travelling to and in France, consult the following government websites:

Australian Department of Foreign Affairs ⓦwww.dfat.gov.au.
British Foreign & Commonwealth Office ⓦwww.fco.gov.uk.
Canadian Department of Foreign Affairs ⓦwww.dfait-maeci.gc.ca.
Irish Department of Foreign Affairs ⓦwww.irlgov.ie/iveagh.
New Zealand Ministry of Foreign Affairs ⓦwww.mft.govt.nz.
US State Department ⓦhttp://travel.state.gov.

Tourism and recreation

Brittany Tourist Board ⓦwww.brittanytourism.com. High-tech English-language edition of the official Breton site. Unless you're careful, you're liable to stray into French-language areas, but everything is translated somewhere. Although it holds plenty of information on the region as a whole, its strongest feature is the easy search facility for local hotels.
CybeVasion ⓦwww.cybevasion.com. General travel-related French portal, bursting with connections to hotels, campsites, agencies, and operators throughout the country. You never quite know whether a link will take you anywhere worthwhile, but there's masses of stuff here. The detailed maps of each *département* in Brittany and Normandy are especially useful.
Maison de la France ⓦwww.franceguide.com. The English-language section of the French Government Tourist Office's website offers up-to-the-minute news and details of forthcoming events, and links to local and regional tourist offices, historic monuments and the like. The "Practical Information" section is packed with destination and transport information.
Monum ⓦwww.monum.fr. Site of the Centre des Monuments Nationaux. Good starting point for information on 200 national monuments and museums across France, including news on special events.
Normandy Tourist Board ⓦwww.normandy-tourism.org. The helpful, well-illustrated official site for tourism in Normandy covers all aspects of visiting the region.

French Government Tourist Offices

Australia Level 20, 25 Bligh St, Sydney, NSW 2000 ⓣ02/9231 5244, ⓔinfo.au@franceguide.com.
Canada 1981 Avenue McGill College, Suite 490, Montréal, QC H3A 2W9 ⓣ514/876 9881, ⓔcanada@franceguide.com.
Ireland 10 Suffolk St, Dublin ⓣ1560/235 235, ⓔinfo.ie@franceguide.com.
New Zealand contact the office in Australia.
UK 178 Piccadilly, London W1J 9AL ⓣ09068/244 123 (60p/min), ⓔinfo.uk@franceguide.com.
USA 9454 Wilshire Blvd, Suite 715, Beverly Hills, CA 90212 ⓣ310/271 6665, ⓔinfo.losangeles@franceguide.com; 1 Biscayne Tower, Suite 1750, 2 South Biscayne Blvd, Miami, FL 33131 ⓣ305/373 8177, info.miami@franceguide.com; 205 North Michigan Ave, Suite 3770, Chicago, IL 60601 ⓣ410/286-8310, info.chicago@franceguide.com; 444 Madison Ave, 16th Floor, New York, NY 10022 ⓣ410/286-8310, ⓔinfo.us@franceguide.com.

Regional tourist boards

Brittany

Brittany Tourist Board 1 rue Raoul Ponchon, 35069 Rennes Cedex ⓣ02.99.28.44.30.
La Maison de la Bretagne 203 bd St-Germain, 75007 Paris ⓣ01.53.63.11.50.

Normandy

Comité Régional du Tourisme de Normandie Le Doyenné, 14 rue Charles Courbeau, 27000 Évreux ⓣ02.32.33.79.00.
Normandy Tourist Board (UK Branch) 44 Bath Hill, Keynsham, Bristol BS31 1HG ⓣ0117/986 0386.

Departmental tourist offices

Each individual *département* in Brittany and Normandy has its own Comité Départemental du Tourisme, which can provide detailed information on its own region. All have their own websites.

Brittany

Côtes d'Armor 29 rue des Promenades, BP 4620, St Brieuc Cedex 22046 ⓣ02.96.62.72.00, ⓦwww.cotesdarmor.com.
Finistère 11 rue Théodore Le Hars, BP 1419, Quimper 29104 ⓣ02.98.76.20.70, ⓦwww.finisteretourisme.com.
Ille-et-Vilaine 4 rue J-Jaurès, BP 60146, Rennes Cedex 35060 ⓣ02.99.78.47.47, ⓦwww.bretagne35.com.
Morbihan Allée Nicolas Leblanc, Vannes 56010 ⓣ02.97.54.06.56, ⓦwww.morbihan.com.

Normandy

Calvados 8 rue Renoir, Caen Cedex 14054 ⓣ02.31.27.90.30, ⓦwww.cg14.fr.
Eure 3 rue du Commandent Letellier, BP 367, Évreux Cedex 27003 ⓣ02.32.62.04.27, ⓦwww.tourisme-eure.com.
Manche Maison du Département, Route de Villedieu, St Lô Cedex 50008 ⓣ02.33.05.98.70, ⓦwww.manchetourisme.com.
Orne 88 rue St Blaise, BP 50, Alençon 61002 ⓣ02.33.28.88.71, ⓦwww.ornetourisme.com.
Seine Maritime 6 rue Couronné, BP 60, Bihorel les Rouen 76420 ⓣ02.35.12.10.10, ⓦwww.seine-maritime-tourisme.com.

Tourisme.fr ⓦwww.tourisme.fr. Handy database of France's municipal and local tourist offices arranged by *région* and *département* (click on "Discover your destination"), plus plenty of other information for a trip to France. A good complement to the Maison de la France site.

News and information

Bretagne.com ⓦwww.brittany-bretagne.com. The English-language section of this specialist Brittany site, run by *Le Télégramme* newspaper among others and featuring up-to-the-minute listings and news, offers a large searchable directory of English-language websites relevant to the region.
Encyclopaedia Britannica D-Day ⓦhttp://search.eb.com/normandy. Copious and absorbing multimedia site dedicated to retelling the story of the D-Day invasions in gripping detail, with special reference to the movie *Saving Private Ryan*.
France 2 ⓦwww.france2.fr. The latest news, weather, and road conditions, as well as cinema listings and the like, from the France 2 TV channel. In French only.
Governments on the Web ⓦwww.gksoft.com/govt/en/fr.html. English-language portal site listing all French government websites, including embassies, departmental and regional authorities, political parties and state media.
Le Monde ⓦwww.lemonde.fr. The online version of one of France's most reputable daily newspapers. Includes national and international news, culture and sports – all in French.
Radio France ⓦwww.radio-france.fr. National and international news coverage, current affairs, as well as music and culture. French language only.

Arts and culture

Breizh.net ⓦwww.breizh.net. A true labour of love, written in Breton, but with French and English translations, and offering excellent sections on learning the language and Breton music.
Bretagnenet ⓦwww.bretagnenet.com. The largest Breton portal hosts an enormous array of websites that cover all aspects of regional culture.
Festivalissimo ⓦwww.festivalissimo.com. Now in English, this is the single best site for information on festivals. You can search by date, theme or location.
IRMA (Information et Ressources pour les Musiques Actuelles) ⓦwww.irma.asso.fr. The French music industry's promotional organization provides information and links to groups representing every genre and style. In French only.
Ministry of Culture ⓦhttp://web.culture.fr. Information (in French) on cultural events and a comprehensive list of links to organizations related to the whole gamut of artistic media.
Via France ⓦwww.viafrance.com. Bilingual events database (including exhibitions, festivals, music and sports) organized by category and region.

Maps

Though their town maps are often very good, tourist office handouts rarely contain usable regional maps. To supplement them – and the maps in this guide – you will probably want a reasonable **road map**. Rough Guides offers its own very detailed map of Brittany (ⓦwww.roughguides.com/store/details.html?ProductID=488), printed on waterproof and rip-proof paper. Otherwise, the *Michelin* 1:200,000 area maps of Brittany (230) and Normandy (231) are more than adequate for driving and other purposes. Virtually every road they show is passable by any car, and those that are tinged in green are usually reliable as "scenic routes".

A useful free map for car drivers, obtainable from filling stations and traffic information kiosks in France, is the *Bison Futé*, showing alternative back routes to avoid the congested main roads, which are clearly signposted on the ground by special green Bison Futé road signs.

If you're planning to **walk or cycle**, check the *IGN* maps – either the green (1:100,000 and 1:50,000) or the more detailed purple (1:25,000) series. The *IGN* 1:100,000 is the smallest scale available with contours marked, though the bizarre colour scheme makes it hard to read. *Michelin* maps have little arrows to indicate steep slopes, which is all the information most cyclists will need.

Anyone planning to visit the battlefields of northern France will find Major and Mrs Holt's *Battle Map Series* invaluable (ⓣ01293/455300), ⓦwww.battletours.co.uk).

Map outlets

UK and Ireland

Blackwell's Map Centre 50 Broad St, Oxford, OX1 3BQ ⓣ01865/793 550, ⓦhttp://maps.blackwell.co.uk. Branches in Bristol, Cambridge, Cardiff, Leeds, Liverpool, Newcastle, Reading and Sheffield.
The Map Shop 30a Belvoir St, Leicester LE1 6QH ⓣ0116/247 1400, ⓦwww.mapshopleicester.co.uk.

National Map Centre 22–24 Caxton St, London SW1H 0QU ⓣ020/7222 2466, ⓦwww.mapsnmc.co.uk.
National Map Centre Ireland 34 Aungier St, Dublin ⓣ01/476 0471, ⓦwww.mapcentre.ie.
Stanfords 12–14 Long Acre, London, WC2E 9LP. ⓣ020/7836 1321, ⓦwww.stanfords.co.uk. Also at 39 Spring Gardens, Manchester ⓣ0161/831 0250, and 29 Corn St, Bristol ⓣ0117/929 9966.
The Travel Bookshop 13–15 Blenheim Crescent, London W11 2EE ⓣ020/7229 5260, ⓦwww.thetravelbookshop.co.uk.
Traveller 55 Grey St, Newcastle-upon-Tyne NE1 6EF ⓣ0191/261 5622, ⓦwww.newtraveller.com.

US and Canada

110 North Latitude US ⓣ336/369-4171, ⓦwww.110nlatitude.com.
Book Passage 51 Tamal Vista Blvd, Corte Madera, CA 94925 and in the historic San Francisco Ferry Building ⓣ1-800/999-7909 or ⓣ415/927-0960, ⓦwww.bookpassage.com.
Distant Lands 56 S Raymond Ave, Pasadena, CA 91105 ⓣ1-800/310-3220, ⓦwww.distantlands.com.
Globe Corner Bookstore 28 Church St, Cambridge, MA 02138 ⓣ1-800/358-6013, ⓦwww.globercorner.com.
Longitude Books 115 W 30th St #1206, New York, NY 10001 ⓣ1-800/342-2164, ⓦwww.longitudebooks.com.
Map Link 30 S La Patera Lane, Unit 5, Santa Barbara, CA 93117 ⓣ1-800/962-1394 or 805/692-6777, ⓦwww.maplink.com. Has a useful list of specialist map/travel bookstores in every US state, as well as some worldwide; click on Retail Partners.
Map Town 400 5 Ave SW #100, Calgary, AB, T2P 0L6 ⓣ1-877/921-6277 or ⓣ403/266-2241, ⓦwww.maptown.com.
Travel Bug Bookstore 3065 W Broadway, Vancouver, BC V6K 269 ⓣ604/737-1122, ⓦwww.travelbugbooks.ca.
World of Maps 1235 Wellington St, Ottawa, ON K1Y 3A3 ⓣ1-800/214-8524 or 613/724-6776, ⓦwww.worldofmaps.com.

Australia and New Zealand

Map Shop 6–10 Peel St, Adelaide ⓣ08/8231 2033, ⓦwww.mapshop.net.au.
Map World (Australia) 371 Pitt St, Sydney ⓣ02/9261 3601, ⓦwww.mapworld.net.au. Also at 900 Hay St, Perth ⓣ08/9322 5733, Jolimont Centre, Canberra ⓣ02/6230 4097 and 1981 Logan Road, Brisbane ⓣ07/3349 6633.
MapWorld (New Zealand) 173 Gloucester St, Christchurch ⓣ0800/627 967, ⓦwww.mapworld.co.nz.
Mapland 372 Little Bourke St, Melbourne ⓣ03/9670 4383, ⓦwww.mapland.com.au.

Insurance

Even EU citizens, who are entitled to health care privileges in France, would do well to take out an insurance policy before travelling to cover against theft, loss and illness or injury. Before paying for a new policy, however, check whether you are already covered: some all-risks home insurance policies may cover your possessions when overseas, and many private medical schemes include cover when abroad. In Canada, provincial health plans usually provide partial cover for medical mishaps overseas, while holders of official student/teacher/youth cards in Canada and the US are entitled to meagre accident coverage and hospital in-patient benefits. Health coverage for North American students often extends during the vacations and for one term beyond the date of last enrolment.

After exhausting these possibilities, contact a specialist travel insurance company, or consider Rough Guides' own travel insurance (see opposite). A **typical travel insurance policy** usually provides cover for the loss of baggage, tickets and – up to a cer-

Rough Guides travel insurance

Rough Guides Ltd offers a low-cost **travel insurance policy**, especially customized for our statistically low-risk readers by a leading British broker, provided by the American International Group (AIG) and registered with the British regulatory body, GISC (the General Insurance Standards Council).

There are five main Rough Guides insurance plans: **No Frills** for the bare minimum for secure travel; **Essential**, which provides decent all-round cover; **Premier** for comprehensive cover with a wide range of benefits; **Extended Stay** for cover lasting four months to a year; and **Annual Multi-Trip**, a cost-effective way of getting Premier cover if you travel more than once a year. Premier, Annual Multi-Trip and Extended Stay policies can be supplemented by a "Hazardous Pursuits Extension" if you plan to indulge in sports considered dangerous, such as scuba diving or trekking.

Call the Rough Guides Insurance line on UK freefone ⓣ08001 015 0906, or get an online policy quote at www.roughguides.com/insurance.

tain limit – cash or cheques, as well as cancellation or curtailment of your journey. Most of them exclude so-called dangerous sports unless an extra premium is paid. Many policies can be chopped and changed to exclude coverage you don't need.

If you take **medical coverage**, ascertain whether benefits will be paid as treatment proceeds or only after return home, and whether there is a 24-hour medical emergency number. When securing baggage cover, make sure that the per-article limit – typically under £500 and sometimes as little as £250 – will cover your most valuable possession. If you need to make a **claim**, keep receipts for medicines and medical treatment, and in the event you have anything stolen, you must obtain an official statement from the police (called a *constat de vol*).

Health

No visitor to France requires vaccinations of any kind, and general health care in the country is of the highest standard. Citizens of all EU and Scandinavian countries are entitled to take advantage of French health services under the same terms as residents, providing they carry the correct documentation. British citizens need form E111, available in the UK from post offices or downloadable from the UK Department of Health website (ⓦwww.dh.gov.uk), or in France from offices of the health authorities, the Caisse Primaire d'Assurance Maladie (CPAM). The E111 is due to be replaced by a new European Health Insurance card during the course of 2005; see the website above for details. North American and other non-EU citizens have to pay for most medical attention and are strongly advised to take out some form of medical insurance (see above).

Under the French health system, every hospital visit, doctor's consultation, prescribed medicine and even ambulance call-out incurs a charge, which you have to pay upfront. EU citizens carrying the correct documents are entitled to a partial refund (usually between 70 and 100 percent) of any medical and dental expenses they incur, providing the doctor is government registered (a *médecin conventionné*). This can still leave a hefty shortfall, however, especially after a stay in hospital.

For minor complaints go to a **pharmacie**, signalled by an illuminated green cross. You'll find at least one in every small town and even some villages. They keep normal shop hours (roughly 9am–noon & 3–6pm), though some stay open late and, in larger towns, at least one (known as the *pharmacie de garde*) is open 24 hours according to a rota; details are displayed in all pharmacy windows.

For anything more serious you can get the name of a **doctor** from a pharmacy, local police station, tourist office or your hotel. Alternatively, look under "Médecins" in the Yellow Pages of the phone directory. The average consultation fee is €20–25. You'll be given a *Feuille de Soins* (Statement of Treatment) for later insurance claims. Any prescriptions will be fulfilled by the pharmacy and must be paid for; little price stickers (*vignettes*) from each medicine will be stuck on another *Feuille de Soins*.

In **emergencies** you will always be admitted to the nearest general **hospital** (Centre Hospitalier), whether you arrive under your own power or by ambulance. The national number for calling an ambulance is ⓣ15.

Costs, money and banks

Although the changeover to the euro saw a fair amount of "rounding up" of prices, Brittany and Normandy are not, on the whole, expensive places to visit. Distances (and transport costs) are relatively small; the price of food and accommodation is consistently lower than in Britain and much of northern Europe; and access is straightforward.

On a shoestring level, camping and eating at least one picnic meal a day, taking buses or cycling, two people travelling together could get by easily enough on €50 (£33 per person per day. Moving slightly more upmarket, staying in modest hotels, spending a bit on restaurants and driving, you should reckon on around €80 (£53) per person per day.

Accommodation is likely to represent the bulk of your expenditure. Hotels average around €35 for the simplest double room in the cheapest places (note that in this book all hotels are given price codes, as explained on p.43). If you're sharing, that works out at little more per person than the €10–20 per person charged by hostels. **Camping**, of course, can cut costs dramatically, so long as you avoid the plusher private sites; the local *Camping municipal* rarely asks for more than €6 a head.

Eating out is the real bargain. You should always be able to find a good three-course meal for around €15, or a takeaway for a lot less (though crêperies seldom work out as cheap as they might appear). Fresh food from shops and markets is surprisingly expensive in relation to low restaurant prices, but it's always possible to save money with a basic picnic of bread, cheese and fruit. More sophisticated meals – takeaway salads and ready-to-heat dishes – can be put together for reasonable prices if you shop at charcuteries (delis) and the equivalent counters of many supermarkets. On the other hand, **drinks** in cafés and bars can make a severe hole in your pocket. Nowhere in the region matches Paris prices, but €5 cups of coffee are not unheard of, and a cognac costs double that; you have to accept that you're paying for somewhere to sit. Note, however, that drink prices in most cafés are lower when ordering and drinking at the bar as opposed to occupying a table and being served by a waiter.

Transport costs obviously depend entirely on how (and how much) you travel. Bikes cost nothing if you bring them, or up to around €15 per day if you rent them. Trains and buses normally operate on a fixed tariff of a maximum of €0.09 per kilometre, and there are no savings to be made by buying a return ticket instead of two one-ways. Petrol prices have been rising steadily; at the time of writing they were around €1.07 a litre for unleaded (*sans plomb*), €1.29 a litre for super and €0.90 a litre for diesel; there are 3.8 litres to the US gallon, which makes it about €3.50 per gallon.

As for sites and museums, admission charges can be high enough to make you picky as to what you visit – even with a student card to soften the blow (many museums have reduced admission for all under-26s, and not just students). But this is no special hardship: the region's attractions lie as much in its towns and landscapes as in anything fenced off or put in a showcase.

Currency

France was one of the twelve European Union countries that changed over to a single currency, the **euro** (€), in January 2002. The euro is divided into 100 cents (often referred to in France as *centimes*). There are seven euro notes – in denominations of 500, 200, 100, 50, 20, 10, and 5 euros, each a different colour and size – and eight different coin denominations, including 2 and 1 euros, then 50, 20, 10, 5, 2, and 1 cents. Euro coins feature a common EU design on one face, but different country-specific designs on the other. No matter what the design, all euro coins and notes can be used in any of the twelve member states which have adopted the euro (Austria, Belgium, Finland, France, Germany, Greece, Ireland, Italy, Luxembourg, Portugal, Spain and The Netherlands).

At the time of writing, the exchange rate hovered around €1.50 to the pound, €0.80 to the US dollar, €0.60 to the Canadian and the Australian dollar, and €0.50 to the New Zealand dollar. For up-to-date exchange rates, consult the currency converter website Ⓦwww.oanda.com.

Banks and exchange

While banks in Paris are typically open from Monday to Friday and closed at the weekend, elsewhere in France many banks close on Mondays, but are open on Saturdays. Standard **banking hours** are 9am to 4pm or 5pm during the week (some close at lunchtime – noon/12.30pm–2/2.30pm) and 9am to noon on Saturdays; all are closed on Sunday and public holidays. They will have a notice on the door if they exchange currency. **Rates and commission** vary from bank to bank, so it's worth shopping around; the usual procedure is a 1–2 percent commission on travellers' cheques and a flat rate charge on cash. Be wary of banks claiming to charge no commission at all; often they are merely adjusting the exchange rate to their own advantage.

There are **money-exchange** counters (*bureaux de change*) at the airports and at the train stations of all the larger towns, with usually one or two in town centres as well, often keeping much longer hours than the high-street banks.

Plastic cards and travellers' cheques

By far the easiest way to handle your money while visiting France is to use plastic. You will usually be able to use your debit card – especially if it bears the symbol of the Cirrus, Plus or Link networks – to withdraw money from French **ATM machines**, which are every bit as ubiquitous as in Britain or North America. Check with your bank before you leave home if you're in any doubt.

Similarly, all major **credit cards** are almost universally accepted in hotels, restaurants and shops, usually for a minimum purchase of around €15, though small-scale local businesses such as B&Bs or snack bars may well prefer cash. Visa – often called Carte Bleue in France – is almost universally recognized, followed by MasterCard (also known as EuroCard). American Express ranks a bit lower. Remember, however, that all cash advances using credit cards are treated as loans, with interest accruing daily from the date of withdrawal; there may be a transaction fee on top of this.

It's worth noting that many French credit cards incorporate a microchip (*puce*) that contains security information. British, American, Australasian and other cards with no such strip are sometimes rejected by card-reading machines in French shops and restaurants. French tourist authorities recommend that travellers who experience difficulties should say (or show) the following words to the retailer:

"les cartes anglaises ne sont pas des cartes à puce, mais à bande magnétique. Ma carte est valable et je vous serais reconnaissant d'en demander la confirmation auprès de votre banque ou de votre centre de traitement."

Though convenient, it's obviously not a wise idea to rely on a single ATM or credit card as your sole source of money on a long trip far from home – a lost, stolen or malfunctioning card leaves you with nothing. For that reason, it's always worth carrying some form of backup. Obtaining some euros in advance, whether from your local bank or simply at the air- or ferry port as you travel, is always worthwhile, and you may also prefer to bring some **travellers' cheques**, which are available from almost any major bank. The most widely recognized brands are Visa, Thomas Cook and American Express, which most banks will change.

In the event that cheques are lost or stolen, most companies claim to be able to replace them within 24 hours. Call the following 24-hour numbers to report your loss: American Express ☎08.00.90.86.00; Diners' Club ☎08.10.31.41.59; MasterCard ☎08.00.90.13.87; Visa ☎08.00.90.43.49.

Getting around

The best way to travel around Brittany and Normandy is with a car or a bike. Public transport is not very impressive. SNCF trains are efficient, as ever in France, and the Atlantique TGV has reduced the Paris–Rennes journey to a mere two hours fifteen minutes, but the rail network circles the coast and, especially in Brittany, barely serves the inland areas.

Buses do complement the trains to some extent – SNCF buses often pick up routes that the trains no longer follow – but on the whole their timetables are geared much more to market, school or working hours than to meeting the needs of tourists, and it can take a very long time indeed to get where you want to go. If you come without your own transport, the ideal solution is to make longer journeys by train or bus, then to rent a bike (never a problem) to explore a particular locality.

Approximate journey times and frequencies for trains, buses and boats can be found under "Travel details" at the end of each chapter in this book; local peculiarities are also pointed out in the text.

Driving

Travelling by car has its disadvantages: the expense, most obviously, but also the strong likelihood of reducing your contact with people. However, you do gain freedom of movement and, especially if you're camping, you can be a lot more self-sufficient.

Car rental in France costs upwards of €250 per week (from around €90 a day); few British travellers tend to see it as an economic alternative to bringing their own vehicle across the Channel. However, the major international rental chains are found

Road information

For information on traffic and road conditions on autoroutes throughout France, ring the multilingual service Autoroutel (☎08.92.68.10.77, €0.34/min), tune in to FM 107.7 or consult Ⓦwww.autoroutes.fr. Traffic information for non-motorway routes can be obtained 24 hours a day at ☎08.26.02.20.22 (French only).

throughout the region, including at the ferry ports. Note that booking online, either through the websites of the major chains (see below) or dedicated car rental sites such as Ⓦwww.auto-europe.co.uk, is usually much cheaper than renting on the spot.

North Americans and Australians in particular should be forewarned that it is very difficult to rent a car with **automatic transmission**; if you can't drive a stickshift, you should try to book an automatic well in advance, possibly before you leave home, and be prepared to pay a much higher price for it. Most rental companies will only rent cars to customers aged under 25 on payment of a young driver surcharge of around €20–23 per day; you still must be over 21 and have driven for at least one year. OTU Voyage (☎08.20.81.78.17, €0.12/min, Ⓦwww.otu.fr), the student travel agency, can arrange car rental for young drivers, with prices beginning at €129 for a weekend.

Petrol/gas (*essence*) or diesel fuel (*gazoil*) is least expensive at out-of-town superstores, and most expensive on the autoroutes. At night, when some stations are unmanned, you might only be able to pay for petrol using a French credit card. Typical fuel prices as this book went to press were around €1.07 a litre for unleaded (*sans plomb*), €1.29 for four-star (*Super*) and €0.90 for diesel. Be warned, it can be difficult to purchase petrol at night as some petrol stations will only accept automatic payment by French credit card.

Autoroute driving, if fast, is boring when it's not hair-raising, and the tolls in Normandy are expensive. The helpful *Bison Futé* map, free from service stations, details lesser-known routes to steer clear of the crowds – invaluable for avoiding the endless traffic jams over the weekends between July 15 and August 15.

If you run into **mechanical difficulties**, all the major car manufacturers have garages and service stations in France. You can find them in the Yellow Pages (*Pages Jaunes*) of the phone book under "Garages d'automobiles". For breakdowns, look under "Dépannages". If you have an accident or break-in, you should make a report to the local police (and keep a copy) in order to make an insurance claim. In case of a breakdown on the motorway, there are orange emergency telephones every 2km. The government-regulated charge for either on-the-spot repairs (up to 30 minutes) or a towing service is €68.60.

For motoring vocabulary, see Language on p.455.

Car rental agencies

UK

Avis ☎0870/606 0100, Ⓦwww.avis.co.uk.
Budget ☎01442/276 266, Ⓦwww.budget.co.uk.
Europcar ☎0870/607 5000, Ⓦwww.europcar.co.uk.
Hertz ☎0870/844 8844, Ⓦwww.hertz.co.uk.
Holiday Autos ☎0870/400 00 99, Ⓦwww.holidayautos.co.uk.
National ☎0870/5365 365, Ⓦwww.nationalcar.co.uk.
Suncars ☎0870/500 5566, Ⓦwww.suncars.com.
Thrifty ☎01494/751 600, Ⓦwww.thrifty.co.uk.

Ireland

Argus ☎01/490 4444, Ⓦwww.argus-rentacar.com.
Avis ☎021/428 1111, Ⓦwww.avis.co.uk, Northern Ireland ☎028/9024 0404.
Budget ☎09/0662 7711, Ⓦwww.budget.ie.
Cosmo Thrifty Northern Ireland ☎028/9445 2565, Ⓦwww.thrifty.co.uk.
Europcar ☎01/614 2888, Ⓦwww.europcar.ie, Northern Ireland ☎028/9442 3444.
Hertz ☎01/676 7476, Ⓦwww.hertz.ie.
Holiday Autos ☎01/872 9366, Ⓦwww.holidayautos.ie.
SIXT ☎1850/206 088, Ⓦwww.irishcarrentals.ie.

North America

Alamo US ☎1-800/462-5266, Ⓦwww.alamo.com.
Auto Europe US & Canada ☎1-888/223-5555, Ⓦwww.autoeurope.com.

Avis US ⓣ1-800/230-4898, Canada ⓣ1-800/272-5871, ⓦwww.avis.com.
Budget US ⓣ1-800/527-0700, Canada ⓣ1-800/472-3325, ⓦwww.budget.com.
Europe by Car US ⓣ1-800/223-1516, ⓦwww.europebycar.com.
Hertz US ⓣ1-800/654-3131, Canada ⓣ1-800/263-0600, ⓦwww.hertz.com.
Kemwel Holiday Autos US ⓣ1-877/820-0668, ⓦwww.kemwel.com.
National ⓣ1-800/962-7070, ⓦwww.nationalcar.com.
Thrifty US & Canada ⓣ1-800/847-4389, ⓦwww.thrifty.com.

Australia

Avis ⓣ13 63 33 or 02/9353 9000, ⓦwww.avis.com.au.
Budget ⓣ1300/362 848, ⓦwww.budget.com.au.
Hertz ⓣ13 30 39 or 03/9698 2555, ⓦwww.hertz.com.au.
National ⓣ13 10 45, ⓦwww.nationalcar.com.au.
Thrifty ⓣ1300/367 227, ⓦwww.thrifty.com.au.

New Zealand

Apex ⓣ0800/93 95 97 or 03/379 6897, ⓦwww.apexrentals.co.nz.
Avis ⓣ0800/655 111 or 09/526 2847, ⓦwww.avis.co.nz.
Budget ⓣ0800/652 227 or 09/976 2222, ⓦwww.budget.co.nz.
Hertz ⓣ0800/654 321, ⓦwww.hertz.co.nz.
National ⓣ0800/800 115 or 03/366 5574, ⓦwww.nationalcar.co.nz.
Thrifty ⓣ09/309 0111, ⓦwww.thrifty.co.nz.

Motoring organizations

UK and Ireland

RAC UK ⓣ0800/55 00 55, ⓦwww.rac.co.uk.
AA UK ⓣ0800/44 45 00, ⓦwww.theaa.co.uk.
AA Ireland ⓣ01/617 9988, ⓦwww.aaireland.ie.

North America

AAA ⓣ1-800/222-4357, ⓦwww.aaa.com.
CAA ⓣ613/247-0117, ⓦwww.caa.ca.

Australia and New Zealand

AAA Australia ⓣ02/6247 7311, ⓦwww.aaa.asn.au.
AA New Zealand ⓣ09/377 4660, ⓦwww.aa.co.nz.

Legal requirements

British, Irish, Australian, Canadian, New Zealand and US **driving licences** are valid in France, though an International Driver's Licence makes life easier. If the vehicle is rented, its registration document (*carte grise*) and the insurance papers must be carried. The **minimum driving age** is 18, and provisional licences are not valid.

The vehicle registration document and the **insurance papers** must be carried; only the originals are acceptable. It's no longer essential for motorists from other EU countries to buy a green card to extend their usual insurance. If you have insurance at home then you have the minimal legal coverage in France; whether you have any more than that, and (if not) whether you want to buy more, is something to discuss with your own insurance company, so check to see what they recommend.

If your car is right-hand drive, you must have your **headlight dip** adjusted to the right before you go and as a courtesy change or paint them to yellow or stick on black glare deflectors. Shops at the ferry terminals sell special headlight deflectors which achieve both aims – you basically pay £6 for two small pieces of sticky yellow plastic, but they do the job.

Similarly, you must also affix **GB plates** if you're driving a British car, and carry a red warning triangle and a spare set of headlight bulbs in your vehicle.

Seat belts are compulsory for the driver and all passengers, and children under 10 can only sit in the front seat if they're in approved rear-facing child seats.

Rules of the road

The main rule of the road to remember in France is that the French **drive on the right**. Most drivers used to driving on the left find it easy to adjust. The biggest problem tends to be visibility when you want to overtake; it's possible to buy special forward-view mirrors that may help.

The law of *priorité à droite* – which says you have to give way to traffic coming from your right, even when it is coming from a minor road – is being phased out, having long been a major cause of accidents. However, it still applies on some roads in built-up areas, so it pays to be vigilant at junctions. A sign showing a yellow diamond on a white background indicates that you have **right of way**, while the same sign with an oblique black slash warns you that vehicles emerging from the right have priority. **Stop signs** mean stop completely; *Cédez le passage* means "Give way". Other signs warning of potential dangers include *déviation* (diversion), *gravillons* (loose chippings), *boue* (mud) and *chaussée déformée* (uneven surface).

The main French national **speed limits**, which apply unless otherwise posted, are 130kph (80mph) on the tolled autoroutes; 110kph (68mph) on dual carriageways; and 90kph (56mph) on other roads. In wet weather, and for drivers with less than two years' experience, these limits are 110kph (68mph), 100kph (62mph), and 80kph (50mph) respectively. There's also a ceiling of 50kph (31mph) in towns and on autoroutes when fog reduces visibility to less than 50m. There are increasingly stiff **penalties** for driving violations, which can mean fines of up to €4500 in the most serious cases. You will have to go to court for exceeding the speed limit by anything above 30kph, with maximum fines of €135 (30kph), €750 (40kph) and €1500 (50kph). The legal **blood alcohol limit** is 0.05 percent (0.5 grams per litre, which is lower than in the UK and North America), and random breath tests are becoming increasingly common.

Moped and motorbike rental

Mopeds and scooters are relatively easy to find: everyone in France, from young kids to grandmas, seems to ride one, and, although they're not built for any kind of long-distance travel, they're ideal for shooting around town and nearby. Places which rent out bicycles will often also rent out mopeds; you can expect to pay around €30 a day for a 50cc Suzuki, for example. No licence is needed for 50cc-and-under bikes (built not to exceed 45kph), but for anything larger you'll need a valid **motorbike licence**. Rental **prices** are around €55 for a 125cc; also expect to leave a hefty **deposit** by cash or credit card – over €1000 is not unusual. **Crash helmets** are compulsory on all mopeds and motorbikes, and the headlight must be switched on at all times.

Trains

French trains, operated by the nationally owned SNCF (Société National des Chemins de Fer), are by and large clean, fast and frequent, and their staff both courteous and helpful. **For national train information**, you can either phone (Ⓣ08.92.35.35.35 from abroad or Ⓣ36.35 in France; €0.34 per minute) or check on the Internet at Ⓦwww.sncf.fr. All but the smallest stations (*gares SNCF*) have an information desk, while many in larger towns operate some form of **left-luggage service**, or provide lockers (*consignes automatiques*). Some also rent out bicycles.

Fares are reasonable, with children under 12 travelling half-price, and under-4s free. The ultra-fast **TGVs** (*Trains à Grande Vitesse*) require a supplement at peak times and a compulsory reservation charge (included in the ticket price). The slowest trains are those marked *Autotrain* in the timetable, stopping at all stations.

Try to use the counter service for buying **tickets**, rather than the complicated computerized system; the latter changes the price of TGV tickets depending on the demand, and you may find you've bought an expensive ticket without realizing that a later train is cheaper.

All tickets – but not passes – must be date-stamped in the orange machines at station platform entrances. It is an offence not to follow the instruction to *Compostez votre billet* ("Validate your ticket"). Train journeys may be broken for up to 24 hours at a time for as long as the ticket is valid (usually two months); if you plan longer stopovers, it's best to indicate this when buying your ticket.

Regional **rail maps** and complete **timetables** are on sale at tobacconist shops (*tabacs*). Leaflet timetables for individual lines are available free at stations. "Autocar" at the top of a column means it's an SNCF bus service, on which train tickets and passes are valid.

For details on taking your **bicycle** by train, see p.41.

Discounts and rail passes

Anyone intending simply to visit Brittany and Normandy – or even to explore all of France – is very unlikely to make enough train journeys for it to be worth purchasing a Europe-wide rail pass. Within France, however, SNCF itself offers a range of **train passes**, which can be purchased online (Ⓦwww.voyages-sncf.com), through most travel agents in France, or from main *gares SNCF*, and are valid for one year. Over-60s can get the Carte Senior, which costs €50 and offers up to 50 percent off tickets on TGVs, subject to availability, or other journeys starting in blue periods *(période bleue)*, a 25 percent reduction on white period *(période bleue)* journeys, as well as a 25 percent reduction on through international journeys involving most countries in western and central Europe. The same percentage reductions are available for under-26s with a Carte 12–25 pass, which costs €49. Under-12s can obtain the same advantages for themselves and up to four travelling companions of any age by purchasing the Carte Enfant Plus (€65).

In addition, the SNCF offers a whole range of **discounted fares** within France on standard rail prices on *période bleue* and *période blanche* days, depending on exactly when you want to travel. A leaflet showing the precise calendar is given out at *gares SNCF*. Any two people travelling together, or a small group of up to nine people – whether a married couple, friends, family, whatever – are entitled to a 25 percent discount on return tickets on TGVs, subject to availability, or on other trains if they start their journey during a blue period. This fare is known as a Découverte à Deux; the same reduction applies to a group of up to four people travelling with a child under 12 (Découverte Enfant Plus), to under-26-year-olds (Découverte 12–25), over-60s (Découverte Senior), and for anyone who books a return journey of at least 200km in distance, including a Saturday night away (Découverte Séjour). Two types of ticket which you can only purchase online can save you more than 50 per cent on regular fares. With a Prem's ticket, which must be bought two weeks in advance, you can get a one-way ticket from Cherbourg to Paris for €20 and from Rennes to Paris for €30, for example. Once paid for, you can print the ticket from the Internet and board the train with it and valid ID. Meanwhile, the *Offres de dernière minute* (last minute offers) are published each Tuesday on the SNCF website and likewise represent considerable savings. Both of these types of tickets are non-refundable and changes are not allowed.

Buses

Buses cover far more Breton and Norman routes than the trains – and even when towns do have a rail link buses are often quicker, cheaper and more direct. They are almost always short distance, however, requiring you to change if you're going further than from one town to the next. And **timetables** tend to be constructed to suit working, market and school hours – often dauntingly early when they do run, and prone to stop just when tourists need them most, becoming virtually nonexistent on Sundays.

Larger towns usually have a central *gare routière* (bus station), most often found next to the *gare SNCF*; *gare routières* either have their own dedicated phone line or are contactable through the major bus operator in the area – all numbers are given in the text. However, the private bus companies (who provide most of the Breton services) don't always work together and you'll frequently find them leaving from an array of different points. The most convenient lines are those run as an extension of rail links by SNCF; these always run to/from the SNCF station (assuming there is one).

Cycling

Bicycles have high status in France. The car ferries and SNCF trains carry them for a minimal charge, and the French (Parisians excepted) respect cyclists – both as traffic, and, when you stop off at a restaurant or hotel, as customers. French drivers normally go out of their way to make room for you; it's the great British caravan you might have to watch out for.

Most importantly, however, **distances** in Brittany and Normandy are not great, the hills are sporadic and not too steep, cities like Rennes and Nantes have useful networks of **cycle lanes**, and the scenery is nearly always a delight. Even if you're quite unused to it, cycling sixty kilometres per day soon becomes very easy – and it's a good way of keeping yourself fit enough to enjoy the rich regional food.

These days most cyclists seem to use **mountain bikes**, which the French call VTTs (*Vélos Touts Terrains*), for touring holidays, although if you've ever made a direct comparison you'll know it's much less effort, and much quicker, to cycle long distances and carry luggage on a traditional touring or racing bike. Whichever you prefer, do use cycle panniers; a backpack in the sun is unbearable.

Restaurants and hotels along the way are nearly always obliging about looking after your bike, even to the point of allowing it into your room. Most large towns have well-stocked retail and **repair shops**, where parts are normally cheaper than in Britain or the US. However, if you're using a foreign-made bike, it's a good idea to carry spare tyres, as French sizes are different. Neither is it easy to find parts for mountain bikes, the French enthusiasm being directed towards racers instead. Inner tubes are not a problem, as they adapt to either size, though you should always be sure that you get the right valves. The best places to find foreign parts are in Raleigh stockists – at Rouen, Rennes and scattered around both provinces.

SNCF run various **schemes for cyclists**, all of them covered in the free leaflet *Guide du Train et du Vélo*, available from most stations. Trains marked with a bicycle in the timetable, and certain TGVs, allow you to take a bike as free accompanied luggage. Otherwise, you can take your dismantled bike, packed in a carrier, on TGVs and other trains with sufficiently large luggage racks. Another option is to send your bike parcelled up as **registered luggage** for a fee of €33.30; delivery should take two days, bearing in mind that the service doesn't operate at weekends. **Eurostar** allows you to take your bicycle as part of your baggage allowance provided it's dismantled and stored in a special bike bag, and the dimensions don't exceed 120cm by 90cm. Otherwise it needs to be sent on unaccompanied, with a guaranteed arrival of 24 hours (you can register it up to ten days in advance; book through Esprit Europe ⓣ08705/850 850); the fee is £20 one-way. **Ferries** either take bikes free (though you must remember to register it) or charge a maximum of £5 one-way, while **airlines** such as British Airways and Air France also carry bikes free – contact the airlines first however.

Bikes are often available to **rent** from campsites and hostels, as well as from specialist cycle shops, some tourist offices and train stations, and from seasonal stalls on islands such as Belle-Île and Ouessant, from around €10 to €15 per day. Bikes are seldom insured, however, and you will be presented with the bill for its replacement if it's stolen or damaged. Check whether your **travel insurance policy** covers you for this if you intend to rent a bike.

For advice on which **maps** to take, see p.31. In the UK, the Cyclists' Touring Club (ⓣ0870/873 0060, ⓦwww.ctc.org.uk), will suggest routes and supply advice for members (£30.50 a year or £18.50 for unemployed, and £11 for under 26 years). They run a particularly good insurance scheme. Companies running specialist bike touring holidays are listed on p.25.

For cycling vocabulary, see Language on p.456.

Boat trips and inland waterways

Boat trips on many of Brittany and Normandy's rivers, as well as out to the islands, are detailed throughout this book. More excitingly, you can **rent a canoe**, **boat** or even **houseboat** and make your own way along sections of the Nantes–Brest canal. French Government Tourist Offices can also provide lists of French and foreign operators who arrange boat rental, or for a full list write to the Syndicat National des Loueurs de Bateaux de Plaisance, Port Javel, Paris 75015 (ⓣ01.44.37.04.00). The Comité Départmental du Tourisme d'Ille-et-Vilaine (see p.30) issues a brochure and map detailing a north–south barge route from the Channel to the Atlantic.

If you are adventurous enough to take your own boat, there is no charge for use of the waterways in Brittany or Normandy, and you can travel without a permit for up to six months in a year. For information on maximum dimensions, documentation, regulations, and so forth, ask at a French Government Tourist Office for the free booklet *Boating on the Waterways*.

Walking

Neither Brittany nor Normandy is serious hiking country. There are no mountains or extensive areas of wilderness, and casual rambling along the clifftops and beside the waterways is the limit of most people's aims. However, if you're into **long-distance walking**, 21 of the French **GR trails** – the *sentiers de grande randonnée* – run through the area. The GRs are fully signposted and equipped with campsites and rest huts along the way. The most interesting are the GR2 (*Sentier de la Seine*), which runs from Le Havre to Les Andelys; the GR341 (*Sentier de Bretagne*) along the Granit-Rose coast between Lannion and St-Brieuc; and the GR347 (*Val d'Oust au pays Gallo*) between Josselin and Redon.

Each GR path is described in a *Topoguide*, which gives a detailed account of the route (in French), including maps, campsites, sources of provisions, and so on. These are produced by the principal French walkers' organization, the Fédération Française de la Randonnée Pédestre, 14 rue Riquet, Paris 75019 (Ⓣ01.44.89.93.90, Ⓦwww.ffrp.asso.fr), and can be ordered through good map shops overseas, such as those listed on p.31.

In addition, many tourist offices provide guides to their local footpaths.

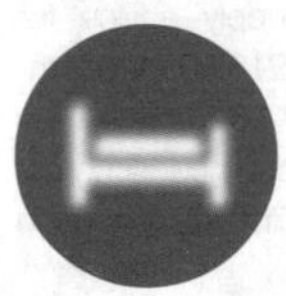

Accommodation

Most of the year, accommodation is plentiful in both Brittany and Normandy, and visitors can expect to be able just to turn up in a town and find a room or a place on a campsite. Booking a couple of nights in advance can, however, be reassuring: it spares you the risk of having to trudge around to find a place and ensures that you know what you'll be paying.

Hotels, hostels and campsites are recommended throughout this book, and their phone numbers provided. The Language section at the back should help you make the necessary phone call if you're uncertain of your French, though many hoteliers and campsite managers, and almost all hostel managers, speak some English.

Problems arise mainly between **July 15 and the end of August**, when the French take their own vacations en masse – the first weekend of August is the busiest time of all – although the whole of July and August, and in the more touristy areas from mid-June to mid-September, is **high season** for the hotels, when prices and availability will be at their highest and lowest respectively. During this period, hotel and hostel accommodation can be hard to come by – particularly in the coastal resorts – and you may find yourself falling back on local tourist offices for help and ideas. With campsites, which are generally open from around Easter to October or November, you can be more relaxed, unless you're touring with a caravan or camper van.

The **tourist season** in Brittany and Normandy runs roughly from Easter until the end of September; while hotels in the cities remain open all year, those in smaller towns and, especially, seaside resorts often close for several months during the winter (November to March, for instance). It's quite possible to turn up somewhere in January or February to find that every hotel is closed; in addition, many family-run places close each year for two or three weeks sometime between May and September, and some hotels in smaller towns and villages close for one or two nights a week, usually Sunday or Monday. Opening dates for each establishment are indicated throughout the book, but it's worth checking ahead if you're in any doubt, and because these dates are prone to change without notice.

Hotels

French **hotels** tend to be consistently better value than they are in Britain and much of northern Europe, but not as good as in North America. Recommendations are given in the guide for almost every town or village mentioned, with their prices indicated by the symbols ❶, ❷, ❸, etc., as explained in the box below. In most towns, you'll be able to get a double room for around €30 (£20), or a single for around €26 (£15), though this will typically mean sharing either a shower or a toilet, or both.

All French **hotels are graded** from zero to five stars. The price more or less corresponds to the number of stars, though the system is a little haphazard, having more to do with ratios of bathrooms per guest than genuine quality; ungraded and single-star hotels are often very good. North American visitors accustomed to staying in hotel rooms equipped with such luxuries as coffee-makers, safes and refrigerators should not automatically expect the same facilities in French hotels however, even the more expensive ones. Lifts are also very much the exception rather than the rule in Normandy and Brittany.

At the cheapest level, what makes a difference in **cost** is whether a room contains a shower: if it does, the bill will be around €6–10 higher. **Breakfast**, too, can add €5–8 per person, though there is no obligation to take it. The cost of eating dinner in a hotel's restaurant can be a more important factor to bear in mind when picking a place to stay. Officially hotels are not supposed to insist that you take meals, but they often do, and in busy resorts you may not find a room unless you agree to *demi-pension* (half-board). If you are unsure, ask to see the menu before checking in; cheap rooms aren't so cheap if you have to eat a €20 meal.

Genuine **single rooms** are rare; lone travellers normally end up in an ordinary double let at a slightly reduced rate. On the other hand most hotels willingly equip rooms with extra beds, for three or more people, at a good discount.

Especially if you're travelling in peak season, try to pick up the full **accommodation lists** available from any French Government Tourist Office (see p.30) or local tourist office. Look out too for the **Logis et Auberges de France**, which are independent hotels, promoted together for their consistently good food and reasonably priced rooms; they're recognizable on the spot by a green-and-yellow logo of a hearth. They have a central reservation number (Ⓣ01.45.84.83.84) and website (Ⓦwww.logis-de-france.fr), which you can contact to obtain their free yearly

Accommodation price codes

All **hotel prices** in this book have been coded using the symbols below. The price shown is for the **least expensive double room in high season**, which, for categories ❶ and sometimes ❷, often means a room without private bath, shower or toilet, though there's usually a washbasin. Most hotels in those categories also have a number of rooms with en-suite facilities, which typically cost around €6–10 extra. In the ❸ category and above, all rooms tend to be equipped with private facilities.

Although many hotels offer rooms at differing prices, ranges (such as ❷–❼) are only indicated when the spectrum is especially broad, or where there are relatively few rooms in the lowest category.

❶ Under €30	❹ €55–70	❼ €100–125
❷ €30–40	❺ €70–85	❽ €125–150
❸ €40–55	❻ €85–100	❾ Over €150

guide (or write to 88 av d'Italie, Paris 75013). Two other, more upmarket federations worth mentioning are Châteaux & Hôtels de France (84 av Victor Cresson, Issy-Les-Moulineaux Cedex 92441, ⓣ01.58.00.22.00, ⓦwww.chateauxhotels.com) and the Relais du Silence (17 rue d'Ouessant, Paris 75015, ⓣ01.44.49.79.00, ⓦwww.silencehotel.com).

One of the great pleasures of travelling in the region is the sheer quality of village hotels. The fixtures and fittings may not always date from the twentieth century, let alone the twenty-first – at the bottom of the range, you'll find corduroy carpets creeping up the walls, blotchy linoleum curling from buckled wooden floors, and clanking great brass keys that won't quite turn in the ill-fitting doors. However, the standards of service are consistently high, and it's rare indeed to stay in a hotel that doesn't take pride in maintaining a well-appointed and good-value restaurant serving traditional local food.

In recent years, outlets of several French **motel chains** have begun to proliferate, usually located alongside major through-routes on the outskirts of larger towns. Other than close to the ferry ports, there are fewer of these in Brittany and Normandy than elsewhere in the country, but those that do exist make a good alternative option for motorists, especially late at night. Among the cheapest is the one-star **Formule 1** chain, which tends to be characterless, but provides rooms for up to three people from €25 (brochures available from Accor central reservation service: ⓣ08.92.68.56.85, ⓦwww.hotelformule1.com). With a Visa, MasterCard or American Express credit card, you can let yourself into a room at any hour of the day or night. Other inexpensive chains include B&B Hotel (ⓣ08.92.78.29.29, ⓦwww.hotel-bb.com), and the slightly more upmarket Première Classe (ⓣ01.64.62.46.46, ⓦwww.premiereclasse.fr) and Etap Hôtel (ⓣ08.92.68.89.00, ⓦwww.etaphotel.com). More comfortable but still affordable options include Campanile (ⓣ08.25.00.30.03 or ⓣ01.64.62.46.46, ⓦwww.campanile.fr), and Ibis (ⓣ08.92.68.66.86, ⓦwww.ibishotel.com), where en-suite rooms with cable TV and direct dial phones cost around €55–65.

Several cities in Brittany and Normandy take part in the "*Bon Weekend en Villes*" programme, whereby you get two nights for the price of one at certain hotels at weekends. The participating towns in this guide are currently Rennes, Nantes, Rouen, Le Havre and St-Nazaire; only St-Nazaire has restricted the offer to the winter period (Nov–March), while the others participate the year round. Further details are available from tourist offices or online at ⓦwww.tourisme.fr/week_end.

Bed and breakfast, rented accommodation and gîtes

In country areas, in addition to standard hotels, you will come across *chambres d'hôtes*, bed-and-breakfast accommodation in someone's house or farm. These vary in standard, but are rarely an especially cheap option; they usually cost the equivalent of a two-star hotel. However, if you strike lucky, they can be good sources of traditional home cooking. Average prices range between €40 and €70 for two people including breakfast; payment is almost always expected in cash. Some offer meals on request (*tables d'hôtes*), usually evenings only. Tourist offices will have lists of **chambres d'hôtes** in their area.

If you're planning to stay a week or more in any one place it's worth considering **self-catering accommodation**. You can do this by checking adverts on the Internet (ⓦwww.frenchconnections.co.uk and ⓦwww.bvdirect.co.uk are well-established sites, or try one of the agents listed on the Maison de la France website, ⓦwww.franceguide.com), while British travellers can check the adverts from private and foreign owners in Sunday newspapers (the *Observer* and *Sunday Times*, mainly). Holiday firms across the world that market accommodation/travel packages are listed on pp.23, 25 and 27 of this book.

Alternatively, contact **Gîtes de France**, 59 rue St-Lazare, Paris Cedex 75439 (Mon–Fri 10am–6.30pm, Sat 10am–1pm & 2–6.30pm; ⓣ01.49.70.75.75, ⓦwww.gites-de-france.fr), a government-funded agency that promotes and manages bed-and-breakfast and self-catering accommodation in France; the latter usually consists of a self-contained country cottage, known as a *gîte rural* or *gîte de séjour*. Further details can be found in their very useful national guides, including *Nouveaux Gîtes Ruraux* (€20), listing new addresses, *Chambres et Tables d'Hôtes* (€22) and *Chambres d'Hôtes de Charme* (€20). Since the national guides are not exhaustive, for complete listings (with photos) you need to buy the relevant regional or departmental guide (around €4–17). All these guides are available from the Paris headquarters and departmental offices of Gîtes de France, as well as from local bookstores and tourist offices.

Hostels, foyers and gîtes d'étape

Auberges de Jeunesse – youth hostels – are invaluable for single travellers on a budget, costing anything from €8 up to €20 per night for a dormitory bed. For couples, however, and certainly for groups of three or more people (see p.43), they'll not necessarily work out less than the cheaper hotels – particularly if you've had to pay a bus fare out to the edge of town to reach them. However, many of the hostels in Normandy and Brittany are beautifully sited, and they do allow you to cut costs by preparing your own food in their kitchens, or eating in cheap canteens.

Slightly confusingly, there are three rival French hostelling associations. The main two are the **Fédération Unie des Auberges de Jeunesse** (FUAJ; 170 hostels), whose hostels are detailed in the International Handbook, and the **Ligue Française pour les Auberges de Jeunesse** (LFAJ; 100 hostels). To stay at hostels run by either, you must show a current **Hostelling International** (HI) membership card. It's usually cheaper and easier to join before you leave home, provided your national Youth Hostel association (see next coloum) is a full member of HI. Alternatively, you can purchase an HI card in certain French hostels for €15.25 (€10.70 under 26 years), or buy individual "welcome stamps" at a rate of €2.90 per night; after six nights you are entitled to the HI card. The third organization is the **Union des Centres de Rencontres Internationales de France** (UCRIF), with 60 hostels in France; membership is not required.

A few large towns provide a more luxurious standard of hostel accommodation in **Foyers des Jeunes Travailleurs/euses**, residential hostels for young workers and students, where you can usually get a private room for around €10. On the whole they are more luxurious than youth hostels and normally have a good cafeteria or canteen.

A further hostel-type alternative exists in the countryside, especially in hiking or cycling areas, in the form of the **gîtes d'étape**. These are less formal than the hostels, often run by the local village or municipality (whose mayor may well hold the key), and provide basic hospital-style beds and simple kitchen facilities from around €8. They are marked on the large-scale IGN walkers' maps and listed in individual GR *Topoguides*. More information can be found in the guides *Gîtes d'Étape et Séjours* (€10), published by Gîtes de France (see opposite), and *Gîtes d'Étape et Refuges*, published by Rando Éditions, available in French bookshops for €19.90, or online at ⓦwww.gites-refuges.com.

Youth hostel associations

France

Fédération Unie des Auberges de Jeunesse (FUAJ) 9 rue Brantôme, Paris 75003 ⓣ01.48.04.70.40, ⓦwww.fuaj.org.

Ligue Française pour les Auberges de Jeunesse (LFAJ) 67 rue Vergniaud Bat K, 75013 Paris ⓣ01.44.16.78.78, ⓦwww.auberges-de-jeunesse.com.

Union des Centres de Rencontres Internationales de France (UCRIF) 27 rue de Turbigo BP 6407, 75064 Paris ⓣ01.40.26.57.64, ⓦwww.ucrif.asso.fr.

UK

Youth Hostel Association (YHA) ⓣ0870/770 8868, ⓦwww.yha.org.uk. Annual membership £13.50; under-18s £6.70; lifetime £195 (or five annual payments of £41).

Scottish Youth Hostel Association ⓣ0870/155 3255, ⓦwww.syha.org.uk. Annual membership £6, for under-18s £2.50.

Ireland

Hostelling International Northern Ireland ⓣ028/9032 4733, ⓦwww.hini.org.uk. Adult membership £13; under-18s £6; family £25; lifetime £75.

Irish Youth Hostel Association ⓣ01/830 4555, ⓦwww.irelandyha.org. Annual membership €25; under-18s €10.50; family €50; lifetime €75.

US

Hostelling International-American Youth Hostels ⓣ301/495-1240, ⓦwww.hiayh.org. Annual membership for adults (18–55) is US$28, for seniors (55 or over) is US$18, and for under-18s and groups of ten or more, is free. Lifetime memberships are US$250.

Canada

Hostelling International Canada ⓣ1-800/663 5777 or 613/237 7884, ⓦwww.hihostels.ca. Rather than sell the traditional 1- or 2-year memberships, the association now sells one individual adult membership with a 16- to 28-month term. The length of the term depends on when the membership is sold, but a member can receive up to 28 months of membership for just Can$35 plus tax. Membership is free for under-18s and you can become a lifetime member for Can$175.

Australia

Australia Youth Hostels Association ⓣ02/9261 1111, ⓦwww.yha.com.au. Adult membership rate Aus$52 (under-18s, Aus$19) for the first twelve months and then Aus$37 each year after.

New Zealand

Youth Hostelling Association New Zealand ⓣ0800/278 299 or 03/379 9970, ⓦwww.yha.co.nz. Adult membership NZ$40 for one year, NZ$60 for two and NZ$80 for three; under-18s free; lifetime NZ$300.

Camping

Practically every village and town in the country has at least one **campsite**, to cater for the thousands of French people who spend their holiday under canvas. The tourist boards for both Brittany and Normandy produce full lists of sites in their regions.

The cheapest – at around €6–8 per person per night – is usually **the Camping municipal**, run by the local municipality. In season or when they are officially open, they are always clean, with plenty of hot water, and often situated in the prime local position. Out of season, many of them don't even bother to have someone around to collect the overnight charge.

On the coast especially, there are **superior categories** of campsite, where you'll pay prices similar to those of a budget hotel for the facilities – bars, restaurants, sometimes swimming pools. These have a rather less transitory population than the Camping municipals, with people often spending a whole holiday in the one base. If you plan to do the same – particularly if you've a caravan, camper van or substantial tent – book ahead. Reckon on paying at least €7 per head with a tent, €9 with a camper van.

Inland, **camping à la ferme** – on somebody's farm – is another (generally facility-less) possibility. Lists of sites are available at local tourist boards and in the guide *Campings et Chalets-Loisirs* (€10) published by Gîtes de France (see p.44).

If you're planning to do a lot of camping, an **international camping carnet** (CCI) is a good investment. The carnet serves as useful identification, covers you for third party insurance when camping, and helps you get ten percent reductions at campsites listed in the CCI information booklet that comes with your carnet. It's available in the UK from the the RAC (to members only) and the Camping and Caravanning Club (ⓣ02476/694 995, ⓦwww.campingandcaravanningclub.co.uk) who also book inspected camping sites in Europe and arrange ferry crossings, and in the US and Canada from Family Campers and RVers (FCRV; ⓦwww.fcrv.org).

Lastly, a **word of caution**: never camp rough (*camping sauvage*, as the French call it) on anyone's land without first asking permission. If the dogs don't get you, the guns might – farmers have been known to shoot before asking any questions. In many parts of France *camping sauvage* on public land is not tolerated – Brittany is the notable exception. On beaches it's best to camp out where there are other people doing so.

Eating and drinking

The superb range of food available has to rank among the principal reasons to visit Brittany and, especially, Normandy. Restaurant quality is consistently high, prices remain reasonable and, to be honest, there are towns and villages where just about the only source of excitement is their gastronomic output.

With no wine production in Normandy, and only the Muscadet-style whites coming from the southeast of Brittany, the most interesting **local alcohol** is derived from the region's orchards. **Cider** is made everywhere, along with its pear equivalent, poiré; and there is of course Norman **Calvados** (apple brandy), as well as numerous local firewaters.

Breton food

Brittany's proudest addition to world cuisine has to be the (white-flour) crêpe, and its savoury (buckwheat) equivalent, the *galette*. Crêperies throughout the region attempt to pass them off as satisfying meals, served with every imaginable filling. However, few people seriously plan their holidays around eating pancakes, and gourmets are more likely to be enticed to Brittany by its magnificent array of **seafood**, and above all its shellfish – mussels, oysters, clams, and scallops, to name but a few. Restaurants in resorts such as St-Malo and Quiberon jostle for the attention of fish fanatics, while smaller towns – such as Cancale, which specializes in oysters (*huîtres*), and Erquy, with its scallops (*Coquilles St-Jacques*) – go so far as to depend on a single specific mollusc for their livelihood.

Although they can't claim to be uniquely Breton, two appetizers feature on every self-respecting menu. These are *moules marinières*, giant bowls of succulent orange mussels steamed open in white wine, shallots and parsley (and perhaps enriched with cream or crème fraîche to become *moules à la crème*), and *soupe de poissons*, served with a pot of the garlicky mayonnaise known as *rouille* (coloured with pulverized sweet red pepper) and a bowl of croûtons. Jars of *soupe de poissons* – or crab, or lobster – are always on sale in seaside *poissonneries*, and make an ideal way to take a taste of France home with you. Paying a little extra in a restaurant – typically on menus costing €25 or more – brings you into the realm of the *assiette de fruits de mer*, a mountainous heap of langoustines, crabs, oysters, mussels, clams, whelks and cockles, most of them raw and all (with certain obvious exceptions) delicious. **Main courses** tend to be plainer than in Normandy, with fresh local fish being prepared with relatively simple sauces. Skate served with capers, or salmon baked with a mustard or cheese sauce, are typical dishes, while even the *cotriade*, a stew containing such fish as sole, turbot or bass, as well as shellfish, is distinctly less rich than the Mediterranean *bouillabaisse*.

Brittany is also better than much of France in maintaining its respect for fresh **green vegetables**, thanks to the extensive local production of peas, cauliflowers, artichokes and the like. Only with the desserts can things get rather too heavy; *far Breton*, considered a great delicacy, is a stodgy baked concoction of sponge, custard and chopped plums, while *îles flottantes* are meringue icebergs adrift in a sea of crème brûlée or custard.

Norman food

The food of **Normandy** owes its most distinctive characteristic – its gut-bursting, heart-pounding **richness** – to the lush orchards and dairy herds of the region's agricultural heartland, and most especially the area southeast of Caen known as the Pays d'Auge. Menus abound in **meat** such as veal (*veau*) cooked in vallée d'Auge style, which consists largely of the profligate addition of cream and butter. Many dishes also feature orchard fruit, either in its natural state or in successively more alcoholic forms

Weekly markets

The list below features the biggest and best of the markets of Brittany and Normandy, with a particular emphasis on those specializing in **fresh food** and **local produce**.

Bear in mind that in addition to the specific days listed here, most large cities – **Rennes, Rouen and Caen**, for example – tend to have markets every day (with the occasional exception of Mondays).

	Normandy	Brittany
Monday	Bricquebec, Cany-Barville, Carentan, Pont-Audemer, Pont-L'Évêque, St-Pierre-sur-Dives, Vimoutiers	Auray, Combourg, Concarneau, Douarnenez, Moncontour, Ploërmel, Questembert, Redon, Vitré
Tuesday	Argentan, Bagnoles, Barfleur, Brionne, Lessay, Portbail, St-Lô, Villedieu-les-Poêles	Dinard, Le Conquet, Locmariaquer, Paimpol, Pont-Aven, St-Malo, St-Pol, La Trinité
Wednesday	Arromanches, Carrouges, Évreux, Falaise, Honfleur, Orbec, Pontorson, Sées, Yvetot	Carnac, Douarnenez, Guérande, Isigny-sur-Mer, Quimper, Roscoff, St-Brieuc, Tréguier, Vannes
Thursday	Alençon, Bellême, Carteret, Cherbourg, Conches-en-Ouche, Coutances, Deauville, Étretat, Forges-les-Eaux, Ste-Mère-Église	Binic, Dinan, Dinard, Hennebont, Lamballe, Lannion, Malestroit
Friday	Argentan, Domfront, Eu, Pont-Audemer, St-Valery, Valognes, Vimoutiers, Vire	Concarneau, Douarnenez, Guingamp, Jugon-les-Lacs, Perros-Guirec, Quimper, Quimperlé, St-Malo, Le Val-André
Saturday	Alençon, Avranches, Bagnoles, Bayeux, Caudebec, Cherbourg, Dieppe, Domfront, Falaise, Granville, Honfleur, Le Tréport, Lisieux, Mortagne-au-Perche, Orbec, Ry, Sées, St-Lô, St-Vaast	Audierne, Dinard, Dol, Douarnenez, Erquy, Fougères, Guérande, Guingamp, Josselin, Locmariaquer, Morlaix, Quimper, Rennes, St-Brieuc, Vannes, Vitré
Sunday	Alençon, Argentan, Brionne, Caen, La Ferrière-sur-Risle, St-Valery (summer)	Auray, Cancale, Carnac, Quimper

– either as apple or pear cider, or perhaps further distilled to produce brandies (Calvados in the case of apples, *poiré* for pears).

Normans have a great propensity for blood and guts. In addition to **game** such as rabbit and duck (a speciality in Rouen, where the birds are strangled to ensure that all their blood gets into the sauce), they enjoy such intestinal preparations as *andouilles*, the blood sausages known in

English as chitterlings, and tripes, stewed for hours *à la mode de Caen*, but rendered no less palatable.

A full blowout at country restaurants in the small towns of inland Normandy – places like Conches, Vire and towns in the Suisse Normande – will also traditionally entail one or two pauses between courses for the *trou normand* – a glass of Calvados while you catch your breath before struggling on with the feast.

Normandy's long coastline ensures that it too is a great destination for **seafood**, serving up much the same range of shellfish as detailed for Brittany. Many of the larger ports and resorts have long waterfront lines of competing restaurants, each with its "*copieuse*" *assiette de fruits de mer*. **Honfleur** is probably the most enjoyable of these, but **Dieppe**, **Cherbourg** and **Trouville** also spring to mind as offering endless eating opportunities. The menus tend to be much the same as those on offer in Brittany, if perhaps slightly more expensive.

The most famous products of Normandy's meadow-munching cows are of course its **cheeses**. The best-known cheeses from the area covered by this book – such as Pont-l'Evêque, Livarot and, most famous of all, Camembert – all come from the Pays d'Auge region of Normandy, and are discussed in detail in the box on p.201.

Cafés and snacks

The days when hotels gave you mounds of croissants or *brioches* for **breakfast** seem to be long gone; now it's virtually always bread, jam and a jug of coffee or tea for at least €5. It makes more sense to pick up a croissant, *pain au chocolat* (a chocolate-filled croissant) or sandwich in a bakery, for a fraction of the price, and wash it down with hot chocolate or coffee.

For **midday meals** and **light snacks**, most bars and cafés – there's no real difference – advertise *les snacks*, or *un casse-croûte* (a bite), with pictures of omelettes, fried eggs, hot dogs, or various sandwiches. Even when they don't, they'll usually make you a half or third of a baguette (French bread stick), buttered (*tartine*) and filled. Likely ingredients include *jambon* (ham), *fromage* (cheese), *thon* (tuna), *saucisson* (sausage) or *poulet* (chicken). **Toasted sandwiches** – most commonly *croques-monsieur* (cheese and ham) or *croques-madame* (cheese and bacon or sausage) – are also invariably on offer. Especially in rural areas, small bars may serve a moderate-priced *plat du jour* (chef's daily special) or *formule* (a limited or no-choice menu).

Many people also recommend **crêpes** for lunch. However, while they may taste nice enough, unless you buy from a market stall crêpes can be poor value compared to a restaurant meal; you need to eat at least three, normally at around €5 each, to feel even slightly full. That they seem to excite children – presumably because they can drench them in chocolate syrup – shouldn't fool parents into thinking of a crêperie as a cheap alternative.

For **picnic and takeaway food**, nothing beats buying fresh ingredients in one of the numerous local **markets**, details of which are given in the box opposite. If there isn't a market around on the day you need it, you'll find charcuteries everywhere – even in small villages. These sell cooked meats, prepared snacks such as *bouchées de la reine* (seafood vol-au-vents), ready-made dishes and assorted salads. You can buy by weight or ask for *une tranche* (a slice), *une barquette* (a carton) or *une part* (a portion). The cheapest, in towns, are the supermarkets' charcuterie counters.

Salons de thé, which open from mid-morning to late evening, serve brunches, salads, quiches, etc., as well as cake and ice cream and a wide selection of teas. They tend to be a good deal pricier than cafés or brasseries – you're paying for the ritzy surroundings.

Patisseries, of course, have impressive arrays of cakes and pastries, often using local cream to excess. In addition to standard French pastries, the Bretons specialize in heavy, pudding-like affairs, dripping with butter, such as *kouïgn-amann*, and *gaufres* – cream-drenched waffles.

Restaurants

Brittany and Normandy have an abundance of **restaurants**, and in many towns **brasseries** add to the choice. There's no

Vegetarians

On the whole, **vegetarians** can expect a somewhat lean time in Brittany and Normandy. One or two towns have specifically vegetarian restaurants (detailed in the text), but elsewhere you'll have to hope you find a sympathetic restaurant (crêperies can be good standbys). Sometimes they're willing to replace a meat dish on the *menu fixe* with an omelette; other times you'll have to pick your way through the carte. Remember the phrase "*je suis végétarien(ne); il y a quelques plats sans viande?*" (I'm a vegetarian; are there any non-meat dishes?).

Many vegetarians swallow a few principles and start eating fish and shellfish on holiday; that of course is a matter for your conscience. If you are a **vegan**, however, you should probably forget about eating in French restaurants altogether and try to cook your own food.

distinction between the two in terms of quality or price range, though brasseries, which resemble cafés, serve quicker meals at most hours of the day; restaurants tend to stick to the traditional meal times of noon until 2pm and 7pm to 9.30pm. After 9pm or so, restaurants often serve only à la carte meals – invariably more expensive than eating the set menu. For the more upmarket places it's wise to make reservations – easily done on the same day. In small towns it may be impossible to get anything other than a bar sandwich after 10pm; in major cities, central brasseries will serve until 11pm or midnight and one or two may stay open all night. Restaurants will usually be closed on one day of the week (often Mondays), in addition perhaps to the odd lunchtime or evening. During low season (in other words, outside of July and August) in seasonal resorts, closing times might extend to a couple of days of the week. Don't forget that hotel restaurants are open to nonresidents, and are likely not only to offer the best food in town but also to do so at good-value prices; the green-and-yellow Logis de France symbol is always worth looking out for. On the road, keep an eye open too for the red-and-blue sign of the **Relais Routiers** – always reasonably priced and gastronomically sound.

Prices and what you get for them are posted outside. Normally there's a choice between one or more *menus fixes* (set menus), where the number of courses has already been determined, the choice is limited, and service is included, and the *carte*, the full menu.

At the bottom price range, say below €12, *menus fixes* revolve around standard dishes, such as steak and chips (*steak frites*), chicken and chips (*poulet frites*), or various offal concoctions, though it's always worth looking out for the *plat du jour*, which may be more appealing. For €12 to €25, virtually any of the restaurants recommended in this guide will serve you a good three-course meal, while four-course blowouts, including a starter as well as separate meat and fish courses, cost from €25 to €50. Most expensive of the lot are the special seafood menus, offering giant platters of assorted crustaceans; away from the big centres such as Cancale and St-Malo, it pays to be wary of these, as the stuff may have been waiting around for several days for someone foolhardy enough to order it. Note that the price of menus can rise by €2 or so in the evenings and sometimes at weekends.

Going à la carte offers greater flexibility and, in the better restaurants, access to the chef's specialities, but you can expect to pay heavily for the privilege. A simple and perfectly legitimate ploy is to have just one course instead of the expected three or four. You can share dishes or just have several starters – a useful strategy for vegetarians. There's no minimum charge.

North American visitors should bear in mind that in France an *entrée* is an appetizer or starter; the main course of the meal is the *plat principal*. In the French sequence of courses, any salad (sometimes vegetables, too) comes separate from the main dish, and cheese precedes a dessert. You will be offered coffee, which always costs extra, to finish off the meal.

Service compris (s.c.) means the **service charge** is included, which is usually the case on all set menus; *service non compris* (s.n.c.), or *service en sus*, means that it isn't, and you need to calculate an additional fifteen percent. **Wine** (*vin*) or a **drink** (*boisson*) is unlikely to be included, although a glass is occasionally thrown in with cheaper menus. When ordering wine, ask for *un quart* (quarter-litre), *un demi-litre* (half-litre) or *une carafe* (a litre). You'll be given the house wine if you don't specify otherwise; if you're worried about the cost, ask for *vin ordinaire*.

The French follow the North American rather than the British line in their attitude towards **children** in restaurants, not simply by offering reduced-price children's menus but in creating an atmosphere, even in otherwise fairly snooty establishments, that positively welcomes kids. It is regarded as self-evident that large family groups should be able to eat out together. A rather murkier area is that of **dogs** in the dining room; it can be quite a surprise in a provincial hotel to realize that the majority of your fellow diners are attempting to keep dogs concealed beneath their tables. One final note is that you should always call the waiter or waitress *Monsieur* or *Madame* (*Mademoiselle* if a young woman), never *garçon*, no matter what you've been taught in school.

Drinking

Where you can eat you can invariably **drink**, and vice versa. Drinking is done at a leisurely pace, whether as a prelude to food (*apéritif*), a sequel (*digestif*), or the accompaniment.

Every bar or café is obliged to display a full **price list**, which will usually show progressively increasing prices for drinks at the bar (*au comptoir*), sitting down (*la salle*), and on the terrace (*la terrasse*).

Wine (*vin*) is the regular drink. Red is *rouge*, white is *blanc*, or there's *rosé*. *Vin de table* – plonk – is generally drinkable and always cheap; it may be disguised (and priced up) as the house wine, or *cuvée*. Restaurant mark-ups for quality wines can be outrageous, in a country where wine is so cheap in the shops. In bars, you normally buy by the glass, and just ask for *un rouge* or *un blanc*; *un pichet* gets you a quarter-litre jug.

> For a comprehensive glossary of French food and drink terms, see p.457.

Strictly speaking, no wine is produced in Brittany or Normandy. However, along the lower Loire Valley, the *département* of Loire-Atlantique, centred on Nantes, is still generally regarded as "belonging" to Brittany – and is treated as such in this book. Vineyards here are responsible for the dry white **Muscadet** – which is what normally goes into *moules marinières* – and the even drier Gros-Plant. You'll find a brief account of how to visit some of the vineyards where they are made on p.374.

Cider (*cidre*) is extremely popular. In Brittany it's a standard accompaniment to a meal of crêpes and may be offered on restaurant *menus fixes*. Normans more often consume it in bars. Most of the many varieties are very dry and very wonderful. *Poiré*, pear cider, is also produced, but on a small scale and is not commercially distributed.

The familiar Belgian and German brands account for most of the **beer** you'll find. Draught (*à la pression*, usually Kronenbourg) is the cheapest drink you can have next to coffee and wine – ask for *un demi* (defined as 25cl). Bottled beer is exceptionally cheap in supermarkets.

British-style ales and stouts are also popular. Every town seems to have some Celtic-affiliated bar that sells Guinness, and specialist beer-drinking establishments can be found in cities like Brest, Rennes and Quimper. There are even home-grown Breton beers, such as Coreff from Morlaix, and Britt, a white beer brewed in Concarneau.

Strong alcohols are drunk from 5am as pre-work fortifiers, right through the day; Bretons have a reputation for commitment to this. Brandies and dozens of *eaux de vie* (spirits) and liqueurs are always available. The most famous of these in Normandy are **Calvados**, brandy distilled from apples and left to mature for anything upwards of ten years, and **Benedictine**, distilled at Fécamp from an obscure mix of ingredients (see p.87). Measures are generous, but they don't come cheap, especially in restaurants (where Calvados is traditionally drunk as a *trou*, or "hole", between courses). The same applies to imported spirits like whisky (Scotch).

On the **soft drink** front, you can buy cartons of unsweetened fruit juice in supermarkets, although in cafés the bottled nectars such as apricot (*jus d'abricot*) and blackcurrant (*cassis*) still hold sway. Some cafés serve tiny glasses of fresh orange and lemon juice (*orange/citron pressé*); otherwise it's the standard fizzy cans. Bottles of **mineral water** (*eau minérale*) and spring water (*eau de source*) – either sparkling (*pétillante*) or still (*eau plate*) – abound, from the best-seller Perrier to the obscurest spa product. But there's not much wrong with the tap water (*eau du robinet*).

Coffee in Normandy is invariably espresso and very strong; in Brittany, particularly in villages, it is sometimes made in jugs, very weakly. *Un café* or *un express* is black, *un crème* is white, *un café au lait* (served at breakfast) is espresso in a large cup or bowl filled up with hot milk. Most bars will also serve *un déca*, decaffeinated coffee. Ordinary tea (*thé*) is Lipton's, nine times out of ten; to have milk with it, ask for "*un peu de lait frais*".

After overeating, **herb teas** (*tisanes*), served in every café, can be soothing. The more common ones are *verveine* (verbena), *tilleul* (lime blossom) and *tisane* (camomile). Unlike tea, *chocolat chaud* (**hot chocolate**) lives up to the high standards of French food and drink, and can be ordered in any café.

Communications

You should have no problem keeping in contact with people at home while you are in France. The country has an efficient postal system and letters and packages can be sent *poste restante* to any of the official branches. The Internet is widely accessible, while if you need to call home, you can use cheap prepaid phone cards or access home-country operators via free numbers.

Mail

As a rule, **post offices** (*bureaux de poste* or PTTs) in Brittany and Normandy are open from around 8am until noon and 2pm to 6pm on weekdays, and 8am until noon only on Saturday; look for bright yellow *La Poste* signs. However, in the larger towns you'll find a main office open throughout the day (8am–7pm), while lunch hours and closing times in the villages can vary enormously. Most larger offices also offer **Internet access**.

You can have letters sent to you *poste restante* at any post office in the country. For whatever town you choose, always specify the main post office (*Poste Centrale*) to avoid possible confusion. The addresses of the two largest in the region covered by this book are:

Poste Restante, Poste Centrale, 76000 **ROUEN**.

Poste Restante, Poste Centrale, 44000 **NANTES**.

To collect mail you'll need a passport, and should expect to pay a charge of €0.50 per item. If you're expecting mail, it's worth asking the clerk to check under your surname (which ideally should be written in capital letters), and all possible Christian names as well – filing systems tend to be erratic.

Sending letters, the quickest international service is by *aérogramme*, sold at all post offices. You can buy ordinary stamps (*timbres*) at any *tabac* (tobacconist). When this book went to press, the current rates for standard letters (*lettres*, weighing 20g or less) and **postcards** (*cartes postales*) were €0.50 for the UK and Europe, €0.90 for North America, and €0.90 for Australia and New Zealand. If you're sending **parcels** abroad, remember that small *postes* don't often send foreign mail and may need reminding of, for example, the huge reductions for printed papers and books. To post your letter on the street, look for the bright yellow postboxes. For further information on postal rates, among other things, log on to the post office website ⓦwww.laposte.fr.

Phones

You can make domestic and international phone calls from any **call box** (or *cabine*), and can also receive calls – you'll find the number in the top right-hand corner of the information panel. Most payphones only take **phone cards** (*télécartes*). These are sold in *tabacs* and newsagents as well as post offices and some train station ticket offices, and come in two sizes: €7.50 for 50 units, and €15 for 120 units. You can also use credit cards in many call boxes. Coin-only boxes still exist in cafés, bars, hotel foyers and rural areas; they take coins of 10, 20 and 50 cents and €1. Certain digital British mobile phones also work in France.

For calls **within France** – local or long-distance – simply dial all ten digits of the number (plus the International code if calling from a mobile phone). Numbers beginning with ⓣ08.00 are free-dial numbers; those beginning ⓣ08.10 are charged as a local call; anything else beginning ⓣ08 is premium-rate (typically charged at €0.34 per minute). Numbers starting with ⓣ06 are mobile and therefore also expensive. At the time of writing, peak-rate local calls from public phones were charged at €0.15 for four minutes; long-distance calls within France cost up to roughly €1.20 for four minutes depending on the distance. You'll pay less when calling from a private phone and usually much more from a hotel. Off-peak rates (between 30 and 50 percent cheaper depending on whether you're calling from a public or private phone) apply on weekdays between 7pm and 8am and all day Saturday and Sunday.

When **phoning abroad**, cheap rates (a reduction of between 20 and 47 percent depending on the country and whether you're calling from a public or private phone) apply on weekdays between 7pm and 8am and all day Saturday and Sunday to most other countries. At the time of writing it costs €0.47 for a one-minute call to the UK (*Royaume-Uni*) from a public phone at peak rates; €0.65 to the USA (*États-Unis*) and Canada; and €1.90 to Australia and New Zealand.

By far the most convenient way to make international calls is to use a **calling card**; the standard *télécartes* make calling from public phone boxes straightforward, but most *tabacs* also sell a wide range of cut-price cards that can be used from both call boxes and private phones. To avoid payment altogether, make a reverse charge or collect call (*téléphoner en PCV*). You can also do this through the operator in the UK, by dialling the Home Direct number ⓣ08.00.89.00.33; to get an

International calls

To place an international **call to France**, dial the following access code followed by the last nine digits of the ten-digit French number (thus omitting the inital 0).

UK ⓣ00 33 | **Ireland** ⓣ00 33 | **USA** & **Canada** ⓣ011 33
Australia ⓣ011 33 | **New Zealand** ⓣ00 44 33

To make an international **call from France**, dial ⓣ00, wait for a tone, and then dial the relevant country code, followed by the number you want minus its initial 0.

UK ⓣ00 44 | **Ireland** ⓣ00 353 | **USA** & **Canada** ⓣ00 1
Australia ⓣ00 61 | **New Zealand** ⓣ00 64

English-speaking operator for North America, dial ⓣ00.00.11.

To speak to the **operator** dial ⓣ13; **directory enquiries**, both national and international, are on ⓣ12; **medical emergencies**, ⓣ15; the **police**, ⓣ17; **fire**, ⓣ18.

Mobile phones

Visitors from the UK who want to use their **mobile phones** while in France should check with their phone providers to see whether the phone will work in France, and what the call charges are; for all but the very top-of-the-range packages, the phone provider will probably have to switch on international access. You're also likely to be charged extra for **incoming calls** when abroad, as the people calling you will be paying the usual rate. For further information about using your phone abroad, check out ⓦwww.telecomsadvice.org.uk/features/using_your_mobile_abroad.htm.

Unless you have a GSM tri-band phone, it's unlikely that a cellphone bought for use inside the US will work abroad. Those that do tend to be very expensive as users are billed for both incoming and outgoing calls. For details of which phones will work outside the US, contact your service provider.

Most mobiles in Australia and New Zealand use GSM, which works well in Europe.

Email

Email is the cheapest and easiest way to stay in touch with home while in France. Practically every reasonable-sized town has a **cyber café** or connection point of some sort, and in less populated areas, the need is being filled by post offices, many of which now have rather expensive public Internet terminals, which are operated with a prepaid card (€7 for the first hour). We have given details of cyber cafés and other Internet access points in the Guide so you can stay online while travelling. Prices range from €3 to €6 per hour, so it can be worth shopping around. It's easy to open a free **email account** to use while you're away with Hotmail or Yahoo: go to ⓦwww.hotmail.com or ⓦwww.yahoo.com to find out how. The website ⓦwww.kropla.com gives details of how to plug your laptop in when abroad, phone country codes around the world, and information about electrical systems in different countries.

The media

For anyone who can read French, or understand it when spoken, the print and electronic media in France match any in the world. If you need your information in English, imported newspapers are available in larger towns, many hotels offer English-language TV, and BBC radio can easily be picked up.

Newspapers and magazines

British and North American **newspapers** – at the very least, the *International Herald Tribune* – are intermittently available. In the larger resorts, and in cities such as Nantes and Rouen, you should find reasonable selections of foreign-language papers. Elsewhere, it's mostly down to the British *Times*, *Daily Mail* or *Sun*.

As for the **French press**, the widest circulations are enjoyed by the **regional dailies**. Throughout Normandy and Brittany, the most important and influential paper is *Ouest-France*. This is based in Rennes but has numerous local editions – worth picking up for their listings supplements, if nothing else. Of the **national dailies**, *Le Monde* is the most intellectual and respected, with no concessions to entertainment (such as pictures), but a correctly styled French that is probably the easiest to understand. *Libération (Libé* for short; daily except Mon), is moderately left-wing, independent and colloquial with good, if choosy, coverage.

Weeklies, on the *Newsweek/Time* model, include the wide-ranging left-leaning *Le Nouvel Observateur*, its right-wing counterpoint *L'Express* and the centrist with bite, *Marianne*. The best, and funniest, investigative journalism is in the satirical *Canard Enchaîné*, unfortunately almost incomprehensible to non-native speakers. **Monthlies** include the young, trendy – and cheap – *Nova*, which has excellent listings of cultural events, and *Actuel*, which is good for current events.

TV and radio

French TV has six channels: three public (France 2, Arte/France 5 and France 3); one subscription (Canal Plus – with some unencrypted programmes); and two commercial open broadcasts (TF1 and M6). Of these, TF1 and France 2 are the most popular channels, showing a broad mix of programmes. In addition, some hotels in Brittany and Normandy offer a limited **range of cable and satellite channels**, which usually includes at least CNN or BBC World, and Eurosport (though not normally in English).

If you've got a **radio**, you can tune into various English-language broadcasts. BBC (Ⓦwww.bbc.co.uk/worldservice), Radio Canada (Ⓦwww.rcinet.ca), and Voice of America (Ⓦwww.voa.gov) list all the world service frequencies around the globe. On top of that, Brittany and Normandy are sufficiently close to British transmitters that BBC Radio 4 from 5am to 11.45pm GMT, and the World Service from 11.45pm to 5am GMT, on 198 kHz long wave, can usually be picked up clearly. For radio news in French, there's the state-run France Inter (87.8 FM), Europe 1 (104.7 FM) or round-the-clock news on France Info (105.5 FM).

Opening hours and holidays

The basic hours of business in France are from 8am or 9am until noon or 1pm, and from 2pm or 3pm to 6.30pm or 7.30pm. In big city centres, shops and other businesses stay open throughout the day, while in July and August most tourist offices and museums are open without interruption. Otherwise almost everything – shops, museums, tourist offices, most banks – closes for a couple of hours at midday.

If you're looking to buy a picnic lunch, you'll need to get into the habit of buying it before you're ready to eat. Small food shops often don't reopen until halfway through the afternoon, closing around 7.30pm or 8pm just before the evening meal.

The standard **closing days** are Sunday and Monday. **Food shops** tend to close on Monday rather than Sunday, but in smaller towns you may well find everything except the odd boulangerie (bakery) – including banks – shut on both days.

Museums are not very generous with their hours, tending to open at around 10am, close for lunch at noon until 2pm (sometimes 3pm) and then run through until only 5pm or 6pm. Summer opening times, usually applicable between mid-May or early June and mid-September, but sometimes only during July and August, often differ from winter times; all variations are indicated in the listings given in this book. The closing days are usually Monday or Tuesday, sometimes both. Admission charges can be quite high, though most state-owned museums have one or two days of the week when they're free, and you can get a big reduction at most places by showing a student card (or passport if you're under 18 or over 60).

Churches and cathedrals are almost always open all day, with charges only for the crypt, treasuries or cloister, and little fuss about how you're dressed. Where they are closed you may have to go during Mass to take a look, on Sunday morning, or at other times which you'll see posted up on the door. In small towns and villages, however, getting the key is not difficult – ask anyone nearby or hunt out the priest, whose house is known as the *presbytère*.

Festivals and events

The most interesting Breton events are without doubt the region's cultural festivals. At the largest of these, the Lorient Festival Inter-Celtique (August), music, performance, food and drink of all seven Celtic nations are featured in a completely authentic gathering that pulls in cultural nationalists (and ethnic music fans) from Ireland to Spain. If you can't get to Lorient, there are two smaller – and more particularly Breton – alternatives in the Nantes Quinzaine Celtique (June/July) and Quimper's Festival de Cornouaille (July).

Look out also for local club events put on by individual **Celtic folklore groups** – Cercles, Bagadou or, best of the lot, Fests-Noz. These are most prolific in Nantes, though wherever you are in the province, listings pages of the Ouest-France can be worth scrutiny. The "Breton music" section at the end of this book has detailed recommendations of clubs and venues to check out in the province.

Religious pardons, sometimes promoted as tourist attractions in Brittany, are rather different affairs. These are essentially church processions, organized by a particular community on the local saint's day. Though generally small-scale, some, like that at Ste-Anne-d'Auray, have over the centuries taken on more region-wide status as pilgrimages. Rather than being carnivals or fêtes, they are primarily very serious occasions, centred on lengthy and rather gloomy church services. If you're not interested by the religious aspects, only the food and drink stalls are likely to hold any great appeal.

By and large, **Normandy** lacks any specific cultural traditions to celebrate, doing its best to make up with celebrations of related **historic events** – births and deaths of William the Conqueror, Ste Thérèse, etc. The **D-Day** (June 6) landings along the Invasion Beaches are always marked in some way. The regional and *départemental* tourist boards listed on p.30 are the best source of information.

In both Normandy and Brittany, avoid the *Spectacles*, camp and overpriced outdoor shows on some mythical theme or other, held most regularly (and most tackily) at Bagnoles and Elven.

On the more mainstream **cultural side**, the larger cities – Rouen, Rennes and Nantes – have active theatre, opera and classical music seasons, though little happens during the summer. **Cinema** is most interesting in these cities, too, and the region is host to perhaps the most accessible French film festival – Deauville's American Film Festival (September). Almost all foreign films will be dubbed into French; "v.o." in the listings signifies original language.

Both Rennes and Rouen have laid recent claim to be "the capital of French rock";

Calendar of events

Early April	**Erquy**	Scallop Festival
Whitsun	**Honfleur**	Seamen's Festival
Second weekend in May	**Binic**	Cod Festival
Third Sun in May	**Tréguier**	St-Yves Pardon
Mid-May	**St-Brieuc**	Art Rock Festival
End May/start June	**St-Malo**	Étonnants Voyageurs
June 6	**Invasion Beaches**	D-Day Ceremonies
Third week in June	**Balleroy**	Balloon Festival (odd-numbered years only)
Last Sun in June	**Le Faouët**	Pardon
End June/start July	**Nantes**	Quinzaine Celtique
Early July	**Lamballe**	Golden Broom Folk Festival
Early July	**Alençon**	Global Folklore Festival
First ten days of July	**Rennes**	Tombées de la Nuit theatre and music festival
Second Sun in July	**Locronan**	Troménie Pardon
July 16	**La Haye du Routot**	Fête de Ste-Claire
Third week in July	**Quimper**	Festival de Cornouaille
Third weekend in July	**Dinan**	Fête des Remparts (even-numbered years only)
July 26	**Ste-Anne-d'Auray**	Pardon
Late July	**Carhaix**	Les Vieilles
Late July	**Charrues**	Rock festival
End July/ start Aug	**Vannes**	Jazz Festival
Last Sun in July	**Locquirec**	Festival of the Sea
Last Sun in July	**Paimpol**	Fête des Terres-Neuvas
Aug 2	**Le Tréport**	Blessing of the Sea
First full week in Aug	**Lorient**	Festival InterCeltique
First fortnight in Aug	**Quimper**	Semaines Musicales
First fortnight in Aug	**Île de Fedrun**	Fête de la Brière
Early Aug	**Dives**	Puppet Festival
Second Sun in Aug	**Lizio**	Festival Artisanal
Mid-Aug	**Crozon peninsula**	Festival du Bout de Monde rock festival
Mid-Aug	**Concarneau**	Fête des Filets Bleus
Mid-Aug	**Guingamp**	Saint Loup Breton Dance Festival
Mid-Aug	**Lamballe**	Horse Festival
Mid-Aug	**Le Roche**	Jagu Jazz Festival
First Sun in Sept	**Le Pin**	Horse Show
First Sun in Sept	**Le Folgoët**	Pardon
Early Sept	**Dieppe**	Kite-flying festival (even-numbered years only)
First week in Sept	**Deauville**	American Film Festival
Second weekend in Sept	**Lessay**	Holy Cross cattle and animal fair
Sun nearest Sept 29	**Mont St-Michel**	Archangel Michael Festival
Last Sun in Sept	**Caudebec**	Cider Festival (even-numbered years only)
Late Sept	**Bellême**	Mycology Festival
Late Sept	**Tinteniac**	Balloon Festival
First week in Oct	**Dinard**	British Film Festival
Last Sun in Oct	**Beuvron-en-Auge**	Cider Festival
Mid-Nov	**St-Valery**	Herring Festival
First week in Dec	**Rennes**	Les Transmusicales international rock festival

Public holidays

There are thirteen national holidays (*jours fériés*), when most shops and businesses (though not necessarily restaurants), and some museums, are closed. May in particular is a big month for holidays: as well as May Day and Victory Day, Ascension Day normally falls then, as sometimes does Pentecost.

January 1 New Year's Day
Easter Sunday
Easter Monday
Ascension Day (forty days after Easter)
Pentecost or Whitsun (seventh Sunday after Easter, plus the Monday)
May 1 May Day/Labour Day
May 8 Victory in Europe Day
July 14 Bastille Day
August 15 Assumption of the Virgin Mary
November 1 All Saints' Day
November 11 1918 Armistice Day
December 25 Christmas Day

Rennes is increasingly the one to watch, with its December *Transmusicales* attracting international stars to share the stage with local groups. St-Brieuc's rival Art Rock Festival caters to more specialist tastes, while Carhaix's Vieilles Charrues festival has established itself very rapidly in just a few years.

Crime and safety

Compared to Paris or the south of France, crime is a low-key problem in Brittany and Normandy. However, you still need to take normal precautions against petty theft – keep your wallet in your front pocket or your handbag under your elbow. If you should be attacked, hand over the money and start dialling the cancellation numbers for your credit cards and travellers' cheques (see p.36).

If you need to report a **theft**, go to the local *gendarmerie* (police station), and try to persuade them to give you the requisite piece of paper (the *constat de vol*) for a claim; the first thing they'll ask for is your passport. The two main types of French **police**, the Police Nationale and the Gendarmerie Nationale, are for all practical purposes indistinguishable; you can go to either.

Drivers are one of the most obviously vulnerable groups, with the ever-present risk of a break-in. Vehicles are rarely stolen, but stereo systems as well as luggage left in cars make tempting targets, and foreign number plates are easy to spot. Good insurance is the only answer – see p.38 – but, whether you have it or not, make sure you don't leave your valuables in sight.

If you have an **accident** while driving, you have to fill in and sign a *constat à l'aimable* (jointly agreed statement); car insurers are

Emergencies

Medical emergencies ⓣ15
Police ⓣ17
Fire Service ⓣ18
Rape crisis (SOS Viol) ⓣ08.00.05.95.95
It's common to call the fire brigade (*les sapeurs pompiers*) for medical problems; they all have paramedical training and equipment.

supposed to give you this with a policy, though in practice few seem to have heard of it.

For non-criminal **driving violations** such as speeding, the police can impose on-the-spot fines. Should you be arrested on any charge, you have the right to contact your nearest consulate. Although the police are not always as cooperative as they might be, it is their duty to assist you – likewise in the case of losing your passport or all your money.

As for offences of your own making, treatment by the police is little different from anywhere else in Europe. **Camping** outside unauthorized sites can bring you into contact with the authorities, though it's more likely to be the landowner who tells you to move off. **Topless sunbathing** is acceptable within reason, but nudity is limited to a few specifically naturist beaches.

Officially, you're supposed to carry **identification documents** at all times, and the police are entitled to stop you and demand it. In practice this doesn't happen much to tourists, at least to whites. If you're black it can be a different matter; the French police have a reputation for racism. In fact, being black can make entering the country difficult, and immigration officers can be obstructive to black holidaymakers.

Sexual harassment is generally no worse than in North America or the UK, though cultural and linguistic differences can make it difficult to judge a situation correctly. Women who need help may prefer to contact women's organizations in the larger cities – Femmes Battues, Femmes en Détresse or SOS Femmes, all reachable through the Hôtel de Ville – before trying the police, while a consulate is likely to be of most immediate assistance.

From a safety point of view, **hitching** is definitely not advisable.

Travellers with disabilities

France does not have an exceptional record for providing facilities for disabled travellers. For people in wheelchairs, haphazard parking habits and stepped village streets are serious obstacles, and public toilets with disabled access are rare. However, in the major cities and coastal resorts, ramps or other forms of access are gradually being added to hotels, museums and theatres. APF, the French paraplegic organization (see p.60), which has an office in each *département*, will be the most reliable source of information on accommodation with disabled access and other facilities.

Public transport is certainly not wheelchair-friendly; although many train stations now have ramps to enable wheelchair-users to board and descend from carriages, at others it's still up to the guards to carry the chair. The high-speed **TGVs** (including Eurostar) all have places for wheelchairs in the First Class saloon coach, for which you must book in advance, though no higher fee is charged; on other trains, a wheelchair symbol within the timetable denotes whether that service offers special features, and you and your

Useful contacts

France

APF (Association des Paralysés de France) 17 bd Auguste-Blanqui, 75013 Paris ⓣ01.40.78.69.00, ⓦwww.apf.asso.fr. National association which can answer general enquiries and put you in touch with their departmental offices, which are also listed on the website.

Association France-Handicaps 9 rue Luce-de-Lancival, 77340 Pontault-Combault ⓣ & ⓕ01.60.28.50.12. Produces the French-language *Guide Rousseau* (€25 plus postage) detailing accessible hotels, museums and other tourist sites.

The UK and Ireland

Access Travel ⓣ01942/888 844, ⓦwww.access-travel.co.uk. Small tour operator that can arrange flights, transfers and accommodation; self-catering in *gîtes* in Normandy from around £280 per person per week, including ferry crossing.

Holiday Care ⓣ0845/124 9971 or 020/8760 0072, ⓦwww.holidaycare.org.uk. Provides free lists of accessible accommodation and information on financial help for holidays.

Irish Wheelchair Association ⓣ01/818 6400, ⓦwww.iwa.ie. Irish organization that provides useful information about travelling abroad with a wheelchair.

Tripscope ⓣ0845/7585 641, ⓦwww.tripscope.org.uk. Charity providing phone-in travel information service, with free advice on transport for those with mobility problems.

North America

Access-Able ⓦwww.access-able.com. Online resource for travellers with disabilities.

Directions Unlimited ⓣ1-800/533-5343 or 914/241-1700. Travel agency specializing in customized tours for people with disabilities.

Mobility International ⓣ541/343-1284, ⓦwww.miusa.org. Information and referral services, access guides, tours and exchange programmes.

Society for the Advancement of Travelers with Handicaps (SATH) ⓣ212/447-7284, ⓦwww.sath.org. Non-profit educational organization representing travelers with disabilities. Annual membership $45; $30 for students and seniors.

Wheels Up! ⓣ1-888/389-4335, ⓦwww.wheelsup.com. Discounted air fares and tour prices for disabled travellers, plus a comprehensive website.

Australia

ACROD (Australian Council for Rehabilitation of the Disabled) ⓣ02/6282 4333 (also TTY), ⓦwww.acrod.org.au. Lists of agencies and tour operators.

New Zealand

Disabled Persons Assembly ⓣ04/801 9100 (also TTY), ⓦwww.dpa.org.nz. Details of tour operators and travel agencies.

companion are again upgraded to First Class with no extra charge. The *Mémento du Voyageur à Mobilité Réduite*, available free at main train stations, details all facilities.

Taxis are obliged by law to carry you and to help you into the vehicle, also to carry your guide dog if you are blind. Specialist taxi services are available in some towns: these are detailed in the Ministry of Transport and Tourism's pamphlet *Guide des Transports à l'Usage des Personnes à Mobilité Réduite*, available at airports, main train stations and some tourist offices. The guide also gives some indication of the accessibility of urban public transport systems, and the availability of cars for rent with hand controls. For **self-drive**, Hertz (ⓣ01.41.91.95.25) and Europcar (ⓣ08.25.35.83.58) can provide automatic cars and cars with hand controls in certain locations, if notified well in advance. Drivers with disabilities are eligible for reduced fees on toll motorways.

Most of the **cross-Channel ferry companies** offer good facilities, though up-to-date information about access is difficult to get hold of. For wheelchair-users, **Le Shuttle** makes a particularly good way to get across the Channel, because there's no need to leave your vehicle during the journey. **Eurostar** too is convenient, in that it provides two special spaces in the First Class carriages for wheelchairs, with an accompanying seat for a companion, both at ordinary second-class fares. No advance bookings are necessary, though the limited spaces might make it wise to reserve ahead of time and also to arrange the special assistance which Eurostar offers at either end. As far as **airlines** go, British Airways has a better-than-average record for treatment of disabled passengers; while from North America, Virgin and Air Canada come out tops in terms of disability awareness (and seating arrangements) and might be worth contacting first for any information they can provide.

Up-to-date **information** is best obtained from organizations at home before you leave or from the French disability organizations. Some tourist offices have information but, again, it is not always very reliable. The Holiday Care Service has an information sheet on accessible **accommodation** in France, while guides produced by Logis de France (see p.43) and Gîtes de France (see p.44) indicate places with specially adapted facilities, though it's advisable to check in advance that these are adequate for your needs.

Read your **travel insurance** small print carefully to make sure that people with pre-existing medical conditions are not excluded. And use your travel agent to make your journey simpler: airline or bus companies can cope better if they are expecting you, with a wheelchair provided at airports and staff primed to help. A **medical certificate** of your fitness to travel, provided by your doctor, is also extremely useful; some airlines or insurance companies may insist on it. Make sure that you have extra supplies of drugs – carried with you if you fly – and a prescription including the generic name in case of emergency. Carry spares of any clothing or equipment that might be hard to find; if there's an association representing people with your disability, contact them early in the planning process.

Work and study

Although EU citizens are in theory free to move to France and find jobs with exactly the same pay, conditions and trade union rights as French nationals, for anyone who isn't a specialist, casual work in Brittany or Normandy is hard to come by. Furthermore, while the French minimum wage (the SMIC) is currently around €7.61 per hour, employers are likely to pay lower wages to temporary foreign workers who don't have easy legal resources. Any foreigner staying in France for over three months must have a *carte de séjour*, or residency permit – in theory, citizens of the EU are entitled to one automatically, but the application process can be long and stressful.

The region has just one wine harvest (around Nantes), almost wholly automated, and there is little chance of picking up any other kind of short-term employment. Visitors from North America or Australasia without a prearranged job offer would be foolish to imagine they have any chance of finding paid employment.

For EU citizens who arrange things in advance, however, there are work possibilities in au-pairing, teaching English as a foreign language, and in the holiday industry. And if you're just looking for an interesting way to fill the summer, assorted archeological schemes, mostly on Brittany's megalithic sites, sometimes have space for foreign volunteers.

Finding work

Whatever you are looking for, it's important to plan well ahead. A couple of **books** which might be worth consulting are *Work Your Way Around the World* by Susan Griffith, *Live and Work in France* by Victoria Pybus and *Summer Jobs Abroad*, all published by Vacation Work (9 Park End St, Oxford OX1 1HJ; ⓣ01865/241 978, ⓦwww.vacationwork.co.uk). **In France**, check out the "Offres d'Emploi" (Job Offers) in *Le Monde*, *Le Figaro* and the *International Herald Tribune*, and try the youth information agency CIDJ (Centre d'Information et de Documentation Jeunesse), 101 quai Branly, 75740 Paris Cedex (ⓣ01.44.49.12.00, ⓦwww.cidj.com), or CIJ (Centre d'Information Jeunesse) offices in other main cities, which sometimes have temporary jobs for foreigners and produce all sorts of useful information about working in France. The national employment agency, ANPE (Agence Nationale pour l'Emploi; ⓦwww.anpe.fr), with offices all over France, advertises temporary jobs in all fields and, in theory, offers a whole range of services to job-seekers open to all EU citizens, but is not renowned for its helpfulness to foreigners. Non-EU citizens have to show a work permit to apply for any of their jobs.

Teaching English

Teaching English is one of the easiest ways to find a job in France. Such posts are frequently advertised in Britain; check the *Guardian*'s "Education" section (every Tuesday), or the weekly *Times Educational Supplement*. Late summer is usually the best time. You don't need fluent French to get a post, but a degree and a TEFL (Teaching English as a Foreign Language) qualification may well be required.

For a thorough breakdown of available TEFL courses, see the annual *EL Gazette Guide to English Language Teaching*, (ⓣ020/7481 6715, ⓦwww.elgazette.com; £13.95 plus postage), or the monthly *EL Gazette*, filled with job ads (same phone and website; subscription for 12 issues £33 within Europe, £44 rest of the world).

If you apply from home, most schools will fix up the necessary papers for you. It's also quite feasible to find a teaching job when you're in France, but you may have to accept semi-official status and no job security. For the addresses of schools, look under "Enseignement: Langues" in the local yellow pages. Offering private lessons (via university noticeboards or classified ads), you'll have lots of competition, and it's hard to reach the people who can afford it, but it's always worth a try. The best places to live and teach are probably St-Malo, Quimper, Rennes and Rouen.

Becoming an au pair

Au pair work is usually arranged through an agency, such as those listed in *Living and Working in France*, published by Vacation Work (see previous column), and on the International Au Pair Association (IAPA) website (ⓦwww.iapa.org). In Britain, *The Lady* is the magazine for **classified adverts** for such jobs, arranged privately. **Terms and conditions** are never very generous, but you shouldn't accept less than €260 a month (on top of board and lodging), and make sure you have an escape route (such as a ticket home) in case you find the conditions intolerable – many people have had bad experiences.

Travel industry jobs

Temporary jobs in the travel industry revolve around **courier work** – supervising and working on bus tours and summer campsites. You'll need **good French** (and maybe even another language) and should write to as many tour operators as you can, preferably in early spring. Ads occasionally appear in the *Guardian*'s "Media" section (every Monday), while travel magazines like the very reliable *Wanderlust* have a "Job Shop" section which often advertises job opportunities with tour companies. Working on a campsite usually involves putting up tents at the start of the season, taking them down again at the end, and general maintenance and troubleshooting work in the months between; **experienced teachers** are also in demand to provide childcare. Canvas Holidays (see p.23) are worth approaching.

Archeological digs

Volunteer work on archeological sites varies from year to year, according to available grants and priorities. Recently, there have been opportunities to work on a number of Breton Gallo-Roman and megalithic sites – including Locmariaquer – and on Neolithic sites in Normandy. Food and campsite or student-hall accommodation is generally provided, though there may be a small weekly charge; travel costs are not normally paid. It's best to write a number of letters to potential authorities asking for details of any projects. Excavations are regularly organized by the following:

Laboratoire d'Anthropologie Préhistorique write c/o Dr Jean Laurent Monnier, Charge de Recherche au CNRS, Université de Rennes I, Campus de Beaulieu, 35042 Rennes.
Ministère de la Culture Circonscription des Antiquités Historiques et Préhistoriques de Bretagne 6 rue du Chapitre, BP 927, 35011 Rennes Cedex.
Musée d'Histoire Naturelle write c/o Jean Pierre Watte, Archéologue Municipal, place du Vieux Marché, 76600 Le Havre.

Organic farming

One final offbeat possibility if you want to discover green rural life is being a working guest on an organic farm. This is unpaid employment for a period of anything from a week to a couple of months and the work may involve cheese-making, market gardening, bee-keeping, cider producing or building. For details of the scheme and a list of French addresses, contact World-Wide Opportunities on Organic Farms (WWOOF; Ⓦwww.wwoof.org/home.asp), which has branches in Britain, the US, Canada, Australia and New Zealand, among other places.

Studying in France

It's relatively easy to be a student in France, and many foreign students perfect their fluency in the language while studying. Foreigners pay no more than French nationals to enrol for a course, and the only problem then is to support yourself. Your *carte de séjour* and – if you're an EU citizen – social security will be assured, and you'll be eligible for **subsidized accommodation**, meals and all the student reductions. In general, French universities are relatively informal; strict entry requirements, including an exam in French, apply only for undergraduate degrees, not for postgraduate courses. For full **details and prospectuses**, contact the Cultural Service of any French embassy or consulate (see p.28).

If you're a full-time non-EU student in France, you can get a non-EU work permit for the following summer so long as your visa is still valid.

Language schools

Language schools all along the coast provide intensive French courses for foreigners. Many of these are listed in the handout *Cours de Français pour Étudiants Étrangers*, obtainable from embassy or consular cultural sections, with the most popular being those organized each summer at St-Malo by the University of Rennes (Ⓦwww.uhb.fr).

The École des Roches, in Verneuil-sur-Avre in Normandy (see p.189), is a well-equipped institute that runs intensive three- to nine-week summer courses in French for pupils aged 11 to 19; contact BP 710, 27137 Verneuil-sur-Avre (Ⓣ02.32.23.40.00, Ⓦwww.ecoledesroches.com).

Directory

Beaches are public property within 5m of the high-tide mark, so you can walk past the private villas, and set foot on islands. Another law, however, forbids you to camp.

Cameras and film Film is considerably cheaper in North America than in France or Britain, so stock up if you're coming from that direction. There are also plenty of shops, including the FNAC, where you can order prints of your digital pictures. If you bring a camcorder, make sure any tapes you buy in France are compatible.

Children and babies are generally welcome everywhere, including most bars and restaurants. Hotels charge by the room, with a small supplement for an additional bed or cot, and many family-run places will babysit or offer a listening service while you eat or go out. Especially in the seaside towns, most restaurants have children's menus or cook simpler food on request. You'll have no difficulty finding disposable nappies (*couches à jeter*), but nearly all baby foods have added sugar and salt, and French milk powders are very rich indeed. SNCF charge nothing on trains and buses for under-4s, and half-fare for 4–11s (see p.40 for other reductions). If you're renting a car, however, baby seats will normally cost extra. Most Syndicat d'initiatives have details of specific activities for children – in particular, many resorts supervise "clubs" for children on the beach. Almost every town also has a children's playground with a good selection of activities. Something to be aware of – not that you can do much about it – is the difficulty of negotiating a child's buggy over the large cobbles that cover many of the older streets in town centres.

Contraceptives Condoms (*préservatifs* or *capotes* in French slang) are available in supermarkets and pharmacies, as well as from many clubs and street dispensers. Note that the Pill (*la pillule*) is only available on prescription.

Electricity is almost always 220V, using plugs with two round pins. If you haven't bought the appropriate transformer before leaving home, the best place in France to find the right one is the electrical section of a department store, where someone is also more likely to speak English; it should cost around €10.

Fishing You get fishing rights by becoming a member of an authorized fishing club – tourist offices have details. The main areas for river fishing are in Brittany, in the Aulne river around Châteaulin and in the Morbihan.

Gay and lesbian travellers France is more liberal on homosexuality than most European countries. The legal age of consent is 16, and gay communities thrive in Paris and many southern towns, though lesbian life is rather less upfront. Brittany and Normandy, however, have little conspicuous gay life; the best source for clubs and meeting places is the *Gai Pied Guide*, widely available in French newsagents and bookshops (or online at ⓦwww.gaipied.fr). The English-language *Spartacus International Gay Guide* has an extensive section on France and contains some info for lesbians. *Têtu* (ⓦwww.tetu.com) is a highly rated gay/lesbian magazine (€5) with events listings and contact addresses; you can buy it in bookshops or through their website, which is also an excellent source of information. Other useful websites include Gay Friendly France (ⓦhttp://us.franceguide.com, click on Gay Friendly France), maintained by Maison de la France in the US, and the French-language sites Gay.com (ⓦwww.fr.gay.com, for online personals) and DykeplaNET (ⓦwww.dykeplanet.com), which produces the *Dyke Guide Lesbien* (€11), containing articles and Lesbian-friendly addresses.

Laundry Laundries/laundromats – *laveries automatiques* – are not all that common in Breton or Norman towns, although some are listed in this guide. The alternative *blanchisserie* or *pressing* services are likely to be expensive, and hotels in particular charge very high rates. If you're staying in hotels, only wash a few items yourself as most places officially forbid doing any laundry in your room.

Smoking is banned on public transport and in museums in France, while all restaurants and bars are obliged to have nonsmoking areas. This said, smoking is still widespread.

Swimming pools (*piscines*) are well signposted in most French towns, and reasonably priced. Tourist offices have addresses.

Tax-free shopping Visitors to France from non-EU countries are entitled to a twelve per cent reduction on duty tax on certain items provided that the amount of the purchase is equal to or higher than €175. Ask for the relevant forms when you buy, then present them to Customs officials as you leave the country.

Time France is one hour ahead of the UK, six hours ahead of Eastern Standard Time, nine hours ahead of Pacific Standard Time, ten hours behind eastern Australia and twelve hours behind New Zealand. This also applies during daylight saving seasons, which are observed in France from the end of March through to the end of October.

Tipping Since restaurants add a service charge to your bill, you only need to leave an additional cash tip if you feel you have received service out of the ordinary. It's customary to tip porters, tour guides, taxi drivers and hairdressers between one and two euros.

Toilets Ask for *les toilettes* or look for signs to the WC (pronounced "vay say"); when enquiring about hotel facilities, don't confuse *lavabo*, which means washbasin, with lavatory. Standards of cleanliness in public toilets are often poor and many tend not to have toilet paper. Toilets in railway stations and department stores are usually okay; most have an attendant and charge a small fee. You'll occasionally come across automated toilet booths in town centres; note that children under 10 aren't allowed in them on their own.

TV and video French TV broadcasts using a different system to the British; only black-and-white portable British TVs work in France. Make sure that any videotapes you buy in France, whether blank for use in a camcorder, or prerecorded, are compatible with your own system.

Vaccinations are neither required nor necessary.

Water The tap water is always safe to drink, though bottled mineral water, always available, may taste better. A litre bottle can cost under €1 in a supermarket, but considerably more in a *tabac*.

Guide

Guide

NORMANDY

BRITTANY

Normandy

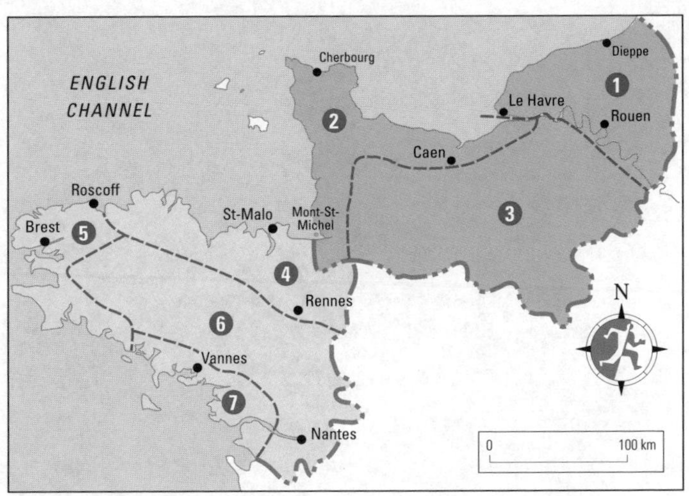

ENGLISH CHANNEL
Cherbourg
Dieppe
Le Havre
Rouen
Caen
Roscoff
Brest
St-Malo
Mont-St-Michel
Rennes
Vannes
Nantes
N
0
100 km
1
2
3
4
5
6
7

1

Seine Maritime

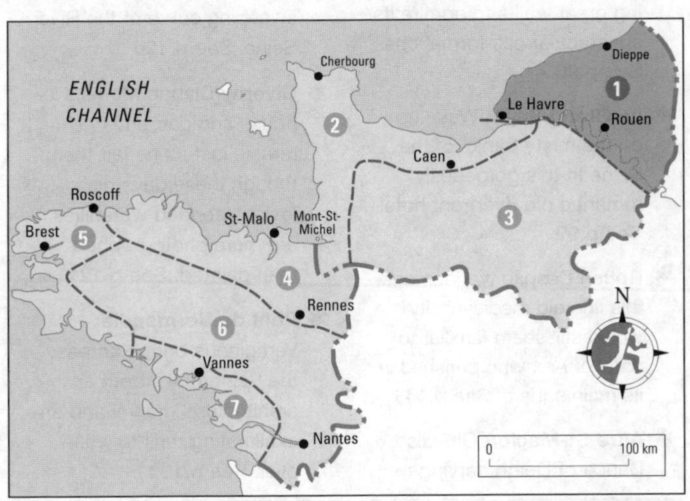

CHAPTER 1 Highlights

✱ **Hôtel de la Terrasse** Lovely clifftop hotel that makes a perfect first- or last-night stopover for ferry passengers. See p.84

✱ **Étretat** Normandy's most attractive little resort, offering great walks to admire its spectacular cliff formations. See p.90

✱ **Le Grand Sapin** Wake up on the misty banks of the Seine in this gorgeously romantic old riverfront hotel. See p.99

✱ **Rouen** Despite war damage, this fine old medieval city would still seem familiar to Joan of Arc, who perished in its main square. See p.103

✱ **Aître St-Maclou** Ghoulish Dance of Death carvings adorn this centuries-old courtyard in central Rouen. See p.111

✱ **Château Gaillard** The atmospheric ruins of Richard the Lionheart's mighty fortress dominate a sweeping curve of the River Seine. See p.120

✱ **Giverny** Claude Monet's house and garden remain just as he left them, though these days his lovingly tended waterlilies are more photographed than painted. See p.121

✱ **Pont de Normandie** Vertiginous bridge across the Seine that's both an architectural marvel and an exhilarating thrill to walk over. See p.130

△ Sunset over the Seine

1

Seine Maritime

The *département* of **Seine Maritime** makes a somewhat atypical introduction to Normandy. Though scattered with the usual Norman half-timbered houses and small farms, the landscape is stark along the coastline and verges on the monotonous in the chalky flatlands of the Caux plateau behind. Only along the sheltered ribbon of the **Seine Valley** do you find the greenery, and profusion of flowers and fruit, that you might expect of the province.

Nonetheless, there's no need to neglect the region or race through it. Arriving at **Dieppe**, you can take advantage of the low-key resorts along the **Côte d'Albâtre**, which hold occasional surprises behind their windswept and tide-chased walks. At **Fécamp**, you'll encounter an absurd "Hammer House of Horror" Benedictine distillery; at **Étretat**, spectacular stacks and arches of rock, to either side of one of the nicest little coastal towns in Normandy; and at **Varengeville**, the wonderful house designed by architect Edwin Lutyens at **Bois des Moutiers**. And while motorists tend to find little to detain them in the hinterland that lies just south of the coastal cliffs, for **cyclists** the gentle valleys and expansive grain fields offer an immediate dose of undemanding pedalling through pastoral French countryside. Even **Le Havre**, on the Seine estuary – the least conventionally enticing of all the Norman Channel ports – is worth attention all the same, not only for its modern architecture and art collections but, as France's second port after Marseille, for its liveliness.

The extravagant meanders of the **River Seine**, however, determine most people's travels in this region. **Rouen**, scene of the trial and execution of Joan of Arc, is one of the major provincial capitals of France; a combination of contemporary verve with its heavily but effectively restored medieval centre makes it by far the most interesting city in Normandy. Along the valley and riverbanks there is plenty to delay your progress: tranquil villages such as **Villequier** and **La Bouille**; the evocatively ruined Romanesque abbeys of **St-Wandrille** and **Jumièges**; the English frontier-stronghold of **Château Gaillard** looming above **Les Andelys**; and, an unmissable last stop before Paris, **Monet's garden** and waterlilies at **Giverny**.

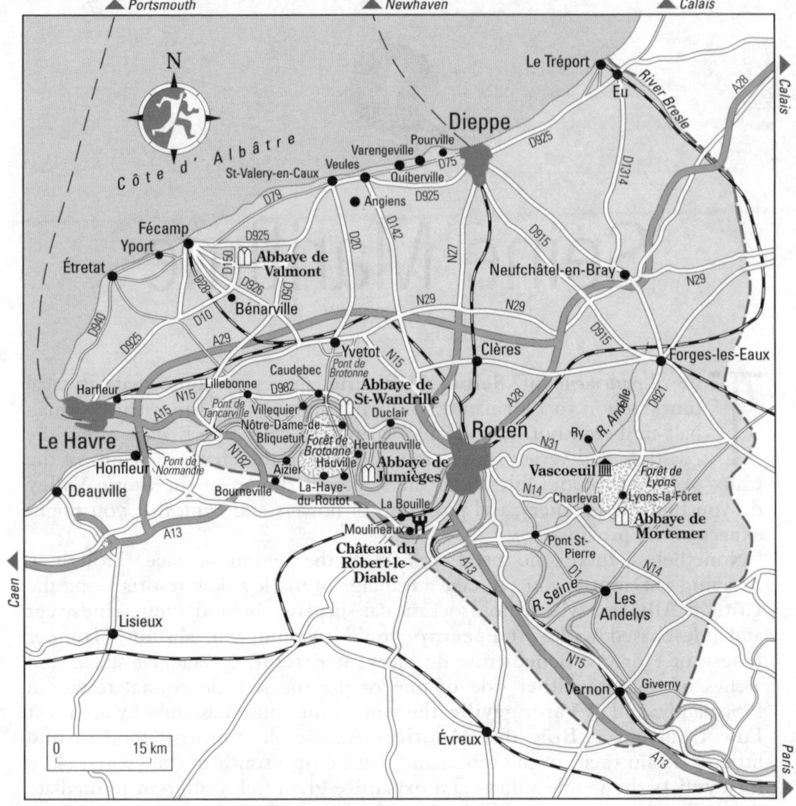

The northern ports

There is no confusing the northern ports of Normandy, **Dieppe and Le Havre**, with their rivals to the east. Each has managed to retain a distinct individual identity in a way that Calais and Boulogne, which have to cope with ten times the number of passengers, simply have not; if you're using either port, there's no need to rush on out as soon as you arrive, or to dice with time to coincide to the minute with the ferries back.

Both offer the same obvious choice of **routes**: inland towards Rouen, or along the coast. If you're setting off from Dieppe with your own transport, the **coast road** is the most immediately gratifying. Harbour towns such as **Le Tréport** to the east, and **Étretat** and **Fécamp** to the west, make diverting overnight stops, whereas the plains of the Caux plateau inland hold few diversions until you get as far south as Rouen. Both Étretat and Fécamp are also within easy reach of Le Havre, the point where you start the route along the Seine. As well as the river towns, places such as Honfleur (see p.130) on the lower Norman coast, covered in Chapter Two, only take a few minutes to get to from Le Havre, via the huge Seine bridges.

Dieppe

Crowded between high cliff headlands, **DIEPPE** is an enjoyably small-scale port at which to arrive, very French but with a long and intimate association with England. As the closest harbour and beach to Paris, 170km southeast, it has had an eventful history. Its existence was first recorded in 1030, when the abbey of Mont Ste-Catherine-de-Rouen acquired the area for an annual rent of 5000 smoked herrings. The port was regularly used by William the Conqueror when he was king of England, and passed into French hands in 1195 when Philippe Auguste burned Richard the Lionheart's fleet in the harbour. Having changed ownership several more times during the Hundred Years War, Dieppe was finally taken for France by the future Louis XI in 1443.

Adventurers from Dieppe were at the forefront of French **naval explorations**. It has been claimed that Dieppois navigators reached the coast of Guinea in 1384, and Brazil in 1488; less questionably, the Italian Giovanni da Verrazzano sailed from the city in 1524 to found the settlement that later became New York. Early emigrants to Canada used the port, too, and the strong links established with the French colony there were to endure long after the French lost Canada to the British in 1759.

When the Edict of Nantes was revoked in 1685, Dieppe was one of the principal escape routes used by Protestant refugees; similarly, during the French Revolution, three Brighton captains of the Channel Packet Service ran a regular – and profitable – service for the *noblesse* who found themselves obliged to flee. In 1848, the railway from Paris reached Dieppe and, from the 1850s, the Newhaven Packet operated a daily cross-Channel service. The town became a fashionable **seaside resort**, attracting French aristocracy and British royalty; the French would promenade along the seafront, while the English colony indulged in the peculiar pastime of bathing.

Modern Dieppe has a population of just under 36,000. While not a place many travellers go out of their way to visit, it is one of the nicer ferry ports in northern France, and you're unlikely to regret spending an afternoon or evening here. With kids in tow, the aquariums of the **Cité de la Mer** museum complex (see p.80) are the obvious attraction; otherwise, you could settle for admiring the cliffs and the castle as you stroll the seafront lawns.

Arrival and information

Daily **ferry** services between Newhaven in England and Dieppe's **gare maritime**, east of the town centre, are operated by Hoverspeed, whose SuperSeaCats take just over two hours, weather permitting (June–Sept only, 2–3 daily; in France, call free on Ⓣ00800.1211.1211, Ⓦwww.hoverspeed.com), and Transmanche Ferries, using conventional vessels that take four hours (1–3 daily; Ⓣ08.00.65.01.00, Ⓦwww.transmancheferries.com). Motorists coming off the boats are directed away from the town, and have to double back west to reach it; foot passengers can easily walk the 500m to the tourist office (see below).

Dieppe's **gare SNCF** is another 500m south of the tourist office, on boulevard Clemenceau, 1km from the beach. Trains are by far the quickest way to get to Rouen or Paris, but to travel along the coast you'll have to catch

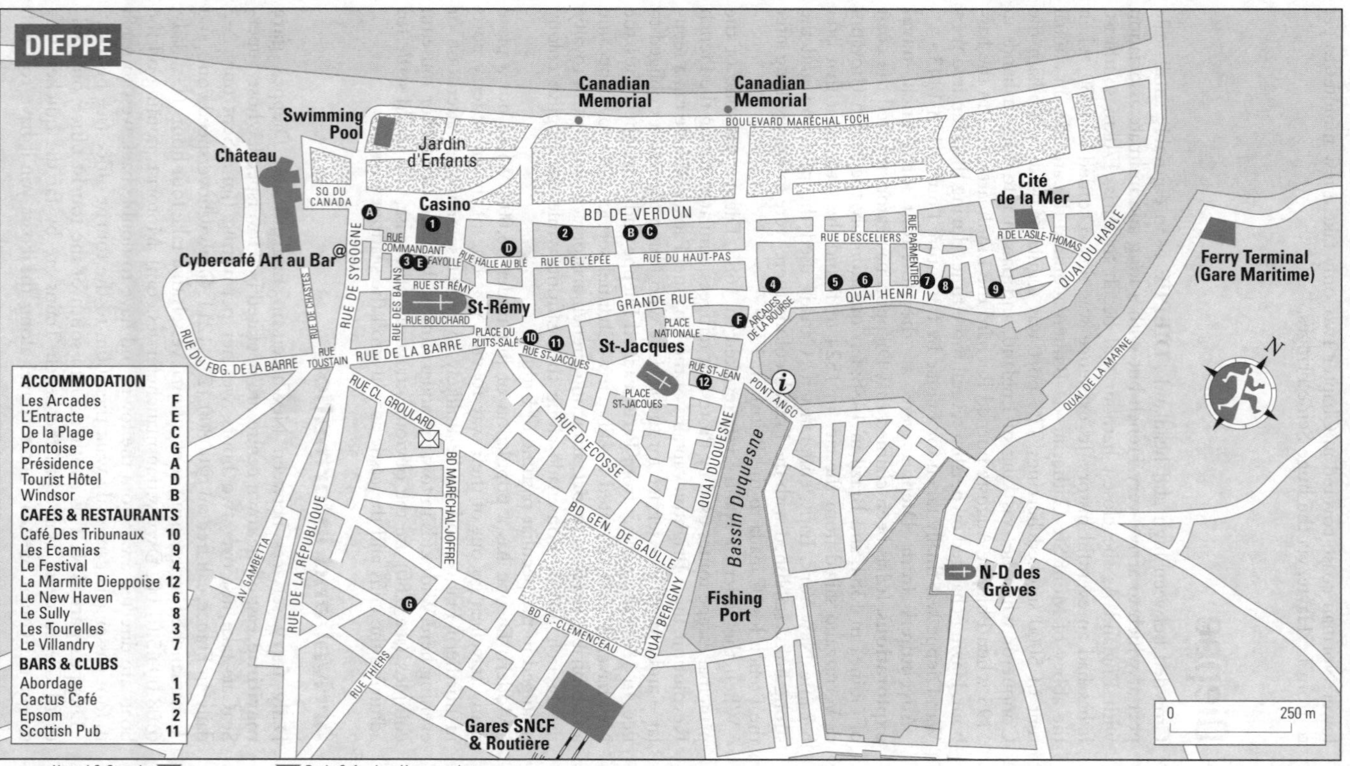
DIEPPE
Canadian Memorial
Canadian Memorial
Swimming Pool
Jardin d'Enfants
Château
Casino
Cité de la Mer
Ferry Terminal (Gare Maritime)
Cybercafé Art au Bar
St-Rémy
St-Jacques
Fishing Port
Bassin Duquesne
N-D des Grèves
Gares SNCF & Routière
BOULEVARD MARÉCHAL FOCH
BD DE VERDUN
SQ DU CANADA
RUE DE SYGOGNE
RUE COMMANDANT FAYOLLE
RUE HALLE AU BLÉ
RUE DE L'ÉPÉE
RUE DU HAUT-PAS
RUE DESCELIERS
RUE PARMENTIER
R DE L'ASILE-THOMAS
QUAI DU HABLE
QUAI HENRI IV
ARCADES DE LA BOURSE
GRANDE RUE
RUE ST RÉMY
RUE DES BAINS
RUE BOUCHARD
PLACE DU PUITS-SALÉ
PLACE NATIONALE
RUE ST-JACQUES
RUE ST-JEAN
PLACE ST-JACQUES
PONT ANGO
QUAI DE LA MARNE
RUE DE CHASTES
RUE TOUSTAIN
RUE DE LA BARRE
RUE DU FBG. DE LA BARRE
RUE CL. GROULARD
BD MARÉCHAL-JOFFRE
RUE D'ECOSSE
BD GEN. DE GAULLE
QUAI DUQUESNE
QUAI BERIGNY
BD G.-CLEMENCEAU
RUE DE LA RÉPUBLIQUE
AV GAMBETTA
RUE THIERS
N
0
250 m
ACCOMMODATION
Les Arcades F
L'Entracte E
De la Plage C
Pontoise G
Présidence A
Tourist Hôtel D
Windsor B
CAFÉS & RESTAURANTS
Café Des Tribunaux 10
Les Écamias 9
Le Festival 4
La Marmite Dieppoise 12
Le New Haven 6
Le Sully 8
Les Tourelles 3
Le Villandry 7
BARS & CLUBS
Abordage 1
Cactus Café 5
Epsom 2
Scottish Pub 11
Pourville & Varengeville
Hostel & Camping
Paris & Auchan Hypermarket

a bus from the **gare routière** alongside. For information on bus departures – basically to Le Tréport or Fécamp – either call the CAN bus company (Ⓣ08.25.07.60.27) or ask at the tourist office for timetables. All **Local buses** stop at the *gare SNCF*, as well as next to the tourist office on pont Ango. In a more touristy vein, a "**petit train**" makes one-hour narrated tours of Dieppe (April to early Sept nine daily 10.30am–7.30pm, leaving on the half hour; adults €6, under-10s €4), starting from the tourist office and heading first to the Cité de la Mer, then back along the full length of the beach and up to the Auchan hypermarket.

Dieppe's **tourist office** (May, June & Sept Mon–Sat 9am–1pm & 2–7pm, Sun 10am–1pm & 3–6pm; July & Aug Mon–Sat 9am–1pm & 2–8pm, Sun 10am–1pm & 3–6pm; Oct–April Mon–Sat 9am–noon & 2–6pm; Ⓣ02.32.14.40.60, Ⓦwww.dieppetourisme.com), is on the pont Ango, which separates the ferry harbour from the pleasure port. **Bicycles** can be rented very cheaply from Vélo Service, operating out of a bus just across the bridge (Ⓣ06.24.56.06.27; €1 per hr, €5 per day). The main **post office** is at 2 bd Maréchal-Joffre (Mon–Fri 8am–6pm, Sat 8am–12.30pm; Ⓣ02.35.04.70.14); **Internet access** is available here, and also at Cybercafé Art au Bar, 19 rue de Sygogne (Mon–Thurs 10–12.30am, Fri & Sat 10–2am; Ⓣ02.35.40.48.35; €4 per hr).

Accommodation

You're unlikely to experience much difficulty finding accommodation in Dieppe, even at the height of summer. It has plenty of **hotels**, with the dearer ones concentrated along the seafront – which is actually among the quietest areas of town – and especially at the western end of the boulevard de Verdun, closest to the château. Room rates on the whole get progressively cheaper as you head further inland, though hotels with their own restaurants like to insist on half-board, or even full-board, in season, which can mean they work out expensive.

There is a welcoming and comfortable **hostel**, somewhat inconveniently located 2km southwest of the *gare SNCF* in the *quartier* Janval at 48 rue Louis Fromager (Ⓣ02.35.84.85.73, Ⓔdieppe@fuaj.org; closed Oct–Feb, plus weekends during May & June; reception 5–10pm; €7.70), offering two-, four-, sixteen- and eighteen-bed dorms. To get there, take bus #2 from the tourist office (direction "Val Druel", stop "Château Michel"). The closest **campsite** is the three-star *Camping Vitamin* on chemin des Vertus, well south of town in an unremarkable setting in St-Aubin-sur-Scie that's really only convenient for motorists, even if it is served by the #2 bus route (Ⓣ02.35.82.11.11; closed mid-Oct to March).

Hotels

Hôtel Les Arcades 1–3 arcades de la Bourse Ⓣ02.35.84.14.12, Ⓦwww.lesarcades.com. Long-established hotel, under the eponymous arcades facing the port; you couldn't ask for a more central location, nor one closer to the ferry. Restaurant with full, good-value menus from €17. ❹

Hôtel L'Entracte 39 rue du Commandant Fayolle Ⓣ02.35.84.26.45. Extremely inexpensive, no-frills rooms above a little bar behind the casino, plus some en-suite ones at slightly higher rates. ❶

Hôtel de la Plage 20 bd de Verdun Ⓣ02.35.84.18.28, Ⓦwww.plagehotel.fr.st. Slightly upmarket rooms, all en suite with cable TV, facing the sea but set back somewhat from the street, alongside the *Windsor*. No restaurant. ❹

Hôtel-Restaurant Pontoise 10 rue Thiers Ⓣ02.35.84.14.57. A basic, inexpensive option, not far from the *gare SNCF* and well away from the beach. ❶

Hôtel Présidence bd de Verdun Ⓣ02.35.84.31.31, Ⓦwww.hotel-la-presidence.com. This ugly grey modern block, below the château at the far west end of the seafront, holds 89 spacious and well-equipped rooms, plus a rooftop restaurant, the *Panoramic*. Rooms with sea views cost almost double. ❹

Tourist Hôtel 16 rue de la Halle au Blé ⓣ02.35.06.10.10, ⓕ02.35.84.15.87. Plain en-suite rooms with phone and TV in a converted town house one block from the beach behind the Casino. No restaurant. ❸

Hôtel Windsor 18 bd de Verdun ⓣ02.35.84.15.23, ⓦwww.hotelwindsor.fr. You pay much higher rates for the superior sea-facing rooms in this *logis*, where the glass-fronted first-floor dining room has lunch menus from €18. The cheaper ones, facing inwards, can be pretty grim, even if they do have baths and cable TV. ❷

The Town

Dieppe remains a busy port, and the sheer bustle and verve of the place cannot fail to strike any visitor. Vast quantities of fruit from all over the world – and forty percent of all shellfish eaten in France – are unloaded at its commercial docks, but the quayside fish stalls near the tourist office are what really grab the eye. Each morning the previous night's catch is displayed with all the usual mouthwatering French flair, an appetizing profusion of sole, turbot and the local speciality, scallops.

Modern Dieppe is still laid out along the three axes dictated by its eighteenth-century town planners, though these central streets have become a little run-down. The **boulevard de Verdun** runs for over a kilometre along the seafront, from the fifteenth-century château in the west to the port entrance, and passes the Casino, along with the grandest and oldest hotels. A short way inland, parallel to the seafront, is the **rue de la Barre** and its pedestrianized continuation, the **Grande Rue**. Along the harbour's edge, an extension of the Grande Rue, **quai Henri IV** has a colourful backdrop of cafés, brasseries and restaurants.

The place du Puits-Salé and around

At the heart of the old town, the **place du Puits-Salé** is dominated by the half-timbered *Café des Tribunaux*, looking sprucer than ever following a lavish restoration. The Café was built as an inn towards the end of the seventeenth century, and briefly became Dieppe's town hall after the previous one was bombarded by the British in 1694. In the late nineteenth century, it was favoured by painters such as Renoir, Monet, Sickert, Whistler and Pissarro. It's now the haunt of college students, a cavernous café with sombre wooden panels and dark-brown velveteen walls, open until after midnight (ⓣ02.32.14.44.65). For English visitors, its most evocative association is that the exiled and unhappy Oscar Wilde drank here regularly. He lived (as M. Melmouth) at Berneval, 10km east of Dieppe, which was where he wrote *The Ballad of Reading Gaol*.

From the Café, rue St-Jacques leads to the **church** of the same name, built in the twelfth century to greet English pilgrims embarking on the trail to the shrine of St James at Santiago de Compostella in Spain. The original church burned down a hundred years later, so its oldest part today is the fourteenth-century lantern tower. Inside, a chapel to the "Canadian Martyrs" neighbours the usual ones to Ste-Thérèse and the Sacred Heart. Dedicated in 1951, this has nothing to do with World War II; instead it's devoted to two Dieppe priests, shown in modern stained glass being hacked to death by "Mohawks" in 1648. Nearby, the **Mur de Trésor** bears intricate and potentially fascinating carvings of Brazilian Indians dating from the seventeenth century. Unfortunately they're too high up to see clearly, and all but indecipherable.

Northwest of the place du Puits-Salé, **rue Bouchard** heads to the sixteenth-century **church of St Rémy**, which was partly destroyed when, used as an arms dump by the Germans, it was blown up the day before the town was liberated in August 1944. Now finally restored, organ and all, it is occasionally open to the public for special events, such as a Festival of Ancient Music, held each August.

The beach

Dieppe's wide, steeply shelving **shingle beach** was deposited by a freak tide long after the rest of the town took shape. Hence the extravagant amount of clear space between the seafront and the first buildings, taken up partly by the windswept grassy lawns that make an ideal venue for the town's biennial **kite festival** (spread across two weekends in early September of even-numbered years), and partly by car parks where departing ferry passengers munch last-minute picnics and twiddle their thumbs. Here you will also find a heated saltwater **swimming pool** (May to early Sept 10am–7.30pm; €3.40).

The château

The most obvious and conspicuous sight in Dieppe is the medieval **Château** that overlooks the seafront from the west. The entrance is not via the square du Canada, as it might first seem, but via rue de Chastes on the southwestern side of the château. Most of those visitors who bother to make the stiff climb up do so simply to enjoy the view, but the château also serves as home to the **Musée de Dieppe** (June–Sept daily 10am–noon & 2–6pm; Oct–May Mon & Wed–Sun 10am–noon & 2–5pm; €3). In addition to its exhibition on local history – and Dieppe's maritime past means that "local history" can encompass pre-Columbian pottery from Peru – the museum houses two showpiece collections. The first is a group of **Dieppe carved ivories** – virtuoso specimens of sawing, filing and chipping of the plundered riches of Africa. The ivory was shipped back to the town by early Dieppe "explorers", in such quantities that during the seventeenth century over three hundred craftsmen-carvers lived here. Earlier pieces, displayed upstairs, tend to be exquisite miniature portraits and classical scenes; by the nineteenth century, the sculptors were concentrating instead on souvenirs, and producing an abundance of model ships.

The other permanent exhibition is made up of a hundred or so prints by the co-originator of Cubism, **Georges Braque**, who went to school in Le Havre, spent his summers in Dieppe, and is buried just west of the town at Varengeville-sur-mer (see p.84). Only perhaps a quarter tend to be displayed at any one time, but in theory you can see the rest if you ask. Other galleries upstairs hold paintings of local scenes by the likes of Pissarro, Renoir, Dufy, Sickert and Boudin, while a separate, much newer wing of the château stages temporary exhibitions.

The square du Canada

At the foot of the château, the **square du Canada** originally commemorated the role played by sailors from Dieppe in the colonization of Canada. After the last war, however, it acquired an additional significance, for it was at Dieppe in August 1942 that the Allied commando raid, **Operation Jubilee**, took place. The first large-scale assault on the continent after Dunkerque, the operation claimed over 3000 Canadian casualties in a near-suicidal series of landings and attacks up sheer and well-fortified cliff faces. Many were cut down as soon as they left their landing craft, before they even touched dry land, while some German defenders are reputed not to have bothered with firing their weapons, and simply dropped projectiles over the edge.

The Allied Command later justified the carnage as having taught valuable lessons for the 1944 invasion. The Channel ports were shown to be too heavily defended to be vulnerable to frontal attack, and the invasion plan was changed to one that required the amphibious landing armies to bring their own harbour with them.

The Cité de la Mer

Dieppe's most ambitious attempt to keep tourists in town for longer than it takes to get to or from the ferry terminal is the **Cité de la Mer** ("Museum of the Sea") at 37 rue de l'Asile-Thomas (daily 10am–noon & 2–6pm; €5). The museum is housed in a featureless white concrete block in the tangle of streets just west of the mouth of the harbour. Setting out simultaneously to entertain children and to serve as a centre for scientific research, it succeeds in both without being all that interesting for the casual adult visitor.

Kids are certain to enjoy learning the principles of navigation by operating radio-controlled boats (€2 for 3min). The museum then traces the history of seagoing vessels, leading from maps of the great Norman voyages of exploration and conquest, via a Viking *drakkar* under construction following methods depicted in the Bayeux Tapestry, right up to a sketchy account of the insides of a nuclear-powered submarine. Next comes a very detailed geological exhibition covering the formation of the local cliffs, from which we learn how to go about converting shingle into sandpaper.

Visits culminate with the large **aquariums**, filled with the marine life of the Channel: flatfish with bulbous eyes and twisted faces, retiring octopuses, battling lobsters, and hermaphrodite scallops (a caption helpfully explains that the white part is male, and the orange, female).

Eating

The most promising area to look for **restaurants** in Dieppe is along the quai Henri IV, which, although it overlooks the port rather than the open sea, makes a lovely place to stroll and compare menus of a summer's evening. As well as a fine array of seafood restaurants, it also holds plenty of cheaper alternatives, selling sandwiches and snacks. The beach itself, by contrast, offers no formal restaurants, but there are a couple of open-air bistro-type cafés selling plates of mussels, salads, and so on, and a handful of crêpe stands. More restaurants can be found all over town – and note that many of the hotels reviewed also have good dining rooms. Competition for ferry passengers keeps prices relatively low, meaning that Dieppe is one of the few towns in Normandy where you can still find a good menu for under €15.

As well as the daily spectacle of the fish on sale in the "port de pêche", described on p.78, there's an all-day open-air **market** in the place Nationale and Grande Rue on Saturday. Otherwise, the main shopping streets in Dieppe are rue de la Barre and the Grande Rue, and there's a Shopi supermarket at 59 rue de la Barre. L'Épicier Oliver at 18 rue St-Jacques has more specialist items such as wines and cheeses. The largest of several **hypermarkets** in the area is Auchan (Mon–Sat 8.30am–10pm), out of town at the Centre Commercial du Belvédère on the route de Rouen (RN 27) or reached by local bus #2 from the tourist office.

Restaurants

Les Écamias 129 quai Henri IV ☎02.35.84.67.67. Small, friendly traditional French restaurant, at the quieter, seaward end of the main quay not far from the Cité de la Mer, where the €13.50 option includes *moules* *marinières*, and they also offer skate with capers. Less touristy feel than the restaurants at the inland end of the quay. Closed Mon.

Le Festival 11 quai Henri IV ☎02.35.40.24.29. Quick-fire brasserie at the busiest end of the quayside that delivers its fishy goods at top speed without skimping on quality. *Moules frites* is a mere €6 and comes in blue china ships, while the €13.50 and €16.50 menus are also dominated by seafood.

La Marmite Dieppoise 8 rue St-Jean ☎02.35.84.24.26. Rustic, busy little restaurant between St-Jacques church and the arcades de la Bourse. Menus are on the pricey side at €32 or €40, but do feature the local speciality *marmite Dieppoise* (seafood pot, with shellfish and white fish). Closed Sun eve & Mon, plus Thurs eve out of season.

Le New Haven 53 quai Henri IV ☎02.35.84.89.72. Reliable seafood specialist, towards the quieter end of the quayside, with good menus from €15.50. The €20.50 *menu de la Jetée* is fine if you hanker after fish livers, the house speciality, while €18 buys you a *choucroute de la mer* (seafood sauerkraut). Closed Tues eve, plus Wed in winter.

Le Sully 97 quai Henri IV ☎02.35.84.23.13. Some of the finest seafood on the quayside – none of it frozen – served either on bargain menus, including attractive options under €15, such as a €13 vegetarian menu, or in lavish platters.

Les Tourelles 43 rue du Commandant Fayolle ☎02.35.84.15.88. Welcoming little local restaurant just behind the Casino, serving the standard seafood dishes. Menus at €14 with moules and steak, or €19 including the famous *trou Normand* and a mid-meal glass of Calvados. Closed Sun eve, all Mon, & Tues eve.

Le Villandry 85 quai Henri IV ☎02.35.82.55.49. Harbourfront restaurant that has an indoor dining room, but is at its best in summer, when tables spread onto its large, uncovered pavement patio. It's €14.95 menu features oysters and mussels, followed by solid fish courses and basic desserts.

Bars and entertainment

Things tend to shut early in Dieppe. Apart from the **Cinema Rex** on the place Nationale (☎08.92.68.69.02) and the tacky appeal of the slot machines at the **Casino** at the western end of boulevard de Verdun, the incentive to abandon your comfortable restaurant terrace of an evening is minimal. The most enticing venue is the *Epsom*, 11 boulevard de Verdun (☎02.35.84.12.27), a *café littéraire* where poets and writers come to discuss their latest works, and there is sometimes **live jazz** on Thursdays. For reggae and Latin music, try the *Cactus Café*, wedged between the glut of restaurants on quai Henri IV (☎02.35.82.59.38), while the *Scottish Pub*, 14 rue St-Jacques (☎02.35.84.13.16), caters to a mainly Anglo-Saxon clientele in search of beer and football. For **dancing**, the *Abordage* nightclub at the Casino (☎02.32.14.48.00) is the only central option. Friday and Saturday nights, when it remains open until 4am, represent your best chance of meeting Dieppes's young and beautiful; the Sunday afternoon tea dance (3–7pm) is positively prehistoric.

The Côte d'Albâtre

The high white cliffs that characterize the Norman coast from Picardy in the east to Le Havre in the west have earned it the name of the **Côte d'Albâtre** – the Alabaster coast. This whole shoreline is eroding at a ferocious rate, and it's conceivable that the small resorts here, tucked in at the mouths of a succession of valleys, may not last more than another century or so. For the moment, however, they are quietly prospering, with casinos, sports centres and yacht marinas ensuring a modest but steady summer trade.

It might seem counter-intuitive for travellers embarking on a tour of Normandy to head **east** along the coast from Dieppe towards Calais and Boulogne, but doing so gives the opportunity to see a couple of surprising old towns: venerable **Le Tréport** and, just inland, the village of **Eu** with its thick forest surround. Head **west**, on the other hand, and the coast road dips into a series of pretty little ports, with **Étretat** the pick of the bunch.

Le Tréport

Thirty kilometres east of Dieppe, at the mouth of the River Bresle which serves as the border with Picardy, **LE TRÉPORT** is a seaside resort that, while busy in summer, has clearly seen better days. It was already something of a bathing spot when the railways arrived in 1873, and was duly promoted as "the prettiest beach in Europe, just three hours from Paris". It remained the capital's favoured resort until the 1950s, but these days its charms are definitely fading.

Le Tréport divides into three distinct sections: the flat wedge-shaped seafront area, bounded on one side by the Channel, on another by the harbour at the canalized river mouth, and on the third by imposing hundred-metre-high white chalk cliffs; the old town, higher up the slopes on safer ground; and the modern town further inland. The **seafront** itself is entirely taken up by a hideous pink and orange concrete 1960s apartment block, with one or two snack bars but no other sign of life, facing the casino and a drab grey shingle beach. It's the more sheltered harbourside **quai François 1er** around the corner that holds most of the action, lined with restaurants, souvenir shops and cafés. A venerable little brick fish market stands across the road by the water, alongside a hundred-year-old carousel. The assorted stone jetties and wooden piers around the harbour are enjoyable to stroll around, as you watch the comings and goings of the fishing boats that still keep Le Tréport bustling. In its heyday it was possible to ride up the cliffs on a *téléphérique*; the tunnel through which it pierced the cliff face is still open to the air at either end, but the cables have rusted away and the facilities are abandoned.

Climbing up from the *quai*, you come to the heavily nautical **Église St-Jacques**, built in the fifteenth century to replace an eleventh-century original that crumbled into the sea, along with the cliff on which it stood. Nearby, next to the fortified former town hall that is now the local library, successive flights of steps, 365 of them in all, climb to the top of the cliffs. As well as views to either side of the decaying mansions of Le Tréport, you can see across to the longer beach of **Mers-les-Bains**, which, being in Picardy, falls outside the scope of this book.

Practicalities

Both **trains** and **buses** arrive in Le Tréport on the far side of the harbour, a short walk from the main *quai*. Turning left as you hit the main drag will bring you to the town's **tourist office**, on quai Sadi-Carnot (April–June & Sept Mon–Thurs 10am–noon & 3–6pm, Fri & Sat 10am–12.30pm & 2.30–7pm, Sun 10am–1pm & 3–5pm; July & Aug daily 10am–7pm; Oct–March Mon–Sat 10am–noon & 3–6pm; ⓣ02.35.86.05.69). Here you can pick up a schedule of activities if you happen to be around for Le Tréport's major annual **festival**, the Blessing of the Sea on August 2.

Of the **hotels** in town, the best option is the *Riche Lieu* at 50–51 quai François 1er (ⓣ02.35.86.26.55; ❷), with en-suite facilities in all the rooms – those with sea views are particularly pleasant – and well-priced, top-quality food served in the restaurant downstairs. The other, consistently tempting seafood **restaurants** along the *quai* are too numerous to review in detail, each boasting of its fresh *assiette de fruits de mer* and serving similar meals from around €15. The one with the highest gourmet reputation is the *Matelote*, 34 quai François 1er (Ⓣ02.35.86.01.13; closed Tues in winter), where dining on the first floor gives you a panoramic overview of all the life of the port.

Eu

Queen Victoria twice visited Le Tréport with Albert; she didn't come to play on the beach, though, but to stay at the château at **EU**, a couple of kilometres inland. When she did so the first time, in the original "Entente Cordiale" in 1843, she became the first English monarch to make an official state visit to France since Henry VIII arrived for the Field of the Cloth of Gold.

Today, Eu is something of a backwater, consisting of a few pedestrian streets at the top of a hill, and a straggle of newer districts reaching down the slopes. The **château** (mid-March to early Nov Wed, Thurs & Sat–Mon 10am–noon & 2–6pm, Fri 2–6pm; €3) that stands at its heart was constructed in the sixteenth century, and served between 1830 and 1848 as the summer residence of the French monarch Louis Philippe. Of Eu's previous château, deliberately burned in 1475 to forestall its capture by the English, only the tiny chapel remains, which was the site of William the Conqueror's marriage to Mathilda.

Unlikely as it may sound, Eu's Gothic church, **Notre-Dame et St-Laurent**, is dedicated to St Lawrence O'Toole, an archbishop of Dublin who died here in 1181 while en route to visit Henry II of England in Rouen, to intercede on behalf of the Irish. His effigy still lies in the brightly lit and eerie crypt.

If you find yourself staying in Eu, you can spend an enjoyable afternoon by venturing into the **forest of Eu**, a mysterious and ancient tangled woodland dominated by tall beeches, with a lost Roman city supposedly hidden in its depths. A good way to explore it more thoroughly, assuming you have your own transport, is to follow the **River Bresle** upstream, along the border between Normandy and Picardy.

Practicalities

Eu is on the Lé Treport rail line, with its **gare SNCF** 500m down the hill from the centre, and its **tourist office** up in the pedestrianized section at 41 rue Bignon (May–June & Sept to mid-Nov Mon–Sat 9.30am–12.30pm & 2–6.30pm, Sun 10am–1pm; July & Aug Mon–Sat 9am–7pm, Sun 10am–1pm; mid-Nov to April Mon–Sat 9.30am–noon & 2–6.30pm; Ⓣ02.35.86.04.68). The best-value central **hotel** is the *Maine* at 20 avenue de la Gare (Ⓣ02.35.86.16.64, Ⓦwww.hotel-maine.com; ❸; restaurant closed Sun eve), a Logis de France in a slightly dilapidated red-brick town house next to the *gare SNCF*, which offers menus from €15. There's also an *FUAJ* **hostel** in the former royal kitchens in rue des Fontaines, the *Centre des Fontaines* (Ⓣ02.35.86.05.03, Ⓔcentredesfontaines@wanadoo.fr; HI members €12.10), which serves meals, and acts as a general resource for local youngsters. Eu is generally rather short of places to **eat**, but *La Bragance*, housed in what used to be an icehouse in the gardens of the château (Ⓣ02.35.50.20.01; closed Sun eve & Mon), serves good-value alfresco lunches on its terrace.

Pourville-sur-mer

Heading **west** from Dieppe along the coastal D75, you come after 3km to the resort of **POURVILLE-SUR-MER**, an extremely tranquil last- or first-night stop for ferry passengers. No more than a simple curving bay that briefly interrupts the line of cliffs, it lacks any form of port, but the wave conditions are enough to attract hordes of **surfers**. The beach itself was painted by Monet, a reproduction of whose *La Plage à Pourville* is displayed at the centre of the promenade.

Most of the few buildings lining the road through Pourville are **hotels**, including a logis confusingly named *Produits de la Mer* (ⓣ02.35.84.38.34; ❷), where all eight rooms have showers or baths, and the plainest seafood menu costs €13 on weekdays, €19.50 at weekends. Next to it is a crazy-golf course. The two-star *Le Marqueval* **campsite** (ⓣ02.35.82.66.46; closed Oct to mid-March) is set in the fields further back from the sea.

Varengeville-sur-mer and around

The straggling clifftop community of **VARENGEVILLE-SUR-MER**, 8km west of Dieppe, has long been popular with **artists**, including at different times Monet, Dufy, Miró, and the painter parents of British Prime Minister Anthony Eden, who was born here. Its greatest devotee, however, was the pioneer Cubist **Georges Braque** (1882–1963), whose **grave** is situated outside a church perched spectacularly above the cliffs a couple of kilometres north of the centre, a smooth marble tomb topped by a sadly decaying mosaic of a white dove in flight. More impressive is his vivid-blue *Tree of Jesse* stained-glass window inside the church, through which you can see the sun rise in summer.

Back along the road towards town from the church, the house at the **Bois des Moutiers**, built for Guillaume Mallet from 1898 onwards and un-French in almost every respect, was one of architect **Edwin Lutyens**' first commissions. Lutyens, then aged just 29 and heavily influenced by the "Arts and Crafts" ideas of William Morris, was at the start of a career that was to culminate during the 1920s when he laid out most of the city of New Delhi. The real reason to visit, however, is to enjoy the magnificent **gardens**, designed by Mallet in conjunction with Gertrude Jekyll, and at their most spectacular in the second half of May (mid-March to mid-Nov daily 10am–noon & 2–6pm; €7 during May & June, otherwise €6). Enthusiastic guides lead you through the highly innovative engineering of the house and grounds, full of quirks and games. The colours of the Burne-Jones tapestry hanging in the stairwell were copied from Renaissance cloth in William Morris's studio; the rhododendrons were chosen from similar samples. Paths lead through vistas based on paintings by Poussin, Lorrain and other eighteenth-century artists; no modern roses, with their anachronistic colours, are allowed to spoil the effect.

Also in Varengeville, 300m south of the D75, is the **Manoir d'Ango**, the "summer palace" of sixteenth-century Dieppe's leading shipbuilder (mid-March to mid-Nov daily 10am–12.30pm & 2–6.30pm; €5). Jean Ango outfitted such major expeditions as Verrazzano's, which "discovered" the site of New York in 1524, and made his riches from pillaging treasure ships out on the Spanish Main. His former home consists of a rectangular ensemble of fine brick buildings arranged around a central courtyard. The intricate patterning of red bricks, shaped flint slabs, stone blocks and supporting timbers is at its finest in the remarkable central **dovecote**, topped by a dome that rises to an elegant point, which is aflutter with pigeons. The rooms of the various houses are all but empty except for cases of damp books, and in the absence of labelling or guidance you may find you've had enough after a few minutes' wandering.

While the village of Varengeville offers little choice of **accommodation**, its one available option is absolutely irresistible – the lovely *Hôtel de la Terrasse*, a logis set amid the pines on the route de Vastérival, (ⓣ02.35.85.12.54; closed mid-Oct to mid-March; ❸). Reached via a right turn off the main highway as you head west of town, it's perched high above the cliffs, with great sea views.

Fish menus in its panoramic dining room cost from €17, and you can follow footpaths down through narrow cracks in the cliffs to reach the rocky beach below.

Varengeville is served by regular **buses** en route between Dieppe and St-Valery.

On from Varengeville

The coastal road immediately beyond Varengeville is not very interesting. **Quiberville**, the main name on the map, is popular with windsurfers, but in itself is little more than an overgrown caravan park; at **Veules**, you pass a couple of ludicrous folk-sculptures, including a seashell-encrusted snowman; and **Angiens** is a pretty village, but with nothing much to linger over.

St-Valery-en-Caux

The first sizeable community west of Dieppe, **ST-VALERY-EN-CAUX**, is a rebuilt but still attractive port where open-air stalls along the quayside of the narrow harbour sell fresh-caught fish daily. St-Valery provides a clear reminder of the fighting – and massive destruction – during the Allied retreat of 1940. To either side of the shingle beach rise crumbling brown-stained cliffs. A monument on the western heights pays tribute to the French division who faced Rommel's tanks on horseback, brandishing their sabres with hopeless heroism, and beside the ruins of a German artillery emplacement on the opposite cliffs a second monument commemorates a Scottish division, the 51st Highlanders, rounded up while fighting their way back to the boats home.

There's now a characterless new Casino in the centre of the seafront, and an even newer church a little way behind, on the northern edge of the main market square. Made almost entirely of stained glass, it holds a giant sailing boat motif above its entrance.

Practicalities

By far the most attractive house to survive in St-Valery is the Renaissance **Maison Henri IV** on the quai d'Aval, with its intricately carved wooden facade. It's now the **tourist office** (May to mid-Sept daily 10am–12.30pm & 2.30–6.30pm; mid-Sept to April daily 10am–1pm & 3–7pm; ⓣ02.35.97.00.63, ⓦwww.ville-saint-valery-en-caux.fr). Although no trains serve the town, around sixteen SNCF **buses** connect each day with trains to and from Rouen at Yvetot, 27km south.

The *Terrasses*, 22 rue le Perrey (ⓣ02.35.97.11.22; ❷–❹; closed Sun eve & Mon, plus Christmas & Jan), is the only **hotel-restaurant** actually facing the sea; rooms with en-suite facilities cost around double those without, and dinner menus cost €15 or €30. A cheaper *logis*, the seven-room *La Marine*, 113 rue St-Léger (ⓣ02.35.97.05.09; ❷; closed Fri in low season, plus Dec & Jan), is tucked away in a backstreet on the west side of the harbour, and several more small hotels surround the market square, including the *Eden*, above a brasserie at 21 place du Marché (ⓣ02.35.97.11.44; ❶; closed Sun eve & Mon in low season). Otherwise, head for the huge *Relais Mercure*, 500m back along the pleasure port at 14 avenue Clemenceau (ⓣ02.35.57.88.00; ❹). Its 149 rooms are faultlessly comfortable, if also characterless, and can be a godsend in high season, when the few resources along this stretch of coast are strained to the limit.

St-Valery holds two municipal **campsites**, the one-star *Falaise d'Amont* (ⓣ02.35.97.05.07; closed mid-Nov to mid-March), on the eastern cliffs, and the larger four-star *d'Étennemare* (ⓣ02.35.97.15.79), open year-round and set back from the sea southwest of the harbour. The best of its **restaurants** is the *Restaurant du Port*, overlooking the harbour at 18 quai d'Amont (Ⓣ02.35.97.08.93; closed Mon, plus Sun eve in low season), which offers a simple but delicious €19 menu, and a more extravagant five-course €33 one, centring on grilled turbot. **Markets** take place on Fridays and summer Sundays, and the town plays host to both a **festival of the sea** in mid-August, and a **herring festival** in mid-November.

Fécamp

FÉCAMP, roughly halfway between Dieppe and Le Havre, is, like Dieppe, a serious fishing port, albeit one with a more frivolous modern sideline as a holiday resort. Its name first features in a charter of 875 AD, as Fiscannum, from the Germanic *fisc* meaning "fish", and it has been a centre for shipbuilding ever since the Vikings set up a boatyard here in 911 AD. These days, it's a striking town, surrounded by high cliffs so that, approaching from inland, you don't see the sea until you're right upon it. It was fortunate enough to sustain very little damage during World War II, though the Germans did destroy its reportedly magnificent Belle-Époque casino, fearing it could serve as a landmark for Allied invaders. The current, much uglier replacement was completed in 1958.

Fécamp still has its **railway link**, the tracks running right up to the small harbour, where fishing boats and yachts jostle for position. The town's long promenade fronts a uniform steep beach of shingle, framed by crumbling and overhanging cliffs. As ever along this coast, windsurfing is more appealing than bathing. In the absence of any major attraction out to sea, the tourist boats or *vedettes* offer cruises to watch the sun set.

Arrival and information

Trains from the south and buses along the coast from Dieppe pull in at the **gares SNCF** and **routière** respectively, both of which lie between the port and the town centre on boulevard de la République. Buses from Le Havre arrive on avenue Gambetta, opposite the St-Étienne church. Steps opposite the *gare SNCF* lead up to avenue Gambetta; the Le Havre stop is on your left. The main **tourist office** is in an inconvenient location, tucked away a few hundred metres from either the *gare SNCF* or the seafront, opposite the distillery at 113 rue Alexandre-le-Grand (Jan–March & Sept–Dec Mon–Fri 9am–6pm, Sat 9.30am–12.30pm & 2–6pm; April–June Mon–Fri 9am–6pm, Sat & Sun 10am–6.30pm; July & Aug daily 9am–6.30pm; Ⓣ02.35.28.51.01, Ⓦwww.fecamptourisme.com). However, there's another summer-only office occupying the blue and white "Point Plage" kiosk in the middle of the seafront promenade (May & June Mon–Fri 10am–6.30pm, Sat & Sun 10am–1pm & 2–6.30pm; July & Aug daily 10am–6.30pm; Ⓣ02.35.10.85.96). Both can provide details of the regular programme of guided tours in and around Fécamp. The **post office** is near the St-Étienne church at 1 place Bellet (Mon 8.30am–noon & 1.30–5.30pm, Tues–Fri 8.30am–12.30pm & 1.30–5.30pm, Sat 8.30am–12.30pm).

Accommodation

Fécamp's **hotels** tend to be set back away from the sea, on random side streets. It's a popular place, so you'll need to reserve a room in summer. A lovely **campsite** with beautiful views of the coast, the *Camping de Reneville* (Ⓣ02.35.28.20.97; closed Jan & Feb), is a short walk out of town on the western cliffs; it also has a handful of simple two-bedroom chalets, rented by the week in summer for €360–500 per week.

Hôtel d'Angleterre 91–93 rue de la Plage Ⓣ02.35.28.01.60, Ⓦwww.hotelangleterre.com. Long-established hotel just back from the sea, which looks unattractive from the outside but has nicely refurbished rooms, all en suite, as well as its own reasonable restaurant (see p.88) and an "English pub" (see p.89). ❷

Hôtel du Commerce 26–28 place Bigot Ⓣ02.35.28.19.28, Ⓦwww.hotel-lecommerce.com. Peaceful, appealing hotel near St-Étienne church in the old town. Some rooms have en-suite facilities; a few are in individual motel-style cabins beyond the courtyard, while the restaurant downstairs (closed Sat lunch & Sun) serves tasty menus from €13 up to €28. ❷

Hôtel de la Mer 89 bd Albert 1er Ⓣ02.35.28.24.64 or 02.35.28.01.57, Ⓕ02.35.28.27.67. Simple but good-value hotel on the seafront, adjoining *La Frégate* bar (see p.89) where boulevard Albert 1er stops just short of the Casino. It's nicer inside than it looks from the outside, with some of the bright rooms having balconies overlooking the sea. Closed first three weeks of Feb. ❷

Hôtel de la Plage 87 rue de la Plage Ⓣ02.35.29.76.51, Ⓦperso.wanadoo.fr/hoteldelaplagefecamp. The smartest option close to the beach; only the higher rooms have sea views, but almost all have been well refurbished and the location is quiet. ❸

The Town

Arriving in Fécamp from the south, whether by road or rail, you'll come into town alongside the Valmont river. With the coastline running roughly north to south at this point, however, the river is in fact flowing westward. By the time it reaches the port it has disappeared into the first of a succession of canalized channels and artificial harbours. The *gare SNCF* is on its left bank at this point, with the town proper, focused on the venerable **Église de la Trinité**, sprawling up the slopes to the south. The sea, however, lies a few hundred yards further west, along a harbourside promenade that holds most of Fécamp's best restaurants. A sturdy sea wall shields the main road from the Channel itself. On the far side, you'll find a steeply shelving shingle beach, while the main feature of the seafront here is the intriguing **Musée des Terres-Neuvas et de la Pêche**.

The Benedictine Distillery

Fécamp owes much of its popularity to an utterly bizarre tourist attraction – the **Benedictine Distillery** at 110 rue Alexandre-le-Grand (daily: early Feb to March & Oct–Dec 10.30–11.45am & 2–5pm; April to early July & early Sept to Oct 10am–noon & 2–5.30pm; early July to early Sept 10am–6pm. Admission on guided tours only, lasting 1hr 30min; €5.20). Set amid the narrow streets that run parallel to the port towards the town centre, this mock-Gothic monstrosity may look like a decaying mansion that has survived nightmarish aeons, but was in fact built at the end of the nineteenth century for the manufacture of the sweet liqueur known as Benedictine. To see inside, you have to join a rather dismal guided **tour**, the first part of which treks through a museum of local antiquities and oddments. Most visitors are frantic to get to the alcohol at the end, but the tour does have its moments. These include headless statues (mostly of bishops), serpentine musical instruments, carved wood and ivory, and – a kitsch treat – a stained-glass window in which Alexandre le Grand, former owner of the Benedictine company (no relation to Alexander the Great), is being treated to a bottle of his liqueur by a passing angel.

Eventually you pass on to the distillery section (although commercial operations have moved to a new factory outside town), where bucket-loads of exotic herbs are thrown into great copper vats and distillation vessels. There is then a massive surge drinkwards, for the (disappointingly modest) *dégustation* across the road; it must be said it's nice stuff, especially the "B&B", Benedictine and brandy, served either neat or on crêpes. Make sure you hang on to your admission ticket to get the free drink.

Église de la Trinité

If your aesthetic sensibilities need soothing after the distillery, head away from the sea to the **Église de la Trinité**. This medieval abbey church is light and almost frail with age, its bare nave echoing to the sound of birds flying free beneath the high roof. The wooden carvings are tremendous, in particular the dusty wooden bas-relief *Dormition of the Virgin*. The abbey also has a fine selection of saintly fingers and sacred hips, authenticated with wax seals, and even a drop of the Precious Blood itself, said to have floated all the way here in a fig tree dispatched by Joseph of Arimathea. Until Mont-St-Michel was built, this was the religious centre of Normandy; Edward the Confessor is more reliably known to have made extensive gifts to the abbey, and may have lived here at some point before his coronation as king of England.

Opposite the main entrance on place des Ducs Richard, the few vestiges that remain of the palace of the early dukes of Normandy – both Richard I and Richard II are buried in the abbey – have been landscaped to create an attractive little public garden. William, bastard son of Duke Robert, was presented here at the age of seven to the assembled lords and bishops of Normandy when his father went away to war, and returned here as William the Conqueror to celebrate Easter 1067.

Musée des Terres-Neuvas et de la Pêche

Just south of the river mouth, though sealed from view of the Channel by the high sea wall, the modern **Musée des Terres-Neuvas et de la Pêche** is at 27 boulevard Albert 1er (July & Aug daily 10am–7pm; Sept–June Wed–Mon 10am–noon & 2–5.30pm; Adults €3, under-18s free). It commemorates Fécamp's association with the sea from the Viking invasions onwards. Spreading across two floors, with lots of miniature model boats and amateur paintings, it focuses in particular on the long tradition whereby the fishermen of Fécamp decamped en masse each year to catch cod in the cold, foggy waters off Newfoundland. Life on board was both brutal and lonely, and the work was hard, with the fish being cleaned and salted on deck, and then sold in Spain or Portugal rather than being carried back to France. Sailing vessels continued to make the trek from the sixteenth century right up until 1931; today, vast refrigerated container ships have taken their place.

Upstairs, there's a fascinating scale model of the port and town as it looked in 1830, shortly before Fécamp was transformed by the arrival of the first railway. At that point, it entirely lacked docks and warehouses; in fact nothing stood on the far side of the river, and the whole town was still surrounded by agricultural land.

Non-French speakers should ask at the front desk for the excellent folder of English translations of all the museum's captions.

Eating

In summer, Fécamp welcomes enough visitors to keep several **restaurants** in business – not surprisingly, the fish tends to be good – but things get rather quieter in winter. The best area to look for somewhere to eat is along the *quais* fronting the harbour; the seafront boulevard Albert 1er, meanwhile, has a relatively meagre choice.

La Manche 91–93 rue de la Plage ⓣ02.35.28.01.60. This simple restaurant at *Hotel Angleterre* is only open for dinner and offers just one menu containing a limited and standard choice of dishes, but at €12, you will be hard pressed to find a cheaper three-course dinner anywhere else. Closed Sun.

La Marée 77 quai Bérigny ⓣ02.35.29.39.15. Very good fish restaurant, enjoying harbour views from a grand upstairs dining room above a wonderful fish shop. Menus from €18 to €34, featuring all kinds of pescatorial pleasures – the only meat anywhere is foie gras – plus an apple caramel *tartellette Bénédictine* for dessert. Closed Sun eve & Mon.

La Marine 23 quai de la Vicomté ⓣ02.35.28.15.94. Friendly little quayside restaurant, not far from the beach, but with indoor seating only. It's open daily for mainly seafood €14 lunches and dinners up to €23; €16 buys an excellent *choucroute de la mer* plus dessert.

Le Vicomté 4 rue Coty ⓣ02.35.28.47.63. Cheery old-fashioned bistro near the distillery and port. It serves just one €14.90 menu, which changes daily and includes hearty traditional meat and fish dishes. Closed Wed eve & Sun.

Bars and entertainment

The hotels generally offer the most promising place to go for a **drink**, although it must be said that the choice is limited and highly conducive to getting an early night. *La Frégate* at *Hotel de la Mer* (ⓣ02.35.28.24.64; closed first three weeks of Feb) is the pick of the bunch, especially in summer when drinkers take advantage of a large terrace facing the sea. One hundred metres north along boulevard Albert 1er, at no. 65, *Le Drakkar* (ⓣ02.35.29.33.63) has a rowdier atmosphere, but does offer **live music** every two weeks during summer and once a month at other times. The *Pub Anglais* at *Hotel Angleterre* (ⓣ02.35.28.01.60) is the one to go for if your idea of fun is darts, beer, quiz nights and more beer. Along with the slot machines, the **Casino** also has a bar-cum-discotheque, which, with its karaoke nights and concerts by local crooners, is awfully kitsch.

Yport

The tiny fishing port of **YPORT**, tucked into a narrow gap in the chalky cliffs 6km west of Fécamp, is something of a cross between Fécamp and Étretat. It's much smaller and more attractive than Fécamp, from which it's actually visible along the shoreline, without being nearly as photogenic (or crowded) as Étretat. Local legend has it that Yport was colonized over two thousand years ago by Greek fishermen from Asia Minor, who for some reason were not deterred by its complete lack of a harbour. Their descendants have remained ever since, meaning that Yport has a reputation for being an insular community. While it's not a place to spend your entire holiday, it makes an appealing and very peaceful overnight stop.

Practicalities

Yport's **tourist office**, just back from the sea at 18 place J-P Laurens (July & Aug daily 9.30am–12.30pm & 2.30–7pm; Sept–June Tues–Sat 10am–noon & 3–6.30pm; ⓣ02.35.29.77.31, ⓦwww.yport.net), can provide details of clifftop hiking trails.

Both the main **hotels** are painted to look as though they're half-timbered. The *Hôtel Normand*, also on place J-P Laurens, at no. 2 (ⓣ02.35.27.30.76; ❸; closed mid-Nov to mid-Dec, plus Tues eve & Wed in winter) is a Logis de France with menus from €14; *La Sirène*, 7 boulevard Alexandre-Dumont (ⓣ02.35.27.31.87; ❸; closed Mon, Tues eve & mid-Dec to mid-Jan), enjoys sweeping beachfront views, and serves the usual seafood menus at €18 and upwards. *La Falaise*, near the *Normand* at 32 rue Émmanuel Foy (ⓣ02.35.29.35.07), is a traditional little French **restaurant**, with pale blue decor, which offers good-value menus from €14 at lunchtime.

On to Étretat

The minor road **D28** runs from Fécamp through a thickly wooded and idyllic valley to **Benarville** – a good cycling route, even though it manages to lose the river somewhere along the way. The **D150** is less pastoral, but leads to the remains of the **Abbaye de Valmont** (April–Sept Wed–Mon 2–5pm). In its spacious grounds you can feast your eyes on a Renaissance chapel, grass-floored and open to the sky, and an intact Gothic Lady Chapel.

Étretat

The delightful little town of **ÉTRETAT**, another 20km west towards Le Havre, is very different to Fécamp. Here the alabaster cliffs are at their most spectacular – their arches, tunnels and the solitary "needle" out to sea will doubtless be familiar from tourist brochures long before you arrive – and the town itself has grown up simply as a pleasure resort.

Étretat doesn't even have a port of any kind; the seafront consists of a sweeping unbroken curve of concrete above the shingle beach. Traditionally, wooden boats were hauled up onto the promenade each summer and thatched over to serve as seasonal bars. These days, the boats are permanently beached, cemented into place and roofed over, but they still add a charming touch. However, what makes Étretat truly special is not the waterfront, but its central core of characterful old timber buildings, grouped around the market square a few metres inland, along with the breathtaking clifftop walks on offer immediately to the north and south of the town (as is the case at Fécamp, the coastline at Étretat runs roughly north to south).

Arrival and information

Étretat's **tourist office** is alongside the main through road in the centre of town, on place M. Guillard (mid-June to mid-Sept daily 9.30am–7pm; mid-Sept to mid-June Mon–Sat 10am–noon & 2–6pm; ⓣ02.35.27.05.21, ⓦwww.etretat.net). Coastal **buses** stop just outside, while **mountain bikes** are available for rent at Le Biclou, one hundred metres south of the tourist office at 5 rue Alphonse-Karr (daily 8am–8pm; ⓣ02.35.27.78.55; €16 per day). From the tourist office, rue Monge leads down to place Foch, the town's main square, and the beach.

Accommodation

Though Étretat is hardly short of **hotels** – four crowd onto the corners of place Foch alone – they struggle to cope with demand during high season. It makes a lovely place to stay, however, so it's well worth booking in advance. **Campers** will find the *Camping Municipal* 1km out on rue Guy-de-Maupassant (ⓣ02.35.27.07.67; closed mid-Oct to late March).

Le Corsaire rue du Général Leclerc ⓣ02.35.10.38.90, ⓦwww.lecorsaire-etretat.com. The most affordable of the seafront hotels, in the thick of things alongside the Casino. All the rooms are en suite, but those that enjoy sea views have been thoroughly renovated, meaning they're considerably more expensive than their plainer counterparts that face inland. The beach terrace restaurant serves good menus from €12.50. ❸–❺

Taverne des Deux Augustins place Foch ⓣ02.35.27.06.99, ⓦwww.les-2-augustins.com. Hybrid structure on the main square, with the pink brick of the hotel proper rising above the sprawling wood-panelled frontage of the *choucroute* restaurant downstairs. Reasonable central rooms. ❹

Dormy House route du Havre ⓣ02.35.27.07.88, ⓦwww.dormy-house.com. Grand, modern establishment perched above town on the coastal road to the west, situated as much for the golf course as the beach. Comfortable rooms with superlative views, and a good restaurant. ❸–❾

L'Escale place Foch ⓣ02.35.27.03.69, ⓕ02.35.28.05.86. Twelve simple but pleasant rooms on the main square, above a snack restaurant specializing in *moules frites* and crêpes. ❸

Hôtel des Falaises 1 bd René-Coty ⓣ02.35.27.02.77. Dependable central hotel, from whose modernized but widely varying rooms – shared bathrooms to four-person suites – you get a nice view of the picturesque *Résidence* across the street.. ❷–❹

Hôtel la Résidence 4 bd René-Coty ☎02.35.27.02.87. Dramatic half-timbered old mansion just off place Foch, moved in its entirety from Lisieux a century ago, with beautiful wooden carvings decorating its every nook and cranny. The quality of rooms, however, is variable; the solitary, cheapest option lacks en-suite facilities, while others are positively luxurious, but few are anything like as elegant as the facade. The organic *Brasserie Bio* restaurant downstairs is run by separate management. ❷–❼

The Town

Étretat is a very pretty little place, thanks partly to its superb setting, and also to the lovely architectural ensemble that surrounds its central **place Foch**, just back from the sea. The old wooden market *halles* still dominate the main square, the ground floor now converted into souvenir shops, but the beams of the balcony and roof are bare and ancient. **Market** day locally is Thursday, with most of the stalls spreading across the larger car park to the west.

As soon as you step onto the beach you're confronted by the cliff formations to either side. The largest arch, and the lone needle, thrust out to the south, is known as the **Falaise d'Aval**. A straightforward if precarious walk leads up the crumbling side of the cliff. On the inland side are the lush lawns and pastures of the local golf course, while on the shore side down at the foot of the cliff, German fortifications extend to the point where the turf abruptly stops. From the windswept top you can see further rock formations and possibly even glimpse Le Havre, but the views back to the town sheltered in the valley, and the **Falaise d'Amont** on its northern side, are what stick in the memory.

Maupassant compared the profile of the smaller arch at the base of the northern cliffs – as painted by Monet, among others – to an elephant dipping its trunk into the ocean. At any time other than high tide, it's possible to stroll along the shingles beyond the town proper to within a few metres of the arch. Alternatively, an extraordinarily picturesque footpath winds to the top of the cliff on this side as well, another demanding climb up the green hillside that leads to the little chapel of **Notre Dame**. Just beyond that is the futuristic white arch erected to commemorate the French aviators **Nungesser and Coli**, who set out from Paris in the *Oiseau Blanc* in May 1927, hoping to make the first east–west transatlantic flight, and were last seen over Étretat. What happened to them is not known – there are suggestions that they crashed somewhere in deepest Maine, New England – but a mere eighteen days later Charles Lindbergh arrived coming from the opposite direction (see p.171) and went into the history books. In the turf alongside the arch, a life-size aeroplane is set in concrete relief, and there's a museum nearby.

Eating

Fierce competition keeps **restaurant** prices in Étretat appealingly low. Even the succession of seafront terraces offer good value for money, while away from the sea there are bargains to be had at both ends of the spectrum.

Le Clos Lupin 37 rue Alphonse-Karr ☎02.35.29.67.53. Small, intimate dining room, a little way back from the seafront bustle at the western end of town, with a wide range of quality fish menus from €16.50 up to €26.50. Veal and steak are the main meat alternatives.

Le Galion 4 bd René-Coty ☎02.35.29.48.74. Probably the best restaurant in Étretat, adjoining the *Résidence* hotel and with a similar antique-filled ambience. The €22 menu makes a definitive introduction to all that's best in Norman cuisine, while the €29 and €41 options are increasingly more refined. Closed Tues & Wed in low season.

La Huitrière place de Gaulle ☎02.35.27.02.82. Panoramic first-floor dining room, at the foot of the steps up the Falaise d'Aval, which makes the perfect setting for an absolute blow-out on seafood. As well as menus from €19, it offers an enormous range of seafood platters, from €15 up to the €69.50 per person *Abondance*, which comes with half a lobster each and a scattering of caviar.

Les Roches Blanches rue Général-Leclerc ☎02.35.27.07.34. Although the modern concrete edifice that houses this seafood brasserie/restaurant at the northern end of the seafront is perhaps the drabbest along the promenade, the views out are great, especially when it's fine enough to dine on the terrace. The food itself is dependably good, with just one menu at €25. *À la carte* choices are cheaper in the brasserie section next to the more formal restaurant. Closed Tues eve & Wed in low season.

Le Havre

Most ferry passengers head straight out of the port of **LE HAVRE**, at the mouth of the Seine, as quickly as the traffic will allow, to escape a city that guidebooks tend to dismiss as dismal, disastrous and gargantuan. While Normandy's largest town, home to a population of 191,000, may not be the most picturesque or tranquil place in the region, neither is it the soulless urban sprawl the warnings suggest – even if the port, the second largest in France after Marseille, does take up half the Seine estuary, extending way beyond the town – and its stature is reflected in its fine contemporary array of "twin" cities, including such ports as Southampton and St Petersburg.

The city was originally built on the orders of François I in 1517. Its function was to replace the ancient ports of Harfleur and Honfleur, then already silting up, and its name was soon changed from Franciscopolis to Le Havre – "the Harbour". After serious flooding in 1540, it was redesigned and rebuilt to a grid pattern by Girolamo Bellarmato, an exiled Italian engineer who had experience of working with the unstable soil of Venice. It became the principal trading post of the northern French coast, prospering especially during the American War of Independence and thereafter, importing cotton, sugar and tobacco. In the years before the outbreak of war in 1939, it was the European home of the great luxury liners such as the *Normandie*, *Île de France* and *France*.

Le Havre suffered heavier damage than any other port in Europe during World War II. Following its all but total destruction, it was rebuilt to the specifications of a single architect, **Auguste Perret**, between 1946 and 1964 – which makes it a rather rare entity, and one that with its utter dependence on **reinforced concrete** is visibly circumscribed by constraints of time and money. Nonetheless, the sheer sense of space can be exhilarating, the showpiece monuments have a dramatic and winning self-confidence, and the few churches and other relics of the old city to survive have been sensitively integrated into the whole. The skyline has been kept deliberately low – there are no tower blocks, and even the mirrored World Trade Centre only manages five storeys – but the endless mundane residential blocks, which simply had to be erected as economically and swiftly as possible after the war, do get dispiriting after a while. However, with the sea visible at the end of almost every street, and open public space and expanses of water at every turn, even those visitors who ultimately fail to agree with Perret's famous dictum that "concrete is beautiful" may enjoy a stroll around his city.

Arrival and information

Three daily P&O **ferries** sail from Portsmouth to the **Terminal de Grande Bretagne**, not far from the train and bus stations in the Bassin de la Citadelle

(Ⓣ08.25.01.30.13). The terminal has a tourist information kiosk, open in summer.

Shuttle buses connect the ferry terminal with the **gare SNCF**, 1.5km east of the Hôtel de Ville on cours de la République. Fast **trains** (though not TGV) timed to connect with the ferries go to Rouen (1hr) and Paris (a further 1hr 15min). If you're travelling west, you have to change at Rouen – a very circuitous route. Commuter services run regularly to Harfleur in around five minutes. Right alongside the *gare SNCF* stands the **gare routière**, which is the base for local bus services in the Bus Océane network (Ⓣ02.35.22.34.00). Heading further afield, express **buses** from here, run by Bus Verts du Calvados (Ⓣ08.10.21.42.14; Ⓦwww.busverts14.fr), take advantage of the Pont du Normandie to connect Le Havre with Honfleur seven times daily, with two services continuing as far as Caen. Les Autocars Gris (Ⓣ02.35.22.34.08) run regular services to Fécamp and Étretat, while CNA (Ⓣ08.25.07.60.27) run down to Rouen via Caudebec-en-Caux.

Le Havre's modern, helpful **tourist office** is in an inconspicuous and not very central location on the main seafront drag, at 186 boulevard Clemenceau, near its intersection with avenue Foch (Easter–Oct Mon–Sat 9am–7pm, Sun 10am–12.30pm & 2.30–6pm; Nov–Feb Mon–Fri 9am–6.30pm, Sat 9am–12.30pm & 2–6.30pm, Sun 10am–1pm; Feb–Easter Mon–Sat 9am–6.30pm, Sun 10am–1pm Ⓣ02.32.74.04.04, Ⓦwww.lehavretourisme.com).

Accommodation

One consequence of the lack of idiosyncratic old buildings in the city is that its **hotels** tend to be hidden away behind indistinguishable concrete facades. There are two main concentrations of hotels: one group faces the *gare SNCF*,

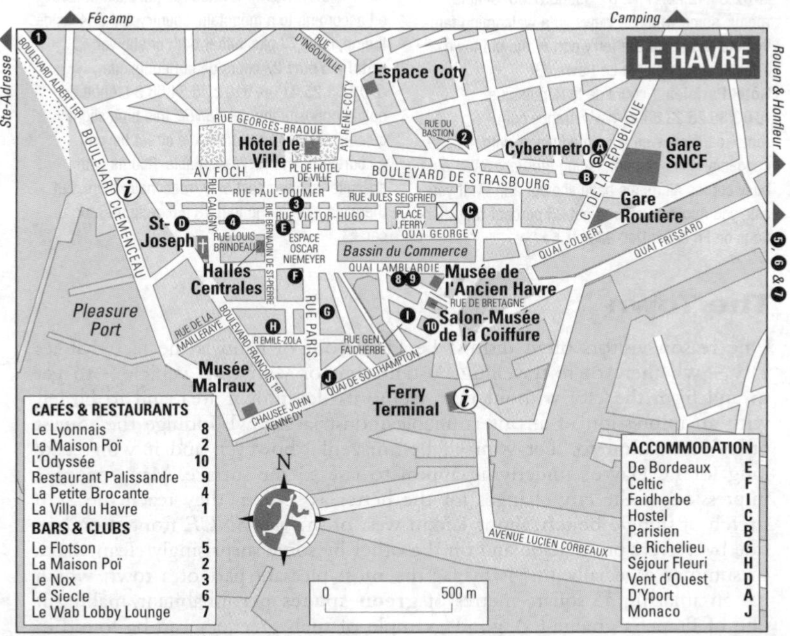

while most of the rest lie within walking distance of the ferry terminal. Many hotels in Le Havre participate in the "Bonne Weekend en Villes" programme (see Basics), offering two nights for the price of one at weekends. Ask at the tourist office for a leaflet detailing which hotels are taking part.

At the time of writing, a new **hostel** was set to open near the *gare SNCF*. Once operational, the *Centre de Loisirs et d'Hébergement "Sans Detour"*, 94 rue Jules Siegfried (ⓣ02.35.54.54.34, Esansdetour@wanadoo.fr) should offer two- and four-bed rooms for €8–10 per person. The closest **campsite** to the port is the surprisingly attractive four-star *Forêt de Montgeon* (ⓣ02.35.46.52.39, ⓔchlorophil€1@wanadoo.fr), just a couple of kilometres north of the town centre in a seven-hundred-acre forest. Take bus #1 from the Hôtel de Ville or *gare SNCF*, direction "Jacques-Monod", getting off at "Ste Cécile".

Hotels

Hôtel de Bordeaux 147 rue Louis-Brindeau ⓣ02.35.22.69.44, ⓦwww.bestwestern.com/fr/debordeaux. Smart, comfortable hotel, affiliated to the Best Western chain, on the north side of the Espace Oscar Niemeyer, facing the Volcano cultural centre. All rooms have cable TV and phone. ❺

Hôtel Celtic 106 rue Voltaire ⓣ02.35.42.39.77, ⓦwww.hotel-celtic.com. Facing the *Bordeaux*, in the long buildings that flank the Espace Oscar Niemeyer, this hotel has some much cheaper rooms (with shared toilets), which are nonetheless good value. Internet access in the lobby. ❷

Hôtel Faidherbe 21 rue Général-Faidherbe ⓣ02.35.42.20.27, ⓕ02.35.42.57.03. Simple rooms, some with sea views, in a welcoming family hotel very near the ferry port in the old town. The cheapest hotel in Le Havre. ❶

Hôtel Parisien 1 cours de la République ⓣ02.35.25.23.83, ⓦwww.ifrance.com/hotel-parisien. Well appointed place, with congenial management, facing the *gare SNCF* on a busy corner. All rooms have shower and TV. If you ask, you might be able to get 25 percent reductions on Fri & Sat Dec–March. ❸

Hôtel Le Richelieu 135 rue de Paris ⓣ02.35.42.38.71, ⓔhotel.lerichelieu@wanadoo.fr. For a friendly mid-priced hotel in a very central location with comfortable rooms – many of which have been recently renovated – this hotel is hard to beat. ❸

Hôtel Séjour Fleuri 71 rue Émile-Zola ⓣ02.35.41.33.81, ⓕ02.35.42.26.44. On a side road off rue de Paris, close to the ferry terminal; not exactly "*fleuri*", but cheered up by some bright red shutters and a couple of window boxes. ❶

Hôtel Vent d'Ouest 4 rue de Caligny ⓣ02.35.42.50.69, ⓦwww.ventdouest.fr. Plain, cream-coloured cement building, beside the main entrance to the St-Joseph church, where all the good-quality, well-renovated rooms, each decorated according to a mountain, countryside or seaside theme, have TV plus either bath or shower. ❺

Hôtel d'Yport 27 cours de la République ⓣ02.35.25.21.08, ⓕ02.35.24.06.34. Another option opposite the *gare SNCF*, this time slightly quieter, set well back from the street beyond a courtyard, and very hospitable. Rooms with en-suite facilities cost only fractionally more, but there's a €3 charge to park a bicycle, €6 for a car. ❷

The Town

One reason visitors often dismiss Le Havre out of hand is the fact that it's easy – whether you're travelling by train, bus or your own vehicle – to get to and from the city without ever seeing its downtown area, and to be left with an impression of an interminable industrial sprawl. Indulge the tourist office's invitation to "Let yourself be amazed!", however, and it won't take long for Le Havre's underlying appeal to rise to the surface. Many people's impression of the city changes for the better as soon as they reach the 2km stretch of shingle **beach**, about 1.5km west of the *gare SNCF*, fronted on one side by a lively promenade and on the other by some surprisingly clean water. In summer especially, this is by far the most pleasant part of a town which has an amazing 32 square metres of **green spaces** per inhabitant, making it one of France's greenest. A good example of such greenery can be found in the pergola walkways, flowerbeds and fountains that surround the Auguste Perret-designed **Hôtel de Ville**, roughly halfway between the beach and the *gare SNCF*: a low, flat-roofed building stretching for over 100m and topped by a seventeen-storey concrete tower,

Perret's other major creation is the church of **St-Joseph**, the steeple of which is clearly visible some way southwest of the town hall. Instead of the traditional elongated cross shape, the four arms of the cross on which this church is built are equally short. From the outside, it's a very plain mass of speckled concrete, almost Egyptian in its simplicity, the main doors thrown open to the street to hint at dark interior spaces that resemble an underground car park. Once you get inside, however, it all makes sense. The altar is right in the centre, with the hundred-metre bell tower rising directly above it. Very simple patterns of stained glass, all around the church and right the way up the tower, produce a bright interplay of coloured light, all focusing on the altar to create the effect of a church "in the round".

Le Havre's boldest example of modern architecture is considerably more recent – the cultural centre known as the **Volcano** (or less reverentially as the "yoghurt pot"), which stands at the end of the Bassin du Commerce dominating the **Espace Oscar Niemeyer**. The Brazilian architect after whom the *espace* is named designed this slightly asymmetrical smooth gleaming white cone, cut off abruptly just above the level of the surrounding buildings, so that its curving planes are undisturbed by doors or windows; the entrance is concealed beneath a white walkway in the open plaza below. A large green copper hand emerges from the Volcano just above its base, slightly cupped and pouring out water as a fountain, inscribed with the sentiment that "One day, like this water, the land, beaches and mountains will belong to all". A smaller white building alongside also forms part of the centre.

The **Bassin du Commerce**, which stretches away from the Espace Oscar Niemeyer, is in fact of minimal commercial significance; a couple of larger boats are moored permanently to serve as clubs or restaurants. It's all surprisingly quiet, existing mainly as an appropriate stretch of water for the graceful white footbridge of the Passarelle du Commerce to cross.

Musée Malraux

The modern **Musée Malraux** (Mon & Wed–Fri 11am–6pm, Sat & Sun 11am–7pm; €3.80, under-18s free), at chausée John Kennedy overlooking the harbour entrance, ranks among the best designed art galleries in France. It uses natural light to full advantage to display an enjoyable assortment of nineteenth- and twentieth-century French paintings. The principal highlight upstairs is a collection of over two hundred canvases by **Eugène Boudin**. Two years after the painter's death, his brother Louis gave the museum the entire contents of Eugène's studio. Although many of the works were neither signed nor dated, and some are no bigger than postcards, they range from throughout the artist's career. Most are arranged by theme, so one wall consists almost entirely of miniature cows, but there are also greyish landscapes from all along the Norman and Breton coastlines, including views of Trouville, Honfleur and Étretat.

Downstairs, the focus shifts to a lovely set of works by **Raoul Dufy** (1877–1953). In his case, the artist's widow left two hundred of his paintings to be divided between three museums – the national modern art museum in Paris, the one in Nice, and this gallery in Dufy's home town. Each curator was allowed to pick a single piece in turn, with the result that Le Havre ended up with a collection of images of itself that make it seem positively radiant. Dufy depicts his native city at play, with drawings and paintings of festivals and parades, and even a panorama of the whole city framed beneath an arching rainbow. Among other treasures are a Gauguin from Tahiti, several Monets – including scenes of Westminster and Varengeville, plus a few waterlilies and a snowscape sunrise – as well as works by Corot, Courbet, Pissarro (including one painted within a few metres of this spot), Sisley, Léger, Braque and Lurçat.

Musée de l'Ancien Havre

If you have the time, you might like to see what old Le Havre looked like in the prewar days when **Jean-Paul Sartre** wrote *La Nausée* here. He taught philosophy for five years during the 1930s in a local school, and his almost transcendent disgust with the place cannot obscure the fascination he felt in exploring the seedy dockside quarter of St-François, in those spare moments when he wasn't visiting Simone de Beauvoir in Rouen. Little survives of the city Sartre knew, but pictures and bits gathered from the rubble are on display in one of the very few buildings that remain from that era, the **Musée de l'Ancien Havre** (Wed–Sun 10am–noon & 2–6pm; €1.50). It looks somewhat incongruous amid the new concrete, just south of the Bassin du Commerce at 1 rue Jerome Bellarmato. Just opposite the museum at 60 rue de Bretagne take a look at the bizarre **Salon-Musée de la Coiffure**, a working barber's shop where much of the premises has been turned into a hairdressing shrine full of bottles of ancient shampoos and aftershaves, rusty cut-throat razors, and gruesome curling and drying machines presided over by some sadistic-looking stylist mannequins. You can see everything from the street without having to enter the salon itself, unless of course you want a haircut.

Harfleur

The once-great port of **Harfleur** is now no more than a suburb of Le Havre, 6km upstream from the centre. While visibly older than the modern city that engulfs it, it's no longer sufficiently distinctive to be worth visiting. It earned an undying place in history, however, as the landing place of Henry V's English army in 1415, en route to victory at Agincourt. During a month-long siege of the town, two thousand English soldiers died from eating contaminated seafood from the surrounding marshes. Harfleur surrendered in late September, following a final English onslaught spurred on – according to Shakespeare – by Henry's cry of "Once more unto the breach, dear friends..."

Eating

Few of the **restaurants** in Le Havre are worth making a fuss about, except perhaps for some near the suburb of **Ste-Adresse**, northwest along the coast towards Étretat, which is no longer quite as picturesque as you might imagine from Monet's depictions of it. There are, however, lots of bars, cafés and brasseries around the *gare SNCF*, and all sorts of crêperies and ethnic offerings – North African, South American, Caribbean – in the backstreets of the St-François quarter opposite the ferry terminal.

If you're shopping for food to take home, possibilities include the central market, just west of place Gambetta and ideal for fresh produce. The larger of the two local Auchan **hypermarkets** (both Mon–Sat 8.30am–10pm) is at the Mont Gaillard Centre Commercial; reached by following cours de la République beyond the *gare SNCF*, through the tunnel, it holds an outlet of the chain self-service cafeteria, *Flunch*. The other, at Montivilliers, is signposted off the Tancarville road, east of the centre. In the town centre, on rue Bernadin de St-Pierre just east of the Espace Oscar Niemeyer, the **Halles Centrales** is a good place to buy fresh fruit and vegetables, fish and meat.

Restaurants

Le Lyonnais 7–9 rue de Bretagne
☎ 02.35.22.07.31. Small, cosy restaurant with chequered tablecloths and an English-speaking owner (hence the menu translated into English). The house speciality is baked fish, though dishes from Lyon, such as *andouillettes*, are also available on menus which start at €15. Closed Sat eve & Sun.

La Maison Poï 25 rue du Bastion
☎ 02.35.22.99.45. Trendy, Parisian-style "café-brunch" place where fixed menus are replaced by *poïchonas de Poï* – fried snacks roughly equivalent to tapas – and some good salads for around €12. Art or photo exhibitions are held once a month; also a good place for an evening drink (see below). Closed Sun & Mon.

L'Odyssée 41 rue Général-Faidherbe
☎ 02.35.21.31.42. First-rate seafood restaurant close to the ferry terminal in the old town, serving a reliable €21 weekday lunch menu and a more adventurous €26 dinner option. Closed Sat lunch, Sun eve, Mon & mid-July to mid-Aug.

Restaurant Palissandre 33 rue de Bretagne
☎ 02.35.21.69.00. Wood-panelled Italian restaurant in the St-François quarter, where most pasta main courses cost around €10, while grilled meats and fish are more like €14. Closed Sat lunch & Sun lunch.

La Petite Brocante 75 rue Louis Brindeau
☎ 02.35.21.42.20. Lively central bistro, where the set menus are a little pricey at €24 and up, but there's always a good-value *plat du jour*, as often as not fresh fish. Closed Sun & first three weeks in Aug.

La Villa du Havre 66 bd Albert 1er
☎ 02.35.54.78.80. A magnificent 1890s villa facing the sea, just before arriving at the suburb of St-Adresse, provides a suitably grandiose setting for chef Jean-Luc Tarfarin's menus, which start at €32 for lunch and rise to €185 for an unforgettable dinner. Closed Sun eve, Mon & Wed eve.

Nightlife and entertainment

Depending on the time of the year, nightlife in Le Havre tends to be based either along the seaside promenade, where in summer numerous seasonal **bars** and brasseries are open for business, or in the St-François quarter close to the ferry terminal, which has a good deal of hostess bars interspersed among the homogenous selection of watering holes where the company, though no less dubious, at least comes free of charge. The best places to go of an evening are dotted around town, including the industrial area near the *gare SNCF*.

Bars and clubs

Le Flotson 34 rue Eugène Mopin
☎ 02.35.51.41.17. A few kilometres east of the centre, but worth the trek if you're looking for a good gay-friendly discotheque. Expect to hear disco, house and techno. Thurs–Sat 10.30pm–4am, Sun 6pm–4am.

La Maison Poï 25 rue du Bastion
☎ 02.35.22.99.45. At night at least, this part of town makes for a peaceful spot to enjoy a refreshing cocktail and munch on a few "poïchonas de Poï", either indoors or at tables outside, while listening to lounge music and the like. Closed Sun & Mon.

Le Nox 21 rue de la Villehervé. Small, very central bar with good music, albeit a little loud for the size of the premises, mainly of the electronic variety. Gay-friendly. Tues–Sun 7pm–2am.

Le Siecle 17 rue des Magasins Généraux
☎ 02.35.24.55.67. Despite being tucked away in an industrial area just east of the *gare SNCF*, surrounded by warehouses, this is the standard bearer of Le Havre nightclubs, attracting DJs from Paris very adept at working the twenty- and thirty-something crowd into a frenzy, either in the R&B or techno room. Thurs–Sat 11pm–5am.

Le Wab Lobby Lounge 31 rue d'Iena
☎ 02.35.27.55.45. Opened in autumn 2004 around the corner from the *Siecle* and the latest attempt to use the city's industrial image for monetary gain, this time by using plenty of brick, iron and leather to transform a 300-square-metre warehouse into Le Havre's first "industrial chic" venue – and the current place to be seen. Mon–Sat 10–2am.

Entertainment

If you're looking to pass an evening or two in Le Havre, the tourist office will be happy to provide information on **cultural events** in and around town.

For all events sponsored by the municipality (a wide and impressive range), book at the Théâtre de l'Hôtel de Ville (box office: Tues–Sat 1.30pm–7.15pm; ⓣ02.35.19.45.74). The most likely venue for **music concerts** has to be the Agora, the performance venue at the Volcano in the Espace Oscar Niemeyer, described on p.95 (box office: Tues–Sat 2–7pm; ⓣ02.35.19.10.10), though you may also hear music performed in the cathedral and other churches. Note that you can book tickets for a wide range of concerts – music, dance, comedy – at the FNAC in the Centre Commercial Espace Coty on avenue René-Coty (ⓣ08.92.68.36.22).

Listings

Banks and exchange Crédit Agricole, 29 ave René-Coty ⓣ02.35.19.71.19; Crédit Lyonnais, 106 bd de Strasbourg ⓣ08.20.82.45.00; Caisse d'Épargne, 57 place de l'Hôtel de Ville ⓣ08.20.85.02.70.
Bicycle rental Vélo Océane, at the tourist office (see p.93) ⓣ02.32.74.04.04 (Mon–Sat 9am–6.30pm, Sun 10am–noon & 2.30–5.30pm).
Cinemas Eden, Espace Oscar Niemeyer ⓣ02.35.19.10.11; Sirius, 5 rue Duguesclin ⓣ08.92.68.00.29 – usually programmes *v.o.* (undubbed) films.
Hospital Groupe Hospitalier du Havre, 55bis rue Gustave Flaubert ⓣ02.32.73.32.32.
Internet access Cybermetro, facing the *gare SNCF* at 15 cours de la République ⓣ02.32.73.04.28 (daily 10am–midnight; €4 per hr).
Post office 62 rue Jules Siegfried ⓣ02.32.92.59.00 (Mon–Fri 8am–7pm, Sat 8am–noon).
Shopping Centre Commercial Espace Coty, ave René-Coty – over 80 shops, including FNAC and Monoprix.
Swimming pool Club Nautique Havrais, bd Clemenceau, opposite the tourist office ⓣ02.35.43.47.65. Buy day passes (€9) at the tourist office.

The Seine valley

As far back as the Bronze Age, the **River Seine** was a crucial part of the "Tin Road" linking Cornwall to Paris. Fortresses and monasteries lined its banks from the time of the Romans onwards. Now, with the threat of its tidal bore and treacherous sandbanks very much a thing of the past, heavy ships make their serene way up its sinuous course from the Channel to the provincial capital of **Rouen**.

Travelling by car, bus or bicycle, it's worth taking this journey equally slowly, savouring such highlights as the riverside towns of **Villequier** and **Caudebec** or the abbey of **Jumièges**. Rouen itself is the major attraction, nonetheless, as one of the most vibrant medieval cities to be found anywhere in France. Beyond it, en route to Paris, things if anything get even better, in the shape of the dramatic castle fortress above **Les Andelys** and Monet's celebrated water-lily-filled gardens at **Giverny**.

Along the Seine to Rouen

Even though the modern cities of Le Havre and Rouen have become vast industrial conglomerates, long stretches of the riverbank between the two remain remarkably unspoiled and tranquil. Leaving Le Havre, however, the refineries and cement works seem to go on forever; to reach the river, drivers have first to negotiate a long approach road that twists its way over the Canal du Havre. Beyond that, the huge humpback span of the **Pont de Normandie** has since 1995 spanned the mouth of the Seine to connect Le Havre with Honfleur, making access between the coasts of Upper and Lower Normandy much more direct. Crossing either that bridge – which incurs a one-way toll of €5 – or the similarly immense and expensive **Tancarville** suspension bridge, 20km upriver, brings you to the **south (left) bank** of the Seine. This holds the vast majority of the **Parc Naturel Régional de Brotonne**, where peaceful rolling hillsides are evenly divided between bucolic agricultural fields and dense woodlands.

By far the quickest route up the Seine valley, however, is to follow the dramatic chalky bluffs along the **north (right) bank**. This side offers richer scenic and historic rewards, with the road that sticks firmly to the riverbank leading past such sights as the venerable towns of **Villequier** and **Caudebec**, and the magnificent ruined abbey of **Jumièges**. It's also, fortunately, the route taken by buses from Le Havre to Rouen (#20 from Le Havre to Caudebec, which connects with #30 to Rouen).

Only one more bridge crosses the river in the extravagant loops that lie between Tancarville and Rouen – the **Pont de Brotonne**, near Caudebec, which leads to the heart of the park. Further upstream, however, there are also intermittent *bacs* (car **ferries**) across the river, which charge smaller tolls, and tend to leave on the hour (and to have long lunch breaks).

Villequier

The first of the riverbank towns you come to on the **D982 along the north bank** is quite undeservedly one of the least known – **VILLEQUIER**. As a stop on the way to or from Le Havre it's ideal, featuring a quite exceptional **hotel**: the *Grand Sapin*, 12 rue Louis le Gaffrie (ⓣ02.35.56.78.73; ❸), is a gorgeous rambling old building, where three of the well-equipped rooms have rickety balconies overlooking the river. It's absolutely magical on a misty morning – and not bad in the evening, when the wood-panelled restaurant (closed Tues eve & Wed except July & Aug) is in full swing (menus range from €20 up to €34). Tables in the riverside garden are laid out under the shade of the eponymous *grand sapin* itself – a rather frail pine that's dwarfed by a giant blossoming lilac nearby.

There's no **entertainment** whatsoever in Villequier, while its principal "sight" is a mournful statue of Victor Hugo peering out into the Seine, across a helpfully marked concrete arrow, to the spot where his daughter and her husband drowned in 1843, just six months after their marriage. So weathered as to make the author appear naked, the statue stands several hundred metres upstream from the centre, reached by an attractive waterfront promenade. The couple's former home, back in town, now serves as the **Musée Victor Hugo**, probably of interest only to fluent French speakers with a passion for Hugo's writings (April–Sept Mon & Wed–Sat 10am–12.30pm & 2–6pm, Tues & Sat 2–6.30pm; Oct–March Mon & Wed–Sat 10am–12.30pm & 2–5.30pm, Tues & Sat 2–5.30pm; €3, under-18s free).

Caudebec-en-Caux

Just over 4km on from Villequier is the bigger and more popular **CAUDEBEC-EN-CAUX**. Few traces of this old town's past survived the firestorm devastation of World War II, but the local tourist authorities extend a rather sad invitation to visitors to join a "heritage trail" of places that used to be attractive. The damage – and previous local history – is chronicled in the museum at the thirteenth-century **Maison des Templiers** on rue Thomas Bassin, 100m back from the river, one of the handful of buildings spared (July & Aug Fri–Wed 11am–12.30pm & 3.30–6.30pm; June & Sept Mon & Fri 11am–12.30pm & 3.30–6.30pm, Sat 10am–noon & 3.30–6.30pm, Sun 3.30–6.30pm; April, May & Oct Wed & Sun 3.30–6.30pm, Sat 10am–noon & 3.30–6.30pm; €3). As well as enjoying "one of the most important collections of chimney plaques in France", you can take a look at pictures of the Seine's regular tidal swell, which still threatens at this narrow point in the river to swamp unwary promenaders. The magnificent flamboyant **Notre Dame church**, with its octagonal spire circled by three separate *fleurs-de-lis* crowns, still dominates the main square, which has been the site of a **market** every Saturday since 1390.

A little way south of town, a **stone aeroplane** propels itself out of the cliff face across the water – a memorial to another curious episode of aviation history, contemporary to that commemorated at Étretat (see p.91). In 1928, a plane was being prepared here for an attempt at what would have been the first east–west transatlantic flight. But shortly before it was due to set off, the Norwegian polar explorer Amundsen issued a worldwide appeal for help to rescue some Italian sailors who had been shipwrecked off Spitzbergen in the Arctic. The French government offered the plane, and its four crewmen left with Amundsen. Two days later they were lost.

Practicalities

Caudebec's **tourist office** is slightly south of the centre, in place Charles de Gaulle by the river (April–Nov daily 10am–12.30pm & 1.30–6.30pm; call for low-season hours; ⓣ02.32.70.46.32, ⓦwww.caudebec-en-caux.com). Two absolutely indistinguishable Logis de France stand side by side facing the river on quai Guilbaud, identical buildings with identical balconies, and all but identical prices and even phone numbers – the *Normotel La Marine* at no. 18 (ⓣ02.35.96.20.11; ❸; restaurant closed Fri eve, Sat lunch & Sun eve), and the *Normandie* at no. 19 (ⓣ02.35.96.25.11; ❸; restaurant closed Sun eve). Both hotels offer en-suite rooms with phone, TV and free parking, while the on-site restaurants have menus ranging from €11 to €38 and are slightly more formal than the several other brasseries and cafés which line the quai. Another logis, the *Cheval Blanc*, is a little way back from the river at 4 place René-Coty, 200m north of the Hôtel de Ville on the western edge of town (ⓣ02.35.96.21.66; ❸; closed late Dec), and there's a riverside **campsite** halfway to Villequier, the two-star *Barre Y Va* (ⓣ02.35.96.26.38; closed Oct–March).

On the last Sunday in September of every even-numbered year (2004, 2006, etc), Caudebec comes alive with a large **Cider Festival**.

The Pont de Brotonne

Slightly upstream from Caudebec, the magnificent span of the **Pont de Brotonne**, completed in 1977 as the world's highest and steepest humpback bridge (charging a €2.50 toll for motorists), climbs out above the Seine. It has an unexpectedly appealing colour scheme – the suspension cables are custard yellow, the rails pastel green, the walkway maroon, and the vast concrete columns left bare. If you don't lose both heart and hat to the sickening drop and the seaborne winds, walking across it is one of the big treats of Normandy.

From a distance, its stays refract into strange optical effects, while far below small tugs flounder in the wash of mighty cargo carriers.

Parc Naturel Régional de Brotonne

Even if the **Parc Naturel Régional de Brotonne** – most but not quite all of which lies south of the Seine – is no longer entirely rural, it ranks among the most beautiful tracts of the Norman countryside. The park shelters a wide range of conservation projects and traditional industry initiatives, run by local people, as well as its more obvious abbey and château sites. Full details on all its aspects can be obtained from the very helpful Maison du Parc in the small village of **NÔTRE-DAME-DE-BLIQUETUIT**, immediately east of the southern end of the Pont de Brotonne (April–June & Sept Mon–Fri 9am–6pm, Sat & Sun noon–6pm; July & Aug Mon–Fri 9am–6.30pm, Sat & Sun 10am–6.30pm; Oct–March Mon–Fri 9am–6pm; ⓣ02.35.37.23.16).

The most compelling section of the park is concentrated into a mighty meander on the southern bank of the Seine, across from Caudebec. Here the slopes are covered by the deep thick woods of the **Forêt de Brotonne**, perfect for cyclists and hikers. The pretty little village of **AIZIER** nestles beside the river at the western limit of the forest, with the edges of the Vernier marshes, grazed by Camargue horses and Scottish Highland cattle, just beyond.

Hauville

The southern border of the Forêt de Brotonne marks the dividing line between the *départements* of Seine-Maritime and Eure, but still under the auspices of the park, outside the small community of **HAUVILLE** (and signposted off the road to the even tinier village of La Mare-Guérard), it's possible to look round what's said to be the oldest still-functioning **windmill** (*moulin*) in France. One of six owned by the monks of Jumièges, who farmed and forested all this area in the Middle Ages, its outline – based on contemporary castle towers – looks like a kid's drawing (mid-April–June & first three weeks in Sept Sun 2.30–6.30pm; July & Aug daily 2.30–6.30pm; €2.30).

La Haye du Routot and around

The churchyard in the neighbouring village of **LA HAYE DU ROUTOT**, 4km west of Hauville, is a real oddity, featuring a pair of 1000-year-old yew trees that are still alive but have been sufficiently hollowed out to shelter a chapel and grotto. Every year, on July 16, the feast day of St Clair, the village stages the dramatic **Fête de St-Clair**. Its centrepiece is a towering, conical bonfire, topped by a cross which must survive to ensure a good year. The smouldering logs are taken home to serve as protection against lightning. Should you miss the big day, a video-recording of the goings-on is featured in the local crafts **museum**, which numbers among its separate sections a traditional functioning bread oven, adjacent to the church, and a clog-specialist shoemaker opposite (both April–June & Sept Sun 2–6.30pm; July & Aug daily 2–6.30pm; March, Oct & Nov Sun 2–6pm; combined admission €3.80).

For a **meal** nearby, the *Auberge de l'Écurie* is a good restaurant in the main square of the slightly larger village of **ROUTOT**, 7km southeast of La Haye du Routot (ⓣ02.32.57.30.30; closed Mon, Sun eve & Wed eve), with menus from €19.90.

Abbaye de St-Wandrille

Just beyond the Pont de Brotonne on the north bank of the Seine, a side road (marked "St-Wandrille-Rançon") climbs two kilometres up to the **Abbaye**

de St-Wandrille. So legend has it, the abbey was founded by a seventh-century count who, with his wife, renounced all earthly pleasures on the day of their wedding. It remains an active monastery, home to fifty or so Benedictine monks who, in addition to their spiritual duties, turn their hands to money-making tasks that range from candle-making to running a modern reprographic studio. It's not such an obvious tourist destination as nearby Jumièges (see below), but the abbey complex nonetheless makes an attractive if curious architectural ensemble: part ruin, part restoration and, in the case of the main buildings, part transplant – a fifteenth-century barn brought in a few years ago from another Norman village miles away.

Throughout the year, monks show visitors around the abbey on **guided tours** (Easter–Oct Tues–Sat 3.30pm, Sun 11.30am & 3.30pm; Nov–Easter Sat 3.30pm, Sun 11.30am & 3.30pm; €3.50; Ⓦwww.st-wandrille.com); in addition, in summer only, it's possible to wander through the grounds on your own for no charge (July & Aug Tues–Sun 10.45am–12.30pm & 3–5pm). You can also hear **Gregorian chanting** in their new church at morning and evening services (Mon–Sat 9.45am & 5.30pm, Sun 10am & 5pm).

For something to **eat**, there's a crêperie opposite the abbey, while the more upmarket *Deux Coronnes* restaurant (Ⓣ02.35.96.11.44; closed Sun eve & Mon), a few doors along in the place de l'Église, is a half-timbered seventeenth-century inn, where delicious menus start at €14.50 for lunch and €21.50 for dinner.

Abbaye de Jumièges

In the next loop of the Seine, 12km upstream from St-Wandrille, squats the more famous **Abbaye de Jumièges** (daily: mid-April to mid-Sept 9.30am–7pm; mid-Sept to mid-April 9.30am–1pm & 2.30–5.30pm; €4, under-18s free). A haunting ruin, it was destroyed – as a deliberate act of policy – during the Revolution. It's said to have been founded by St Philibert in 654 AD, just five years after St-Wandrille, burned by marauding Vikings in 841, and then rebuilt a century later. Its main surviving shell, however, as far as it can still be discerned, dates from the eleventh century; William the Conqueror himself attended its reconsecration in 1067. The twin towers, over 52m high, are still standing. So too is one arch of the roofless nave, while a one-sided yew tree stands in the centre of what were once the cloisters.

How evocative you find these bleached stone ruins will depend on your mood. Visits consist of an unescorted ramble across the lawns; for the most part, you're obliged to keep well clear of the precarious walls themselves. Though it survived the Revolution intact, the grand château-like **abbot's residence** that commands a nearby eminence – built in the seventeenth century, by which time the abbot was appointed directly by the king rather than being elected by his fellow monks – is not open to visitors. The grounds, however, are sometimes used for temporary art exhibitions.

The *Auberge des Ruines* at 17 place de la Mairie in Jumièges (Ⓣ02.35.37.24.05; closed Sun eve, Tues eve, Wed and over Christmas and New Year), is a truly superb **restaurant**. Its menus start at €18 for lunch and go up to €55 for a gastronomic dinner.

The river itself now flows roughly a kilometre west of the ruins. A tiny *bac* (ferry) crosses the Seine at this point to Heurteauville on the left bank, half-hourly in summer and hourly in winter; the riverbank *Auberge du Bac* (Ⓣ02.35.37.24.16; closed Mon & Tues) makes a lovely lunchtime halt, serving excellent €18.60, €21.60 and €25.60 menus.

Duclair

If you want to **cycle** beside the river for any distance, the D982 tends to be forever climbing and descending, and in any event is a bit busy. However, the stretch from Le Mesnil (just beyond Jumièges) as far as Duclair is long, quiet and flat, and has a wonderful view of the lush riverbanks. **DUCLAIR** itself holds a nice riverside **hotel**, in the shape of the *Hôtel de la Poste* opposite the landing stage for the town's little *bac*, at 286 quai de la Libération (☎02.35.05.92.50; ❷; closed second fortnight of Feb and first fortnight of July).

As you continue from here towards Rouen, you get a first panoramic prospect, from beside the church at Canteleu, of the docks, the island and the city. The road onwards coasts endlessly down into the maelstrom of city traffic. Don't attempt to cycle *out* of Rouen in this direction, as the gradient – and the fumes – are unbearable.

Rouen

ROUEN, the capital of Upper Normandy, is one of France's most ancient and historic cities. Standing on the site of Roman Rotomagus, which was the lowest point on the river then capable of being bridged, it was laid out by the Viking Rollo shortly after he became the first duke of Normandy in 911. Captured by the English in 1419, after a long siege, it became the stage in 1431 for the trial and execution of Joan of Arc, before returning to French control in 1449.

Over the centuries, Rouen has suffered repeated devastation; there were 45 major fires in the first half of the thirteenth century alone. It has had to be almost entirely rebuilt during the last sixty years, and now you could spend a whole day wandering around the city without realizing that the Seine ran through its centre. Wartime bombs, specifically during the fierce onslaught that coincided with the D-Day landings, destroyed all its bridges, the area between the cathedral and the *quais*, and much of the left bank's industrial quarter. The immediate riverside area has never been adequately restored, and what you might expect to be the most beautiful part of this venerable city is in fact something of an abomination.

Enormous sums have, however, been lavished on an upmarket restoration job on the streets a few hundred metres north of the river, which turned the centre into the closest approximation to a medieval city that modern imaginations could come up with. The project was supervised by Louis Arretche, who redesigned postwar St-Malo so successfully (see p.234). The suggestion that for historical authenticity the houses should be painted in bright, clashing colours was not deemed appropriate by the city authorities, but, so far as it goes, the whole of this inner core can be very seductive, and its churches are extremely impressive by any standards.

Outside the renovated quarters, things are rather different. The city spreads deep into the loop of the Seine, with its docks and industrial infrastructure stretching endlessly away to the south, and it is increasingly expanding up into the hills to the north as well, while the riverbank itself is lined with a fume-filled, multi-laned motorway. As the nearest point that large container ships can get to Paris, even in decline this remains the fourth largest port in the country.

Arrival, information and city transport

The main **gare SNCF** set high above the river at the top end of Rouen's main thoroughfare, rue Jeanne d'Arc, is Gare Rive Droite; Gare Rive Gauche on the south bank only handles goods traffic. The passenger station is not immediately conspicuous on most maps, because the train lines run underground, but on the ground you can't miss it. From the outside, its minaret makes it resemble a nineteenth-century confection, intended perhaps for Algiers or Istanbul; in fact, it was completed in 1928. The main hall is decorated with garish murals. Rouen is roughly halfway between Paris and the Channel ports; both **Le Havre** and **Dieppe** are one hour away on different train routes, while the journey to **Paris** takes an hour and a quarter. You can also get trains west to **Lisieux** (1hr 15min) and **Caen** (2hr). From the *gare SNCF*, it's a ten-minute walk down rue Jeanne d'Arc to the town centre.

At the bottom end of rue Jeanne d'Arc just before it crosses the Seine, the **gare routière** is located in the Espace Métrobus (see below) opposite the Théâtre des Arts, where the CNA bus company have an information desk (Mon–Fri 8am–6.30pm; ⓣ08.25.07.60.27). The buses themselves leave from various stops along the quais du Havre and de la Bourse. The number of out-of-town buses has been scaled down considerably, with services to **Évreux** (1hr), **Clères** (50min), **Caudebec-en-Caux** (1hr – via **Jumièges** and **St-Wandrille**) and **Le Havre** (2hr 30min) the only ones of potential interest for tourists to survive.

Rouen's **airport** at **Boos** is nine kilometres southeast of the centre (ⓣ02.35.79.41.00) and served by Air France. A shuttle bus leaves twice daily during the week and only once at weekends from the *gare SNCF* and takes thirty minutes to get to the airport; otherwise you must take a taxi – try Radio Taxi (ⓣ02.35.88.50.50). Budget (ⓣ02.35.98.64.38), Europcar (ⓣ02.32.08.39.09) and Hertz (ⓣ02.35.98.16.57) offer **car rental** both in the terminal and in town.

Information

Rouen's **tourist office**, opposite the cathedral at 25 place de la Cathédrale, stands in the early sixteenth-century "House of the Exchequer" (May–Sept Mon–Sat 9am–7pm, Sun 9.30am–12.30pm & 2–6pm; Oct–April Mon–Sat 9am–6pm, Sun 10am–1pm; ⓣ02.32.08.32.40, ⓦwww.rouentourisme.com). It serves as the starting point for daily two-hour **walking tours** of the city, departing at 2pm – a tour in English leaves on Fridays at 5pm. Both cost €6.50. For more sedate visitors, a motorized "**petit train**" makes a forty-minute-loop tour from the tourist office at regular intervals (April–Oct daily 10am, 11am, noon, 2pm, 3pm, 4pm & 5pm; €5.50).

City transport

The city centre of Rouen, north of the Seine, is small enough to stroll around with little effort, and there's also an efficient **bus** network. For information on routes, visit the **Espace Métrobus** opposite the Théâtre des Arts at 9 rue Jeanne d'Arc (Mon–Sat 7am–7pm; ⓣ02.35.52.52.52, ⓦwww.tcar.fr). With an ever-expanding network of pedestrianized streets, it's not a city you can drive around with any ease; far better to park in one of the many underground car parks as soon as you arrive.

Rouen's pride and joy, the multibillion-franc **métro** system unveiled in 1998, is on the whole more useful to commuters than tourists. From the Gare-Rue Verte, at the SNCF station, trains follow the line of rue Jeanne d'Arc,

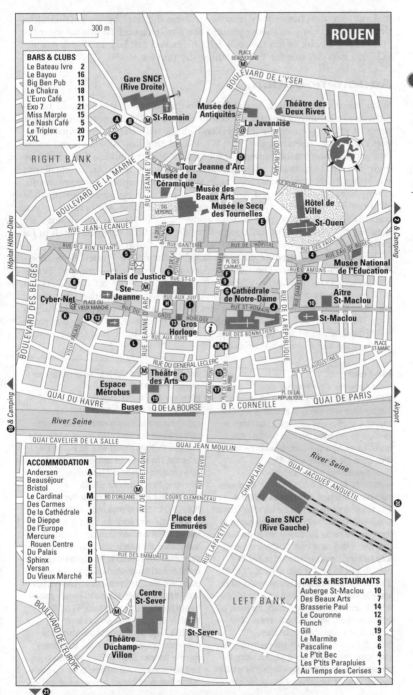

ROUEN

0 300 m

BARS & CLUBS

Le Bateau Ivre 2
Le Bayou 16
Big Ben Pub 13
Le Chakra 18
L'Euro Café 11
Exo 7 21
Miss Marple 15
Le Nash Café 5
Le Triplex 20
XXL 17

ACCOMMODATION

Andersen A
Beauséjour C
Bristol I
Le Cardinal M
Des Carmes F
De la Cathédrale J
De Dieppe B
De l'Europe L
Mercure Rouen Centre G
Du Palais H
Sphinx D
Versan E
Du Vieux Marché K

CAFÉS & RESTAURANTS

Auberge St-Maclou 10
Des Beaux Arts 7
Brasserie Paul 14
Le Couronne 12
Flunch 9
Gill 19
Le Marmite 8
Pascaline 6
Le P'tit Bec 4
Les P'tits Parapluies 1
Au Temps des Cerises 3

RIGHT BANK
LEFT BANK
Place Beauvoisine
Boulevard de l'Yser
Gare SNCF (Rive Droite)
St-Romain
Musée des Antiquités
Théatre des Deux Rives
La Javanaise
Rue Pouchet
Rue Jeanne d'Arc
Rue Bouvreuil
Rue du Donjon
Rue Beauvoisine
Rue Louis Ricard
Tour Jeanne d'Arc
Musée de la Céramique
Musée des Beaux Arts
Musée le Secq des Tournelles
Sq. Verdrel
Boulevard de la Marne
Rue Bourg l'Abbé
Hôtel de Ville
St-Ouen
Rue Jean-Lecanuet
R. des Basnages
Rue Ganterie
Rue de l'Hôpital
Rue des Faulx
Rue Eau de Robec
Musée National de l'Education
Rue des Bon Enfants
Recuyère
R. de la Poterne
Pl. des Carmes
Rue des Carmes
Rue d'Amiens
Rue Damiette
Palais de Justice
Rue St-Lo
Ste-Jeanne
Cathédrale de Notre-Dame
Aître St-Maclou
Cyber-Net
Place du Vieux Marché
Rue aux Juifs
Rue du Gros Horloge
Rue St-Romain
St-Maclou
Boulevard des Belges
Vieux Palais
Gros Horloge
Rue des Bonnetiers
Rue aux Ours
Rue de la République
Place St-Marc
Rue du General Leclerc
Rue des Augustines
Théâtre des Arts
Espace Métrobus
Rue Grand Pont
Rue de la Tour de Beurre
Pl. de la République
Quai du Havre
Buses
Q de la Bourse
Q P. Corneille
Quai de Paris
River Seine
Quai Cavelier de la Salle
Quai Jean Moulin
Quai Jacques Anquetil
Champlain
Av de Bretagne
Rue St-Sever
Bd d'Orleans
Cours Clemenceau
Place des Emmurées
Rue Lafayette
Gare SNCF (Rive Gauche)
Rue des Emmurees
Boulevard de l'Europe
Centre St-Sever
St-Sever
Théatre Duchamp-Villon

Hôpital Hôtel-Dieu
2 & Camping
18 & Camping
Airport
20
21

making two stops before they resurface to cross the river by bridge; thereafter, the tracks dip below and above ground like a rollercoaster. Individual journeys cost €1.30; a book of ten tickets is €10.40, or you can buy an all-day pass for €3.50, a two-day one for €5, or a three-day one for €6.50.

Accommodation

With more than three thousand **hotel** rooms in town, there should be no difficulty in finding appropriate accommodation in Rouen, even at the busiest times. If you're coming for the weekend, check with the tourist office to see if any hotels are operating the "Bon Week-End en Villes" scheme (a red leaflet lists participating establishments), under which guests booking for a Saturday night at least 24 hours in advance, and confirming by letter, fax or email, can stay either Friday night or Sunday night free. Few of the hotels have restaurants, chiefly because there's such a wide choice of places to eat around town, while all those listed below remain open throughout the year. Motorists who just want to spend a day or two looking at the sights of Rouen should seriously consider the possibility of staying at one of the delightful riverside hotels in **La Bouille** (see p.117), or in the woods at **Lyons-la-Forêt** (see p.118).

There are two **campsites** within reasonable distance of Rouen, both accessible by public transport. The *Camping Municipal* on rue Jules-Ferry in Déville-lès-Rouen, 4km northwest of town (Ⓣ02.35.74.07.59 or Ⓣ02.32.82.34.80) is a surprisingly small site that's geared towards caravans rather than tents; take bus #8 or T2 from the Théâtre des Arts. *Camping de l'Aubette*, 23 rue du Vert Buisson in St-Léger du Bourg-Denis, 4km east of town on bus route #20 (Ⓣ02.35.08.47.69) is a basic site in a more rural, but much less accessible, setting than the *Camping Municipal*.

Hotels

Hôtel Andersen 4 rue Pouchet Ⓣ02.35.71.88.51, Ⓕ02.35.07.54.65. Very friendly place with plenty of character, set back beyond a small gravel yard and a short walk to the right as you come out from the Gare Rive Droite. Large, light and colourful rooms – shared showers in the cheaper ones. ❸

Hôtel Beauséjour 9 rue Pouchet Ⓣ02.35.71.93.47, Ⓕ02.35.98.01.24. Good-value place near the station (turn right as you come out), though once you're past the attractive orange facade with its window boxes, and nice garden courtyard, the rooms themselves are on the plain side, even if they do all have TV, phone and en-suite facilities. Closed second half of July. ❸

Hôtel Bristol 45 rue aux Juifs Ⓣ02.35.71.54.21, Ⓕ02.35.52.06.33. Clean, pretty nine-room hotel, above its own little brasserie (Ⓣ02.35.71.66.35) in a half-timbered house overlooking the Palais de Justice. All rooms are en suite, and have TV. ❷

Le Cardinal 1 place de la Cathédrale Ⓣ02.35.70.24.42, Ⓦwww.hotels-rouen.com. Very good-value hotel in a stunning location facing the cathedral; the rooms have excellent en-suite facilities and views of the cathedral (the higher ones from balconies), and ample buffet breakfasts are served for €6.80. ❸

Hôtel des Carmes 33 place des Carmes Ⓣ02.35.71.92.31, Ⓕ02.35.71.76.96. Twelve-room hotel in a beautifully decorated nineteenth-century house in a quiet central square, complete with blue shutters, a short walk north from the cathedral. The rooms are on the small side, but have benefited from recent renovation. "Normandy" breakfasts for €6. ❸

Hôtel de la Cathédrale 12 rue St-Romain Ⓣ02.35.71.57.95 Ⓦwww.hotel-de-la-cathedrale.fr. One of the most attractive and conveniently located hotels in Rouen, alongside the cathedral and archbishop's palace, though the plain rooms themselves don't live up to the appealing facade and quaint old flower-filled courtyard. Set in a quiet pedestrianized street – so parking is a problem – that's lined with fourteenth-century timber-framed houses. Buffet breakfasts €7.50. ❹

Hôtel de Dieppe place Bernard Tissot Ⓣ02.35.71.96.00, Ⓦwww.bestwestern.com/fr/ledieppe. Grand traditional hotel, immediately opposite the *gare SNCF*, which is affiliated to the Best Western chain and is home to the top-notch *Quatre Saisons* restaurant, where menus start at €27. Prices for the well-equipped rooms are greatly discounted at weekends. ❻

Hôtel de l'Europe 87–89 rue aux Ours ⓣ02.32.76.17.76, ⓦwww.h-europe.fr. Situated just south of the place du Vieux-Marché, where the staff are helpful and eager to please and the rooms modern, all en-suite with TV and phone – plus a minibar in the more expensive ones – and spotlessly clean. There is also a small restaurant serving good food from a simple menu. ❸

Mercure Rouen Centre 7 rue Croix de Fer ⓣ02.35.52.69.52, ⓔh1301@accor-hotels.com. Large chain hotel in the heart of the old city, offering a reliably high standard of accommodation, although the hefty room rates mean that this is not the best value in town, especially since extras such as parking and breakfast can add considerably to the bill. ❼

Hôtel du Palais 12 rue du Tambour ⓣ02.35.71.41.40. Very inexpensive central hotel, tucked away just north of the Gros Horloge, offering stylish though not fancy rooms at unbeatable prices. While some rooms are en suite, the cheapest options involve sharing a toilet and shower. ❶

Hôtel Sphinx 130 rue Beauvoisine ⓣ02.35.71.35.86. Very basic, even grim, accommodation, near the Musée des Antiquités, but this is possibly the only hotel left in Normandy where you can get a room for €16, and that's enough to keep the budget travellers coming. None of the rooms has its own shower – which cost €2 a time – while an extra bed is €10. ❶

Hôtel Versan 3 rue Jean Lecanuet ⓣ02.35.07.77.07, ⓦwww.lerapporteur.fr/versan. Modern en-suite rooms at reasonable prices, close to the Hôtel de Ville and the museums. Buffet breakfasts €7.50. ❸

Hôtel du Vieux Marché 15 rue de la Pie ⓣ02.35.71.00.88, ⓦwww.hotelduvieuxmarche.com. Very modern place, set around a venerable old courtyard, just a few steps from the place du Vieux-Marché. A high standard of comfort has quickly made this the most popular upmarket hotel in town. ❻

The Town

Rouen has traditionally spent a higher proportion of its budget on **monuments** than any other provincial town, which maddens many a Rouennais. As a tourist, your one complaint may be the lack of time to visit them all. Certainly there are some great sights to be seen – the **Cathédrale de Notre Dame**, the **Gros Horloge**, the **Aître St-Maclou**, all the delightful twisting streets of timbered houses – and there's history aplenty too, most notably the links with **Joan of Arc**.

Place du Vieux-Marché

One obvious place to start exploring the city is the **place du Vieux-Marché**, where a small plaque and a huge cross, 20m high, adorn the public square in which Joan of Arc was burned to death on May 30, 1431. The architect, Louis Arretche, was commissioned to design a memorial **church** to the saint in 1969, and the result was dedicated in 1979 (Mon–Sat 10am–12.30pm & 2–6pm, Sun 2–6pm). A wacky, spiky-looking thing, said to represent either an upturned boat or the flames that consumed Joan, it's indisputably an architectural triumph, part of an ensemble of buildings that manages to incorporate in similar style a covered food market (open daily except Mon), designed more for show than practical shopping. The theme of the church's fish-shaped windows is continued in the scaly tiles that adorn its roof, which is hugely elongated to form a covered walkway across the square. Part of Arretche's brief was to incorporate some sixteenth-century stained glass, removed from the church of St-Vincent that stood on this site before it was destroyed in the war. It's now displayed beautifully, all on one facade of the new church, despite the fact that the windows that hold it are an entirely different shape. The outline of the foundations of the vanished old church is visible on the adjacent lawns, where a flowerbed marks the precise spot of Joan's martyrdom. The square itself is surrounded by fine old brown and white half-timbered houses; many of those on the south side now serve as restaurants.

Joan of Arc

Joan of Arc stands alone, and must continue to stand alone... There is no one to compare her with, none to measure her by... There have been other young generals, but they were not girls; young generals, but they have been soldiers before they were generals; she began as a general; she commanded the first army she ever saw; she led it from victory to victory, and never lost a battle with it; there have been young commanders-in-chief, but none so young as she: she is the only soldier in history who has held the supreme command of a nation's armies at the age of seventeen.

Mark Twain, *Joan of Arc*

When the 17-year-old peasant girl known to history as **Joan of Arc** arrived at the French court in Chinon early in 1429, the Hundred Years War had already dragged on for over ninety years. Most of northern France was in the grip of an Anglo-Burgundian alliance, whose major strongholds were the châteaux of the Loire. Since 1425, Joan had been hearing voices in her native village of Domrémy, in Lorraine near France's eastern frontiers. Convinced that she alone could save France, she came to Chinon to present her case to the as-yet-uncrowned Dauphin. Partly through recognizing him despite a simple disguise he wore to fool her at their first meeting, she convinced him of her divine guidance; and after a remarkable three-week examination by a tribunal of the French *parlement*, she went on to secure command of the armies of France. In a whirlwind campaign, which culminated in the raising of the siege of Orléans on May 8, 1429, she broke the English hold on the Loire Valley. She then escorted the Dauphin deep into enemy territory, with town after town rallying to her standard as they advanced, so that in accordance with ancient tradition he could be crowned King Charles VII of France in the cathedral at Reims, on July 17.

Within a year of her greatest triumph, Joan was captured by the Burgundian army at Compiègne in May 1430, and held to ransom. Chivalry dictated that any offer of payment from the vacillating Charles must be accepted, but in the absence of such an offer Joan was handed over to the English for 10,000 ducats. On Christmas Day 1430, she was imprisoned in the château of Philippe-Auguste at Rouen.

Charged with heresy, on account of her "false and diabolical" visions and refusal not to wear men's clothing, Joan was put on trial for her life on February 21, 1431. For three months, a changing panel of 131 assessors – only eight of whom were English-born – heard the evidence against her. Condemned, inevitably, to death, Joan recanted on the scaffold in St-Ouen cemetery on May 24, and her sentence was commuted to life imprisonment. The presiding judge, Bishop Pierre Cauchon of Beauvais, reassured disappointed English representatives that "we will get her yet". The next Sunday, Joan was tricked into breaking her vow and putting on male clothing, and taken to the archbishop's chapel in rue St-Romain to be condemned to death for the second time. On May 30, 1431, she was burned at the stake in the place du Vieux-Marché; her ashes, together with her unburned heart, were thrown into the Seine.

Charles VII finally recaptured Rouen in 1449. Seeing the verdict against Joan as reflecting on the legitimacy of his own claim to the French throne, he instigated a *Procés en Nullité*, which took evidence from all the surviving witnesses, and resulted in a papal declaration of Joan's innocence in 1456. Joan herself passed into legend, until the discovery and publication of the full transcript of her trial in the 1840s. The forbearance and devout humility she displayed throughout her ordeal added to her status as France's greatest religious heroine. She was canonized as recently as 1920, and soon afterwards became the country's patron saint.

Also on the south side of the *place*, the privately owned **Musée Jeanne d'Arc**, in an ancient cellar in the back of a gift shop at no. 33, draws large crowds to its collection of tawdry waxworks and facsimile manuscripts (daily: mid-April to mid-Sept 9.30am–1pm & 1.30–7pm; mid-Sept to mid-April 10am–noon & 2–6.30pm; €4). Among the bric-a-brac is a page from the records of the Paris *parlement*, dated May 10, 1429, which refers to reports reaching Paris that, on the previous Saturday, the French had trounced the English at Orléans. A sketch in the margin, possibly by a bored clerk, depicts a young woman, with her hair tied back, a banner in one hand and a sword in the other. This, the only other contemporary portrait of the "Maid of Orléans" was not drawn from life, so there's no reason to think it any more authentic than the movie stills on display in the museum, showing Ingrid Bergman as Joan in both 1948 and 1954, and Jean Seberg in the role in 1957.

Gros Horloge

From place du Vieux-Marché, rue du Gros-Horloge leads east towards the cathedral. Just across rue Jeanne d'Arc you come to the **Gros Horloge** itself. A colourful one-handed clock, it used to be on the adjacent Gothic belfry until it was moved down by popular demand in 1529, so that people could see it better. When the ongoing restoration work is finished (current predictions are for some time in 2005), you should be able to pay a small fee to climb up rather too many steps to see the clock's workings and, if the sponginess of the lead roofing agrees with your nerves, totter around the top for a marvellous view of the old city, and the startling array of towers and spires around. The bell up there, cast in 1260, still rings what's known as the "Conqueror's Curfew" at 9pm daily. A block to the north is the Renaissance splendour of the former **Palais de Justice**, which was largely destroyed during World War II, only to be rebuilt as good as new. It is not open to tourists however, so you'll have to content yourself with admiring the magnificently ornate exterior.

Cathédrale de Notre Dame

The **Cathédrale de Notre Dame** (Mon 2–7pm, Tues–Sun 8am–7pm), a couple of hundred metres east of the Gros Horloge, stands on the site of a Roman place of worship, erected in the third century AD at a major crossroads. Despite the addition of all sorts of different towers, spires and vertical extensions, it remains at heart the Gothic masterpiece that was built in the twelfth and thirteenth centuries. Later accretions include the flamboyant **Tour du Beurre**, named for what was probably the erroneous belief that it was paid for by the granting of dispensations that allowed wealthy churchgoers to eat butter during Lent, and the nineteenth-century iron **spire** of the central lantern tower, known in French as the *flèche* or "arrow". Cast in the foundries of Conches, it was built to replace a tower that burned down in 1822, and was at the time, at 151m, the highest in France.

The cathedral has undergone extensive **restoration work** in recent years, an immense task which was added to when one of the spire's four greenish supports was detached by the hurricane of late December 1999, and fell, piercing the roof of the cathedral itself and destroying a section of the medieval choir stalls below. Intricately sculpted like the rest of the exterior, the west facade of the cathedral was **Monet's subject** for over thirty studies of changing light, which now hang in the Musée d'Orsay in Paris. Monet might not recognize it now, however – in the last few years, it's been scrubbed a gleaming white, free from the centuries of accreted dirt he so carefully recorded. For that matter, Monet would be equally nonplussed by the melange of postmodern buskers who now congregate in the

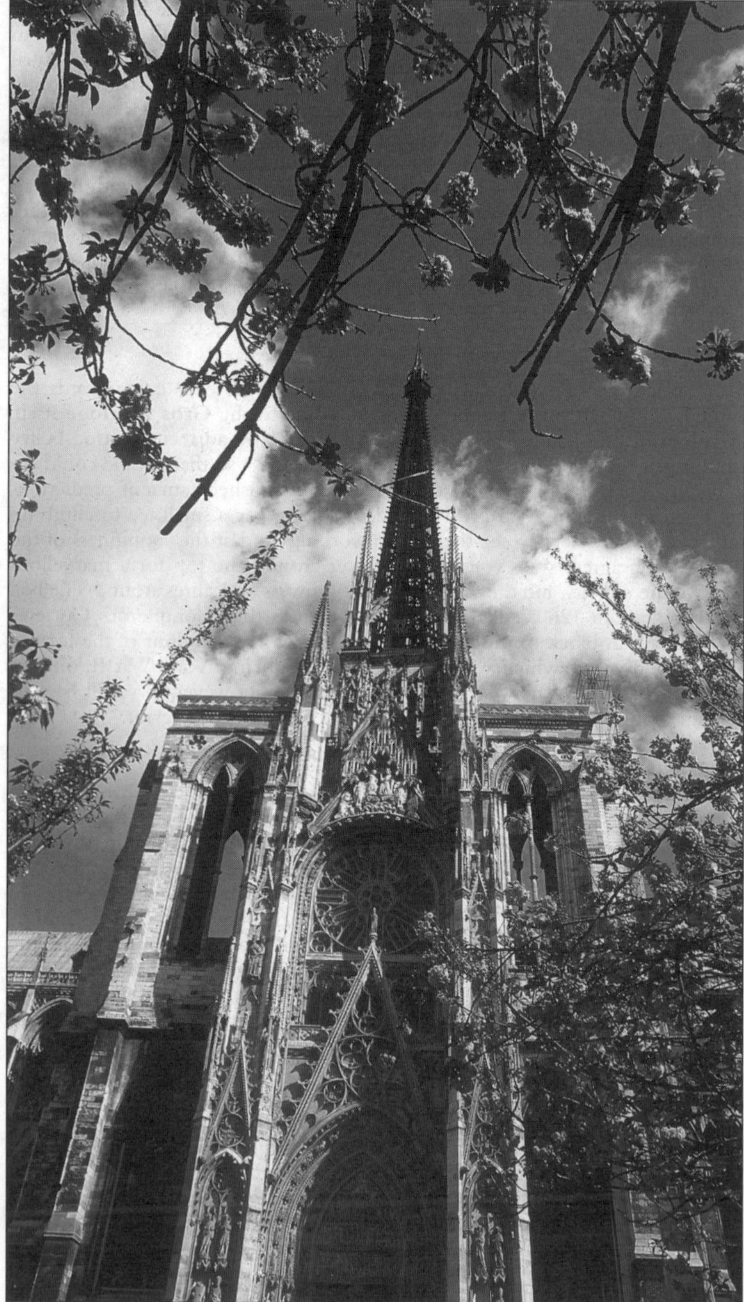

△ Rouen Cathedral

square in front, such as Andean pan-pipers playing medleys of Abba hits. In an attempt to make up for this neglect, the town has laid on a thirty-minute light show, **La Cathédrale de Monet aux Pixels** (daily: late June to mid-September 10.45pm; free), whereby colours inspired by Monet's cathedral paintings are projected onto the church's façade, transforming it quite magnificently into a series of giant Monet-esque canvases.

Inside the cathedral, the carvings of the misericords in the choir depict fifteenth-century life, in secular scenes, as well as the usual mythical beasts. The chapel dedicated to Joan of Arc, and paid for by an English commitee in 1956, contains a statue of Joan at the stake. The **ambulatory** and **crypt** – closed on Sunday mornings and during services – hold the assorted tombs of various recumbent royal figures, stretching back as far as **Duke Rollo**, who died "enfeebled by toil" in 933 AD. Rollo's effigy was destroyed by the bombs of 1944, and has now been replaced by a nineteenth-century copy of someone else's. Both he and **Richard the Lionheart** – whose heart reposes beneath a similar figure nearby – seem to have detachable feet, which are occasionally removed for cleaning.

Église St-Maclou and Aître St-Maclou

A short way east of the cathedral, the intricate wooden panelling in the porch of the fifteenth-century church of **St-Maclou** is the highlight of what is often cited as the most spectacular example of Gothic flamboyant architecture in France (Mon–Sat 10am–5pm, Sun 10.30am–5.30pm). The whole building was so badly damaged by bombs on June 4, 1944 that it could only reopen in 1980; thankfully, the ornate stone stairway up to the organ inside remains as ethereal as ever. The interior is so light partly because most of its stained glass was destroyed, and the windows are now clear. St Maclou himself – perhaps more familiar as St Malo – was a seventh-century missionary from Wales.

Nearby, with its entrance a little hard to find in between nos. 184 and 186 rue Martainville, is the **Aître St-Maclou** (daily 8am–8pm; free). This was built between 1526 and 1533, in an era of mass plague deaths, as a cemetery and charnel house. The ground floor was used as an open cloister and, in the rooms above, the bare bones of countless victims were exposed to view. At first sight it looks very picturesque – a tranquil garden courtyard of half-timbered houses – but look closely at the carvings on the beams of the one open lower storey of the surrounding buildings and you see traces of a macabre **Dance of Death**, while in the case to the right of the entrance is a mummified cat. The buildings are still in use, and still stimulating morbid imaginations, not as a morgue but as Rouen's Fine Arts school. In the square outside are several good antique bookshops and a few art shops.

St-Ouen

The last of Rouen's great churches is **St-Ouen**, next to the Hôtel de Ville in a large open square to the north (mid-Jan to mid-March and Nov to mid-Dec Tues, Sat & Sun 10am–noon & 2–5pm; mid-March to Oct Tues–Sat 10am–12.15pm & 2–6pm, Sun 9am–12.15pm & 2–6pm). It's larger than the cathedral and has far less decoration; as a result, its Gothic proportions and the purity of its lines have that instant impact with which nothing built since the Middle Ages can compete. Originally, it was an abbey church, founded in the seventh century before the Viking invasion. The present building was begun in 1318 and completed in the fifteenth century. Inside, it holds some stunning fourteenth-century stained glass, though much was destroyed during the Revolution – hence the 1960 *Crucifixion* in the choir, by Max Ingrand.

Immediately north of St-Ouen is the city's **Hôtel de Ville**, outside which parades an equestrian statue of Napoléon, weathered to an eerie green and looking like death incarnate.

Rue Eau de Robec

The **rue Eau de Robec**, which runs east from rue Damiette just south of St-Ouen, was described by one of Flaubert's characters in an earlier age as a "degraded little Venice". It's now a textbook example of how Rouen has been restored. Where once a shallow stream flowed beneath the raised doorsteps of venerable half-timbered houses, a thin trickle now makes its way along a stylized cement bed crossed by concrete walkways. It remains an attractive ensemble, if a rather ersatz one, and the houses themselves are now predominantly inhabited by antique dealers, interspersed with the odd café.

In a fine old mansion at no. 185, the **Musée National de l'Éducation** (Mon & Wed–Fri 10am–12.30pm & 1.30–6pm, Sat & Sun 2–6pm; €3) tells the story of the last five centuries of schooling in France, with photos, paintings, ancient textbooks and a mocked-up schoolroom. Unless you read French well, however, it's unlikely to hold your interest.

Tour Jeanne d'Arc

The pencil-thin **Tour Jeanne d'Arc** (April–Sept Mon & Wed–Sat 10am–12.30pm & 2–6pm, Sun 2–6.30pm; Oct–March Mon & Wed–Sat 10am–12.30pm & 2–5pm, Sun 2–5.30pm; €1.50), a short way southeast of the *gare SNCF* at the junction of rue du Donjon and rue Bouvreuil, is all that remains of the castle of Philippe-Auguste, built in 1205 and scene of the imprisonment and trial of Joan of Arc. It served as the castle's keep and entranceway, and was itself fully surrounded by a moat. It was not, however, Joan's actual prison – that was the Tour de la Pucelle, demolished in 1809. The trial took place first of all in the castle's St-Romain chapel, and then later in its great central hall, both of which were destroyed in 1590.

Joan came to this building only once, on May 9, 1431, to be confronted with the fearsome torture chamber in its lowest level. Threatened by Bishop Cauchon with the words "There is the rack, and there are its ministers. You will reveal all, now, or be put to the torture", she responded: "I will tell you nothing more than I have told you; no, not even if you tear the limbs from my body. And even if in my pain I did say something otherwise, I would always say afterwards that it was the torture that spoke and not I".

The tall, sharp-pointed tower was bought by public subscription in 1860, and restored to its present state. After seeing a small collection of Joan-related memorabilia, you can climb the steep spiral staircase to the very top (on the way up there are photos of some of Philippe-Auguste's other castles in Normandy), but you can't see out over the city, let alone step outside into the open air.

Musée des Beaux Arts

Rouen's imposing **Musée des Beaux Arts** commands the square Verdrel from just east of the central rue Jeanne d'Arc (Wed–Mon 10am–6pm; €3). Even this grand edifice is not quite large enough to display some of its medieval tapestries, which dangle inelegantly from the ceilings to trail along the floor, but the collection as a whole is consistently absorbing. Unexpected highlights include dazzling Russian icons from the sixteenth century onwards, and an entertaining three-dimensional eighteenth-century Nativity from Naples.

Many of the biggest names among the **painters** – Caravaggio, Velázquez, Rubens – tend to be represented by a single minor work. However, there are

Museum admission charges

Under the **carte-musées** scheme, you can gain admission to the Beaux Arts, Céramique and Secq Tournelles museums on a single ticket costing €5.35 and valid for two days. If you need more time, consider the €9.15 option, which gives you unlimited access to the three museums for the whole year, plus reductions for temporary exhibitions.

several Monets, including a Rouen Cathedral from 1894, Paris's rue St-Denis aflutter with flags in 1894, and a recently acquired *Vue Générale de Rouen*, as well as canvases by Blanche Hoschedé-Monet, who was both the daughter of Claude Monet's mistress Alice and the wife of his son Jean. The central sculpture court, roofed over but very light, is dominated by a wonderful three-part mural of the course of the Seine from Paris to Le Havre, prepared by Raoul Dufy in 1937 for the Palais de Chaillot in Paris.

Musée de la Céramique

Rouen's history as a centre for *faïencerie*, the manufacture of earthenware pottery, is recorded in the **Musée de la Céramique**, facing the Beaux Arts from rue Faucon to the north (Wed–Mon 10am–1pm & 2–6pm; €2.30). A series of beautiful rooms, some of which incorporate sixteenth-century wood panelling rescued from the demolished nunnery of St-Amand, display specimens from the seventeenth century onwards. Until polychrome appeared in 1698, everything was blue; at that time, Rouen's main rivals and influences were the cities of Delft and Nevers, well represented in this collection. Assorted tiles and plates reflect the eighteenth-century craze for chinoiserie, although the genuine Chinese and Japanese pieces nearby possess a sophistication contemporary French craftsmen could only dream of emulating. The mood changes abruptly in the Revolutionary era, as witnessed by a fascinating collection of plates bearing slogans from both sides of the political fence.

Musée Le Secq des Tournelles

Behind the Beaux Arts, housed in the old and barely altered church of St-Laurent on rue Jacques-Villon, stands an interesting and unusual museum of ironmongery, the **Musée Le Secq des Tournelles** (Wed–Mon 10am–1pm & 2–6pm; €2.30). It consists of a collection of wrought-iron objects of all dates and descriptions, among them nutcrackers and door knockers, locks and gates, nineteenth-century toys and jewellery, spiral staircases that lead nowhere, and hideous implements of torture.

Musée des Antiquités

The **Musée des Antiquités** (Mon & Wed–Sat 10am–12.15pm & 1.30–5.30pm, Sun 2–6pm; €3), a short walk north of the town centre at the top of rue Beauvoisine, provides a dry but comprehensive run-through of ancient artefacts found in or near Rouen. Starting with an impressive pointed helmet from the Bronze Age and an assortment of early iron tools, it continues with some remarkably complete Roman mosaics from villas unearthed in Lillebonne and the Forêt de Brotonne. Then come a long gallery filled with woodcarvings rescued from long-lost Rouen houses – including a lovely bas-relief of sheep that served as the sign for a medieval draper's shop – and some fine fifteenth-century tapestries.

The Musée Flaubert et de l'Histoire de la Médicine

For an insight into the Rouen that Flaubert knew, don't go to the **Pavillon Flaubert** at Croisset-Canteleu, nine kilometres from Rouen along the D982 in the direction of Duclair. Like Rouen's two other literary museums – the two homes of Pierre Corneille – it only proves the pointlessness of the genre. Visit, instead, the **Musée Flaubert et de l'Histoire de la Médicine**, at the Hôtel-Dieu Hospital (Tues 10am–6pm, Wed–Sat 10am–noon & 2–6pm; €2.20). This stands on the corner of rue de Lecat and rue du Contrat-Social, a five-minute walk west from the place du Vieux-Marché (or bus #5 stop "Préfecture", or bus #T, T2, T3, stop "Louis-Pasteur"), and it's infinitely more relevant to Flaubert's writings than the manuscript copies and personal mementos in the Pavillon museum.

Flaubert's father was chief surgeon and director of the medical school, living with his family in this house within the hospital; Gustave himself was born here in 1821. Even during the cholera epidemic when he was 11, the young Gustave and his sister were not stopped from running around the wards or climbing along the garden wall to look into the autopsy lab. Some of the medical exhibits would certainly have been familiar objects to him – a phrenology model, a childbirth demonstrator resembling a giant ragdoll, and the sets of encyclopedias. There's also one of his stuffed parrots, as featured in Julian Barnes' novel *Flaubert's Parrot*.

Eating

Rouen has a good reputation for **food**, with its most famous dish being *canard rouennais* – a crossbreed of duck from the Seine Valley with a more meaty taste than usual. Unlike the hotels, which sometimes have cheaper weekend rates, the city's **upmarket restaurants** tend to charge more over weekends, when families eat out. The greatest concentration of restaurants is in place du Vieux-Marché, an area in which, ironically, there are few hotels.

There's a daily **food market** in the same square where you can buy fresh fish, fruit and cheese, while the area just north is full of Tunisian **takeaways**, **crêperies**, and so forth. There are also sumptuous **patisserie** shops everywhere, and if you've had enough of all things continental, the rue du Gros-Horloge holds a half-timbered *McDonald's*. More or less opposite, Rouen's most central **supermarket** is the Monoprix.

Restaurants

Auberge St-Maclou 224–226 rue Martainville ⓣ02.35.71.06.67. Half-timbered building in the shadow of St-Maclou church, with tables on the street outside and an old-style ambience inside. The pedestrian street gets crowded in summer, but the menus are far from overpriced – the €11.50 set lunch includes mussels as starter and/or main course. Prices to suit all budgets, and excellent desserts. Closed Sun (except March–June), Mon, 3 weeks in Aug & 2 weeks in Feb.

Des Beaux Arts 34 rue Damiette ⓣ02.35.70.17.15. Located on a pretty pedestrianized street north of St-Maclou church, this place serves very good-value North African cuisine: couscous from €8 or tajine from €11, with all kinds of sausages and assorted meats. Closed Mon & Tues eve.

Brasserie Paul 1 place de la Cathédrale ⓣ02.35.71.86.07. The definitive address for Rouen's definitive bistro, an attractive Belle-Époque place with seating both indoors and on a terrace in full view of the cathedral. Daily lunch specials, such as the goats' cheese and smoked duck salad that was Simone de Beauvoir's favourite in the 1930s, cost under €10.

Flunch 60 rue des Carmes ⓣ02.35.71.81.81. Large and good self-service on a street running north from the cathedral, with many fresh dishes, starters and desserts, and a €5.60 daily *formule*. Unlimited vegetables with any hot dish. A much healthier alternative to *McDonald's* and the like.

Gill 8–9 quai de la Bourse ⓣ02.35.71.16.14. Absolutely classic French restaurant, chosen for well over ten years in a row as the best in

Normandy by a local magazine on account of such Gilles Tournadre specialities as lobster grilled with asparagus and pigeon baked in puff pastry. Weekday lunch menus start at €32 (not bad value considering the quality), while the most expensive dinner menu will set you back €78. Closed Sun & Mon.

Le Marmite 3 rue de Florence ☎02.35.71.75.55. Romantic little place just west of the place du Vieux-Marché, offering beautiful, elegantly presented gourmet dishes on well-priced menus at €22, €32 (featuring hot foie gras) and €48. Closed Sun eve, Mon & Tues lunch.

Le Couronne 31 place du Vieux-Marché ☎02.35.71.40.90. Claims to be the oldest *auberge* in France, serving food since well before Joan of Arc's time. Over the years it has become one of the city's finest restaurants, and definitely the eatery of choice on the place du Vieux-Marché. If you find the interior a little too stuffy and formal, there are a few tables on the square itself. Menus range from €23 for lunch and €28 or €43 for dinner.

Pascaline 5 rue de la Poterne ☎02.35.89.67.44. Classic bistro, located to the north of the Palais de Justice, near the flower market, with a green wooden enclosure attached to the front of a half-timbered house. As well as two set menus costing €16 or under, they offer a full list of à la carte specialities and occasionally have live jazz music.

Le P'tit Bec 182 rue Eau de Robec ☎02.35.07.63.33. Friendly brasserie-cum-tea-room which has become Rouen's most popular lunch spot. Two simple menus at €11.50 and €14 include a fish or meat main course, plus plenty of vegetarian options; also serves afternoon tea. There's seating both indoors and outside on the pedestrianized street beside the running water and in view of a fine blue half-timbered mansion next door. Closed eves except for Fri & Sat; closed all day Sun.

Les P'tits Parapluies 46 rue Bourg l'Abbé, place de la Rougemare ☎02.35.88.55.26. Elegant, secluded half-timbered restaurant not far north of the Hôtel de Ville, on the edge of an attractive little square. Counting your calories (or your pennies) is not really an option; the trio of menus, some of which change weekly, start at €24 and include such delights as foie gras and oysters, and come with two glasses of wine. Closed Sat lunch, Sun eve & Mon.

Au Temps des Cerises 4–6 rue des Basnages ☎02.35.89.98.00. If you've come to Normandy for the cheeses, this is the place to get it all out of your system. Turkey breast in Camembert, goats' cheese crêpes, and above all fondues of every description. Lunch menus from €10.50, dinners from €15.50. Trendy if slightly overstyled. Closed Mon & Sat lunch, & Sun.

Nightlife and entertainment

As a city with a strong student population, and one renowned for its (largely rock-oriented) **music scene**, Rouen enjoys a far-from-provincial nightlife, with new clubs springing up all the time. Some of the city's most appealing **bars** lie in the maze of streets between rue Jean-Lecanuet and place du Vieux-Marché. Incoming sailors used to head straight for this area of the city – the small bars are still there, even if the sailors aren't. Unfortunately, most of the **nightclubs** are some distance from the centre and hard to reach unless you have your own transport.

Bars and music venues

Le Bateau Ivre 17 rue des Sapins ☎02.35.70.09.05. Low-key but atmospheric hangout a long way northeast of the centre which puts on a mostly rock-oriented programme of music and performance, with an open-mike night on Thursdays that seems to attract lovers of traditional French chansons. Tues & Wed 10pm–2am, Thurs–Sat 10pm–4am. Closed Sun, Mon & all Aug.

Le Bayou 26 rue St-Étienne-des-Tonneliers ☎02.35.88.77.18. Formerly the Latin music club *La Luna*, it remains to be seen what the new management will make of this large nightclub right in the town centre. The location is a definite plus for tourists, although the current 1980s playlist might be a little tepid for serious clubbers. Tues–Sat 6pm–4am.

Big Ben Pub 95 rue du Gros-Horloge ☎02.35.88.44.50. Right under the big clock – hence the name – this busy pub in a splendid half-timbered house has the air of a medieval tavern, given a modern twist by the Karaoke evenings on Thurs, Fri and Sat evenings (except during summer). There are two floors inside and some tables on the busy street outside – a perfect vantage point for people watching. Mon 6pm–2am, Tues–Sat noon–2am.

Le Chakra 4 bd Ferdinand-de-Lesseps ☎02.32.10.12.02. Formerly known as *Le Traxx*, but still playing plenty of house and techno to an especially young clientele. Next to the Seine a couple of kilometres west of the centre. Fri–Sat 11pm–4am.

L'Euro Café 41 place du Vieux-Marché. Justifiably popular bar occupying a multistorey half-timbered building on the western corner of the place du Vieux-Marché. House music predominates on the ground floor, where you can drink at tables on the square, and music from the 1980s on the first. There is a space for dancing on the second floor. Daily 10pm–2am.

Exo 7 13 place des Chartreux ☎02.35.03.32.30. Traditionally the centre of Rouen's heavy-rock scene, a long way south of the centre, the Exo 7 (pronounced "Exocet") is these days becoming a bit more eclectic, with the odd techno dance night as well. Fri & Sat 11pm–5am.

Miss Marple 35 rue de la Tour de Beurre ☎02.35.88.47.32. Small and friendly bar for lesbians, where, if you are new, the owner will make a special effort to introduce you to people. If no one captures your interest, there is always the pinball machine and, occasionally, organized debates on various women's issues to keep you drinking. Tues–Sat 6pm–2am.

Le Nash Café 97 rue Écuyère. Relaxed bar popular with locals. The interior has a lounge-like feel with its moody lighting and zebra-striped upholstery, while the outdoor terrace is much more akin to a classic French café. Music ranges from ambient house to Latin. Mon–Fri 11.30am–2pm & 6pm–2am, Sat 6pm–2am.

Le Triplex 177 rte de Paris, Amfreville-la-Mivoie ☎02.35.07.40.30. Mixed, but gay-friendly, disco a few kilometres east of Rouen. Plays host to visiting DJs playing mainly electronic music, but also has a "disco-latino" room and various theme nights where costumes, wigs and plenty of glitter are required. Fri & Sat 10pm–4am.

XXL 25–27 rue de la Savonnerie ☎02.35.88.84.00. Well known gay (male) bar near the river, just south of the cathedral, which has regular theme nights and a small dance floor in the basement. Although unambiguously geared to men looking for men, women will not be turned away. Tues & Wed 9pm–2am, Thurs–Sat 9pm–4am, Sun 10pm–2am.

Entertainment

As you would expect in a conurbation of 400,000, there's always plenty going on in Rouen, from classical concerts in churches to alternative events in community and commercial centres. The city has several **theatres**, which mainly work to winter seasons. The most highbrow venue for big spectacles is the **Théâtre des Arts**, 7 rue de Dr-Rambert (box office: Tues–Sat 1–8pm; ☎08.10.81.11.16), which puts on opera, ballet and concerts. The more adventurous repertory company of the **Théâtre des Deux Rives** (☎02.35.70.22.82), based opposite the Antiquités museum at the top end of rue Louis-Ricard, at the junction with rue de Joyeuse, presents work by playwrights such as Beaumarchais, Shakespeare, Beckett and Gorky.

Major **concerts** often take place in the **Théâtre Duchamp-Villon** in the St-Sever complex (☎02.32.18.28.10), accessible by metro (stop "St-Sever"). Also south of the river and on the metro (direction "Georges Braque"), albeit a long way further out, are the **Théâtre Charles Dullin**, allée des Arcades, Grand Quévilly (☎02.35.69.51.18), and the **Théâtre Maxime-Gorki**, 24 rue Joseph Lebas, Petit Quévilly (☎02.35.03.29.78), which specializes in contemporary and traditional music from around Europe.

Shopping

Most of the classier **shops** in Rouen are in the pedestrian streets near, and slightly north of, the cathedral. If you are looking for fancy foodstuffs, patisserie, chocolates and the like, there are shops on rue Jeanne d'Arc around and just above rue du Gros-Horloge. For **hypermarkets** and cheap clothes, however – or just for something to do on a rainy day – go south of the river to the modern multistorey St-Sever complex. There's an open-air antiques and bric-a-brac **market** nearby in the place des Émmurées.

The largest **bookshop** in Rouen can be found at the all-purpose FNAC, underground in the Espace du Palais mall immediately north of the Palais de Justice; it stocks a fine selection of local maps and guides, largely in French, and English-language titles, as well as a wide range of CDs, videos and computer paraphernalia. The ABC Bookshop, 9–11 rue des Faulx, near the St-Ouen church, specializes in English titles. There's also a Virgin Megastore at 14 rue Guillaume Le Conquérant.

Listings

American Express in the tourist office at 25 place de la Cathédrale ⓣ02.35.89.48.60 (May–Sept Mon–Sat 9am–1pm & 2–7pm, Sun 9.30am–12.30pm & 2–6pm; Oct–April Mon–Sat 9am–1pm & 2–6pm).
Banks and exchange Most of the major banks can be found along rue Jeanne d'Arc, such as Société Générale at no. 34 (ⓣ02.35.52.58.00). All have ATMs.
Bicycle Rental Rouen Cycles, 45 rue St-Éloi ⓣ02.35.71.34.30 (Tues–Sat 8.30am–noon & 2–7pm).
Cinemas Gaumont, 28 rue de la République ⓣ02.35.07.31.32; Melville, 75 rue du Général Leclerc ⓣ02.35.07.18.48; UGC CinéCité, Centre Commercial St-Sever ⓣ08.92.70.00.00 ext 760.
Hospital CHU du Rouen, 1 rue de Germont ⓣ02.32.88.89.90.
Internet access *Cyber-Net*, 47 place du Vieux-Marché ⓣ02.35.07.73.02 (daily 10am–11pm; €4 per hr); *La Javanaise*, 174 rue Beauvoisine ⓣ02.35.89.25.24 (daily 10–1am; €4 per hr, €1 15 min);.
Pharmacy Grande Pharmacie du Centre, 29 place de la Cathédrale ⓣ02.35.71.33.17 (Mon 10am–7.30pm, Tues–Fri 9am–7.30pm, Sat 9am–7pm).
Post office 45bis rue Jeanne d'Arc, in the centre of town (post code 76000) ⓣ02.35.15.66.73 (Mon–Fri 8am–7pm, Sat 8.30am–12.30pm).
Swimming pools Centre Sportif du Docteur Duchêne, Île Lacroix ⓣ02.35.07.94.70; Piscine Diderot, 112 bd de l'Europe ⓣ02.35.63.59.14.

Around Rouen

Though it only takes a few minutes of travelling along the river from Rouen in either direction to reach pleasant small towns well worth an overnight stop – such as Villequier or Les Andelys, both described elsewhere in this chapter – a number of places only just outside the city proper make **good day-trips** while you are based in Rouen. Some are also worth considering as **alternative bases** for visits to the city; note, however, that **public transport** connections are generally poor.

La Bouille

Ten kilometres southwest from central Rouen along the southern riverbank, the small village of **LA BOUILLE** stands near a magnificent sweeping bend in the Seine. Little more than a couple of narrow twisting lanes lined with gnarled half-timbered houses, pressed hard against the steep hillside, it's a complete contrast to the noise and bustle of the city, and makes a perfect place to spend a couple of nights for anyone not dependent on public transport. Not far north, a little *bac* (ferry) crosses the river (14 daily, Mon–Sat) to the small Forêt de Roumare, which makes for a pleasant stroll

Two expensive but exquisite **hotels**, the *Bellevue*, 13 quai Hector-Malot (ⓣ 02.35.18.05.05; ⓦwww.hotel-le-bellevue.com; ❸), and the luxurious *St-Pierre*, place du Bateau (ⓣ02.35.67.00.86; ❹), overlook the main road through the village, and both have superb dining rooms.

Clères

Roughly 16km northeast of Rouen, and reachable on bus #29 from the *gare routière*, trains from the *gare SNCF*, or via the D6 if driving, the pretty village of **CLÈRES** has centred since the eleventh century on an imposing **Château**, though the stout walls that now remain date back a mere five hundred years. The spacious and beautifully landscaped grounds are home to a popular **zoo**; while not holding a very wide range of species, it displays them in idyllic surroundings (March–Nov daily 10am–7pm; €4.60). The whole place is something of a Garden of Eden, in that peacocks, antelope and wallabies can wander at will in the absence of predators; families with pushchairs, however, may well struggle with some of the steeper gravel footpaths. Exotic birds kept in ageing aviaries include emus, rheas and kookaburras, while the château itself plays host to changing temporary art exhibitions. The infamous French writer Colette made the impenetrable but presumably complimentary remark that "at Clères, in the zoo park, it is easy to lose the melancholy feeling of inevitability".

The Forêt de Lyons

Around 25km east of Rouen, the **Forêt de Lyons** was a thousand years ago a favoured hunting ground of William the Conqueror and other dukes of Normandy. In 1135, Henry I of England died in the central village of Lyons-la-Forêt of a surfeit of lampreys consumed after a late-November hunting expedition. The village itself is a picturesque place, while a few kilometres to the north and south of it respectively, there are a château and abbey worth visiting. Parts of the forest feel as though they have changed little in the intervening millennium – remarkable considering its proximity not only to Rouen but also to Paris. Almost any of the little roads through these dense woods rewards exploration by cyclists or walkers.

Lyons-la-Forêt

At the heart of the forest, the little hill village of **LYONS-LA-FORÊT**, actually situated not in Seine-Maritime but the neighbouring *département* of Eure, was the site of William's now completely indiscernible castle, but has retained a superb ensemble of half-timbered Norman houses dating from around 1610. In the centre of the village stand the plain old wooden *halles*, often used as a film set, while the roads around abound in splendid rural mansions. One such, the house named *Le Fresne* on rue d'Enfer, was much used by the composer Ravel in the 1920s.

Lyons' central **tourist office**, 20 rue de l'Hôtel de Ville (April–Sept Tues–Sat 10am–noon & 2–5pm, Sun 10am–noon & 2–4pm; Oct–March Tues–Sat 10am–noon & 2–5pm; ⓣ02.32.49.31.65), has information on the whole forest area. Of the **hotels** in the village, your best bets are the brick-fronted *Grand Cerf*, right next to the *halles* on place Bensérade (ⓣ02.32.49.60.44; ❸; closed Tues eve & Wed, plus Feb) – which has a secluded garden tucked away behind the archway and serves *moules marinières* for €7 and full menus from €15 – and the pink-painted *Licorne* nearby at 27 place Bensérade (ⓣ02.32.49.62.02; ❹; no restaurant). There are also a couple of reasonably priced **restaurants** with outdoor seating in the main square.

Abbaye de Mortemer

Half-a-dozen kilometres south of Lyons, clearly signed off a main road, the ruins of the twelfth-century Cistercian **Abbaye de Mortemer** amount to little more than heaps of rubble scattered across gentle lawns, amid a landscape of rolling parklands (park daily 1.30–6pm; guided tours half-hourly May–Aug daily 2–6pm, Sept–April Sat & Sun 2–5.30pm; €5 admission, €7 with tour). Plenty of outbuildings survive, however, including a round stone *pigeonnier*, with a spider's-web tangle of wood inside, and little niches for hundreds of pigeons (reared by the monks for food); a cast-iron pigeon stands permanently on top.

The highlight of the standard visit is the **museum** in the eighteenth-century château that dominates the grounds, where you see models of the abbey as it is now, and an audiovisual show of life as it used to be, complete with plenty of tales of hauntings and bumps in the night. Beyond the abbey, which was quarried after the Revolution to build the nearby village of Lisors, a couple of marshy lakes are populated by geese and swans and surrounded by woods and lawns that accommodate free-roaming deer.

Vascoeuil

The small but graceful **Château de Vascoeuil**, on the northwest edge of the forest 12km from Lyons (March–June & Sept to mid-Nov 2.30–6.30pm, July & Aug 11am–7pm; €7), is known to have existed as early as 1050, and was home during the nineteenth century to the historian Michelet. These days, it's renowned for staging top-quality temporary **art exhibitions** (March to mid-April Fri–Sun 2.30–6.30pm; mid-April to mid-June, Sept & Oct daily 2.30–6.30pm; mid-June to Aug daily 11am–7pm; ⓣ02.35.23.62.35).

Ry

The village of **RY**, 4km northwest of the château, is immortalized in literary history as the real-life home of Flaubert's fictionalized Madame Bovary. A monument in its churchyard commemorates Delphine Couturier, who committed suicide in Ry in 1849 having married a local doctor ten years previously, at the age of 17.

Ry consists of one main street, with green hills rising at either end, and a church to one side with an unusual carved wooden porch. Delphine's husband is buried in the churchyard, and Madame Bovary is evident throughout the village, which seems to have had little else to celebrate for a century or so. The local florist is Emma's, the video shop is Bovary, while the pharmacy was her real house.

An expensive **Musée des Automates**, appealing largely to young children, though some of its mannequins jerkily act out the less explicit moments of Madame Bovary's career, stands next to a pretty bridge over the River Crevon (Easter–June, Sept & Oct Mon, Sat & Sun 11am–noon & 2–7pm; July & Aug Mon, Sat & Sun 11am–noon & 2–7pm, Tues–Fri 3–6pm; €5). There are no hotels, but the *Rôtisserie Bovary* (ⓣ02.35.23.61.46) serves reasonable lunches in the town's smartest building, near the church at 14 rue de l'Eglise.

Upstream from Rouen

Upstream from Rouen towards Paris, high cliffs on the north bank of the Seine imitate the coast, looking down on waves of green and scattered river islands. By the time you reach **Les Andelys**, 25km outside Rouen and officially in the *département* of Eure, you're within 100km of the capital, meaning that accommodation and eating prices tend to be geared towards affluent weekend- and day-trippers. Large country estates abound in this agreeable countryside, while public transport is minimal – it's assumed any visitor has, if not a residence, then at least a car. There are two buses daily from Rouen to both Petit and Grand Andely, while trains from Rouen call at Vernon, which is the closest station to **Giverny**, renowned as both home and inspiration to Claude Monet.

Pont St-Pierre

The first point south of Rouen at which the Seine begins to be enticing again is **PONT ST-PIERRE**, where it's joined by the River Andelle. Any surplus money you may have could be enjoyably spent on a stay at the pink-and-brown *Hostellerie la Bonne Marmite*, 10 rue René Raban (Ⓣ02.32.49.70.24, Ⓦwww.la-bonne-marmite.com; ❹; closed Sun eve, Mon lunch & Tues lunch, plus late Feb to late March), set around a little courtyard a little way south of the eponymous bridge on the main road. Duck-and-lobster-loaded menus in the restaurant start at €16.50.

At the junction of the two rivers, you are confronted with the spectacularly sharp **Côte des Deux Amants**. This sheer escarpment, leading to a plateau high above the Seine, takes its name from a twelfth-century legend, in which a cruel king stipulated that the man who would marry his daughter must first run with her in his arms to the top of this hill. Noble Raoul sprinted up carrying the fair Caliste, but then dropped dead and out of sympathy, so did she. That story provides precious little incentive for anyone else to make the climb – but rumour has it that the view from the top does.

Les Andelys

The next town of any size is **LES ANDELYS**, which, as the name implies, consists in fact of two towns, overshadowed by the magnificent Château Gaillard. **Petit Andely**, which was the birthplace in 1594 of Nicolas Poussin, is a gorgeous little place. Its main street, parallel to the Seine, is lined with ancient half-timbered houses, while from the grassy riverbank behind you can see north to some imposing white bluffs as well as south to the château. **Grand Andely**, at the end of a 1.5-kilometre-long boulevard stretching inland, is the centre for shops, bars, and a **market** on Saturday.

Château Gaillard

The single most dramatic sight anywhere along the Seine short of Paris – especially awesome and magical by night – has to be **Château Gaillard**, perched high above Les Andelys. The château was constructed in the space of a single year, 1196–97, under the auspices of Richard the Lionheart. A previous truce had expressly forbidden the construction of a castle here, but Richard went ahead and seized the rock on which it stands from Archbishop Walter of Rouen, and then bribed the pope for permission to build. His object was to deny the king of France access to Rouen by establishing total control of traffic along the Seine, by both road and river. That was successful until after Richard's death, when Philippe-Auguste managed to capture the château in 1204 (his soldiers gaining access via the latrines). It might well have survived intact into this century, though, had Henry IV not ordered its destruction in 1603. Even then, it would have taken more recent devices to reduce Château Gaillard to rubble. The stout flint walls of its keep, roughly 4m thick, remain reasonably intact, and the outline of most of the rest is still clear, arranged over assorted green and chalky knolls. The castle was originally divided into two separate segments, linked by a bridge across a moat that was never intended to be filled with water – you can still explore the storage caves hidden in its depths.

Visits to the château are permitted between mid-March and mid-November only (Wed–Mon 10am–1pm & 2–6pm; €3). On foot, you can make the steep climb up via a path that leads off rue Richard Coeur-de-Lion in Petit Andely. The only route for motorists is extraordinarily convoluted, following a long-winded one-way system that starts opposite the church in Grand Andely. An alternative would be to park your car in Petit Andely and follow the route from there up the steep path on foot.

Practicalities

The **tourist office** for Les Andelys is below the château at 24 rue Philippe-Auguste in Petit Andely (Feb–April, Oct & Nov Mon–Fri 2–5.30pm, Sat 9.30am–12.30pm & 2.30–5.30pm, Sun 10am–noon & 2–5pm; May–Sept Mon–Fri 9.30am–12.30pm & 2–6pm, Sat 9.30am–12.30pm & 2.30–5.30pm, Sun 10am–noon & 2–5pm; Ⓣ02.32.54.41.93).

The nicest places to **stay** have to be the two attractive Seine-side hotels in Petit Andely: the eighteenth-century *Chaîne d'Or*, opposite the thirteenth-century St-Sauveur church at 27 rue Grande (Ⓣ02.32.54.00.31; ❺; closed Sun eve, Mon lunch & Tues lunch, plus Jan), and the *Normandie* at 1 rue Grande (Ⓣ02.32.54.10.52, Ⓦwww.hotelnormandie-andelys.com; ❶–❸; closed Wed eve & Thurs, plus Dec), where a couple of rooms are much cheaper than the rest. Both have high-quality expensive restaurants – even breakfast at the *Chaîne d'Or* costs €12, while the cheapest dinner menu is more than double that. If you can't get a room at either of those, the *Hôtel de Paris*, further back from the river at 10 avenue de la République in Grand Andely (Ⓣ02.32.54.00.33; ❷; restaurant closed Sun eve, Wed eve & Thurs lunch), is a good alternative, with yet another top-notch dining room. There's also a lovely riverside **campsite**, far below the château, the *L'Île des Trois Rois* (Ⓣ02.32.54.23.79; closed Nov–March).

Giverny

Had it not caught the eye of Claude Monet from a passing train carriage, the little village of **GIVERNY** might by now have decayed into insignificance; instead, it ranks among the most-visited tourist attractions in Normandy. Standing a few hundred metres back from the right bank of the Seine, 20km south of the ancient fortifications of Les Andelys and a mere 40km from Paris, it welcomes a constant stream of traffic in summer. Between November and March, however, when Monet's house and gardens are closed to visitors, everything else seems to close down too.

The road south to Giverny from Les Andelys crosses a flat plain dotted with lovely little hamlets. **Port Mort** in particular, where the road is lined by an almost unbroken stone wall, is well worth a stop. The closest **trains** come to **Vernon** (see p.124), 4km north of Giverny across the river and on the Rouen–Paris-St-Lazare line. Either rent a bike for €12 per day at *Café du Chemin de Fer*, directly opposite the *gare SNCF*, or catch the connecting bus to Monet's gardens which is operated by Vernon Cars (Ⓦwww.vernoncars.com).

Fondation Claude Monet

The Fondation Claude Monet (gardens and house open April–Oct Tues–Sun 9.30am–6pm; last ticket sold 5.30pm, no advance sales; €5.50 house and gardens, €4 gardens only) is situated in the former home of Claude Monet. If anything, art lovers who make the pilgrimage here are outnumbered by garden enthusiasts. None of Monet's original paintings is on display – most are in the Orangerie and Musée d'Orsay in Paris – whereas the **gardens** that

Claude Monet at Giverny

Claude Monet first rented the Giverny home that now houses the Fondation Claude Monet in 1883. At the age of 43, he was exactly halfway through his life. Born in Paris in 1840, he had grown up in Le Havre, and had spent the previous decade living in Argenteuil, Vétheuil and Poissy. Although his reputation as a painter was already established – the movement known as **Impressionism** had taken its name from a critic's somewhat contemptuous response to his work *Impression, Sunrise*, shown in Paris in April 1874 as part of the First Impressionist Exhibition – his personal and financial circumstances were far from settled.

The Monet ménage, whose houseboat arrived in Giverny on April 29, 1883, consisted of ten people. As well as Claude's two sons by his wife Camille, who had died in 1879, he was now also responsible for the six children of his long-term mistress **Alice Hoschedé**. Her husband Ernest was a former patron of the Impressionists who had fallen on hard times; she finally married Monet after his death in 1891.

Monet was to find both artistic and commercial success in Giverny. In his early years, he continued to travel to paint landscapes not only throughout Normandy but also in Brittany, on the Riviera and in England. As time went by, however, his advancing physical frailty and failing eyesight made extended trips increasingly daunting, while his growing prosperity enabled him to tailor his immediate environment to meet his needs as a painter.

In 1890, Monet began to produce sequences of reworkings and renditions of the same scene, shown at different times of the day or seasons of the year. The first such series consisted of 25 views of the **haystacks** on a neighbouring farm; all were arranged side by side in his studio, to be worked on simultaneously. Designed to be seen en masse, they went on show in Paris early in 1891, and proved hugely popular. The individual paintings sold out quickly, and from then on visiting American collectors – and would-be students – were a constant feature of life at Giverny.

In 1891, Monet painted a sequence showing the poplar trees that stood along the banks of the River Epte, about 1.5km south of his home. By now he was rich enough to buy the trees, for as long as his work was in progress, from a local timber merchant who was due to fell them. Having purchased his house outright, for 22,000F, he went on to buy a further plot of land, across the main road. With permission from the local authorities, he dammed the stream known as the Ru to feed an artificial pond, which he planted with **waterlilies** and spanned with a Japanese footbridge.

A team of gardeners worked to keep different sections of his **flower gardens** in bloom as much of the year as possible, so he would always have a suitable subject on which to work. One man had the full-time responsibility of tending the waterlilies to Monet's specifications, depending, for example, on whether he planned to use square or rectangular canvases. Monet would work outdoors for around six hours each day, avoiding the midday sun, and went on to paint over 250 versions of his waterlilies (*nymphéas*), not to mention the canvases he destroyed in disgust. One set of 48 waterlily pictures is said to have hung in his studio for six years, being constantly reworked, before it was exhibited in 1909.

Photographs of Monet in his later years show him as very much the white-bearded patrician, not only presiding over his studio and household but also playing host to leading painters and politicians. Despite a series of operations on his eyes, he continued to work almost until his death in December 1926. The house at Giverny passed to his son, Jean Monet, who left it in turn to the Académie des Beaux Arts in 1966. After restoration, it reopened as a museum in 1980.

many of his friends considered to be his masterpiece are still lovingly tended in all their glory.

Visits start in the huge **studio**, built in 1915, where Monet painted the last and largest of his many canvases depicting waterlilies (in French, *nymphéas*). It now serves as a well-stocked book and gift shop. A gravel footpath leads from there to the actual **house**, a long two-storey structure facing down to the river, and painted pastel pink with green shutters. Monet's bedroom is bedecked with family photos and paintings by friends and family, while among the washed-out reproductions in his *salon* are a depiction by Renoir of Monet at work in his earlier, less perfect garden at Argenteuil in 1875, and one by Monet himself of his dream closer to realization in the garden at Vétheuil in 1881. All the other main rooms are crammed almost floor-to-ceiling with his collection of Japanese prints, especially works by Hokusai and Hiroshige. Most of the original furnishings are gone, but you do get a real sense of how the dining room used to be, with all its walls and fittings painted a glorious bright yellow; Monet designed his own yellow crockery to harmonize with the surroundings. By contrast, the stairs and upstairs rooms are a pale blue.

More enticing than the house are the colourful flower gardens, with trellised walkways and shady bowers, stretching down from the house. Originally, the main footpath here led straight down to the **waterlily pond**; now, however, visitors have to reach the *jardin d'eau* by burrowing beneath the main road in a dank underpass. Once there, paths around the perimeter of the pond, as well as arching Japanese footbridges of course, offer differing views of the waterlilies themselves, cherished by gardeners in rowing boats. May and June, when the rhododendrons flower, and the wisteria that winds over the Japanese bridge is in bloom, are the best times to visit. Whenever you come, however, you'll have to contend with camera-happy crowds jostling to capture their own impressions of the waterlilies. These same crowds are the cause of long waits to enter the house during the busy summer period.

There's free parking close to the house; don't be fooled by signs for private car parks elsewhere in Giverny.

Musée d'Art Américain

A few minutes' walk up Giverny's village street, to the left as you leave Monet's house, stands the **Musée d'Art Américain** (April–Oct Tues–Sun 10am–6pm; €5.50, free first Sun of each month). The exterior is far from attractive, but inside you'll find a spacious and well-lit gallery devoted to American artists resident in France between 1865 and 1915, and in particular those who congregated in Giverny from 1887 onwards. Although Monet accepted no formal pupils, some, such as Theodore Robinson, joined his circle of intimates. Some took their admiration to a point that now seems embarrassing, painting many of the same scenes as Monet himself. As well as the waterlilies, for example, John Leslie Brech produced a series of twelve haystacks within a year of Monet's.

Mary Cassatt, who lived in a château at Le Mesnil-Thérebus, is represented by a far more interesting series of woodcuts, heavily influenced by *ukiyo-e* Japanese woodcuts, as well as canvases that focus on the domestic life of women while clearly belonging to the Impressionist movement. John Singer Sargent and Winslow Homer both contribute scenes of Brittany, especially Cancale, while James Henry Whistler's paintings include views of Dieppe and Étretat.

Practicalities

Heading right for a hundred metres as you leave Monet's house brings you to Giverny's one **hotel**, the *Musardière*, at 123 rue Claude-Monet (☎02.32 .21.03.18,

Ⓔiraymonde@aol.com; ❸); dinner menus in its restaurant start at €26, but they also serve crêpes and snacks during the day and the terrace, with plenty of shade provided by the surrounding trees, makes a nice spot for lunch. Alternatively, a former café at 1 rue du Colombier, a hundred metres to the right as you leave the Musée d'Art Américain, has been converted into a very friendly **B&B** called *Au Bon Maréchal* (Ⓣ02.32.51.39.70; ❸), which has three colourful rooms surrounded by an attractive garden.

A pleasant little tearoom and **restaurant** serving mainly salads, *Les Nymphéas* (Ⓣ02.32.21.20.31; closed Nov–March), is located opposite the Fondation Claude Monet; and there's another restaurant inside the Musée d'Art Américain with a peaceful garden terrace. Otherwise, the charcuterie at 60 rue Claude-Monet, a few doors down from *Au Bon Maréchal*, makes delicious sandwiches. If you've brought a picnic, eating in the grounds of Monet's house and the American art museum is forbidden, and the surrounding countryside is not particularly appealing.

Vernon

VERNON straddles the Seine just before it leaves Normandy altogether, with walks laid out along either bank. Were it not for the proximity of Giverny, there'd be no real reason to visit here, let alone stay; as it is, the central *Hôtel d'Évreux*, 11 place d'Évreux (Ⓣ02.32.21.16.12; Ⓦwww.hoteldevreux.fr; ❷), has **rooms** at assorted prices – the cheapest with shared bathrooms – and a good restaurant, and you can also eat well at *Restaurant de la Poste*, near the hotel at 26 avenue Gambetta (Ⓣ02.32.51.10.63; closed Tues eve & Wed), where menus start at €20 and include veal and snails.

Travel details

Buses

Dieppe to: Fécamp (4 daily; 2hr 20min); Le Tréport (4 daily; 30min); St-Valery (5 daily; 1hr).
Fécamp to: Étretat (8 daily; 30min), with connections to Le Havre (8 daily; 1hr 30min) and Yport (8 daily; 15min).
Le Havre to: Caen (2 daily express services; 1hr 25min); Étretat (9 daily; 50min); Fécamp (8 daily; 1hr 30min); Honfleur (7 daily; 30min).
Rouen to: Clères (6 daily; 45min); Évreux (hourly; 1hr); Le Havre (hourly; 2hr 45min), via Jumièges and Caudebec; Lisieux (2 daily; 2hr 30min).

Trains

Dieppe to: Paris-St-Lazare (19 daily; 2hr 10min) via Rouen (19 daily; 50min).
Fécamp to: Bréauté-Beuzeville (10 daily; 25min) with connections to Le Havre (total journey 1hr) or Rouen (total journey 1hr 30min).
Le Havre to: Paris (11 daily; 2hr 15min); Rouen (11 daily; 1hr).
Rouen to: Caen (9 daily; 2hr); Clères (11 daily; 20min); Lisieux (9 daily, 1hr 15min); Paris-St-Lazare (19 daily; 1hr 15min); Vernon (12 daily; 30min); Yvetot (18 daily; 20min) with connecting bus to St-Valery (total 1hr 20min).

International ferries

Dieppe to: Newhaven with Hoverspeed (June–Sept only, 2–3 daily; 2hr 15min; Ⓣ00800.1211.1211, Ⓦwww.hoverspeed.com) and Transmanche Ferries (1–3 daily; 4hr; Ⓣ08.00.65.01.00, Ⓦwww.transmancheferries.com).
Le Havre to: Portsmouth (3 daily; 5hr 30min) with P&O (Ⓣ08.25.01.30.13, Ⓦwww.poef.com).
For more details, see Basics.

2

The Lower Normandy Coast

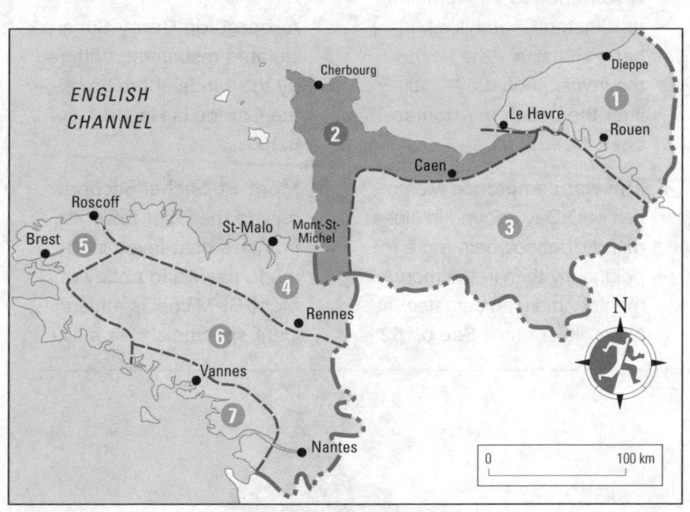

CHAPTER 2

Highlights

- ✱ **Les Maisons Satie** Surreal museum devoted to the avant-garde composer in the beautiful harbour town of Honfleur. See p.133
- ✱ **La Ferme Auberge des Aulnettes** Spend a tranquil night in an old-fashioned clifftop country-house hotel. See p.137
- ✱ **Arromanches** The remains of Winston Churchill's Mulberry Harbour – the key to the invasion of 1944 – still litter the beach at Arromanches. See p.151
- ✱ **The war cemeteries** Memories of D-Day abound in Normandy, but nowhere more poignantly than in the monumental American cemetery at Colleville-sur-mer. See p.152
- ✱ **The Bayeux Tapestry** An extraordinary historical document, embroidering the saga of William the Conqueror in colourful detail. See p.157
- ✱ **Le Conquérant** Delightful, inexpensive old hotel in ancient Barfleur, which makes a great stop for ferry passengers. See p.166
- ✱ **Auberge de Goury** Superb isolated restaurant, battered by the winds at the tip of the Cap de la Hague. See p.169
- ✱ **Mont-St-Michel** Second only to the Eiffel Tower as France's best-loved landmark, the island abbey of Mont-St-Michel is a magnificent spectacle. See p.177

△ Mont-St-Michel

2

The Lower Normandy Coast

The **coast of Lower Normandy** progressively changes in character as you move from east to west. Along the **Côte Fleurie**, from Honfleur to Cabourg, it is moneyed and elegant, with the **Norman Riviera** styling itself as a northern counterpart to the Côte d'Azur. Then, through the much flatter **Côte de Nacre** and into the area known as the **Bessin**, around Caen and Bayeux, the shoreline is much lower key: though the coastal strip remains predominantly built up, few towns amount to more than slender ribbons sandwiched between the broad sandy **Invasion Beaches** used by the Allies in 1944, and the featureless scrub that lies inland. West again, separated from the bulk of the mainland by a series of marshes, is the **Cotentin Peninsula**, with low-key harbour villages along its east front, cliffs across the north, and vast dunes and wild beaches to the west. Finally, there is the southern bay of **Mont-St-Michel**, where the island abbey is swept by treacherous tides.

The most enjoyable destination along the Côte Fleurie is **Honfleur**, a real gem of a harbour town, familiar from the paintings of Eugène Boudin, Monet and other Impressionists. Elsewhere, the prevailing atmosphere tends to be one of wealthy sterility. **Trouville**, **Deauville** and **Cabourg** preoccupy themselves with such events as vintage car rallies, and forever seem to hark back to a nineteenth-century past of leisured aristocrats, albeit with twenty-first-century prices.

Thanks to their lack of over-developed resorts, the Côte de Nacre and the Bessin are much more likeable. This region's pivotal role in the **D-Day Landings** is commemorated not only in numerous cemeteries and memorials, but also in the many museums that set out to explain aspects of its wartime history. Only a small proportion of the tourists and veterans who flock here during the day stay the night, however, so the small-scale seaside towns remain for the most part charmingly atmospheric places to spend a few days. Just inland, the venerable cathedral city of **Bayeux** would be a destination to savour even without the bonus of its world-famous **tapestry**, while its much larger neighbour, **Caen**, although less immediately captivating, also boasts an abundance of impressive medieval architecture, and rivals Rouen as a centre for contemporary culture.

The main city of the Cotentin Peninsula, **Cherbourg**, may not be a port to linger over, but ferry passengers who arrive here can choose between the lovely little villages that lie to the east, and the magnificent beaches and dunes of the peninsula's western coastline (popular with windsurfers). Such distractions

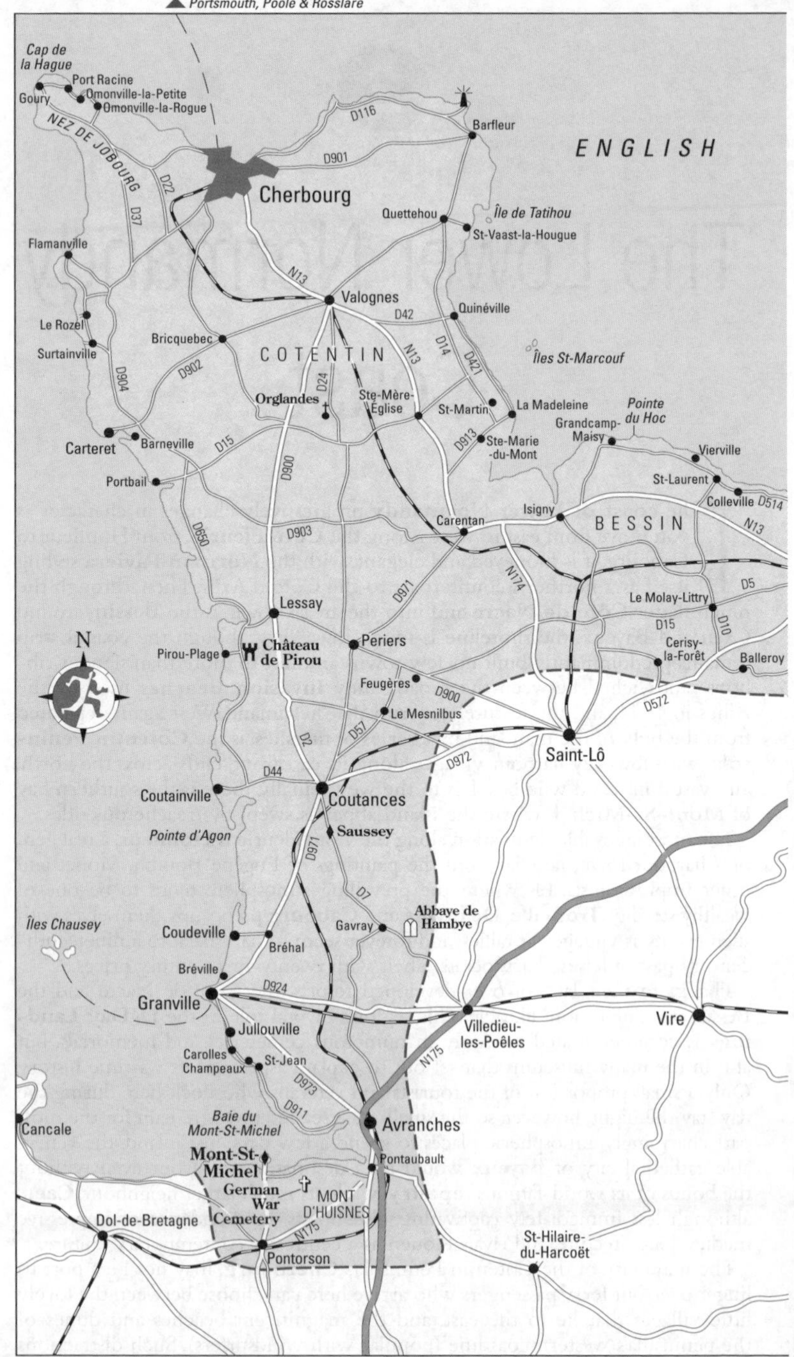
Portsmouth, Poole & Rosslare
Cap de la Hague
Port Racine
Goury
Omonville-la-Petite
Omonville-la-Rogue
NEZ DE JOBOURG
D116
Barfleur
ENGLISH
D901
D22
D37
Cherbourg
Quettehou
Île de Tatihou
St-Vaast-la-Hougue
Flamanville
N13
Valognes
Quinéville
D42
Le Rozel
Bricquebec
COTENTIN
N13
D14
D421
Surtainville
D902
Îles St-Marcouf
D904
D24
Orglandes
Ste-Mère-Église
St-Martin
La Madeleine
Pointe du Hoc
Grandcamp-Maisy
Carteret
Barneville
D15
D913
Ste-Marie-du-Mont
Vierville
Portbail
D900
St-Laurent
Colleville
D514
Isigny
Carentan
BESSIN
N13
D650
D903
N174
D971
D5
Le Molay-Littry
Lessay
D15
D10
N
Pirou-Plage
Château de Pirou
Periers
Cerisy-la-Forêt
Balleroy
Feugères
D900
D572
Le Mesnilbus
D2
D57
Saint-Lô
D972
D44
Coutainville
Coutances
Saussey
Pointe d'Agon
D971
D7
Abbaye de Hambye
Îles Chausey
Gavray
Coudeville
Bréhal
Bréville
D924
Granville
Villedieu-les-Poêles
Vire
Jullouville
N175
Carolles
Champeaux
St-Jean
D973
D911
Baie du Mont-St-Michel
Cancale
Avranches
Mont-St-Michel
Pontaubault
German War Cemetery
MONT D'HUISNES
Dol-de-Bretagne
N175
St-Hilaire-du-Harcoët
Pontorson

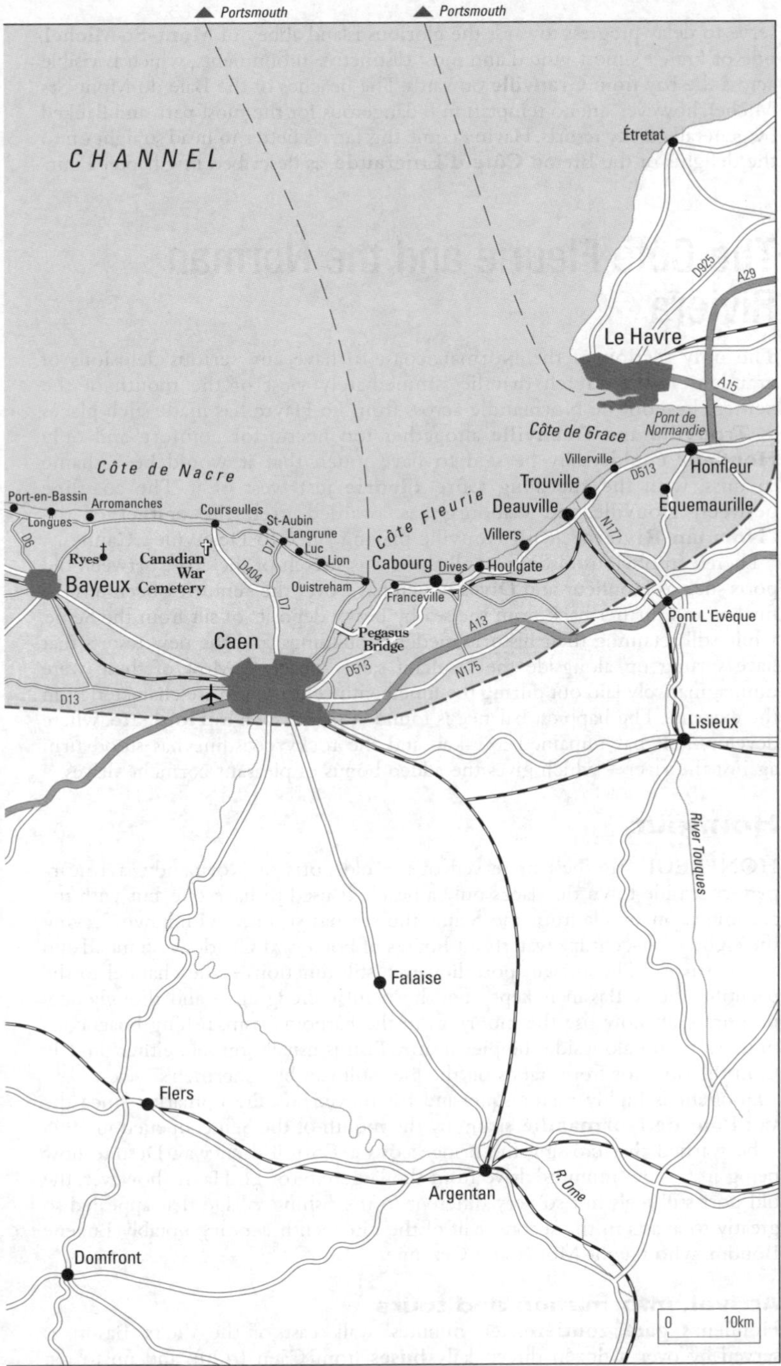

Portsmouth
Portsmouth
CHANNEL
Étretat
D925
A29
Le Havre
A15
Pont de Normandie
Côte de Grace
Villerville
D513
Honfleur
Trouville
Equemauville
Deauville
N177
Villers
Côte Fleurie
Côte de Nacre
Port-en-Bassin
Arromanches
Longues
Courseulles
St-Aubin
Langrune
Luc
Lion
D6
D7
D404
Ryes
Canadian War Cemetery
Bayeux
Ouistreham
Cabourg
Dives
Houlgate
Franceville
Pont L'Evêque
Pegasus Bridge
Caen
A13
D513
N175
D13
Lisieux
River Touques
Falaise
Flers
Argentan
R. Orne
Domfront
0
10km

serve to delay progress towards the glorious island abbey of **Mont-St-Michel**, one of France's most visited and most distinctive monuments, which is visible across the bay from **Granville** onwards. The beaches of the Baie du Mont-St-Michel, however, are no temptation – dangerous for the most part, and flanked by generally tacky resorts. Having come this far, it's better to head straight on to the delights of the Breton **Côte d'Émeraude**, as described in Chapter Four.

The Côte Fleurie and the Norman Riviera

The only section of the Norman coast to have any serious delusions of grandeur is the stretch that lies immediately west of the mouth of the Seine. The Pont de Normandie across from Le Havre has made such places as **Trouville** and **Deauville** altogether too hectic for comfort, and only **Honfleur** could really be said to have much that it would be a shame to miss, with the appealing **Côte Fleurie** just west of it. The coastline between Trouville and Cabourg has awarded itself the epithet of the "**Norman Riviera**", with Trouville playing Nice to Deauville's Cannes.

There's an obvious distinction all along this stretch of the coast between old ports such as Honfleur and **Dives** which have, over the centuries, been pushed further and further back from the sea by heavy deposits of silt from the Seine, while still retaining their historic medieval buildings, and the new resorts that have sprung up alongside the resultant sandy beaches. Most of these were unimaginatively laid out during the nineteenth century, and are characterless in the extreme. The happiest balance is found at places such as **Houlgate**, where development has remained low-key and the rocky coastline has stood firm against the river – which gives the added bonus of pleasant corniche drives.

Honfleur

HONFLEUR, the best preserved of the old ports of Normandy, is a near-perfect seaside town that lacks only a beach. It used to have one, but with the accumulation of silt from the Seine, the sea has steadily withdrawn, leaving the eighteenth-century waterfront houses of boulevard Charles V stranded and a little surreal. The ancient port, however, still functions – the channel to the beautiful Vieux Bassin is kept open by regular dredging – and though only pleasure craft now use the moorings in the harbour basin, fishing boats continue to tie up alongside the pier nearby. Fish is usually on sale either directly from the boats or from stands on the pier, still run by fishermen's wives.

Honfleur is highly picturesque, and has moved steadily upmarket since the vast **Pont de Normandie**, spanning the mouth of the Seine, opened in 1995 – be warned that crossing the bridge costs a €5 toll each way. Despite now being just a few minutes' drive from the large city of Le Havre, however, the old port still feels not so very different to the fishing village that appealed so greatly to artists in the second half of the nineteenth century, notably Eugène Boudin, who taught Monet and Cézanne.

Arrival, information and tours

Honfleur's **gare routière**, ten minutes' walk east of the Vieux Bassin, is served by over a dozen direct daily **buses** from Caen (#20), and up to ten

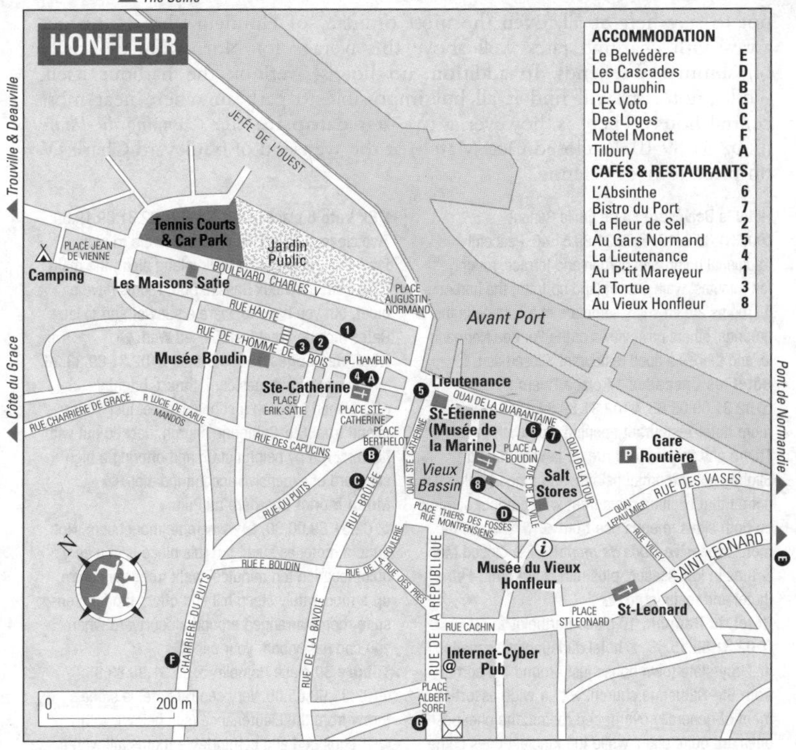

services from Le Havre (Bus Verts; ⓣ08.10.21.42.14, ⓦwww.busverts14.fr). However, the nearest **train station** is at Pont-l'Évêque (see p.195), connected to Honfleur by the Lisieux bus #50 (20min ride).

The **tourist office** adjoins the glass-fronted Mediathèque library on quai Le Paulmier, between the Vieux Bassin and the *gare routière* (Easter–June & Sept Mon–Sat 10am–12.30pm & 2–6.30pm, Sun 10am–5pm; July–Aug Mon–Sat 10am–7pm, Sun 10am–5pm; Oct–Easter Mon–Sat 10am–12.30pm & 2–6pm; ⓣ02.31.89.23.30, ⓦwww.ot-honfleur.fr). During July and August, the tourist office conducts worthwhile evening **guided tours** of the old town. Also in summer, several fifty-minute **cruises** sail upriver each day from either side of the Avant-Port from well-signposted departure points, for a closer look at the Pont de Normandie (€6.50).

The **post office** is a few hundred metres inland along rue de la République, just beyond place Albert-Sorel (Mon–Fri 8.30am–noon & 1.45–5.30pm, Sat 8.30am–noon). Just before place Albert-Sorel at 53 rue de la République, you can get **Internet access** at Internet-Cyber Pub (Mon–Wed 9am–noon & 2–8pm, Fri & Sat 10am–noon & 2–10pm, Sun 10am–noon & 2–8pm; ⓣ02.31.89.95.83; €3.50 per hr).

Accommodation

It's not as easy to live the bohemian life in Honfleur as it used to be. If finding budget **accommodation** is one of your main priorities, you may decide not to stay here at all. Even the most ordinary of Honfleur's hotels can get away with charging rates well above the average for Normandy, especially on summer weekends. In addition, no hotels overlook the harbour itself, while motorists will find it all but impossible to park anywhere near most central hotels. There is, however, a two-star **campsite**, the *Camping du Phare* (ⓣ02.31.89.10.26; closed Oct–March) at the west end of boulevard Charles V on place Jean-de-Vienne.

Hôtel le Belvédère 36 rte Emile Renouf ⓣ02.31.89.0813, ⓕ02.31.89.51.40. Peaceful traditional hotel, with garden and terrace, roughly ten minutes' walk east of (and up from) the harbour. All rooms are en suite; some are in a cottage in the grounds, others have views of the Pont de Normandie, and there's a good restaurant. Closed Jan. ❹

Hôtel les Cascades 17 place Thiers ⓣ02.31.89.05.83, ⓕ02.31.89.32.13. Seventeen-room hotel-restaurant opening onto both place Thiers and the cobbled rue de la Ville behind. Slightly noisy rooms upstairs, and a good-value if not all that exciting restaurant with outdoor seating on both sides; menus rise from €13 towards the more expensive *fruits de mer* at €29. Closed Mon & Tues in low season, plus mid-Nov to mid-Feb (hotel and restaurant). ❷

Hôtel du Dauphin 10 place Berthelot ⓣ02.31.89.15.53, ⓔhotel.dudauphin@wanadoo.fr. Grey-slate town house just around the corner from Ste-Catherine church, with a wide assortment of generally overpriced rooms; the cheapest ones are quite plain, while the fanciest ones come with Jacuzzis. The creaky floorboards and thin walls are universal, however. Closed Jan. ❹

L'Ex Voto 8 place Albert-Sorel ⓣ02.31.89.19.69. Two clean, well-priced rooms above a friendly family-run bar, a short walk inland along the main road from the Vieux Bassin. Both rooms have a bidet, but you have to share a shower and toilet. Rates include breakfast. Closed Wed. ❷

Hôtel des Loges 18 rue Brûlée ⓣ02.31.89.38.26, ⓦwww.hoteldesloges.com. Smart, brightly refurbished hotel on a cobbled street just 100m inland from Ste-Catherine church, decked out with flowers, run by helpful staff, and offering a high standard of expensive accommodation. ❻

Motel Monet Charrière du Puits ⓣ02.31.89.00.90, ⓦwww.motelmonet.com. Not quite a motel as such, but this place is in a very quiet location ten minutes' walk from the centre up a moderately steep hill and offers modern, en-suite rooms arranged around a courtyard where you can easily park your car. ❹

Tilbury 30 place Hamelin ⓣ02.31.98.83.33, ⓕ02.31.98.85.06. Very central hotel, a stone's throw from the Lieutenance (see below), with well-equipped and comfortable rooms, all with bath, above a crêperie. There are also three suites, suitable for families. ❸

The Town

Visitors to Honfleur inevitably gravitate towards the old centre, around the **Vieux Bassin**. At the *bassin*, slate-fronted houses, each of them one or two storeys higher than seems possible, harmonize despite their tottering and ill-matched forms into a backdrop excelled only by the **Lieutenance** at the harbour entrance. The latter was the dwelling of the King's Lieutenant, and has been the gateway to the inner town since at least 1608, when Samuel Champlain sailed from Honfleur to found Québec (just one of eight expeditions Champlain launched from here).

The church of **St-Étienne** on the eastern side of the *bassin* is now the **Musée de la Marine**, which combines a collection of model ships with several

Museum admission charges

As detailed in the text, each of Honfleur's principal museums charges its own admission fee, but it's also possible to buy a €4.20 **combination ticket** on sale at each museum which offers admission to both the Musée de la Marine and the Musée du Vieux Honfleur, or a €9 one that covers both those museums plus the Boudin and Satie museums as well.

rooms of antique Norman furnishings (mid-Feb to March & Oct to mid-Nov Tues–Fri 2.30–5.30pm, Sat & Sun 10am–noon & 2.30–5.30pm; April–Sept Tues–Sun 10am–noon & 2–6.30pm; closed mid-Nov to mid-Feb; €3). Next to the church on tiny rue de la Prison the old prison building serves as the **Musée de Vieux Honfleur** (same hours and entrance fee), filling ten rooms with a fascinating assortment of everyday artefacts from old Honfleur. Just behind these two museums on rue de la Ville, two seventeenth-century **salt stores** used to contain the precious commodity during the days of the much-hated *gabelle*, or salt tax, but are now used for art exhibitions and the like.

Honfleur's artistic past, and its present concentration of galleries and painters, owes most to Eugène Boudin, forerunner of Impressionism. Born in Honfleur in 1824 – his father worked on the ferries between Honfleur and Le Havre – Boudin continued to paint here throughout his life. He taught the 18-year-old Monet and was joined for various periods by Pissarro, Renoir and Cézanne. Boudin was among the founders of what's now the **Musée Eugène Boudin** (mid-March to Sept Wed–Mon 10am–noon & 2–6pm; Oct to mid-March Mon & Wed–Fri 2.30–5pm, Sat & Sun 10am–noon & 2.30–5pm; €5.10), west of the port on place Erik-Satie, and left 53 works to it after his death in 1898. His pastel seascapes and sunsets in particular are quite appealing in context – some are juxtaposed with nineteenth-century photographs of the same scenes – while modern works such as Fernand Herbo's hellish vision of workers streaming out of Le Havre's Shell refinery add a more contemporary edge. The museum also houses a few ethnographic displays and plays host to changing temporary exhibitions.

Honfleur's most remarkable building has to be the church of **Ste-Catherine** (daily 9am–6pm), with its distinctive detached **belfry**, which ranked among Monet's favourite subjects in his younger days. The church was built almost entirely of wood, during the Hundred Years War; all stone was at that time reserved for military use, and so the town's shipbuilders, experienced in working with wood, took responsibility for its construction. All the timbers inside are now exposed to view, having been sheathed in white plaster during the nineteenth century, when an incongruous four-columned porch (long since removed) was added to the front. The changing patterns on its tiles, both along the main body and the belfry, delineate Christian symbols. It all makes a change from the great stone Norman churches, and has the added peculiarity of being divided into twin naves, with one balcony running around both. The belfry itself (mid-March to Sept Wed–Mon 10am–noon & 2–6pm; Oct to mid-Nov Mon & Wed–Fri 2.30–5pm, Sat & Sun 10am–noon & 2.30–5pm; closed mid-Nov to mid-March; €2) now holds the **religious paintings** of the Musée Eugène Boudin.

Just down the hill from the Musée Boudin, at 67 boulevard Charles-V, is **Les Maisons Satie** (May–Sept Wed–Mon 10am–7pm; Oct–April Wed–Mon 11am–6pm; last entry 1hr before closing time; €5), the red-timbered house of Érik Satie. From the outside, it looks unchanged since the composer was born there in 1866. Step inside, however, and you'll find yourself in Normandy's most unusual and enjoyable museum. As befits a close associate of the Surrealists, Satie is commemorated by means of all sorts of weird interactive surprises. It would be a shame to give too many of them away here; suffice it to say that you're immediately confronted by a giant pear, bouncing into the air on huge wings to the strains of his best-known piano piece, *Gymnopédies*, and said to represent Satie's soul leaving his body after his death in Paris on July 1, 1925. You also get to see a filmed reconstruction of *Parade*, a ballet on which Satie collaborated with Picasso, Stravinsky and Cocteau, and which created a furore in Paris in 1917.

Satie's home forms part of a row of stately shipbuilders' residences that once lined the Honfleur waterfront; now they look across reclaimed flatlands to the industrial desert of Le Havre's docks in the distance. Over the road, and beyond the public gardens by the place Augustin-Normand, you can follow the **shipping channel** out towards the mouth of the Seine and the sea. A rusty old pipeline runs alongside, inside which you can hear rats and mice scampering to and from the sea. However, it would not occur even to the most hard-nosed mud-caked sewer rat to swim in the sea once it got there – the shore is a slimy grey wasteland, the water foul and sluggish. Nonetheless, it's possible to slip and squirm your way onto the shingle and then walk along the Côte de Grace, the name of the stretch of coast immediately to the west of Honfleur before it becomes the Côte Fleurie, with beautiful wooded hills sitting tantalizingly above you. Inland, the grand old houses of ancient aesthetes, and the **Chapelle Notre Dame de Grâce** in Équemauville, beloved of the Impressionists, nestle dry-footed in the forests.

Eating and drinking

With its abundance of day-trippers and hotel guests, Honfleur supports an astonishing number of **restaurants**, most naturally specializing in seafood and many of them very good at it indeed. Surprisingly few restaurants actually face onto the harbour itself; the narrow buildings around the edge seem to be better suited to snack bars, crêperies, cafés and ice-cream parlours (including a *Ben & Jerry's*). Instead, you'll find extensive arrays both east, along the quai de la Quarantaine, and west, on place Hamelin and rue Haute. Few of the town's hotels attempt to compete with the restaurants; the *Cascades* (see p.132) is probably the best of those that do.

One local speciality, available in October and November, is *crevettes grises* – tiny shrimp eaten with an unsalty Spanish-style bread, *pain brié*. If you're buying your own food, look out for the excellent *Panatérie*, a **boulangerie** selling granary and wholemeal breads, on the corner of the rue des Prés and rue de la République.

The profusion of restaurants hides the fact that there are very few **bars**. If you fancy a drink without having to order some food, head for the harbour, where on the western side of quai Ste-Catherine, at no. 32, the *Albatros* is the obvious choice for a tea or a coffee and the *Perroquet Vert*, at no. 52 (closed Dec to mid-Jan), for something alcoholic. Both have outdoor seating.

L'Absinthe 10 quai de la Quarantaine ☎02.31.89.39.00. This eighteenth-century mansion houses the most imaginative and gastronomic of the row of five restaurants that stand just around the corner from the *bassin*, with such dishes as smoked salmon *carpaccio* or foie gras in ginger on menus ranging from €29 up to a seven-course €58 extravaganza. Closed mid-Nov to mid-Dec.

Bistro du Port 14 quai de la Quarantaine ☎02.31.89.21.84. The middle of five adjacent and substantially similar restaurants, all with outdoor seating but in a not very picturesque setting beside the main road just east of the harbour. The *Bistro* has solid, conventional seafood menus, with the cheapest at €16, and more fancy ones at €20 and €25 (featuring a *pavé de thon*).

La Fleur de Sel 17 rue Haute ☎02.31.89.01.92. Elegant, formal option, with indoor seating only, offering gourmet menus at €22, €29, €39 and €49 that are equally strong on meat and fish. Closed Tues & Wed.

Au Gars Normand 8 quai des Passagers ☎02.31.89.05.28. Right in the thick of things, two small dining rooms crammed into a little house all but next door to the Lieutenance. Menus from €15, with clams and mussels, but very unadventurous main courses. Closed Sun eve, Mon & Dec.

La Lieutenance 12 place Ste-Catherine ☎02.31.89.07.52. Not in fact by the Lieutenance, despite the name. Plenty of outdoor seating on the cobbled pedestrian square, facing both church and belfry. Gourmet dining with a heavy emphasis on oysters; menus start at €23, while a seafood feast for two, consisting of a giant double platter followed by dessert, costs €85. Closed Sun eve & Mon in low season.

Au P'tit Mareyeur 4 rue Haute ⓣ02.31.98.84.23. No distance from the centre, but all the seating is indoors and there are no views. Very good fish dishes, such as red crab soup with garlic, plus plenty of creamy *pays d'Auge* sauces and superb desserts. Local diners appreciate the restaurant's policy of listing its suppliers of meat, fish, vegetables and even salt. Closed Mon, Tues & Jan.

La Tortue 36 rue de l'Homme de Bois ⓣ02.31.89.04.93. A welcoming place near the Musée Boudin, where €16 buys a great-value five-course meal, and there's even a €12 vegetarian menu, consisting of apple soup, a couple of salads, vegetables and dessert. Closed Tues, plus mid-Jan to mid-Feb.

Au Vieux Honfleur 13 quai St-Étienne ⓣ02.31.89.15.31. The best of the restaurants around the harbour itself, with spacious alfresco dining – in shade at lunchtime – on its pedestrianized eastern side. Simple menus, but the seafood is very good, as befits prices starting at €29. The only other set menu, at €48.50, offers lobster or turbot, with no meat options other than foie gras.

Along the Côte Fleurie

For the 15km **west along the corniche** from Honfleur to Trouville, green fields and fruit trees line the land's edge, and cliffs rise from sandy beaches. The **resorts** aren't cheap, but they're relatively undeveloped, and if you want to stop by the seaside this is the place to do it.

The most conspicuous community is **VILLERVILLE**, 10km west of Honfleur, a coastal village whose narrow twisting streets, filled with old mansions, front onto a huge sandy beach that unfortunately faces straight across the mouth of the Seine to the refineries of Le Havre. The grand old *Bellevue*, dropping down the hillside from the main D513 just east of town (ⓣ02.31.87.20.22, ⓦwww.bellevue-hotel.fr; ❹), has some very comfortable but rather anonymous **rooms** in its seafront annexe, and cheaper ones in its main building, and serves good fish menus in its sea-view **restaurant** – the €25 option also has *canard à l'orange*.

Trouville and Deauville

The towns of Trouville and Deauville lie within a stone's throw of each other to either side of the mouth of the River Touques, sharing many of their amenities, and also their rather exclusive reputations.

TROUVILLE retains at least some semblance of a real town, with a constant population and industries other than tourism. But it is primarily a resort, and has been ever since Napoléon III started bringing his court here for the summer in the 1860s (his empress, Eugénie, fled France from here in 1870 in the yacht of an English admirer). A long promenade marks the boundary between the sands and the succession of spectacular villas that line the beach, including the former **Hôtel des Roches Noires** (now a private residence), a chic turn-of-the-nineteenth-century resort patterned with complex brickwork and topped by ornate turrets; several were painted by Monet during a visit in 1870. Slightly further back, a tangle of busy pedestrian streets are alive with restaurants and hotels. Assuming you're not offended by conspicuous consumption, the whole place has a charming Belle-Époque feel, and the beach is both enormous and packed with activities for children. The only paying attraction, the **Natur'Aquarium**, is a rather sorry little aquarium that's only accessible from the beachfront boardwalk (daily: Easter–June, Sept & Oct 10am–noon & 2–7pm; July & Aug 10am–7.30pm; Nov–Easter 2–6.30pm; adults €7, under-15s €4.50) and also holds assorted tarantulas, stick insects and boa constrictors besides its apathetic sharks.

One of Emperor Napoléon's dukes, looking across the river, saw not marshlands but money, and lots of it, in the form of a **racecourse**. His vision materialized, and villas appeared between the racecourse and the sea to become **DEAUVILLE**, which likes to style itself as the "*21e arrondissement*" of Paris. Now you can lose money on the horses, cross five streets to lose more in the casino, where Winston Churchill spent the summer of 1906 gambling every night until 5am, and finally lose yourself in the broad band of private bathing huts that intervene before the *planches*. Beyond this stretch of boardwalk, rows of primary-coloured parasols obscure the sea.

If you're tempted to **gamble** in Deauville's Casino, formal attire is compulsory, and you have to pay a temporary membership fee of around €15 to be allowed anywhere near the tables. One more congenial reason to visit is the **American Film Festival,** held in Deauville in the first week of September – a festival that's the antithesis of Cannes, with public admission to a wide selection of previews, but which still attracts big-name stars. For information, visit ⓦwww.festival-deauville.com.

Practicalities

Trouville and Deauville share their **gare SNCF** (served by trains from Paris via Lisieux) and **gare routière** (ⓣ08.10.21.42.14), in between the two just south of the marina. Each day, ten of the hourly buses from Caen continue along the coast to Honfleur.

Deauville's **tourist office** is on place de la Mairie (May & June Mon–Fri 9am–12.30pm & 2–6.30pm, Sat 9am–6.30pm, Sun 10am–1pm & 2–5pm; July to mid-Sept Mon–Sat 9am–7pm, Sun 10am–1pm & 3–6pm; mid-Sept to April Mon–Sat 9am–12.30pm & 2–6.30pm, Sun 10am–1pm & 2–5pm; ⓣ02.31.14.40.00, ⓦwww.deauville.org). Trouville's equivalent can be found at 32 quai F. Moureaux (April–June, Sept & Oct Mon–Sat 9.30am–noon & 2–6.30pm, Sun 10am–1pm; July & Aug Mon–Sat 9.30am–7pm, Sun 10am–4pm; Nov–March Mon–Sat 9.30am–noon & 1.30–6pm, Sun 10am–1pm; ⓣ02.31.14.60.70, ⓦwww.trouvillesurmer.org). Both supply the usual lavish brochures.

As you might imagine, **hotels** here tend to be either luxurious or overpriced. The *Hôtel des Sports*, 27 rue Gambetta (ⓣ02.31.88.22.67; ❹; closed Sun in winter), behind Deauville's fish market, is among the least expensive, while *Le Trouville*, 50m from the beach at 1 rue Thiers (ⓣ02.31.98.45.48; ❸; closed Jan), is Trouville's closest equivalent. If you fancy staying right on the seafront, it's hard to beat the *Flaubert*, rue Gustave-Flaubert (ⓣ02.31.88.37.23, ⓦwww.flaubert.fr; ❹), a grand faux-timbered mansion at the start of Trouville's boardwalk, which is home to the excellent *Le Vivier* restaurant. Deauville, meanwhile, has a **campsite**, *La Vallée de Deauville*, 3km from the centre on route de Beaumont-en-Auge in St-Arnoult (ⓣ02.31.88.58.17; ⓦwww.camping-deauville.com; closed Dec–Jan).

A good **place to eat** in Deauville is *Chez Miocque* at 81 rue Eugène-Colas (ⓣ02.31.88.09.52), a top-quality Parisian-style bistro where a full meal costs around €40. Trouville also has its fair share of good fish restaurants, including *Les Vapeurs* at 160 boulevard F. Moureaux (ⓣ02.31.88.15.24) – one of several lively brasseries opposite the attractive old half-timbered fish market – and *La Petite Auberge*, 7 rue Carnot (ⓣ02.31.88.11.07; closed Tues all year, plus Wed except in Aug), though both get very crowded at weekends.

Villers-sur-mer and Houlgate

To the west of Deauville, the shoreline at first stays flat, and the main coast road passes through a succession of what are almost suburban resorts – significantly less snobbish than Trouville and Deauville, but equally crowded and equally short of inexpensive hotels. The largest of these is **VILLERS-SUR-MER**, noteworthy for straddling the Greenwich Meridian, which runs right through the three-star local **campsite**, *Camping Bellevue* (Ⓣ02.31.87.05.21, Ⓦwww.campingbellevue.com; closed Nov–March).

A hundred years ago, **HOULGATE**, 7km west of Villers-sur-mer, was every bit as glamorous and sophisticated a destination as its neighbours. What makes it different today is that it has barely changed since then. Its long straight beach remains lined by a stately procession of ornate Victorian villas, with what few commercial enterprises the town supports confined to the narrow parallel street, the **rue des Bains**, around 50m inland. As a result, Houlgate is the most relaxed of the local resorts, ideal if you're looking for a peaceful family break where the only stress is deciding whether to paddle or play mini-golf.

So long as you keep an eye on the tides, it's possible to walk between Villers and Houlgate along the foot of the **Vaches Noires** (Black Cows) cliffs, which force the main road at this point up and away from the sea. However, industrial Le Havre is a bit too visible across the water for it to be an especially picturesque stroll. Arriving in Houlgate by **bus**, get off at the stop named "Stop" for the tourist office or "Imbert" for the beach.

Practicalities

Houlgate's **tourist office** is set back from the sea, by the main roundabout as you come into town from the east, on boulevard des Belges (April–June Mon–Sat 10am–1pm & 2–6pm, Sun 10–noon & 2–6pm; July & Aug daily 10am–1pm & 2.30–6.30pm; Nov–March Mon–Sat 10am–1pm & 2–6pm; Ⓣ02.31.24.34.79, Ⓦwww.ville-houlgate.fr). The *Hostellerie Normande*, just off the rue des Bains at 11 rue E-Deschanel (Ⓣ02.31.24.85.50; ❹; closed Sept–April), is a pretty but rather impersonal little **hotel** covered with ivy and creeping flowers, with a €13 lunch menu on which you can follow fish soup with a plate of *moules frites* or tripe. Nearby, at 17 rue des Bains, the more formal but friendlier red-brick *Le 1900* (Ⓣ02.31.28.77.77, Ⓦwww.hotel-1900.fr; ❸; closed last two weeks of Nov & mid-Jan to mid-Feb) holds a glassed-in Belle-Époque bistro where dinner menus start at €18.50.

Set well back from the corniche road above the cliffs east of town, *La Ferme Auberge des Aulnettes* (Ⓣ02.31.28.00.28; ❷), is a lovely half-timbered country house in pleasant gardens, with a good restaurant and room to sit outside in the evening. The best **campsite** in the area, the four-star *Les Falaises* (Ⓣ02.31.24.81.09, Ⓦwww.lesfalaises.com; closed Nov–March), is not far away, though technically it's in the separate community of Gonneville-sur-Mer.

Dives

Immediately west of Houlgate, the main D513 is forced to detour away from the open sea when it reaches the mouth of the River Divette. Just a kilometre along, the venerable little port of **DIVES** was the spot from which William the Conqueror sailed for Hastings, by way of St-Valery; contemporary chronicles tell of vast stockpiles of supplies accumulating on the beach in the days preceding the invasion. Now, like Honfleur, pushed well back from the sea, Dives is an older and more authentic place than Cabourg, its haughty aristocratic neighbour across the river, although Marcel Proust's dream vision "land's end church of Balbec" is the town's **Notre Dame** church.

A lively **Saturday market** focuses around the ancient wooden *halles*, tucked away south of the main through road. The steep tiled roof of the *halles* must be five times the height of its walls, and its venerable weather-beaten timbers are held together by tight metal bands; it's crammed with mouthwatering delicacies and Norman specialities, while more mundane produce and imported jeans are sold in the square alongside and up and down the narrow streets. The town hosts a **puppet festival** in early August.

Dives is home to a large, inexpensive *Étape* **hotel**, on voie nouvelle de Port-Guillaume (☎02.31.28.13.97; ❷), as well as the summer-only municipal **campsite**, *Les Tilleuls* (☎02.31.91.25.21; closed mid-Sept to March).

Cabourg

At **CABOURG**, you are confronted not so much by a seaside resort as an exercise in applied geometry, created at much the same time as Deauville for the same elderly clientele. There's an awful lot of town planning, but not really any town.

At the centre of the straightest promenade in France, the **Grand Hôtel**, which once regularly accommodated Marcel Proust (see box, below) and remains today Cabourg's smartest place to stay – now operating under the auspices of the Mercure hotel chain – looks out towards the sea, while behind it the crescent that defines the formal **Jardins du Casino** is the first of several concentric crescents, spreading out like ripples and lined with large, placid, undistinguished houses. Cabourg makes an unlikely twin town for the raucous, downmarket gambling mecca of Atlantic City, New Jersey; for example, notices request that you "avoid noise on the beach", where picnicking is forbidden.

Practicalities

Trains run all the way from Paris Gare St-Lazare, via Trouville-Deauville, to the **gare SNCF** that Cabourg shares with Dives (see p.137) every day in July and August, and otherwise at weekends only. Arriving by **bus** – it's on the Caen–Honfleur route (#20) – you'll be dropped off at the gardens on avenue Pasteur; walk through them and turn right down avenue de la Mer to reach the Jardins du Casino.

The **tourist office** in the Casino gardens (July & Aug daily 9.30am–7pm; Sept–June Mon–Sat 9.30am–noon & 2–5.30pm, Sun 10am–noon & 2–4pm; ☎02.31.91.20.00, ⓦwww.cabourg.net) has full details on **hotels**. The best value, and the quietest, is the *Oie qui Fume*, 18 avenue de la Brèche-Buhot (☎02.31.91.27.79; closed Jan to mid-Feb, plus Mon eve, Tues & Wed in low season; ❸), 100m back from the sea on a peaceful road half a dozen streets west of the centre. The similarly half-timbered *Hôtel de Paris*, 39 avenue de la

Proust at the Grand Hôtel, Cabourg

As both child and adult, between 1881 and 1914, Marcel Proust stayed repeatedly at the *Grand Hôtel* in Cabourg. The town is the "Balbec" of *Du Côté de Chez Swann*, and the hotel itself – now officially located on the boulevard Marcel-Proust – thrives on its Proustian connection. All guests are served with a *madeleine* for breakfast, and Proust's own room is available at a cost of a little under €200 per night (which is considerably less than the price of the most expensive room in the hotel). The rock star Sting stayed in that very room in 1991. The main dining room, which has a superb sea view, is now called *Le Balbec*. The ambivalent Proust referred to it as "the aquarium"; each night locals would press their faces to its window in wonder at the luxurious life within, "as extraordinary to the poor as the life of strange fishes or molluscs".

Mer (Ⓣ02.31.91.31.34, Ⓦwww.hotel-de-paris-cabourg.fr; ④), is more central, on Cabourg's only commercial (semi-pedestrianized) street, and offers slightly smarter rooms. It has no restaurant, but its bottom floor holds a **café** that serves juices and snacks. In any case, *La Crémaillère*, two doors down at no. 41 (Ⓣ02.31.91.14.40), has menus at all prices, and there are plenty of pizzerias and snack bars nearby. If money is no object, you can always stay in the famous seafront *Grand Hôtel Mercure*, promenade Marcel-Proust (Ⓣ02.31.91.01.79; ⑨), where both the views and the prices are tremendous, and you can even stay in Proust's own room (see box, p.138).

Franceville

Continuing along the coast towards Caen, in **FRANCEVILLE** the main road passes a half-timbered logis, the *Hôtel le Vauban*, 8 route du Cabourg (Ⓣ02.31.24.23.37; closed Tues eve & Wed; ③), with adequate en-suite rooms and good food on menus from €13, and the bizarre *The Bunker*, a disco concealed in a former German radar station. Rusty cars and camper vans parked haphazardly to either side of the main coast road betray the proximity of good **surfing** beaches just beyond the dunes.

A little further on, you can turn right, across what used to be Pegasus Bridge (see p.149), for direct access to Ouistreham and the Landing Beaches.

Caen

Appropriately enough for a city that has been fought over throughout its long history, the name of **CAEN**, capital and largest city of Basse Normandie, originally came from a Celtic word meaning "battlefield". This site was first fortified in 1060 by **William the Conqueror**, who preferred it to Rouen because it was further from the marauding Franks, and because the navigable River Orne afforded him safe access to the Channel. Over the next centuries Caen repeatedly changed hands, and was twice sacked by the English: first by Edward III in 1346, and then by Henry V in 1417. It was Henry VI of England who founded the university here in 1432, but Caen has been French since Charles VII took it back in 1450.

The modern city began to take shape when a canal to the sea was completed in 1850, running parallel to the heavily silted Orne. At the same time, the Bassin St-Pierre was built, creating a central marina that is now reminiscent of the "port" in Vannes. The smaller River Odon was covered over, and the number of bridges across the Orne was doubled. **World War II**, however, devastated the city. It was the prime target of the Allied Invasion in June 1944, and historians still argue as to quite why it took so long to capture. The "Battle of Caen" lasted two full months – even after the Canadians entered the city four weeks after D-Day, the southern bank of the river remained in enemy hands. Three-quarters of the town had to be destroyed before they were finally dislodged.

Caen today is not a place where you're likely to spend much time, though in parts it remains highly impressive. The central feature is a ring of ramparts that no longer has a castle to protect, and, though there are the scattered spires and buttresses of two abbeys and eight old churches, roads and roundabouts fill the wide spaces where prewar houses stood. Approaches are along thunderous dual-carriageways through industrial suburbs, now prospering once more following an influx of high-tech newcomers.

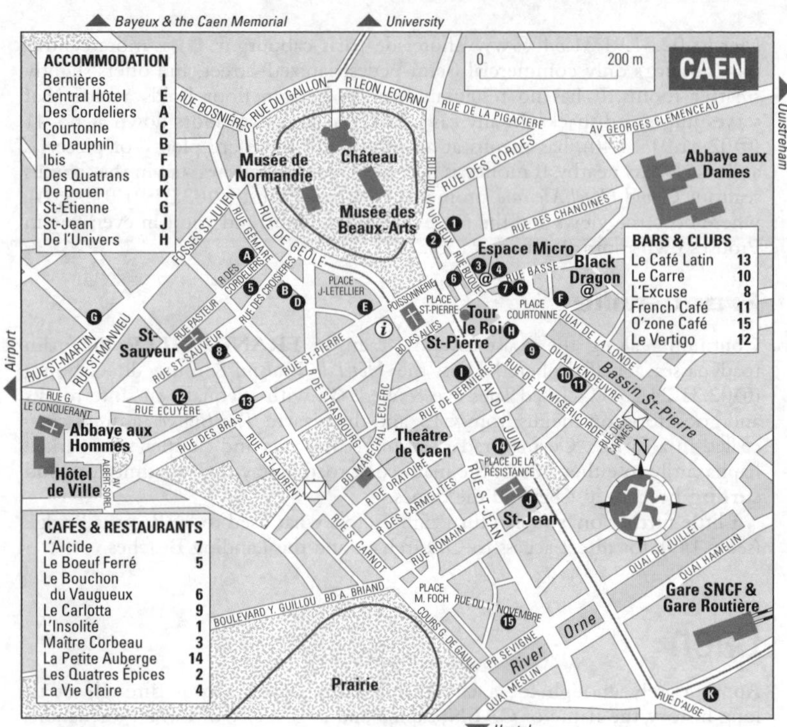

Arrival, information and tours

Caen's small, modern **airport** is on the D9 just outside **Carpiquet**, 7km west of the city centre (ⓣ02.31.71.20.10). **Buses** from the airport (route #1; €1.05) take 25 minutes to reach the Tour-le-Roi stop in place Courtonne. Avis (ⓣ02.31.84.73.80), Budget (ⓣ02.31.83.70.47), Europcar (ⓣ02.31.84.61.61), Hertz (ⓣ02.31.84.64.50), National (ⓣ02.31.82.66.10) and Rent A Car (ⓣ02.31.84.10.10) provide car rental both in the terminal and in town.

An extensive network of **local buses** and **trams** is run by TWISTO (ⓣ02.31.15.55.55, ⓦwww.twisto.fr), which has ticket and information centres at 15 rue de Geôle (just north of the tourist office), and on boulevard Maréchal Leclerc next to the theatre. The main tram route, inaugurated in 2002, connects the southern and northern suburbs, cutting through the heart of the city, passing the *gare SNCF* and running up avenue du 6 Juin to the university and beyond.

The **tourist office** (April–June & Sept Mon–Sat 9.30am–6.30pm, Sun 10am–1pm; July & Aug Mon–Sat 9am–7pm, Sun 10am–1pm & 2–5pm; Oct–

The Brittany Ferries service from Portsmouth, promoted as sailing to Caen, in fact docks at **Ouistreham**, 15km north (see p.148). Buses from Caen's *gare routière* connect with each sailing, and Bus Verts' express bus #1 runs the same route.

March Mon–Sat 9.30am–1pm & 2–6pm, Sun 10am–1pm; ⓣ02.31.27.14.14), on place St-Pierre across from the church of St-Pierre, holds a large model of the city (April–June & Sept Mon–Sat 9.30am–6.30pm, Sun 10am–1pm; July & Aug Mon–Sat 9am–7pm, Sun 10am–1pm & 2–5pm; Oct–March Mon–Sat 9.30am–1pm & 2–6pm, Sun 10am–1pm; ⓣ02.31.27.14.14). The official local **website**, ⓦwww.caen.fr/tourisme, has unusually thorough and well-illustrated listings of local restaurants and attractions. From around mid-July to late August, the tourist office offers a series of excellent **guided tours** (in French and English) focusing mainly on William the Conqueror's connections with Caen. The best tours, however, are unfortunately reserved for French-speakers, and involve witnessing a series a short historical sketches by actors as you tour either the château by day or the city's older and more atmospheric streets by night.

Accommodation

Caen has a great number of **hotels**, though as so often in the bomb-damaged cities of Normandy, few could be called attractive; even those that advertise their antiquity tend to have been totally rebuilt. They're not particularly concentrated in any one area, though you'll find clusters just west of the château and tourist office – a convenient location for motorists heading to or from the ferry – as well as around the pleasure port, and a handful facing the *gare SNCF*. A number of charmless motel-type places are also scattered on the ring road around town. With plenty of dedicated restaurants in town, few hotels other than those specifically mentioned below bother to provide food.

In the absence of a nearby campsite, the *Auberge de Jeunesse de Caen*, 68 rue Eustache-Restout, Grâce-de-Dieu (ⓣ02.31.52.19.96, ⓕ02.31.84.29.49; closed Oct–May; reception open 5–9pm) is a lively and welcoming **hostel**, situated in an otherwise sleepy area about 2km southwest of the *gare SNCF*, where beds in four- or five-bed dorms cost €10 per person. Take tram #B from the town centre or the train to the end of the line at "Grâce-de-Dieu".

Hotels

Hôtel Bernières 50 rue de Bernières ⓣ02.31.86.01.26, ⓦwww.hotelbernieres.com. Bright, central hotel, offering appealing en-suite rooms above a brasserie halfway between the churches of St-Pierre and St-Jean. ❸

Central Hôtel 23 place J. Letellier ⓣ02.31.86.18.52, ⓦwww.centralhotel-caen.com. A budget hotel, by Caen standards; not as quiet as it used to be, but very central. Good views of the château from the balconies of the higher rooms. All rooms are en suite. ❷

Hôtel des Cordeliers 4 rue des Cordeliers ⓣ02.31.86.37.15, ⓕ02.31.39.56.51. Friendly hotel in small side street near the castle. The very cheapest rooms have showers but no toilet, but fully en-suite ones are only a few euros more. ❷

Hôtel Courtonne 5 rue des Prairies St-Gilles ⓣ02.31.93.47.83, ⓕ02.31.93.50.50. Very welcoming modernized hotel, overlooking place Courtonne and the pleasure port, though the building is so narrow it's easy to miss. All rooms have bath or shower, phone and TV. ❸

Hôtel-Restaurant le Dauphin 29 rue Gémare ⓣ02.31.86.22.26, ⓦwww.le-dauphin-normandie.com. Upmarket Best Western hotel, tucked away behind the tourist office. Part of it was a priory during the eighteenth century, not that you'd guess. The rooms are comfortable without being exciting in any way, although a sauna and fitness centre are positive attributes. Grand restaurant, with an €18.50 weekday dinner menu; weekend menus €29 and €51 (closed Sat lunch & Sun, plus mid-July to early Aug). ❹

Hôtel Ibis 6 place Courtonne ⓣ02.31.95.88.88, ⓔh1183@accor-hotels.com. Smart modern chain hotel overlooking the port de Plaisance, offering reliable creature comforts plus its own brasserie (open until 10.30pm nightly) and bar. ❹

Hôtel des Quatrans 17 rue Gémare ⓣ02.31.86.25.57, ⓦwww.hotel-des-quatrans.com. Fully renovated hotel in an anonymous modern setting, a very short walk from the tourist office and the château. The pastel theme of the facade continues inside; some might find it a bit cloying, but the service is friendly, and everything works well. All rooms are en-suite. ❸

Hôtel de Rouen 8 place de la Gare ⓣ02.31.34.06.03, ⓕ02.31.34.05.16. Reasonably smart budget option, furthest to the west (right) in the parade that faces you as you exit the *gare SNCF*, and offering rooms with and without en-suite facilities. Worth considering if there is no room at the more central hotels. ❷

Hôtel St-Étienne 2 rue de l'Académie ⓣ02.31.86.35.82, ⓦwww.hotel-saint-etienne.com. Friendly, inexpensive hotel in an old stone house in the characterful St-Martin district, not far from the Abbaye des Hommes. The cheapest rooms have no showers, but en suite ones cost little more. ❶

Hôtel St-Jean 20 rue des Martyrs ⓣ02.31.86.23.35, ⓕ02.31.86.74.15. Simple but well-equipped rooms – all have shower or bath – facing St-Jean church across from the *Petite Auberge* restaurant (see p.145). Half of the rooms have views of the church and there is free parking. ❷

Hôtel de l'Univers 12 quai Vendeuvre ⓣ02.31.85.46.14, ⓕ02.31.38.21.33. Small, plain but perfectly acceptable budget option, above a café near the port de Plaisance. All rooms have showers. ❷

The City

A virtue has been made of the necessity of clearing away the rubble of Caen's medieval houses, which formerly pressed up against its ancient **château ramparts**. The resulting open green space means that those walls are now fully visible for the first time in centuries. In turn, walking the circuit of the ramparts gives a good overview of the city, with a particularly fine prospect of the reconstructed fourteenth-century facade of the nearby church of **St-Pierre**. Some magnificent Renaissance stonework has survived intact at the church's east end.

Within the castle walls, it's possible to visit the former Exchequer – which dates from shortly after the Norman Conquest of England, and was the scene of a banquet thrown by Richard the Lionheart en route to the Crusades – and inspect a garden that has been replanted with the kind of herbs and medicinal plants that would have been cultivated here during the Middle Ages. Also inside the precinct, though not housed in original structures, are two **museums**. Most visitors will probably prefer the **Beaux Arts**, housed in a light 1960s stone building, kept deliberately low to avoid topping the castle walls (Wed–Mon 9.30am–6pm; €3.20, free on Sun). Its upstairs galleries trace a potted history of European art from Renaissance Italy through such Dutch masters as Brueghel the Younger (whose *Census of Bethlehem* includes boys throwing snowballs) up to grand portraits from eighteenth-century France. Downstairs brings things up to date with a diverse range of twentieth-century and contemporary art – though there are few big-name works – as well as paintings by Monet, Bonnard and Gustave Doré (represented by a spectacular Scottish landscape). The other museum, the **Musée de Normandie** (Wed–Mon 9.30am–6pm; €1.60, free on Sun), provides a surprisingly cursory overview of Norman history, ranging from archaeological finds like stone tools from the megalithic period and glass jewellery from Gallo-Roman Rouen to artefacts from the Industrial Revolution.

Just to the north of the château lies the complex of **university** buildings, originally founded in 1432 by Henry VI of England, and now the proud home of the largest nuclear particle accelerator in Europe. The only reason for tourists to pass this way is to see the large-scale **model of Ancient Rome**, as it stood around 300 AD, which has been laid out in the Maison de la Recherche en Sciences Humaines (Mon–Fri 8am–7pm, free; also a 20min "son et lumière" show (Mon–Fri 8.30am–4pm, €1.80).

When William the Conqueror married Mathilda in Eu (see p.83), in 1051, both incurred excommunication. Historians argue as to the precise nature of their offence – they may have been distant cousins – but Pope Nicholas II only agreed to sanction their marriage and readmit them to the church in 1059 upon the solemn vow that each would build an abbey in Caen. William's, the **Abbaye aux Hommes** to the west of the city centre, is focused on the Romanesque church known as the Abbatiale Ste-Étienne (daily 8.30am–12.30pm & 1.30–7pm; free); 1hr 15min guided tours of the abbey leave from the adjacent Hôtel de Ville daily 9.30am, 11am, 2.30pm & 4pm; tours in English mid-July to Aug only daily 11am, 1.30pm & 4pm; €2, free on Sun). The abbey was originally designed to hold William's tomb, but his burial here, in 1087, was hopelessly undignified. The funeral procession first caught fire and was then held to ransom, as various factions squabbled over his rotting corpse for any spoils they could grab. A further interruption came when a man halted the service to object that the grave had been constructed without compensation on the site of his family house, and the assembled nobles had to pay him off before William could finally be laid to rest. His tomb still occupies pride of place in front of the main altar, though the church was subsequently ransacked both by Protestants in 1562 and during the Revolution, so it now holds at most a solitary thighbone rescued from the river. Still, the building itself serves as a wonderful monument – although not enhanced by the latest desecration, "multilingual, computerized audiovisual visits" – and is also home to a fine collection of seventeenth- to nineteenth-century paintings. As you explore, look out for the huge wooden clock to the left of the altar.

The **Hôtel de Ville** alongside, which all but obscures the abbey, is housed in what used to be its convent buildings – hence the surprising harmony with which the two blend together.

William's queen, Mathilda, lies across the town in the **Abbaye aux Dames** at the end of rue des Chanoines. She had commissioned the building of the abbey church, La Trinité, well before the Conquest. It's starkly impressive, with a gloomy pillared crypt, superb stained glass behind the altar, and odd sculptural details like the fish curled up in the holy-water stoup (daily 2–5.30pm; guided tours 2.30pm & 4pm; free).

The nineteenth-century **Bassin St-Pierre**, a short walk south of the Abbaye aux Dames, now serves as Caen's pleasure port, and marks the end of the canal that links the city to the sea. In summer, it's one of the liveliest areas in town, although, considering the crowds, it holds surprisingly few pavement cafés. Also in summer, a pleasure boat, the *Hastings*, sets off four times daily on **cruises**, from the quai Vendeuvre here, up to Pegasus Bridge (see p.149) and back (9am, 12.15pm, 3.15pm & either 7pm or 7.30pm; 2hr 30min; €12; ⓣ02.31.34.00.00, ⓦperso.wanadoo.fr/bateau.lhastings).

The Caen Memorial

The **Caen Memorial** (daily: mid-Jan to early Feb, Nov & Dec 9am–6pm; early Feb to mid-July & late Aug to Oct 9am–7pm; mid-July to late Aug 9am–8pm; last entry 1hr 15min before closing time; ⓣ02.31.06.06.44, ⓦwww.memorial-caen.fr; mid-Jan to March €16.50; April–Aug €18; Sept–Dec €17) is a war museum with a big and very welcome difference, in that it proclaims itself to be a "Museum for Peace". For the most part, it succeeds admirably in that intention. Located on a plateau named after General Eisenhower, just north of Caen at the end of avenue Marshal-Montgomery, it was funded by the governments of the US, Britain, Canada, Germany, Poland, the former Czechoslovakia and the former USSR, as well as France, and stands immediately above the headquarters used by the German army during June and July 1944.

All visitors have to follow a prescribed route through the ultramodern building, which, with a slightly heavy-handed literalism, leads on a downwards spiral from World War I and the Treaty of Versailles towards the maelstrom of World War II. Hitler's image recurs with increasing size and frequency on screens beside you as the events of the 1920s and 1930s are recounted.

The war itself is superbly documented, with a greater emphasis on the minutiae of everyday life in occupied France than on military technology. Nothing is glossed over in the attempt to provide a fully rounded picture of the nation under occupation and at war. The collaborationist Vichy government is set in its context without being excused, with such statements as Pierre Laval's "I wish for the victory of Germany, because without it Bolshevism will spread everywhere" on prominent display alongside a book of the "99 most touching answers of French schoolchildren to the question 'Why do you love Maréchal Pétain?'". Secret Nazi reports show how Resistance activity in Normandy grew as the war continued, and what reprisals were taken.

Visits to the **upper section** of the memorial culminate with two **films**, each in a separate auditorium. The first is a harrowing account of D-Day itself and the ensuing battle to liberate Normandy; in the first part of the film the screen is split in two to show, on one side, the preparations of the Allied forces on the eve of the invasion and, on the other side, those of the Germans; the second part of the film traces the course of the Battle of Normandy using maps and photographs. In keeping with the Memorial's theme of peace and reconciliation, the second film, *Espèrance* (hope) is a mosaic of the world's problems since World War II: a compilation of harrowing images of the Vietnam war and starvation in Africa, interspersed with more optimistic moments such as the fall of the Berlin Wall and the ending of apartheid. Both films depend on visual stimuli more than words, while most of the captions throughout the museum, though not always the written exhibits themselves, are well translated into English.

The former German bunkers at the foot of the hillside, reached by a short lift ride from the Memorial proper, have been refurbished as the **Nobel Peace Prizewinners' Gallery**. Portraits and short essays commemorate each recipient in turn, placing their achievements in context, and also point out notable omissions from the list, such as Mahatma Gandhi. Outside, various formal **gardens** have been laid out to honour the different Allied nations.

All in all, this museum creates something new in a genre which can occasionally seem morally suspect, and the display cannot be recommended too highly for anyone with a serious interest in the war and its lasting legacy. Allow at least two hours for a visit, as the films alone occupy a whole hour. In summer, especially when the weather is not so good, queues can be very long, so make allowances for the wait when planning your time. If you feel like a break, there's a good-value self-service restaurant upstairs.

The museum is served by bus #2 from Tour le Roi; the Memorial is at the end of the route. See p.148 for details of tours of the Landing Beaches.

Eating

The centre of Caen offers two major areas for **eating**. The attractive pedestrianized **quartier Vaugueux** (around rue du Vaugueux) features cosmopolitan restaurants such as the *Kouba*, serving up couscous dishes, *Sauveurs de Persie* from Iran, and even *À l'Âge de Pierre*, which prepares "stone age" food by cooking slabs of horse meat on super-heated stones, as well as a wide array of pizzerias and crêperies. Streets such as rue des Croisiers and rue Gémare off **rue de Geôle**, near the western ramparts, on the other hand, house rather more traditional French restaurants.

Restaurants

L'Alcide 1 place Courtonne ⓣ02.31.44.18.06. Large but rather anonymous-looking bistro-style place, which turns out to be surprisingly good, serving classic rich French dishes cooked with great attention to detail. Menus from €15.20 up to €23.50. Closed Sat.

Le Boeuf Ferré 10 rue des Croisiers ⓣ02.31.85.36.40. Gourmet restaurant, all indoors, with stone walls and timbered ceiling, serving rich and substantial meals; foie gras is the house speciality, as featured on the no-choice €20.60 menu, and there's always plenty of duck and red meat. Midday menu €14.50 on weekdays, dinners from €17.50. Closed Mon lunch & Sun eve, plus the first two weeks in March and the second two weeks of July.

Le Bouchon du Vaugueux 12 rue du Graindorge ⓣ02.31.44.26.26. Intimate little brasserie in the Vaugueux quarter, offering only two menus: one at €16 featuring steak tartar and another at €21 where you can choose from veal, duck or roast pork. Closed Mon & Sun, plus first three weeks of Aug.

Le Carlotta 16 quai Vendeuvre ⓣ02.31.86.68.99. Smart, busy, fashionable Paris-style brasserie beside the pleasure port, which serves good Norman cooking both à la carte and on menus from €21. Closed Sun.

L'Insolité 16 rue du Vaugueux ⓣ02.31.43.87.87. Attractive half-timbered restaurant with terrace and indoor seating in the Vaugueux district. The main emphasis is on seafood, with a €15 menu that features a trio of steamed fish, and a knock-out €45 *Prestige* menu where lobster stew with cider takes pride of place. Closed Sun, plus Mon in low season.

Maître Corbeau 8 rue Buquet ⓣ02.31.93.93.00. Fondue is the speciality in this eccentric little place, and they won't let you forget it, festooning the whole place with cheesy iconography. A typical fondue costs around €13, while non-fondue menus start from €15. Closed Sat lunch, Sun, Mon lunch & three weeks in Aug.

La Petite Auberge 17 rue des Équipes-d'Urgence ⓣ02.31.86.43.30. Plain and simple restaurant, with a nice view of the St-Jean church. Very good-value Norman specialities served on a €12 menu (daily except Sat eve) that doesn't force you to eat tripe, or a wide-ranging €19 one. Closed Sun, Mon & first three weeks of Aug.

Les Quatres Épices 25 rue Porte-au-Berger ⓣ02.31.93.40.41. Lively West African restaurant, just off rue du Vaugueux. Everything is à la carte – prawns with sweet potato for €17, grilled fish with ginger and spices for €14, plus plantains and meat galore – and African music plays nonstop.

La Vie Claire 4 rue Basse ⓣ02.31.93.66.72. Vegetarian cafeteria-style restaurant, attached to a pricey health-food shop, that serves pasta and salad specials – and also some fish – for €5–8. Open Tues–Sat for lunch only.

Nightlife and entertainment

Caen represents your best chance in Lower Normandy of finding something to do of an evening. There are several good and, for the most part, busy **bars**, found mainly along the pleasure port and in the town centre a few hundred metres west of the port. A few of the most enticing of these serve tapas and have convivial, laid-back atmospheres. The **Théâtre de Caen**, at 135 boulevard Maréchal Leclerc (ⓣ02.31.30.48.00, ⓦwww.theatre.caen.fr), offers a complete programme of music, dance and drama, while several **cinemas** show the latest film releases, usually dubbed into French for the benefit of the local audience.

Bars and clubs

Le Café Latin 135 rue St-Pierre. A convivial and invariably packed tapas bar in the town centre. Upstairs the theme of the décor is Mexican; downstairs, both inside and on the street terrace, it is much more French. The huge plates of tapas are very good and the music is not so loud as to drown out conversation. Mon–Sat 10am–1am.

Le Carre 32 quai Vendeuvre ⓣ02.31.38.90.90. A very central discotheque which has the rare policy of admitting only those over 27. The resulting crowd tends to be in its 30s, 40s and even 50s, making a refreshing change from the majority of clubs heaving with spotty adolescents. Tues–Sun 10.30pm–5am.

L'Excuse 20 rue Vauquelin ⓣ02.31.38.80.89. Tiny bar in a side street next to St-Sauveur church, primarily for girls looking for girls, but not off-limits to those of other persuasions. The music tends to be loud, no doubt in an attempt to encourage patrons to grace the small dance floor. Wed–Sat 11pm–3am.

French Café 32 quai Vendeuvre ⓣ02.31.50.10.02. Trendy, antique-filled bar directly next to the *Carre* nightclub facing the pleasure port, serving cocktails and reasonable tapas, all you can eat on some evenings. A lot of 1980s music and rock, with the occasional French golden oldie thrown in for good measure. Tues–Sun 7pm–3am.

O'zone Café 22 rue du 11 Novembre ⓣ02.31.84.11.22. Promoted as a mixed bar, but primarily gay for all that. The interior is barely lit by fluorescent lights, which gives the place a sleazy appearance, set off by ambient house and other electronic music. Tues–Thurs 6pm–2am, Fri & Sat 6pm–4am.

Le Vertigo 14 rue Écuyère ⓣ02.31.85.43.12. A popular local hang-out, especially among rock music-loving students. The narrow bar leads to a drinking room with attractive stone walls, several tables, but not much ventilation. Claustrophobics will prefer the outside terrace. Mon–Wed 10–1am, Thurs–Sat 10–2am.

Shopping

Most of the centre of Caen is taken up with busy new shopping developments and pedestrian precincts, where the cafés are distinguished by such names as *Fast Food Glamour Vault*. The shops are good, possibly the best in Normandy or Brittany, if Parisian style is what you're after. Outlets of the big Parisian **department stores** – and of the aristocrats' grocers, Hédiard, in the Cours des Halles – are here, along with good local rivals. Rue Écuyère has a fine assortment of shops full of unusual and cheap oddments, **antiques**, stuff for collectors and jokes.

The main city **market** takes place on Sunday, filling place Courtonne by the Bassin St-Pierre, while another large one spreads along both sides of Fossés St-Julien every Friday. If you're looking for **books**, **CDs** or **tickets** for local events, call in at the branch of FNAC (ⓣ02.31.39.41.00) in the Centre Paul-Doumer, on the corner of rue Doumer and rue Bras.

Listings

Banks and exchange Banque de France, 14 av Verdun ⓣ02.31.38.33.00; Crédit Agricole 1 bd Maréchal-Leclerc ⓣ02.31.85.90.56.

Cinemas Pathé Lumière, 15 bd Maréchal-Leclerc ⓣ08.36.68.22.88; Pathé Malherbe, 55 rue des Jacobins ⓣ08.36.68.22.88; AEP Cinéma Lux, 6 av Ste-Thérèse ⓣ08.36.68.00.43.

Hospitals C.H.U. av Côte de Nacre ⓣ02.31.06.31.06; C.H.R. av Georges-Clemenceau ⓣ02.31.27.27.27.

Internet access Espace Micro, on place Courtonne at 1 rue Basse ⓣ02.31.53.68.68 (Mon–Thurs 10am–11pm, Fri & Sat 10–1am, Sun 10am–1pm & 3–9pm; €3.80 per hr); Black Dragon, 11 rue Courtonne ⓣ02.31.94.00.33 (Mon–Fri 11–12.30am, Sat & Sun 1pm–2.30am; €3 per hr).

Launderette Lavomatique, rue Écuyère (daily 7am–8pm).

Pharmacie Grande Pharmacie du Progrès, 2 bd des Alliés ⓣ02.31.27.70.10 (Mon–Sat 8am–8pm).

Post office The main local branch is on place Gambetta (postcode 14000); Mon–Fri 8am–7pm, Sat 8.30am–12.30pm; ⓣ02.31.39.35.76.

Swimming pools Chemin Vert, 42 rue Champagne ⓣ02.31.73.08.79. Stade Nautique, av Albert Sorel ⓣ02.31.30.47.47.

The Invasion Beaches

Despite the best efforts of *Saving Private Ryan*, it remains all but impossible now to picture the scene at dawn on **D-Day**, June 6, 1944, when Allied troops

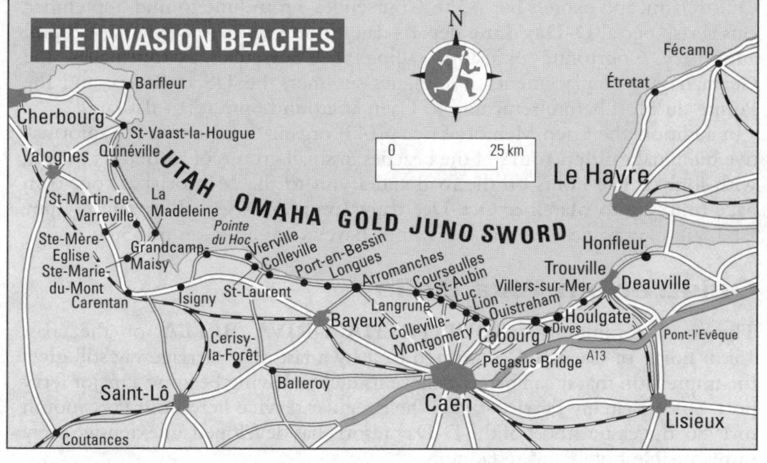

landed at points along the Norman coast from the mouth of the Orne to the eastern shore of the base of the Cotentin Peninsula. For the most part, these are innocuous beaches backed by gentle dunes, and yet this foothold in Europe was won at the cost of 100,000 lives. That the invasion happened here, and not nearer to Germany, was partly due to the failure of the Canadian raid on Dieppe in 1942. The ensuing **Battle of Normandy** killed thousands of civilians and reduced nearly 600 towns and villages to rubble, but within a week of its eventual conclusion, Paris was liberated.

The **beaches** are still often referred to by their wartime code names. The British and Commonwealth forces landed on **Sword**, **Juno** and **Gold** beaches between Ouistreham and Arromanches; the Americans, further west on **Omaha** and **Utah** beaches (the latter, the westernmost beach, is on the Cotentin Peninsula, and is therefore covered on p.168 onwards). Bits of shrapnel can still be found in the sands, six decades later, but more substantial traces of the fighting are rare. At Arromanches, the remains are visible of one of the prefabricated Mulberry harbours that made such large-scale landings possible, while at Pointe du Hoc the cliff heights are still deeply pitted with German bunkers and shell-holes. Elsewhere, the reminders are **cemeteries** – British and Commonwealth, American and German, each highly distinct in character – and **war museums**, examples of which you'll find in almost every coastal town.

The D-Day events provide a focus for most foreign visitors to this part of the coast; travelling through, you're bound to come across veterans and their descendants paying their respects. Taken simply as holiday territory, however, the towns and villages offer their own rewards. They are traditional seaside resorts, without the inflated prices or flashiness of the Deauville area – old-fashioned villages, with rows of boarding houses and little wooden bathing huts that must have been kept in storage somewhere during the war. Increasingly, there is also **windsurfing** on offer – better suited to these north-facing resorts than chilly bathing.

Bus Verts (ⓣ08.10.21.42.14, ⓦwww.busverts14.fr) run all along this coast. From Bayeux, bus #75 goes to Arromanches, Courseulles, and Ouistreham, and bus #70 to the Pointe du Hoc, the US cemetery at Colleville-sur-mer, and Port-en-Bessin. From Caen, bus #30 runs inland to Bayeux, express bus #1 to

Ouistreham, and express bus #3 to Courseulles. From June to mid-September, Bus Verts' special **D-Day Line** departs daily from Caen's *gare routière* (9.20pm) and place Courtonne (9.35am), calling at Courseulles, Arromanches, the German gun emplacements at Longues-sur-mer, the US cemetery and the Pointe du Hoc, before returning to Caen at around 6pm (€14 flat fare).

In addition, the Caen Memorial (see p.143) organizes expensive but informative bilingual **guided tours** of the beaches in small groups of around six people, with four or five hours on the road and a visit to the Memorial at your own pace (mid-Jan to March & Oct–Dec daily 1pm; April–Sept daily 9am & 2pm; €67.50). Companies that run tours from Bayeux are listed on p.155.

Ouistreham-Riva Bella

The small community of **OUISTREHAM-RIVA BELLA**, on the coast 15km north of Caen and connected to it by a fast dual carriageway, still gives the impression that it can barely believe its luck at having become a major ferry port. Since Brittany Ferries started their regular service here from Portsmouth in 1986, the easternmost of the D-Day resorts has developed an extensive array of reasonable hotels and restaurants.

The town itself is not especially appealing, and most arriving passengers choose to press on out – this is one of the Channel's simpler ports to leave, as boats dock just a few hundred metres from the small central square, **place Courbonne**. However, Ouistreham's road system, at least in summer, is still not quite up to the task of coping with the volume of traffic, and motorists should allow plenty of time to catch their boats. All services are connected by bus with Caen.

If instead of setting off for Caen you head directly west along the coast from the ferry terminal, after a few hundred metres you come to the long straight main drag of beach – the **Riva Bella** itself. This is progressively shedding its somewhat run-down image; the large casino has been remodelled as a 1930s passenger liner, housing an expensive restaurant and cocktail bar, and even the old-fashioned bathing huts have had a fresh lick of paint. Nearby, the **Musée du Mur de l'Atlantique** (daily: Feb, March & Oct to mid-Nov 10am–6pm; April–Sept 9am–7pm; €6) is housed in a lofty bunker, the headquarters of the several German batteries which defended the mouth of the River Orne, and which, after brief resistance, fell to Allied forces on June 9, 1944. Inside the heavily restored bunker, displays re-create living conditions, with newspapers, cutlery and packets of cigarettes adding a welcome human touch to the moderately interesting explanations of the workings of the generators, gas filters and radio room. The semi-pedestrianized **Avenue de la Mer**, which connects the casino and tourist office with the main highway back from the sea, is lined with inexpensive snack bars and restaurants.

Practicalities

Brittany Ferries (Ⓣ08.03.82.88.28, Ⓦwww.brittany-ferries.com) services are detailed in Basics. The **tourist office** is in place Alfred-Thomas, alongside the Casino on the beach (April–June & Sept daily 10am–12.30pm & 2–5.30pm; July & Aug daily 10am–1pm & 2–7pm; Oct–March Mon–Sat 10am–12.30pm & 2.30–6pm, Sun 10am–12.30pm; Ⓣ02.31.97.18.63, Ⓦwww.ville-ouistreham.fr). **Bikes** can be rented from Riva Loisir, 77 avenue Foch (Ⓣ02.31.97.19.04), or the Cyclorama on the seafront (Ⓣ02.31.96.47.47), which also offers family-sized pedal cars for group excursions. If you're **cycling**, the obvious direction to take for a gentle start to your holiday is west along the coast, but if you head south towards Caen, the designated cycle path that follows the canal all the way to Caen city centre is far more pleasant than the main road. Access to the path is signposted once you reach the canal, which stretches south from place de Gaulle. **Internet access** is available at the tourist office (€0.10 per min).

Several cafés and brasseries in the place Courbonne, immediately outside the *gare maritime*, are eager to liberate passengers from their spare change, while *Le Channel*, just around the corner at 79 avenue Michel-Cabieu (ⓣ02.31.96.51.69; ❶), is the best value for both **eating and accommodation**. Menus in the restaurant start with the €10.50 *menu du port*, which includes mussels, while the €13.75 and €30 options increase in splendour; the guest rooms, which are cheap for en-suite facilities, are in a separate building across the street. Alternatively, try the smart *Le Normandie*, a few doors down at 71 avenue Michel-Cabieu (ⓣ02.31.97.19.57, ⓦwww.lenormandie.com; ❹; closed mid-Dec to mid-Jan, plus Sun eve & Mon Nov–March), which has pleasant, quiet rooms. Its "Normand" menu at €21 features *boudin noir*, while the €35 option makes an excellent last-night blowout. Good-value hotels near the beach include the *Hôtel de la Plage*, an imposing red-brick mansion in a peaceful location barely 100m from the Casino at 39–41 avenue Pasteur (ⓣ02.31.96.85.16, ⓦwww.hotel-plage-ouistreham.com; closed Nov–Feb; ❸), and the *St-Georges* at 51 avenue Andry (ⓣ02.31.97.18.79; closed Jan; ❸).

Pegasus Bridge

Roughly 5km south of Ouistreham, the main road towards Caen passes close by the site now known as **Pegasus Bridge**. On the night before D-Day, the twin bridges here that cross the Caen canal and the River Orne were the target of a daring **glider assault** just after midnight. Capturing them intact was a crucial objective for the Allied forces, because it both enabled the invaders to advance east along the coast and blocked the Germans from sending reinforcements. Three of the six Horsa gliders launched from the *Halifax*, six miles offshore, landed close enough for what was then Bénouville Bridge to be captured within half an hour, although Lieutenant Brotheridge, leading the charge, became the first British casualty of D-Day in the process.

Despite protests from veterans, the original bridge was replaced in 1994, but it has been preserved as the focus of the **Mémorial Pegasus** immediately to the east (daily: Feb–April & Oct–Nov 10am–1pm & 2–5pm; May–Sept 9.30am–6.30pm; €5). This vaguely glider-shaped museum, which opened in 2000, holds the expected array of helmets, goggles, medals and other memorabilia, most helpfully captioned in English, as well as various model bridges used in planning the attack. The bridge itself spans a hole in the lawns outside, behind which stands a life-sized replica of the type of glider used in the assault, inaugurated in June, 2004, by none other than Prince Charles and 85-year-old Jim Wallwork, one of the surviving glider pilots.

Ouistreham to Arromanches: Sword and Juno beaches

While the coast along Sword and Juno beaches is generally featureless, the towns themselves are welcoming. A long promenade curves by the sea all the way from Ouistreham to Lion – it's built up, though always in a low-key way, and makes a pleasant walk straight from the ferry. **Colleville-Montgomery**, the first village after the port, is one of the few "Montgomeries" in the area really to be named after the British general rather than his Norman ancestors. It's not otherwise distinguished.

Luc-sur-mer

If you're looking for atmosphere – albeit sedate – **LUC-SUR-MER**, 11km from Ouistreham, has much to recommend it. It's a gentle resort with a small wooden pier, neon-lit crêpe-stands, and tearooms along the promenade, with the **hotel** *Beau Rivage*, right on the seafront at 1 rue Docteur Charcot (Ⓣ02.31.96.49.51, Ⓦwww.hotel-beaurivage-lucsurmer.fr; closed mid-Dec to mid-Jan; ❹), as its most reasonably priced, where the rooms are comfortable enough, albeit not decorated in the most modern of styles. Menus here start at €18; options on the €26 one include a spectacular salad of smoked fish, *langoustines* and foie gras. A couple of hundred metres further west, several rooms at the newer and much grander *Hôtel des Thermes*, at 3 rue Guynemer (Ⓣ02.31.97.32.37, Ⓦwww.hotelresto-lesthermes.com; closed Nov–Easter; ❼), have large sea-view balconies. There's also a huge four-star **campsite** near the beach, *La Capricieuse* (Ⓣ02.31.97.34.43, Ⓦwww.campinglacapricieuse.com; closed Oct–March).

Langrune and St-Aubin-sur-mer

Attractive individual seaside **hotels** are scattered all along the D-Day coast – typically with simple rooms upstairs above a large glass-fronted sea-view dining room – so ferry passengers have a choice of several logis for a first- or last-night stop. The *Hôtel de la Mer*, boulevard Aristide-Briand (Ⓣ02.31.96.03.37; ❷), in **Langrune** is particularly inexpensive for simple rooms and decent if unexceptional food, while further on, facing the beach across the pedestrian-only promenade at **St-Aubin-sur-mer**, *Le Clos Normand* (Ⓣ02.31.97.30.47, Ⓦwww.closnormandhotel.com; closed mid-Nov to mid-Feb; ❹;) may be large, but it's extremely peaceful. Its **restaurant** has a seafront terrace and offers a series of four- to eight-course *table d'hôte* menus, where the price depends on your choice of main course and ranges from €20.90 to €57.

Courseulles and Juno Beach

COURSEULLES, 3km west of St-Aubin, is a bit more of a town, with an enjoyable Friday **market** in an old square set back from the sea, and, allegedly, the best oysters in Normandy. The town is fronted by **Juno Beach**, the section of Norman coast allocated to the 14,000 Canadian soldiers who took part in the D-Day landings; within ten days of its capture, Winston Churchill and King George VI visited the beach on morale-boosting excursions. Opened in June, 2003, the **Centre Juno Beach**, next to the beach itself (April–Sept 9am–7pm; Oct–March 10am–1pm & 2–6pm; €6.50), commemorates the Canadian contribution to World War II, focusing not so much on what happened at Juno itself as on all things Canadian, from that country's role in some of the war's most important battles to its quirky passion for curling. The beautiful **Canadian Cemetery** is about 3km inland from Courseulles at Bény-sur-mer, on flat ground from which you can see the sea.

Courseulles' main function these days is as a yachting port, and apart from an excellent crêperie, *du Moulin*, on the outskirts, there's not much choice of hotels and restaurants. The *Crémaillère-Le-Gytan*, boulevard de la Plage (Ⓣ02.31.37.46.73, Ⓦwww.la-cremaillere.com; ❸), is the best option for both **sleeping** and **eating**, with rooms boasting sea views and menus costing from €16.50.

Arromanches

At **ARROMANCHES**, 13km west of Courseulles and a total of 31km from Ouistreham, the artificial **Mulberry harbour**, "Port Winston", facilitated the landings of two and a half million men and half a million vehicles during the Invasion. Two of these prefab concrete constructions were built in segments in Britain, while "doodlebugs" blitzed overhead, then submerged in rivers away

The war cemeteries

The World War II **cemeteries** that dot the Norman countryside are filled with foreigners; most of the French dead are buried in the churchyards of their home towns. After the war, some felt that the soldiers should remain in the makeshift graves that were dug where they fell. Instead, commissions gathered the remains into purpose-built cemeteries devoted to the separate warring nations.

The **British** and **Commonwealth** cemeteries are magnificently maintained, and open in every sense. They tend not to be screened off with hedges or walls, or to consist of endless expanses of manicured lawn, but are instead intimate, punctuated with bright flowers. The family of each soldier was invited to suggest an inscription for his tomb, making each grave very personal, and yet part of a common attempt to bring meaning to the carnage. Some epitaphs are questioning – "One day we will understand"; some are accepting – "Our lad at rest"; some matter-of-fact, simply giving the home address; some patriotic, quoting the "corner of a foreign field that is forever England". Interspersed among them all is the chilling refrain of the anonymous: "A soldier... known unto God". Thus the cemetery outside **Ryes**, northeast of Bayeux, where so many of the graves bear the date of D-Day, and so many of the victims are under 20, remains immediate and accessible – each grave clearly contains a unique individual. Even the monumental sculpture is subdued, a very British sort of fumbling for the decent thing to say (to reach it, head 2km southeast of the village on the D87 towards Bazenville). The understatement of the memorial at **Bayeux**, with its contrived Latin epigram commemorating the return as liberators of "those whom William conquered", conveys an entirely appropriate humility and deep sadness.

An even more eloquent testimony to the futility of war is afforded by the **German** cemeteries, filled with soldiers who died for a cause that largely precludes talk of "nobility" or "sacrifice". What such cemeteries might have been like had the Nazis won doesn't bear contemplation. As it is, they are sombre places, inconspicuous in order to minimize the bitterness they still arouse. At **Orglandes**, 10km south of Valognes (see p.167) on the Cotentin peninsula, 10,000 are buried, three to each of the plain headstones set in the long flat lawn, almost hidden behind an anonymous wall. There are no noble slogans and the plain entrance is without a dedicatory monument. At the superb site of **Mont d'Huisnes**, 6km east of Mont-St-Michel, the circular mausoleum holds another 10,000, filed away in cold concrete tiers. There is no attempt to defend the indefensible, and yet one feels an overpowering sense of sorrow – that there is nothing to be said in such a place bitterly underlines the sheer waste.

The largest **American** cemetery, at **Colleville-sur-mer** near the Pointe du Hoc, may already be familiar to you from the opening sequences of *Saving Private Ryan*. Neat rows of crosses cover the tranquil clifftop lawns, with no individual epitaphs, just gold lettering for a few exceptional warriors. At one end, a muscular giant dominates a huge array of battlefield plans and diagrams, covered with surging arrows and pincer movements. George W. Bush is the latest of many US presidents to have paid his respects here.

Companies that offer guided tours of the D-Day beaches and cemeteries are detailed on p.148 and p.155.

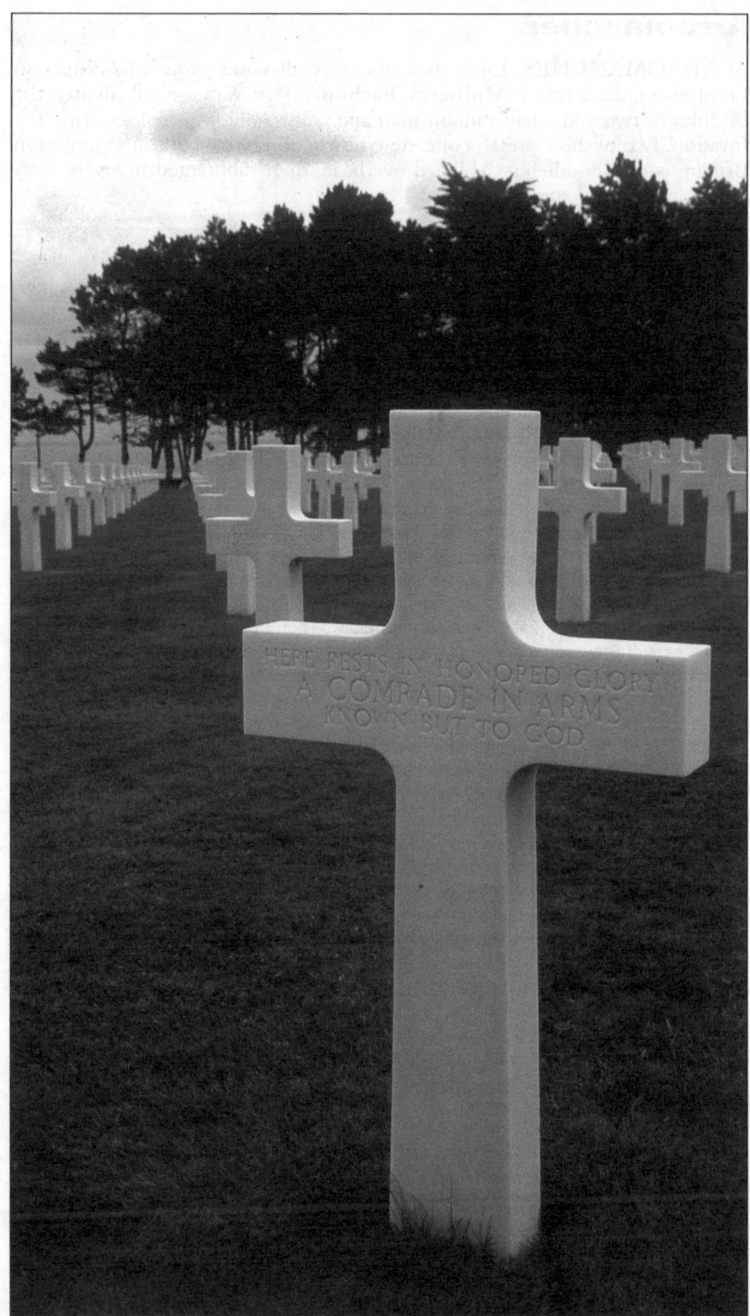

△ War cemetery

from the prying eyes of German aircraft, and finally towed across the Channel at 6kph as the Invasion began. Meanwhile, the British 47 Royal Marine Commando were storming Arromanches itself to clear the way.

The seafront **Musée du Débarquement**, in Arromanches's main square (Feb & Nov–Dec daily 10am–12.30pm & 1.30–5pm; March & Oct Mon–Sat 9.30am–12.30pm & 1.30–5.30pm, Sun 10am–12.30pm & 1.30–5.30pm; April Mon–Sat 9am–12.30pm & 1.30–6pm, Sun 10am–12.30pm & 1.30–6pm; May Mon–Sat 9am–7pm, Sun 10am–7pm; June–Aug daily 9am–7pm; Sept Mon–Sat 9am–6pm, Sun 10am–6pm; closed Jan; €6; Ⓦwww.normandy1944.com), recounts the whole story by means of models, machinery and movies – and the evidence of your own eyes. A huge picture window runs the length of the museum, staring straight out to where the bulky remains of the harbour stretch away along the coast, making a strange intrusion on the beach and shallow sea-bed. Its sheer scale is impossible to appreciate at this distance; for three months after D-Day, this was the largest port in the world. (The other such harbour, slightly further west on Omaha Beach, was broken up within two weeks by a huge storm, but this one was repairable; see p.433.)

Several other war memorials are scattered throughout Arromanches, including a crucifix and a statue of the Virgin Mary, high up on the cliffs above the invasion site. Alongside, a steel dome contains **Arromanches 360** (daily: Feb & Dec 10.10am–4.40pm; April, Oct, first week in May & second week in Sept 10.10am–5.40pm; second week in May & first week in Sept 10.10am–6.10pm; June–Aug 9.40am–6.40pm; €4; Ⓦwww.arromanches360.com), a wraparound cinema which at half-hourly intervals, under the slogan of "eighteen minutes of total emotion", plunges viewers into the heart of the fighting. There's not all that much contemporary footage, but with the action running simultaneously on separate screens, the effect is undeniably impressive.

Practicalities

Arromanches somehow manages to be quite a cheerful place to stay, with a lively pedestrian street of bars and brasseries, and a long expanse of sand where you can rent windsurf boards. The local **tourist office** is just back from the sea at 2 rue Maréchal-Joffre (daily: July & Aug 9am–12.30pm & 2–6pm; Sept–June 10am–noon & 2–5pm; Ⓣ02.31.22.36.45, Ⓦwww.arromanches.com).

La Marine, 1 quai Canada (Ⓣ02.31.22.34.19, Ⓦwww.hotel-de-la-marine.fr; closed mid-Nov to early Feb; ❹), is a slightly expensive **hotel**, with well-appointed rooms – many of which enjoy superb sea views – and an excellent restaurant serving fish menus from €19; there's also a cheaper brasserie, the *Winston*, alongside. Across the main square, opposite the tourist office, the *Arromanches*, 2 rue du Colonel René Michel (Ⓣ02.31.22.36.26, Ⓦwww.hoteldarromanches.fr; closed Tues, Wed & Jan to mid-Feb; ❹), is less well situated but just as comfortable; here, the *Pappagall* restaurant has menus from €16 to €26. The cheaper *Normandie* stands nearby at 5 place du 6 Juin (Ⓣ02.31.22.34.32; ❸). The town's spacious three-star municipal **campsite** is located 200 metres back from the seafront (Ⓣ02.31.22.36.78; closed Nov–March).

West to the Cotentin: Omaha Beach

Six kilometres west of Arromanches, a minor road leads 1.5km north of the village of **LONGUES-SUR-MER** to the best-preserved German defensive post to survive the war. **La Batterie de Longues-sur-mer** consists of four concrete Nazi pillboxes, from which mighty gun barrels still point out across the Channel. Visitors are free to wander in and over the bunkers, and there are guided tours in English, French and German in summer (April–Sept daily 10am–6pm; €5).

PORT-EN-BESSIN, 11km west of Arromanches, and the nearest point on the coast to Bayeux (on the #70 bus route), has a thriving fishing industry and – rare on this coast – a sheltered, enclosed site. The fish, caught off Devon and Cornwall, are auctioned three times a week. It's not, however, desperately attractive, though the *de la Marine* (☎02.31.21.70.08; ❸) is a classic seaside **hotel** on quai Letourneur, with menus from €15. The squalid *La Prairie* **campsite**, on the other hand, is definitely one to avoid.

The coastline west of Port-en-Bessin becomes steadily hillier, and as **Omaha Beach** it presented a stiff challenge to the American forces on D-Day. The clifftop village of **COLLEVILLE-SUR-MER**, 10km along, marks the start of the long approach road to the larger of the two **American war cemeteries**, a sombre place, described on p.152. Unlike the British and Commonwealth forces, the Americans repatriated over half of their dead. **ST-LAURENT**, 2.5km further on and the next point where road access to the sea becomes possible, holds the small **Omaha Beach Museum** (daily: mid-Feb to mid-March 10am–12.30pm & 2.30–6pm; mid-March to mid-May & mid-Sept to mid-Nov 9.30am–6.30pm; mid-May to June & first fortnight of Sept 9.30am–7pm; July & Aug 9.30am–7.30pm; €5.20), 100m inland, which displays a fine assortment of photos taken on D-Day itself, but few artefacts of any interest.

Just beyond St-Laurent, **VIERVILLE**, like Arromanches (see p.152), was chosen as a site for the building of an artificial harbour, this time codenamed "Gooseberry" to Arromanches' "Mulberry", which lasted just thirteen days before breaking up in an unprecedented storm. A memorial to the US National Guard stands atop a ruined German pillbox at the west end of town; nearby, the weatherbeaten Hôtel du Casino (☎02.31.22.41.02; closed mid-Nov to Feb; ❸;) whilst a Logis de France, surveys the scene.

Further along, the most dramatic American landings took place along the cliff heights of the **POINTE DU HOC**, still today deeply pitted with German bunkers and shell-holes. Standing amid the scarred earth and rusty barbed wire, looking down to the rocks at the base of the cliff, it seems inconceivable that the first US sergeant was at the top five minutes after landing, and the whole complex taken within another quarter of an hour.

Grandcamp-Maisy and Isigny

GRANDCAMP-MAISY, 3km west of Pointe du Hoc, centred on a compact fishing harbour, was too severely damaged in the war to make much of a holiday destination now. It does, however, offer a couple of reasonably priced **hotels**, the *Duguesclin*, 4 quai Crampon (☎02.31.22.64.22; closed mid-Jan to mid-Feb; ❷), which has a panoramic sea-view dining room, though most of the accommodation is in the modern annexe behind, and *Au Petit Mareyeur*, a long way back from the sea on avenue Marcel Destors (☎02.31.22.65.91, Ⓦwww.hotelrestaurantaupetitmareyeur.com; ❷). It also has a good **campsite**, the *Camping du Joncal* (☎02.31.22.61.44; Ⓦwww.campingdujoncal.com; closed Oct–March). **Cruises** of the landing beaches to both the north and the east, on the sixty-passenger *Colonel Rudder*, cost from €10 for a one-hour trip to the Pointe du Hoc, and €16 for a two-and-a-half-hour trip to Omaha Beach; for a full schedule, call ☎02.31.21.42.93. Boats leave from quai Nord in Grandcamp's port, and departure times depend on the tides.

The nearby town of **ISIGNY** is renowned for its dairy products, butter in particular, which you can see being made, and purchase afterwards, at the

Coopérative Laitière Isigny-Ste-Mère, 2 rue du Docteur Boutrois (guided tours July & Aug Mon–Sat 10am, 11am, 2pm, 3pm & 4pm; rest of year by appointment only; €4; ⓣ02.31.51.33.88, ⓦwww.isigny-ste-mere.com). Though once again of no great beauty or interest, it does have a **hotel**, *De France*, 13 rue É. Demagny (ⓣ02.31.22.00.33, ⓔhotel.france.isigny @wanadoo.fr; closed mid-Nov to mid-Feb; ❷), if you're stuck.

Bayeux

BAYEUX, with its perfectly preserved medieval ensemble, magnificent **cathedral** and world-famous **tapestry**, is 23km west of Caen – a mere twenty -minute train ride. It's a smaller and much more intimate city, and, despite the large crowds of summer tourists, a far more enjoyable place to visit. Just ten kilometres in from the coast, Bayeux was the first French city to be liberated in 1944, the day after the D-Day landings. It was occupied so quickly – before the Germans had got over their surprise – that it escaped serious damage, and briefly became capital of Free France.

Arrival, information and tours

Bayeux's **gare SNCF** is fifteen minutes' walk southeast of the town centre, just outside the "ring road", while **buses** operated by Bus Verts du Calvados stop at both the *gare SNCF* and on the other side of town, on the north side of place St-Patrice; tickets are sold at the *gare SNCF* and on the actual buses.

The **tourist office** stands in the very centre of town, in what used to be the fish market on the arched pont St-Jean (Jan–Feb & Nov–Dec Mon–Sat 9.30am–12.30pm & 2–5.30pm; April–May & Sept–Oct Mon–Sat 9.30am–12.30pm & 2–5.30pm; June–Aug Mon–Sat 9am–7pm, Sun 9am–1pm & 2–6pm; ⓣ02.31.51.28.28, ⓦwww.bayeux-tourism.com). The **post office** is just around the corner at 14 rue Larcher (Mon–Fri 8.15am–6.30pm, Sat 8.15am–noon; ⓣ02.31.51.24.90), where **Internet access** is also available. **Bicycles** can be rented from the Family Home (see p.156), or Tandem, 2 hameau de la Rivière, off boulevard Winston-Churchill (Tues–Sat 9.30am–noon & 2–6.30pm; ⓣ02.31.92.03.05).

Travellers without cars who plan to visit the landing beaches and/or the war cemeteries are better advised to join a **minibus trip** with a local operator such as D-Day Tours (ⓣ02.31.51.70.52, ⓦwww.d-daybeaches.com), or Normandy Tours, 26 place de la Gare (ⓣ02.31.92.10.70, ⓦwww.d-daybeachtours.com). Prices for half-day tours start from €35. Details of tours organized through the Caen Memorial can be found on p.148.

Accommodation

As one of Normandy's most important tourist destinations, Bayeux is well equipped with accommodation. On the whole, however, the **hotels** are more expensive than elsewhere. Bayeux also has both a municipal **hostel** and municipal **campsite**. *Camping Municipal* is a large, three-star campsite on boulevard d'Eindhoven (ⓣ02.31.92.08.43; closed Oct–April), on the northern ring road (RN13) near the river – and the local sewage works. In addition, the *Centre d'Accueil Municipal*, 21 rue des Marettes (ⓣ02.31.92.08.19, ⓕ02.31.92.12.40), 1.5km west of the *gare SNCF* near the Musée de la Bataille de Normandie, remains open all year, and charges €14.50 for a tiny,

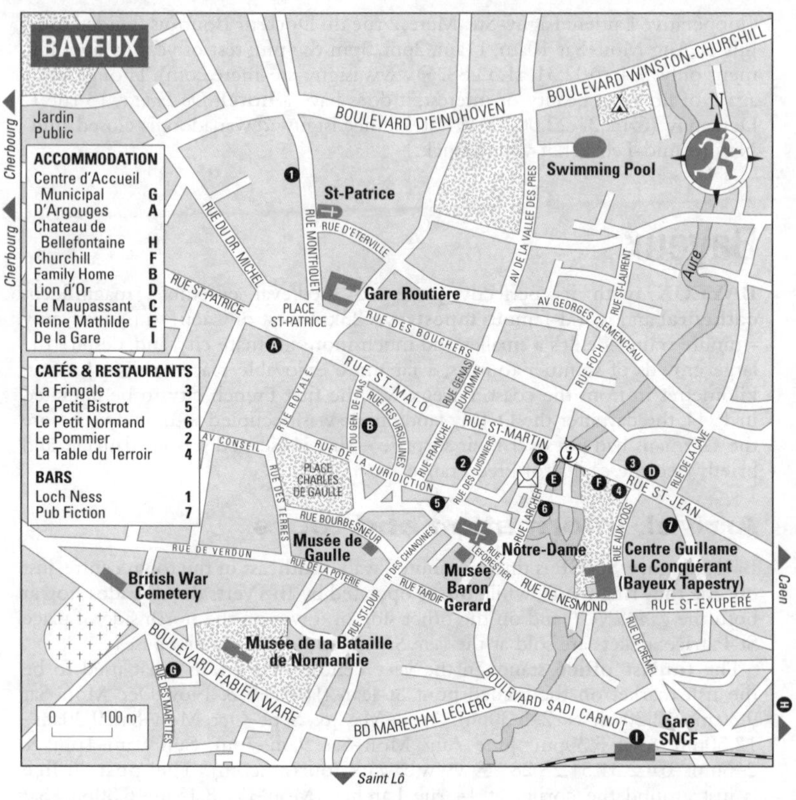

single private room plus breakfast. Bayeux's other, privately-run, hostel is more central (see below).

Hôtel d'Argouges 21 rue St-Patrice ⓣ02.31.92.88.86, ⓔdargouges@aol.com. Quiet, central and very stylish eighteenth-century building, with an imposing courtyard entered via an archway on the west side of place St-Patrice, and a well-kept garden around the back. Several rooms are very grand, with magnificent exposed wooden beams, and the rates are very reasonable for what you get. ④

Chateau de Bellefontaine 49 rue de Bellefontaine ⓣ02.31.22.00.10, ⓦwww.hotel-bellefontaine.com. Rooms with high ceilings and fireplaces in a beautiful chateau surrounded by a duck-filled garden, a fifteen-minute walk from the town centre and five minutes from the *gare SNCF*. There are also rooms in the old granary which are ultra-modern with designer decor. Closed Jan. ⑦

Churchill Hôtel 14–16 rue St-Jean ⓣ02.31.21.31.80, ⓦwww.hotel-churchill.com. Relatively large, completely renovated, 32-room hotel, which often has rooms when elsewhere is full), and whose size does not preclude personal and friendly service. Perfectly situated in the heart of the town centre, with free parking directly behind the hotel. ⑤

Family Home 39 rue du Général de Dias ⓣ02.31.92.15.22, ⓕ02.31.92.55.72. Hostel in a central, seventeenth-century house, which is more convenient than the *Centre d'Accueil Municipal* (see p.155). Its prices are a little over the usual odds – €18 each for members, €20 for non-members, while private doubles are €30. It's a bit self-consciously jolly, but people return again and again. Room prices include breakfast. Communal dinners, served at 7.30pm nightly with Madame Lefèvre presiding at the head of a long table in an old oak-beamed dining room, cost €12 per person. They also rent bikes and can find you a bed in their other property, about 1km from the centre, if the *Family Home* is full – which it often is during summer. ❶

Hôtel de la Gare 26 place de la Gare ⓣ02.31.92.10.70, ⓕ02.31.51.95.99. Old but perfectly adequate basic hotel, with a simple brasserie, beside the station, on the ring road fifteen minutes' walk from the cathedral. Tours of D-Day beaches arranged through Normandy Tours (see p.155), who are based here but offer tours to guests and non-guests alike. ❶

Hôtel-Restaurant Lion d'Or 71 rue St-Jean ⓣ02.31.92.06.90, ⓦwww.liondor-bayeux.fr. Grand old coaching inn – affiliated to the quiet "Relais du Silence" organization – that's set back behind a courtyard just beyond the pedestrianized section of rue St-Jean, opposite the Halles des Grains (now the assembly rooms). The rooms themselves are brighter and newer than the exterior suggests. Closed mid-Dec to late Jan. Menus from €20. ❺

Hôtel Le Maupassant 19 rue St-Martin ⓣ02.31.92.28.53, ⓔmaupassant14@hotmail.com. Basic rooms not far from the river in the heart of town, with a bar-cum-brasserie downstairs. Can be an icebox in winter. ❷

Hôtel Reine Mathilde 23 rue Larcher ⓣ02.31.92.08.13, ⓕ02.31.92.09.93. Simple but well-equipped rooms – all have showers and TV – backing onto the canal, between the tapestry and the cathedral. The nice open-air, lunch-only brasserie downstairs, *Le Guillaume* (closed Tues), has menus from €9.50. Closed mid-Nov to early Feb. ❸

The Town

Within the confines of a busy ring road, the core of Bayeux is surprisingly small. It consists largely of one long street, which starts from the place St-Patrice in the west (scene of a Saturday **market**). As the rue St-Malo and rue St-Martin, this is lined with the busy little shops of a typical Norman town; it then crosses the attractive canalized River Aure, passing the tourist office and the old **watermill**, Moulin Crocquevieille, to become rue St-Jean (which is pedestrianized June–Sept) on the east side, filled with cafés, brasseries, restaurants and souvenir shops (and itself the site of a market on Wednesdays).

Both Bayeux's principal attractions lie south of this main thoroughfare. The **Cathedral (Notre Dame)** is in an attractive tangle of old streets, best reached along rue des Cuisiniers – look out for the magnificent fourteenth-century half-timbered house that overhangs the street at no. 1, on the corner with rue St-Martin. The **tapestry** is on the other side of the river, housed in an impressive eighteenth-century seminary, remodelled as the **Centre Guillaume le Conquérant** (daily: mid-March to April & Sept–Oct 9am–6.30pm; May–Aug 9am–7pm; Nov to mid-March 9.30am–12.30pm & 2–6pm; last admission 45min before closing; €7.40), and clearly signposted on rue de Nesmond.

The Bayeux Tapestry

The **Bayeux Tapestry** – also known to the French as the *Tapisserie de la Reine Mathilde* – is a seventy-metre strip of linen that recounts the story of the Norman Conquest of England. Although created over nine centuries ago, the brilliance of its coloured wools has barely faded, and the tale is enlivened throughout with scenes of medieval life, popular fables and mythical beasts. Technically, it's not really a tapestry at all, but an embroidery; the skill of its draughtsmanship, and the sheer vigour and detail, are stunning. The work is thought to have been carried out by nuns in England, commissioned by Bishop Oddo, William's half-brother, in time for the inauguration of Bayeux Cathedral in 1077; recent suggestions by an English historian that the tapestry is considerably newer, in view for example of the "kebabs" being grilled in one beach scene, are discounted by most authorities.

The tapestry looks – and reads – like a modern comic strip. While it's generally considered to be historically accurate, William's justification for his invasion – his contention that during an enforced sojourn after being shipwrecked on the Normandy coast, Harold had sworn to accept William as King of England – remains in dispute. In the tapestry itself, Harold is every inch the villain, with his dastardly little moustache and shifty eyes. At the point when he breaks his oath and takes the throne for himself, Harold looks extremely pleased with himself; however, his comeuppance swiftly follows, as William, the noble hero, crosses the Channel and defeats the English armies at Hastings.

Visits are well planned and highly atmospheric, if somewhat exhausting. You can't actually touch or linger over the tapestry itself, which is in any case kept for its preservation under very dim light. However, the display is excellent. First you pass along a photographic replica of the tapestry, with enlargements and detailed commentaries in both French and English. These set the expedition in its historical context, as a continuation in a sense of the Viking raids that had created Normandy a century before. Dioramas and models also cover the aftermath of the conquest of England, which is absent from the tapestry itself.

If you feel you know the 1066 story well enough by now, you can skip the film that follows, which goes over much of the same ground. Beyond this, you finally approach the real thing, which has a strong three-dimensional presence you might not expect from all the flat reproductions.

Although the tapestry makes such a bullish and effective piece of propaganda that Napoléon exhibited it in Paris – to show that a successful invasion of England was indeed possible – much of the pleasure of viewing it comes from the incidental vignettes of contemporary life that parallel the main story. The preparation of William's forces is shown in sufficient detail that museums such as those in Dieppe and Douarnenez have constructed boats using the same methods, while the depiction of Halley's Comet blazing in the sky helped astronomers to establish its orbit. Only the faintest smattering of Latin is required to be able to follow the captions that accompany each major scene, and in any case, you file past the tapestry with headsets giving a concise commentary on what is laid before your eyes. The saga comes to an abrupt end immediately after the turmoil, carnage and looting of the Battle of Hastings, and of course the death of Harold (who may or may not be the figure with an arrow in his eye).

Cathédrale Nôtre Dame

The **Cathédrale Nôtre Dame** (daily: Jan–March 9am–5pm; April–June 8am–6pm; July–Sept 8.30am–7pm; Oct–Dec 8.30am–6pm), the first home of the tapestry, is a short and very obvious walk away from its latest resting place. Despite such eighteenth-century vandalism as the monstrous fungoid baldachin that flanks the pulpit, Bishop Oddo's original Romanesque plan is still intact, for the most part sensitively merged with Gothic additions. The crypt, entirely original, is particularly wonderful, with its frescoes of angels playing trumpets and bagpipes, looking exhausted by their eternal performance. Along the nave is some tremendous twelfth-century sculpture, and you shouldn't miss the beautifully carved wooden choir stalls. The tiled floor of the chapterhouse features a fifteenth-century maze depicting the road to Jerusalem. To get access to both crypt and chapterhouse, you may have to seek out the sacristan.

Musée Baron Gerard

The courtyard that adjoins the western facade of the cathedral is dominated by the **Liberty Tree**, a 200-year-old plane tree planted with much Revolutionary rejoicing in 1797. In its shadow to the north, the former palace of the archbishops of Bayeux has over the centuries received a considerable quantity of porcelain and lace donated by local families, which is now displayed in the **Musée Baron Gerard** (daily: July & Aug 10am–12.30pm & 2–7pm; Sept–June 10am–12.30pm & 2–6pm; €2.60, free on presentation of your ticket for the tapestry), named in honour of its most generous patron.

The Musée-Mémorial Général de Gaulle and place de Gaulle

Although the **Musée-Mémorial Général de Gaulle** (mid-March to mid-Nov daily 9.30am–12.30pm & 2–6.30pm; €3.50) at 10 rue de Bourbesneur, near place de Gaulle, is aimed squarely at French devotees of the great man, it makes an interesting detour for foreign visitors. The sheer obsession of the displays, which focus on the five separate day-trips de Gaulle made to Bayeux during the course of his long life, somehow illuminates the extent to which he came to epitomize the very essence of a certain kind of Frenchness – which to foreigners seems scarcely removed from self-parody.

Over three floors, the life of the general is traced from his days as a dashing cadet, first seen in a magnificent plumed hat before he was united with his trademark flat-topped *képi*. He was wounded three times in World War I, including at both the Somme and Verdun. Having argued in vain that France should prepare for the new era of mechanized warfare, he became a general on the battlefield in 1940 just in time to be swept aside by the Nazi Blitzkrieg, and was in London by June 18 to launch his famous (but unrecorded) radio appeal to the "Free French"; the indecipherable manuscript is on display.

Then come his visits to Bayeux. The first and most significant was the day his exile ended; we see him addressing French sailors on the destroyer *Le Combattant*, then landing on French soil at Courseulles, with an incredible haunted look in his eyes, and finally declaiming before a delirious crowd in Bayeux, conducting them in the *Marseillaise*. De Gaulle is hailed throughout the museum as the embodiment of France, not least by the *sous-prefet* who welcomed him in 1944, narrates the closing video and who was still alive to chair the fiftieth-anniversary celebrations in 1994. The general returned in 1945 to welcome the first deportees to come home from Germany, and again on June 16, 1946, no longer in power, to proclaim his vision of a new constitution.

A monument in **place de Gaulle**, just along from the museum, commemorates the spot where General de Gaulle made his first emotional speech after returning to French soil on June 14, 1944. That visit was a day-trip undertaken in the face of opposition from the Allied commanders; his arrival was so unexpected that the first two civilians he encountered, two policemen wheeling their bicycles, failed to recognize him.

The Musée Mémorial 1944 de la Bataille de Normandie

Set behind massive guns, next to the ring road on the southwest side of town, Bayeux's **Musée Mémorial 1944 de la Bataille de Normandie** (daily: May to mid-Sept 9.30am–6.30pm; mid-Sept to April 10am–12.30pm & 2–6pm; €5.50) is one of the old school of war museums, with its emphasis firmly on hardware rather than humans. Much of its former heavy-handedness seems to have disappeared since the end of the Cold War, and it shows some evocative film footage of the landings, by both sea and air, but nonetheless the obsession with technical minutiae remains a little disconcerting.

By way of contrast, the understated and touching **British War Cemetery** stands immediately across the road (see box on p.152).

Eating and drinking

Several of Bayeux's hotels have acceptable **restaurants** or brasseries, while the *Family Home* serves a good-value dinner each evening (see p.156); non-guests should phone ahead to reserve a place. Otherwise, most restaurants are in the rue St-Jean leading east from the river, or near the main door of the cathedral. On Sundays, virtually everywhere is shut. Away from the terraces along rue St-Jean, there are basically two **bars** worth considering when looking for somewhere to have a drink, both with pool tables and a steady stream of mainly rock and pop music. The *Loch Ness* at 67 rue Montifiquet, just north of the place St-Patrice, is the busier and more attractive of the two, though the *Pub Fiction*, 14 rue du Petit Rouen, just south of rue St-Jean, is not a bad alternative.

La Fringale 43 rue St-Jean ⓣ02.31.21.34.40. The nicest of the many pavement restaurants along rue St-Jean, offering lunch menus from €13.80, and also generous salads and snacks, as well as more formal fish dinners. Closed Wed, plus mid-Dec to mid-Feb.

Le Petit Bistrot 2 rue Bienvenue ⓣ02.31.51.85.40. Tiny old place opposite the cathedral, where the menus from €18 upwards boast a fine assortment of terrines and foie gras. Closed Sun & Mon.

Le Petit Normand 35 rue Larcher ⓣ02.31.22.88.66. Sixteenth-century house by the cathedral, offering good traditional cooking, with seafood specialities and local cider. Lunch menus from €9.50, dinner from €17.50. Closed mid-Dec to mid-Jan.

Le Pommier 38–40 rue des Cuisiniers ⓣ02.31.21.52.10. Ever-expanding traditional restaurant near the cathedral, with a tiny terrace. Meat- and dairy-rich Norman cuisine on menus from €10 (lunch only) to the €25.50 "D-Day Menu", which aims "to build up the strength of the soldiers". There's also an €13.50 vegetarian option. Closed Feb, plus Tues & Wed in low season.

La Table du Terroir 42 rue St-Jean ⓣ02.31.92.05.53. A rendezvous for closet meat freaks, tucked away behind a butcher's shop and serving the freshest, bloodiest flesh on a well-judged triplet of menus, at €16, €20 and €26. Seating at communal tables. Closed Sun eve & Mon eve, plus mid-Oct to mid-Nov.

Southwest from Bayeux

Travellers heading **southwest from Bayeux**, towards St-Lô, pass close to two remarkable buildings: the **Abbaye de Cerisy-la-Forêt** and the **Château de Balleroy**. Neither is easy to get to without transport, but if you have a bike or car they shouldn't be missed.

Cerisy-la-Forêt

The village of **CERISY-LA-FORÊT** stands at the edge of its forest 6km west of the D572 and a total of 22km southwest of Bayeux. Its eleventh-century Romanesque **abbey** (Easter–Nov daily 9am–6.30pm; €3; guided tours Easter–Sept daily 10.30am–12.30pm & 2.30–6.30pm; Oct–Nov Sat & Sun 10.30am–noon & 2.30–6pm; €4) was founded by William the Conqueror's father on the site of an already venerable monastery. Set on a hill, overlooking an attractive pond just east of Cerisy itself, its triple tiers of windows and arches, lapping light onto its cream stone, can make you sigh in wonder at the skills of medieval Norman masons.

Balleroy

At **BALLEROY**, 8.5km south of Cerisy across the D572, you switch to an era when architects ruled over craftsmen. The main street of the village leads straight to the **Château** (both château and museum mid-March to June & Sept to mid-Oct Wed–Mon 10am–6pm; July & Aug daily 10am–6pm; ⓦwww.

chateau-balleroy.com; €6.86), masterpiece of the celebrated seventeenth-century architect François Mansard. In keeping with its ostentatious past, its most recent purchaser was the late American press magnate Malcolm S. Forbes, pal of presidents Nixon, Ford and Reagan, not to mention Elizabeth Taylor. You can tour the house to see its eclectic furnishings, pieces of modern sculpture and an original *salon* – with superb royal portraits by Mignard.

The focus, however, is on Forbes himself. Forbes was an acquisitor untrammelled by financial restraint – he owned the world's largest collection of Fabergé jewelled eggs (which were almost scrambled by a fire early in 1990), and his palace in Tangier, containing 100,000 lead soldiers, was the scene of a notoriously extravagant seventieth birthday party. At Balleroy, he created a museum to his principal passion, **ballooning**. It's all a bit absurd, beginning with some interesting history, but degenerating into egomania: photos of Malcolm S. Forbes in various Forbes balloons winning various Forbes prizes (as seen, of course, in his own *Forbes Magazine*). Admission is expensive, and seems a poor substitute for indulging in the real thing, which unlike, say, running for the US presidency – his son Steve's bid for world fame in 1996 – is more than a hobby for self-publicizing millionaires. Every two years, in the third week of June, Balleroy's magnificent grounds host Europe's largest **balloon festival**.

The Cotentin Peninsula

Hard against the frontier with Brittany, and cut off from the rest of Normandy by difficult marshy terrain, the **Cotentin Peninsula** has traditionally been seen as something of a backwater, far removed from the French mainstream. The local *patois* has a special pejorative word for "stranger", applied indiscriminately to foreigners, Parisians and southern Cotentins alike, while official disdain for the region might explain why the Cap de la Hague, the peninsula's westernmost tip, was chosen as the site for a controversial nuclear reprocessing plant. The Cotentin nonetheless makes a surprisingly rewarding goal for travellers, and one that by sea at least is very easily accessible. Regular ferries from both England and Ireland still dock at the peninsula's major port, **Cherbourg**, with a plethora of attractive little villages nestled amid the hills to both east and west.

Geographically, this is an area of transition. Little ports such as **Barfleur** and **St-Vaast** on the indented northern headland presage the rocky Breton coast, while inland the meadows resemble the farmlands of the Bocage and the Bessin. The long western flank with its flat beaches serves as a prelude to **Mont-St-Michel**, with hill towns such as **Coutances** and **Avranches** cherishing architectural and historical relics associated with the abbey. Halfway down, the approaches to the Baie du Mont-St-Michel are guarded by the walled port of **Granville**, an extremely popular destination with French holiday-makers and a sort of small-scale mirror-image of Brittany's St-Malo.

Cherbourg

If the murky city of **CHERBOURG** is your port of arrival in France, the best advice is probably to head straight out and on. Despite some busy pedestrian streets and lively bars, the town itself lacks anything of substantial interest, and there are some much more appealing places within a few kilometres to either side. Napoléon inaugurated the transformation of what had been a rather poor, but perfectly situated, natural harbour into a major transatlantic port, by means of massive artificial breakwaters. An equestrian statue commemorates his boast that in Cherbourg he would "re-create the wonders of Egypt". As yet, however, there are no pyramids nearer than the Louvre in Paris.

Arrival and information

The days of the great transatlantic liners may be over, but cross-Channel **ferries** still sail into Cherbourg's *gare maritime* (daily 5.30am–11.30pm; ⓣ02.33.44.20.13), not far east of the town centre. Services from Poole are operated by Brittany Ferries (1–3 daily; 4hr 30min; ⓣ08.03.82.88.28, ⓦwww.brittany-ferries.com). Irish Ferries also sail to Cherbourg, from Rosslare (2–3 weekly; ⓣ02.33.23.44.44, ⓦwww.irishferries.com). Regular €1 **shuttle buses** connect the terminal with the tourist office and *gare SNCF*.

The **gare SNCF**, on avenue François-Millet/place Jean-Jaurès, is served by regular trains to Paris, Bayeux and Caen. Buses to Coutances (ⓣ02.33.98.13.38) and St-Lô, Valognes and Barfleur (ⓣ02.33.44.32.22) run from the **gare routière** opposite.

Cherbourg's **tourist office** is at 2 quai Alexandre III (June Mon–Sat 9am–12.30pm & 2–6.30pm; July & Aug Mon–Sat 9am–6.30pm, Sun 10am–12.30pm; Sept–May Mon–Sat 9am–12.30pm & 2–6pm; ⓣ02.33.93.52.02, ⓦwww.ot-Cherbourg-cotentin.fr). In summer there's also a tourist information kiosk at the ferry terminal, open to coincide with sailings (ⓣ02.33.44.39.92). The **post office** is at 1 rue d'Ancien Quai (Mon–Fri 8am–7pm, Sat 8.30am–noon; ⓣ02.33.08.87.01), while the Forum Espace Culture, on place Centrale, is a large book and record shop that also offers **Internet** access (Mon 2–7pm, Tues–Sat 10am–7pm; €4.70 per hr; ⓣ02.33.78.19.30).

Cycles can be rented from Station Nautique at the *gare maritime* (ⓣ02.33.78.19.29; €12 per day), National, 25 rue du Val de Saire (ⓣ02.33.20.34.20), and Europcar, 4 rue des Tanneries (ⓣ02.33.44.53.85), provide **car rental**.

Accommodation

By the standards of the rest of Normandy, **room** rates in Cherbourg are very reasonable. If you do find yourself obliged to spend the night here, it makes a lively enough place to pass an evening – though the crowds and traffic can get a bit much, and the lack of parking space during the day is a real problem for motorists. Few of the hotels, however, bother to maintain their own restaurant.

There is a refurbished, well-equipped **youth hostel** fifteen minutes' walk west of the centre at 55 rue de l'Abbaye (ⓣ02.33.78.15.15, ⓔcherbourg@fuaj.org), which offers dorm beds for €16.05 (members) or €18.95 (non-members), including breakfast. The nearest **campsite** to the ferry terminal is the three-star *Camping de Collignon* in Tourlaville, 3km east towards Barfleur (ⓣ02.33.20.16.88; closed Oct–April).

Hôtel Croix de Malte 5 rue des Halles ⓣ02.33.43.19.16, ⓔhotel.croix.malte@wanadoo.fr. Simple hotel on three upstairs floors, one block back from the harbour and around the corner from the theatre. Clean renovated rooms – all have TV and at least a shower – with the cheapest rates being for the perfectly acceptable, windowless ones in the attic. ❶

Hôtel de la Gare 10 place Jean-Jaurès ⓣ02.33.43.06.81, ⓕ02.33.43.12.20. Very convenient for the *gares SNCF* and *routière*, if not exactly stunning in itself. The cheapest rooms have a shower but no toilet. ❷

Hôtel Moderna 28 rue de la Marine ⓣ02.33.43.05.30, ⓦwww.moderna-hotel.com. Reasonable, well-priced rooms, slightly back from

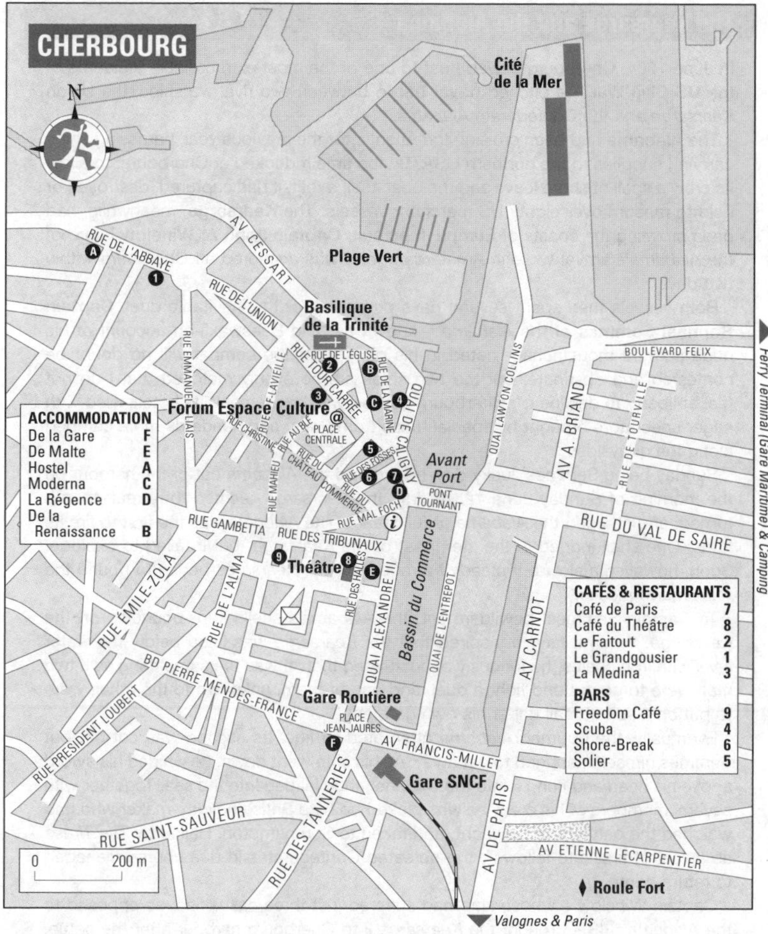

the harbour and tourist office; the cheapest have only sinks, while the pricier ones have phones, good showers and cable TV. ❶

Hôtel La Régence 42–44 quai de Caligny ⓣ02.33.43.05.16, ⓦwww.laregence.com. Small, neat rooms with balconies overlooking the harbour, in a *Logis de France* just around the corner from the tourist office. The restaurant downstairs starts with a reasonable €16 menu, and ranges up to €29.50; it's not the best along the *quai*, but there's something to be said for eating where you sleep. ❸

Hôtel de la Renaissance 4 rue de l'Église ⓣ02.33.43.23.90, ⓕ02.33.43.98.10. Nicely refurbished rooms, all en suite and some with sea views, in a friendly hotel facing the port in the most appealing quarter of town. The *Église* of the address is the attractive Trinité. ❸

The Town

The only area of Cherbourg that really encourages a ramble is over by the Basilique de la Trinité and the former town beach, now grassed over to form the "Plage Vert". Over to the south, you could alternatively climb up to **Roule Fort** for a view of the whole port. The fort itself contains the **Musée de**

The Kearsarge and the Alabama

In June 1864, Cherbourg played host to one of the most extraordinary incidents of the **US Civil War** – a pitched **naval battle** between two rival warships, the Union *Kearsarge* and the Confederate *Alabama*.

The **Alabama** had been cruising the Atlantic for the previous year, harassing ships carrying supplies to the northern USA. By the time it docked at Cherbourg, to allow its crew a spell of shore leave and the boat itself a refit, it had captured, destroyed or held to ransom over eighty US merchant vessels. The **Kearsarge**, meanwhile, had been prowling the coasts of Europe in pursuit; **Captain John A. Winslow** heard of the *Alabama*'s arrival while in Amsterdam, and was anchored off Cherbourg within two days.

Both vessels then spent several days preparing for the inevitable duel. **Captain Raphael Semmes** of the *Alabama* – known as "Old Beeswax" on account of his huge pointed moustache – noted in his diary that "the combat will no doubt be contested and obstinate, but the two ships are so evenly matched that I do not feel at liberty to decline it". Cherbourg buzzed with excitement: its hotels filled with eager spectators brought by special trains from Paris, and hundreds more camped along the quaysides.

Sunday being Semmes' lucky day, he ordered the *Alabama* out of the harbour on the morning of Sunday June 12. At first, the *Kearsarge* seemed to retreat; then it turned, and charged the *Alabama* at full steam. The *Alabama* was the first to fire its guns. One shell lodged in the sternpost of the *Kearsarge*, but it failed to explode. Soon, however, a slow but steady barrage from the *Kearsarge* began to pound the *Alabama* to pieces.

To Captain Semmes' bewilderment, the *Alabama*'s shells kept bouncing off the *Kearsarge*. When it later transpired that the *Kearsarge* was lined below the water level with iron chains, he furiously expostulated that "It was the same thing as if two men were to go out and fight a duel, and one of them, unknown to the other, were to put on a suit of mail under his own garment."

Eventually, the doomed *Alabama* attempted to flee. Its escape was cut off, but Semmes himself managed to get away. As his ship went down, he whirled his sword above his head and flung it into the Channel, then leaped into the sea. Together with several members of his crew, he was picked up by a British holiday-maker who had watched the battle from his yacht, and taken to Southampton. Hailed by *The Times* as a "set of first-rate fellows", the defeated Confederates in due course managed to return home.

Captain Winslow – whose ship had suffered just three casualties, as opposed to the *Alabama*'s 43 – brought the *Kearsarge* into Cherbourg harbour after the battle. Their previous Confederate sympathies conveniently forgotten, the local citizens hailed him as a hero, before he made his way to a celebration banquet arranged by the American community in Paris.

la Libération, which, with the usual dry maps and diagrams but plenty of contemporary newsreel – much of it, for once, in English – commemorates the period in 1944 when Cherbourg was briefly the busiest port in the world (May & Sept daily 10am–noon & 2–6pm; June–Aug Tues–Sat 11am–6pm & Sun & Mon 2–6pm; Oct–April Wed–Sun 2–6pm; €3).

In 2002, the city unveiled a major new attraction, **La Cité de la Mer**, combining a large aquarium with a visitable nuclear submarine (daily: June–Aug 9.30am–7pm; Sept–May 10am–6pm; last entry 1hr before closing; May–Sept €13, Oct–April €11.50; Ⓦwww.citedelamer.com). Though the complex centres on the grand former Transatlantic ferry terminal, in fact the old terminal simply houses its ticket offices. Displays in a new building behind tell the story of underwater exploration in history and fiction, starting with an image of Alexander the Great in 352 BC descending into the Bay of Bengal in the first diving bell, then moving swiftly via Jules Verne and H.P. Lovecraft to Jacques Cousteau, pictured with his diving saucer "shaped like a giant lentil" in 1959. Separate fish tanks hold species such as jellyfish, seahorses, and large (though sadly not giant) squid, while walkways enable you to peer into a vast cylindrical aquarium at ever greater depths. In a dry dock alongside, the *Redoutable* was France's first ballistic missile submarine. With an audio commentary from its former Captain Prudhomme, visitors can scramble through its labyrinth of tube-like walkways and control rooms, though as the nuclear generator that once powered it has been removed, there's a cavernous empty space at its heart. The cramped crew quarters will feel very familiar if you've just shared a cabin on an overnight ferry crossing, while the plush carpeting and moulded chairs in the living room are remarkably reminiscent of Elvis's Graceland.

Eating

Restaurant options in Cherbourg divide readily into the glass-fronted seafood places along the quai de Caligny, each with its copious *assiette de fruits de mer*, and the more varied, more adventurous and less expensive little places tucked away in the pedestrianized streets and alleyways of the old town.

If you want to stock up on food, Cherbourg also boasts some lively **markets**, held on Tuesday and Thursday around the rue des Halles, and on Wednesday next to the church of St-Pierre. Your best bets for large-scale shopping, however, are the Auchan **hypermarket** at the junction of RN13 and N13, south of town, or the Carrefour, on the southeast corner of the Bassin du Commerce. For **wine**, check out the extensive selection at the British-run Normandie Wine Warehouse, 71 avenue Carnot (Ⓣ02.33.43.39.79).

Café de Paris 40 quai de Caligny Ⓣ02.33.43.12.36. Work your way up through the ranks of *assiettes de fruits de mer*, from the €14.50 *Matelot* to the *Amiral* at €110 for two; there's also a selection of menus from €21, featuring a few meat dishes along with the predominately fishy selection. Closed Sun eve, plus Mon lunch in low season.

Café du Théâtre 8 place de Gaulle Ⓣ02.33.43.01.49. Attractive setup adjoining the theatre, with a café behind plate-glass windows on the ground floor and a full-scale brasserie upstairs, arranged on three sides of the central opening. It's a place used by the community as a whole rather than a typical tourist restaurant. The varied menus, from €12.50, offer more than just seafood; the €22 one features snails. Closed Sun.

Le Faitout 25 rue Tour-Carrée Ⓣ02.33.04.25.04. Shopping-district restaurant that offers traditional French cuisine, including bowls of mussels, originally prepared with celery, apples and the like, generally for under €10. Most dishes are à la carte with meat and fish dishes priced around €10–13. Closed Sun & Mon.

Le Grandgousier 21 rue de l'Abbaye Ⓣ02.33.53.19.43. Formal, definitive French fish restaurant, well worth the walk to its unprepossessing location at the west end of town. Menus start at €16, but this is a place to expect to spend a lot and dine well. Imagine any combination of fish, throw in a few oysters, crab claws and a leavening of foie gras, and you'll find it somewhere on the menu. Closed Sun eve & Mon.

La Medina 54 rue Tour-Carrée Ⓣ02.33.93.25.01. Smart, attractive Tunisian restaurant, decked out like a snake charmer's boudoir with little mosaic tables, and serving meaty couscous dishes from €17 or vegetarian *tajines* for €14, plus Tunisian wine. Closed Sun.

Bars and nightlife

While the **bars and cafés** on place Centrale itself are not overly appealing, there are several more promising establishments on the small streets around it, most notably rue des Fosses, where you will find the psychedelic *Shore-Break* and a decent pub in the *Solier* (the main entrance is at 55 Grande Rue). Also close to the place Centrale, on rue de la Marine, the *Scuba* (closed Sun) offers pool tables and darts as its main selling points, while the *Freedom Café* at 9 rue Charles Blondeau is the best of the few **gay-friendly bars** in Cherbourg.

East from Cherbourg

East from Cherbourg, the D901, which switchbacks through a series of pretty valleys, is the most direct route to the old ports of **Barfleur** and **St-Vaast**. Following the D116 along the coast, however – signposted throughout as the **Route du Val de Saire** – takes you past a succession of stunning viewpoints and some really lovely quasi-fortified villages, shielded from the sea winds by stout stone walls.

Barfleur

The pleasant little harbour village of **BARFLEUR**, 25km east of Cherbourg, was the biggest port in Normandy seven centuries ago. The population has since dwindled from nine thousand to around six hundred, and fortunes have diminished alongside – most recently through the invasion of a strain of plankton, which poisoned all the mussels. It's now a low-key place, whose grey granite quayside and formal main street retain an appealing elegance. Although the sweeping crescent of the main harbour sees little tourist activity, clusters of tiny fishing vessels tie up alongside, and fresh fish is often for sale.

Barfleur's small **tourist office** (July & Aug Mon–Sat 10am–2.30pm & 3.30–6.30pm, Sun 10am–5pm; Sept–June Tues–Sun 10am–12.30pm & 3–6pm; ⓣ02.33.54.02.48) is located near the church at the far left-hand end of the harbour. A lichen-covered rock on the shoreline nearby commemorates the fact that, when William the Conqueror embarked for southern England in 1066, it was in a ship constructed at Barfleur – the *Mora* – and piloted by a Barfleurais, Étienne. On November 25, 1120, William's descendant – also called William – set out from here to return home after a visit to France. He was travelling in a separate vessel to his father, Henry I of England: according to a contemporary account, "she flew swifter than the winged arrow, sweeping the rippling surface of the deep; but the carelessness of the intoxicated crew drove her onto a rock, which rose above the waves not far from the shore". William (recently "outed" by historians as being gay) reached the safety of a small lifeboat, but turned back to sea upon hearing the cries of his sister, and was drowned together with 300 of his companions.

Since 1834, the rock upon which William came to grief, north of Barfleur, has been guarded by the **Gatteville lighthouse**. A pleasant footpath leads there in thirty minutes from town, starting beside what was in 1865 the first lifeboat station to be built in France. At 75m, the lighthouse is the second tallest in France, with a beam that in reaching 50km overlaps with that of its opposite number on the Isle of Wight. Energetic visitors can climb the 365 steps to the top (daily: Feb, first two weeks in Nov & last two weeks in Dec 2–4pm; March & Oct 2–7pm; April & Sept 2–6pm; May–Aug 2–7pm; €2).

Barfleur has a fine brace of **hotels**. By far the better is *Le Conquérant*, a short distance back from the sea at 16–18 rue St-Thomas-à-Becket (ⓣ02.33.54.00.82; closed mid-Nov to mid-March; ❷); its nicest rooms face onto a lovely garden courtyard, and it has its own summer-only crêperie. Accommodation at *Le Moderne*, tucked away south of the main road at 1 place de Gaulle (ⓣ02.33.23.12.44; ❷), is not quite as appealing, but the **restaurant** is quite superb, with the €24.50 menu including the house speciality, oysters – stuffed or raw.

For a lighter **snack**, *Chez Buck*, at 1 rue St-Thomas-à-Becket where the main road meets the port (Ⓣ02.33.54.02.16; closed mid-Nov to mid-Jan), is a cosy, busy little crêperie that also serves cheap conventional menus.

St-Vaast

ST-VAAST-LA-HOUGUE, 11km south of Barfleur, is more of a resort, with lots of tiny Channel-crossing yachts moored in the bay where Edward III landed on his way to Crécy. The narrow spit of sand called **La Hougue**, south of the centre, holds various sporting facilities, such as tennis courts and a diving club, although the tip itself is a sealed-off military installation; the fortifications are graceful, courtesy (as ever) of the celebrated seventeenth-century military architect Vauban. The whole area is at its best at high tide; low tide reveals, especially on the sheltered inland side, bleak muddy flats dotted with some of the country's best-loved **oyster beds**.

In 1692, a French and Irish army gathered at St-Vaast and set sail for Britain in an attempt to restore the deposed Stuart King James II to the English throne. However, the fleet was destroyed by a combined Anglo-Dutch force, before it could get any further than La Hougue. The battle took place just off the sandy flat island of **Tatihou**, very close to the mainland, which now doubles as a bird sanctuary and the location of an ecologically minded Musée Maritime. A limited number of visitors each day are carried across by amphibious mud-wallowing "**ferries**" from St-Vaast; the exact schedule is determined by the state of the tides (April–June & Sept daily 10am–6pm; July & Aug daily 10am–7pm; Oct–March Sat & Sun 1.30–5pm; €4.60 return, €7.60 including admission; Ⓣ02.33.23.19.92, Ⓦwww.tatihou.com).

The **hotel** *de France* just back from the sea in St-Vaast at 20 rue du Maréchal Foch (Ⓣ02.33.54.42.26, Ⓦwww.france-fuchsias.com; ❶–❻; closed Jan–Feb, plus Tues & Mon in winter), with its splendid gardens, is an ideal stopover for ferry passengers – in fact both it and the annexe at the end of the garden are packed throughout the season with British visitors. The **restaurant**, *Fuchsias*, is also excellent, with a €17 weekday menu and gourmet four-course dinners of local produce from €24. If you can't get a room there, *La Granitière*, down the road at 74 rue du Maréchal Foch (Ⓣ02.33.54.58.99, Ⓦwww.hotel-la-granitiere.com; closed mid-Dec to mid-March; ❹) is an appealing alternative, with attractive gardens, and there are more rooms at the harbourside *Hôtel le Café du Port*, 5 quai Vauban (Ⓣ02.33.23.42.42; closed mid-Nov to mid-Dec; ❷). It's also possible to stay overnight in some very comfortable rooms on Tatihou island; contact *Accueil Tatihou* on quai Vaubon (Ⓣ02.33.23.19.92; ❷–❹).

Valognes

VALOGNES, around 18km through the woods from St-Vaast on the main road south from Cherbourg, is described in tourist handouts, with a dose perhaps of wishful thinking, as "the Versailles of Normandy". The description might have had some meaning before the war, when the region was full of aristocratic mansions, but now only a scattering of fine old houses remain, along with the very scant ruins of a Gallo-Roman settlement called Alauna.

All Valognes has to show for itself is a **cider museum** housed in an old watermill (April–June, Sept & Oct Mon & Wed–Sat 10am–noon & 2–6pm, Sun 2–6pm; July & Aug Mon–Sat 10am–noon & 2–6pm, Sun 2–6pm; Nov–March groups by appointment; €4; Ⓣ02.33.40.22.73), crammed with bizarre old wooden implements and ancient warped barrels – including a particularly obscene example upstairs – a little public garden, and a big empty square, enlivened only for the Friday **market**. But it's a quiet, convenient alternative to waiting around in Cherbourg, and the surounding country lanes around make for a pleasant stroll.

The rambling, ivy-coated *Hôtel du Agriculture* at 16–18 rue L-Delisle (Ⓣ02.33.95.02.02, Ⓦwww.hotel-agriculture.com; closed Sun eve & Mon eve; ❷) is the best of several inexpensive **hotels**, and serves top-quality food on menus that start at €12.50.

Utah Beach

The westernmost of the main Invasion Beaches, **Utah Beach** stretches for approximately 30km south from St-Vaast. Operations here on D-Day started at 4.30am, with the capture of the uninhabited **Îles St-Marcouf**, clearly visible 6km offshore; from 6.30am onwards, 23,000 men and 1700 vehicles landed on the beach itself. A minor coast road, the D421, traces the edge of the dunes and enables visitors to follow the course of the fighting, though in truth there's precious little to see these days. Ships that were deliberately sunk to create artificial breakwaters are still visible at low tide, while markers along the seafront commemorate individual fallen heroes.

Quinéville

At the point where the D421 commences its coastal run, in **QUINÉVILLE**, the **Musée de la Liberté** (daily: mid-March to May & Oct to mid-Nov 10am–6pm; June & Sept 9.30am–7pm; July & Aug 9.30am–7.30pm; €5) focuses on the everyday life of the people of Normandy under Nazi occupation. Its central reconstruction of a village street is adorned with German posters announcing the strict nightly curfew, or offering a 30,000-franc reward for anyone turning in a saboteur. Displays covering their American liberators include some fine shots of aircrews sporting Mohican haircuts.

A short way back from the beach, the *Hôtel de la Plage*, at 7 avenue de la Plage (Ⓣ02.33.21.43.54; closed Mon in winter, plus 3 wks in Oct and 1 wk in March; ❷), offers six pleasant guest **rooms** and serves well-priced **meals**.

St-Martin-de-Varreville and Ste-Marie-du-Mont

Another 12km south of Quinéville, a monument at **ST-MARTIN-DE-VARREVILLE** honours the French General Leclerc, who landed here with his 2nd Armoured Division on August 1, 1944; see also p.206. However, the single best opportunity to learn about the Utah Beach landings comes at the southern end of the D421, in **STE-MARIE-DU-MONT**. Housed in a former German stronghold, the **Musée du Débarquement d'Utah-Beach** (Feb, March & Nov daily 10am–12.30pm & 2–5.30pm; April & May daily 10am–6pm; June–Sept daily 9.30am–7pm; Oct daily 10am–12.30pm & 2–6pm; mid-Nov–Dec Sat, Sun & hols 10am–12.30pm & 2–5.30pm; Ⓦwww.utah-beach.org; €4.50) explains operations in exhaustive detail, with huge sea-view windows to lend immediacy to its copious models, maps, films and diagrams.

Ste-Mère-Église

The church of the market town of **STE-MÈRE-ÉGLISE**, a short way inland from Utah Beach on the main road between Valognes and Carentan, was immortalized in the film *The Longest Day*, thanks to scenes of an unfortunate US paratrooper dangling from its steeple during the heavy fighting. That incident was based on fact, and the man in question, John Steele, used to return occasionally to re-enact and commemorate his ordeal. He's now dead, but a uniformed mannequin is permanently entangled on the roof in his stead. The new stained glass above the main door of the church also depicts American parachutists, surrounding the Virgin with Child.

Just behind and to the right of the church, Ste-Mère's approximately parachute-shaped **Musée Airborne** (Airborne Troops Museum) tells the story of the landings, complete with tanks, jeeps, and even a troop-carrying plane (daily: Feb, March, Oct & Nov 9.30am–noon & 2–6pm; April–Sept 9am–6.45pm; €5).

Ste-Mère-Église has two **hotels**. The ivy-covered *Auberge John Steele*, just north of the church at 4 rue du Cap de Laine (Ⓣ02.33.41.41.16; ❷), serves a couple of cheap menus, while the ugly modern logis *Le Ste-Mère*, south of the centre at the intersection of the main street with N13 (Ⓣ02.33.21.00.30, Ⓔhotel-le-ste-mere@wanadoo.fr; closed Fri eve, Sat lunch & Sun; ❸), offers €12.50 buffet dinners and set menus from €14. The small *Café Au Domino* is just outside the museum entrance, facing the church; and its outdoor seating makes it a good spot for lunch.

West from Cherbourg

The stretch of coast immediately west of Cherbourg is similar to that to the east, although it holds no harbour town to compare with Barfleur or St-Vaast. The main goal for most visitors is the windswept Cap de la Hague at its westernmost tip. However, the old villages of **Omonville-la-Petite** and **Omonville-la-Rogue**, 20km out of Cherbourg, are lovely places to stroll around, while all the way along you'll find wild and isolated countryside where you can lean against the wind, watch waves smashing against rocks or sunbathe in a spring profusion of wild flowers.

Cap de la Hague and Goury

The real drawback of the area around **Cap de la Hague** is that the discharges of "low-level" radioactive wastes from the **nuclear reprocessing plant** may discourage you from swimming. In 1980, the Greenpeace vessel *Rainbow Warrior* chased a ship bringing spent Japanese fuel into Cherbourg harbour. The *Rainbow Warrior's* crew were arrested, but all charges were dropped when 3000 Cherbourg dockers threatened to strike in their support. In the spring of 1985, the French secret service finally took their revenge on the *Rainbow Warrior* by sinking it in Auckland harbour, killing a member of the crew in the process. As detailed in Contexts, controversy continues to surround the plant, which has no longer welcomed visitors since September 11, 2001.

The main road, the D901, continues a couple of kilometres beyond the plant to **GOURY**, where the fields finally roll down to a craggy pebble coastline. Almost the only building amid the windswept splendour, the *Auberge de Goury* (Ⓣ02.33.52.77.01; closed Mon), is a really excellent **restaurant**, facing the octagonal lifeboat station and looking out towards a slate-grey lighthouse. It specializes in charcoal-grilled fish and meat, with a wide-ranging cheeseboard that includes the extraordinary *voluptueuse*, and is (not surprisingly) very popular at lunchtimes.

From the cape of **La Hague** itself, the northern tip of the peninsula, bracken-covered hills and narrow valleys run south to the cliffs of the Nez de Jobourg, claimed in wild local optimism to be the highest in Europe. South of La Hague, a great curve of sand – some of it military training ground – takes the land's edge to **Flamanville** and another nuclear installation. On the other side, facing north, **Port Racine** declares itself rather ludicrously to be the smallest port in France.

Barneville and Carteret

The next two sweeps of beach down to Carteret, with sand dunes like miniature mountain ranges, are among the best **beaches** in Normandy if you have transport and want solitude. **CARTERET** itself, sheltered by a rocky headland, is the nearest harbour to the English-speaking island of **Jersey**, just 25km away across seas made treacherous by the fast Alderney current. Hugo Express (ⓣ02.33.01.10.11) runs **ferries** there from May to September, charging €35 for a 72-hour return.

Carteret's old port area is not especially attractive, but does have several seafront **hotels**, including the *Hôtel de la Marine* at 11 rue de Paris in the little shopping street (ⓣ02.33.53.83.31; closed mid-Nov to mid-March; ❺) and the *Hôtel du Cap et de la Plage* on the quayside promenade A. Lebouteiller a bit further out (ⓣ02.33.53.85.89; ❸).

Visitors who prefer to be beside a beach should head instead for Carteret's twin community of **BARNEVILLE**, directly across the mouth of the bay but a few kilometres away by road. Here an endless (and quite exposed) stretch of clean, firm sand is backed by a long row of weather-beaten villas and the odd hotel, including the *Hôtel les Isles* near the northern end at 9 boulevard Maritime (ⓣ02.33.04.90.76; closed mid-Nov to mid-March; ❷), which has a superb **restaurant** that offers views clear to the Channel Islands on fine evenings. Menu prices start at €15 and include oysters stewed in *pommeau*.

There are two **campsites** in the dunes north of town: the two-star *Le Ranch* at **Le Rozel** (ⓣ02.33.10.07.10, ⓦwww.camping-leranch.fr; closed Nov–March), and the three-star *Les Mielles* at **Surtainville** (ⓣ02.33.04.31.04).

Portbail

Five kilometres further down the coast from Barneville, the dunes are interrupted once again by the broad estuary of the Ollonde River. Set slightly back from the sea, **PORTBAIL** is a delightful village with a tiny Romanesque church. Its streets are thronged on summer Tuesdays with a bustling **market**, where as well as buying spit-roasted chickens and fresh oysters you can pick up a dining table or have your chairs re-upholstered. Access to two fine beaches is by way of an old stone bridge, beneath which crowds of fishermen wade thigh-deep in the river.

The small **hotel** in Portbail's main square – *Les Pléiades*, place E-Laquaine (ⓣ02.33.04.84.18; closed Jan to mid-Feb; ❷) – also holds, by default, the town's best **restaurant**, even if it's just a basic affair that specializes in *moules frites*. Two attractive cafés face off nearby, close to the bridge, but while both make pleasant places to sit and watch the world go by, the food at neither *Aux XIII Arches* nor *Au Rendezvous des Pêcheurs* is recommended.

Bricquebec

Fifteen kilometres inland from Carteret, halfway to Valognes, the old market town of **BRICQUEBEC** is dominated by the well-preserved twelfth-century castle at its heart. Part of this attractive edifice, centred around a peaceful courtyard, is run as the upmarket *Hostellerie du Vieux Château* (ⓣ02.33.52.24.49; closed Jan; ❹). Queen Victoria once stayed here (in room 2), but unfortunately while the tacky furnishings and slapdash service make it feel at first like a treasurable piece of kitsch, the restaurant is so bad that there's not much point in coming; they also impose hefty parking fees for cars and even bicycles. Across the main square in front of the castle – scene of a busy Monday **market** – the unassuming *Donjon*, 2–4 place Ste-Anne (ⓣ02.33.52.23.15, ⓦwww.hotel-le-donjon.com; ❷; restaurant closed Sun; ❷), is by contrast a very welcoming little **hotel**, with a good bistro **restaurant**.

Lessay

Heading south from Carteret, the road around the headland joins the main D900 at **LESSAY**, where an important Romanesque **monastery** stands right in the heart of town. Until the war it was one of the few early Norman churches still intact. When it had to be rebuilt from scratch afterwards, guided by photographs, the job was done using not only the original stone but also authentic tools and methods.

The square central tower of Lessay is similar to that which collapsed centuries ago on Mont-St-Michel. The abbey hosts a series of evening concerts, under the umbrella title **Heures Musicales**, in July and August (for details call ⓣ02.33.46.90.27), while its monks sing Gregorian chants each Sunday. They're also very much in evidence at the **Holy Cross Fair** in the first half of September, which celebrates cattle and other animals (more information from the tourist office on ⓣ02.33.45.14.34). The town is served by **buses** en route between Cherbourg and Coutances.

Lessay's tiny aerodrome, south of town, was where **Charles Lindbergh** landed on completing the first solo transatlantic flight in 1927; the first beach he crossed is now called plage Lindbergh.

Pirou

Off the main coastal road, the D650, roughly 2km south of the junction for Lessay, turns inland for a few hundred metres to reach the **Château de Pirou** (April–June & Sept Wed–Mon 10am–noon & 2–6.30pm; July & Aug daily 10am–noon & 2–6.30pm; Oct–March 10am–noon & 2–5pm; €4). Although you see nothing from the road, once you've passed through its three successive fortified gateways you are confronted by a ravishing little castle. Some historians have suggested that this is the oldest castle in Normandy, dating back to the earliest Viking raids; it's thought to have taken its current form around the twelfth century.

Considering that it was converted into a farm, and then for centuries forgotten and all but submerged in ivy, it remains remarkably complete. Originally built of wood, on the coast, it was later remodelled in stone and now stands encircled by a broad moat, its towers rising sheer from the water. At your own risk, you can pick your way up to the top of the keep and look out over the surrounding fields. In summer, a tapestry depicting the Norman invasion of Sicily is on display in a barn opposite the drawbridge.

Heading towards the sea instead of inland at the turn-off for the Château de Pirou brings you to a dead end in a couple of hundred metres at the tiny community of **PIROU-PLAGE**. When the tide is low, you can see the *buchôts*, poles used in the cultivation of shellfish, poking up from the six-kilometre strip of sand that stretches away to either side. To sample the local produce, call in at the seafront **restaurant** *De la Mer*, 2 rue Ferdinand Desplanques (ⓣ02.33.46.43.36; closed Mon & Tues eve, plus Wed in winter and mid-Jan to mid-Feb).

Feugères and Le Mesnilbus

If you have time, it's worth straying east of the main roads towards Coutances, to spend a while on the **D57** and to enjoy the magnificent countryside, with undulating meadows filled with rich flowers and sleek animals placidly waiting to be eaten. The village square of **FEUGÈRES** is almost completely taken up by an amazing tangle of warped wood, once some sort of cider press and mill.

From there on to tiny **LE MESNILBUS** – where the four-room, delightfully rural *Auberge des Bonnes Gens* (ⓣ02.33.07.66.85; ❷; closed Sun eve &

Mon in low season) offers menus to suit every palate and pocket, as well as arranging **horse-riding** expeditions.

Coutances

The old hill town of **COUTANCES**, 65km south of Cherbourg and confined by its site to just one main street, has on its summit a landmark for all the surrounding countryside – the **Cathédrale de Notre Dame**, whose twin towers stand in magnificent silhouette against the sky. Essentially Gothic, it is very Norman in its unconventional blending of architectural traditions; Louis XIV's master architect Vauban said the lantern tower must be "the work of a madman". Pleasantly illuminated on summer nights (and left open) are the fountained **Jardins Publiques**, highly formal gardens with smooth rolling lawns, a well of flowers, a fountain of obelisks and an odd pyramid of hedges. They enclose a small **Musée Municipal** (July & Aug Mon & Wed–Sat 10am–noon & 2–6pm, Sun 2–6pm; Sept–June Mon & Wed–Sat 10am–noon & 2–5pm, Sun 2–5pm; €2.30), which has a rather dull collection of permanent paintings but a nice line in pretentious temporary art exhibitions.

Practicalities

Coutances's **gare SNCF** is about 1.5km southeast of the town centre (at the bottom of the hill), and also serves as the stop for **buses** heading both north and south. The **tourist office** is housed in a new wing behind the Hôtel de Ville in place Georges-Leclerc (July & Aug Mon–Fri 9.30am–6pm, Sat 10am–noon & 2–6pm, Sun 10am–1pm; Sept–June Mon–Sat 9.30am–12.30pm & 2–6pm, Sun 10am–12.30pm & 2–5pm; ⓣ02.33.19.08.10).

The cream-coloured *Rose des Sables*, behind and below the cathedral at 2 place du Gaulle (ⓣ02.33.45.01.40; closed Mon; ❷), has **rooms** of varying quality, as well as an à la carte-only restaurant. A better alternative for motorists is the *Relais du Viaduc*, at 25 avenue de Verdun (ⓣ02.33.45.02.68; closed first fortnight of July & second fortnight of Dec, plus Fri eve & Sat in low season; ❶) – the junction of the D7 and D971, south of town – which can be a little noisy but serves some fine food, with menus starting at €9.90 on weekdays. The excellent year-round municipal **campsite**, *Les Vignettes* (ⓣ02.33.45.43.13), halfway up the hill west of town that's climbed by the D44 towards Agon, stands next to a large, comfortable chain hotel, the *Cositel* (ⓣ02.33.19.15.00; ⓦwww.hotelcositel.com; ❸).

Coutainville

COUTAINVILLE, at 10km west the nearest resort to Coutances, is crammed in summer with bronzed and glamorous posers and their turbo-charged status symbols. This is an utterly nondescript stretch of coast, where the open sea batters against an endless, featureless beach. Huge tides expose massive sandflats, while behind the line of dunes dull holiday homes are punctuated by the occasional snack bar, campsite or motel.

A long walk south from town, fighting against the wind, brings you to the **Pointe d'Agon** after 3–4km, where a lighthouse commands a view of the dune environment at its most ecologically unspoiled.

Rooms at the *Hôtel Neptune*, right on the seafront (ⓣ02.33.47.07.66; closed Oct–March; ❹), are a bit expensive, but several enjoy magnificent sea views. Otherwise, there are several shorefront **campsites** on boulevard Lebel Jehenne, including two municipal ones, the three-star *Marais* (closed Sept–June) and the two-star *Martinet* (closed Nov–March), which share the same phone number and email address (Ⓣ02.33.47.05.20, Ⓔmartinetmarais@wanadoo.fr).

Abbaye de Hambye

What's left of the **Abbaye de Hambye** stands in a very sylvan setting 20km southeast of Coutances and 10km northwest ofVilledieu , with little lawns laid out in front, an orchard alongside, and cows grazing in the adjacent meadows (April–Oct daily 10am–noon & 2–6pm; €4). The abbey, which is very reminiscent of such Yorkshire abbeys as Rievaulx, was constructed as a Cistercian monastery in the second half of the twelfth century, at a time when builders were about to abandon the Romanesque tradition in favour of the new Gothic style. Much of the structure was quarried for stone and left in ruins after the Revolution; nineteenth-century prints show the walls drowning in rampant ivy. However, the central tower still stands foursquare above the high narrow walls of the nave, and a few delicate buttresses remain in place, the whole ensemble crammed in tight against a wooded hillside and inhabited mostly by crows. Beyond the little exhibition in the entrance room above the ancient gateway, visitors are guided around and among the ruins, with an optional pause to examine the rather dull displays of vestments in what was once the lay brothers' dormitory.

A luxurious rural **hotel**, the *Auberge de l'Abbaye*, is located 100m from the abbey at the turning off the D51 (Ⓣ02.33.61.42.19; ❸; closed Mon, plus mid-Feb to mid-March & first half of Oct). There being few alternative ways to pass an evening here, its restaurant serves up extravagant and expensive gourmet **dinners**.

Granville

From Coutances, the D971 runs down to the coast at **GRANVILLE**, the Norman equivalent to Brittany's St-Malo, with a similar history of piracy and a stark citadel – the **haute ville** – guarding the approaches to the bay of Mont-St-Michel across from Cancale. Thanks in part to the long beach that stretches away north of town, which disappears almost completely at low tide, it's the most popular resort in the area. However, it simply doesn't match the appeal of its Breton rival, with its nightmarish traffic and hordes of tourists milling around in summer in the vain hope of finding some way of amusing themselves.

Granville had an unexpected brush with destiny on March 9, 1945, when it was overrun for an hour and a half by German commandos from Jersey, long after the invading Allied forces had swept on to Germany.

Arrival and information

Trains between Paris and Cherbourg arrive well to the east of the town centre at the **gare SNCF** on avenue Maréchal-Leclerc, which doubles as the **gare routière** (Ⓣ02.33.50.77.89). **Ferry** services from the harbour to Jersey and Sark (both €35 for a 72-hour return) are operated by Hugo Express (Ⓣ02.33.61.08.88), and to the Îles Chausey (see p.175) by both Jolie France (Ⓣ02.33.50.31.81) and Compagnie Corsaire (Ⓣ08.25.16.80.50, Ⓦwww.compagniecorsaire.com). The **tourist office** is down below the citadel at 4 cours Jonville (July & Aug daily 9am–1pm & 2–7.30pm; Sept–June Mon–Sat 9am–12.15pm & 2–6.30pm; Ⓣ02.33.91.30.03, Ⓦwww.ville-granville.fr).

Bikes can be rented from Gérard Marchand Cycles, 35 avenue Maréchal-Leclerc (Ⓣ02.33.61.53.62).

Accommodation

With so many visitors in summer, Granville is a place where it's well worth booking **accommodation** in advance. There are no hotels in the *haute ville*; most of the possibilities are concentrated in the new town, either beneath the walls near the casino on the seaward side, or near the station. The modern, oceanfront *Centre Régional de Nautisme* (Ⓣ02.33.91.22.60; closed Sat & Sun Nov–Feb; ❶), 1km south of the station on boulevard des Amiraux, just south of the town centre, serves as Granville's **hostel**. Dorm beds cost €10.50 (members) or €13 (nonmembers), while a private double is €14.60 per person (members) or €17 (nonmembers); they also offer sailing lessons.

Hôtel des Bains 19 rue G-Clemenceau Ⓣ02.33.50.17.31, Ⓕ02.33.50.89.22. Very central upmarket hotel, facing the casino just below the old town, with four floors of good quality, mostly sea-view rooms. Closed two weeks in Jan. ❹

Hôtel de la Mer 74 rue du Port Ⓣ02.33.50.01.86, Ⓕ02.33.50.67.56. Simple hotel in front of the piles of rusting ironmongery of the commercial port, a short walk from the town centre. The restaurant has a dull €15.90 menu, but gets interesting at €24.90 where the likes of squid and sole join the mussels and stuffed sardines; there's a small streetside terrace, but you have to sit upstairs to get a view. Closed Mon, plus Tues in low season. ❷

Hôtel Michelet 5 rue Jules-Michelet Ⓣ02.33.50.06.55, Ⓕ02.33.50.12.25. White-fronted hotel, very near the sea and facing towards the high crags of the old town. It offers reasonably well-equipped but rather characterless rooms, the very cheapest of which lack en-suite facilities, and there's no restaurant. ❶

Hôtel Terminus 5 place de la Gare Ⓣ02.33.50.02.05. Simple, inexpensive hotel, immediately across from the station. ❶

The Town

The great difference between Granville and St-Malo is that Granville's walled, fortified **citadel** stands separate from the modern town, and has very few shops or restaurants, no hotels, and indeed hardly any attractions of interest to tourists. Sheltered behind a rocky outcrop that juts out into the Channel, it's reached by steep stairs from alongside the beach and casino, or circuitous climbing roads from the port. Once up there, you'll find three or four long narrow parallel streets of forbidding grey-granite eighteenth-century houses that lead to the church of Notre Dame. The views up and down the coast, across to Mont-St-Michel and out to the Îles Chausey, are dramatic, but no more so than in many other towns along the Cotentin coast. Ornamental gardens close to the headland boast a statue of the city's best-known pirate, **Georges Pléville le Pellay**, splendidly complete with peg leg and cutlass.

Set into the citadel walls directly above the port, the **Musée du Vieux Granville**, 2 rue le Carpentier (April–Sept daily except Tues 10am–noon & 2–6pm; Oct–March Wed, Sat & Sun 2–6pm; €2.55, or €4 with admission to the Musée Anacréon), holds three floors of rather dry displays on local history. The main feature downstairs, amidst old postcards and paintings, is a model of Granville as it appeared in 1912; higher up, antique coiffes and costumes jostle for space with hefty wooden Norman furniture, while the top level is devoted to the history of the Newfoundland cod fisheries.

In pride of place at the inland end of the *haute ville*, the **Musée d'Art Moderne Richard Anacréon** (Wed–Mon 11am–6pm; €2.50, or €4 with Musée du Vieux Granville) houses art accumulated by the eponymous Monsieur Anacréon, who was born in Granville in 1907 and opened his L'Originale bookshop in Paris in 1940. Filled with sketches and autographs from the likes of Jean Cocteau and André Derain – and one or two Picasso *eau-fortes* – it's not all that compelling, but the gallery itself is impressive and hosts interesting temporary exhibitions.

The family home of a more famous Granvillais contemporary of Anacréon, the couturier **Christian Dior**, who was responsible for the "New Look", overlooks the beach a few hundred metres northeast of the citadel. A striking orange-and-pink-painted mansion, it can be reached along a coastal footpath that continues another 6.5km to St-Martin de Bréhal. Its tranquil, flower-filled gardens enjoy sweeping views, while the interior of the actual house has been stripped bare and is refitted each summer for changing annual exhibitions on aspects of twentieth-century fashion, focusing on Dior in particular (late May to late Sept daily 10am–12.30pm & 2–6.30pm; €5).

Eating

Granville's best **restaurants** are of the seafood variety, situated hard below the citadel walls with waterfront views – albeit of a gritty commercial port rather than a delightful harbour.

La Citadelle 34 rue du Port ⓣ02.33.50.34.10. The closest to the town centre of the port's top-notch seafood places. The €16 *Menu du Terre et Mer* has haddock as its main course, while the superb €31 option features veal or fried sea bass. Closed Feb.

L'Échauguette 24 rue St-Jean ⓣ02.33.50.51.87. Cosy, stone-walled old-town crêperie, which serves good simple meals, grilled over an open fire. *Galettes* cost under €8, meat main courses more like €12.

Le Phare 11 rue du Port ⓣ02.33.50.12.94. Sea-front fish restaurant facing the small-boat harbour towards the end of the peninsula, which has the standard mussels and fish soup on its €16.50 menu, and an extraordinarily copious *assiette de fruits de mer* on the €27.50 one. Closed Tues & Wed.

Restaurant du Port 19 rue du Port ⓣ02.33.50.00.55. Top-quality seafood place, just along from the *Phare* at the small-boat harbour, with a mouthwatering assortment of very fishy menus, and an unbelievably garlicky fish soup as its speciality. Menus range from €14.50 up to €29.90; the good-value €25 menu features stuffed oysters and a delicious parcel of duck in Camembert sauce. Closed Sun eve, plus Mon in low season, and Jan–mid-Feb.

The Îles Chausey

Nowadays visited for their long beaches of fine sand, the sparsely inhabited **Îles Chausey** were the site of the quarries that provided the granite that built Mont-St-Michel. They originally formed part of the ancient Forest of Scissy, until exceptional tides at the spring equinox of 709 AD, combined with strong north winds, flooded the entire region. There is just one (summer-only) **hotel**, the lonely *Hôtel du Fort et Îles* (ⓣ02.33.50.25.02; closed Oct–April, restaurant closed Mon; ❸), which insists on a minimum stay of two nights. Other accommodation is available in either private or municipal *gîtes*, the latter run by the tourist office in Granville (see p.173). The only **restaurant** on the island is the modest crêperie, the *Bellevue* (ⓣ02.33.51.80.30).

Two **ferry** companies operate services out to the islands from Granville's *gare maritime*: Jolie France II (March–Oct up to 3 daily, Nov–Feb 1–3 weekly; ⓣ02.33.50.31.81) and Compagnie Corsaire (April–Sept 1–2 daily; ⓣ08.25.16.80.50, ⓦwww.compagniecorsaire.com). Precise timings and frequencies depend on the tides; the trip takes just under an hour each way, and day returns cost around €17.

Around Granville

If you prefer to be out of town, the coastal countryside is best to the **north**, although the villages tend to be nonevents. As well as the ubiquitous wind-surfers, the huge flat sands attract hordes of sand-yachters. Among accommodation possibilities, **Coudeville** has a good campsite on its long beach, the two-star *Dunes* (☎02.33.51.76.07; closed Nov–March), and a large (and highly unrecommended) hotel in a converted sanatorium, the *Relais des Îles*.

Eight kilometres south of Granville, **Jullouville** is younger, more upbeat and very tacky, with an endless drag of amusements, fast-food joints and soda bars, while **Carolles** has a good beach, but little more; its one hotel is uninviting. However, in the clifftop village of **Champeaux**, a short steep climb further on from Carolles, the *Hôtel les Hermelles* (☎02.33.61.85.94; closed Tues eve & Wed, plus second half of Nov; ❸), enjoys a truly spectacular view out across the bay, and has a superb restaurant.

Another kilometre downhill, at **St-Jean-Le-Thomas** – which promotes itself as "le Petit Nice de la Manche", but is remarkably *unlike* Nice in that it consists of a single street leading up to a beach – the sea retreats so far at low tide that it's possible to walk across to Mont-St-Michel. However, this is not a walk to take on a drunken, or any other, impulse; as the notices advise, "It's dangerous to risk you in the bay during the rising tide. This can surprise you at each time."

Avranches

AVRANCHES, perched high above the bay on an abrupt granite outcrop, is the nearest large town to Mont-St-Michel. It has always had close connections with the abbey. The Mont's original church was founded by an eighth-century bishop of Avranches, spurred on by the Archangel Michael, who supposedly became so impatient with the lack of progress that he prodded a hole in the bishop's skull (later gold-plated, the skull now forms part of the *trésor* of Avranches's St-Gervais basilica). Robert of Torigny, a subsequent abbot of St-Michel, played host in the town on several occasions to Henry II of England, the most memorable being when Henry – bare-footed and bare-headed – did public penance for the murder of Thomas à Becket, on May 22, 1172. Henry's act of contrition took place in **Avranches Cathedral**. Designed by Robert himself, though without expertise, it eventually "crumbled and fell for want of proper support"; all that now marks the site of Henry's humbling is a fenced-off platform.

A more vivid evocation of the area's medieval splendours comes from the illuminated manuscripts, mostly created on the Mont, on display in the library of the **town hall** close to the tourist office (daily: June & Sept 10am–noon & 2–6pm; July & Aug 10–6pm; €3.10, or €4.60 with municipal museum). If that piques your curiosity, the **municipal museum** nearby, in what was once the bishop's palace, holds a re-creation of a scriptorium where monks would have carried out the laborious study of these manuscripts, as well as archeological finds from the area and more recent local costumes (June–Sept daily 10am–noon & 2–6pm; €2.30).

The ruins of the old **castle** dominate this whole central area of the town; the highest point of all is the former keep, which, together with the vestiges of a small section of ramparts, has been landscaped into a small garden. From the very top, you get long views over Avranches itself, and the Mont away to the west. The terrace of Avranches's large formal public gardens, the **Jardin des Plantes** across town, is another good vantage point for the Mont.

A monument to General George Patton, southeast of the town centre, commemorates the spot where he stayed the night before his crucial Avranches breakthrough, at the end of July 1944. This small plot of land was ceded to the USA, so technically the statue stands on US soil – and literally it does, earth having been brought across the Atlantic to create a memorial garden.

Practicalities

Avranches' **gare SNCF** is a long way below the town centre; the walk up is enough to discourage most rail travellers from stopping here at all. The **tourist office** is located in the central square – scene of a lively market on Thursdays – at 2 place Général-de-Gaulle (July & Aug Mon–Sat 9.30am–12.30pm & 2–7pm, Sun 9.30am–12.30pm & 2–6pm; Sept–June Mon–Fri 9.30am–12.30pm & 2–7pm, Sat & Sun 9.30am–12.30pm & 2–6pm; ⓣ02.33.58.00.22, ⓦwww.ville-avranches.fr). In high summer, one **bus** per day runs to Mont-St-Michel from right outside.

The nicest **hotel** has to be the gloriously old-fashioned *Croix d'Or*, near the Patton monument at 83 rue de la Constitution (ⓣ02.33.58.04.88; closed Jan, plus Sun eve in winter; ❸), which boasts beautiful hydrangea-filled gardens and the best **restaurant** in town. Reasonable alternatives include *Le Jardin des Plantes*, near the Église Notre-Dame des Champs at 10 place Carnot (ⓣ02.33.58.03.68; ⓦwww.le-jardin-des-plantes.fr; ❸), where the restaurant is more basic but very good value. For a quick meal, the *Union*, a busy spot opposite the tourist office at 2 place Littré (ⓣ02.33.58.00.44; closed Sun), serves a tasty *choucroute* and a good-value €10.50 lunch menu.

If you're **camping**, a better base for the Mont than Avranches would be the two-star, English-owned *Vallée de la Sélune* site (ⓣ02.33.60.39.00; closed mid-Oct to March) at **Pontaubault**, 7km to the south.

Mont-St-Michel

The island at the very frontier of Normandy and Brittany, which for over a millennium has housed – indeed, all but consisted of – the stupendous abbey of **MONT-ST-MICHEL**, was once known as "the Mount in Peril from the Sea". Many were the pilgrims in medieval times who were drowned or sucked under by quicksand while trying to cross the bay to this eighty-metre-high rocky outcrop. The Archangel Michael was its vigorous protector, the most militant spirit of the Church Militant, with a marked tendency to leap from rock to rock in titanic struggles against Paganism and Evil.

The abbey dates back to the eighth century, when the archangel appeared to a bishop of Avranches, Aubert, who duly founded a monastery on the island poking out of the Baie du Mont-St-Michel. Since the eleventh century – when work on the sturdy church at the peak commenced – new buildings have been grafted onto the island to produce a fortified hotchpotch of Romanesque and Gothic buildings, piled one on top of the other and clambering to the pinnacle of the graceful church, to form the most recognizable silhouette in France after the Eiffel Tower.

Over the course of its long history, the island has many times been besieged. However, unlike all the rest of northern France, it was never captured, not even during the 27 years, from 1423 to 1450, when the English had a permanent fort on nearby Tombelaine. It took the Revolution to close the monastery down, rename the island "Free Mount", and convert it into a prison. Although the abbey was home to a large community – a fortress town, even at its twelfth-century peak it never housed more than sixty monks, who said Mass

for pilgrims and ran their own school of art. In 1966, exactly a thousand years after Duke Richard the First originally brought the order to the Mont, the Benedictines were invited to return, but they departed again in 2001, having found that the present-day island does not exactly lend itself to a life of quiet contemplation. In their place, a dozen nuns and monks from the Monastic Fraternity of Jerusalem now maintain a presence.

For many years, the Mont has not, strictly speaking, been an island – the causeway (*digue*) that leads to it is never submerged, and is continuing to silt up to either side. Current plans envisage that the causeway will soon be cut away and replaced by a bridge, perhaps with a tram service to spare visitors the two-kilometre walk from the mainland. Currently scheduled for completion in 2009, this should not only make tourist numbers easier to control but also enable the sea to wash away much of the accumulated silt.

Arrival and information

In addition to the regular **bus** service from the nearest *gare SNCF* at Pontorson (see p.181), Les Courriers Bretons (Ⓣ02.99.19.70.80, Ⓦwww.lescourriersbretons.fr) run scheduled services to Mont-St-Michel from the *gare SNCF* in **Rennes** and from **St-Malo**, all arriving in front of the lowest gateway, which is also the location of Mont-St-Michel's **tourist office** (daily: April–June & Sept 9am–12.30pm & 2–6.30pm; July & Aug 9am–7pm; Oct–March 9am–noon & 2–6pm; Ⓣ02.33.60.14.30, Ⓦwww.ot-montsaintmichel.com), and **post office** (Mon–Fri 7am–5.30pm, Sat 9am–4pm). The tourist office offer **currency exchange**, albeit at disadvantageous rates, or there is an **ATM** machine next door.

Visiting Mont-St-Michel

Access to the island of Mont-St-Michel is free and unrestricted, although there's a €4 fee to **park** on either the causeway or the sands below it, from where it's about a 500m walk to the entrance. If you're visiting by car in summer, you might prefer to park on the mainland around 2km short of the Mont, both to enjoy the walk across the causeway and to avoid the dense traffic jams.

Between May and August, the **abbey** is open daily from 9am to 7pm, with last admission at 6pm; from September to April, it's open daily from 9.30am until 6pm, last admission at 5pm. It's closed on Jan 1, May 1, and Dec 25. Paying the standard €7 **admission fee** (ages 18–25 €4.50, under-18s free) entitles you to wander the generally accessible areas, and to join an expert-led **guided tour** in the language of your choice. Tours last 45 minutes between mid-June and mid-Sept, and a full hour the rest of the year; the daily schedule for each language is displayed at the entrance to the abbey and at the tourist office. There are also a number of more detailed two-hour tours, in French only, which take you both higher and deeper (July & Aug daily 10.30am, 11.30am, 2pm & 4pm; Sept–June Sat & Sun 10.30am & 2pm; €4 extra).

In July and August, the Mont typically stays open **after hours**, both in the early evening when visitors are free to stroll in the gardens, and at night when the abbey itself reopens for musical and video installations. At the time of writing, these events were subject to confirmation. Contact the tourist office for the latest information.

Tours

Walking tours across the bay to Mont-St-Michel set off from **Genêts** on a schedule that varies according to the tides. Quite how far you go, and how much time you spend once you get there, changes daily. The standard guided trip, from the beach at Genêts to the Mont and back (a total of 13km), takes 4hr 30min and costs €5.50 without a commentary, while narrated themed tours, aimed at explaining various aspects of the Mont's history or wildlife, are available in English, and can take anything up to ten hours and cost up to €20. Contact Chemins de la Baie (Ⓣ02.33.89.80.88, Ⓦwww.cheminsdelabaie.fr) for a full programme.

Accommodation

The island holds a surprising number of **hotels**, but nothing like enough to cope with the sheer number of visitors. Most are predictably expensive, though virtually all seem to keep a few cheaper rooms (presumably there just isn't the space to refit and expand them in order to put the prices up); all charge extra if you want a view of the sea.

The most famous, *La Mère Poulard* (Ⓣ02.33.89.68.68, Ⓦwww.mere-poulard.com; ❼–❾), uses the time-honoured legend of its fluffy omelettes, as enjoyed by Leon Trotsky and Margaret Thatcher (not simultaneously), to justify extortionate charges. Higher up the Mont, room prices fall to more realistic levels. The cheapest option is the *Du Guesclin* (Ⓣ02.33.60.14.10; ❹), where all the rooms have TV; the nicest is the *Hôtel La Croix Blanche* (Ⓣ02.33.60.14.04; closed mid-Nov to mid-Feb; ❺); and the *Mouton Blanc* (Ⓣ02.33.60.14.08; ❹) falls somewhere in between.

In addition, the main approach road to the island, the D976, is lined shortly before the causeway by around a dozen large and virtually indistinguishable hotels and motels, each with its own brasserie or restaurant. Typical among these are the *Motel Vert* (Ⓣ02.33.60.09.33, Ⓦwww.le-mont-saint-michel.com; closed mid-Nov to mid-Feb; ❷), the *Hôtel Formule Verte* (Ⓣ02.33.60.14.13,

ⓦwww.le-mont-saint-michel.com; closed Nov to mid-Feb; ❸) and the *Hôtel de la Digue* (ⓣ02.33.60.14.02, ⓦwww.ladigue.fr; closed mid-Nov to mid-March; ❹). The three-star, 350-pitch *Camping du Mont-St-Michel* (ⓣ02.33.60.22.10, ⓦwww.le-mont-saint-michel.com; closed Nov to mid-Feb) is also on the mainland just short of the causeway.

For accommodation in nearby Pontorson, see p.181.

The Island

The base of Mont-St-Michel rests on a primeval slime of sand and mud. Just above that, you pass through the heavily fortified **Porte du Roi** onto the narrow **Grande Rue**, climbing steadily around the base of the rock, and lined with medieval gabled houses and a jumble of overpriced postcard and souvenir shops, maintaining the ancient tradition of prising money out of pilgrims. A plaque near the main staircase records that Jacques Cartier was presented to King François I here on May 8, 1532, and charged with exploring the shores of Canada.

The rather dry **Musée Maritime** offers an insight into the island's ties with the sea, while the Archangel Michael manages in just fifteen minutes to lead visitors on a voyage through space and time in the **Archéoscope**, with the full majestic panoply of multimedia trickery. Further along the Grande Rue and up the steps towards the abbey church, next door to the eleventh-century **church of St-Pierre**, the absurd **Musée Grévin** contains such edifying specimens as a wax model of a woman drowning in a sea of mud (all open Feb to mid-Nov daily 9am–6pm; €15 for all, or €7 each one).

Large crowds gather each day at the **North Tower** to watch the tide sweep in across the bay. During the high tides of the equinoxes (March & Sept), the waters are alleged to rush in like a foaming galloping horse. Seagulls wheel away in alarm, and those foolish enough to be wandering too late on the sands toward Tombelaine have to sprint to safety.

Amazingly enough, less than a third of the three million visitors who come to Mont-St-Michel each year climb up to visit the abbey itself, so the higher you go the more the crowds thin out. If you're impatient to escape all the jostling, you can duck through St-Pierre church to reach the **gardens**. From the various footpaths here, popular with picnickers, you can see the giant ramp up the side of the hill, up which prisoners used to haul supplies for the abbey by walking around a treadmill at the top.

The Abbey

The **abbey** (for hours and prices, see box p.179), an architectural ensemble which incorporates the high-spired archangel-topped church and the magnificent Gothic buildings known since 1228 as the **Merveille** ("The Marvel") – incorporating the entire north face, with the cloister, Knights' Hall, Refectory, Guest Hall and cellars – is visible from all around the bay, but it becomes if anything more awe-inspiring the closer you approach. In Maupassant's words:

> **I reached the huge pile of rocks which bears the little city dominated by the great church. Climbing the steep narrow street, I entered the most wonderful Gothic building ever made for God on this earth, a building as vast as a town, full of low rooms under oppressive ceilings and lofty galleries supported by frail pillars. I entered that gigantic granite jewel, which is as delicate as a piece of lacework, thronged with towers and slender belfries which thrust into the blue sky of day and the black sky of night their strange heads bristling with chimeras, devils, fantastic beasts and monstrous flowers, and which are linked together by carved arches of intricate design.**

The Mont's rock comes to a sharp point just below what is now the transept of the **church**, a building where the transition from Romanesque to Gothic is only too evident in the vaulting of the nave. In order to lay out the church's ground plan in the traditional shape of the cross, supporting crypts had to be built up from the surrounding hillside, and in all construction work the Chausey granite has had to be sculpted to match the exact contours of the hill. Space was always limited, and yet the building has grown through the centuries, with an architectural ingenuity that constantly surprises in its geometry – witness the shock of emerging into the light of the **cloisters** from the sombre Great Hall. The statue of St Francis of Assisi here commemorates the fact that 1228, when the cloisters were completed, was the same year that Francis was canonized.

Not surprisingly, the building of the monastery was no smooth progression; the original church, choir, nave and tower all had to be replaced after collapsing. The style of decoration has varied, too, along with the architecture. That you now walk through halls of plain grey stones is a reflection of modern taste, specifically that of the director of the French Department of Antiquities. In the Middle Ages, the walls of public areas such as the refectory would have been festooned with tapestries and frescoes, while the original coloured tiles of the cloisters have long since been stripped away to reveal bare walls.

All visitors exit the abbey on its north side; as you follow the circling footpath back to the mayhem below, you pass beneath what Victor Hugo described as "the most beautiful wall in Europe".

To get a clearer sense of the abbey's historical development, be sure to take a look at the intriguing scale models in the reception area, which depict it during four different epochs.

Eating

Sadly, the **restaurants** on Mont-St-Michel, both independent and in the hotels, are consistently worse than almost anywhere in France. It's impossible to make any confident recommendations, other than ideally you should aim to eat elsewhere – for example, Cancale (see p.243), which has a fabulous selection of restaurants.

Pontorson

Many visitors to Mont-St-Michel find themselves lodging either at Avranches or **PONTORSON**, 6km inland. The latter has the nearest **gare SNCF**, connected to the Mont by regular buses. Nothing much about Pontorson itself is worth staying for, although the café attached to the station isn't bad.

The **hotels** are not especially interesting, but both the *Montgomery*, in a fine old ivy-covered mansion at 13 rue du Couesnon (Ⓣ02.33.60.00.09, Ⓦwww.hotel-montgomery.fr; closed 2 weeks in Feb & Nov; ❹), and the *Bretagne*, just along the main road at 59 rue du Couesnon (Ⓣ02.33.60.10.55, Ⓦwww.lebretagnepontorson.com; closed Feb; ❷), have very distinguished **restaurants**. The *Hôtel de France et Vauban*, 50 bd Clemenceau (Ⓣ02.33.60.03.84, Ⓦwww.hotel-france-vauban.com; ❷), oddly consists of two formerly separate hotels on either side of the level crossing beside the station, while the *Tour Brette*, at the western end of the central drag at 8 rue de Couesnon (Ⓣ02.33.60.10.69; ❷; restaurant closed Wed in low season), is a friendly and inexpensive logis with good lunch menus from €10.50. A renovated **hostel** stands near the cathedral, a kilometre west of the station, in the *Centre Duguesclin* at 21 rue du Général-Patton (Ⓣ02.33.60.18.65, Ⓔaj@ville-pontorson.fr); dorm beds cost €8.70 per night for members, €9.70 for nonmembers.

Along the bay

The most direct **route from Pontorson to the Mont** runs alongside the River Couesnon, which marks the Normandy–Brittany border. The sands at the mouth of the Couesnon are those from which Harold can be seen rescuing two floundering soldiers in the Bayeux Tapestry, in the days when he and William were still getting on with each other. The sheep that graze on the scrubby pastures of the marshes at the sea's edge provide meat for the local delicacy, *mouton pré-salé*.

A more roundabout road to the abbey can take you to the **German war cemetery** at **MONT D'HUISNES**, a grim and unforgettable concrete mausoleum on a tiny hill (see p.152).

Travel details

Trains

Caen to: Cherbourg (10 daily; 1hr 15min), via Bayeux (20min) and Valognes (1hr); Le Mans (5 daily; 2hr), via Argentan (45min) and Alençon (1hr 15min); Lisieux (21 daily; 30min); Paris-St-Lazare (11 daily; 2hr 10min); Rennes (4 daily; 3hr), via Bayeux (20min), St-Lô (50min), Coutances (1hr 15min) and Pontorson (2hr); Rouen (6 daily; 2hr); Tours (1 daily; 3hr).
Cherbourg to: Paris (8 daily; 3hr) via Valognes (15min) and Caen (1hr 15min).
Coutances to: Caen (6 daily; 1hr 15min) with connections to Paris; Lison (12 daily; 45min) via St-Lô (15min), with connections for Cherbourg.
Dives-Cabourg to: Trouville-Deauville (July & Aug 6 daily, rest of year 2 daily Sun & national hols only; 30min) via Houlgate (6min) and Villers (20min).
Granville to: Coutances (7 daily; 30min).
Trouville-Deauville to: Lisieux (6 daily in winter, much more frequently in summer; 20min); Paris (6 daily in winter, much more frequently in summer; 2hr).

Buses

Bayeux to: Arromanches (4 daily; 30min); Courseulles (4 daily; 40min); Grandcamp-Maisy (6 daily; 1hr); Ouistreham (3 daily; 1hr 15min); Port-en-Bessin (5 daily; 20min).
Caen to: Arromanches (1 daily; 1hr 10min); Bayeux (3 daily; 50min); Clécy (4 daily; 50min); Falaise (7 daily; 1hr); Honfleur (13 daily; 2hr) via Cabourg (50min), Houlgate (1hr) and Deauville (1hr 15min), of which 5 continue to Le Havre (2hr 30min); Le Havre (3 daily express services; 1hr 40min) via Honfleur (1hr); Luc-sur-mer (12 daily; 40min); Ouistreham (20 daily; 30min); Pont-L'Évêque (3 daily; 1hr 10min); Thury-Harcourt (5 daily; 40min); Vire (connections for Brittany; 3 daily; 1hr 30min).
Cherbourg to: St-Lô (3 daily; 1hr 45min) via Valognes (30min) and Carentan (1hr); St-Vaast (2–3 daily; 1hr) via Barfleur (45min).
Mont-St-Michel to: St-Malo (4 daily; 1hr 30min); Rennes (5 daily; 1hr 20min).

Ferries

Caen (Ouistreham) to: Portsmouth (2–3 daily; 6hr) with Brittany Ferries (☎08.03.82.88.28, Ⓦwww.brittany-ferries.com).
Cherbourg to: Poole (1–3 daily; 2hr 15min–4hr 30min), with Brittany Ferries; Rosslare (2–3 weekly; 19hr 30min), with Irish Ferries (☎02.33.23.44.44, Ⓦwww.irishferries.com).
Granville to: Jersey and Sark (1–2 daily; 1hr–1hr 50min) with Hugo Express (☎02.33.61.08.88) and to the Îles Chausey (1–2 daily; 50min) with Jolie France (☎02.33.50.31.81) and Compagnie Corsaire (☎08.25.16.80.50, Ⓦwww.compagniecorsaire.com).

Inland Normandy

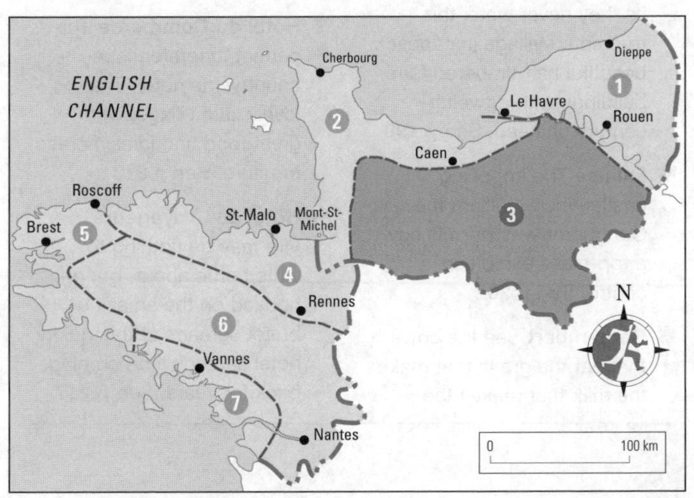

3 INLAND NORMANDY

CHAPTER 3

Highlights

* **Abbaye de Bec-Hellouin** One of the most venerable monasteries in Christendom sets the tone for an idyllic rural valley. See p.194
* **Crèvecoeur-en-Auge** Evoking the Middle Ages as they never were, this re-created village juxtaposes beautiful half-timbered farm buildings with a twelfth-century château. See p.199
* **Falaise** The imposing castle where William the Conqueror was born is now a top-class exhibition centre. See p.202
* **Camembert** See the cows that eat the grass that make the milk that makes the cheese that made the name of Normandy. See p.203
* **Le Pin-au-Haras** If you love horses, you won't be able to resist the French National Stud, laid out in the eighteenth century. See p.205
* **Hôtel du Commerce** The perfect, unpretentious countryside hotel, in a lovely little village, with great food and idiosyncratic furniture. See p.213
* **Hôtel des Voyageurs** Vire may be nothing to write home about, but get hooked on the amazing buffet spreads at this quirky hotel and you'll be coming back for years. See p.217

△ Camembert Village

3

Inland Normandy

Specific highlights are hard to pin down in **inland Normandy**. The pleasures lie not so much in show-stopping sights, or individual towns, as in the feel of the landscape – the lush meadows, orchards and forests of the Norman countryside. On top of that, of course, there's the **food**, always a major draw in these rich dairy regions. To the French, the **Pays d'Auge**, **Calvados** and the **Suisse Normande** are synonymous with cheeses, creams, apple and pear brandies, and ciders.

However, the territory is not devoid of other sensory pursuits. There are spas, forests, rivers and lakes for lazing or stretching the muscles in, and, everywhere, classic half-timbered houses and farm buildings. If you are staying on the Norman coast, trips inland – even just ten to twenty kilometres – will pay dividends, while if you arrive at a Norman port intending to head straight for Brittany or southern France you may find yourself tempted to linger, or at least to take a circuitous route.

Travelling from **east to west**, you pass through a succession of distinct regions. **South of the Seine**, a natural target from Le Havre, Dieppe or Rouen, lie the **river valleys** of the **Eure**, **Risle** and **Charentonne**. While certain areas – especially along the Charentonne – have been disfigured by industrial development, the valleys remain for the most part rural and verdant. The occasional château, castle ruin or abbey provides a focus, most memorably at **Bec-Hellouin**, near Brionne, and at the country town of **Conches**. Further south lie the wooded hills and valleys of **the Perche**, home of the mighty Percheron horse and also of the original Trappists (see p.190).

Following the rivers northwest, on the other hand, as they flow towards the sea near Honfleur or Cabourg, brings you into the classic cheese and cider country of the **Pays d'Auge**, all rolling pastoral hills, grazing meadows and orchards. **Livarot**, **Pont-l'Évêque** and **Camembert** here are renowned throughout the world for their cheeses, while **Lisieux**, as the home barely a century ago of Ste Thérèse, has become one of the major pilgrimage towns of France. To the **south** of the Pays d'Auge extend the forests of the **Parc Naturel Régional de Normandie-Maine**, with the sedate and famous spa at **Bagnoles** and the national stud at **Le Pin**.

Further west, on the routes inland from either Caen or Cherbourg and the Cotentin, there is something of a shift. Around Thury-Harcourt and stretching south to Pont-d'Ouilly and Putanges is the area dubbed the **Suisse Normande**, for its "alpine" valleys and thick woods; fine walking country, if not genuinely mountainous. To its west, the **Bocage** begins with grim memories of war around **St-Lô** – this was the main 1944 invasion route – but subsides into a pastoral scene once more as you hit the gastronomic centres of the **Vire**.

South from the Seine

South across the Seine from Rouen lies the long and featureless **Neubourg plain** – intensive agricultural land where the crumbling barns, Tudor-style houses and occasional grazing horses look oddly out of place. It's not an area where you can expect to find hidden charms, and the first sizeable town you come to, war-ravaged **Évreux**, provides little incentive to stop. Most visitors choose instead to press on as far as the attractive medieval towns of **Conches**, with its snug surrounding of forest, and **Verneuil**.

While regular **buses** link Rouen with Évreux, elsewhere public transport is at a minimum, and you'll need a car or bicycle to make the most of the region.

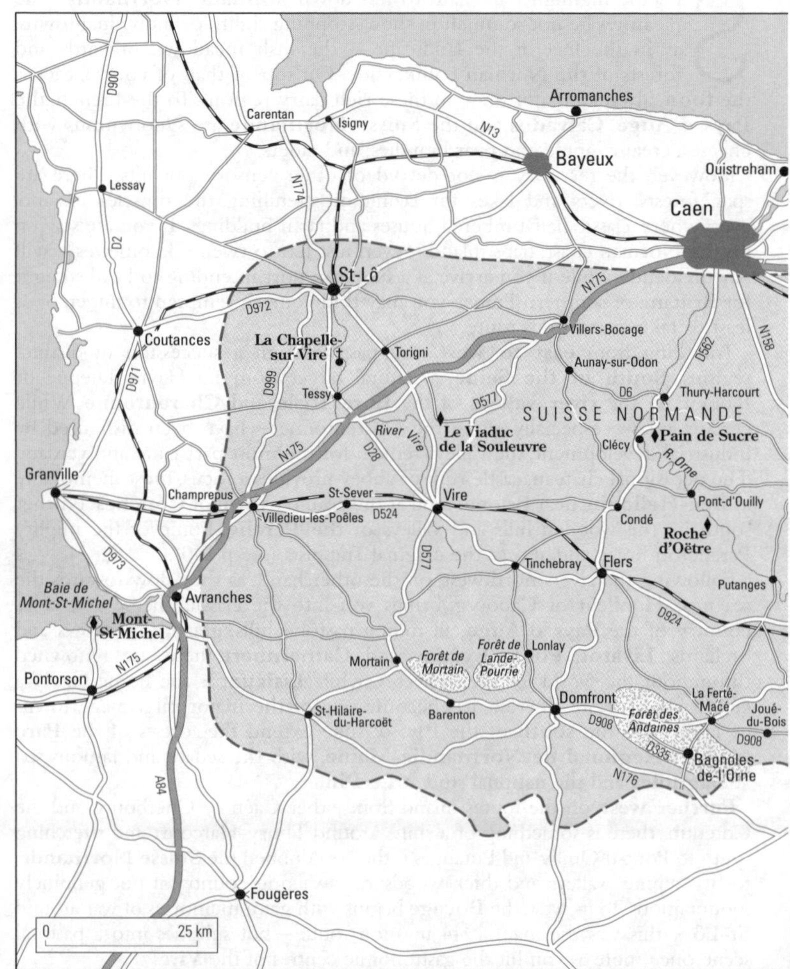

Le Neubourg

The only town of any size on the Neubourg plain is **LE NEUBOURG** itself, which blows any possibility of being charming by festooning its streets with deafening loudspeakers. It holds little of interest to the traveller, but, 5km northwest on the D83, the seventeenth-century **Château du Champ-de-Bataille**, with its dramatic entrance arch, is worth a look (April & Oct Sat & Sun 2–6pm; May–Sept daily 2–6pm; €6).

If you do need to spend the night here, Le Neubourg does at least offer a good **hotel-restaurant**, the central logis *Au Grand St-Martin*, at 68 rue de la République (Ⓣ02.32.35.04.80; ❸), where sumptuous menus start at €15.

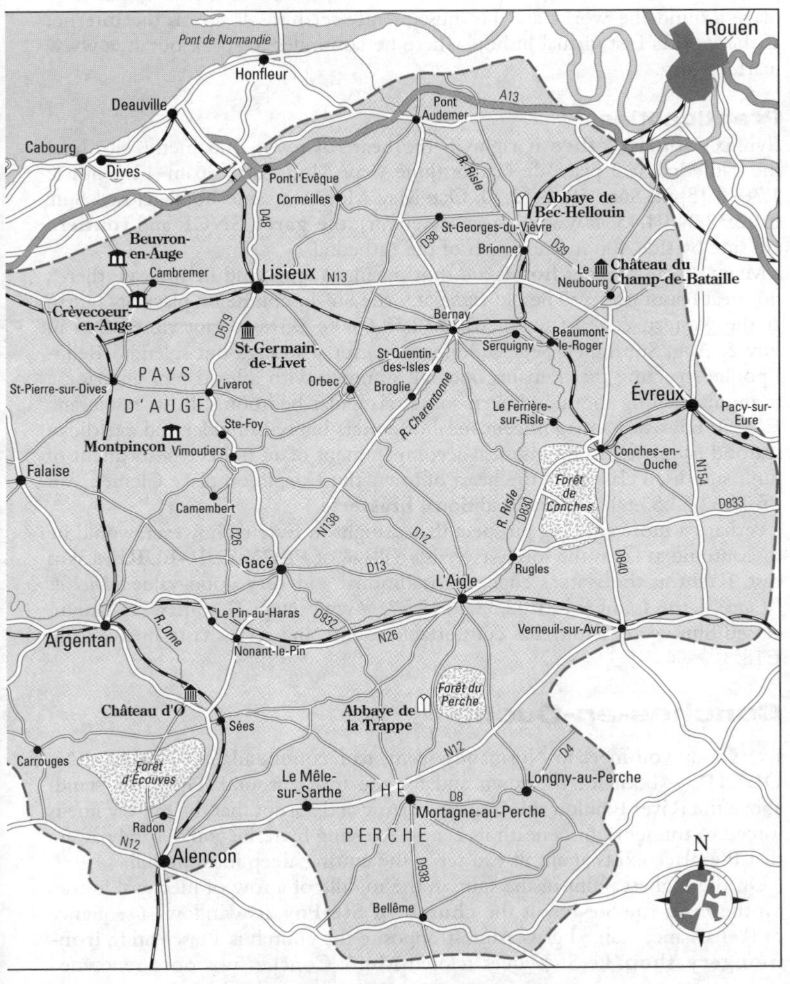

Évreux

Twenty kilometres south of Le Neubourg you come to **ÉVREUX**, which is capital of the Eure *département*, despite not being on the Eure River itself. It's an extremely venerable place that throughout history has suffered violent reversals of fortune – as early as the fifth century, its affluent Gaulish community made an inviting target for rampaging Vandals.

Bombing raids by both sides during World War II reduced much of the city to rubble, however, and Évreux today is disconcertingly lifeless. Even so, an afternoon's wander in the vicinity of the **cathedral** – a minor classic with its flamboyant exterior decoration and original fourteenth-century windows – and along the ramparts by the Iton riverbank is pleasant enough. In 1995, Évreux's bishop, Jacques Gaillot, was dismissed by the pope for his advocacy of the use of condoms to prevent AIDS, and his statement that "homosexuals will precede us into the kingdom of heaven". Demonstrations on his behalf took place around the world, and he subsequently set himself up on the Internet as the world's first virtual bishop, where he continues to speak out at Ⓦwww.partenia.org.

Practicalities

Évreux's **tourist office** is right in the heart of town, 300 metres north of the cathedral at 3 place de Gaulle (June–Sept Mon–Sat 9.30am–12.30pm & 1.30–6.15pm, Sun 10am–12.30; Oct–May Mon–Sat same hours, closed Sun; Ⓣ02.32.24.04.43, Ⓦwww.ot-pays-evreux.fr); the **gares SNCF** and **routière** are side by side 400 metres south of the cathedral.

Many of the cheaper **hotels** are shut during August, and in any case there's no great reason to stay. The old *Biche*, at 9 rue Ste-Joséphine on place St-Taurin at the western edge of town (Ⓣ02.32.38.66.00; ❷; restaurant closed Sun in July & Aug, Sun lunch Sept–June), is, however, a strange but splendid Belle-Époque structure that remains open all summer, with a lurid pink interior, a triangular dining room and even some triangular bedrooms. In its restaurant, €22.50 buys you a magnificent meal of oysters braised in cider and a garlicky seafood *pot-au-feu*, to the musical accompaniment of an unlikely assortment of funk and disco classics. In the heart of town, the *Français* on place Clemenceau (Ⓣ02.32.33.53.60) is a fine traditional **brasserie**.

Perhaps a more enticing prospect than a night in Évreux, however, would be to continue as far as the lovely riverside village of **PACY-SUR-EURE**, 13km east. Right at the water's edge, the traditional and very good-value *Hôtel de l'Étape*, 1 rue Isambard (Ⓣ02.32.36.12.77, Ⓦwww.etape27.com; ❸; restaurant closed Sun eve & Mon), has comfortable rooms, and serves tasty menus from €18.

Conches-en-Ouche

Everybody you meet in Normandy seems to recommend **CONCHES-EN-OUCHE** – both for the town and for the forest around. The town stands above the River Rouloir on a spur so narrow and abrupt that the railway line is forced to tunnel right beneath its centre. Arriving by train, you're barely aware that the place exists at all; all you see is the cutting, deep into the hill.

On the highest point of the spur, in the middle of a row of medieval houses on the main rue Ste-Foy, is the **church of Ste-Foy**, its windows a sequence of Renaissance stained glass. Almost opposite the church is a fascinating **iron-mongery shop**, Le St-Jacques (closed Mon); Conches was once renowned for its metal foundries, which cast the iron spire of Rouen Cathedral in 1876, but the shop is the only vestige of that heritage you're likely to encounter. It's a building with an unlikely secret; descend the stone spiral staircase in the back room, and you'll find yourself in a labyrinth of eleventh-century cellars that extends under most of its neighbours.

Behind the church, in the gardens of the **Hôtel de Ville**, a robust, if anatomically odd, stone boar gazes proudly out over a spectacular view, raising its eyes to the horizon far beyond the sewage works. Next to the Hôtel de Ville, you can scramble up the slippery steps of the ruined twelfth-century **castle**, one of the many haunts of the ubiquitous Bertrand du Guesclin (see Contexts) and twice captured by the English during the Hundred Years War. Such sights ensure that Conches remains firmly rooted in the past, but the town is given an added contemporary flavour, too, by the pieces of modern sculpture that you come upon around seemingly every corner.

On the other side of the main road from the castle, you'll find a long and subtly formal **park**, with parallel avenues of trees, a large ornamental lake and fountain.

Practicalities

Conches' **tourist office**, close to the castle 200m south of the church in place Aristide-Briand (July & Aug Tues–Sat 10am–12.30pm & 2–6pm, Sun 10am–noon; Sept–June same hours, closed Sun & Mon; ⓣ02.32.30.76.42, ⓦwww.conches-en-ouche.fr), rents out mountain **bikes** by the hour or day. The best **accommodation** option is *Le Cygne*, a Logis de France at 2 rue Paul Guilbaud at the north end of town (ⓣ02.32.30.20.60; ❸; closed Sun eve & Mon). There's also a two-star **municipal campsite**, *La Forêt* (ⓣ02.32.30.22.49; closed Oct–March). The *Grand'Mare* is a classy **restaurant** in a green and quiet location beside the park at 13 avenue Croix de Fer (ⓣ02.32.30.23.30), serving a good €20 menu; the *Bistro* in the same building is a less formal place to have lunch. On Thursday the whole town is taken up by a **market**

The Forêt de Conches

The wild and open woodland of the **Forêt de Conches**, which stretches southwest of Conches, is very popular with hikers and **horse-riders**. The Village Equestre de Conches (ⓣ02.32.30.22.56) which caters specifically for young riders up to the age of eighteen, is based in the hamlet of Le Fresne, 1km east of town.

If you feel the need for a direction in your wanderings around Conches, head for the village of **LA FERRIÈRE-SUR-RISLE**, a stately array of old buildings around a spacious central square that holds both a beautiful **church**, with a garish altar but some fine wooden statues, and a restored fourteenth-century covered **market hall**. Paddocks and meadows lead down to the river, while on the quiet square you'll find a small and inviting **hotel**, the *Vieux-Marché* (ⓣ02.32.30.25.93; ❶), with a daily set menu at €10.

Verneuil-sur-Avre

Southwest of Conches, the towns of Rugles and L'Aigle are both industrial and uninteresting. However, 25km due south on the D840 you come to the pretty little hilltop town of **VERNEUIL-SUR-AVRE**. While now marking nothing more significant than the transition from the Ouche to the Perche, this was, during the Hundred Years War, a crucial fortified outpost between (English-held) Normandy and France proper. Traces of its former ramparts and deep moat can still be seen along boulevard Casati on the west side of town, while the three main streets and numerous alleyways are lined with venerable half-timbered houses.

As you approach along the arrow-straight D840 from the north, the solid bell tower of **La Madeleine** is perfectly framed for several kilometres' distance by the avenue of trees. The actual church of La Madeleine, to which it is somewhat inelegantly attached, stands in the main square, completely dwarfed by the belfry. Owing to damage incurred during the major storm of December 1999, it's not currently possible to go up the tower.

Following the pedestrian lanes that lead away from the square will bring you out at the **Notre Dame** church in the southeast, built of crude red agglomerate stone in the twelfth century, or to the sixteenth-century **Tour St-Jean** to the southwest, a former church spire separated by wartime bombing from its Gothic porch.

Practicalities

Verneuil's **gare SNCF**, five minutes' walk north of the centre, is served by four daily trains from Paris. The local **tourist office** is at no.129 on the main place de la Madeleine (May–Sept Mon 2–6pm, Tues–Fri 10am–noon & 2–6pm, Sat & Sun 10am–noon & 2.30–6pm; Oct–April Mon & Tue–Fri same hours, Sat 10am–noon only, closed Sun; ⓣ02.32.32.17.17).

Virtually next door to the tourist office, the cream-coloured **hotel** *Le Saumon*, 89 place de la Madeleine (ⓣ02.32.32.02.36, ⓦwww.hoteldusaumon.fr; ❸; closed Sun eve Nov–March), which glows an inviting pink at sunset, offers well-equipped and comfortable rooms at very reasonable rates. A tankful of live lobsters nervously await patrons of the more expensive menus; in mid-week especially, the lower-priced menus are very good value, though you need to spend at least €25 to be sure of avoiding a surfeit of innards. The *Hostellerie Le Clos*, 98 rue de la Ferté-Vidame (ⓣ02.32.32.21.81; ❽; closed mid-Dec to mid-Jan), a bizarre little château near the Notre Dame church, has an even better restaurant and phenomenally expensive rooms. The best stand-alone **restaurant** in town is the half-timbered *Grand Sultan*, tucked in behind La Madeleine at 30 rue de la Poissonnerie (ⓣ02.32.32.13.14; closed Mon), where traditional menus start at €15.50.

Nine kilometres southwest of Verneuil is the glass-covered dome of a family holiday complex, the *Hôtel-Résidence du Lac*, run by **Center Parcs** (ⓣ08.25.80.28.04), which insists on a three-night minimum booking with rates from €230 to €435 for a chalet.

The Perche

All roads south of Verneuil start to undulate alarmingly as you enter the region known as the **Perche**, which lies within the *département* of Orne. This offers some of Normandy's most bucolically appealing countryside, with green valleys nestled between heavily forested hills. Despite its apparent fertility, however, it has never been a particularly rich area: in the seventeenth century, times were hard enough for a large proportion of the population to emigrate to Canada. It's well known for the mighty **Percheron horses**, the strongest workhorses in the world, while its remoteness and seclusion made it an ideal home for the first **Trappist** monks, who took their name from the Forêt de la Trappe.

The Trappists

The **Abbaye de la Trappe** is set in open rolling fields on the fringes of the Forêt de la Trappe – a minor western appendage of the Forêt du Perche – just beyond a popular fishing lake and 10km north of Mortagne. This was the original home of one of the world's most famous – yet deliberately self-effacing, and consistently misunderstood – Christian monastic orders. Although the abbey was founded in the thirteenth century, and suffered the vicissitudes of the Hundred Years War, it was not until the reforms instigated by the **Abbé Rancé** in 1664 that its monks began to follow the principles for which the Trappists are known today. The Abbé reacted against the excesses of his time by setting out to re-create the lives of the "**Desert Fathers**" of the first few centuries after Christ, who lived in contemplative isolation in the Sinai, and to follow St Benedict's precept that true monks should live by the labour of their own hands.

The monks were driven out by the Revolution, successively to Switzerland, Poland, Russia and as far as the United States, but succeeded in returning to their utterly devastated abbey in 1815, still under the leadership of Dom Augustin l'Estrange – which made them the only order of monks in France not to be wiped out.

The abbey as it exists today is entirely a nineteenth-century creation. The monks live communally – they don't have individual cells – and not literally in the absolute silence of popular myth, but speaking only for the necessities of work and community life and spending the rest of their time in quiet reflection. Not surprisingly, tourists are not encouraged to disturb them, but anyone with a genuine interest can watch a video in a reception room beside the main entrance. There's also an unusual **shop** (Mon–Sat 10.30am–noon & 2–5.30pm, Sun after 10am Mass until noon & 2–5.30pm) which sells all things monk-made: herbal teas, muesli, metal polish, shampoo, furniture wax – even local *boudin* (a pork blood sausage) and coffee grown in Cameroon.

Mortagne-au-Perche

MORTAGNE-AU-PERCHE, the largest town of the Perche region, stands on a hill set in the heart of the forests. Although it has lost virtually all of its fortifications, it remains an appealing country town, with a pleasant ensemble of stone town houses. The one part of the ramparts to survive is the **Porte St-Denis**, a fifteenth-century arch topped in the sixteenth century by two ordinary storeys of rooms that now contain an exhibition about Percheron horses (mid–June to mid–Sept Tues–Sat 3–6pm; free).

Mortagne's liveliest square is the **place de Gaulle**, where the nineteenth-century market hall has been imaginatively converted into a cinema, with some postmodern spiral staircases attached to either side. Nearby stands an unusual modern fountain, looking like an open mummy case made of copper. If you cross from here through the main gates of the Hôtel de Ville to reach the flower-filled gardens around the back, which are filled with sculpture old and new, you can enjoy fine views over the Perche hills.

Practicalities

Mortagne's former market hall, described above, is also the site of the local **tourist office** (mid-May to mid-June & last fortnight of Sept Tues–Sat 9am–12.30pm & 2.30–6pm; mid-June to mid-Sept Mon 10am–12.30pm & 2.30–6pm, Tues–Sat 9am–12.30pm & 2.30–6pm, Sun 10am–12.30pm; Oct to mid-May Tues–Sat 10am–12.30pm & 3–6pm; Ⓣ02.33.85.11.18, Ⓦwww.officemortagne61.fr.st). The nicest **hotel** in town has to be the *Hôtel du*

Tribunal, a *logis* on the sleepy little tree-lined place du Palais (Ⓣ02.33.25.04.77, Ⓔhotel.du.tribunal@wanadoo.fr; ❸), which consists of two or three old stone buildings with a few exposed timbers, crammed together on the corner of an alleyway leading to Porte St-Denis. This is where Yves Montand chose to stay when filming locally; the comfortable bedrooms are in an annexe at the back, while the restaurant at the front has a reasonable €17 menu and gets exotic if you pay more, with such dishes as scallops in orange butter.

The *Genty-Home*, just off place de la République at 4 rue Notre-Dame (Ⓣ02.33.25.11.53; ❸; closed Sun eve & Mon), has a handful of very plush rooms upstairs and a couple of restaurants; the less formal *Grillade* downstairs, and another upstairs serving traditional menus costing up to €30. Both offer Mortagne's speciality – the black *boudin noir*, a crumbly black pudding or blood sausage with a healthy dose of fat and tripe thrown in.

By far the nicest **campsite** in the vicinity of Mortagne is the year-round *Camping Monaco Parc* (Ⓣ02.33.73.59.59), in a gorgeous wooded valley roughly 15km east of town outside **Longny-au-Perche**, which has a huge, opulent swimming pool.

Bellême

Tiny **BELLÊME**, 17km due south of Mortagne on the switchback D938, is actually the capital of the Perche despite being very much smaller. In many ways it's more attractive, too, crammed so tightly onto the top of a sharp hill that the views are consistently superb. Like Mortagne, hardly anything survives of the fortifications that once ringed the very crest of the hill. The one exception is the forbiddingly thick **Porche** – now the home of the local library, but still equipped to take a portcullis if things turn bad – reached by an alleyway leading off from a corner of the place de la République near the St-Sauveur church.

Practicalities

The grand white facade of Bellême's best **hotel**, the *Relais St-Louis*, 1 bd Bansard des Bois (Ⓣ02.33.73.12.21; ❹; closed Sun eve & Mon), may be in a slight state of disrepair, but it's elegant enough inside, and the seven guest rooms are even spacious enough to boast proper armchairs. The light dining room downstairs, serving menus from €15 to €33, looks out on one side to a flowery garden, and across the town's diminutive ring road on the other to a small vestige of moat overlooked by an imposing eighteenth-century mansion. There's also a tiny two-star municipal **campsite**, *Le Val*, on the edge of town (Ⓣ02.33.85.31.00; closed mid-Oct to mid-April).

The local **tourist office** (Mon & Sun 2–6.30pm, Tues–Sat 9.30am–12.30 & 2–6.30pm; Ⓣ02.33.73.09.69, Ⓔtourisme.belleme@wanadoo.fr), all but next door to the *Relais St-Louis*, doubles appealingly as the headquarters of the adjoining miniature golf course. It can also provide details of Bellême's annual five-day **Mycology Festival**, held at the end of each September to celebrate the more obscure mushrooms of the surrounding forests.

The Charentonne and the Risle

The **River Risle** drains down from the Ouche region, north of the Perche, and passes initially through traditional and now very faded ironworking towns such as L'Aigle. Roughly 30km northwest of Conches, it's joined by a fast-flowing tributary, the **Charentonne**. In the area to either side of the confluence, and from then on northwards as the newly strengthened Risle heads towards the sea near Honfleur, there are several small riverside towns worth visiting.

Broglie

The southernmost town of any size along the Charentonne is **BROGLIE**, pronounced *Broy*, 12km east of Orbec (see p.200). The impressive private **château** that stands on the brow of the hill above Broglie is the ancestral home of the de Broglie family. Its last but one owner, Prince Louis, won the Nobel Physics Prize for demonstrating that matter, like light, has wavelike properties. His work – to "seek the last hiding places of reality", as he put it – subsequently formed the foundation of the whole discipline of quantum mechanics. Originally a medieval historian, Louis was supposed to have been attracted to his great theory "purely on the grounds of intellectual beauty".

Across Broglie's charming little central square, the place des Trois Maréchaux, from the half-Roman, half-Gothic church of **St-Martin**, the local **tourist office** (May to mid-Oct Tues–Fri 3–6pm Sat 10.30am–12.30pm & 3–6pm, Sun 9.30am–12.30pm; ⓣ02.32.46.27.52) can offer several useful maps and brochures detailing cycling and sightseeing tours of the region. The town does not, however, currently have either a hotel or a campsite.

Downstream from Broglie

Immediately downstream from Broglie, the Charentonne sprawls between its banks on a wide flood plain. It is classic inland Normandy, uneventful and totally scenic; the one flaw in the whole thing is the unseemly preponderance of porcelain donkeys in people's front gardens.

Not far short of Bernay, a couple of kilometres north of **ST-QUENTIN-DES-ISLES** on the D33, the sixteenth-century riverside windmill *Moulin Fouret* (ⓣ02.32.43.19.95; ❸; closed Sun eve & Mon), is primarily a **restaurant**, with two pricey menus for €30 or €60, but also has a few **rooms**, making it the nicest place to stay in the vicinity.

Bernay

As you approach **BERNAY**, 11km northeast of Broglie, more and more factories and warehouses line both sides of the river. The town itself, however, has a few humpback footbridges and picturesque half-timbered old streets interspersed between the more serious traffic routes, and one of those churches typical of the region with a spire that looks like a stack of inverted octagonal ice-cream cones. After extensive restoration work, you can now admire the impressive Romanesque twelfth-century **abbey church** (mid-June to mid-Sept Tues–Sun 10am–noon & 2–7pm; mid-Sept to mid-June 2–5.30pm; €3.20).

Bernay has few other claims to renown, though Edith Piaf lived here as a child, and a local baker found fame for *running* each stage of the Tour de France during the night before the cyclists raced over it. The *Lion d'Or*, at 48 rue Général-de-Gaulle (ⓣ02.32.43.12.06, ⓔhotelliondor@wanadoo.fr; ❸), is a conventional, good-quality **hotel-restaurant** in the heart of town, while the municipal **campsite** is a short way southwest (ⓣ02.32.43.30.47; closed mid-Sept to mid-May).

Beaumont-le-Roger

BEAUMONT-LE-ROGER is set beside the Risle 25km northwest of Conches and 17km east of Bernay, shortly before the Risle meets the Charentonne. Its ruined thirteenth-century priory **church** is gradually crumbling to the ground, the slow restoration of one or two arches unable to keep pace. Little happens in the village beyond the hourly hammering of the church bell – next door to the abbey – by a nodding musketeer; and with each passing hour, the ruins crumble a little more. Just across the Risle from here, on the D25 near Le Val-St-Martin, huge **stables** are spread across an almost absurdly sylvan setting, and horses are available for hire (ⓣ02.32.45.23.25; closed Mon).

Beaumont-le-Roger is not exactly an exciting place to stay, but it is home to a sixteenth-century **coaching inn** with some quiet courtyard rooms – the *Lion d'Or*, 91 rue St-Nicolas (ⓣ02.32.46.54.24; ❸) – and also a top-quality and very friendly **restaurant**, *La Calèche*, nearby at 54 rue St-Nicolas (ⓣ02.32.45.25.99; closed Tues & Wed), which offers menus from €17.

At **SERQUIGNY**, not only the two rivers but also several roads and rail lines converge, and the banks are once again briefly industrial, clogged with factories and fumes.

Brionne

The small town of **BRIONNE**, 10km north of Serquigny and the first stop on the rail line to Rouen, plays host to large regional **markets** on Tuesday and Sunday. The fish hall is on the left bank; the rest by the church on the right bank. Above them both, with panoramic views, is a **donjon**, or old castle keep, spotlit by the setting sun. Should you decide to climb up the hill to reach it, you'll find a *table d'orientation* with arrows pointing out local landmarks.

Brionne holds two good but pretty expensive **hotels** which also contain excellent restaurants: the lovely old half-timbered *Auberge du Vieux Donjon*, facing the marketplace at 19 rue de la Soie (ⓣ02.32.44.80.62, ⓦwww.auberge-vieux-donjon.com; ❸; closed Mon, plus Sun eve in low season & last fortnight in Oct), where the food is significantly better than the accommodation, and the much more modern *Logis de Brionne*, close to the *gare SNCF* but a long way west of the centre at 1 place St-Denis (ⓣ02.32.44.81.73, ⓔlelogisdebrionne@free.fr; ❹; closed second half of Feb & first half of Aug).

The Abbaye de Bec-Hellouin

Following the Risle on towards Honfleur and the sea, the **D39** is lined with perfect timbered farmhouses. Four kilometres from Brionne, the size and tranquil setting of the **ABBAYE DE BEC-HELLOUIN** give a monastic feel to the whole valley. Bells echo between the hills and white-robed monks go soberly about their business. From the eleventh century onwards, the abbey was one of the most important centres of intellectual learning in the Christian world; an intimate association with the court of William the Conqueror meant that three of its early abbots – Lanfranc, the philosopher Anselm, and Theobald – became archbishops of Canterbury. Recent archbishops of Canterbury have maintained tradition by coming here on retreat.

Owing to the Revolution, most of the monastery buildings are relatively new – the monks only returned in 1948 – but there are some survivals and appealing clusters of stone ruins, and fragments of medieval lettering are still visible on the solitary tower, topped by a beehive spire. Visitors are welcome to wander through the grounds for no charge (daily 8am–9pm), though if you want to understand what you're seeing it's best to join one of the regular **guided tours** (June–Sept Mon & Wed–Sat 10am, 11am, 3pm, 4pm & 5pm, Sun & hols noon, 3pm, 3.30pm, 4pm & 6pm; Oct–May Mon & Wed–Sat 11am, 3.15pm & 4.30pm, Sun & hols noon, 3pm & 4pm; €4.60; Ⓦwww.abbayedubec.com).

The tiny and rather twee adjacent village of **Bec-Hellouin** has a **museum of mechanical music**, visitable on 45-minute guided tours only (April, May & Sept daily 3pm, 4pm & 5pm; June–Aug daily 3pm, 4pm, 5pm & 6pm; €4.60). There are also a couple of **restaurants**; the ivy-covered *Canterbury* (Ⓣ02.32.44.14.59; closed Sun eve, Tues eve, Wed & all Feb), which serves regional specialities on menus from €13.57 up to €31.25, and the rather cheaper *Restaurant de la Tour* on place Guillaume-le-Conquérant (Ⓣ02.32.44.86.15; closed Wed eve & Thurs, plus two weeks in Nov), which has some outdoor tables.

Pont-Audemer

Continuing north, the last major crossing point over the Risle is at **PONT-AUDEMER**, where medieval houses lean out at alarming angles over the crisscrossing roads, rivers and canals. It's an attractive little place, the scene of busy markets on Mondays and Fridays. Inexpensive rooms can be found at the basic riverside *Hôtel de l'Agriculture* at 84 rue de la République (Ⓣ02.32.41.01.23; ❶; closed Sun eve in winter). Across the river from there, the *Erawan*, 4 rue de la Seule (Ⓣ02.32.41.12.03; closed Wed), must be Normandy's only traditional half-timbered Thai **restaurant**, with a €19.80 set menu.

From Pont-Audemer you have the choice of making for the sea at Honfleur (see p.130), passing some tottering Giacometti-style barns on the way to St-Georges-du-Vièvre 15km or so to the south along the thickly wooded valleys of the D38, or going on towards the Seine. If you plan to cycle north across the Forêt de Brotonne towards Caudebec, be warned that, to discourage motorists from spoiling the nicest part of the forest, the road signs direct you the long way round via La Mailleraye.

Pont-l'Évêque

There was little left after the war of the old **PONT-L'ÉVÊQUE**, 35km west of Pont-Audemer and technically the northernmost town of the Pays d'Auge (see p.196). One or two ancient houses remain, most notably along rue St-Michel where some have been repainted in the bright colours of the middle ages, but the town as a whole has become such a turmoil of major roads it seems a rather odd place to linger in for too long.

A couple of kilometres south of town on the D48, an impressive medieval barn at the twelfth-century Château de Betteville is home to a **vintage car museum**, while there's a karting circuit laid out in the grounds (daily: April–June & Sept 10am–12.30pm & 1.30–7pm; July & Aug 10am–7pm; Oct to mid-Nov 2–6pm; €6). Immediately opposite, the *Hôtel-Restaurant Eden Park* (Ⓣ02.31.64.64.00, Ⓦwww.edenparkhotel.com; ❸), is a large new Logis de France, housed in a sprawling complex of buildings beside its own lake, that makes an ideal overnight stop for families.

Cormeilles

The village of **CORMEILLES**, 17km southeast of Pont-l'Évêque, makes a more appealing destination for a day out, having been left relatively unscathed by fighting. Each Friday sees a **market** in its tiny centre, and there are several half-timbered restaurants scattered around.

On the southern edge of town, the *Auberge du Président*, 70 rue de l'Abbaye (Ⓣ02.32.57.80.37; ❸; closed Wed eve in low season), is an efficient hybrid, featuring motel-style rooms around the back and a very traditional, formal and good plush-velvet restaurant in the old building facing the street, with menus from €16.

The Pays d'Auge

The pastures of the **Pays d'Auge**, the region that extends south from the ancient cathedral city of **Lisieux** – itself now almost entirely preoccupied with the cult of Ste Thérèse – are the lushest in all of Normandy, renowned for producing the world-famous cheeses of Camembert, Livarot and Pont-l'Évêque. Its rolling hills and green twisting valleys are scattered with magnificent half-timbered manor houses. Each sprawling farm is liable to consist of a succession of such "Tudor" (in fact the Norman tradition predates the English) treasures, each family house, as it becomes too dilapidated to live in, being converted for use as a barn, and replaced by a new one built alongside. In addition to grazing land, the area has acres of orchards, which yield the best of Norman ciders, both apple and pear (*poiré*), as well as Calvados apple brandy.

Much of the appeal of this area lies in the scope just to wander, and it's easy to fill the days following signs down the back roads to farms where you can sample home-made **ciders** and **cheeses**. In addition, the manor houses of **Beuvron-en-Auge**, **Crèvecoeur-en-Auge** and **Montpinçon** are well worth finding, while at **Cambremer** there is a special crafts market on Sunday morning in July and August.

Unlike many other areas of inland Normandy, the Pays d'Auge is somewhat accessible by **public transport**, although the limited bus service operated by Bus Verts (Ⓣ08.10.21.42.14, Ⓦwww.busverts14.fr) is no replacement for exploring the area with your own transport. Buses run from Caen (see p.139) to Falaise (7 daily, 1hr), and from Lisieux to Orbec (6 daily, 35min), Livarot (4 daily, 30min) and Vimoutiers (4 daily, 40min). Regular trains also run between Caen and Lisieux.

Lisieux

LISIEUX, the main town of the Pays d'Auge, was a regional capital successively under the Gauls, the Romans and the Franks. However, it was obliterated by barbarians in 275 AD, and again by the Allies in 1944, with the result that what had once been a beautiful market town is now for the most part nondescript. Although it still boasts a Norman Gothic cathedral built in 1170, which holds a chapel erected by Pierre Cauchon, the judge who sentenced Joan of Arc to death, these days Lisieux's identity is thoroughly wrapped up in the life and death of **Ste Thérèse** (see box, opposite) – the most influential French spiritual figure of the last hundred years.

Pilgrims come to Lisieux in considerable numbers, and even a casual visitor will find the Thérèse cult inescapable. The garish and gigantic **Basilique de Ste-**

Sainte Thérèse

Born at Alençon in 1873, **Thérèse Martin** lived for the last nine years of her short life in the Carmelite convent in Lisieux, until she died of TB at the age of 24. She had felt the call to take holy orders when only 9, but it took a pilgrimage to Rome and a special dispensation from the pope before she was allowed into the convent at the age of fifteen. The prioress said then that "a soul of such quality should not be treated as a child".

Thérèse owes her fame to her book *Story of a Soul*, in which she describes the approach to life she called her "Little Way" – a belief that all personal suffering, thankless work and quiet faith is made holy and worthwhile as an offering to God. What to modern sensibilities might appear as meekness and lack of worldliness verging on the selfish proved astonishingly popular after her death, particularly in trying to make sense of the vast suffering of World War I, and Thérèse was rapidly beatified. In 1945, she was declared France's second patron saint, after her heroine Joan of Arc. In fact, Thérèse wrote several poems to Joan, and there are even photographs of her dressed as the imprisoned saint chained to a wall. Her continuing contemporary relevance to Catholics has been celebrated by Pope John Paul II, who not only made his own pilgrimage to Lisieux but also declared Thérèse in 1997 to be the thirty-third "Doctor of the Church". This highest of theological honours had only previously been conferred on two women, Catherine of Siena and Theresa of Avila.

Thérèse, on a slope to the southwest of the town centre, was modelled on the Sacré-Coeur in Paris. Completed in 1954, it was the last major religious building in France to be erected solely by public subscription. Thérèse is in fact buried in the chapel of the Carmelite convent roughly opposite the tourist office on rue du Carmel, though her presence in the Basilica is ensured by selected bones from her right arm (in a reliquary given by Pope Pius XI) and by countless photographs, Thérèse being one of the very few saints to have lived since the invention of the camera. The huge modern mosaics that decorate the nave are undeniably impressive, but the overall impression is of a quasi-medieval hagiography.

In summer, a white, flag-bedecked funfair "train" runs fifty-minute tours around the holiest sites, chugging through the open, wide streets and squares, and past the delightful flower-filled park, raised above street level behind the restrained and sober Cathédrale St-Pierre (departures from the Basilica: July & Aug daily 11am, 2pm, 3pm, 4pm, 5pm & 6pm; Sept Sat & Sun same times; €5.10).

For an idea of Lisieux's former glories, take a look at the fading photos in the **Musée d'Art et d'Histoire**, 38 boulevard Pasteur (Wed–Mon 2–6pm; €2.50).

Practicalities

Lisieux is 35 minutes by train from Caen, en route to Paris or Rouen; the **gare SNCF** is on the south side of town, below the Basilica. On exiting the station, walk down rue de la Gare then turn right, to reach the **tourist office**, at 11 rue d'Alençon (mid-June to Sept Mon–Sat 8.30am–6.30pm, Sun 10am–12.30pm & 2–5pm; Oct to mid-June Mon–Sat 8.30am–noon & 1.30–6pm; ⓣ02.31.48.18.10), which can help with finding accommodation in Lisieux itself, and provides information on the rural areas further inland.

The number of pilgrims means that Lisieux is full of good-value places to stay. Among its **hotels** are the *Terrasse*, a Logis de France up on the hill near the Basilica at 25 avenue Ste-Thérèse (ⓣ02.31.62.17.65; ❸; closed Jan, plus Mon

△ Dovecote at Crèvecoeur

in winter), which serves good menus from €16 on its pleasant terrace; and the exceptionally cheap *Hôtel des Arts*, backing onto the Bishop's Gardens at 26 rue Condorcet (Ⓣ02.31.62.00.02; ❶). There is also a large two-star **campsite**, *de la Vallée* (Ⓣ02.31.62.00.40; closed Oct–March), but campers would probably be better off somewhere more rural, such as Livarot or Orbec.

Most of the hotels are equipped with tempting **restaurants**, and you can also get a reasonable lunch for under €10 at *Au Vieux Normand*, in one of Lisieux's few surviving half-timbered houses, at 14 rue H-Chéron (Ⓣ02.31.62.03.35; closed Sun eve & Mon). If Thérèse isn't your prime motivation, Saturday is the best day to visit, for the large **street market** – stacked with Pays d'Auge cheeses.

Crèvecoeur-en-Auge

While it's always fun simply to stumble across dilapidated old half-timbered farms in the Pays d'Auge, here and there it's possible to visit prime specimens that have been beautifully restored and preserved. An especially fine ensemble has been gathered just west of **CRÈVECOEUR-EN-AUGE**, 17km west of Lisieux on the N14, in the grounds of a small twelfth-century **Château** (April–June & Sept daily 11am–6pm; July & Aug daily 11am–7pm; Oct Sun 2–6pm; guided tours July & Aug Sun 2.30–6pm to no fixed times; €4.60). Around the pristine lawns of a re-created village green, circled by a shallow moat, this photogenic group of golden adobe structures includes a manor house, a barn and a tall thin dovecote that date from the fifteenth century. They were brought here by the Schlumbergers, a local family of German origin, who made their fortune from the 1920s onward by pioneering the use of electricity in prospecting for petroleum. That process is described in exhaustive detail in the barn, while the manor house explains exactly what's involved in restoring these kinds of buildings. By far the most interesting displays are in the little twelfth-century chapel that adjoins the château, which holds a fascinating exhibition on the music and instruments of the Middle Ages. Unfortunately, almost all the explanatory captions are in French.

For **accommodation**, at 44 route de St-Pierre-sur-Dives in the actual village of Crèvecoeur-en-Auge, the five-room *Auberge du Cheval Blanc* (Ⓣ02.31.63.03.28, Ⓔaubchevalblanc@aol.com; ❸; hotel closed mid-Jan to mid-Feb, restaurant closed Mon & Wed), is a welcoming hotel that serves fine regional food.

Beuvron-en-Auge

No village has any right to be as pretty as **BEUVRON-EN-AUGE**, 7km north of the N13 halfway between Lisieux and Caen, which consists of an oval central *place*, ringed by a glorious ensemble of multicoloured half-timbered houses. The largest of these, the yellow and brown sixteenth-century **Vieux Manoir** at the south end of the village, backs onto a stream and open fields. The beams around its first storey bear weather-beaten carvings, including one of a Norman soldier. A map in the main square details suggested **walking routes** through the countryside nearby, while if you step off the square into the alleyway known as **rue de la Catouillette**, opposite the Vieux Manoir, you'll find another set of lovely half-timbered structures clustered around a tiny courtyard.

Beuvron-en-Auge stages its own **Cider Festival**, with a huge local market in the square, on the last Sunday in October each year.

Practicalities

Accommodation comes in the form of a *chambre d'hote*, with the former farmhouse opposite the Vieux Manoir (☎02.31.39.00.62; ❸; closed Nov–Easter) a friendly and comfortable option. The very centre of the *place* is taken up by the *Pavé d'Auge* **restaurant** (☎02.31.79.26.71; closed Mon, plus Tues Sept–June), where regularly changing menus start at €28.50.

St-Germain-de-Livet

Around 7km south of Lisieux, and clearly signposted off the D579, the **château** of **ST-GERMAIN-DE-LIVET** (Feb–Sept & mid-Oct to Nov Wed–Mon 11am–6pm; closed first half of Oct, plus Dec & Jan; €6) – owned and operated by the town of Lisieux – is an appealing blend of fifteenth- and sixteenth-century architectural elements. From the main gate, its half-timbered older wing – home to some stirring military frescoes – is largely concealed by the more imposing later addition, with its cheerful checked facade of coloured stones and brick. The whole edifice is topped by classic pointed grey-slate turrets, circled by a moat, and surrounded by scrupulously maintained lawns.

If you want to explore some of the surrounding countryside, you can do so by horse-drawn **carriage rides** operated by the farm next to the château (€25 per hr for four people, €5 per extra person up to a maximum of eight; ☎02.31.31.08.68); when not in use, the carriage is housed in an amazing tumbledown barn next door.

Orbec

The most attractive of the larger Pays d'Auge towns, **ORBEC** lies just a few kilometres along a valley from the source of its river, the Orbiquet, 19km southeast of Lisieux. Consisting of little more than its main road, the rue Grande, with the huge tower of Notre Dame church at its southern end, it epitomizes the simple pleasures of the region.

Along the Rue Grande, you'll see several houses in which the gaps between the timbers are filled with intricate patterns of coloured tiles and bricks. Debussy composed *Jardin sous la Pluie* in one of these, and the oldest and prettiest of the lot – a tanner's house dating back to 1568, and once again called the **Vieux Manoir** – holds a museum of local history (April–June & Oct Sat 10am–noon & Sun 2–6pm; July–Sept Wed–Fri & Sun 2–6pm, Sat 10am–noon; free, or €2 for a guided tour). On the whole, though, it's more fun just to walk down behind the church to the river, and its watermill and paddocks.

Practicalities

In the absence of any **hotels** in Orbec, contact the tourist office (☎02.31.32.56.68) for a list of *chambres d'hôtes*. The best **restaurant** in town is at the narrowest point of rue Grande, where *Le Caneton* (☎02.31.32.73.32) in the half-timbered house at no. 32 serves top-quality menus for under €20. Orbec also has a two-star municipal **campsite**, *Les Capucins* (☎02.31.32.76.22; closed Oct to late May).

Livarot

The centre of the cheese country is the old town of **LIVAROT**, 18km south of Lisieux, where the recently opened **Fromagerie de Livarot**, 42 rue du Général Leclerc (April–Sept Mon–Sat 9am–5.30pm; free), gives you a closer look at how Livarot's eponymous cheese is made, with free samples doled

The cheese of the Pays d'Auge

The tradition of cheesemaking in the Pays d'Auge is thought to have been started in monasteries during the Dark Ages. The characteristics of the local product seem to have become fairly standard by the eleventh century. At first, it was variously known as either *Augelot* or *Angelot*; the *Roman de la Rose* in 1236 referred to *Angelot* cheese, which was identified with a small coin depicting a young angel killing a dragon. This cheese was the forerunner of the principal modern varieties, which began to emerge in the seventeenth century – **Pont-l'Évêque**, which is square, with a washed crust, and is soft but not runny, and **Livarot**, which is round, thick and firm, with a stronger flavour.

Although Marie Herel is generally credited with having invented **Camembert** in the 1790s, a smaller and stodgier version of that cheese had already existed for some time. Apparently, one Abbé Gobert, a priest fleeing the Revolutionary Terror at Meaux, stayed in Mme Herel's farmhouse at Camembert and watched the methods she used for making cheese. He suggested modifications in line with the techniques he'd seen employed to produce Brie de Meaux – a slower process, gentler on the curd and with more thorough drainage. The rich full cheese thus created was an instant success in the market at Vimoutiers, and the development of the railways (and the invention of the chipboard cheesebox in 1880) helped to give it a worldwide popularity.

out at the end of each visit. For the best views of the valley, climb up to the thirteenth-century church of **St-Michel de Livet**, just above the town.

Practicalities

Livarot's **tourist office**, 1 place Georges-Bisson (Tues–Sat 9am–noon & 2–6pm; ⓣ02.31.63.47.39, ⓔotsi.livarot@wanadoo.fr), is almost next door to the appealing **hotel** *Du Vivier* (ⓣ02.31.32.04.10, ⓔvivier14@club-internet-fr; ❷; closed Fri, plus Sun eve Oct–Easter), whose restaurant *Le Cottage* serves menus from €15 and up. The enjoyable *Café de la Paix* is further east, up from the central traffic lights, and there's also a tiny one-star municipal **campsite** (ⓣ02.31.63.53.19; closed Sept–April). The local **cheese fair** falls on the first weekend of each August.

St-Pierre-sur-Dives

ST-PIERRE-SUR-DIVES, 16km west of Livarot, is noteworthy for two fine old architectural treasures, both of which date back to the twelfth century. The wooden *halles* in its vast open marketplace – which still plays host to a large **market** every Monday – were burned to the ground in 1944, but had been rebuilt by 1949. Only traditional techniques were used: there's not a single nail or screw in the place – the timber frame rests on low stone walls and is held together by chestnut pegs alone.

Just across the central street stands a Gothic-Romanesque **church**, whose windows depict the history of the town. The Benedictine abbey of which it forms part is progressively being restored, and its former convent buildings now house a slightly academic complement to the practical-minded *fromagerie* at Livarot (see opposite), the **Musée des Techniques Fromagères** (mid-April to mid-Oct Mon–Fri 9.30am–12.30pm & 1.30–6pm, Sat 10am–noon & 2–5pm; mid-Oct to mid-April Mon–Fri 9.30am–12.30pm & 1.30–5.30pm, €2.30).

St-Pierre's **tourist office** shares the convent on rue St-Benoist with its cheesy neighbours (same hours; ⓣ02.31.20.97.90, ⓦwww.mairie-saint-pierre-sur-dives.fr). The best bet for both **accommodation** and **food** is *Les Agriculteurs*, a Logis de France at 118 rue de Falaise (☎02.31.20.72.78, ⓔles.agriculteurs@wanadoo.fr; ❶; restaurant closed Sun eve). Its two-star, summer-only **campsite** (☎02.31.20.97.90; closed Oct–April) is 1km south of town.

Falaise

William the Conqueror, or William the Bastard as he is more familiarly known to Normans, was born in **FALAISE**, 40km southwest of Lisieux. His mother, Arlette, a laundress and daughter of a tanner, was spotted by his father, Duke Robert of Normandy, at the washing place below the château. She was a shrewd woman, who scorned secrecy in her eventual assignation by riding publicly through the main entrance to meet him. During her pregnancy, she is said to have dreamed of bearing a mighty tree that cast its shade over Normandy and England.

From a distance, the sheer wall of the **castle keep**, firmly planted on the massive rocks of the cliff (*falaise*) that gave the town its name, and towering over the **Fontaine d'Arlette** down by the river, looks all but impregnable. Nonetheless, it was so heavily damaged during the war that it took over fifty years to reopen the castle for regular visits (mid-Feb to June & Sept to mid-Dec daily 10am–6pm; July & Aug daily 10am–7pm; English-language tours daily 11.30am, with another at 3.30pm in July & Aug; €6). Huge resources have been lavished on restoring the central *donjon* – reminiscent of the Tower of London, with its cream-coloured Caen stone – in accordance with cutting-edge contemporary concepts. A guiding principle was to avoid any possible confusion as to what is original and authentic, and what is new. Steel slabs, concrete blocks, glass floors and tent-like canvas awnings have been slapped down atop the bare ruins, and metal staircases even squeezed into the wall cavities. The raw structure of the keep, down to its very foundations, lies exposed to view, while the newly created rooms are used for changing exhibitions that focus on the castle's fascinating past. Add the superb views of the town and surroundings from the battlements, and you have one of Normandy's most rewarding historical sites.

The whole of Falaise was devastated in the course of the struggle to close the "Falaise Gap" in August 1944 – the climax of the Battle of Normandy, as the Allied armies sought to encircle the Germans and cut off their retreat. By the time the Canadians entered the town on August 17, they could no longer tell where the roads had been and had to bulldoze a new four-metre strip straight through the middle. Set in almost derelict wilderness right next to the town centre on chemin des Roches is an isolated survivor, the **Château de la Fresnaye**, housing a rather earnest local museum focusing on the battle (April to mid-Nov 10am–noon & 2–6pm; €5.35).

Opposite the tourist office (see below), the **Musée des Automates**, also known as "Automates Avenue", preserves mechanical window displays that graced the department stores of Paris between the 1920s and 1950s (April–Sept daily 10am–12.30pm & 1.30–6pm; Oct–March Sat 10am–12.30pm & 1.30–6pm, Sun 2–6pm; €4.60). The highlight is a mock-up of a real-life collision that took place in a tiny village between the cyclists of the Tour de France and a herd of pigs.

Practicalities

Falaise's modern, well-stocked **tourist office** is located in the Forum, on the boulevard de la Libération (May–Sept Mon–Sat 9.30am–12.30pm &

1.30–6.30pm, Sun 10am–noon & 3–5pm; Oct–April Mon–Sat 9.30am–12.30pm & 1.30–5.30pm; ⓣ02.31.90.17.26, ⓦwww.otsifalaise.com).

Most of Falaise's few **hotels** stand along the main Caen–Argentan road, which can make them rather noisy. The *Poste*, not far from the tourist office at 38 rue Georges-Clémenceau (ⓣ02.31.90.13.14, ⓔhotel.delaposte@wanadoo.fr; ❸; restaurant closed Sun eve & Mon) serves good food on menus from €15, while rooms and meals at the *Hôtel de la Place*, next to the church at 1 place St-Gervais (ⓣ02.31.40.19.00; ❶; closed Sun eve & Wed), are significantly cheaper. The three-star **campsite**, *Camping du Château* (ⓣ02.31.90.16.55; closed Oct to mid-April), next to Arlette's fountain and the municipal swimming pool, is in a much better location.

Vimoutiers and Camembert

The war-ravaged and consequently rather ugly town of **VIMOUTIERS**, 10km south of Livarot, contains a quirky **cheese museum** at 10 avenue Général de Gaulle (April–Sept Mon 2–6pm, Tues–Sat 9am–noon & 2–6pm, Sun 10am–noon & 2.30–6pm; Nov–March Mon 2–5pm, Tues–Sat 10am–noon & 2–5.30pm; €3 or €4 with free samples), featuring a glorious collection not to be missed by tyrosemiophiles – cheese-label collectors (they do exist) – who will find Camembert stickers ranging from remote Chilean dairies to Marks & Spencer. Most of the cheese on display, however, turns out to be polystyrene.

A statue in the main square honours Marie Harel, who, at the nearby village of **CAMEMBERT**, developed the original cheese early in the nineteenth century, promoting it with a skilful campaign that included sending free samples to Napoléon. There's a photo in the museum of the statue with its head blown off after a US air raid in June 1944; its replacement was donated by the cheesemakers of Ohio. Marie is confronted across the main street by what might be called the statue of the Unknown Cow.

Camembert itself, 3km southeast of Vimoutiers, is tiny, hilly and very rural, home to far more cows than humans. On one side of its little central square, the largest local cheese producers, La Ferme Président, run their own **cheese museum** (March–May, Sept & Oct daily 10am–5.30pm; June–Aug 10am–6pm; €5), where the forty-minute tour adds little to anything you may have learned in Vimoutiers. On the other side, the rival Le Maison du Camembert is a British-run cheese and souvenir stall with another ramshackle free cheese museum (same dates and hours as La Ferme Président).

Practicalities

Vimoutiers is the venue of a **market** on Monday afternoons. Its **tourist office**, in the town cheese museum (same hours as museum; ⓣ02.33.39.30.29), has piles of information on local cheese-related attractions. Of its **hotels**, the very central but far from welcoming *Soleil d'Or*, 3 rue de Chatelet (ⓣ02.33.39.07.15; ❶; hotel closed 2 wks in Feb & 2 wks in Oct; restaurant closed Fri eve & Sun eve), has a reasonable €15 menu and a better €20 one.

A short way south of Vimoutiers, en route to Camembert, the beautifully sited lake known as the **Escale du Vitou** offers everything you need for windsurfing, swimming and horse-riding, as well as its own new, comfortable, rural hotel, *L'Escale du Vitou* (ⓣ02.33.39.12.04; ❷). There's also a clean and very cheap **campsite** nearby on boulevard Docteur-Dentu, the two-star *La Campière* (ⓣ02.33.39.18.86; closed Nov–Feb).

Ste-Foy de Montgommery

A couple of kilometres north of Vimoutiers, towards Livarot, the D579 passes through the village of **STE-FOY DE MONTGOMMERY**. Outside the *Café La Gosselinais* here, on the night of July 17, 1944, **Field-Marshal Rommel** was seriously injured when RAF Typhoons attacked his Mercedes. This prevented Rommel from taking a key role in the July 20 attempted assassination of Hitler – although his involvement in the plot was still sufficient for Hitler to force him to commit suicide three months later. That Rommel's nemesis should overtake him in a place called "Holy Faith of Montgommery" became part of the legend surrounding the British field-marshal.

South to Gacé

The **D26** runs along the **valley of the Vie** south of Vimoutiers – a route that is something of a microcosm of Norman vernacular architecture, lined along the way with ramshackle old barns, outhouses and farm buildings. Faded orange clay crumbles from between the weathered wooden beams of these flower-covered beauties.

GACÉ itself, 18km from Vimoutiers, is not wildly exciting, but it does have a handful of reasonable **hotels**. The imposing red-brick *Hostellerie les Champs* on the route d'Alençon south of the centre (Ⓣ02.33.39.09.05; ❹; closed Jan, plus Wed in low season), offers several well-priced menus.

Nonant-le-Pin, 12 km south of Gacé, was the birthplace in 1824 of Alphonsine Plessis, a celebrated courtesan who served as the inspiration for Dumas' *La Dame aux Camélias* and Verdi's *La Traviata*.

Argentan and around

ARGENTAN centres on a **ruined castle** – the site where Henry II of England received the news on New Year's Day 1171 that four of his knights had taken him at his word and murdered Thomas à Becket. In fact, the entire town was comprehensively ruined during General Patton's bid to close the "Falaise pocket" in August 1944, and there's virtually nothing to see; the **church of St-Germain** which dominates all approaches has been under continuing restoration ever since, but remains closed to visitors. Even the castle ruin takes a bit of finding, atop the hill nearby. Although Argentan makes an enjoyable enough halt when the central market square, place du Marché, is in full swing on Tuesdays, or for boat trips on the River Orne, the main reason anyone comes here is not monuments but **horses**. Outside the town are numerous equestrian centres, with riding schools, stables, racetracks and studs.

Trains to Argentan pull in at the **gare SNCF**, across the Orne a short way southwest of the centre. Full information on the area is available from the **tourist office** in the old chapel at 6 place du Marché (July & Aug Mon–Sat 9am–7pm; Sept–June Mon & Sat 9.30am–12.30pm & 1.30–5.30pm, Tues–Fri 9.30am–12.30pm & 2–6pm; Ⓣ02.33.67.12.48, Ⓦwww.argentan.fr). Of the **hotels** in town, the best budget option is the *Donjon*, right by the castle keep and above a brasserie at 1 rue de l'Hôtel-de-Ville (Ⓣ02.33.67.03.76; ❶; restaurant closed Sun eve), while the *France*, 8 boulevard Carnot (Ⓣ02.33.67.03.65; ❸; hotel closed Fri eve & Sun eve; restaurant closed Fri eve, Sun eve & Mon), has an excellent dining room, with menus from €13.50.

Le Pin-au-Haras

LE PIN-AU-HARAS, 15km east of Argentan on the N26, is an essential stop for horse lovers: it's the home of the **National Stud** (*Haras National*). The plan for the stud was originally conceived by Louis XIV's minister, Colbert, and the ground subsequently laid out by the famous garden and landscape designer André Le Nôtre from 1715 to 1730. It can be approached via a number of woodland avenues, but the most impressive is the D304, which climbs slowly from the hippodrome and is lined with jumps and hedges.

While the buildings are magnificent, they're nowhere near as sumptuous as the residents – around eighty of them – incalculable investments that include champions of Epsom and Longchamp, as well as prize specimens of the indigenous Norman Percheron.

Tours of the stud leave every thirty minutes from the main entrance (daily: April to mid-Oct 9.30am–6pm; mid-Oct to March 2–5pm; €4; arrive one hour before closing for the last tour). You are escorted by a groom through stables full of stomping, snorting, glistening stallions, rooms of polished harnesses and fine carriages, and great doorways labelled in stone, until eventually you come out to a pastoral vision of the horses grazing in an endless succession of gardens and paddocks. Each tour lasts for around an hour; if you find it hard to follow the rapid French-only commentary, you can amuse yourself by watching the way everybody scrupulously affects not to notice the rampant sexuality – which, of course, is the *raison d'être* of the whole place.

Between June and September, displays of horsemanship are held on Thursdays at 3pm (€3), while there are also special events on three or so Sundays during September and October, as well as a few other summer weekends. Between February 15 and July 15, most of the horses are away. The **château** itself is only open during school holidays (Feb–May & Oct–Dec Thurs 2–5pm; €4.60 or €8 with the stud), but not the summer holidays.

The Château d'O

Just outside Mortrée, 15km southeast of Argentan on the N158, and 6.5km northwest of Sées (see below), you will pass the postcard-perfect **Château d'O**. This turreted château, whose grey-slate roof rises to a cluster of sharp pencil-points, is in perfect condition, with a full moat that widens out into a lake. The house dates from the end of the fifteenth century and, unusually, was designed purely as a domestic residence, with no military pretensions. Unfortunately, public visits were stopped when the owner died and the house became the subject of disputed – and ongoing – hereditary claims.

Sées

SÉES, midway between Argentan and Alençon, has long had an air of being lost in its own history. A succession of dusty and derelict squares, all with medieval buildings intact, surround the great Gothic, white-ceilinged **cathedral**, which is the fifth to stand on the site and is magnificently illuminated every summer evening. One of its predecessors was burned down by its own bishop, attempting to smoke out a gang of thieves – much to the scorn of the pope.

However, Sées does hold several tasteful, long-established **hotels**. The *Cheval Blanc* overlooks the pretty little place St-Pierre on the main road south (Ⓣ 02.33.27.80.48; ❶; closed Nov, plus Thurs eve & Fri), and offers menus from €10.50, with a good €14 menu of regional specialities. The *Dauphin*, a Logis de France, is hidden away a little further west, in a quiet location at 31 place des Halles next to the old covered marketplace (Ⓣ02.33.80.80.70; ❸; closed Sun eve all year, plus Mon in winter), and has an equally good (if more expensive) restaurant, while the *Garden Hôtel* at 12bis rue des Ardriers (Ⓣ02.33.27.98.27; ❶) is a peaceful, elegant refuge reached via an ivy-covered gatehouse in the northwest corner of another sleepy square, nearer the cathedral.

Le-Mêle-sur-Sarthe

LE-MÊLE-SUR-SARTHE, 20km southeast of Sées on the minor D42, holds another logis worth stopping at. The *Hotel de la Poste,* 27 place de Gaulle (Ⓣ02.33.81.18.00; ❷; closed Sun eve & Mon eve, plus Fri eve in low season), offers very good-value €7.80 and €15.50 **brasserie** menus for both lunch and dinner, and the latter includes drinks and coffee in the price. The *Café du Commerce* across the square (Ⓣ02.33.27.60.38) is an excellent alternative, open for lunch only daily except Sundays, with a four-course set menu, again including drinks and coffee, for €9.50.

Alençon and around

ALENÇON, a fair-sized and busy town, is best known for its traditional – and now pretty much defunct – **lacemaking** industry. The **Musée des Beaux Arts et de la Dentelle**, housed in a former Jesuit school (July & Aug 10am–noon & 2–6pm; Sept–June Tues–Sun 10am–noon & 2–6pm; €2.95 or €5.10 with a 90min guided tour), has all the best trappings of a modern museum. However, the highly informative history of lacemaking upstairs, with examples of numerous different techniques, can be rather deadly for anyone not already fascinated by the subject. The temptation to leave without a visit to the "Minor Lace Exhibition Room" is almost overwhelming; but the room beyond it holds a collection of gruesome Cambodian artefacts, spears and lances, tiger skulls and elephants' feet, gathered by a "militant socialist" French governor at the turn of the twentieth century. The paintings in the Beaux Arts section downstairs are fairly nondescript, except for a touching Nativity by the Norman artist, Latouche, and a few works by Courbet and Géricault.

Stained glass in the **Notre Dame** church on the place de la Magdeleine shows the medieval guilds of craftsmen who paid for each specific window, and the baptism of **Ste Thérèse** is commemorated in the chapel in which it took place. If you haven't already had a surfeit of the saint at Lisieux, you can also wander over to her **birthplace**, on rue St-Blaise, just in front of the *gare routière* (Feb–May & Oct–Dec daily except Tues 9.30am–noon & 2.30–5pm; June–Sept daily 9am–noon & 2–6pm; free).

The **Château des Ducs**, the old town castle, looks impressive but doesn't encourage visitors – it's a prison. People in Alençon have nightmare memories of its use during the war by the Gestapo.

Thanks to wartime bombardment, little is left of the buildings that once stood on the banks of the River Sarthe. Alençon was the first town in France to be liberated by French forces alone, and a monument right next to the Pont-Neuf honours their leader, the aristocratic **Général Leclerc** (whose headmaster at school was General de Gaulle's father). Directly behind the general's statue the movements of his army are chronicled through the deserts of North Africa, via Utah Beach, to Alençon, on August 12, 1944. Within two weeks he was in Paris; within a year, in Berlin; and by March 1946 he was in Hanoi – he died in a plane crash in North Africa in 1947.

Practicalities

Alençon's **gare routière** and **gare SNCF** are both northeast of the centre, with the train station slightly the further out of the two. If you arrive by **car**, on the other hand, watch out for the town's abysmal one-way system. The **tourist office** is housed in the dramatic fifteenth-century Maison d'Ozé on the central place La Magdelaine (July & Aug Mon–Sat 9.30am–7pm, Sun 10am–12.30pm & 2–5pm; Sept–June Mon–Sat 9.30am–noon & 2–6.30pm; ⓣ02.33.80.66.33, ⓦwww.paysdalencontourisme.com). In summer, they also organize **guided tours** of the town (July & Aug Mon–Wed & Sat 10.30am, Fri 8.30pm; €4). Free **Internet access** is available a short walk west, at both the town hall annexe at 6–8 rue des Filles-Notre-Dame (Mon–Sat 8.30am–7pm; ⓣ02.33.32.40.43) and in the Halle aux Blé (Mon–Sat 2–6pm; ⓣ02.33.80.87.00).

Alençon's prime concentration of **hotels** lies in the immediate environs of the *gare SNCF*. The logis, *L'Industrie*, 20 place Général de Gaulle (ⓣ02.33.27.19.30; ❷; closed Fri eve & Sat), is decent and has fixed-price menus from €10. Another logis a few hundred yards closer to the centre, *Le Grand Cerf*, occupies a Neoclassical town house at 21 rue St-Blaise (ⓣ02.33.26.00.51, ⓦwww.hotelgrandcerf_61.com; ❸; closed Sun) and has large comfortable rooms and a top-quality restaurant, with garden seating in summer. Otherwise, the best place to **eat** has to be the delightful *L'Escargot Doré*, southeast of town on the Le Mans road at 183 avenue Général Leclerc (ⓣ02.33.28.67.67; closed Sun eve & Mon), which serves traditional Norman cooking, much of it prepared on the wood-burning stove in the corner, from €19.

Some good shops and cafés are to be found in the handful of pedestrianized streets in the town centre. Good places to sample the thriving local **bar** scene include *La Caves Aux Boeufs*, spreading across the pedestrian rue de la Caves Aux Boeufs, (ⓣ02.33.82.99.45), and the half-timbered *Café des Sept Colonnes* at 2 rue du Château (ⓣ02.33.26.14.08), both of which also serve simple brasserie menus.

If you're interested in **horse-riding** along the banks of the Orne, contact the Orne Tourist Board, 88 rue St-Blaise (ⓣ02.33.28.88.71, ⓦwww.ornetourisme.com) for their list of local stables.

The Forêt d'Écouves

The **Forêt d'Écouves**, easily reached (under your own steam) from Alençon or Sées (see p.205), is the centrepiece of the Parc Régional Normandie-Maine, an amorphous area stretching from Mortain in the west to within a few kilometres of Mortagne-au-Perche in the east. A dense mixture of old spruce, pine, oak and beech, set on high hills a few kilometres north of Alençon, the Écouves forest is one of the most attractive in Normandy. These commanding heights were bitterly fought over during the war, and a Free French tank still guards the **Croix-de-Médavy** at their very apex.

Unfortunately, the forest is now a favoured spot of the military – and, in autumn, of deerhunters too. To avoid risking life and limb, check with the park's offices to find the safe routes. You can usually ramble freely along the cool paths, happening on wild mushrooms and even the odd wild boar. The nearest accommodation is in either Alençon or Sées.

Carrouges

One alternative base at the western end of the Forêt d'Écouves is the appealing little hilltop town of **CARROUGES**, 28km northwest of Alençon. Down below the centre, at the foot of the hill, a fine fourteenth-century **château** commands spacious landscaped grounds (daily: April to mid-June & Sept 10am–noon & 2–6pm; mid-June to Aug 9.30am–noon & 2–6.30pm; Oct–March 10am–noon & 2–5pm; €6.10). Its two highlights are a superb restored brick staircase, and a room in which hang portraits of fourteen successive generations of the Le Veneur family, an extraordinary illustration of the processes of heredity. In the **Maison de Métiers**, the former castle chapel, local craftsmen sell their produce.

On the narrow rue Ste-Marguerite that runs through the heart of Carrouges – a noisier location than it might look – the *Hôtel du Nord* (☎02.33.27.20.14; ❷; closed mid-Dec to mid-Jan, plus Fri Sept–June) offers a handful of reasonably large en-suite rooms at low rates, and delicious local cuisine on menus that start at €11. Facing the same little square, the even smaller, but otherwise virtually identical *St-Pierre* (☎02.33.27.20.02; ❷; closed Sat lunch & Sun eve) offers five en-suite rooms, and menus from €10.

Bagnoles de l'Orne

The spa town of **BAGNOLES DE L'ORNE**, 17km west of Carrouges, lies at the heart of a long, narrow wood, the Forêt des Andaines. Broad avenues radiate into the forest from the centre of the town. As you approach, you begin to encounter pale figures shuffling slowly outwards, blinking as if unused to the light of day, as though silently fleeing some nameless evil. In fact, the forbidding nineteenth-century building from which they emerge contains nothing more fearsome than **thermal baths**. Bagnoles is a mecca for the sick from all over

France; its springs are such big business that they maintain a booking office next to the Pompidou Centre in Paris.

Although life in the town is conducted at a phenomenally slow pace, it is all surprisingly jolly – redolent with aged flirtations and gallantry. The lakeside gardens are the big scene, with pedalos, horse-drawn *calèches* and an enormous casino. And with so many visitors to keep entertained, and their spending money, there are innumerable cultural **events**, concerts and stage shows throughout the summer; the ostensible high spot, the annual *Spectacle* in July, is one of the less enthralling.

Away from its main roads, the **Forêt des Andaines** is pleasant, with scattered and unspoilt villages, such as Juvigny and St-Michel, and the secluded, private **Château de Couterne**, a visual delight even from the gates, with its lake and long grass-floored avenue approach.

Practicalities

Whether you'd actually want to spend time in Bagnoles depends on your disposable income as well as your health. Furthermore, the town as a whole operates to a season that lasts roughly from early April to the end of October; arrive in winter, and you may find everything shut. The numerous **hotels** are expensive and sedate places, in which it's possible to be too late for dinner at 7pm and locked out altogether at 9pm, while the three-star **campsite**, *de la Vée* (Ⓣ02.33.37.87.45; closed Nov to mid-March), south of town, is rather forlorn.

The **tourist office** on place du Marché (April–Oct Mon–Sat 9.30am–12.30pm & 2–6pm, Sun 10am–12.30pm & 2.30–6.30pm; Nov–March Mon–Sat 9.30am–12.30pm & 2–6pm; Ⓣ02.33.37.85.66, Ⓦwww.bagnolesdelorne.com) will provide details on accommodation in Bagnoles and its adjacent less exclusive sister town of **TESSE-MADELEINE**. Among the cheaper options in Bagnoles proper – all very near the central roundabout, place de la République – are the *Albert 1er* at 7 avenue Dr Poulain (Ⓣ02.33.37.80.97; ❷; closed Jan to mid-Feb), which has excellent menus from €14, and the *Grand Veneur* at 6 place de la République (Ⓣ02.33.37.86.79; ❷; closed Nov–March). Despite its ugly would-be-Deco exterior, the *Cetlos*, on rue des Casinos (Ⓣ02.33.38.44.44, Ⓦwww.le-cetlos.com; ❹), is the biggest and probably the best of the crop, bedecked with balconies and terraces overlooking the lake. **Restaurants**, in both towns, tend to be good value: the *Terrasse* (Ⓣ02.33.37.81.44; closed Dec & Mon all year, plus Sun eve in low season) in Bagnoles is well tried and popular, with a traditional dining room offering menus from €12.10 upwards, and a cheaper crêperie.

If you fancy **taking the waters**, four treatments cost €75, rising to €725 for 36 treatments; you can also arrange an all-inclusive package through the tourist office. For more information, visit Ⓦwww.thermes-bagnoles.com.

Domfront

The road **west through the forest** from Bagnoles, the D335 and then the D908, climbs above the lush woodlands and progressively narrows to a hog's back before entering **DOMFRONT**, 22km on. Less happens here than at Bagnoles, but by way of compensation the countryside is prettier.

A public park, near the long-abandoned former train station, leads up to some redoubtable **castle ruins** perched on an isolated rock. Henry II and his queen, Eleanor of Aquitaine, often visited this castle; their daughter, also called Eleanor, was born here in October 1162. Thomas à Becket came to stay for

Christmas 1166, saying Mass in the Notre-Dame-sur-l'Eau church down by the river, which has sadly been ruined by vandals. The views from the flower-filled gardens that surround the mangled keep are spectacular, including a very graphic panorama of the ascent you've made to get up.

A slender footbridge connects the castle with the narrow little **village** itself, which boasts an abundance of half-timbered houses. Near its sweet little central square, the modern **St-Julien** church, constructed out of concrete segments during the 1920s, is bursting with exciting Byzantine-style mosaics, which culminate in the vast *Christ in Majesty* above the altar. From the outside, it's an odd-looking building, especially when its belfry is swathed in green netting to catch loose stones, which it seems to be pretty much all the time.

Practicalities

The **tourist office** is beside the castle at 12 place de la Roirie (Tues–Sat 9.30am–12.30pm & 2.30–6pm; ⓣ02.33.38.53.97, ⓦwww.domfront.com). On two summer afternoons a week (July & Aug Tues & Thurs 4.30pm), they run free **guided tours** of old Domfront. Closer to the church, there's an unexpected English Bookshop and Internet Café at 25 rue St-Julien (Wed–Sat 10am–5pm, but subject to changes).

Domfront's **hotels**, clustered together at the foot of the hill below the old town, make useful and very pleasant stopovers. Two Logis de France stand side by side: the *Relais St-Michel*, 5 rue du Mont-St-Michel (ⓣ02.33.38.64.99, ⓦwww.hotellerelaisstmichel.com; ❷; closed Fri & Sun eve) has widely varied menus from under €15, while the similarly priced *Hôtel de France*, 7 rue du Mont-St-Michel (ⓣ02.33.38.51.44, ⓦwww.region-normande.com/hoteldefrance; ❷), has a nice bar and garden. Campers should take note that the two-star local **campsite**, *du Champs Passais* (ⓣ02.33.37.37.66; closed early Oct to March), is exceptionally small.

The Suisse Normande

The area known as the **Suisse Normande** lies roughly 25km south of Caen, along the gorge of the River **Orne**, between **Thury-Harcourt** and **Putanges**. While the name, with its allusion to the Alps, may be a little far-fetched – there are certainly no mountains – this is nonetheless a distinctive and highly attractive region, with cliffs and crags and wooded hills at every turn. The energetic race along the Orne in canoes and kayaks, their lazier counterparts contenting themselves with pedalos or a bizarre species of inflatable rubber tractor, while high above them climbers dangle from thin ropes and claw desperately at the sheer rock face. For mere walkers, the Orne can be frustrating: footpaths along the river are few and far between, whatever maps may say, and often entirely overgrown with brambles. At least one road sign in the area warns of unexploded mines, so tread carefully.

The Suisse Normande is most usually approached from Caen or Falaise, and contrasts dramatically with the prairie-like expanse of wheatfields en route. **Bus** Verts #34 can take you to Thury-Harcourt or Clécy on its way from Caen to Flers, and **SNCF** run occasional special summer train excursions from Caen. If you're **cycling**, the least stressful approach is to follow the D212 from Caen, cruising across the flatlands to Thury-Harcourt; although swooping down the D23 from Bretteville, with thick woods to either side of you, is pretty exhila-

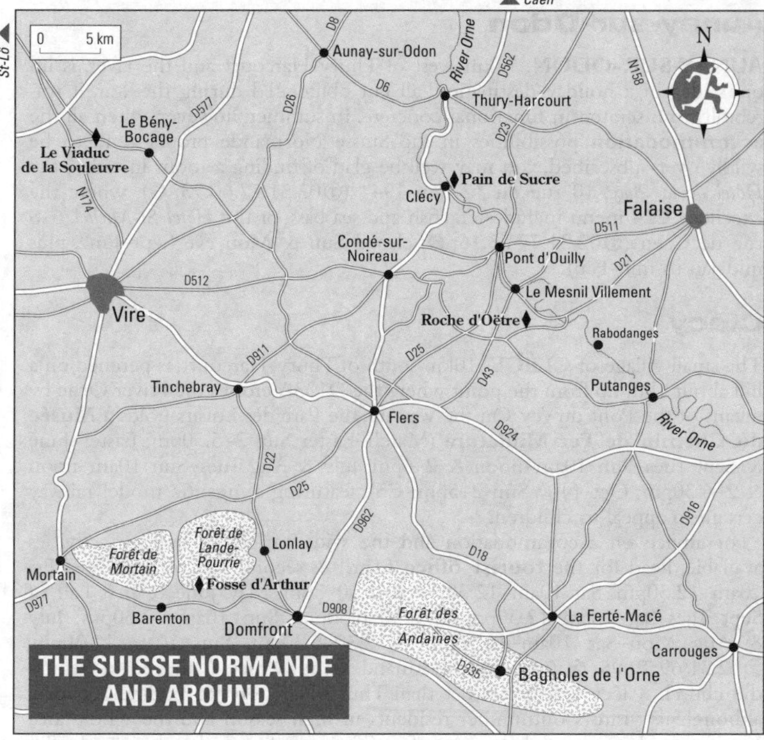

rating. Taking the D235 from Caen, follow signs for Falaise, and head straight on through the town of Ifs. **Touring** the Suisse Normande on a bike, however, is an exhausting business: the minor roads do not follow the gorge floor, but undulate endlessly over the surrounding slopes.

Thury-Harcourt

THURY-HARCOURT is really two separate towns: a little village around a bridge across the Orne, and a larger market town on the hill that overlooks it. In summer, the grounds of the local manor house are open to visitors, giving access to the immediate riverside (April & Oct Sun 2.30–6.30pm; May–Sept daily 2.30–6.30pm; €4).

The **tourist office**, 2 place St-Sauveur (Jan–April & Oct–Dec Mon 2.30–5pm, Tues–Fri 10am–12.30pm & 2.30–5pm, Sat 10am–12.30pm; May, June & Sept Tues–Sat 10am–12.30pm & 2.30–6.30pm, Sun 10am–12.30pm; July & Aug Mon–Sat 10am–12.30pm & 2.30–6.30pm, Sun 10am–12.30pm; ⓣ02.31.79.70.45, ⓦwww.suisse-normande.com), can suggest walks, rides and *gîtes d'étape* throughout the Suisse Normande. Kayak Club Thury-Harcourt at the waterfront Base de Canoe (ⓣ02.31.79.40.59) rent out both bikes and canoes. Despite having an attractive four-star **campsite**, the *Vallée du Traspy* (ⓣ02.31.79.61.80; closed Oct–April), nearby Clécy (see overleaf) is a better location thanThury-Harcourt for hotels.

Aunay-sur-Odon

AUNAY-SUR-ODON, 14km west of Thury-Harcourt and the river, is no one's idea of a holiday destination; all but obliterated during the war, it was rebuilt from scratch in functional concrete. In summer, however, when all the **accommodation** possibilities in the Suisse Normande proper tend to be wildly over-subscribed, you may well be glad of finding a room in either the *Hôtel de la Place*, 10 rue du 12-Juin-1944 (Ⓣ02.31.77.60.73; ❷), where the excellent €24 menu includes crayfish and sea bass, or the *Hôtel St-Michel*, 6–8 rue de Caen (Ⓣ02.31.77.63.16; ❷; closed Sun & Mon eve Sept–June, plus mid-Jan to mid-Feb).

Clécy

The small village of **CLÉCY**, 10km south of Thury-Harcourt, is perched on a hill about 1km up from the point where the D133A crosses the River Orne by means of the Pont du Vey. On the way up, the Parc des Loisirs holds a **Musée du Chemin de Fer Miniature** (March–Easter Sun 2–5.30pm; Easter–June & Sept Tues–Sun 10am–noon & 2–6pm; July & Aug Tues–Sun 10am–noon & 2–6.30pm; Oct–Nov Sun 2–5pm; €5), featuring a gigantic model railway certain to appeal to children.

For advice on accommodation and the wide variety of holiday activities available, head for the **tourist office** (April & second half of Sept Tues–Fri 10am–12.30pm, Sat 10am–12.30pm & 2.30–5pm; May, June & first half of Sept Tues–Sat 10am–12.30pm & 2.30–6.30pm, Sun 10am–12.30pm; July & Aug Mon–Sat 10am–12.30pm & 2.30–6.30pm, Sun 10am–12.30pm; Ⓣ02.31.69.79.95, Ⓦwww.suisse-normande.com), which is tucked in behind the church. Clécy is a better bet than Thury-Harcourt for finding a **room**, although its visitors outnumber residents in high season and the whole area can get much too crowded for comfort. The logis facing the church, *Au Site Normand*, 2 rue des Châtelets (Ⓣ02.31.69.71.05, Ⓦww.ausitenormand-clecy.com; ❸; closed Nov–Feb), consists of an old-fashioned and good-value dining room in the main timber-framed building, and a cluster of newer units opening onto a courtyard around the back.

Down the hill, the *Moulin du Vey* (Ⓣ02.31.69.71.08, Ⓦwww.moulinduvey.com; ❺; hotel closed Dec & Jan, restaurant closed Sun in winter), set in spacious grounds on the far bank of the river, is a luxury hotel that takes its name from the restored watermill right by the bridge, which is itself, confusingly, now a restaurant. The western riverbank continues in a brief splurge of restaurants, takeaways and snack bars as far as the two-star municipal **campsite** (Ⓣ02.31.69.70.36; closed mid-Oct to March).

The Pain de Sucre

Across from Clécy, the **east bank** of the Orne is dominated by the exposed rock face of the giant **Pain de Sucre**, or Sugarloaf, looming above the river. Small footpaths, and the tortuous Route des Crêtes, wind up to its flat top, making for some of the most enjoyable walks in Normandy. Picnic sites and parking places along the crest hold orientation maps so weather-beaten as to be almost abstract, but the views down to the flat fields of the Orne valley are stupendous. This is a prime site for **hang-gliders**; disconcertingly, at two points paved concrete ramps, built to facilitate launches lead right to the edge of the precipice.

Pont-d'Ouilly

If you're planning on walking, or cycling, one good central spot in which to base yourself is **PONT-D'OUILLY**, a dozen or so kilometres upriver from Clécy, at the point where the main road from Vire to Falaise crosses the river. It's a small town, with a few basic shops, an old covered market hall and a promenade (with bar) slightly upstream alongside the weir. Canoes, kayaks and mountain bikes can be rented by the hour or the day at the Base de Plein Air by the river (ⓣ02.31.69.86.02, ⓦwww.pontdouilly-loisirs.com). Alternatively, a pleasant walk leads for 3.5km south along the riverside to the pretty little village of **Le Mesnil Villement**. A Grand Pardon de St-Roch takes place along the river on the third Sunday in August.

As well as its **campsite**, overlooking the river (ⓣ02.31.69.46.12; closed Oct–Easter), Pont-d'Ouilly has an attractive **hotel**, the *du Commerce* (ⓣ02.31.69.80.16; ❷; closed Sun eve & Mon). This is the quintessential French village hotel, with a friendly welcome and attentive service, though the slightly higher-priced en-suite rooms have only been converted rather perfunctorily. Its **restaurant** is very popular with local families, serving superb, definitive Norman cooking, with plenty of creamy *pays d'Auge* sauces, on menus that start at €15; the options at €28 and €34 include a fabulous *assiette de fruits de mer*. Be sure to try the flaming *Bourdelot* for dessert, a sort of incandescent apple turnover. Appropriately enough, the dining room is filled with stuffed animals.

About 1km north of Pont-d'Ouilly, the more upmarket *Auberge St-Christophe*, covered with ivy and geraniums, offers exclusively en-suite rooms in a beautiful setting on the right bank of the Orne (ⓣ02.31.69.81.23; ❸; closed Sun eve, Mon & three weeks in Feb). The cheapest of its imaginative menus costs €20, while the *Menu Gastronomique* is €47.

The Roche d'Oëtre

A short distance south of Pont-d'Ouilly is the **Roche d'Oëtre**, a high rock affording a tremendous view, not over the Orne but into the deep and totally wooded gorge of the Rouvre. The rock itself is private property, though you're under no obligation to visit the café there.

The river widens soon afterwards into the **Lac du Rabodanges**, formed by the many-arched Rabodanges Dam. It's a popular spot, with a multi-facility **campsite**, *Les Retours*, perfectly situated between the dam and the bridge on the D121. There's a play area for kids, and grassy picnic slopes lead down to the water's edge, where the occasional bather risks a swim among the waterskiers, speedboats, windsurfers, canoes and kayaks. The imposing Rabodanges château, higher up the hillside, is now a stud farm.

Putanges

Further-climbing roads bring you to **PUTANGES**, another possible place to stay, with a well-priced **hotel**, the *Lion Verd* (ⓣ02.33.35.01.86; ❷; closed Sun eve & Mon, plus all Jan), very near the river, and a small **campsite**, the *Val d'Orne* (ⓣ02.33.35.04.67; closed Oct–March). The town lies a bit beyond the main attractions of the region, but nevertheless it's a pleasant stop, with a few bars and pavement cafés and, just upstream from the bridge, the weirs over which the Orne appears from its source a short way south.

The Bocage

The region centring on **St-Lô**, west of Caen and just south of the Cotentin, is known as the **Bocage Normande**. The word *bocage* refers to a type of cultivated countryside common in the west of France, in which fields are cut by tight hedgerows rooted into walls of earth well over 1m high.

An effective form of smallhold farming, at least in preindustrial days, it also proved to be a perfect system of anti-tank barricades. When the Allied troops tried to advance through the region in 1944, it was almost impenetrable – certainly bearing no resemblance to the East Anglian plains where they had trained. The war here was hand-to-hand, inch-by-inch slaughter; the destruction of villages often wholesale.

St-Lô

The city of **ST-LÔ**, a transport junction 60km south of Cherbourg and 36km southwest of Bayeux, was crucial in the war to the Allied breakout of the Cotentin, and is still known as the "Capital of the Ruins". Black-and-white postcards of the wartime devastation are on sale everywhere, and you come across memorial sites at every turn. In the main square, the gate of the old prison commemorates Resistance members executed by the Nazis, people deported east to the concentration camps and soldiers killed in action. When the bombardment of St-Lô was at its fiercest, the Germans refused to take any measures to protect the prisoners; the gate was all that survived. In similar vein, behind the cathedral, a monument to the dead of World War I is pitted with shrapnel from World War II. Less depressingly, at the foot of the rock under the castle you can see the entrance to caves where citizens sheltered from the onslaught, while somewhere far below are great vaults used by the German command. In Studs Terkel's book, *The Good War*, a GI reminisces about the huge party thrown there after the Americans found vast stockpiles of champagne; Thomas Pynchon's *Gravity's Rainbow* has a crazed drinking scene based on the tale. Samuel Beckett was here during the battle and after, working for the Irish Red Cross as interpreter, driver and provision-seeker – for such things as rat poison for the maternity hospitals. He said he took away with him a "time-honoured conception of humanity in ruins".

The newness of so much in St-Lô reveals the scale of fighting. Between the *gare SNCF* and the castle rock, for example, a walk leads along the canalized channel of the Vire – an attractive course, but unmistakeably an attempt to patch over the ravages of war. All the trees in the city are the same height, too, all planted to replace the battle's mutilated stumps. But the most visible – and brilliant – reconstruction is the **Cathédrale de Notre Dame**. The main body of this, with its strange southward-veering nave, has been conventionally repaired and rebuilt. Between the shattered west front and base of the collapsed north tower, however, a startling sheer wall of icy green stone makes no attempt to mask the destruction.

By way of contrast to such memories, a lighthouse-like 1950s folly spirals to nowhere on the main square, place Général-de-Gaulle. Should you feel the urge to climb its 157 steps, make your way into the brand-new and even more pointless labyrinth of glass at its feet, which now houses St-Lô's tourist office (for hours, see opposite), and pay the €1.50 admission fee. More compelling, around the back of the Mairie, is a **Musée des Beaux Arts** (Wed–Mon 10am–noon & 2–6pm; €2). This is full of treasures: a Boudin sunset; a Lurçat tapestry of his dog Nadir and the Pirates; works by Corot, van Loo, Moreau; a

Léger watercolour; a fine series of unfaded sixteenth-century Flemish tapestries on the lives of two peasants; and sad bombardment relics of the town.

Practicalities

St-Lô makes an interesting pause, but it's virtually abandoned at night. Full information on what it has to offer can be obtained from the **tourist office** in place Général-de-Gaulle, described above (July & Aug Mon–Sat 9am–6pm; Sept–June Mon 2–6pm, Tues–Fri 9.30am–12.30pm & 2–6pm, Sat 9.30am–1pm; ⓣ02.33.77.60.35, ⓦwww.mairie-saint-lo.fr). The **gare routière** is on the rue des 80e and 136e, a short way south.

Most of the **hotels**, restaurants and bars, however, are just across the river, near the **gare SNCF**. Overlooking the river from the brow of a ridge beside the station, the upmarket logis *Hôtel des Voyageurs*, 5–7 avenue Briovère (ⓣ02.33.05.08.63, ⓦwww.hoteldesvoyageurs50.com; ❹), is home to the *Tocqueville* **restaurant**, which has menus from €19. If you'd rather be up in town, try *La Crémaillère*, 10 rue de la Chancellerie (ⓣ02.33.57.14.68; ❷; closed Fri eve & Sat in low season).

The Vire Valley

Once St-Lô was taken in the Battle of Normandy, the armies moved speedily on to their next confrontation. Consequently, the **Vire Valley**, trailing south from St-Lô, saw little action – and indeed its towns and villages have rarely been touched by any historic or cultural mainstream. The motivation in coming to this landscape of rolling hills and occasional gorges is essentially to consume the region's cider, Calvados, and butter-rich fruit pastries.

Although the countryside is filled with orchards of apples and pears, the land is less fertile than elsewhere in Normandy – and has suffered heavily from the recent depression in the fruit market. A booming trade, however, has grown up around illicit Calvados, bolstering the faltering economy of many Vire farmers. Bootleggers smuggle hundreds of thousands of litres throughout France, using the hydraulic suspension of their Citröen cars to obscure the heavy loads they are carrying from the eyes of watching taxmen. One much-arrested smuggler has such James Bond accessories as automatically rotating licence plates, smoke screens and even oil jets for use against pursuing motorcycles.

Between St-Lô and Vire

The best section of the Vire is the valley that comes down from St-Lô through the Roches de Ham to Tessy-sur-Vire. The **Roches de Ham** are a pair of sheer rocky promontories high above the river. They are promoted as a "viewing table", though the pleasure lies as much in the walk up, through lanes lined with blackberries, hazelnuts and rich orchards.

Just downstream from the Roches, and a good place to stop over for a night, is **LA CHAPELLE-SUR-VIRE**. Its church, towering majestically above the river, has been an object of pilgrimage since the twelfth century. There's a weir nearby and a scattering of grassy islands. Next to the bridge on the lower road is the *Auberge de la Chapelle* (ⓣ02.33.56.32.83; ❷), a good but rather expensive **restaurant** that also offers a few cheap **rooms** (which include breakfast). Menus are priced at €22 and €28, and feature plenty of fresh river fish.

An alternative base for the Roches, 5km northeast of La Chapelle, is **TORIGNI-SUR-VIRE**, which was the base of the Grimaldi family before they achieved quasi-royal status upon moving on to the principality of Monaco. A spacious country town, it boasts a few grand buildings and an attractive **campsite**, *Camping du Lac* (Ⓣ02.33.56.91.74). The *Auberge de l'Orangerie*, 3 rue Victor-Hugo (Ⓣ02.33.56.70.64; ❷; hotel closed mid-Nov to mid-Feb; restaurant closed Sun eve & Mon) is a good **restaurant**, with menus starting at €13, and also offers five rooms.

At the eastern end of the sinuous Vire gorge, 10km north of Vire and 6km west of Le Bény-Bocage, stands the former railway viaduct of **Le Viaduc de la Souleuvre**, designed by Gustave Eiffel. Only the six supporting granite pillars of Eiffel's original structure remain – the railway closed down in 1970 – but in 1990 a wooden boardwalk was relaid across half the span of the bridge, on which visitors can cross to the deepest part of the gorge. Once there, 61m up, they are expected to jump off – this is A.J. Hackett's **bungy-jumping** centre (hours vary, but open daily late June to mid-Sept; late March to late June and mid-Sept to mid-Nov Sat, Sun & hols only; reservations essential Ⓣ02.31.66.31.66, Ⓦwww.ajhackett.fr). Jumpers have to be aged at least 13, and for one to three people to make a single jump each costs €76 per person; you also have to pay €3 for the privilege of parking in the adjacent field. Less intrepid souls can walk down to the meadows immediately beneath the viaduct and watch the plummeting from there.

Vire

The pride and joy of the people of the hill town of **VIRE** are their *andouilles*, the blood sausages known in English as chitterlings. If you can avoid these hideous parcels of pigs' intestines, and the assortment of abattoirs that produce them, it's possible to have a good time; in fact, Vire is a town worth visiting specifically for its food.

The only problem is what to do when you're not eating. As testified by a memorial in the **belfry** that stands alone in the town centre, the town was all but destroyed on D-Day, at a cost of five hundred lives. That stunted tower houses temporary exhibitions each summer (July & Aug Mon–Thurs 2–6pm, Fri & Sat 10am–noon & 2–6pm; free), while down the hill towards the river, the town museum in the place Ste-Anne holds furniture, costumes and paintings by regional artists (Wed–Mon 10am–noon & 2–6pm; €3.95). Nearby, you can wander by the little scrap of **canal**, equipped with twee floating houses for the ducks, that lies just below the one stark finger that survives of the castle. The only action is at the Friday **market**, again obsessively dedicated to food.

For some exercise, head 6km south along the D76 to **Lac de la Dathée**. Set in open country, the lake is circled by footpaths; in summer it sometimes dries up completely, but when it's wet it can also be crossed by rented sailing boat, kayak or windsurf board (daily June–Sept; Ⓣ02.31.66.01.58).

Incidentally, although the small industrial area immediately north of Vire, where the Vire and Varenne valleys meet, may now appear dull in the extreme, it holds a remarkable place in the history of popular music. As the **Vaux de Vire**, this became a centre during the fifteenth century for the manufacture of cloth. The drinking songs composed by one of the textile workers, Olivier Basselin, acquired such popularity throughout medieval Europe that the district gave its name to a new kind of entertainment – **Vaudeville**.

Practicalities

Vire's **tourist office** is in the square de la Résistance at the heart of town (July & Aug Mon–Sat 9.30am–6.30pm; Sept–June Mon–Sat 9.30am–12.30pm & 1.30–6pm; ⓣ02.31.66.28.50, ⓦwww.vire-tourisme.com). When choosing a **hotel**, it makes sense to go for one with a good dining room. The central *Hôtel de France*, within sight of the tourist office at 4 rue d'Aignaux (ⓣ02.31.68.00.35; ❷), serves several separate menus; the €24 *menu du terroir* is packed with local specialities, including *andouilles*, but no one's going to make you eat it if you don't want to – there's always *tripes a là mode de Caen* instead. The *Hôtel des Voyageurs*, north of the centre near the station at the bottom of avenue de la Gare (ⓣ02.31.68.01.16; ❷), offers basic but acceptable rooms, while its restaurant, the *Welcome*, serves remarkably sumptuous buffets of hors d'oeuvres and desserts; you can sample both for €13. Otherwise, *Au Vrai Normand*, 14 rue Armand-Gasté (ⓣ02.31.67.90.99; closed Tues eve, Wed all day & Sun eve), is the best stand-alone **restaurant**, with lunch from €12.50 and a €17 dinner menu that includes a *Montgolfière de pêcheur*, a sort of fish stew covered with pastry.

West and south from Vire

Once past Vire, the roads towards Brittany present you with the choice either of heading southwest for the frontier towns of **Fougères** and **Vitré** (see pp.255 & 258), or directly to the coast and making the magnificent **Mont-St-Michel** (see p.177) your last port of call in Normandy.

West from Vire, the road to Villedieu passes through **ST-SEVER**, not in itself much to write home about but backed by a dark and magical **forest** in which there's a dolmen, an abbey and a scattering of good picnic spots marked by signs showing a champagne bottle in a hamper.

Villedieu-les-Poêles

VILLEDIEU-LES-POÊLES – literally "City of God the Frying Pans" – is a lively though touristy place, 28km west of Vire. Much of this ancient town still retains significant elements of its medieval appearance, especially in its backstreets where perfectly preserved old courtyards are tucked away behind unprepossessing wooden gateways. Ever since the twelfth century, Villedieu has been a centre for metalworking, despite the fact that with no mines in Normandy the only source of copper came from melting down unwanted artefacts. To this day, copper souvenirs and kitchen utensils gleam from its rows of shops, and the tourist office can provide lists of dozens of local *ateliers* for more direct purchases.

Displays at the **Musée de la Poeslerie**, in a pretty little courtyard at 25 rue Général-Huard (April to mid-Nov Tues 2.30–6.30pm, Wed–Mon 10am–12.30pm & 2.30–6.30pm; €3.60), illustrate the historical development of Villedieu's copperware; the same ticket also gets you into the **Musée de la Dentelle** (lace) in the same building – while paying an extra €1.60 entitles you to admission to the **Musée du Meuble Normand** (Norman furniture) down the street in the place du Pussoir Fidèle (same hours as the Poeslerie). On the road between the museums, you can also watch copper craftsmen at work, and buy the results, in the **Atelier des Cuivres** at 54 rue Général-Huard (Easter–Oct Mon–Sat

9am–noon & 1.30–5.30pm, Sun 10am–noon & 2.30–5.30pm; Nov–Easter Mon–Sat 9am–noon & 1.30–5.30pm; €4.50).

Even if all this emphasis on copper pots and pans is starting to seem obsessive, it's well worth making time to visit the **Fonderie de Cloches** at 13 rue du Pont-Chignon, one of the twelve remaining **bell foundries** in Europe. Work here is only part-time due to limited demand, but you may find the forge lit nonetheless (mid-Feb to June & Sept to mid-Nov Tues–Sat 10am–12.30pm & 2–5.30pm; July & Aug daily 9am–6pm; €4). Expert craftsmen will show you the moulds, composed of an unpleasant-looking combination of clay, goats' hair and horse manure.

Practicalities

Villedieu's **tourist office** is located in a hexagonal glass kiosk on place des Costils (April–June & Sept Mon–Sat 9am–noon & 2–6.30pm; July & Aug daily 9am–6.30pm; Oct–March Mon–Sat 9am–noon & 2–6pm; ⓣ02.33.61.05.69, ⓦwww.ot-villedieu.fr). If you're charmed into **staying**, the very welcoming logis *Hôtel St-Pierre et St-Michel*, in the heart of the main street at 12 place de la République (ⓣ02.33.61.00.11, ⓦwww.st-pierre-hotel.com; ❸; closed mid-Jan to mid-Feb), houses the stylish *Le Sourdin* restaurant, where the €31 menu is seriously gastronomic. There's also a three-star **campsite** by the river, *Jean-Louis Bougourg* (ⓣ02.33.61.02.44; closed Oct–Easter).

By far the nicest **bar** in Villedieu is *Le Pussoir Fidèle*, 2 place du Pussoir Fidèle (ⓣ02.33.51.94.58; closed Mon Oct–May). It offers tables in the cobbled square, Guinness, Rolling Rock and local cider, a good selection of music from around the world (especially the Celtic bits), and attracts a youngish clientele.

Champrepus

Eight kilometres west of Villedieu at **CHAMPREPUS**, an arch across the D924 serves as both a sign announcing, and a bridge between the two sections of Normandy's finest **zoo** (Feb & Oct to mid-Nov daily 1.30–6pm; March Sat & Sun 1.30–6pm; April–June & Sept daily 10am–6pm; July & Aug daily 10am–7pm; €10; ⓣ02.33.61.30.74, ⓦwww.zoo-champrepus.com). It displays a vast array of species in remarkably natural surroundings, starting a little disappointingly with domestic and farm animals such as bunnies and donkeys, but swiftly moving on to tigers and chimps, ostriches and otters. In this typically pastoral Norman landscape, it's oddly shocking to encounter zebras grazing in the meadows, wallabies hopping around the orchards, and lions making their homes amidst dolmens. In the most unusual section, visitors are free to stroll in among large groups of sleepy-eyed lemurs, with nothing to stop you touching them apart from their prominently bared canine teeth. Children are invited to milk an artificial cow or bounce on an inflatable elephant, and there's a little grill restaurant on site.

Mortain and the Forêt de Lande-Pourrie

South from Vire, if you are heading for Fougères (see p.255) or Domfront (see p.209), you pass through the **Forêt de Mortain** and its continuation, the **Forêt de Lande-Pourrie**. The **Fosse d'Arthur**, a remote spot in the forest to the east of Mortain, is one of the many unlikely claimants to King Arthur's death scene. A couple of waterfalls disappear into deep limestone caverns, but really there's little to see.

The war-ravaged town of **MORTAIN** itself perches high above the very deep gorge of the Cance, 24km south of Vire. It's not a place to linger very long, but the views, especially from the south end of the main street, are spectacular. A short walk west out of town leads into some lovely countryside, with two **waterfalls** – known as the Grande Cascade and the Petite Cascade – interrupting the river itself. Head up the high rocky bluff to the east, on the other hand, and from the tiny chapel at the top the neighbouring province of Maine spreads before you. On a clear day, you can even see Mont-St-Michel.

If you want a **place to stay** in Mortain, the *Hôtel de la Poste*, 1 place des Arcades (ⓣ02.33.59.00.05, ⓦwww.hoteldelaposte.fr; ❸; closed Mon & Tues), is the best option, with a restaurant serving good menus from €18.

St-Hilaire-du-Harcoët

The thriving (Wednesday) market town of **ST-HILAIRE-DU-HARCOËT**, 28km north of Fougères, amounts to little more than a crossroads near the big market square. It does, however, hold a few restaurants and **hotels**, such as *Le Cygne et Résidence*, on the main road into town from Fougères at 99 rue Waldeck-Rousseau (ⓣ02.33.49.11.84; ❸; closed first three weeks of Jan, plus Sun eve & Fri eve Oct–March), a comfortable, newly modernized logis with a swimming pool in the garden and an appealing set of menus from €14 up to €38, and the cheaper *L'Agriculture*, higher up at 79 rue Waldeck-Rousseau (ⓣ02.33.49.10.60; ❶), where the €12 menu kicks off with nine fresh oysters in season.

Travel details

Trains

Alençon to: Caen (6 daily; 1hr 20min) via Sées (13min) and Argentan (30min); Tours (1 daily; 2hr 10min); Le Mans (10 daily; 50min).
Argentan to: Granville (5 daily; 1hr 30min) via Vire (50min) and Villedieu (1hr 5min).
Bagnoles to: Briouze (3 daily; 40min) for Argentan (1hr 20min) and Paris (3hr 20min).
Évreux to: Bernay (7 daily; 25min); Caen (7 daily; 1hr 10min); Conches (4 daily; 15min); Lisieux (7 daily; 45min); Paris St-Lazare (18 daily; 1hr); Serquigny (4 daily; 30min).
Lisieux to: Rouen (4 daily; 1hr 30min) via Bernay (20min) and Serquigny (30min); Paris (11 daily; 2hr) via Bernay (15min) and Évreux (1hr); Cherbourg (15 daily; 2hr 40min) via Caen (30min) and Bayeux (50min).
St-Lô to: Caen (4 daily; 50min) via Bayeux (30min); Rennes (4 daily; 2hr 10min) via Coutances (20min) and Pontorson (1hr 15min).
Vire to: Paris (5 daily; 2hr 45min) via Argentan (50min) and L'Aigle (1hr 30min); to Granville (7 daily; 1hr 15min) via Villedieu (40min).

Buses

The main inland bus networks are operated by **Bus Verts**, who cover Calvados in particular from their base in Caen (ⓣ08.01.21.42.14; ⓦwww.busverts14.fr), and **STAO**, whose routes extend across most of the Orne region further south (Alençon ⓣ02.33.26.06.35; Argentan ⓣ02.33.80.09.09; Mortagne ⓣ02.33.25.19.11).
L'Aigle to: Gacé (1–2 daily; 1hr); Vimoutiers (1–2 daily; 1hr 10min); Évreux (2–3 daily; 1hr 20min) via Conches (45min); Mortagne (3 daily; 1hr).
Alençon to: Bagnoles (3 daily; 1hr); Évreux (1 daily; 2hr), via L'Aigle (1hr 40min); Vimoutiers (1–3 daily; 1hr 30min) via Sées (30min); Mortagne (1–3 daily; 1hr); Bellême (1–2 daily; 1hr).
Argentan to: Alençon (1–2 daily; 1hr 15min) via Sées (40min); Carrouges (1–3 daily; 45min); Domfront (1–3 daily; 1hr 50min) via Bagnoles (1hr).
Caen to: Vire (3 daily; 1hr 30min) via Aunay-sur-Odon (1hr); Flers (4 daily; 1hr 20min) via Thury-Harcourt (40min) and Clécy (50min); Falaise (7 daily; 1hr); Pont-L'Évêque (3 daily; 1hr 10min).

Lisieux to: Pont-l'Évêque (4 daily; 25min) and on to Honfleur (50min); Vimoutiers (4 daily; 40min) via Livarot (30min); Orbec (6 daily; 35min); Le Havre (2 daily; 1hr 30min).

Mortagne to: Bellême (1–4 daily; 20min).

St-Lô to: Bayeux (8 daily; 30min); Cherbourg (3 daily; 1hr 40min); Coutances (5 daily; 30min).

Vire to: Condé-sur-Noireau (2 daily; 30min); Fougères (4 daily; 1hr 30min); Avranches (5 daily; 45min).

Brittany

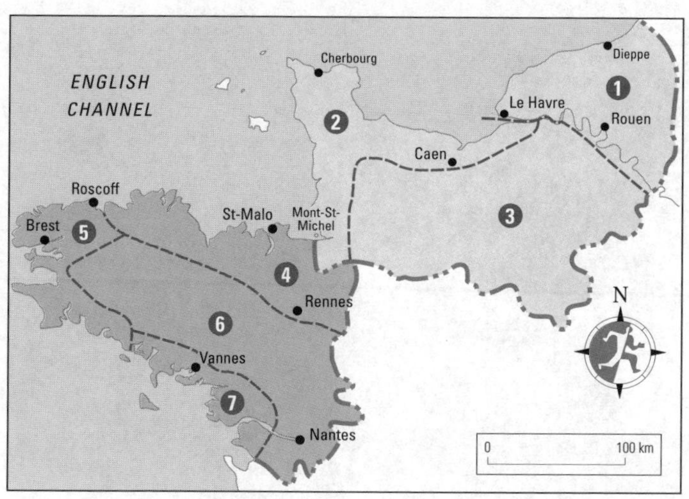

ENGLISH CHANNEL
Cherbourg
Dieppe
Le Havre
Rouen
Caen
Roscoff
Brest
St-Malo
Mont-St-Michel
Rennes
Vannes
Nantes
N
0
100 km
1
2
3
4
5
6
7

The North Coast and Rennes

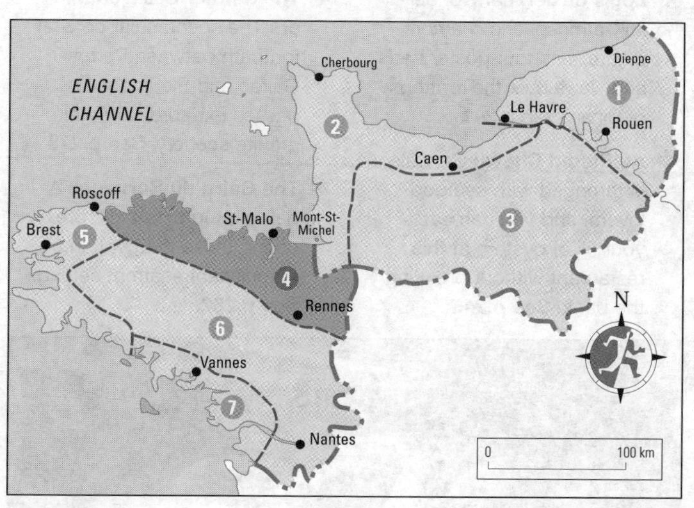

CHAPTER 4

Highlights

- **St-Malo** Over-crowded it may be, but St-Malo's walled *citadelle* still feels like the romantic haunt of pirates and explorers. See p.228
- **Dinan** With its imposing walls and delightful lanes, Dinan is one of France's finest medieval towns. See p.239
- **Logis de Jerzual** Wonderfully atmospheric *chambre d'hote*, with four-poster beds and views over the rooftops of Dinan. See p.241
- **Au Pied d'Cheval** Cancale is thronged with seafood-lovers, and you can eat your fill of oysters at this restaurant without breaking the bank. See p.245
- **Binic** Cute little seafront resort with huge beaches, that's ideal for families and romantic couples alike. See p.267
- **Île de Bréhat** Even in high summer, a boat trip to this beautiful island enables you to escape the traffic and crowds. See p.272
- **The Sentier des Douaniers** The spectacular coastal footpath between Perros-Guirec and Ploumanac'h passes extraordinary pink-granite scenery. See p.278
- **The Cairn du Barnenez** A pair of step pyramids, predating those in Egypt, in a magnificent seafront setting. See p.282

△ Crate of lobsters

The North Coast and Rennes

The **northern coast** of Brittany is varied in the extreme. Long sections, open to the full force of the Atlantic, are spectacular but much too dangerous for swimming; others shelter superb natural harbours and peaceful resorts. The old *citadelle* port of **St-Malo** makes an attractive point of arrival, from which you are well positioned for exploration, even if your ultimate goals lie elsewhere.

The best of the **resorts** are concentrated along two separate stretches of coastline, the Côte d'Émeraude and the Côte de Granit Rose. As green as its name suggests, the **Côte d'Émeraude** remains largely unspoiled, at its wildest on the heather-covered headlands of Cap Fréhel. Thanks to gorgeous beaches, seaside towns such as **Le Val-André** and **Erquy** tend to be dominated by English visitors, but it's always possible to find a secluded campsite for a night or two's stopover.

Further west, beyond the placid **Baie de St-Brieuc** (the town of St-Brieuc itself is, for most holidaymakers, a traffic-crowded nuisance to be avoided), the coastline erupts into a garish labyrinth of pink granite boulders, the famed **Côte de Granit Rose**. This harsher territory was once, at **Paimpol** and elsewhere, the home of cod and whaling fleets that ranged right across the Atlantic. Today it's reliant on tourism, especially at the attractive twin resorts of **Perros-Guirec** and **Ploumanac'h.** There are also plenty of smaller places where you can avoid the crowds, such as **Loguivy** on the mainland, and, just offshore, the **Île de Bréhat** – among the most beautiful of all northern French islands.

The first 20km of the route **inland** from St-Malo take you alongside the delightful **Rance estuary**. Frequent boats connect both St-Malo and Dinard with **Dinan**, a medieval fortress town *par excellence* that, like most of this region, owes its prosperity to an epic saga of trading and piracy on the high seas. Beyond it, to the south of the more ancient community of **Dol** – site of several fascinating prehistoric relics – lies a patchwork of waterways and woodlands, where rivers and canals cut through characteristic Breton **forests** like **Ville-Cartier**. Further **east**, the redoubtable **citadelles** of **Fougères** and **Vitré** still guard the frontier with Normandy.

At the heart of the *département* of Ille-et-Vilaine, just over 60km southeast of St-Malo, the city of **Rennes** has after centuries of rivalry with Nantes finally

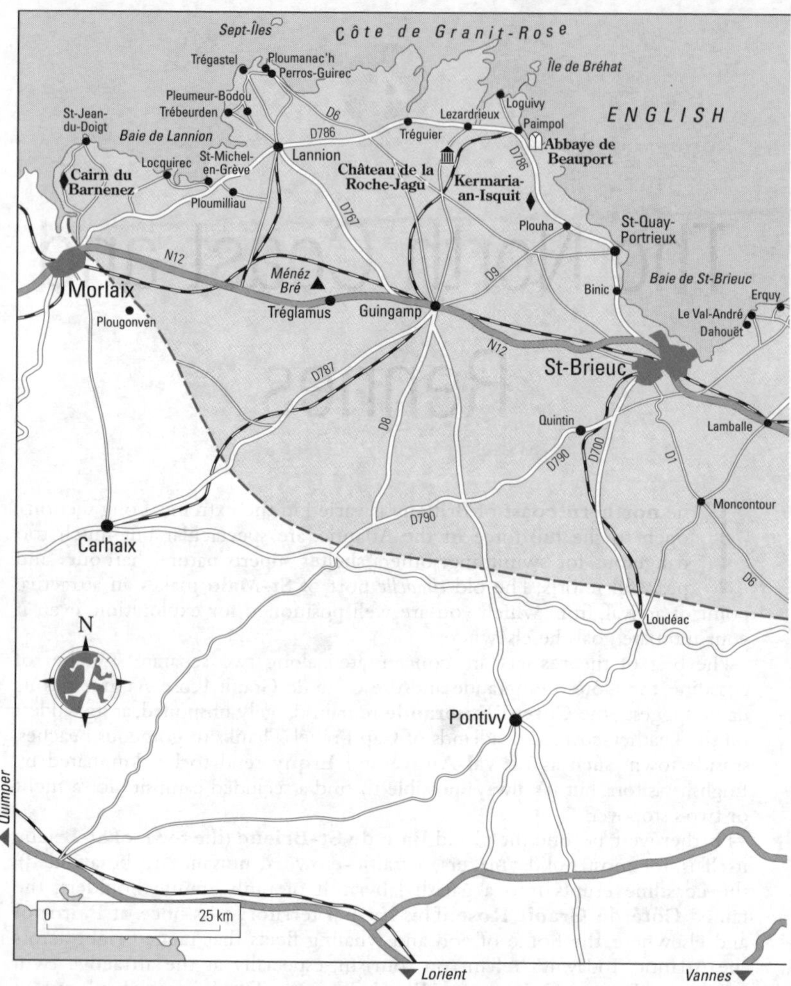

established itself as the indisputable capital of Brittany. Rennes may not be the prettiest town in the province, but it is without doubt the liveliest. It hosts an important university and most of the major Breton political and cultural organizations; it's also renowned for **festivals**, devoting itself to ten days of theatre and music each July during the **Tombées de la Nuit**, and celebrating **Les Transmusicales**, one of the most important events in the calendar of French rock, in December.

Among numerous other annual events in northern Brittany, the biggest and most compelling is the **Breton Music** festival, held each July at **St-Brieuc**. That's also the venue of the ominous-sounding **Art Rock** festival in late May, while the region's largest traditional festival is the *pardon* of St Yves in **Tréguier**, on the third Sunday in May.

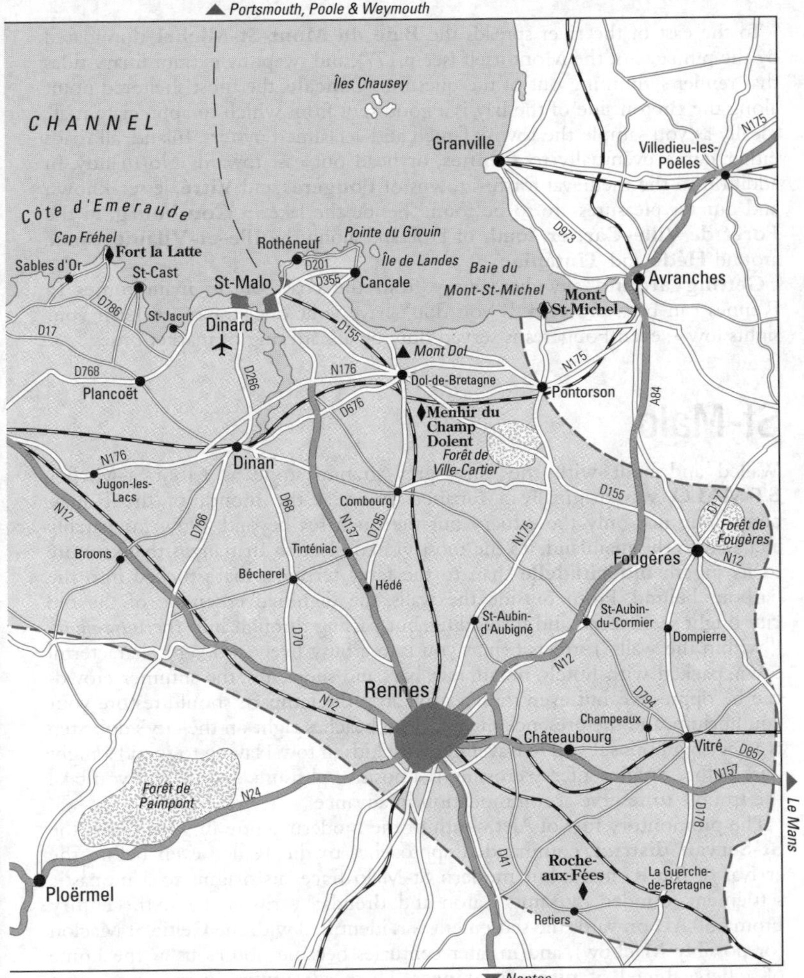

East: the Rance and Rennes

Whether you approach across the Channel by ferry, or along the coast from Mont-St-Michel in Normandy, the wide estuary of the **River Rance** serves as a spectacular introduction to Brittany. The towns of **St-Malo** and **Dinard**, each with its own very distinct ambience, stand to either side of its mouth, while **Dinan** guards the head of the river itself 20km upstream. From those few places where it's possible to cross the Rance (most notably, along the top of the tidal power dam known as the **Barrage de la Rance**), you can enjoy magnificent views of its sheltered banks – rich, fertile and repeatedly pierced by tributaries.

To the east of the river spreads the **Baie du Mont-St-Michel**, dominated by the pinnacle of the Mont itself (see p.177), and swept by extraordinary tides that render swimming out of the question. **Cancale**, the most sheltered point along the Breton side of the bay, is a good spot from which to appreciate it all, ideally as you sample the town's famed and acclaimed oysters. Inland, all roads either curve eventually to **Rennes**, or head out east towards Normandy. In addition to the medieval fortress towns of **Fougères** and **Vitré**, lesser-known and quieter pleasures are to be found beside the lake in **Combourg**, in the **Forêt de Ville-Cartier**, south of Dol, and along the **Ille-et-Vilaine canal**, around **Hédé** and **Tinténiac**.

Getting around anywhere away from the coast or off main routes to Rennes can be a problem. If you don't have your own transport, keep your sights low – even Fougères is served only by a scattering of market buses.

St-Malo

Walled and built with the same grey granite stone as Mont-St-Michel, **ST-MALO** was originally a fortified island at the mouth of the Rance, controlling not only the estuary but the open sea beyond. Now inseparably attached to the mainland, it's the most visited place in Brittany – thanks more to its superb **old citadelle** than to the ferry terminal that's tucked into the harbour behind. From outside the walls, the dignified ensemble of the old city might seem stern and forbidding, but passing through into the *intra-muros* ("within the walls") streets brings you into a busy, lively and very characterful town, packed with hotels, restaurants, bars and shops. Yes, the summer crowds can be oppressive, but even then a stroll atop the ramparts should restore your equilibrium, and the presence of vast, clean beaches right on the city's doorstep is a very big bonus if you're travelling with kids in tow. Having to spend a night here before or after a ferry crossing is a positive pleasure – so long as you take the trouble to reserve accommodation in advance.

The promontory fort of Alet, south of the modern centre in what's now the **St-Servan district**, commanded approaches to the Rance even before the arrival of the Romans, but modern St-Malo traces its origins to a monastic settlement founded by saints Aaron and Brendan early in the sixth century. From 550 AD onwards the settlement was identified with the Celtic St Maclou (or possibly MacLow), and in later centuries became notorious as the home of a fierce breed of **pirate-mariners**. These adventurers were never quite under anybody's control but their own; for four years from 1590, St-Malo even declared itself to be an independent republic, under the motto "*Ni Français, Ni Bretons, Malouins Suis*". Over a period of centuries, the *corsaires* of St-Malo not only forced English ships passing up the Channel to pay tribute, but also brought wealth from further afield. Jacques Cartier, who founded the earliest French colony in Canada, lived in and sailed from St-Malo, as did the first colonists to settle the Falklands – hence the islands' Argentinian name, Las Malvinas. Even when the Duke of Marlborough landed 15,000 men just up the coast near Cancale in 1758, and attempted to take the city by land, St-Malo's defences proved too formidable.

Arrival and city transport

St-Malo is always busy with **boats**. From the **Terminal Ferry du Naye**, Brittany Ferries (Ⓣ02.99.40.64.41, Ⓦwww.brittany-ferries.com) sails to

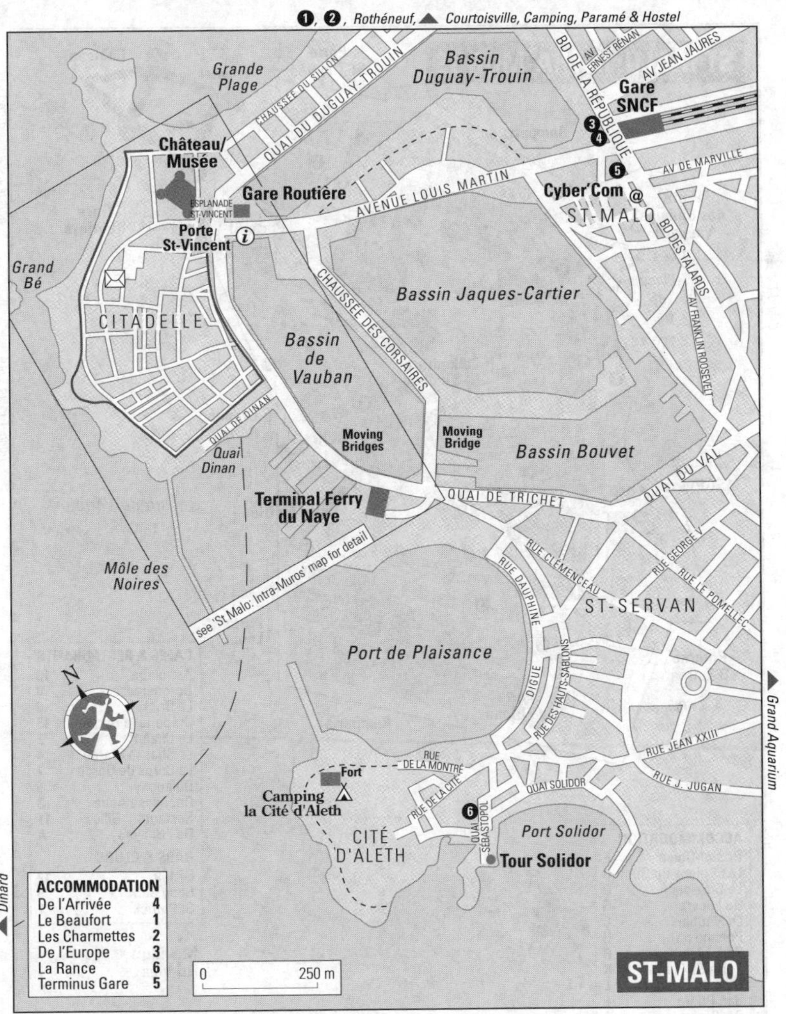

Portsmouth, while Condor Ferries (☎02.99.20.03.00, www.condorferries.com) connects with both Weymouth (via Jersey or Guernsey) and Poole during spring and summer; for full details, see p.21.

Between April and early November, regular passenger **ferries to Dinard** operate from the **quai Dinan**, just outside the westernmost point of the ramparts in front of the port (Compagnie Corsaire; ☎08.25.16.80.35,

> Le Chateaubriand (☎02.99.46.44.40, www.chateaubriand.com) puts on **gastronomic cruises** in the Baie du Mont-St-Michel and up the Rance, costing €50–70, from the Gare Maritime de la Richardais, at the Dinard end of the Barrage de la Rance.

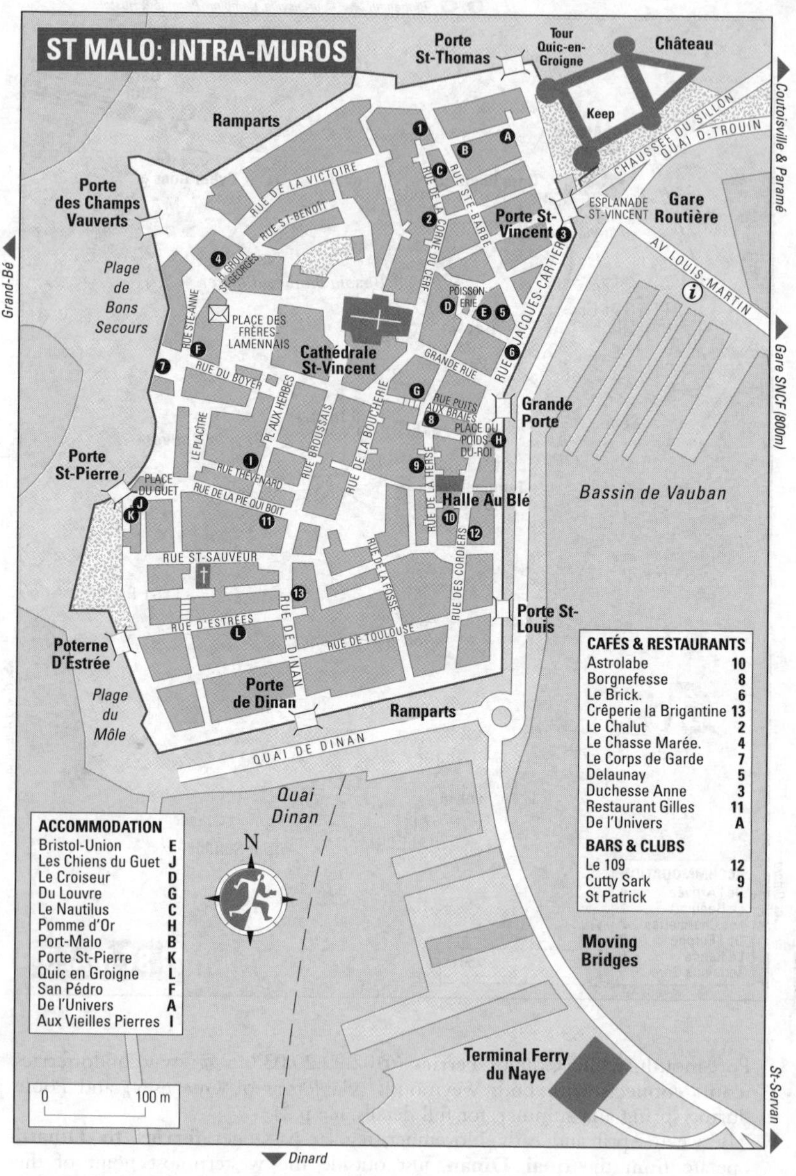

www.compagniecorsaire.com; €3.70 single, €5.90 return, bikes €4.50 or €7.50 return); the trip across the estuary takes an all-too-short ten minutes. Compagnie Corsaire also conduct excursions up the river to Dinan (see p.239), and cruises along the Brittany coast to Cap Fréhel and the Île Cézembre, and out to the Îles Chausey (see p.175). In addition, Emeraude Jersey Ferries (Ⓣ08.25.16.51.80, Ⓦwww.emeraude.co.uk) connect St-Malo with the **Channel Islands**.

St-Malo's **gare SNCF** (☎08.36.35.35.35) is 2km out from the *citadelle* on square Jean Coquelin, and convenient neither for the old town nor the ferry (take care if you're planning a tight connection). All trains to and from St-Malo pass through Dol. Most continue through to Rennes, so if you're heading west towards Dinan and St-Brieuc, or northeast into Normandy, you'll probably have to change at Dol.

Though almost all St-Malo buses – whether local or long-distance – also call at the *gare SNCF*, the **gare routière** – not a building, just an expanse of concrete – is officially located on the esplanade St-Vincent right next to the tourist office (see below). The two main regional bus companies both have ticket offices here. Tourisme Verney act as agents for the Compagnie de Transport d'Ille et Vilaine (TIV; ☎02.99.40.82.00), which run services to Dinard, Dinan, Cancale, Combourg (not in July and August) and Rennes. Les Courriers Bretons (☎02.99.19.70.80, Ⓦwww.lescourriersbretons.com), go to Cancale, Mont-St-Michel, Dol and Fougères. In summer, they also operate a complicated schedule of day-trips and half-day-trips to destinations including Mont-St-Michel, Dinan, Cap Fréhel and the Île de Bréhat.

Approaching central St-Malo or the ferry terminal by **road** can be somewhat dismal; the signposts appear designed to confuse, and all the roads seem to end on tramlined docksides. Lost and bewildered motorists circle the port like seagulls, and finding a place to **park** in high summer can be impossible. Driving in to catch a ferry, keep well clear of the old town; the **Chaussée des Corsaires**, which links the *citadelle* with the ferry terminal, can be closed for long periods while its moveable bridge is opened to let boats out of the Bassin Jacques-Cartier.

Car and **bicycle rental** outlets are detailed on p.237. You can get information on St-Malo's network of **city buses** at the *gare routière* or by calling ☎02.99.56.06.06.

Information

St-Malo's helpful **tourist office** (April–June & Sept Mon–Sat 9am–12.30pm & 1.30–7pm, Sun 10am–12.30pm & 2.30–6pm; July & Aug Mon–Sat 8.30am–8pm, Sun 10am–7pm; Oct–March Mon–Sat 9am–12.30pm & 1.30–6pm; ☎02.99.56.64.48, Ⓦwww.saint-malo-tourisme.com) is housed in a single-storey building on the Esplanade St-Vincent, right in front of the city walls, in between the Bassin de Vauban and the Bassin Duguay-Trouin in the **Port des Yachts**. As well as good detailed city maps, it can provide information on annual festivals such as the **Étonnants Voyageurs** (Amazing Travellers), dedicated to the film and literature of travel and adventure, which takes place for three days in late May and/or early June.

Accommodation

St-Malo boasts over a hundred **hotels**, including the traditional seaside boarding houses located just off the beach, as well as several **campsites** (see p.233) and one of the busiest **hostels** in France, the *Centre Patrick Varangot* (also known as the *Centre des Rencontres Internationales*), 37 avenue du Père-Umbricht, a couple of kilometres northeast of the *gare SNCF* in Paramé, not far from the walled city and only a short way back from the beach, (☎02.99.40.29.80, Ⓦwww.centrevarangot.com; dorm beds €12.20 including breakfast). To get there from the *gare SNCF*, take bus #1 or #5. Facilities include a cut-price cafeteria, a kitchen and even tennis courts, and there is no curfew.

In high season, St-Malo needs every one of its hotel rooms: the demand is phenomenal. Motorists intending to stay the night before catching a summer ferry sailing should make reservations well in advance; if you don't have a reservation, don't demoralize yourself hunting around, and settle for spending the night somewhere else along the coast or nearby. Apart from the obvious alternatives of Dinard and Dinan, it's worth considering peaceful smaller towns such as Combourg, Cancale, Jugon-les-Lacs, St-Jacut, or Erquy.

Hotels in the citadelle

The thirty or so of St-Malo's **hotels** that stand **within the city walls** are able to charge their guests premium rates; it's inside the walls that most of the after-dark activity takes place, and getting there from any of the surrounding suburbs requires a fair walk in through the docks. Those *intra-muros* hotels with their own restaurants tend to take advantage of high summer demand by insisting that all guests eat in.

Hôtel Bristol-Union 4 place de la Poissonnerie ⓣ02.99.40.83.36, ⓦwww.hotel-bristol-union.com. Unexciting but acceptable and recently renovated rooms, some very small, in a relatively quiet little square facing the former fish market, just off the Grande Rue. ❹

Hôtel-Restaurant les Chiens du Guet 4 place du Guet ⓣ02.99.40.87.29, ⓕ02.99.56.08.75. Simple, plain rooms – the cheapest of which lack en-suite facilities – in a friendly little hotel just inside the little Porte St-Pierre, which serves very good-value menus from €15 up to €33.50 on a cosy terrace. Closed mid-Nov to Jan. ❷

Hôtel Le Croiseur 2 place de la Poissonnerie ⓣ02.99.40.80.40, ⓦwww.saint-malo-gallery.com/hotel-lecroiseur. Clean and relatively modern place, near the Grande Porte. All rooms have TV plus bath or shower. ❸

Hôtel du Louvre 2 rue des Marins ⓣ02.99.40.86.62, ⓦwww.hoteldulouvre-saintmalo.com. Pleasant, upmarket place just off Grande Rue, between the Grande Porte and Cathédrale St-Vincent, with fifty refurburbished rooms – some suitable for the handicapped – and good €9 buffet breakfasts. ❺

Hôtel Le Nautilus 9 rue de la Corne de Cerf ⓣ02.99.40.42.27, ⓦwww.lenautilus.com. Colourfully refitted hotel (with a lift) not far in from the Porte St-Vincent, offering small but good-value and bright rooms. ❹

Hôtel-Restaurant Pomme d'Or 4 place du Poids-du-Roi ⓣ02.99.40.90.24, ⓦwww.la-pomme-dor.fr. Twelve modernized rooms in a fine old building, just inside the *citadelle* near the ramparts – take a sharp left after entering through the Grande Porte. Conventional menus start at €14.50, while the breakfast buffet spread is €6.70. Closed Jan to mid-Feb. ❸

Hôtel Port-Malo 15 rue Ste-Barbe ⓣ02.99.20.52.99, ⓕ02.23.18.48.93. Small but clean and comfortable en-suite rooms – above a nice old-fashioned bar, so go for the higher floors – with friendly and helpful management. No restaurant. ❷

Hôtel-Restaurant Porte St-Pierre 2 place du Guet ⓣ02.99.40.91.27, ⓕ02.99.56.09.94. Comfortable Logis de France, peeping out to sea over the walls of the *citadelle*, near the small Porte St-Pierre and very handy for the plage de Bon Secours. Predominantly fish-based dinner menus, in the separate restaurant across the alley, run from €26 upwards. Closed Dec & Jan. ❹

Hôtel Quic en Groigne 8 rue d'Estrées ⓣ02.99.20.22.20, ⓦwww.quic-en-groigne.com. Friendly little hotel at the far end of the *citadelle*, with nicely styled en-suite rooms. ❸

Hôtel San Pédro 1 rue Ste-Anne ⓣ02.99.40.88.57, ⓦwww.sanpedro-hotel.com. Twelve compact but tastefully and stylishly refurbished rooms in a nice quiet setting, just inside the walls in the north of the *citadelle*, near the Porte des Bés. Rooms on the higher floors (reached via a minuscule lift) enjoy sea views. No smoking. Closed mid-Nov to mid-Feb. ❹

Hôtel-Restaurant de l'Univers 10 place Chateaubriand ⓣ02.99.40.89.52, ⓕ02.99.40.07.27. One of the grand hotels that face you immediately upon entering the Porte St-Vincent. The rooms are a little stuffy and overpriced, but there is a good restaurant downstairs (see p.236). ❺

Hôtel-Restaurant aux Vieilles Pierres 9 rue Thévenard ⓣ02.99.56.46.80. Six-room hotel, near place aux Herbes, which remains one of the better bargains within the walls, even if a room with a shower costs €16 extra. Menus at the restaurant cost €21 with fish soup and steak, or €29 for the full spread, which in theory totals six courses – though half of those are just intended to keep you ticking over until the next one arrives. Open all year. ❶

Hotels outside the walls

Lower-priced places can be found near the *gare SNCF*, or in suburban Coutoisville and Paramé, east of the *citadelle*, but there's little pleasure in staying outside the *citadelle* for the sake of saving a few francs. This said, you will probably have a better chance of finding a vacancy in these areas than you would at hotels *intra-muros*.

Hôtel de l'Arrivée 52 bd de la République ⓣ02.99.56.30.78, ⓕ02.99.56.16.05. A good budget option on a corner very near the *gare SNCF*, where the cheapest rooms have en-suite toilets but a shared shower. ❷

Hôtel le Beaufort 25 chaussée du Sillon, Coutoisville ⓣ02.99.40.99.99, ⓦwww.hotel-beaufort.com. Grand sea-view hotel, 30min walk from the *citadelle*, with modernized rooms – some with lovely balconies – and a good restaurant. ❺–❾

Hôtel les Charmettes 64 bd Hébert, Coutoisville ⓣ02.99.56.07.31, ⓔhotel-les-charmettes@wanadoo.fr. One of Coutoisville's cheaper options, not on the front itself (though a few rooms have sea views), but very near the beach and the imposing *Grand Hôtel*. Closed mid-Nov to mid-Feb. ❷

Hôtel de l'Europe 44 bd de la République ⓣ02.99.56.13.42, ⓦwww.hotels-st-malo.com/europe. Year-round cheap but clean rooms in a genuinely friendly (if noisy) hotel near the *gare SNCF*, with a cosy café serving breakfast for €5.50 . ❷

Hôtel la Rance 15 quai Sébastopol, St-Servan ⓣ02.99.81.78.63, ⓦwww.hotelterminus-stmalo.com. Small, tasteful option in sight of the Tour Solidor, with eleven spacious rooms. ❹

Hôtel-Restaurant Terminus Gare 8 bd des Talards ⓣ02.99.56.14.38, ⓕ02.99.56.65.46. Reasonable Logis de France across from the station (not to be confused with the other *Hôtel Terminus*, in distant Rothéneuf), with double glazing and a lift. ❸

Campsites

St-Malo's four municipal **campsites** tend to be full in July and August, and you may have to travel inland to find space; there are several private sites in the vicinity. If in difficulties, you could try contacting the Camping Department of the Mairie (ⓣ02.99.56.98.72, ⓦwww.ville-saint-malo.fr/campings). All of the campsites listed below are reachable on bus #1 from the *gare SNCF* or Porte St-Vincent.

La Cité d'Aleth allée Gaston Buy, St-Servan ⓣ02.99.81.60.91. By far the nearest campsite to the *citadelle*, in a dramatic location on the headland southwest of St-Malo, overlooking the city from within the wartime German fortified stronghold. Closed Oct–April

Les Ilôts av de la Guimorais, Rothéneuf ⓣ02.99.56.98.72. Green little site, located five minutes' walk inland from either of two crescent beaches, roughly 5km east of the *citadelle*. Closed Sept–April.

Le Nicet av de la Varde, Rothéneuf ⓣ02.99.40.26.32. Right on the coast, by the Pointe de Nicet, just beyond the headland that marks the eastern limit of Paramé. Reservations essential. Closed Sept–June.

Les Nielles av John Kennedy, Paramé ⓣ02.99.40.26.35. Right on the beach at the smaller of Paramé's strands, the plage du Minhic, just a short walk from the town's facilities. Closed Sept–June.

The Town

The **citadelle** of St-Malo, very much the prime destination for visitors, was for many years joined to the mainland only by a long causeway, before the original line of the coast was hidden forever by the construction of the harbour basin. Although its cobbled streets of restored seventeenth- and eighteenth-century houses can be packed to the point of absurdity in summer (and the cobbles present quite a challenge to parents pushing buggies), away from the more popular thoroughfares random exploration is fun.

Due to space limitations on this tiny peninsula, the buildings tend to be a little more high-rise than you might expect. Ancient as they may look, they are almost entirely reconstructed – photographs of the damage suffered in 1944, when General Patton bombarded the city for two weeks before the Germans surrendered, show barely a stone left in place. Eighty percent of the city had to be lovingly and precisely rebuilt, stone by stone. Beneath grey skies, the narrow lanes can appear sombre, even grim, but in high summer or at sunset they take on a different, softer hue, much more in keeping with the *citadelle's* romantic atmosphere. In any case, you can always surface to the sunlight on the **ramparts** – first erected in the fourteenth century, and redesigned by the master builder Vauban four hundred years later – to enjoy wonderful views all round, especially to the west as the sun sets over the sea.

The main gate of the *citadelle* as you approach by road is the **Porte St-Vincent**. Until 1770, the whole town was sealed off by a 10pm curfew, and as you walk through the gateway, you pass the small room where latecomers were obliged to spend the night. To the right, as you walk through the gate, you'll see the forbidding stone walls of the **castle**, which now houses the **Musée de la Ville** (April–Sept daily 10am–12.30pm & 2–6pm; Oct–March Tues–Sun 10am–noon & 2–6pm; €4.80), something of a paean to the "prodigious prosperity" enjoyed by St-Malo during its days of piracy, colonialism and slave-trading. Climbing the 169 steps of the castle keep – whose walls are up to 7m thick – you pass a fascinating mixture of maps, diagrams and exhibits. Among them are chilling handbills from the Nazi Occupation, accounts of the "infernal machine" used by the English to blow up the port in 1693, and savage four-pronged *chaussetrappes*, thrown by pirates onto the decks of ships being boarded to immobilize their crews. At the top a gull's-eye prospect takes in the whole *citadelle*.

It is possible to pass **through the ramparts** at a couple of points on the western side of the peninsula, where there are some small, sheltered **beaches**. On the open shore to the east of the *citadelle*, a huge beach stretches away beyond the rather featureless resort-suburbs of **Courtoisville** and **Paramé**. Out to sea stand a procession of rocky islets, many of which still hold traces of medieval fortifications.

When the tide is low, an easy short walk across the sands of the Plage du Bons Secours, past a seawater swimming pool refreshed by each high tide, leads to the small island of **Grand-Bé**. It's such a popular stroll that you may even need to queue to get onto the short causeway. Solemn warnings are posted of the dangers of attempting to return from the island when the tide has risen too far – timetables are displayed by the Porte St-Pierre and elsewhere. If you're caught on the island, there you have to stay. Its one "sight" is the **tomb** of the nineteenth-century writer-politician Chateaubriand (who was born in St-Malo on Sept 4, 1768, and died in 1848). Marx described him as "the most classic incarnation of French *vanité*... the false profundity, Byzantine exaggeration, emotional coquetry... a never-before-seen mishmash of lies". Suitably enough, he features heavily on all the tourist brochures, which – with no apparent irony – extol his "modesty" in choosing so "isolated" a burial spot.

The coast along here is safer for paddlers than for swimmers, but it is very popular for **windsurfing**. Boards are available for rental from Surf School, 2 avenue de la Hoguette (Ⓣ02.99.40.07.47), or the Société Nautique de la Baie de St-Malo, quai de Bons Secours (Ⓣ02.99.40.11.45); most surfers make for the beaches further along the coast towards Cancale, the **plage du Verger** and the larger **Anse du Guesclin**.

St-Servan

The district of **St-Servan**, within walking distance along the corniche to the south of the *citadelle*, is actually older than St-Malo itself. It was on the site of the Gallo-Roman city of Alet that St Maclou established his church, and the seat of the bishopric only moved onto the impregnable island fortress when danger threatened in 1142.

St-Servan curves round several small inlets and beaches to face the tidal power dam across the river. It's dominated by the distinctive **Tour Solidor**, which consists of three linked towers built in 1382, and in cross-section looks just like the ace of clubs. Originally known in Breton as the *Steir Dor*, or "gate of the river", this now holds a **museum** of Cape Horn clipper ships, open all year for ninety-minute guided visits (April–Sept daily 10am–12.30pm & 2–6pm; Oct–March Tues–Sun 10am–noon & 2–6pm; €4.80). Most of the great European explorers of the Pacific are covered, from Magellan onwards, but naturally the emphasis is on French heroes such as Louis Antoine de Bougainville, who was responsible for spreading the brightly coloured bougainvillea plant around the globe. Tours culminate with a superb view from the topmost ramparts.

Follow the main road due south from St-Servan, ignoring signs for the Barrage de la Rance – or take bus #5 from the *gare SNCF* – and at a roundabout high above town you'll come to the **Grand Aquarium** (daily: April–June & Sept 10am–7pm; first two weeks in July & second two weeks in Aug 9.30am–8pm; mid-July to mid-Aug 9.30am–10pm; Oct–March 10am–6pm as a rule, but wide variations day by day, with some closures in Nov & Jan; €13, under-18s €9.50; Ⓣ02.99.21.19.00, Ⓦwww.aquarium-st-malo.com). This postmodern structure can be a bit bewildering at first, but once you get the hang of it it's an entertaining place, where you can either learn interesting facts about slimy monsters of the deep or simply pull faces back at them. Its eight distinct fish tanks include one shaped like a Polo mint, where dizzy visitors stand in the hole in the middle as myriad fish whirl around them. There's actually another aquarium, logically enough named the **Petit Aquarium**, set into the walls of the old city, but this is far superior.

The Barrage de la Rance

The road from St-Malo to Dinard crosses the Rance along the top of the world's first **tidal power dam**. Built in 1966, the Barrage de la Rance alas failed to set a non-nuclear example to the rest of the province, where a century ago there were five thousand working windmills. If you choose to cover the 4km between the centre of St-Malo and the *barrage* on foot or bicycle, try to make your way on the small roads through St-Servan, following the line of the estuary southwards rather than the signposted (circuitous) inland route used by motorists.

Rothéneuf

Just inside the eastern end of St-Malo's city limits, as the D201 winds towards Cancale, signs direct visitors away from the central streets of suburban **Rothéneuf** to the **Roches Sculptées**, or "sculpted rocks" (daily: Easter–Sept 9am–9pm; Oct–Easter 10am–5pm; €2.50). The hermit priest Abbé Fouré spent 25 years, from the 1870s onwards, carving these jumbled boulders into the forms of dragons, giants and assorted sea monsters. Perched on a rocky promontory high above the water line, they're quite weathered now, and not all compelling in themselves, but with the town well out of sight this makes an appealing spot to stop and admire the coastline. The gardens of the site also hold a small, sheltered café, and a shop that sells Breton pottery.

Eating

Even more **restaurants** than hotels are crammed into *intra-muros* St-Malo, with a long crescent lining the inside of the ramparts between the Porte St-Vincent and the Grande Porte. Prices are probably higher than anywhere else in Brittany, however, especially on the open café terraces – the demand is inflated by the numbers of day-trippers, from as far afield as the Channel Islands, and ferry passengers having last-night blowouts. Bear in mind that most of the crêperies also serve *moules* and similar quasi-snacks. If you just fancy an **ice cream**, call in at *Glacier Sanchez*, 9 rue de la Vieille-Boucherie (☎02.99.56.67.17; closed Wed in low season). There are **markets** in the Halle au Blé within the walls of St-Malo on Tuesdays and Fridays, in St-Servan on Mondays and Fridays, and in Paramé on Wednesdays and Saturdays. All the restaurants listed below are in the *citadelle*; and don't forget the various hotel restaurants mentioned on p.232.

Astrolabe 8 rue des Cordiers ☎02.99.40.36.82. Quality cuisine served in a comfy dining room down a few steps not far south of the Grande Porte. The menu costs €19 and changes regularly; otherwise it's *à la carte*. Closed Mon.

Borgnefesse 10 rue du Puits aux Braies ☎02.99.40.05.05. Feels more like the tavern it once was, or a pub, than a restaurant. Pirate-themed dining room with good solid French cooking, where you can have a two-course meal for €16.80 or a three-course one for €20.80. Closed Sun all day & Mon lunch.

Le Brick 5 rue Jacques-Cartier ☎02.99.40.18.88. Perhaps the best of the many seafood restaurants set into the walls near the Grande Porte, with a €14.50 menu that offers fish soup or "big size winkles" followed by skate, and more lavish options up to €33. Closed Mon.

Crêperie la Brigantine 13 rue de Dinan ☎02.99.56.82.82. Sweet and savoury pancakes at very reasonable prices – the seafood fillings are exceptional. An individual crêpe can cost just €1.50, and there's a €9.55 full menu. Closed Tues & Wed in low season.

Le Chalut 8 rue de la Corne de Cerf ☎02.99.56.71.58. Quite an exclusive dining room, in a stylish blue-painted bistro a short way in from the Porte St-Vincent. All the menus offer a limited choice, with perhaps one or two exclusively fishy main courses, and the odd meaty appetizer. The €22 menu centres on the catch of the day; otherwise you can pay €33 or €49 for a gourmet fish dinner, designed to be not quite as rich as the traditional norm. Reservations preferred. Closed Mon all day & Tues lunch.

Le Chasse Marée 4 rue Grout de St-Georges ☎02.99.40.85.10. Nautical decor and *haute cuisine*, just round the corner from the post office, with a few tables out on the quiet street and more upstairs. The €18 menu has an excellent salmon tartare, followed by a choice between skate, sea bream or a steak. Closed Mon all day & Tues lunch.

Le Corps de Garde 3 montée Notre Dame ☎02.99.40.91.46. The only restaurant that's right up on St-Malo's ramparts is unfortunately an ordinary crêperie, serving standard €5–7 crêpes; the views from the terrace are sensational, though, looking out over the beach to the myriad little islets.

Delaunay 6 rue Ste-Barbe ☎02.99.40.92.46. Located between the Porte St-Vincent and Cathédrale St-Vincent, and serving high-quality traditional French cooking. Everything is *à la carte*; reckon on at least €35 for a full meal, though you can easily spend that on a single item such as the *agneau prés-salé*, a regional speciality. Closed Sun.

Duchesse Anne 5–7 place Guy-la-Chambre ☎02.99.40.85.33. Situated right next to the Porte St-Vincent, the best known of St-Malo's upmarket restaurants continues to work hard to keep up its reputation – and its prices. The only set menu is a €67 lobster option; you might manage to get a lunch for under €16, but dinner will cost well over twice that. Whole baked fish is the main speciality. Closed Wed & Mon lunch, Sun eve in low season, plus all Dec & Jan.

Restaurant Gilles 2 rue de la Pie-qui-Boit ☎02.99.40.97.25. Bright, modern, good-value restaurant, just off the central pedestrian axis. The basic €18.70 menu is fine; alternatively, €21 brings you oysters or mussel soup and a rabbit *cuissot* with cider. Closed Wed.

Hôtel-Restaurant de l'Univers 10 place Chateaubriand ☎02.99.40.89.52. This hotel's restaurant serves an excellent €12.50 menu or a €15 vegetarian option, with the option of eating at tables out on the square opposite the château.

Nightlife

Along with the multitude of restaurants *intra-muros*, you'll also find a few decent places to have a **drink**, including the *St-Patrick*, 24 rue Ste-Barbe, a cosy Irish pub, and the *Cutty Sark*, 20 rue de la Herse, with its good choice of beers and cocktails, karaoke nights and occasional **live music**. *Le 109*, at 3 rue des Cordiers (ⓦwww.le-109.com), is a flashy discotheque decked out in fiery reds and yellows and open until 3am.

Listings

Banks & exchange Banque de France, 7 rue d'Asfeld ⓣ02.99.20.53.00; Banque Populaire de l'Ouest, 33 bd de la République ⓣ08.20.85.04.63.
Bicycle rental Les Vélos Bleus, 19 rue Alphonse Thébault ⓣ02.99.40.31.63, ⓦwww.velos-bleus.fr; Espace Nicole, 11–13 rue Robert Schuman, Paramé ⓣ02.99.56.11.06, ⓦwww.cyclesnicole.com.
Car rental Most of the major car-rental companies are represented in town; both Avis (ⓣ02.99.40.58.68) and National (ⓣ02.23.18.00.00) have offices at the ferry terminal and *gare SNCF*.
Hypermarkets Carrefour, Centre Commercial La Madeleine ⓣ02.99.21.10.10 (closed Sun); Centre Leclerc, 55 bd des Déportés, Paramé ⓣ02.99.19.97.97 (closed Sun).
Internet access Cyber' Com, just west of the *gare SNCF* at 29bis bd des Talards (Mon 2–6pm, Tues, Wed & Fri 9am–noon & 2–6pm, Thurs 1–8pm, Sat 9am–noon & 2–5.30pm; ⓣ02.99.56.05.83; €3.80 per hr); also in the tourist office.
Post office The most convenient post office for visitors is within the walls at 4 place des Frères Lamennais (Mon–Fri 8.45am–12.15pm & 1.30–5.45pm, Sat 8.45am–noon). If you want to receive poste restante letters, make sure the address specifies *35402 St-Malo intra-muros*.
Sailing St-Malo's Station Nautique can provide full information on all aspects of sailing in the vicinity, from lessons to rentals and cruises; advisers can be found at the tourist office in summer (ⓣ02.99.40.34.04, ⓦwww.station-nautisme-saint-malo.com).
Scuba diving St-Malo Plongée Émeraude, Centre Bleu Émeraude, Terre Plein du Naye, St-Servan ⓣ02.99.19.90.36, ⓦwww.saintmaloplongee.com.

Dinard

The former fishing village of **DINARD** sprawls around the western approaches to the Rance estuary, just across the water from St-Malo but a good twenty minutes' drive away. It's a town that might not feel out of place on the Côte d'Azur, with its casino, spacious shaded villas and social calendar of regattas and ballet. Here in Brittany it's a little incongruous, though pleasant enough.

The nineteenth-century metamorphosis of Dinard was largely thanks to the tastes of affluent English and Americans, though these days age rather than nationality seems to be the common factor uniting most of its summer influx of tourists. Although Dinard is a hilly town, undulating over a succession of pretty little coastal inlets, it attracts great numbers of older visitors; as a result, prices tend to be high, and pleasures sedate (literally so, with benches scattered in abundance where the weary can rest their legs while admiring the views).

Arrival and information

Dinard has a small **airport** (ⓣ02.99.46.18.46), served by Ryanair flights from London Stansted (see p.22), and is also connected with the Channel Islands by Aurigny Air Services (ⓣ02.99.46.70.28, ⓦwww.aurigny.com). The airport lies 4km southeast of the town centre, off the D168 near Pleurtuit; TIV bus #990, timed to connect with the Ryanair flights, leaves from a poorly marked stop just to the left as you come out of the terminal, and runs via Dinard's tourist office to St-Malo's *gare SNCF* and Porte St-Vincent for a €3.50 flat fare. National have a **rental car** outlet in the terminal (ⓣ02.23.18.00.00).

Many visitors to Dinard simply come over for the day on one of the regular Compagnie Corsaire **boats** from St-Malo; tickets can be bought in Dinard a ten-minute walk east of the tourist office (follow the signs for "Embarcadère Excursions en Mer") on promenade du Clair de Lune, directly above the pleasure port where the ferries actually come in (April to early Nov only; ⓣ08.25.16.81.30, ⓦwww.compagniecorsaire.com; €3.70 single, €5.90 return, bikes €4.50 single or €7.50 return). If the ten-minute crossing only serves to whet your appetite, you can also take a trip down the Rance to Dinan.

Local **buses** run regularly between Dinard and St-Malo, across the dam, while long-distance buses go from the former *gare SNCF* and "Le Gallic" stop (near the tourist office) to Dinan, Rennes, Cancale and St-Brieuc, run by TIV (ⓣ02.99.82.26.26) and TAE (ⓣ02.99.26.16.00).

Dinard's **tourist office** is close to the seafront in the heart of town at 2 boulevard Féart (Easter–June & Sept Mon–Sat 9am–12.15pm & 2–7pm; July & Aug daily 9.30am–7.30pm; Oct–Easter Mon–Sat 9am–12.15pm & 2–6pm; ⓣ02.99.46.94.12, ⓦwww.ot-dinard.com). **Cycles** are available for rental from Cycles Duval, 53 rue Gardiner (ⓣ02.99.46.19.63).

Accommodation

On the whole, Dinard is an expensive place to stay, but it does at least have a wide selection of **hotels** to choose from, many of which can be found on the Web at ⓦwww.dinard-hotel-plus.com. The best positioned of its several **campsites** is the municipal *Port Blanc*, over 1km west of the centre near the plage du Port-Blanc on rue Sergent-Boulanger (ⓣ02.99.46.10.74; closed Oct–March).

Hôtel de la Gare 28 rue de la Corbinais ⓣ02.99.46.10.84. Dinard doesn't have a *gare SNCF* these days, but that doesn't worry the *Hôtel de la Gare*, a basic inexpensive place 500m back from the beach in a rather dull part of town slightly south of the centre. Entrance is via the simple brasserie downstairs, *L'Épicurien*. ❶

Hôtel les Mouettes 64 av Georges V ⓣ02.99.46.10.64, ⓦwww.hotel-les-mouettes.com. Small, inexpensive family-oriented hotel, a short walk from the sea; the rooms are far from fancy, but they're clean, and great value. ❷

Hôtel-Restaurant du Parc 20 av Édouard VII ⓣ02.99.46.11.39, ⓕ02.99.88.10.58. Friendly little hotel on a busy street a short way west of the place de la République. Simple restaurant offering menus from €13.50, and good buffet breakfasts. Closed early Oct to March. ❷

Hôtel-Restaurant Printania 5 av Georges V ⓣ02.99.46.13.07, ⓦwww.printaniahotel.com. Good-value place around 250m east of the centre, on a relatively quiet seafront street near the Port de Plaisance. Menus in the magnificent terrace restaurant, looking over to St-Malo, start at €20, featuring *moules marinières* and sole. Closed mid-Nov to mid-March. ❸

Hôtel des Sables 12 rue des Vergers ⓣ02.99.46.18.10, ⓦwww.hotel-des-sables.com. Reasonable hotel whose main advantage lies in its proximity to the quiet, family-oriented St-Énogat beach. There is also free parking – but no restaurant. Closed Nov–March. ❸

Hôtel-Restaurant la Vallée 6 av Georges V ⓣ02.99.46.94.00, ⓦwww.hoteldelavallee.com. Attractive Logis de France, down at sea level in the pleasure port, but unfortunately facing the wrong way for views of St-Malo. The most basic rooms look straight onto a bare cliff face, but in principle this is a nice spot. Menus start at €20, featuring grilled sardines and skate. ❺–❽

The Town

Central Dinard faces north to the open sea, across the curving bay that holds the attractive **plage de l'Écluse**. As so often in Breton resorts, the buildings that line the waterfront are, with the exception of the casino in the middle, venerable Victorian villas rather than hotels or shops, and so the beach itself has a relatively low-key atmosphere, despite the summer crowds. An unexpected statue of **Alfred Hitchcock**, standing on a giant egg with a ferocious-looking bird perched on each shoulder, dominates its main access point – he was placed here to commemorate the town's annual festival of English-language films, held in early October. Rows of delightful, blue-and-white-striped, tent-like sunshelters, which cost €10.60 to hire for the afternoon, add colour to the sands below. Few casual visitors realize that some of **Pablo Picasso's** most famous images, such as *Deux Femmes Courants sur la Plage* and *Baigneuses sur la Plage* – both of which look quintessentially Mediterranean with their blue skies and golden sands – were painted on the main **beach** at Dinard during the artist's annual summer visits in the 1920s.

Enjoyable **coastal footpaths** lead off in either direction from the beach. The path heading east – which is floodlit each evening between July and early October – leads up to the Pointe du Moulinet for views over to St-Malo, and then (as the **promenade du Clair de Lune**) continues past the tiny and now exclusive port, and down to the estuary beach, the plage du Prieuré. Setting off west, on the other hand, takes you around more rocky outcrops to the secluded strand at neighbouring **St-Énogat**, where windsurfing equipment and kayaks are available for rent in summer (ⓣ02.99.46.83.99).

Eating

All the hotels listed opposite (except the *des Sables*) have reasonable **restaurants**. Good alternatives in town include the busy *Brasserie Le Cancaven*, whose outdoor tables take up most of place de la République (ⓣ02.99.46.15.45); their cheapest menu is not all that interesting, but for €17.50 they offer a real cornucopia of fish and shellfish, from spider crab to squid.

Dinan

The wonderful citadel of **DINAN** has preserved almost intact its three-kilometre encirclement of protective masonry, along with street upon colourful street of late medieval houses. However, for all its slightly unreal perfection (it would make the ideal film set for *The Three Musketeers*), it's seldom overrun with tourists. There are no essential museums, the most memorable architecture is vernacular rather than monumental, and time is most easily spent wandering from crêperie to café, admiring the overhanging half-timbered houses along the way.

Arrival and information

Both the Art Deco **gare SNCF** (ⓣ08.36.35.35.35) and the **gare routière** (ⓣ02.96.39.21.05) are in Dinan's modern quarter (a rather gloomy exile from the rest of the town), on place du 11 Novembre, ten minutes' walk west of the main entrance of the walled town on Grande Rue. Armor Express (TAE) **buses** (ⓣ02.99.26.16.00) go direct to Dinard and to Rennes, which saves changing trains at Dol.

Between mid-April and late September, **boats** along the Rance sail between the port downstream and Dinard and St-Malo. The trip takes two hours 45

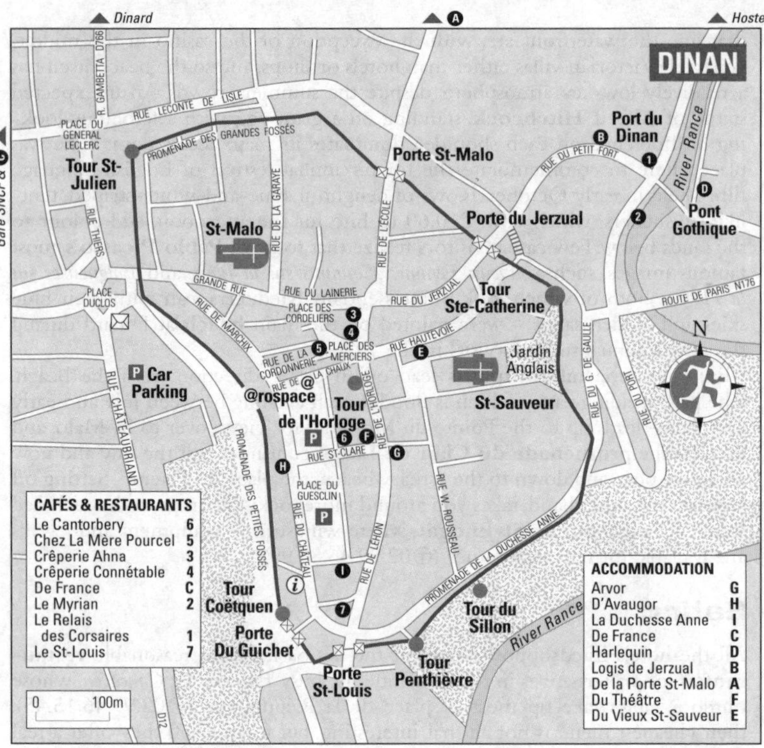

minutes, with the exact schedule varying according to the tides (adults €18, under-13s €11). It's only possible to do a day return by boat (adults €24, under-13s €14.50) if you start from St-Malo or Dinard; starting from Dinan, you'd have to come back by bus or train. For details, contact Compagnie Corsaire on the quai de la Rance (Ⓣ08.25.16.81.20), or check out its website – Ⓦwww.compagniecorsaire.com.

Dinan's modern **tourist office** is at the southwest corner of the place du Guesclin near the Tour Coëtquen, at 9 rue du Château (mid-June to Sept Mon–Sat 9am–7pm, Sun 10am–12.30pm & 2.30–6pm; Oct to mid-June Mon–Sat 9am–12.30pm & 2–6pm; Ⓣ02.96.87.69.76, Ⓦwww.dinan-tourisme.com). A **petit train** sets off from rue de l'Horloge next to the Théâtre des Jacobins on regular town tours (Easter–June & Sept Mon–Wed, Fri & Sat 11am–6pm; July & Aug daily 10am–6pm; €5). **Internet access** is available for €1.50 per fifteen minutes at @rospace, in the heart of the walled town at 9 rue de la Chaux (Tues–Sat 10am–12.30pm & 2–7pm; Ⓣ02.96.87.14.85, Ⓔarospace @wanadoo.fr), while the **post office** is on place Duclos (Mon–Fri 8am–6.30pm, Sat 9am–12.30pm; Ⓣ02.96.39.25.07).

Accommodation

Many of Dinan's **hotels** lie within the walled town or down by the pretty port, which are both convenient locations if you are on foot. Motorists, however, should note that finding parking spaces during summer can be difficult.

Most of the hotels are in the mid-range price category, with only a couple of genuine budget options.

The run-of-the-mill two-star municipal **campsite**, *Camping Chateaubriand*, is in a central position just outside the western ramparts at 103 rue Chateaubriand (Ⓣ02.96.39.11.96, Ⓕ02.96.87.08.40; closed late Sept to late May). Camping is also permitted in the grounds of the beautifully situated **hostel**, set amid green fields below the town centre right next to the river on Moulin de Méen, Vallée de la Fontaine-des-Eaux (Ⓣ02.96.39.10.83, Ⓔdinan@fuaj.org; dorm beds €9.30; closed Jan). Unfortunately, the hostel's not on any bus route; to walk there, follow the quay downstream from the port on the town side, and after a few hundred metres you'll see a small sign to the left – from there it's another 500m.

Hotels

Hôtel Arvor 5 rue Pavie Ⓣ02.96.39.21.22, Ⓦwww.hotel-arvor-dinan.com. Renovated eighteenth-century town house in the heart of town, with some surviving traces of the convent that previously occupied the site. Smart, well-equipped rooms, and free parking. ❸

Hôtel d'Avaugor 1 place du Champ Ⓣ02.96.39.07.49, Ⓦwww.avaugourhotel.com. Smart, elegant hotel, entered from the main square but backing onto the ramparts, with very tasteful renovated rooms and lovely gardens. ❼

Hôtel-Restaurant La Duchesse Anne 10 place du Guesclin Ⓣ02.96.39.09.43, Ⓕ02.96.87.57.26. Comfortable if not luxurious rooms on the quieter side of the square, above a basic crêperie/restaurant where set menus start at €10.50. Closed mid-Nov to mid-Dec. ❷

Hôtel-Restaurant de France 7 place du 11 Novembre Ⓣ02.96.39.22.56, Ⓦwww.hoteldefrance-dinan.com. An excellent logis opposite the *gare SNCF*, with fourteen renovated and well-equipped rooms, the top ones with attractive wooden floors. Friendly, English-speaking management and a good restaurant (see p.243). ❸

Hôtel Harlequin 8 rue du quai Talard Ⓣ02.96.39.68.68, Ⓕ02.96.39.10.16. Distinguished old building in a lovely setting just across the Rance in the port, offering pleasant en-suite rooms and serving reasonable French cooking on its terrace overlooking the river for €15 and up. ❸

Logis de Jerzual 25–27 rue du Petit Fort Ⓣ02.96.85.46.54, Ⓔronssery@wanadoo.fr. *Chambres d'hôte* on the exquisite little lane that leads from the port, halfway up to the Porte du Jerzual. The rooms have wonderful character, with four-poster beds, modern bathrooms and romantic views over the rooftops. The house is surrounded by a lovely garden terrace and the tasty breakfasts (included in the rates) are served by the friendly and talkative owner. ❹

Hôtel de la Porte St-Malo 35 rue St-Malo Ⓣ02.96.39.19.76, Ⓦwww.hotelportemalo.com. Very comfortable rooms in a tasteful small hotel just outside the walls, beyond the Porte St-Malo. ❸

Café-Hôtel du Théâtre 2 rue Ste-Claire Ⓣ02.96.39.06.91. Nine basic rooms (the cheapest come only with a sink) above a bar, right by the Théâtre des Jacobins, and under the same efficient management as the nearby *Restaurant Cantorbery* (see p.243). ❶

Hôtel du Vieux St-Sauveur 21 place St-Sauveur Ⓣ02.96.85.30.20. Ancient edifice facing the St-Sauveur church, which has a slightly noisy bar downstairs, but six nicely equipped and very good-value en-suite rooms upstairs, including a three-person family room. ❸

The Town

Like St-Malo, Dinan is best seen when arriving by boat up the Rance. By the time the ferries get to the lovely **port du Dinan**, down below the thirteenth-century ramparts, the river has narrowed sufficiently to be spanned by a small but majestic old stone bridge. High above it towers the railway viaduct now used by the N176. The steep cobbled **rue du Petit-Fort** twists up from the artisans' shops and restaurants along the quay. Taking advantage of its many stone benches to catch your breath, it makes a wonderful climb, passing ancient flower-festooned edifices of wood and stone, as well as several crêperies and even a half-timbered poodle parlour, before it enters the city through the **Porte du Jerzual**.

Above that imposing gateway, **St-Sauveur** church sends the skyline even higher. It's a real hotchpotch, with a Romanesque porch and an eighteenth-century steeple. Even its nine Gothic chapels feature five different patterns of vaulting in no symmetrical order; the most complex pair, in the centre, would make any spider proud. By contrast, a very plain cenotaph on the left contains the heart of Bertrand du Guesclin, the fourteenth-century Breton warrior (and later Constable of France) who fought and won a single combat with the English knight Thomas of Canterbury, in what is now place du Guesclin, to settle the outcome of the siege of Dinan in 1364. Relics of his life and battles are scattered all over Brittany and Normandy; in death, he spread himself between four separate burial places for four different parts of his body (the French kings restricted themselves to three burial sites).

The **place du Guesclin** only comes alive on Thursdays, when together with the adjoining place du Champ Clos it's the scene of a large **market**; for the rest of the week, it serves as the main central car park. The true heart of town consists of two much smaller squares, the **place des Merciers** and the **place des Cordeliers**. These hold Dinan's finest assortment of medieval wood-framed houses, painted in lively hues and with their upper storeys perching precariously on splintering wooden pillars that appear to buckle beneath the weight.

Unfortunately, you can only walk along one small stretch of the **ramparts**, from the Jardin Anglais behind St-Sauveur church to a point just short of Tour Sillon overlooking the river – although even this stretch was closed for restoration at the time of writing. You can, however, get a good general overview from the wooden balcony of the central **Tour de l'Horloge**, which dates from the end of the fifteenth century (daily: April–June & Sept 2–6pm; July & Aug 10am–6.30pm; €2.60). The original mechanism of the clock here was made in Nantes and put in place in 1498; in 1507, the ubiquitous Duchesse Anne presented the monumental bell. A small and uninteresting shopping mall has been created around the foot of the belfry's stout stone walls.

As you might guess from its blending of two separate towers, the fourteenth-century keep that once protected the town's southern approach was built by Estienne Le Tour, architect of St-Malo's Tour Solidor (see p.235). It's now known as the **Château de Duchesse Anne**, with a small local-history museum housed in the ancient **Tour Coëtquen** (daily: June–Sept 10am–6.30pm; Oct–Dec & Feb–May 1.30–5.30pm; €4). On the lower floor, a group of stone fifteenth-century notables looks for all the world like a medieval time capsule, about to depetrify at any moment.

On the third weekend of July, every other (even-numbered) year, the **Fête des Remparts** is celebrated with medieval-style jousting, banquets, fairs and processions, culminating in an immense fireworks display.

Eating and drinking

All sorts of specialist **restaurants**, including several ethnic alternatives, are tucked away in the old streets of Dinan. Stroll through the town and down to the port, and you'll pass at least twenty places to choose from, with the vast majority offering better value for money than Brittany's seaside resorts. The port itself has a particularly fine assortment of waterfront grills, restaurants and brasseries.

Once you've eaten, the area for **bars** is the series of tiny parallel alleyways between place des Merciers and rue de Marchix. Along rue de la Cordonnerie, the busiest of the lot, the various hangouts define themselves by their taste in music: *À la Truye qui File* at no. 14 is a contemporary folky Breton dive, while *Morgan's Bar*, next door at no. 12 is considerably more raucous and mainstream.

Crêperie Ahna 7 rue de la Poissonnerie ☎02.96.39.09.13. Smart central crêperie with limited outdoor seating and very popular with lunching locals. Savoury pancakes cost €4.50–7.50, and they also serve potato blinis and grilled meats, including nice big sausages. Closed Sun in low season.
Le Cantorbery 6 rue Ste-Claire ☎02.96.39.02.52. Reasonable food served in an old stone house with rafters, a spiral staircase and a real wood fire. Lunch from €12, while traditional dinner menus start with a good €23 option that includes fish soup and roast lamb. Closed Sun eve & Wed in low season.
Chez La Mère Pourcel 3 place des Merciers ☎02.96.39.03.80. Beautiful half-timbered fifteenth-century house in the central square. Lunch menus can be pretty minimal, but the dinners, starting at €28, are gourmet class. Closed Sun eve & Mon in low season.
Crêperie Connétable 1 rue de l'Apport ☎02.96.39.06.74. Magnificent old house diagonally opposite the *Mère Pourcel* beside the place des Merciers. Sit at the pavement tables, and enjoy crêpes and snacks in the perfect spot for people-watching.
Hôtel-Restaurant de France 7 place du 11 Novembre ☎02.96.39.22.56. Carefully prepared French cuisine, including *magret de canard* and steak, on good-value menus starting at €14.50, served in the relaxing dining room of this hotel opposite the *gare SNCF*. Closed Sat & Sun eve.
Le Myrian 3 rue du Port ☎02.96.87.93.36. Attractive and inexpensive pizzeria in a waterfront cottage down by the port, serving €7–12 pizzas, plus assorted salads and wine by the carafe, on its shady terrace immediately next to the river.
Le Relais des Corsaires 7 rue du Quai, port du Dinan ☎02.96.39.40.17. Large but attractive waterfront restaurant, down by the port, which in theory is split between a formal dining room and the less expensive all-hours *Petit Corsaire*, which bills itself as a "grill". Both, however, seem to serve much the same wide range of traditional French cuisine, on menus starting with an €14 option that offers shrimp followed by mussels or cod; the only real difference is that the pricier menus are dropped in winter. Closed Mon & Tues in low season.
Le St-Louis 9–11 rue de Léhon ☎02.96.39.89.50. Good-value restaurant just inside the Porte St-Louis specializing in buffets; a €15 menu entitles you to choose at will from extensive buffets of *hors d'oeuvres* and desserts, while the €17.50 option offers the same deal plus a conventional main course. Closed Sun eve, Tues & Wed in low season.

Around the Baie du Mont-St-Michel

The **coastal road** D201 runs east from St-Malo to **Cancale**, past a succession of coves and beaches, where lines of dunes attempt to hang on against the battering from the sea. At the **Pointe du Grouin** – a perilous and windy height that also overlooks the bird sanctuary of the **Île de Landes** to the east – the line of cliffs turns sharply back on itself at one extremity of the **Baie du Mont-St-Michel**. This is a huge flat expanse of mud and sand, over which the tide – as just about every piece of literature on this region will tell you – can race faster than a galloping horse. It's dangerous to wander out too far, quite apart from the risk of quicksands, and, in the Breton part of the bay at least, the beaches have little appeal for bathers.

The course of the **River Couesnon**, which marks the border between Brittany and Normandy, has shifted repeatedly over the centuries. So too has the shoreline of the bay, in which traces of long-drowned villages can be seen when the tide is out. Bretons like to say that it is just an accident that the river now runs west of Mont-St-Michel; be that as it may, the Mont and Pontorson, the nearest town to it, are both in Normandy (see p.177). The pinnacle of *La Merveille*, however, remains clearly visible from every vantage point along the coast.

Cancale

Just south of the Pointe du Grouin, and less than 15km east of St-Malo, **CANCALE** is not so much a one-horse as a one-mollusc town – the whole place is obsessed with the **oyster**, and with "*ostréiculture*". Its current population is, at around five thousand, less than it was a century ago, but the town looks much bigger than that would suggest – and the reason must be the visitors attracted by its edible hinged bivalves.

Arrival and information

Cancale is not served by any trains, but **buses** from St-Malo arrive in the church square well above the port. The **tourist office** is a short way down the hill at 44 rue du Port (May, June & Sept Mon–Sat 9am–12.30pm & 2–6pm, Sun 9am–12.30pm; July & Aug daily 9am–7pm; Oct–April Mon–Sat 9am–12.30pm & 2–6pm; ⓣ02.99.89.63.72, ⓦwww.ville-cancale.fr), but most visitors prefer to call in at the "Point I" information office (early-July to Aug daily 2.30–7pm; ⓣ02.99.89.74.80) on the waterfront in the heart of the harbour, across from the upmarket glass-fronted hotels and restaurants that line quai Gambetta.

Accommodation

A long sequence of **hotels** lines the quayside down in the port of Cancale. Most insist that you eat if you want to stay, but that's no great problem considering that there's nothing much else to do in town. Budget travellers can head instead for the **youth hostel**, 2km north of town at Port Picain (ⓣ02.99.89.62.62, ⓔcancale@fuaj.org; dorm beds €9.30; closed Jan). The coastal bus to St-Malo operated by Les Courriers Bretons stops at the hostel in July and August; catch it next to the information centre at the harbour (stop "La Houle") and get off at "Port Picain". By far the best **campsite** in the vicinity is the *Pointe du Grouin* (ⓣ02.99.89.63.79; closed Nov–Feb), beyond the hostel, where the views are sensational.

Le Grand Large 4 quai Jacques-Cartier ⓣ02.99.89.82.90, ⓔrietz.alain@wanadoo.fr. Comfortable rooms in an ivy-covered house at the quieter southern end of the port, well away from most of the action but with its own good restaurant (see opposite). ❸

La Houle 18 quai Gambetta ⓣ02.99.89.62.38. Very nice, inexpensive option in the middle of the port; the rooms have excellent bathrooms and those with sea-view balconies are only €7 extra. ❷

Le Phare 6 quai Thomas ⓣ02.99.89.60.24, ⓕ02.99.89.91.75. Appealing logis towards the far end of the harbour, offering good rooms above its top-notch restaurant (see opposite). Closed mid-Nov to mid-Feb, restaurant closed Thurs in low season. ❸

The Town

Cancale is divided into two distinct halves; the old town up on the hill, and the port area of **La Houle** down below, now very pretty and smart. Oysters may have been a cheap working-class staple in the past, but these days they're slurped by the lips of elegant *bourgeois* holidaymakers. In the old church of **St-Méen**, at the top of the hill, a small **Musée des Arts et Traditions Populaires** documents this obsession with meticulous precision (June & Sept Mon & Fri–Sun 2.30–6.30pm; July & Aug Mon 2.30–6.30pm, Tues–Sun 10am–noon & 2.30–6.30pm, and groups by appointment on ⓣ02.99.89.71.26; €3.50). Cancale oysters have been found in the camps of Julius Caesar, were taken daily to Versailles for Louis XIV, and even accompanied Napoléon on the march to Moscow. The most famous symbol of the town – and its oyster cultivation – is the stark rocky pinnacle known as the **Rocher du Cancale** just offshore; the museum lists all the *Rochers du Cancale* restaurants that have ever existed, including ones in Shanghai and Phnom Penh, and one in Moscow which closed in the 1830s.

From the rue des Parcs, next to the jetty of the port, you can see at low tide the **parcs** where the oysters are grown. At one time there was an annual event, *La Caravanne*, when a huge flotilla of sailing vessels dragged nets along the bottom of the sea for wild oysters; now they are farmed like any other crop. The sea bed is divided into countless segments of different sizes, each having an individual owner who has the right to sell what it produces. The oysters are cultivated from year-old "spat" bought in from elsewhere. Behind, the rocks of the cliff are streaked and shiny like mother-of-pearl; underfoot, the beach is littered with countless generations of empty shells.

Follow the corniche road out of Cancale to the southwest, and you'll soon come to the **Ferme Marine**, a working *parc* where the entire oyster-raising process is described on enjoyable guided tours (mid-Feb to mid-June & mid-Sept to Oct Mon–Fri at 3pm; mid-June to mid-Sept daily at 11am, 3pm & 5pm, with an English-language tour at 2pm; €6.10; ⓣ02.99.89.69.99).

Cancale has a **market** on Sunday in the streets behind the main church, the rue de la Marine and the rue Cocar.

Eating

Cancale offers a fabulous range of **restaurants** for seafood lovers; there's no great reason to recommend any one of them above the rest. All serve enticing seafood spreads, with twenty or so options. **Oysters** can also be had for as little as €2.50 per dozen from takeaway stalls.

Au Pied d'Cheval 10 quai Gambetta ⓣ02.99.89.76.95. Very informal little seafront shack, where they'll dish up a dozen oysters from the huge baskets that weigh down their wooden quayside tables for just €4.80, or prepare a massive *fruits de mer* plate for two people for around €35.

Le Grand Large 4 quai Jacques-Cartier ⓣ02.99.89.82.90. This spacious restaurant at the southern end of the port comes into its own in the summer, when its large wedge-shaped wooden terrace makes a great spot for an evening meal. It also offers a change from all that seafood, with lots of meaty couscous options.

L'Huîtrière 14 quai Gambetta ⓣ02.99.89.94.35. Very classy seafood specialist which serves a lovely €26 menu with three fish courses, and an even better €30 option with an *assiette de fruits de mer* followed by grilled scampi, duck or lamb.

Le Phare 6 quai Thomas ⓣ02.99.89.60.24. Another good choice for oysters, seafood platters and lobster, with menus starting at €14 for lunch and €18 for dinner, plus a heated outdoor terrace for end-of-season alfresco dining. Closed Wed & Thurs in low season.

Dol-de-Bretagne and around

The foundation of **DOL-DE-BRETAGNE**, 30km west of Mont-St-Michel, is attributed to St Samson, one of the many Celtic evangelists who flooded into Brittany around the sixth century. The Breton hero King Nominoë appointed its first official bishop during the ninth century, and the city remained an important bishopric throughout the Middle Ages.

Dol is no longer large enough to merit its own bishop, but Samson's name lives on in the fortified thirteenth-century **Cathédrale St-Samson**, with its strange, squat, tiled towers and ornate porches. Housed in a former school in the cathedral square, the highly ambitious **CathédralOscope** (April–Oct daily 10am–7pm; at other times by appointment; €7.50) sets out to explain the construction and significance of not only this example, but medieval cathedrals in general. For all its high-tech presentation and flair, however, non-French speakers may find it heavy going.

An appealing handful of Dol's older streets are still packed with venerable buildings, most notably the pretty **Grande Rue des Stuarts**, just south of the cathedral, where one Romanesque edifice dates back as far as the eleventh century, an assortment of 500-year-old half-timbered houses look down on the bustle of shoppers below, and a laundry claims to have been visited by Victor Hugo in 1836.

Practicalities

Dol's **tourist office** can be found at 3 Grande Rue des Stuarts (June & Sept Mon 2–6pm, Tues–Sat 10am–12.30pm & 2–6pm; July & Aug Mon–Fri 9.30am–7pm, Sat & Sun 9.30am–1pm & 2–7pm; Oct–May Tues–Sat 10am–12.30pm & 2–6pm; Ⓣ02.99.48.15.37, Ⓦwww.pays-de-dol.com). There's little to keep casual visitors in Dol for long, but if you do decide to stay, you'll find a reasonable **hotel**, the *Bretagne*, next to the market at 17 place Chateaubriand (Ⓣ02.99.48.02.03; ❶; closed Oct), east of Grande Rue des Stuarts. This has rooms to suit all budgets – those at the back look out across a vestige of ramparts towards Mont Dol – and menus from €11 to €27.

Among good **campsites** nearby are the four-star *Vieux Chêne* (Ⓣ02.99.48.09.55, Ⓦwww.camping-vieuxchene.fr; closed Oct–March), 3km east towards Baguer-Pican on N176, and the phenomenally luxurious *Castel Camping des Ormes* (Ⓣ02.99.73.53.00, Ⓦwww.lesormes.com; closed mid-Sept to mid-May), set around a lake in the grounds of a château 6km south towards Combourg on the N795, which arranges **horse-riding** for its guests, and boasts its own golf course and even a cricket pitch.

A couple of nice **fish restaurants** stand opposite each other in the ancient houses on rue Ceinte, as it winds its way from Grande-Rue des Stuarts to the cathedral. *Le Porche au Pain* at no. 1, (Ⓣ02.99.48.37.57; closed Wed in low season) has a wood-burning grill and offers menus from €16 to €30, while *La Grabotais* at no. 4 (Ⓣ02.99.48.19.89; closed Mon, plus Sun eve in low season) serves meals from €17.80. After you eat, the *Katédral* **bar**, at the other end of rue Ceinte between the church and museum, is worth a brief pause.

Mont Dol

All approaches to Dol from the bay are watched over by the former island of **Mont Dol** – now eight rather marshy kilometres in from the sea. This abrupt granite outcrop, looking mountainous beyond its size on such a flat plain, was the legendary site of a battle between the Archangel Michael and the Devil. Various fancifully named indentations in the rock, such as "the Devil's Claw", testify to the savagery of their encounter, which was inevitably won by the saint. The site has been occupied since prehistoric times – flint implements have been unearthed alongside the bones of mammoths, sabre-toothed tigers and even rhinoceroses. Later on, it appears to have been used for worship by the druids, before becoming, like Mont-St-Michel, an island monastery.

Traces of the abbey have long vanished, though the mythic battle may recall its foundation, with Christianity driving out the old religion. A plaque proclaims that visiting the small chapel on top earns a Papal Indulgence (presumably on the condition that you don't add to the copious graffiti on its walls). The climb is pleasant, too, a steep footpath winding up among the chestnuts and beeches to a solitary bar.

If you fancy an extended walk, Dol and Mont Dol are in fact located on the long-distance **GR34** trail, which leads east to Mont-St-Michel (reckoned as an eight-hour stroll), and west along the coast way beyond St-Malo.

The Menhir du Champ-Dolent

A short way out of Dol to the south, a small picnic area fenced off among the fields contains the **Menhir du Champ-Dolent**. According to one legend, this

9.6-metre standing stone dropped from the sky to separate two brothers who were on the point of mutual fratricide. Another has it that the menhir is inching its way into the soil, and the world will end when it disappears altogether. It has to be said, this would not be a particularly interesting spot on which to experience the end of the world – the unadorned stone, big though it is in its banal setting, has little of the romance or mystery of the megalithic sites of the Morbihan and elsewhere.

The Forêt de Ville-Cartier

The *Circuit Touristique* signposted from Dol continues beyond the menhir and the village of Trans to the **Forêt de Ville-Cartier**. The pines and beech of the dense forest sweep down to a lake in which it is possible – in fact almost irresistible – to swim. Keeping to the *circuit*, along the D155, would lead eventually to Fougères (see p.255).

Inland to Rennes

Much the most direct route inland from the north coast to Rennes is the **N137**, which takes barely half an hour to drive from St-Malo. The D795 south from Dol however makes an appealing alternative, passing through the castle town of **Combourg**. The twin canalside towns of **Hédé** and **Tinténiac** also merit a brief detour.

Combourg

As well as being a pleasant little town in its own right, **COMBOURG**, 17km south of Dol and 24km southeast of Dinan, has two chief attractions. Perched on a hill and dominating magnificent landscaped gardens, the **Château de Combourg** was the childhood home of the writer Chateaubriand (now buried at St-Malo – see p.234), and remains in the hands of his descendants (château: April–June & Sept Mon–Fri & Sun 2–5.30pm; July & Aug daily 11am–5.30pm; gardens: April–June & Sept Mon–Fri & Sun 10am–12.30pm & 2–6pm; July & Aug daily 10am–6pm; Oct Mon–Fri & Sun 10am–noon & 2–5pm; €5.50 for gardens & chateau). The castle's Tour du Chat is supposedly haunted by a ghost taking the form of a cat; Chateaubriand himself claimed it was haunted by the ghost of the **wooden leg** of a former lord – and that the cat was merely an acquaintance of this phantasmal limb. The entrance to the château is not where you expect it to be: turn right at the end of Combourg's main square instead of continuing straight towards the keep, and it's a short way up on the left.

Below both the château and town, the tranquil cypress-lined **lake** is, if anything, more appealing than the château itself. Misty and quiet early in the morning, busy only with anglers, it provides a welcome opportunity for leisurely countryside walks.

Practicalities

Combourg maintains a small **tourist office** in the Maison de la Lanterne, at 23 place Albert-Parent (April–June & Sept Tues–Sat 9.30am–12.30pm & 2–6pm; July & Aug Mon 10am–1pm, Tues–Sat 10am–1pm & 2–7pm, Sun 10am–12.30pm; Oct–March Tues–Fri 9.30am–12.30pm & 2–6pm; Ⓣ02.99.73.13.93, Ⓦwww.combourg.org). Two superb if somewhat expensive (and not very imaginatively named) **hotels** square off against each other across place Chateaubriand, which squeezes in between château and lake. While the *Hôtel du Château* at no. 1 (ⓣ02.99.73.00.38, ⓔhotelduchateau@wanadoo.fr; ❸; closed Mon lunch, Sat lunch, Sun eve in low season, plus mid-Dec to mid-Jan) is beyond reproach, the *Hôtel du Lac* at no. 2 (ⓣ02.99.73.05.65; ❸; closed Fri eve & Sun eve in low season, plus the last two weeks in Jan) just has the edge, with lake views from most of the rooms, as well as from the restaurant, where menus start at €11.50.

Beside the canal: Hédé and Tinténiac

The D795 south from Combourg meets the N137 roughly twenty kilometres north of Rennes, close to the particularly pleasant stretch of the **Canal d'Ille-et-Vilaine** that connects the two old towns of **HÉDÉ** and **TINTÉNIAC**. There are tempting places to collapse in the sun between the many locks and lock-keepers' cottages, although the towpath isn't consistent enough to follow for any distance on foot, let alone bike.

Both Hédé and Tinténiac are set on hills to the west of the canal. The one **hotel** in the area is situated on the main road just north of Hédé, where the *Hostellerie du Vieux Moulin* (ⓣ02.99.45.45.70; ❸; closed Sun eve & Mon, plus the first two weeks in Jan & the last two weeks in Oct), a Logis de France, stands in a lovely rural setting below the ruined ramparts of the town castle; the guest rooms are pretty minimal for the price, but the food in the restaurant is magnificent, with menus starting at €21.

In addition, a flower-festooned stone cottage just off the highway between Tinténiac and Hédé, a couple of hundred metres north of the *Vieux Moulin*, holds the inexpensive but high-quality *Restaurant le Genty-Home* (ⓣ02.99.45.46.07; closed Tues eve & Wed), whose enthusiastic young chef prepares traditional meats and fish on menus from €22.90 and up; €36 gets you a four-course feast including fois gras, a mixed plate of shellfish and pigeon.

St-Aubin-d'Aubigné and St-Aubin-du-Cormier (see p.257) are other possible bases. The **Forêt de Paimpont** (see p.357), too, is well within reach and allows you to bypass Rennes.

Rennes

For a city that has been the capital and power centre of Brittany ever since it was united with France in 1532, **RENNES** is – outwardly at least – uncharacteristic of the province, with its Neoclassical layout and grandiose major buildings. Much of its potential to be a picturesque tourist destination was destroyed in 1720, when a drunken carpenter managed to set light to virtually the whole city. The fire lasted a week, razing 33 streets and nine hundred houses. Only sections of the area known as **Les Lices**, at the junction of the canalized Ile-et-Rance and the River Vilaine, were left undamaged; fortunately, it was even then the oldest part of Rennes, so some traces of the medieval town survive. After the fire, the remodelling of the rest of the city was handed over to Parisian architects, not in deference to the capital but in an attempt to rival it. The result, on the north side of the river at any rate, is something of a patchwork quilt, consisting of grand eighteenth-century public squares interspersed with intimate little alleys of half-timbered houses. It's quite a pleasant city to stroll

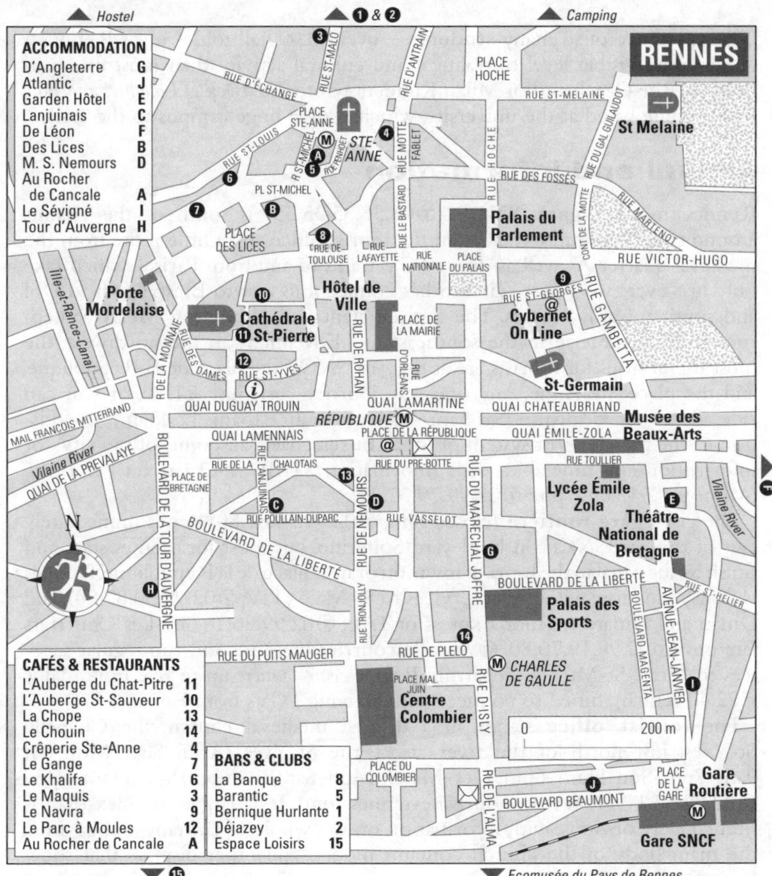

around for half a day, but not one that impresses the casual visitor with much sense of a cohesive personality.

Rennes was first laid out by the **Romans**, at a convenient ford in the Vilaine that was already home to the Celtic community of Condate; over thirty thousand Roman coins have been found in the riverbed, it being traditional for travellers to toss in an offering whenever they crossed water. Although it was ravaged by barbarian invaders in 276, the city subsequently enjoyed around a thousand years of independence before it was captured by Charles VIII of France in 1491. That defeat obliged Duchess Anne to marry Charles, and led to the union of Brittany and France, sealed in 1532 in the Cohue in Vannes (see p.405). From 1561, the Breton parliament met in Rennes and helped to preserve a measure of autonomy for Brittany in the face of growing centralization. To "celebrate" four centuries of the union in 1932, Breton separatists blew up a statue outside the Hôtel de Ville which showed Brittany swearing allegiance to Louis XV. In 1994, during demonstrations staged by fishermen protesting against a visit by Prime Minister Édouard Balladur, a stray firework caused huge damage to the buildings of the Breton parliament.

The presence of so many **students** – over 40,000 all told – gives Rennes a rather more visible level of political and cultural activity than most places in Brittany (the Czech author Milan Kundera wrote *The Book of Laughter and Forgetting* while based at the university, which is on a huge campus to the east).

Arrival and information

Rennes' modern **gare SNCF** (Ⓣ08.36.35.35.35) is south of the Vilaine, around twenty minutes' walk from the tourist office and a little more from the medieval quarter. As well as direct TGV trains to and from Paris – which take only just over two hours – it also has connections east to Brest, north to Dol and south towards Nantes. The fast, efficient and ultra-clean **Métro** system runs from La Poterie in the southeast to J.F. Kennedy in the northwest; the most useful stops for tourists are at the *gare SNCF*, the place de la République, and the place Ste-Anne. Any one-way journey costs just €1.10, or you can ride all day for €3 (Mon–Sat 5am–12.45am, Sun 7.15am–12.45am). In addition to the métro, a vast system of **local buses** covers all points of the city; for information and timetables, visit Information STAR at 12 rue du Pré Botté (Mon–Sat 7.15am–7pm; Ⓣ02.99.79.37.37).

The city's **gare routière** (closed Sun; Ⓣ02.99.30.87.80) stands immediately east of the *gare SNCF* on boulevard Solferino, but most local buses start and finish by the canal in the heart of town, on or near place de la République. Rennes is a busy junction, with direct services to St-Malo (TIV; Ⓣ02.99.30.87.80), and Dinan and Dinard (Armor Express or TAE; Ⓣ02.99.26.16.00). Les Courriers Bretons (Ⓣ02.99.19.70.80, Ⓦwww.lescourriersbretons.com) run regular services to Mont-St-Michel (departing Rennes *gare routière* up to five times daily; €22.40 return), timed to connect with arriving TGVs from Paris.

The **tourist office** stands in a disused medieval church, the Chapelle St-Yves, just north of the river at 11 rue St-Yves (April–Sept Mon–Sat 9am–7pm, Sun 11am–6pm; Oct–March Mon–Sat 9am–6pm, Sun 11am–6pm; Ⓣ02.99.67.11.11, Ⓦwww.tourisme-rennes.com). It's a larger complex than is immediately obvious, with information on the whole of Brittany and beyond; the main body of the church contains models and other displays that show how the city has grown.

Accommodation

There are surprisingly few **hotels** in the old part of Rennes – and those that there are can be hard to find. If you arrive by train or bus, it's easier to settle for staying south of the river, near the *gares SNCF* and *routière*. Rennes' hotels stay open all year round. Contact the tourist office if you plan to spend a **weekend** in Rennes; under the *Bon Week-End en Villes* scheme (Ⓦwww.bon-week-end-en-villes.com), you can get two nights' accommodation for the price of one.

Rennes' **youth hostel**, the *Centre International de Séjour*, 10–12 Canal St-Martin (Ⓣ02.99.33.22.33, Ⓔrennes@fuaj.org; dorm beds €13.55 including breakfast), is attractively positioned 3km north of the centre, next to the Canal d'Ille et Rance. Facilities include a cafeteria and a laundry, and there is a 1am curfew. To get there, catch bus #18 from place Ste-Anne, taking direction "St-Gregoire", and get off at the "Auberge de Jeunesse" stop. For the municipal **campsite**, *des Gayeulles*, 1km east of the centre on rue de Professeur-Maurice-Audin (Ⓣ02.99.36.91.22), take bus #3, direction "St-Laurent", getting off at "Gayeulles".

Hôtel d'Angleterre 19 rue du Maréchal-Joffre ⓣ02.99.79.38.61, ⓕ02.99.79.43.85. Unexceptional but cheap and scrupulously maintained hotel a short way south of the river towards the *gare SNCF*; a full en-suite room costs only €4 extra, while all doubles have shower and TV. ❷

Hôtel Atlantic 31 bd Beaumont ⓣ02.99.30.36.19, ⓕ02.99.65.10.17. Reasonable en-suite rooms with satellite TV in an unprepossessing street very close to the *gare SNCF*. ❸

Garden Hôtel 3 rue Duhamel ⓣ02.99.65.45.06, ⓕ02.99.65.02.62. Comfortable, nicely decorated and very personal Logis de France, north of the *gare SNCF* and not far from the river, with a pleasant little garden café. ❸

Hôtel Lanjuinais 11 rue Lanjuinais ⓣ02.99.79.02.03, ⓕ02.99.79.03.97. Standard, recently refurbished upmarket hotel, on a quiet little street less than 50m south of the river. ❸

Hôtel de Léon 15 rue de Léon ⓣ & ⓕ02.99.30.55.28. Quiet little eleven-room hotel, off the beaten track northeast of the *gare SNCF*, offering old-fashioned but adequate rooms at knockdown rates. ❶

Hôtel des Lices 7 place des Lices ⓣ02.99.79.14.81, ⓦwww.hotel-des-lices.com. Forty-five rooms, all with TV and balcony, in a very comfortable and friendly modern hotel on the edge of the prettiest part of old Rennes, very convenient for the place des Lices car park. ❹

Hôtel M. S. Nemours 5 rue de Nemours ⓣ02.99.78.26.26, ⓦwww.hotelnemours.com. Idiosyncratic nautical-themed hotel south of the river, where all the en-suite rooms are spick and span, and "Commandant Chappey" and his crew say "welcome aboard". ❸

Hôtel-Restaurant au Rocher de Cancale 10 rue St-Michel ⓣ02.99.79.20.83. Four-room hotel on a lively pedestrian street, between place Ste-Anne and place St-Michel, in the heart of medieval Rennes and ideally positioned for the city's nightlife. Beautifully restored frontage and ground floor, but with modern facilities upstairs. There is also a good restaurant (see p.254). ❸

Hôtel Le Sévigné 47 av Jean-Janvier ⓣ02.99.67.27.55, ⓦwww.hotellesevigne.fr. Smart, upmarket establishment 100m north of the *gare SNCF* en route to the centre, with a large brasserie next door. All rooms are en suite, with satellite TV. ❹

Hôtel Tour d'Auvergne 20 bd de la Tour-d'Auvergne ⓣ02.99.30.84.16, ⓕ02.23.42.10.01. A very simple but welcoming option between the *gare SNCF* and the river. Some low-priced rooms have en-suite shower facilities, but the cheapest come only with a sink. ❶

The City

Rennes' original **medieval core** – the "ville rouge", bordered by the canal to the west and the river to the south – is known to have been enclosed by walls well before 1422. Those walls were enlarged in 1440, when the **Porte Mordelaise** was constructed to serve as the ceremonial entrance to the city. The old quarter remains the liveliest part of town and it stays up late, particularly in the area around St-Aubin church and along rue St-Michel and rue de Penhöet.

Just to the northeast of the porte, the **place des Lices**, now dominated by two usually empty market halls, comes alive every Saturday for one of France's largest **street markets**. The place was originally the venue for jousting tournaments, and on this spot in 1337 the hitherto unknown **Bertrand du Guesclin**, then aged 17, fought and defeated several older opponents. This set him on his career as a soldier, during which he was later to save Rennes when it was under siege by the English. However, after the Bretons were defeated at Auray in 1364, he fought for the French and twice invaded Brittany. Thus, while he may be a French hero, some Bretons consider him a traitor; in 1946, Breton separatists destroyed a memorial to him in the Thabor gardens.

Magnificent medieval-style town houses overlook the place des Lices, but they're not as old as they look: most were built in the late seventeenth century to house Brittany's parliamentarians. The streets immediately northeast offer a more genuine glimpse of ancient Rennes. Wander around the back of the excellent crêperie at 5 place Ste-Anne (see p.254), through an archway beside no. 7 rue Motte-Fablet, and you'll find an extraordinary specimen of medieval high-rise housing.

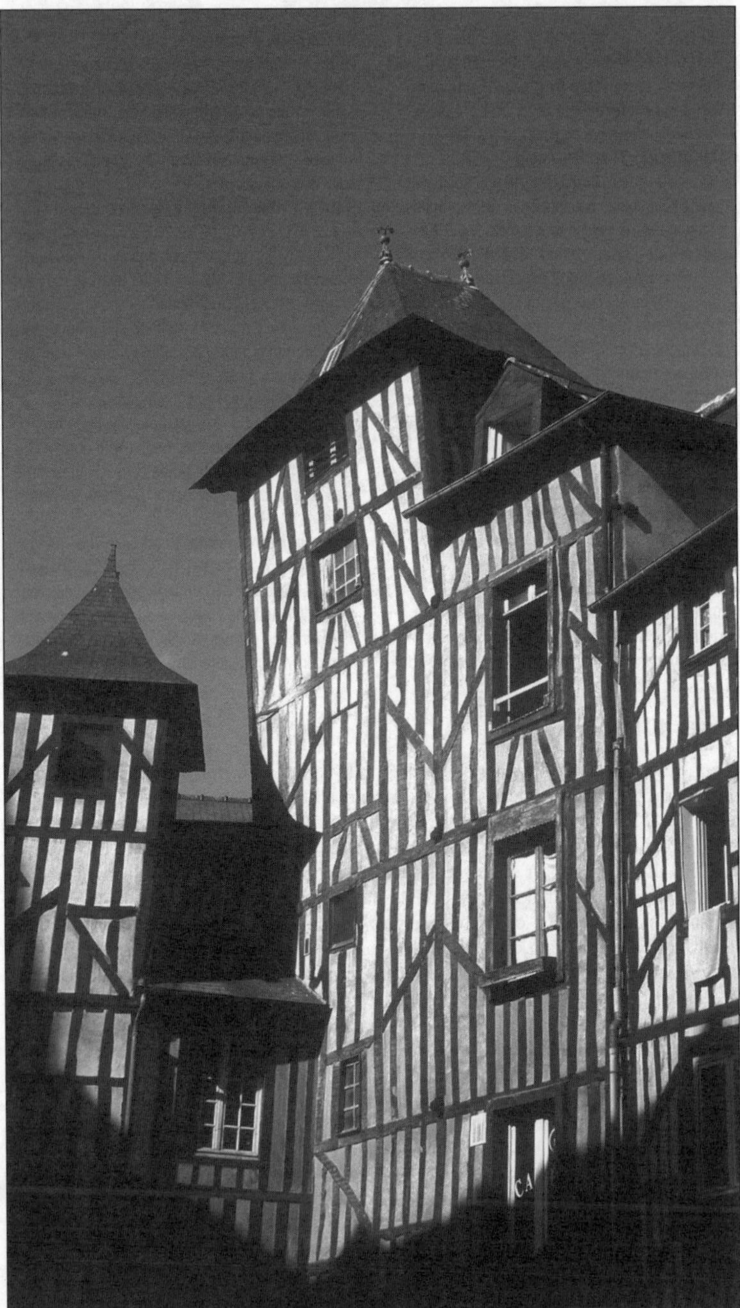

△ Medieval houses

The one central building to escape the 1720 fire was the **Palais du Parlement** on rue Hoche downtown. Ironically, however, the Palais was all but ruined by a major conflagration in 1994. The exact circumstances remain somewhat mysterious, but it's thought the blaze was sparked by a stray flare set off during a demonstration by Breton fishermen. Since then, the entire structure has been rebuilt and restored, and is once more topped by an impressive array of gleaming gilded statues. Inside, its lobby houses a small tourist office and also stages temporary exhibitions.

The **south bank** of the river is every bit as busy as the north. Just west of the *gare SNCF*, the vast **Centre Colombier** is Rennes at its most modern, packed with shops of all kinds, plus cafés and snack bars, and featuring a crystal model of itself in its main entrance hall. Slightly nearer the river, **rue Vasselot** has its own array of half-timbered old houses.

The **Lycée Émile Zola**, just south of the Beaux Arts museum at the corner of avenue Jean-Janvier and rue Toullier, was the scene in 1899 of the retrial of **Captain Alfred Dreyfus**. It had taken three years – and Émile Zola's famous letter "J'accuse" – to secure him the retrial following his wrongful conviction of treason in 1896. The notorious saga is commemorated by a modern steel statue, *La Dégradation de Dreyfus*, by Igael Tumurkin.

The museums

The **Vilaine** flows through the centre of Rennes, narrowly confined into a steep-sided channel, and even forced underground at one point. An imposing former university building at 20 quai Émile-Zola on its south bank houses the city's **Musée des Beaux Arts** (Tues–Sun 10am–noon & 2–6pm; €5.10). Its collection reaches back several millennia, and numbers among its artefacts mummified Egyptian cats and Etruscan urns as well as Greek and Roman statues and ceramics. Many of its finest artworks – which include drawings by Leonardo da Vinci, Botticelli, Fra Lippo Lippi and Dürer – are, however, not usually on public display. Instead you'll find a number of indifferent Impressionist views of Normandy by the likes of Boudin and Sisley, interspersed with the odd treasure such as Pieter Boel's startlingly contemporary-looking seventeenth-century animal studies, Veronese's depiction of a flying *Perseus Rescuing Andromeda*, and Pierre-Paul Ruben's *Tiger Hunt*. Only a few of its many canvases by lesser-known Breton artists tend to be on show at any one time, but if you're lucky they'll include the haunting landscapes of Théodore Aligny, painted in the 1850s but suffused with a delicate Maxfield-Parrish-style glow. Picasso also makes a cameo appearance, with a nude from 1923, a simple *Baigneuse à Dinard* from 1928, and a very late and surprisingly Cubist canvas from 1970.

The same building also used to be home to the **Musée de Bretagne**, covering the history and culture of Brittany, which has been closed for several years while its exhibits are moved to a new, high-tech museum, due to open on the cours des Alliés at the end of 2005; check with the tourist office for the latest.

Also worth a look is the **Ecomusée du Pays de Rennes** (April–Sept Tues–Fri 9am–6pm, Sat 2–6pm, Sun 2–7pm; Oct–March Tues–Fri 9am–noon & 2–6pm, Sat 2–6pm, Sun 2–7pm; €4.60), south of the centre on the route Chatillon sur Seiche (reached on city bus #15 from the place de la République, getting off at the "Tage" stop, or by metro – stop "Triangle"). Formerly the Ferme de la Bintinais, this farmhouse has been preserved as a monument to the rural history of the area. State-of-the-art techniques have been used to recount the minutiae of five centuries of daily life, showing the vital role Rennes has played in the evolution of Breton agriculture; living exhibits range from dairy cattle to honey bees.

Eating

Most of Rennes' more interesting **restaurants** are to be found in the streets just south of the place Ste-Anne, towards the place des Lices, with rues St-Michel and Penhoët – each with a fine assemblage of ancient wooden buildings – at the epicentre. Ethnic alternatives are concentrated along rue St-Malo just to the north, and also on rue St-Georges near the place du Palais. Rue Vasselot is the nearest equivalent south of the river, though if you're just looking for a quick snack, don't forget the various outlets in the Centre Colombier. There are also plenty of brasseries, restaurants and bars both in the *gare SNCF* complex and in the surrounding streets.

L'Auberge du Chat-Pitre 18 rue du Chapitre ⓣ02.99.30.36.36. Enjoyable re-creation of medieval dining, seated at long communal tables in a very pretty red half-timbered mansion close by the cathedral. Everything is à la carte, with hearty stews and roasts; starters cost around €5.80, main courses €10–16. Dinner only. Closed Sun.
L'Auberge St-Sauveur 6 rue St-Sauveur ⓣ02.99.79.32.56. Classy, romantic restaurant, in an attractive medieval house near the cathedral, with light lunches for €12 and richer, meaty dinner menus costing up to €27. Closed for lunch on Sat & Mon, plus all day Sun.
La Chope 3 rue de la Chalotais ⓣ02.99.79.34.54. Classic, busy brasserie serving simple lunches from €11 and dinners from €18 upwards. Closed Sun.
Le Chouin 12 rue d'Isly ⓣ02.99.30.87.86. The set lunch at this fine fish restaurant costs €13.50, while both the €16.50 and €21.50 dinner menus include nine oysters to start. Closed Sun & Mon, plus first two weeks of Aug.
Crêperie Ste-Anne 5 place Ste-Anne ⓣ02.99.79.22.72. Appealing crêperie nicely situated on the place Ste-Anne opposite the church, with plenty of outdoor seating and a good selection of *galettes* for around €5. Closed Sun.
Le Gange 34 place des Lices ⓣ02.99.30.18.37. Quality Indian restaurant offering €8.50 lunches, plus a vegetarian menu at €14.50, and meat-based ones from €18.
Le Khalifa 20 haut de la place des Lices ⓣ02.99.30.87.30. Assorted Moroccan dishes, served outside or in an atmospheric dining room. Couscous and brochettes from €9.95, tajine €11.50, as well as various set *formules*. Closed Mon.
Le Maquis 13 rue St-Malo ⓣ02.99.63.83.06. Very lively, friendly African restaurant, serving lots of Senegalese marinated chicken and fish dishes for around €9, plus Cameroonian beef stew. Dinner only. Closed Mon.
Le Navira 39 rue St-Georges ⓣ02.99.38.88.90. Simple, welcoming French restaurant with outdoor seating on a busy semi-pedestrian alley east of the Palais du Parlement, offering good-value lunch (€14.60) and dinner (€19.10) menus. Closed Sun & Mon.
Le Parc à Moules 8 rue Georges-Dottin ⓣ02.99.31.44.28. Mussels from Mont-St-Michel Bay cooked in 32 different delicious ways for €9.50, *moules* Calvados for €14, plus more expensive fishy dishes. Closed for lunch Sun & Tues, plus all day Mon.
Hôtel-Restaurant au Rocher de Cancale 10 rue St-Michel ⓣ02.99.79.20.83. This hotel restaurant has well-priced lunchtime (€9) and dinner (€14) menus, as well as an excellent – exclusively fish – menu for €20. Closed Sat & Sun.

Nightlife and entertainment

As with restaurants, the prime area for **bars** and **nightlife** in Rennes is around the place Ste-Anne. Leading off the south side of the square, rue St-Michel boasts half a dozen bars within spitting distance, including the *Sympatic* and the *Tennessee* (which plays good electronic music), while the rue St-Malo to the north is if anything even rowdier, and stays up later.

Rennes is seen at its best in the first ten days of July, when the **Festival des Tombées de la Nuit** takes over the whole city to celebrate Breton culture with music, theatre, film, mime and poetry in joyful rejection of the influences of both Paris and Hollywood (information from the tourist office). In the first week of December, the **Transmusicales** rock festival attracts big-name acts from all over France and the world at large, though still with a Breton emphasis.

Over the last decade it has helped to make Rennes an important centre for French rock (information on ⓣ02.99.31.12.10).

The **Théâtre National de Bretagne** (TNB), 1 rue St-Helier (ⓣ02.99.31.12.31), puts on varied events throughout the year, except in August. All year round, in a different auditorium on the same premises, *Club Ubu* (ⓣ02.99.31.12.00) is the venue for large-scale rock concerts. The TNB also has a good **cinema** showing films other than Hollywood blockbusters, often in their original languages. For the film programme at this and other cinemas in Rennes, visit ⓦwww.cine35.com.

Bars and clubs

La Banque 5 allée Rallier du Baty. Just south of the place St-Michel, this labyrinthine Irish pub is on the first floor of a building that once served as Rennes' prison.

Barantic 4 rue St-Michel. One of the city's favourite bars, especially among Breton nationalists and boisterous students. Occasional live performances of Breton music provide the main attraction for others.

Bernique Hurlante 40 rue St-Malo. Rendezvous for local artists and activists, as well as being one of Rennes' more gay-friendly bars. Closed Mon & Tues.

Déjazey 54 rue St-Malo. Friendly bar with live music at least once a week in a variety of styles, including jazz, funk, soul and Latin music. There is a small space for dancing, too.

Espace Loisirs 45 bd de la Tour d'Auvergne. Rennes' best discotheque plays thumping house music and attracts a mixed crowd of straight and gay clubbers.

Listings

Banks Banque de France, rue de la Visitation ⓣ02.99.25.12.12; Crédit Lyonnais, 2 rue d'Orléans ⓣ08.20.82.40.62; Société Générale rue Le Bastard ⓣ02.99.78.84.00;

Bookshops Co-op Breizh, 17 rue Penhoët ⓣ02.99.79.01.87 – has cassettes of Breton and Celtic music along with books and posters; FNAC, Centre Commercial Colombier ⓣ02.99.67.10.10.

Bicycle rental The town council provides **free bikes** for visitors, for up to seven hours on receipt for a deposit of €76, from a kiosk on the quai Duguay-Trouin in the central place de la République (daily 9am–7pm; ⓣ02.99.79.65.88). This is a separate scheme to the one open only to city residents, under which locals are given special identity cards to unlock the free white bicycles you'll see parked all over town.

Car rental Most of the main agencies have offices at the *gare SNCF*, including Avis ⓣ02.23.42.14.14, Hertz ⓣ02.23.42.17.01 and Budget ⓣ02.99.65.41.76.

Cinemas Gaumont, 8 quai Duguay-Trouin ⓣ02.99.31.57.92; films in English at L'Arvor, 29 rue d'Anatrain ⓣ02.99.38.72.40 and Ciné TNB, 1 rue St-Hélier ⓣ02.99.31.12.31.

Hospital Hôtel Dieu, 2 rue de l'Hôtel Dieu ⓣ02.99.28.43.21.

Internet access Cybernet On Line, near the Palais du Parlement at 22 rue St-Georges ⓣ02.99.36.37.41 (Mon 2–8pm, Tues–Sat 10.30am–8pm; €4 per hr); France Telecom shop, next to the post office on the place de la République (Mon–Sat 9am–7pm; €1 per 20min).

Pharmacie Pharmacie Colombia, Centre Commercial Colombier ⓣ02.99.65.08.08 (Mon–Sat 9am–8pm).

Post office Palais du Commerce in the heart of town on the place de la République ⓣ02.99.79.50.71 (Mon–Fri 8am–7pm, Sat 8.30am–12.30pm); 27 bd du Colombier, just west of the *gare SNCF* ⓣ02.99.31.42.72 (Mon–Fri 8am–7pm, Sat 8am–noon).

Fougères and around

FOUGÈRES, 50km short of Rennes on the main road into Brittany from Caen, promotes itself as the "*ville au joli nom*", *fougères* being the French for "fern". Name apart, however, it's not an especially pretty town, and it has a topography impossible to grasp from a map. Streets that look a few metres long turn out to be precipitous plunges down the escarpments of its split-levelled

Balzac's Fougères

The flavour of eighteenth-century Fougères is evoked in Balzac's *Les Chouans* – a bit of a potboiler with its absurd twists, but nonetheless an essentially historical account of the events surrounding the Chouan rebellion in Brittany, the attempt to restore the monarchy after the Revolution. Balzac makes great play of the town's unusual layout and of the various bloodthirsty survivors of the revolt that he met while doing his research: "In 1827, an old man accompanied by his wife was selling cattle at the Fougères market unremarked and unmolested, although he was the killer of more than one hundred persons."

site, and lanes collapse into flights of steps; the only efficient way to get around is on foot.

Perhaps the oddest feature is the positioning of the **castle**, sited in pre-artillery days well below the main part of the town, on a low spit of land that separates two mighty rock faces towering above. The massive structure was laid out in 1166 to replace a wooden fort destroyed by English invaders. Shielded by great curtain-walls, and circled by a hacked-out moat full of weirs and waterfalls, it was also protected in its heyday by the River Nançon. None of this, however, prevented it being captured several times by medieval adventurers such as du Guesclin. Today it remains a spectacular sight; the moat is still filled with water, while every crevice of the surrounding buildings seems to erupt with bright geraniums.

Within the castle keep, a romantic setting in Balzac's *Les Chouans* (see box above), the focus is disappointingly prosaic. Footwear, to this day the main industry of the town, is presented in a **museum** included in the hourly **château tours** (daily: April to mid-June & last two weeks of Sept 9.30am–noon & 2–6pm; mid-June to mid-Sept 9am–7pm; Oct–Dec, Feb & March 10am–noon & 2–5pm; €3.55). Literally the high spot of the tours, in summer only, is the view from the top of its clock tower.

The best approach to the castle is from **place des Arbres** beside St-Léonard's church off rue Nationale, the main street of the old fortified town. Footpaths, ramps and stairways drop down through successive tiers of formal public gardens, offering magnificent views of the ramparts and towers along the way, to reach the water meadows of the River Nançon. You cross the river itself beside a little cluster of medieval houses – the sculpted doorway at 6 rue de Lusignan is particularly attractive.

Up in the town, at 51 rue Nationale, the **Musée de la Villéon** (mid-June to mid-Sept daily 10am–12.30pm & 2.30–6pm; mid-Sept to mid-June Wed–Sun 10am–noon & 2–5pm; free), commemorates the Impressionist Emmanuel de la Villéon. Born in Fougères in 1858, he painted numerous memorable Breton landscapes.

Practicalities

Fougères' old *gare SNCF*, down below the modern town, has long been inactive; the **buses** to and from Vitré and Rennes that use the square beside it are the only form of public transport to pass through. The **tourist office** at 2 rue Nationale (Easter–June, Sept & Oct Mon–Sat 9.30am–12.30pm & 2–6pm, Sun 1.30–5.30pm; July & Aug Mon–Sat 9am–7pm, Sun 10am–noon & 2–4pm; Nov–Easter Mon 2–6pm, Tues–Sat 10am–12.30pm & 2–6pm; ⓣ02.99.94.12.20, ⓦwww.ot-fougeres.fr) is also a stopping-point for the usual motor-driven **petit train**, which runs regular town tours for €5 and is most useful for sparing weary legs the climb back up from the castle.

Not far from the tourist office, on the main road, the renovated *Hôtel les Voyageurs*, 10 place Gambetta (Ⓣ02.99.99.08.20, Ⓔhotel-voyageurs-fougeres@wanadoo.fr; ❷; closed the second two weeks in Aug) is a particularly nice **place to stay**, with TVs in all rooms – ask for one of the quieter rooms at the back. Selecting the cheapest €16 menu in the excellent downstairs restaurant (run by different management, but with the same name as the hotel; closed Sat lunch & Sun eve) can get you a delicious poached fillet of perch; other menus cost up to €37, and there is a well-laden *chariot des desserts*. A central alternative is the *Hôtel Balzac*, in a grey-granite town house at no. 15 in the semi-pedestrianized rue Nationale (Ⓣ02.99.99.42.46, Ⓦwww.balzachotel.com; ❸), with nicely refurbished rooms, while the *Buffet*, down the street at no. 53bis (Ⓣ02.99.94.35.76; closed Wed eve & Sun, plus the first two weeks in Aug), serves great-value food from €10.20, including all-you-can-eat buffets of *hors d'oeuvres*, cheeses and desserts.

There are no hotels in the immediate vicinity of the château, but the squares on all sides are crammed with an abundance of appealing **bars** and **crêperies**. At *Le Mediéval*, 2 place Raoul-II (Ⓣ02.99.94.92.59), which has lots of outdoor seating beside the moat, you can snack on *moules frites* or crêpes, or get a full dinner from €13.50.

The Forêt de Fougères

Northeast of Fougères, the **Forêt de Fougères**, stretching for roughly 8km on either side of the D177, which heads towards Vire (see p.216), is one of the most enjoyable in the province. The beech woods are spacious and light, with various megaliths and trails of old stones scattered among the chestnut and spruce. It's quite a contrast to their normal bleak and windswept haunts to see dolmens in such verdant surroundings. A good walk is to start at **Landéan**, about 8km northeast of Fougeres on the D177, and walk west through the forest for another 8km or so as far as **Le Chatellier**, a village set high in thick woods.

For a **horseback tour** of the Forêt de Fougères, contact the Centre d'Activitiés et Loisirs de Chénedet in **Chénedet**, 2.5km south of Landéan. (Ⓣ02.99.97.35.46).

St-Aubin-du-Cormier

Halfway between Fougères and Rennes on the N12, **ST-AUBIN-DU-CORMIER** makes a peaceful overnight stop. Though nothing much happens here, the town does boast a major sight – the keep of its old **castle**, which was demolished after the great battle here in 1488 in which the forces of Duke Francis were defeated by the French army. Many Breton soldiers were dressed in the English colours of a black cross on white silk, to scare the French into believing that the duke had extensive English reinforcements. The victorious French were told to spare all prisoners except the English, and so the hapless Bretons were massacred. Just one sheer wall of the castle survives, with a fireplace visible halfway up. A small **monument** in a field nearby marks the actual site of the battle.

For **accommodation**, St-Aubin's very cheap *Hôtel du Bretagne*, 68 rue de l'Écu (Ⓣ02.99.39.10.22; ❷), has to be recommended – a rambling old building, with lumpy lino corridors stretching off in random directions upstairs, and good food downstairs. The municipal **campsite** (☎02.99.39.10.42; closed Oct–March) sprawls immediately below the castle, next to a small lake.

Vitré

VITRÉ, just north of the Le Mans–Rennes motorway, 30km east of Rennes, is a lesser rival to Dinan as the best-preserved **medieval town** in Brittany. Occupation of the site dates right back to the Romans, when a certain Vitrius is known to have owned a villa here. While its thirteenth-century walls are no longer quite complete, their effect is enhanced by the fact that what lies outside them has changed so little. To the north are stark wooded slopes, while into the western hillside beneath the castle burrow thickets of stone cottages that must once have been Vitré's medieval slums. This little suburb is called **Rachapt**, a corruption of the French for "repurchase", in memory of the time during the Hundred Years War when the castle's defendants finally paid the English army, by whom they'd been besieged for several years, to go away. By 1589, when the castle successfully resisted a siege by the Catholic League, Vitré had become a Huguenot stronghold.

In best fairy-tale fashion, the towers of the **castle** itself (April–June daily 10am–noon & 2–5.30pm; July–Sept daily 10am–6pm; Oct–March Wed–Fri 10am–noon & 2–5.30pm, Sat–Mon 2–5.30pm; €4), which dominates the western end of the ramparts, have pointed slate-grey roofs that look like freshly sharpened pencils. First erected in 1060, the castle was remodelled to its present appearance two hundred years later. Unfortunately, the **museum** inside throws little light on the town's eventful past; instead, it's a ragbag of pretty much anything some nineteenth-century curator could get his hands on. The highlight amid all the seashells, birds and bugs is a collection of tatty **stuffed frogs** doing amusing things, such as fighting duels and playing billiards.

The admission fee for the castle also includes entry to three other, mediocre museums in the general vicinity, all of which share the same opening hours as the castle. The **Musée St-Nicholas**, on the western outskirts of town, occupies the huge former chapel of a fifteenth-century hospital, with a sober collection of medieval reliquaries and religious paraphernalia; the attractive seventeenth-century manor house of the **Musée de la Faucillonnaie**, 3km northwest of the centre in Montreuil-sous-Pérouse, is more of a draw than the general mishmash of secular artefacts, mostly of more recent origin, housed within; and the **Château des Rochers Sévigné**, 10km southeast, is a place of pilgrimage for French devotees of the seventeenth-century society letter-writer Madame de Sévigné, and holds little interest for anyone not familiar with her work.

Vitré is a market town rather than an industrial centre, with its principal **market** held on Mondays in the square in front of Notre Dame church. The old city is full of twisting streets of half-timbered houses, a good proportion of which are bars. The **rue de la Baudrairie**, between the church and the castle, and formerly the town's leather-working quarter, is the most picturesque of the streets, but the **rue d'en Bas**, which climbs up from Rachapt to the castle, has the best selection of bars; the *Aston* at no. 7 is a nice place to spend an evening.

Practicalities

Vitré's candy-striped **gare SNCF** is on the southern edge of the centre, where the ramparts disappear and the town imperceptibly blends into its newer sectors. As you exit the station, on the left side of place Général de Gaulle you'll find the **tourist office** (July & Aug daily 10am–12.30pm & 2–7pm; Sept–June Mon 2.30–6pm, Tues–Fri 9.30am–12.30pm & 2.30–6pm, Sat 10am–12.30pm & 3–5pm; ⓣ02.99.75.04.46, ⓦwww.ot-vitre.fr), which runs an intricate schedule of guided tours of the town in summer.

Most of the **hotels**, too, are near the *gare SNCF*. The *Petit-Billot*, 5bis place du Général-Leclerc (ⓣ02.99.75.02.10, ⓦwww.petit-billot.com; ❸), is good value, while rooms on the higher floors of the *Hôtel du Château*, 5 rue Rallon (ⓣ02.99.74.58.59; ❸; closed Sun in low season) on a quiet road just below the castle, have views of the ramparts.

Of the **restaurants**, *Le St-Yves*, immediately below the castle at 1 place St-Yves (ⓣ02.99.74.68.76; closed Mon eve, Thurs eve & all day Sun), serves menus from €14 to €23. *La Taverne de l'Ecu*, 12 rue de la Baudrairie (ⓣ02.99.75.11.09; closed Tues eve & Wed, plus Sun eve in low season), is set in a particularly attractive medieval house and serves good fish menus from €16, while *La Soupe aux Choux*, a little higher up at 32 rue Notre-Dame (ⓣ02.99.75.10.86; closed Sat lunch, plus Sun in low season), prepares simple but classic French food on an €11 menu.

Around Vitré

There are several interesting smaller towns in the area. **CHAMPEAUX**, 8km west of Vitré, consists of a central paved square, surrounded by stone houses, with an ornate well in the centre. Its fifteenth-century collegiate **church** contains a superb stained-glass *Crucifixion* by Gilles de la Croix-Vallée, the ornate tombs of its founding family, and some fine carved choir stalls. **CHÂTEAUBOURG**, halfway between Vitré and Rennes, has a wonderful but expensive **hotel**, the *Ar Milin* (ⓣ02.99.00.30.91, ⓦwww.armilin.com; ❻; restaurant closed Sun in low season), straddling the River Vilaine in huge gardens at 30 rue de Paris. Breakfast, at €11, consists of an enormous buffet of fresh pastries.

The Roche-aux-Fées

About 15km south of Châteaubourg, not far from the road just off the D341 near Retiers, the **ROCHE-AUX-FÉES** is the least-visited of the major megalithic monuments of Brittany. The "fairy rock" is a twenty-metre-long covered alleyway of purplish stones, with no apparent funerary purpose or, indeed, any evidence that it was ever buried. It's set on a high and exposed spot, guarded by just a few venerable trees, and it's thought the slabs had to be dragged a good 45km to get here. There's no admission charge. Tradition has it that engaged couples should come to the Roche-aux-Fées on the night of a full moon and separately count the stones; if they agree on the total, things are looking good.

West along the coast

To the west of the Rance, beyond Dinard, stretches the green of the **Côte d'Émeraude**. While this region has its fair share of developed family resorts, such as **St-Jacut**, **Erquy** and **Le Val-André**, it also offers wonderful camping, at its best around the heather-surrounded beaches near **Cap Fréhel** – for once not encroached upon by the military. Further west, the coast becomes wilder and harsher. Beyond **St-Brieuc**, the seaside towns tend to be crammed into narrow rocky inlets or set well back in river estuaries, and only a few beaches manage to break out from the rocks. Once past **Paimpol**, the shoreline is known as the **Côte de Granit Rose** – a literal description of its primeval tangle of vast pink granite boulders. They certainly deserve to be seen, at the very least as a quick detour before catching the ferry at Pointe de l'Arcouest (near Paimpol) for the Île de **Bréhat**.

The Côte d'Émeraude

The coast immediately **west of Dinard** is one of Brittany's most traditional family resort areas, with old-fashioned holiday towns, safe sandy beaches and a plethora of well-organized campsites. None of the towns is of any significant size, and paying attractions or entertainments suitable for whiling away rainy afternoons are almost nonexistent. If you're lucky enough to be here on a fine summer's day, however, **St-Jacut**, **St-Cast**, **Erquy** and **Le Val-André** all make idyllically lazy seaside destinations, while **Cap Fréhel** offers a fine, if bracing, coastal walk.

St-Jacut-de-la-mer

ST-JACUT, which takes up most of the tip of a narrow peninsula roughly 16km west of St-Malo, looks today like a classic nineteenth-century bathing resort, but was in fact founded a thousand years earlier by an itinerant Irish monk. Though not the most exciting of places, it has everything young children could want – good sand, rocky pools to clamber about, and woods nearby to scramble in.

St-Jacut also boasts one of Brittany's most distinctive **hotels**, atop the central spine of the peninsula: the *Hôtel le Vieux Moulin*, 22 rue du Moulin (☎02.96.27.71.02; ❸; closed mid-Oct to March), centres on a fifteenth-century windmill, and as a result two of its guest rooms are completely round and offer sea views in two directions. It also serves good, if eccentric, food, with generous portions on changing dinner menus, priced at €22 and €27, that are apt to include home-made crisps as a vegetable. The *Camping Municipal* is beside the plage de la Manchette (☎02.96.27.70.33; closed Oct–March).

St-Cast-le-Guildo

The pleasant seaside community of **ST-CAST**, on the next promontory along, is a thirty-kilometre drive from St-Malo, and connected by SNCF buses with the nearest train station, at Lamballe (see p.264). Most of its commercial activity takes place in the rather uninspiring **Bourg**, set back from the water, but the seaside area down below is very nice, with a large swathe of **beach** popular with families running parallel to rue du Duc d'Auguillon – the main throughfare with plenty of restaurants – and a quiet, picturesque **port** north of the beach as you approach the headland. There are also good walks along the coast to the headland.

Among medium-price **hotels** in St-Cast is the attractive *Hôtel des Mielles*, 3 rue du Duc d'Auguillon (☎02.96.41.80.95; ❸; closed mid-Sept to April), just a few metres from the beach. The **tourist office** on place Charles-de-Gaulle (July & Aug Mon–Sat 9am–7.30pm, Sun 10am–12.30pm & 3–6.30pm; Sept–June Mon–Sat 9am–noon & 2–6pm; ⓣ02.96.41.81.52, ⓦwww.ot-st-cast-le-guildo.fr) can provide details of local **campsites**, such as the four-star *Châtelet* beside the bay on rue des Nouettes (ⓣ02.96.41.96.33, ⓦwww.lechatelet.com; closed mid-Sept to April). The most popular of St-Cast's **restaurants** is *Le Bonheur est dans le Blé*, 17 rue du Duc d'Auguillon (ⓣ02.96.81.03.99), a crêperie known for its generous portions and imaginative fillings; it's best to reserve in advance during summer. There's a **cybercafé** in town, *@sc2*, at 14 rue de la Mer (Mon–Sat 10–1am, Sun 5pm–1am; ⓣ02.96.81.04.56; €6 per hr).

Cap Fréhel

The one truly exceptional spot along the Côte d'Émeraude is **Cap Fréhel**. This high, warm expanse of heath, cliffs and heather is over-visited – camping is prohibited for 5km around the tip – but the headland itself, 400m walk from the road, remains unspoiled, with no more than a few ruins of old buildings and a small "tearoom" nearby. The rocks sixty metres down at the foot of the cliffs, busy with puffins and guillemots, officially constitute the Fauconnière **seabird sanctuary**. Offshore, the heather-covered islands are grand to look at, although too tiny to visit; the view from the cape's **lighthouse** (July & Aug daily 2–6pm; free) can extend as far as Jersey and the Île de Bréhat.

The **Fort la Latte**, to the east, is used regularly as a film set. Its tower (containing a cannonball factory) is accessible only over two drawbridges, and to visit you must take a guided tour (April–Sept daily 10am–12.30pm & 2.30–6pm; Oct–March Sat, Sun & hols 2.30–6pm; €4.10; ⓣ02.99.30.38.84, ⓦwww.castlelalatte.com).

The nearest places to stay to Cap Fréhel are the ideal, isolated **campsite** 5km inland from the Cap at Plévenon, the *Camping des Grèves d'En Bas* (ⓣ02.96.41.43.34; closed mid-Sept to mid-June), and a basic **hostel** on the D16 just outside Plévenon en route towards the cape at Kérivet-en-Fréhel, *La Ville Hardrieux* (ⓣ02.96.41.48.98; dorm beds €7.70; closed Oct–March) – which also rents out bicycles.

Erquy

The perfect crescent beach at **ERQUY**, around 20km west of Cap Fréhel, curves through more than 180 degrees, and is home to schools of both **sailing** (ⓣ02.96.72.32.62) and **diving** (ⓣ02.96.72.49.67). At low tide, the sea disappears way beyond the harbour entrance, leaving gentle ripples of paddling sand. Adventurers equipped with suitable boots could walk right across its mouth, from the grassy wooded headland on the left side over to the picturesque little lighthouse at the end of the jetty on the right.

In July and August, Les Vedettes de Bréhat (ⓣ02.96.55.79.50, ⓦwww.vedettesdebrehat.com) operate **boat trips** every four or five days, depending on the tides, from Erquy (8.30am or 10am; €25) and in some cases also nearby Dahouët (8.45am; €25) out to the **Île de Bréhat** (see p.272). There are also sporadic sailings in June and September.

Erquy's **tourist office** on the boulevard de la Mer (July & Aug Mon–Sat 10am–7pm, Sun 9.30am–12.30pm & 3.30–6.30pm; Sept–June Mon–Sat 9.30am–12.30pm & 2–6pm; ⓣ02.96.72.30.12, ⓦwww.erquy-tourisme.com) coordinates information for the surrounding area.

The *Hôtel Beauséjour*, 21 rue de la Corniche (Ⓣ02.96.72.30.39, Ⓦwww.beausejour-erquy.com; ❸; closed Sun eve & Mon in low season), has a good view of the bay, and excellent fish dinners from €17, while the more upmarket **restaurant** *l'Escurial* (Ⓣ02.96.72.31.56; closed Sun eve & Mon in low season) by the seafront serves menus from €20 during the week and €29 at weekends, some of which consist entirely of **scallops**, the town's speciality.

There are several **campsites** on the promontory (dotted with tiny coves) that leads to the Cap d'Erquy north of town, including the three-star *de la Plage de St-Pabu* (Ⓣ02.96.72.24.65, Ⓦwww.saintpabu.com; closed mid-Oct to March) right beside the sea.

Le Val-André

The beach in the broader bay of **LE VAL-ANDRÉ**, another 11km down the coast, is on a slightly larger scale than that of Erquy, and composed of finer sand. The endless pedestrian promenade that stretches along the seafront feels oddly Victorian, consisting solely of huge old houses undisturbed by shops or bars. However, Le Val-André is definitely more of a town than Erquy, and rue A-Charner, running parallel to the sea one street back, is busy with holiday-makers in summer.

For an enjoyable scenic **walk**, follow the 2km-long footpath around the headland to the small, secluded lagoon of **Dahouët**. The construction of a large yachting marina here has obliterated all significant traces of its past, but this lagoon is known to have been used by Viking raiders over a thousand years ago.

Le Val-André's helpful **tourist office** (April–June Mon–Sat 9am–12.30pm & 2–6pm; July & Aug Mon–Sat 9am–1pm & 2–7pm, Sun 10.30am–12.30pm & 3.30–6pm; Sept–Dec Mon–Sat 9am–12.30pm & 2.30–6.30pm; Dec–March Mon–Sat 9am–12.30pm & 2–5.30pm; Ⓣ02.96.72.20.55) is located in the modern casino at the very centre of the waterfront.

Of its **hotels**, the tastefully refurbished *Hôtel de la Mer*, 63 rue A-Charner (Ⓣ02.96.72.20.44; ❸), serves magnificent food, including a €23 *Menu de Luxe*. You have to pay a little extra for an en-suite room, and more again for one with a sea view. Bear in mind too that with the success of the business many guests who turn up without a prior reservation find themselves having to sleep in the characterless *Nuit et Jour* motel, run by the same management.

PLÉNEUF, the *bourg* associated with Le Val-André, 1.5km up the hill from the sea, also has a few hotels. The *Hôtel de France*, in its main church square at 4 rue Pasteur (Ⓣ02.96.72.22.52; ❶), has an eccentric block of cheap rooms out the back, all accessed from open balconies and imaginatively marine-themed with knots, canvas and navy-blue trimmings. It also has a good restaurant hidden away, with a recommended €19.50 menu.

Back down close to the beach, the *Restaurant au Biniou*, 121 rue Clemenceau (Ⓣ02.96.72.24.35; closed Tues eve & Wed in low season, plus all Feb), is the best of several adjacent seafood specialists just back from the casino; in addition to the usual choices, its €23.50 menu features various fish in original sauces such as mussel and ginger.

St-Brieuc

The major city on the Côte d'Émeraude, **ST-BRIEUC**, is far too busy being the industrial centre of the north to concern itself with entertaining tourists. It's an odd-looking city, with two very deep wooded valleys spanned by viaducts at its core. The streets are hectic, with the town centre cut in two by what's effectively a motorway, unrelieved by any public parks, and not much improved either by a mega-shopping complex. Motorists and cyclists, unfortunately, have little choice but to plough straight through rather than attempting to negotiate the back roads and steep hills around.

Every July, St-Brieuc makes a concession to summer visitors by organizing a **Festival of Breton Music**, while towards the end of May comes the **Art Rock Festival** (ⓣ02.96.52.59.59); if you're interested, the tourist office (see below) can supply relevant information on both. Also worth checking out is the Comité Départmentale de Tourisme for the *département* of Côtes d'Armor at 29 rue des Promenades (ⓣ02.96.62.72.00, ⓦwww.cotesdarmor.com). Throughout the summer they organize one-day **tours** in the area to visit **craft workshops** of every variety – taxidermists, bakers, farmers, and makers of furniture and of cider.

Practicalities

Trains between Paris, Dol and Brest stop at the **gare SNCF**, around 1km south of the centre of St-Brieuc, and regular **buses** run to the nearby resorts. There's an information desk at the station in summer, though the official **tourist office** is in the town centre, right by the cathedral at 7 rue St-Gouéno (July & Aug Mon–Sat 9am–7pm, Sun 10am–1pm; Sept–June Mon–Sat 9.30am–12.30pm & 1.30–6pm; ⓣ02.96.33.32.50, ⓦwww.baiedesaintbrieuc.com).

The two best-value central **places to stay** are the *Champ-de-Mars*, 13 rue du Général-Leclerc (ⓣ02.96.33.60.99, ⓕ02.96.33.60.05; ❸), where the old-fashioned green-painted brasserie downstairs serves mussels or fish soup for around €8, and the *Duguesclin*, 2 place Duguesclin (ⓣ02.96.33.11.58, ⓦwww.hotel-duguesclin.com; ❸). St-Brieuc also has a **hostel**, 2km northwest of the place du Champ-de-Mars, in the magnificent fifteenth-century Manoir de la Ville-Guyomard (ⓣ02.96.78.70.70, ⓔsaint-brieuc@fuaj.org; €13.75); served by bus #3 from the Champ-de-Mars (take direction "C.Com. Les Villages"), it also offers bicycles and canoes for rent.

Some of the nicest **eating** options in town are in the old quarter, behind the cathedral. The traditional French cooking at *Le Madure*, 14 rue Quinquaine (ⓣ02.96.61.21.07; closed Sat lunch & Sun), is served à la carte, with steaks around €14 and salads half that; the fondues at *Le Chaudron*, 19 rue Fardel (ⓣ02.96.33.01.72; closed Sun), start at around €12 per person.

The inland route: west to Morlaix

While following the coast from Dinard and Dinan is by far the most scenic route westwards across Brittany, it can also be pretty slow. Travellers in a hurry to reach Morlaix and Finistère can choose instead to head **inland**, either by branching onto the D768 just south of St-Jacut if coming from Dinard, or following the N176 west out of Dinan. Both routes pass through the occasional time-forgotten little town or village; few have much in the way of tourist facilities, but all make potentially pleasant opportunities to stretch your legs.

Jugon-les-Lacs

Tiny old **JUGON-LES-LACS** lies 15km southwest of the market town of **Plancoët** (home of a popular brand of mineral water). Jugon is poised at one end of its own artificial lake – the *grand étang* – which was originally created for defensive purposes during the twelfth century. Peculiarly, the central place du Martray – scene of a market each Friday – is well below the water level, and you have to climb uphill to reach the massive cobblestone dyke that shields it from inundation. At the opposite end of town, the N176 crosses high above the valley on a viaduct. Jugon, nestled cosily between the two, has no room to expand even if it wanted to – it's a subdued but atmospheric place, whose few streets are almost deserted in the evenings.

For most of the way around the **lake**, there's no approach road or footpath, only meadows and trees sweeping down to the water. However, just out of town at the *Au Bocage du Lac* campsite (see below), there's a small beach from which you can go swimming.

The local **tourist office** is in the Hôtel de Ville on the main square (July & Aug Mon–Sat 10am–12.15pm & 2.30–6.15pm, Sun 10am–noon; Sept–June Mon–Fri 10am–noon & 2–5pm; ⓣ02.96.31.70.75, ⓦwww.jugon-les-lacs.com). Among the handful of moderately priced **hotels** in Jugon is *La Grande Fontaine*, 7 rue Penthièvre (ⓣ02.96.31.61.29; ❸), a couple of hundred metres east of the centre on the main road towards Dinan, which has a lively bar with a roadside terrace, and menus from €16 – €40 gets you half a lobster, plus a seafood platter. *The Auberge de l'Ecu* is a lovely flower-festooned restaurant on the main square (ⓣ02.96.31.61.41), again with a terrace and serving menus from €11.50 up to €31.

Out of town along the D52 towards Mégrit, the *Au Bocage du Lac* **campsite** (ⓣ02.96.31.60.16; closed Oct–April) is very much a family campsite; it has a heated swimming pool, as well as boats and **windsurf boards** for hire – and tuition available – from its École de Voile (ⓣ02.96.31.64.58).

Lamballe

The main N176 westwards from Jugon brings you after 20km to **LAMBALLE**, an old town crammed into a narrow valley beside a broad river, dominated by a church high up on battlement walls. Its most famous former citizen was the princess of Lamballe, a lady-in-waiting to Marie Antoinette, who was guillotined in 1792.

Lamballe's picturesque main square, the **place du Martray**, is dominated by fourteenth-century half-timbered buildings, the grandest of which is the **Maison du Bourreau**. Formerly home to the town's public executioner – the word "Martray" means "martyr", and so the place du Martray customarily denotes the square where executions took place – it now houses not only the **tourist office** (see opposite), but also the tiny **Musée Mathurin Méheut** (June–Sept Mon–Sat 10am–noon & 2.30–6pm; Easter hols Mon–Sat 10am–noon & 2.30–5pm; Oct–Dec & Feb–May, except for Easter hols Tues, Fri & Sat 2.30–5pm; €2.50). Half the museum explores the town's history, and features a fascinating model of Lamballe as it looked in 1417; the rest focuses on the paintings of local-born Mathurin Méheut (1882–1958), which range from Breton landscapes to illustrations for children's books.

A branch of the **national stud** (the *haras national*) all but adjoins the main square. Though not quite on the same scale as Le Notre's dramatic park near Argentan (see p.205), and specializing in any case more in sturdy Breton workhorses than glossy thoroughbreds, it will still delight any horse-lover (guided tours only: Feb to mid-June and mid-Sept to mid-Nov Wed, Sat & Sun 2.45pm & 4pm; mid-June to mid-Sept daily 11am–5.30pm, with tours at half-hourly intervals; July & Aug tours in English daily 2.30pm &

3.30pm; €5). It's the focus of a big **horse festival** on the first weekend after August 15.

Lamballe's **tourist office** is in the Maison du Bourreau in the main square (same hours as museum; ⓣ02.96.31.05.38). A central **hotel-restaurant** is the *Tour d'Argent*, a Logis de France at no. 2 on rue Dr-Lavagne, the road which becomes the D102 as it leaves town (ⓣ02.96.31.01.37, ⓔlatourdargent@wanadoo.fr; ❸; closed Sat in low season). *La Tête Noire*, near the tourist office on place du Martray (ⓣ02.96.50.88.74), is a glorious medieval tavern-cum-bistro specializing in piping-hot *cassolettes*, which cost around €10.50.

Moncontour

The attractive little hill town of **MONCONTOUR**, 18km southeast of Lamballe and 23km southwest of St-Brieuc, was during the Middle Ages one of the more prosperous towns of the region, thanks to its hemp industry. Having been under no pressure to grow since then, it remains largely enclosed by its medieval fortifications – not that you get much impression of them once you're actually in the town, as the houses all face inwards onto the narrow streets.

Moncontour centres on the pretty, triangular **place du Penthièvre**. Here, the Romanesque tower of the church of St-Mathurin gained a delightfully eccentric new belfry with wooden eaves and grey-slate domes in 1902, and now constitutes the highest point on the hill.

Moncontour's **tourist office** can be found at 4 place de la Carrière, a short way south of place du Penthièvre (daily: June to mid-July 10am–12.30pm & 2.30–6.30pm; mid-July to Aug 10am–6.30pm; Sept 10am–noon & 2–6pm; ⓣ02.96.73.49.57). The village lacks any hotels, but there's a beautifully situated **B&B**, the four-room *Chambres d'hôte à la Garde Ducale*, in a sixteenth-century house at 10 place Penthièvre (ⓣ02.96.73.52.18; ❸). Near the tourist office, the *Chaudron Magique* (ⓣ02.96.73.40.34; closed Mon Oct–May) is a medieval-theme **restaurant** where liveried waiters can serve you a decent meal for €11 and upwards. On the final Sunday of August, Moncontour echoes its days of glory by playing host to a hectic and atmospheric "medieval fair".

Quintin

QUINTIN, 20km southwest of St-Brieuc, is in the official jargon "a little city of character", which prospered as a weaving community in the seventeenth and eighteenth centuries, and remains pretty much intact. Work on the grand **Château de Quintin** began in 1640, and was never completed, but you can tour a few of the rooms in the interior (May to mid-June & second two weeks in Sept daily 2–5pm; mid-June to mid-Sept daily 10.30am–12.30pm & 1.30–5pm; Oct Sun 2–5pm; rest of the year by appointment only; €5). The château is at its most imposing, however, when seen from the River Gouët below.

A twenty-minute stroll up from the river can show you the best of what Quintin has to offer. Follow the rue du Vau-du-Gouët from the east, and climb a stone staircase up through the vestiges of the old town walls, which are overshadowed by the round **Tour des Archives**, covered with creeping wild flowers. At the top is the late nineteenth-century **Basilique Notre Dame**. Beyond that, you enter the central place 1830, with the rue Grande stretching ahead. Most of its houses are made of elegant grey stone, but a few of their half-timbered predecessors still remain.

Turn right at the Hôtel de Ville at the far end of the rue Grande, and you'll soon come to the walled **Parc de Roz Maria**. These attractive formal gardens were laid out in the eighteenth century, and still contain a large public wash-place that's now overgrown with green algae.

Quintin's **tourist office** is at no. 6 on the main place 1830 (July & Aug Mon–Sat 9.30am–12.30pm & 2–6pm, Sun 10.30am–12.30pm & 2.30–4.30pm; Sept–June Tues–Sat 9.30am–noon & 2–5pm; ⓣ02.96.74.01.51, ⓔotsi.pays-de-quentin@wanadoo.fr). The ivy-coated *Hôtel du Commerce*, on the western fringes of the centre at 2 rue Rochenen (ⓣ02.96.74.94.67; ❸; closed Fri eve, Sun eve & all day Mon), is a classic little village **hotel**, tasteful if far from fancy. Its solemn but attractive dining room serves good meals from €14 upwards.

Guingamp and around

Should you choose to skip St-Brieuc and the Côte de Granit Rose, the most direct route west towards Finistère carries across the centre of the northern peninsula. The only town of any size here is the old weaving centre of **GUINGAMP** – its name possibly the source of the striped or checked fabric "gingham". It's an attractive place of cobbled streets, but there's not much to see beyond the main square – where a fountain bedecked in griffins and gargoyles is overlooked by a splendid pair of lopsided old timber-frame houses propping each other up – and the Black Virgin in the thirteenth-century **basilica**. A big *pardon*, featuring a night procession to the basilica, is held on the first Saturday in July, while a ten-day **Festival de la Danse Bretonne** enlivens the middle of August.

Guingamp is the first rail stop west of St-Brieuc; its **gare SNCF** lies southeast of the place Champ-au-Roy, where you'll find the **tourist office** (June–Aug Tues–Sat 10.15am–noon & 2.15–6pm; Sept–May Wed, Fri & Sat 10.15am–noon & 2.15–6pm; ⓣ02.96.43.73.89, ⓦwww.ot-guingamp.org) and the **gare routière**.

Of its **hotels**, the white-painted, modernized *Hôtel d'Armor*, 44–46 bd Clémenceau (ⓣ02.96.43.76.16; ❸), is probably the best value, and has a nice garden around the back. The best **restaurant** in town, however, is in the expensive hotel *Le Relais du Roy*, 42 place du Centre (ⓣ02.96.43.76.62; ❼; restaurant closed Sun mid-Nov to March), where you can dine in the magnificent dining room for a minimum of €22. After football matches, the local team and its supporters congregate in the always lively *Campbell's Pub* in place St-Michel.

The Ménéz Bré

Fifteen kilometres along the road out towards Morlaix is the "mountain" of the **Ménéz Bré**, a rounded and exposed monolith that may be just 302m tall but nonetheless seems a spectacular height amid these plains. In the mid-nineteenth century, the local rector was often observed to climb, laden with books, to the mountain's peak on stormy nights, accompanied only by a donkey. For all his exemplary piety, his parishioners suspected him of sorcery and witchcraft; he was in fact doing early research into natural electrical forces. Modern visitors hike to the top for dramatic views towards the sea to the north and the rolling hills inland. A footpath leads to the Ménéz Bré from the village of **Tréglamus**, 8km west of Guingamp just off the N12; the round-trip walk is 10km.

The Baie de St-Brieuc

St-Brieuc itself may be more of an obstacle to be avoided than an appealing destination, but it serves as a gateway to the series of attractive little resorts that dot its eponymous bay. It also marks the point at which visitors usually begin to become aware that Brittany really does amount to something more than just another indistinguishable corner of the French coastline, and has its own very distinct culture and traditions.

As you move northwest from St-Brieuc along the edge of the V-shaped bay towards Paimpol, the countryside becomes especially rich – it's called the **Goëlo** – while the coast itself grows wilder and harsher. The seaside towns tend to be crammed into narrow rocky inlets or set well back in river estuaries.

Binic

BINIC is probably the nicest place to stay on the Baie de St-Brieuc. The whole place is on an appealingly small scale with sandy beaches, a narrow pleasure port crammed with yachts, a jazzed-up little central shopping and dining district, a paved promenade along the seafront, and to either side Devon-like meadows that roll down to the sea. In the mid-nineteenth century, Binic was one of the busiest ports in all France; these days it's simply a minor but attractive tourist resort, with a lucrative sideline of selling mud from the River Ic for fertilizer.

The main beach at Binic, the **Plage de la Banche**, stretches away east of the road as you come into town from St-Brieuc. Spacious even at high tide, packed in summer with families, swimmers, children's clubs, and groups playing pétanque, at low tide it becomes absolutely vast. On the far side of town, well away from the through highway and out of sight even from the dead-end little road around the harbour, there's another large but much more secluded beach, the **Plage de l'Avant Port**.

Six kilometres west of Binic, just off the D47, the **Jardin Zoologique de Bretagne**, also known as the Zoo de Trégomeur, is a leafy park containing the likes of llamas, ostriches and zebras in deceptively natural surroundings. It was closed for renovation at the time of writing, but is due to reopen sometime in 2005; call the Binic tourist office (see below) for the latest information.

Les Vedettes de Bréhat (Ⓣ02.96.55.79.50, Ⓦwww.vedettesdebrehat.com) run occasional **day-trips** between mid-June and early September from Binic to the **Île de Bréhat** (see p.272), costing €26 and setting off at 8am.

Practicalities

Binic's **tourist office** is in L'Estran, a multipurpose cultural centre well back from the sea on avenue du Général-de-Gaulle (April–June, Sept & Oct Mon–Fri 9.30am–12.30pm & 2–6pm, Sat 10am–12.30pm & 2–5pm; July & Aug Mon–Sat 9.30am–12.30pm & 2–7pm, Sun 10am–12.30pm & 2–5pm; Nov–March Mon–Fri 9.30am–noon & 2–6pm, Sat 10am–noon & 2–5pm; Ⓣ02.96.73.60.12, Ⓦwww.ville-binic.fr).

The only sea-view **accommodation** in town is at the very pleasant *Hôtel Benhuyc*, on the north side of the port at 1 quai Jean-Bart (Ⓣ02.96.73.39.00, Ⓦwww.benhuyc.com; ❸). The cheapest rates are for relatively small rooms, but you don't have to pay much extra to get a good one (including one with a kitchenette). The adjoining restaurant (Ⓣ02.96.65.25.68) is under different management but still highly recommended, with menus from €22 up to €39.

Much plainer and less expensive rooms are available above a bar/brasserie immediately across the street (despite the address), in *Le Neptune*, on place de l'Église (Ⓣ02.96.73.61.02; ❷).

Also on the north side of the port, the quai du Courcy is lined with **restaurants** and **crêperies**. At the most conspicuous, *La Mascotte* (Ⓣ02.96.73.30.77), you pay over the odds for the privilege of being seated beneath colourful blue awnings on board a boat moored in the water, Nearby, *la Batelière* (Ⓣ02.96.73.36.26) is a busy, friendly **brasserie** with pizzas and salads at €6–10.

Of the many **campsites** to be found nearby, the best is the secluded three-star *Les Madières* to the south (Ⓣ02.96.79.02.48, Ⓦwww.campinglesmadieres.com; closed Oct–April), 3km from Binic off the main road near the village of **Pordic**, and set back slightly from the sea. It also has a swimming pool.

St-Quay-Portrieux

ST-QUAY, 5km to the north of Binic, is considerably more upmarket and a bit soulless, though there's a lot of activity going on in its sister town of **PORTRIEUX**, where a yachting marina has encouraged what used to be a slightly seedy waterfront – dating back to the days of the Newfoundland fishing fleets – to smarten itself up. The two towns share no less than seven **beaches**: the Plage du Casino in St-Quay and the fine sandy beach next to the port in Portrieux are both popular with families; while for more seclusion head for the Grève d'Isnain and the Grève de Fontenay, both in small bays surrounded by cliffs.

Between mid-June and mid-September, Les Vedettes de Bréhat (Ⓣ02.96.55.79.50, Ⓦwww.vedettesdebrehat.com) run a few **day-trips**, following an erratic schedule, from Portrieux to the **Île de Bréhat** (see p.272) for €26 (departures 8.30am).

The **tourist office** for St-Quay-Portrieux is at 17bis rue Jeanne-d'Arc (July & Aug Mon–Sat 9am–7pm, Sun 10.30am–12.30pm & 3.30–6pm; Sept–June Mon–Sat 9am–12.30pm & 2–6.30pm; Ⓣ02.96.70.40.64, Ⓦwww.saintquayportrieux.com). In St-Quay itself, the *Gerbot d'Avoine*, 2 boulevard de Littoral, near the Plage du Casino (Ⓣ02.96.70.40.09, Ⓦwww.gerbotdavoine.com; ❸; closed Jan & mid-Nov to mid-Dec, restaurant closed Sun eve & Tues lunch in low season), is an entertaining **logis** worth staying at for its good food (menus from €17) and refreshingly original decor: crimson carpets creep up the corridor walls in a good impression of the hotel in *The Shining*, while in the rooms themselves, washbasins and even showers are discreetly hidden away in cupboards. The *Hôtel le Commerce*, 4 rue Georges-Clemenceau (Ⓣ02.96.70.41.53; ❸; closed Tues in low season, plus 3 weeks in Jan), is a good alternative, and convenient for the beach in Portrieux.

Kermaria-an-Isquit

You may well get your first exposure to spoken Breton (see box, opposite) in smaller villages such as **KERMARIA-AN-ISQUIT**. This is not an easy place to find, especially coming from Lanloup to the north; the best signposted of its approaches is along the D21 from Plouha. Nonetheless, a fairly constant trickle of visitors make their way here throughout the summer to see the village's **chapel** and its extraordinary *Dance of Death*, one of the most striking of all French medieval images (Easter–Sept Mon–Fri 9am–noon & 2–6pm, Sat 9am–noon, Sun 2–6pm; donation).

Into the Breton heartland

At **Plouha**, a short way along the D786 from St-Quay, you cross what was traditionally the boundary between French-speaking "Upper Brittany" and Breton-speaking "Lower Brittany". As a general indication, you can tell which language used to be spoken in a particular area by its place names. Thus, from here on west there is a preponderance of names beginning with the Breton "PLOU" (meaning parish), "TREZ" (sand or beach), "KER" (town) or "PENN" (head). See p.465 for a comprehensive glossary of Breton words that you are likely to come across.

The **Dance of Death** is no delicate miniature. This huge series of frescoes – depicting Ankou, the skeletal death-figure, leading representatives of all social classes in a *Danse Macabre* – covers the arcades all round the chapel. Painted at the end of the plague-fearing fifteenth century, they were subsequently whitewashed over, not to be rediscovered until 1856. Since then, much of the work has vanished altogether, especially on the ceiling, and even in what survives the original colours have faded, and the figures are often no more than silhouettes. However, the fresco has lost little of its power to shock; a look at the hand-drawn copies made in 1861, on show below the real thing, reveals quite how grotesquely menacing the figure of death could be.

In yellow, on a red background, the skeleton alternates with such living characters as a King, a Knight, a Bishop and a Peasant. Verses below, now mostly illegible though available in transcription, have each person pleading for life and lamenting death, while Ankou insists that all must in the end come to him. A wall to the left of the altar holds a barely discernible representation of the classic medieval theme of the encounter between the *Trois Vifs*, three finely apparelled noblemen out hunting, with the *Trois Morts*, three corpses reflecting in a cemetery on the transience of all things human:

Nous avons bien este en chance
Autrefoys, comme estes a present
Mais vous viendrez a nostre dance
Comme nous sommes maintenant.

("We were lucky enough once to be like you, but you'll have to come and join our dance in the end".)

The chapel was originally the property of the lords of the manor of Noë Vert, and is said to be linked by a tunnel, long since flooded, to their manor house 5km away. It was known in Breton as "*Itron Varia An Iskuit*", meaning "Our Lady Who Helps". A small display case behind the altar contains the skull of one of the lords – Jean de Lannion, who died in 1658 – while a couple of grotesque heart-shaped boxes hold the hearts of another and his wife. To the right, a unique statue shows the infant Jesus refusing milk from the Virgin's proffered breast, symbolizing the choice of celestial over terrestrial food.

Abbaye de Beauport

As the D786 north of Kermaria and Binic meanders back towards the shoreline, a couple of kilometres short of Paimpol it passes the substantial ruins of the **Abbaye de Beauport** (daily: mid-June to mid-Sept 10am–7pm, with regular 1hr 30min guided tours; mid-Sept to mid-June 10am–noon & 2–5pm; Ⓦwww.abbaye-beauport.com; €4.50). In summer, the abbey reopens for late-night visits, with imaginative lighting effects (mid-June to Aug, Wed & Sun 10pm–1am; €8).

The abbey of Bellus Portus was established in 1202 by Count Alain de Goëlo, in memory of his parents. Sited halfway between St-Brieuc and Tréguier, its primary function was as a way station for English pilgrims en route to Santiago de Compostela. Much of its income was drawn from thirteen parishes in Lincolnshire, and it never really recovered after the Reformation in England threw the monks here back onto their own resources. A merchant from Paimpol bought the entire estate after the Revolution, and his family owned it until 1992, when they sold it to the State.

The abbey is currently being restored, but the main appeal for visitors is the sheer romance of its setting and semi-dilapidated condition. Its stone walls are covered with wild flowers and ivy, the central cloisters are engulfed by a huge tree, and birds flutter about everywhere. The Norman Gothic **chapterhouse** is the most noteworthy building to survive, but wandering through and over the roofless halls you may spot architectural relics from all periods of its history. The monks' refectory looks out across the **salt meadows** where they raised their sheep, and planted orchards on land that they reclaimed from the sea with an intricate network of dams. Footpaths lead all the way down to the sea, offering the same superb views of the hilltop abbey that must have been appreciated by generations of arriving pilgrims.

Paimpol

Though still an attractive town, with a tangle of cobbled alleyways lined with fine grey-granite houses, **PAIMPOL** has lost something in its transition from working fishing port to pleasure harbour. It was once the base of a cod and whaling fleet that sailed for the fisheries of Iceland each February, sent off with a ceremony marked by a famous *pardon*. From then until August or September, the town would be empty of all young men. Within a few years of the first expedition in 1852, the annual exodus consisted of as many as fifty vessels, with 25 men in each. A haunting glimpse of the way Paimpol used to look can be seen in the silent film of Pierre Loti's book *Pêcheur d'Islande*, made on location here by Jacques de Baroncelli in 1924.

Loti, and the heroine of his book, lived in the **place du Martray** in the centre of town, which is lined with an impressive array of sixteenth century houses. Cobbled streets lead from here down to the port through the peaceful **quartier latin**, an area once filled with bars and *cabarets* relieving returning fishermen of their money and frustrations. Thanks to naval shipyards and the like, the open sea is not visible from Paimpol; a maze of waterways leads to its two separate harbours. Both are usually filled with the high masts of yachts, but still also used by the fishing boats that keep a fish market and a plethora of *poissonneries* busy. From close quarters the tiny port area is a little disappointing, very much rebuilt and quite plain, though it's always lively in summer.

The best **beach** in town, La Tossen, is a short way east of the port, but there are better seaside resorts elsewhere along this stretch of coast, and with its plentiful accommodation Paimpol is more often used as a base from which to visit the Île de Bréhat (see p.272).

Arrival and information

The **gare SNCF** and **gare routière** lie next to each other on avenue du Général de Gualle, close to the pleasure port on the southern edge of the town centre. From late May to late Sept, the restored **steam train** known as **La**

Vapeur de Trieux chugs its way on regular excursions from the *gare SNCF* through the Trieux Valley between Paimpol and Pontrieux to the southwest, passing within view of the Château de la Roche-Jagu (late May to June & Sept departs Paimpol Wed–Sun, with departures at either 9.30am, 11.15am or 11.20am depending on the day; July & Aug departs Paimpol 5–7 days per week, with departures at either 10.15am, 11.15am or 3.40pm depending on the day; reservations essential, ⓣ08.92.39.14.27; €21 return).

Paimpol's **tourist office** is 100m from the pleasure port on place de la République (June–Sept Mon–Sat 9.30am–7.30pm, Sun 10am–6pm; Oct–May Mon–Sat 9.30am–12.30pm & 1.30–6.30pm; ⓣ02.96.20.83.16, ⓦwww.paimpol-goelo.com).

Accommodation

Most of the nicest of Paimpol's many **hotels** are clustered together on the northern side of the port, either right on the waterfront or in the network of semi-pedestrianized little alleyways just behind.

Hôtel Berthelot 1 rue du Port ⓣ02.96.20.88.66. Small but very hospitable family-run hotel, offering a dozen simple rooms – including a good value one for four people (❷) – set slightly back from the pleasure port. ❶

Le Goëlo 4 quai Duguay-Trouin ⓣ02.96.20.82.74, ⓦwww.hotel-legoelo.com. Modern, double-glazed hotel (equipped with a lift) in the ugly new block that lines the inland side of the fishing harbour; some rooms overlook the port. ❹

Hôtel K'Loys 21 quai Morand ⓣ02.96.20.40.01, ⓦwww.k-loys.com. Imposing, very comfortable harbourside mansion, where sea-view rooms cost significantly extra. There's also a little pavement café and oyster bar. ❹–❻

Hôtel de la Marne 30 rue de la Marne ⓣ02.96.20.82.16, ⓔrestaurant.hotel.marne@wanadoo.fr. Smart, twelve-room hotel well up from the port, with a formal restaurant offering menus from €22. They might insist on *demi-pension* during July and August. ❹

Hôtel Origano 7bis rue du Quai ⓣ02.96.22.05.49. Somewhat plain, but very comfortable hotel, on a quiet cobbled street opposite the *Berthelot*. Closed mid-Nov to March. ❸

Le Repaire de Kerroc'h 29 quai Morand ⓣ02.96.20.50.13, ⓔrepair€2kerroch@wanadoo.fr. The most luxurious option in Paimpol, in a grand old house (equipped with a lift) overlooking the small-boat harbour, where the rooms come with safe, mini-bar and the like, and there is a restaurant offering good meals on menus priced at €18 and €25. Restaurant closed Mon. ❹

Eating and drinking

Appealing **restaurants** stand on all sides of the port, as well as in the backstreets of the town proper, near the marketplace. The *Corto Maltese* **bar** at 11 rue du Quai, very near the *Origano* hotel, serves a fine selection of British and other beers.

La Cotriade quai Armand-Dayot ⓣ02.96.20.81.08. Uncompromising gourmet restaurant on the far side of the harbour to the town centre, that's a great bet for authentic fish dishes. Menus from €18 to €42, bursting with crab, scallops and prawns. Closed Wed eve & Thurs.

Crêperie-Restaurant Morel 11 place du Martray ⓣ02.96.20.86.34. Cavernous place just a few steps from the port in the main square in the heart of town, that's popular with locals not only for its inexpensive €4–7 *galettes*, but also for its good-value daily bistro specials and large *terrasse* on the square. Closed Sun.

La Vieille Tour 13 rue de l'Église ⓣ02.96.20.83.18. Cosy but sophisticated upstairs dining room, tucked away from the port in the cobbled pedestrian area, and offering top-quality seafood on a quarter of constantly changing menus; the €24 one is usually good enough, but you can pay up to €65. Closed Sun eve, & Wed in low season.

Loguivy-sur-mer

If Paimpol is too crowded for you, it's well worth continuing a few kilometres further across the headland to reach the little fishing hamlet of **LOGUIVY**.

All of the long river inlets along this northern coast tend to conceal tiny coves – at Loguivy a working harbour manages to squeeze into one such gap in the rocks. **Lenin** holed up here for his summer holidays for two months in 1902, straight from three years of forced labour in Siberia.

Loguivy's one **hotel** is right on the waterfront, looking out towards Bréhat: *Le Grand Large* (☎02.96.20.90.18; ❸; closed Jan, restaurant closed Sun eve & Mon in low season) serves superb fish dinners from €15 – look out for the chef's speciality, a salad of seared scallops – and has a nice little outdoor terrace. However, only four of its six guest rooms have sea views; the others are dark and unpleasant.

The Île de Bréhat

The **ÎLE DE BRÉHAT** – in reality two islands joined by a tiny slip of a bridge – gives the appearance of spanning great latitudes. On the north side are windswept meadows of hemlock and yarrow, sloping down to chaotic erosions of rock; on the south, you're in the midst of palm trees, mimosa and eucalyptus. All around is a multitude of little islets – some accessible at low tide, others *propriété privée*, most just pink-orange rocks. All in all, this has to be one of the most beautiful places in Brittany, renowned as a sanctuary not only for rare species of **wild flowers**, but also for **birds** of all kinds. Individual private gardens are also meticulously tended, so you can always anticipate a magnificent display of colour, for example in summer from the erupting blue acanthus.

As you might expect, a high proportion of the homes on this island paradise now belong to summer-only visitors from Paris and beyond, and young Bréhatins leave in ever-increasing numbers for lack of a place of their own, let alone a job. In winter, the remaining three hundred or so natives have the place to themselves, without even a *gendarme*; the summer sees two imported from the mainland, along with upwards of three thousand temporary residents and a hundred times as many day-trippers.

All boats to Bréhat arrive at the small harbour of **PORT-CLOS**, though depending on the level of the tide passengers may have to walk several hundred metres before setting foot on terra firma. No **cars** are permitted on the island

Getting to Bréhat

Bréhat is connected by regular **ferry** from the Pointe de l'Arcouest, 6km northwest of Paimpol; buses run frequently in summer from Paimpol's *gare SNCF* to the Pointe de l'Arcouest. Sailings, with Les Vedettes de Bréhat (☎02.96.55.79.50, Ⓦwww.vedettesdebrehat.com), are roughly half-hourly in July & Aug, hourly between April and June and in September, and every two hours for the rest of the year, with the first boat out to Bréhat at 8.30am in summer, and the last boat back at 7.45pm. The return trip costs €7.50, while bringing your own bike costs an additional €8; to do so in summer you have to catch a ferry before 10am, and leave the island before 4pm. You can purchase tickets at the tourist office in Paimpol (see p.270). The same company also operates boats in summer from Erquy, Dahouët, Binic and St-Quay-Portrieux.

In addition, guided **boat tours** (45min; €12) circle the island each day (April to mid-July & Sept 5 daily; mid-July to Aug 10 daily; Oct–March 1 daily depending on weather and tides).

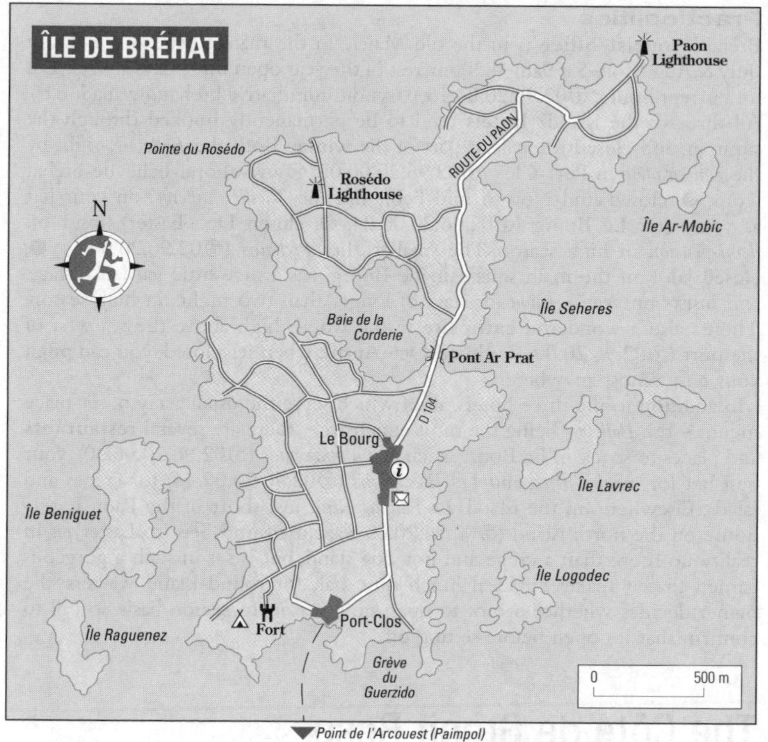

– there's barely a road wide enough for its few light farm vehicles – so many visitors rent **bikes** at the ferry port (€15 per day), although it's easy enough to explore the whole place on foot; walking from one end to the other takes less than an hour.

Each batch of new arrivals invariably heads first to Bréhat's village, **LE BOURG**, which stands 500m up from the port and is the centre of all activity on the island. As well as a handful of hotels, restaurants and bars, it also has a limited array of shops, a post office, a bank (Crédit Agricole), and an ATM machine, and hosts a small **market** most days. In high season, the attractive central square tends to be packed fit to burst, with exasperated holiday-home owners pushing their little hand-wagons through the throngs of day-trippers.

Continue a short distance north of Le Bourg, however, and you'll soon cross over the slender **Pont ar Prat bridge** to the northern island, where the crowds thin out, and countless little coves offer opportunities to sprawl on the tough grass or clamber across the rugged boulders. Though the coastal footpath around this northern half – in theory, banned to bicycles – offers the most attractive walking on the island, the best **beaches** line the southern shores, with the **Grève du Guerzido**, facing the mainland at its southeastern corner, being the pick of the crop.

Bréhat no longer has a castle (it was blown up twice by the English), but it does have a couple of lighthouses and a nineteenth-century **fort**, in the woods near the campsite (see p.274).

Practicalities

Bréhat's **tourist office** is in the old Mairie in the main square in Le Bourg (July & Aug Mon–Sat 9am–4.30pm; rest of the year open three days a week, call for current hours; ⓣ02.96.20.04.15, Ⓔsyndicatdinitiative.brehat@wanadoo.fr). All three of the island's **hotels** tend to be permanently booked through the summer, and closed for at least part of the winter. Both the *Bellevue*, right by the *embarcadère* in Port-Clos (ⓣ02.96.20.00.05, Ⓦwww.hotel-bellevue-brehat .com; ❺; closed mid-Nov to mid-Feb), and the *Vieille Auberge*, on your left as you enter Le Bourg (ⓣ02.96.20.00.24; ❺; closed Dec–Easter), insist on *demi-pension* in high season. The smaller *Aux Pêcheurs* (ⓣ02.96.20.00.14; ❸; closed Jan), on the main square in Le Bourg, has a nice little garden terrace, and insists on *demi-pension* for stays of longer than two nights in high season. There's also a wonderful **campsite** in the woods high above the sea west of the port (ⓣ02.96.20.00.36; closed Oct–April); when it's closed, you can pitch your tent almost anywhere.

In addition to the three hotels, all of which serve the usual array of set-price menus – the *Bellevue* being the most expensive – there are several **restaurants** and places to snack in Le Bourg, such as *La Brazérade* (ⓣ02.96.20.06.30), your best bet for *moules frites*, and *Les Blés Noirs* (ⓣ02.96.20.09.44) for crêpes and salads. Elsewhere on the island, *Le Paradis Rose*, just short of the Paon Lighthouse on the north island (ⓣ02.96.20.03.89; closed mid-Sept to Easter), is in reality no more than a crêpe and hot-dog stand, but is set in such a gorgeous garden that it makes an ideal lunch-time halt for round-island walkers; the owner decides whether or not to open on a season-to-season basis, so call to confirm that it's open before setting off.

The Côte de Granit Rose

The whole of the northernmost stretch of the Breton coast, from Bréhat to Trégastel, has loosely come to be known as the **Côte de Granit Rose**. Great granite boulders are scattered in the sea around the island of Bréhat, and at the various headlands to the west, but the most memorable stretch of coast lies around **Perros-Guirec**, where the pink granite rocks are eroded into fantastic shapes.

Pink granite, glittering sharply but wearing smooth and soft, is an absolutely gorgeous stone – which is just as well, for everything in this area seems to be made of it: the houses are faced with granite blocks, and the streets paved with them; the breakwaters in the sea are granite, and the polished pillars of the banks are granite; the hotels even have overgrown granite mini-golfs with little pink granite megaliths as obstacles; and the markets claim to sell *granit-smith* apples.

Tréguier

The D786 turns west from Paimpol, passing over a green *ria* on the bridge outside Lézardrieux before arriving at **TRÉGUIER**. This is one of the very few hill-towns in Brittany, set at the junction of the Jaudy and Guindy rivers. It was rebuilt on this fortified elevation in 848 AD after an earlier monastery was destroyed by Norman raiders, though it has since spread to include a small commercial and pleasure port by the river.

The central unmissable feature ofTréguier is the **Cathédrale de St-Tugdual**, whose geometric Gothic spire, dotted with holes, contrasts sharply with its earlier Romanesque "Hastings" tower. Its uppermost ten metres were knocked down by the storm of Boxing Day 1999, but have since been restored. Inside, the masonry blocks are appealingly crude, and dripping with damp that has somehow spared the wooden stalls. The most elaborate of several recumbent tombs is that of **St Yves**, a native of the town who died in 1303 and – for his incorruptibility – became the patron saint of lawyers. Attempts to bribe him continue to this day; his tomb is surrounded by marble plaques and an inferno of candles invoking his aid, including one special plea from a group of American lawyers. A *pardon* of St Yves is held each year on the Sunday closest to his feast day, May 19.

The half-timbered houses of the square outside look down on a portly, seated statue of the writer and philosopher **Ernest Renan**, born here in 1823, whose work formed part of the great nineteenth-century attempt to reinterpret traditional religious faith in the light of scientific discoveries. Worthy Catholics were so incensed at the erection of this memorial in 1903 that they soon built their own "Calvary of Reparation" on the quayside.

Practicalities

Tréguier's **tourist office** is at 67 rue Ernest Renan, opposite the commercial port (mid-June to mid-Sept Mon–Sat 9am–1pm & 2–7pm, Sun 10am–1pm & 4–6pm; mid-Sept to mid-June Mon–Sat 10am–12.30pm & 2.30–6pm; ⓣ02.96.92.22.33, ⓦwww.paysdetreguier.com). The *Hôtel-Restaurant d'Estuaire* down on the waterfront (ⓣ02.96.92.30.25; ❶) is a very basic **place to stay** – though the sea views are great – that serves a reasonable €12 menu, with *moules* followed by fish of the day and dessert. You'll pay only slightly more for a better room up in town at the modernized *Hôtel St-Yves* at 4 rue Colvestre near the cathedral (ⓣ02.96.92.33.49; ❶; closed Thurs). The *Poissonnerie Moulinet*, above a fish shop just below the cathedral at 2 rue Ernest Renan (ⓣ02.96.92.30.27), is a sort of tasting room where you can buy superb seafood platters at low prices, though if you fancy a more formal sit-down meal, *Le Canotier*, 5 rue Ernest Renan (ⓣ02.96.92.41.70; closed Thurs & Sat lunch, plus Wed eve in winter), serves several full fish menus.

The town holds a **market** each Wednesday, with clothes and so on spread out in the square up by the cathedral, and food and fresh fish further down by the port. The cafés and delis of the main square save their best displays for that day.

Château de la Roche-Jagu

About 10km inland from Tréguier and Lézardrieux, the fifteenth-century **Château de la Roche-Jagu** (daily: mid-June to mid-Sept 10am–7pm; mid-Sept to mid-June 10.30am–12.30pm & 2–6pm; park access free, château €2, or more during special exhibitions) stands on a heavily wooded slope above the meanders of the Trieux River, just as it starts to widen. It's a really gorgeous building, a harmonious combination of fortress and home. The central solid facade is composed of irregular reddish-granite boulders, cemented together, and incorporating one venerable turreted tower at the front and one at the back.

Both the château and its grounds were devastated by the storm of 1987, but the ensemble has since been turned into a modern landscaped park, traced through by several **hiking trails**. The château itself plays host to lavish **annual exhibitions**, usually on some sort of Celtic theme. The rooms within are bare, but it's well worth climbing right up to the top of the building. Here you can admire the beautiful woodwork of the restored eaves, and walk the two long

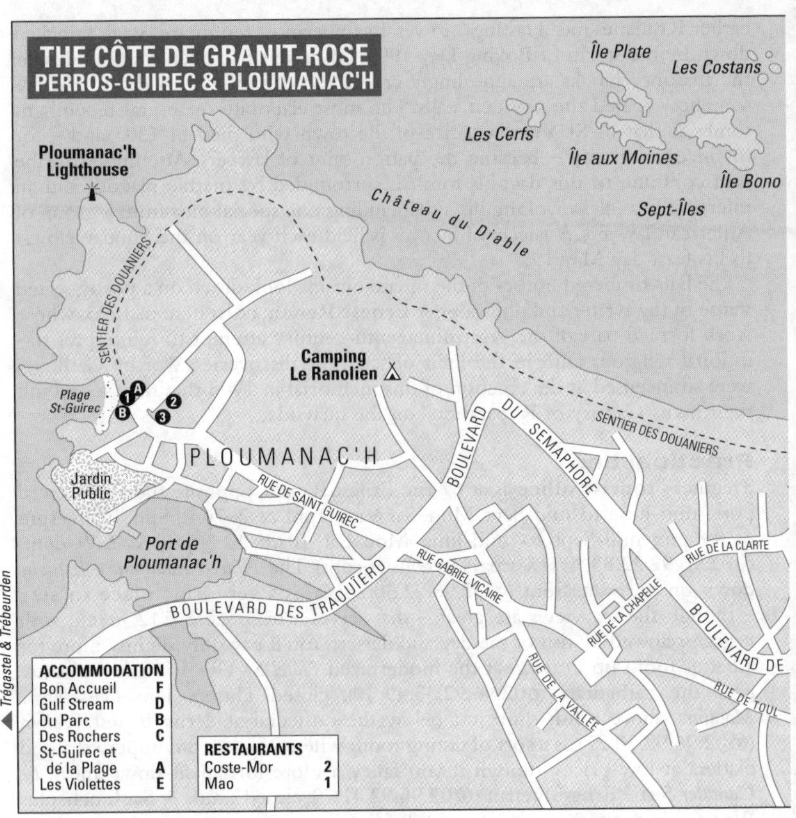

indoor galleries, one of wood and one of stone, to enjoy tremendous views over the river.

The *Restaurant de la Château de la Roche-Jagu* (☎02.96.95.16.08), in the castle gateway, offers lunch menus on the lawns from €13.

Perros-Guirec

PERROS-GUIREC is the most popular resort along this coast, if not perhaps the most exciting. It has a reputation that seems to attract the retired – its tourist brochures list places where you can get a game of bridge or Scrabble – and an array of shops intended to match: antiques, bric-a-brac and pottery with a big line in granite guillemots and puffins. Perros is also a lot less city-like than it looks on the maps: most of its network of roads turn out to be tree-lined avenues of suburban villas.

The commercial streets of the centre (up the hill from the port) hold little of interest, and are often jammed solid with traffic in summer. Much more enjoyable is to take a walk around the headland to see the magnificent view from the **Table d'Orientation** at the sharp curve of the boulevard Clemenceau. The best beach is the **Plage de Trestraou**, on the opposite side of town to

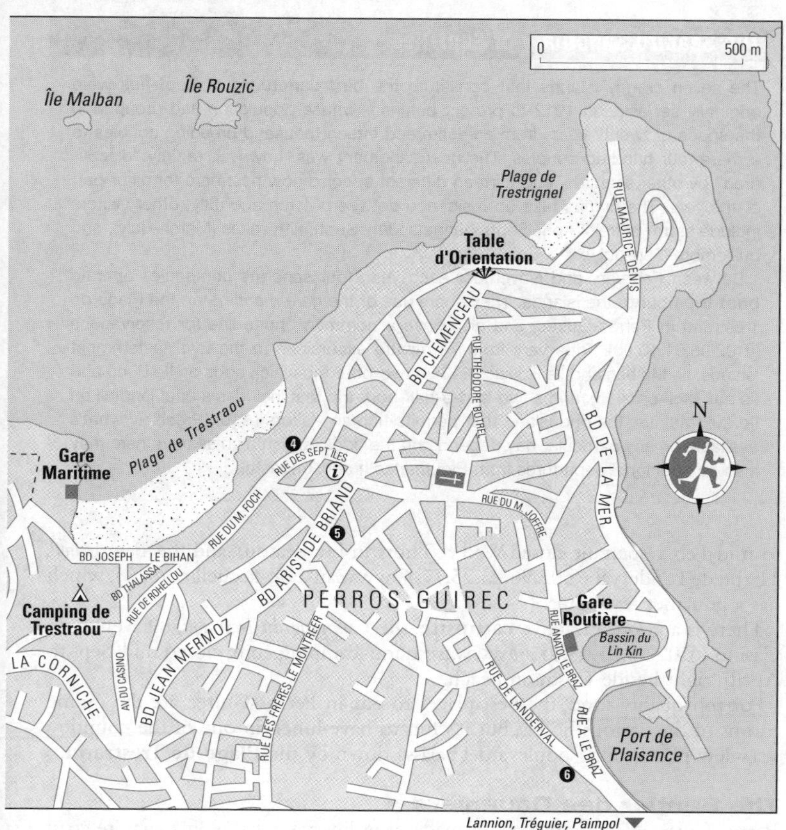

the port, a long curve of sand speckled with bars, snackeries, and crazy-golf courses.

Practicalities

If you're relying on public transport, Perros-Guirec is surprisingly hard to reach. What **buses** there are arrive at and leave from the Bassin du Lin Kin in the port, a few hundred metres down from the town centre. For those without their own transport, a good first move is to rent a **bike**; Perros Cycles, near the *gendarmerie* at 14 boulevard Aristide-Briand (ⓣ02.96.23.13.08), can oblige.

Perros-Guirec's extremely efficient **tourist office** is at 21 place de l'Hôtel-de-Ville (July & Aug Mon–Sat 9am–7.30pm, Sun 10am–12.30pm & 4–7pm; Sept–June Mon–Sat 9am–12.30pm & 2–6.30pm; ⓣ02.96.23.21.15; ⓦwww.perros-guirec.com). Ask for their schedule of **guided walks** in the vicinity.

If you'd rather stay here than in the smaller community of Ploumanac'h a couple of kilometres to the west, good **hotels** include the old-fashioned *les Violettes*, 19 rue du Calvaire (ⓣ02.96.23.21.33; ❷), which has a cheap restaurant with menus from €11, and two places with sea views, the *Gulf Stream*, perched high on the hillside with tremendous views at 26 rue des Sept-Îles (ⓣ02.96.23.21.86, ⓦwww.gulf-stream-hotel-bretagne.com; ❸; closed mid-Jan

The Seabird Sanctuary of Sept-Îles

The seven craggy islands that constitute the **bird sanctuary of Sept-Îles** were originally set aside in 1912 to protect puffins – whose population had dropped in the space of twenty years from an estimated fifteen thousand breeding couples to a mere four hundred couples. The new sanctuary was, however, rapidly "discovered" by other seabirds, and thirteen different species now nest here for all or part of the year. The puffins take up residence between March and July; other visitors include storm petrels (April–Sept), gannets (Jan–Sept), kittiwakes (March–July), and guillemots (Feb–July).

Between February and November each year, four separate companies operate **boat trips** out to the islands. They share use of the *gare maritime* on the Plage de Trestraou in Perros-Guirec, and also have a common phone line for reservations (Ⓣ02.96.91.10.00). Trips vary from 75-minute excursions to the two easternmost islands, Île Malban and Île Rouzic (€13), a two-hour trip which adds on Île Bono and Île aux Moines (€15), and a two-and-a-half-hour trip that includes a brief landfall on Île aux Moines, the one island that permits human visitors (€16). Precisely what's available on any particular day depends on the tides, and in high season there may also be additional departures from Ploumanac'h and Trégastel.

to mid-Feb, restaurant closed Wed & Thurs in low season), and the *Bon Accueil*, 11 rue de Landerval (Ⓣ02.96.23.25.77, Ⓦwww.au-bon-accueil.com; ❸), which has a gourmet restaurant.

There is a good, attractive **campsite**, the *Camping du Trestraou*, 89 avenue du Casino (Ⓣ02.96.23.08.11, Ⓦwww.trestraou-camping.com; closed mid-Sept to April), right beside Trestraou beach.

For top-quality food, the best places to **eat** in Perros-Guirec are the dining rooms of the various hotels, but it's fun to have lunch in one of the countless sea-view places along boulevard Thalassa down by the **Plage de Trestraou**.

The Sentier des Douaniers

Perros-Guirec's Trestraou beach is made of ordinary sand; the pink-granite coast proper starts just beyond its western end. The long **Sentier des Douaniers** pathway winds round the clifftops to **Ploumanac'h** past an astonishing succession of deformed and water-sculpted rocks. Allow around an hour to walk its full length one-way, assuming you take the time to enjoy the many splendours en route – the path ranks among the finest coastal walks in Brittany. Birds wheel overhead towards the sanctuary, and battered boats shelter in the narrow inlets or bob uncontrollably out on the waves. There are patches and brief causeways of grass, clumps of purple heather and yellow gorse. Occasionally the rocks have crumbled into a sort of granite grit to make up a tiny beach.

The rocks, in good French cataloguing fashion, have all been given names based on supposed resemblances in their shapes. The more banal ones – such as the great big *Foot* and the *Pancake* – are in a way the best; you can't help wondering, though, what committee it was, and when, that went along labelling the *Torpedo*, the *Armchair*, the *Tortoise* and *Napoleon's Hat*.

Ploumanac'h

PLOUMANAC'H is a more active resort than Perros-Guirec, though again with a dominant and specific clientele – this time families with youngish children. In fact, few places on earth can offer quite such enchantment for energetic kids, who love to scramble around the surreal sandscape revealed when the long tides draw out. Glinting pink-granite boulders, fringed with green seaweed, erupt from the depths, and rock pools bursting with crabs and other mysteries just wait to be explored. The most obvious focal point is the tiny **Château du Diable**, framing the horizon on one of the countless little islands in the bay – which was where the novel *Quo Vadis* was written around the end of the nineteenth century. When the tide is in, head instead for the pleasantly wild **municipal park** that separates the two halves of Ploumanac'h, the Bourg and the Plage.

Half-day **boat trips** out to the Sept-Îles (see box, opposite) also run from the little port in Ploumanac'h in summer; call ⓣ02.96.91.44.40 for schedules.

Practicalities

The road into Ploumanac'h comes to a dead end at the beach, at the spot where the unfortunately named **restaurant**, *Coste-Mor*, 162 rue St-Guirec (ⓣ02.96.91.65.55; closed Nov–March), enjoys magnificent views across the bay. In the formal dining room indoors, or at the stone tables on its terrace, you can order anything from a cold glass of wine up to a delicious seafood feast; a large *plateau de fruits de mer* costs around €85 for two people, but there are good menus starting at €12.50. The adjoining **hotel**, *St-Guirec et de la Plage* (ⓣ02.96.91.40.89, ⓦwww.hotelsaint-guirec.com; ❷; closed Nov–March), has some lovely sea-view rooms at bargain rates, and serves a simple good-value menu to all guests in a separate dining room.

Just short of the beach, the small lively rue St-Guirec leads to the little square that serves as the main local car park. The *Mao*, at 147 rue St-Guirec (ⓣ02.96.91.40.92; closed Mon, plus Oct–March), is a former snack bar that has expanded to take over several adjacent buildings, including a Polynesian-style thatched hut; it offers bargain menus from €9 (even less for crêpes) and, like most places in Ploumanac'h, it has special cheap menus for children. The *Hôtel du Parc*, on the square itself at 175 place St-Guirec (ⓣ02.96.91.40.80; ❷; closed mid-Nov to March), has reasonably priced rooms, and serves good seafood menus, while *Des Rochers*, slightly further back from the beach at 70 chemin de la Pointe (ⓣ02.96.91.44.49, ⓦwww.hotel-des-rochers.com; ❸; closed Oct–March) verges on the luxurious. Be warned that the emphasis on children does mean that Ploumanac'h goes to bed early – you can find yourself locked out of a slumbering hotel at 9.30pm.

A nice place to **camp** is the four-star *Le Ranolien* (ⓣ02.96.91.65.65, ⓦwww.leranolien.com; closed late Sept to March), which backs on to the Sentier des Douaniers (see opposite) near a little beach about halfway round; it's also directly accessible on the other side by road, and has its own swimming pools and waterslides.

Trégastel

Three kilometres west of Ploumanac'h along a pretty coastal road, **TRÉGASTEL** boasts a delightful sheltered beach with a couple of huge lumps of pink granite slap in the middle. Sadly, however, the village itself is an ugly stretch of concrete, centring on the seafront Forum, a swimming pool and leisure complex. A little way back from the seafront, a rather rudimentary **aquarium** has been squeezed beneath another massive pile of boulders (daily: April–June & Sept 10am–noon & 2–6pm; July & Aug 10am–7pm; Oct 2–5pm; ⓦwww.aquarium-tregastel.com; €4.70).

Of Trégastel's three **hotels**, the *Beau Séjour*, 5 plage du Coz-Pors (ⓣ02.96.23.88.02; ❹; closed mid-Jan to mid-Feb & mid-Nov to mid-Dec) has the best sea views, especially from the terrace of its restaurant, *Le Roof* (closed Mon). **Campsites** include the three-star *Tourony* by the beach (ⓣ02.96.23.86.61, ⓦwww.camping-tourony.com; closed late Sept–Easter).

Trébeurden

Outbreaks of bizarre red rocks have all but petered out by the time you reach **TRÉBEURDEN**, another 11km southwest along the coast from Trégastel, but you do at least come to one more long curving sandy beach, much less developed than most in these parts. The one **hotel** is set on a bluff several hundred metres up from the sea, with fabulous views: the *Ker An Nod*, rue de Pors-Termen (ⓣ02.96.23.50.21; ❸; closed Jan–March), is a Logis de France, serving menus from €15. There's also a lovely seafront **hostel**, *Le Toëno*, 2km north of town at 60 route de la Corniche (ⓣ02.96.23.52.22; dorm beds €9.10; closed Nov–Feb).

Pleumeur-Bodou

Head inland from Trégastel on the **route de Calvaire**, rather than along the coast, and you'll come in a few kilometres to a spectacle stranger than anything the erosions can manage: an old stone saint halfway up a high calvary raising his arm to bless or harangue the gleaming white discs and puffball dome of the Pleumeur-Bodou Telecommunications Centre. A new pink-granite "dolmen" commemorates its opening by de Gaulle in 1962, when it was the first receiving station to pick up signals from the American Telstar satellite. Now that the centre is no longer operational, it has been remodelled as a **Museum of Telecommunications**, which is also known as **Cosmopolis** (Feb Mon–Fri & Sun 2–6pm; April & Sept Mon–Fri 11am–6pm, Sat & Sun 2–6pm; May & June daily 11am–6pm; July & Aug daily 11am–7pm; March & Oct–Dec by appointment only; €7; ⓦwww.leradome.com). Inside the golf ball itself, the **Radôme**, frequent spectacular *son et lumière* shows explain the history of the whole ensemble, and there's also a smaller **planetarium** alongside. One final incongruous note is struck by the reconstructed **Gaulish village** nearby (April–June & Sept Mon–Fri & Sun 2–6pm; July & Aug daily 10.30am–7pm; €4), which is designed to raise money for a French charity working in Africa, and thus incorporates some traditional huts from Togo.

The Bay of Lannion

Despite being located significantly back from the sea on the estuary of the River Léguer, **Lannion** gives its name to the next bay west along the Breton coast – and it's the bay rather than the town that is most likely to impress visitors. One enormous beach stretches from **St-Michel-en-Grève**, which is little more than a bend in the road, as far as **Locquirec**; at low tide you can walk hundreds of metres out on the sands.

Lannion

LANNION, set amid plummeting hills and stairways, is a historic city with streets of medieval housing, and a couple of interesting old churches – but it's also a centre for a burgeoning and extremely hi-tech telecommunications industry, and as such is one of modern Brittany's real success stories – hence its rather self-satisfied nickname, *ville heureuse* or "happy town".

In addition to admiring the half-timbered houses around the place de Général-Leclerc and along rue des Chapeliers (look out for nos. 3 and 4), it's well worth climbing from the town up the 142 granite steps which lead to the twelfth-century Templar **Église de Brélévenez**. This church was remodelled three hundred years later to incorporate a granite bell tower, and the views from its terrace are quite stupendous.

Lannion's **gare SNCF** is across the river from town. Arriving passengers reach the centre across an attractive little bridge, from which you should spot the **tourist office**, next to the post office on the quai d'Aguillon (July & Aug Mon–Sat 9am–7pm, Sun 10am–1pm; Sept–June Mon–Sat 9.30am–12.30pm & 2–6pm; Ⓣ02.96.46.41.00, Ⓦwww.ot-lannion.fr).

The only **accommodation** in the centre of Lannion is the *Ibis*, opposite the station at 30 avenue de Général-de-Gaulle (Ⓣ02.96.37.03.67, Ⓕ02.96.46.45.83; ❹), which has modern rooms, but no **restaurant**; for something to eat, *La Flambée* is an inexpensive fish restaurant west of the tourist office at 67 rue Georges Pompidou (Ⓣ02.96.48.04.85; closed Mon). There's also a year-round **hostel**, *Les Korrigans*, handily near the station and the town centre at 6 rue du 73e Territorial (Ⓣ02.96.37.91.28, Ⓔlannion@fuaj.org; dorm beds €13.25 including breakfast). Its friendly management do not operate a curfew, and they arrange birdwatching and similar expeditions, and rent out bikes – not that you'll necessarily relish cycling around Lannion itself, with its gruelling hills.

Ploumilliau

Taking a four-kilometre detour inland from St-Michel-en-Grève, 11km southwest of Lannion on the D30, brings you to the trim little village of **PLOUMILLIAU**. Here the weathered granite parish **church** (daily 2–6pm), dating from the early seventeenth century and surrounded by beds of colourful flowers, contains a beautiful pulpit and sculpted wooden panelling, but is really worth a visit for its unique white-painted wooden representation of **Ankou**, the skeletal symbol of death. The statue, carrying a scythe to catch the living and a spade to bury them, was once carried in local processions.

Locquirec

LOCQUIREC, across the bay from Lannion and officially just within the *département* of Finistère, boasts some inviting beaches on both sides of its peninsula, although the town itself veers towards being over-twee. Around the main port, smart houses stand in sloping gardens, looking very southern English with their whitewashed stone panels, grey-slate roofs and jutting turreted windows. The small beach here is said to be the only one facing south along the entire northern coastline of Brittany, which prompts some brave souls to test the waters as early as Easter. On the last Sunday in July, Locquirec holds a combined *pardon de St-Jacques* and Festival of the Sea.

None of Locquirec's **hotels** are particularly cheap – although the *Grand Hôtel des Bains*, 15bis rue de l'Église (Ⓣ02.98.67.41.02, Ⓦwww.grand-hotel-des-bains.com; ❾; closed Jan), has so gorgeous a setting (plus an indoor heated swimming pool, Jacuzzi and gym) that perhaps it doesn't matter. It became widely known in France when it was used as the location for *Hôtel de la Plage*, a coming-of-age movie about youngsters summering in

Brittany. If this is outside your budget, the *Sables-Blancs*, 25 rue des Sables-Blancs (ⓣ02.98.67.42.07; ❸; closed Jan & Feb), offers sea views at considerably lower prices, while the municipal **campsite**, the *Toul ar Goue*, 1km south along the corniche (ⓣ02.98.67.40.85; closed mid-Sept to mid-April), is beautifully positioned, too.

St-Jean-du-Doigt

By the direct road, Locquirec is less than 20km northeast of Morlaix, but following the longer coastal route instead enables you to pass through **ST-JEAN-DU-DOIGT**, where the parish church contains an object held in veneration as the finger of John the Baptist. This sanctified digit is dipped into the Sacred Fountain to produce holy water. It was brought here in 1437 and is the principal object of the *pardon* on June 23 and 24 each year. A more recent tradition of pilgrimage made St-Jean the site of massive antinuclear demonstrations in the 1970s when the town was one of four proposed sites in Brittany for the building of nuclear reactors. Opposition was so vehement that plans for the reactor were eventually scrapped.

The Cairn de Barnenez

In a glorious position at the mouth of the Morlaix estuary, 6km north of Plouézoch and a total of 13km north of Morlaix, the prehistoric stone **Cairn de Barnenez** overlooks the waters from the summit of a hill (May–Aug daily 10am–6.30pm; Sept–April Tues–Sun10am–12.30pm & 2–5.30pm; €4.60). As on the island of Gavrinis in the Morbihan (see p.410), its ancient masonry has been laid bare by recent excavations, and provides a stunning sense of the architectural prowess of the megalith builders. Radiocarbon testing has shown the work here to date back to around 4500 BC, which makes this one of the oldest large monuments in the world. In the words of André Malraux, it represents "the Breton Parthenon". There is evidence that it remained in continuous use for around 2500 years; it was probably used repeatedly as a place of burial, then sealed off and abandoned. When it was first built, incidentally, the sea level was much lower than it is now; what was the highest tide then would be the lowest tide today.

The ensemble consists of two distinct **stepped pyramids**, the older one constructed of local dolerite stone, and the other of grey granite from the nearby Île de Sterec. Each rises in successive tiers, built of large flat stones chinked with pebbles (but no mortar); the second was added onto the side of the first, and the two are encircled by a series of terraces and ramps. The whole thing measures roughly 70m long by 15m to 25m wide; the current height of 6m is thought to be smaller than that of the original structure. Both were long ago buried under an eighty-metre-long earthen mound.

While the actual cairns are completely exposed to view, most of the passages and chambers that lie within them are sealed off. Visitors cannot in any case enter the structure, but simply walk around it to admire it from all angles. The two minor corridors that are open simply cut through the edifice from one side to the other, and were exposed by quarrying activities around thirty years ago – which inadvertently provided a good insight into the construction methods, though nothing much of note was found inside. Each is covered with great slabs of rock; in fact most of the familiar dolmens seen all over Brittany and elsewhere are thought to be the vestiges of similarly complex structures. Local tradition has it that one tunnel runs right through this "home of the fairies", and continues out deep under the sea.

Travel details

Trains

Lannion to: St-Brieuc (4 daily; 1hr) via Plouaret (15min) and Guingamp (35min).
Paimpol to: Guingamp (2–4 daily; 45min).
Rennes to: Brest (5 TGVs daily; 2hr 15min, plus 6 daily slower services, 2hr 40min); Caen (4 daily; 3hr) via Dol (35min) and Pontorson (1hr); Morlaix (5 TGVs daily; 1hr 40min); 5 daily slower services to Morlaix (1hr 50min) also stop at Lamballe (40min), Guingamp (1hr 10min) and Plouaret (1hr 25min); Nantes (5 daily; 1hr 30min); Paris-Montparnasse (10 TGVs daily; 2hr 10min); Quimper (9 daily; 2hr 30min); St Brieuc (6 TGVs daily; 50min); Vannes (6 daily; 1hr); Vitré (10 daily; 35min).
St-Malo to: Rennes (4 daily; 1hr; connections for Paris on TGV). All trains pass through Dol (20min).

Buses

Dinan to: St-Cast (3 daily; 1hr 5min); St-Jacut (3 daily; 45min).
Dinard to: Cancale (2 daily, 1hr 30min); Dinan (6 daily; 40min); St-Brieuc (8 daily, 25min).
Fougères to: Vire in Normandy (2 daily; 1hr 30min); Vitré (2 daily; 35min).
Lannion to: Perros-Guirec (7 daily; 20min) and Trégastel (7 daily, 40min); Locquirec (4 daily, 30min) and Morlaix (4 daily; 1hr 20min); Paimpol (3 daily, 1hr).
Rennes to: Dinan (6 daily; 1hr 20min); Dinard (5 daily; 1hr 40min); Fougères (10 daily; 1hr); Mont-St-Michel (5 daily; 1hr 20min).
St-Brieuc to: Carhaix (1 daily; 3hr); St-Malo (2 daily; 2hr); Lamballe (3 daily 1hr 10min), with connections to St-Cast (4 daily, 40min); Cap Fréhel (2 daily, 1hr 25min) via Le Val-André (50min) and Erquy (1hr 10min); Dinan (4 daily; 1hr); Lannion (3 daily; 1hr 40min) via Guingamp (45min); Moncontour (4 daily; 1hr); Rostrenen (2 daily; 2hr 10min); Paimpol (8 daily; 1hr 30min); Vannes (2 daily; 2hr).
St-Malo to: Cancale (4 daily; 45min); Combourg (2 daily; 1hr); Dinan (4 daily; 45min); Dinard (8 daily; 30min); Fougères (3 daily; 2hr 15min); Mont-St-Michel (4 daily; 1hr 30min); Pontorson (4 daily; 1hr 15min); Rennes (3 daily; 1hr 30min) via Tinténiac (1hr) and Hédé (1hr 10min); St-Cast (2 daily; 1hr) via St-Jacut (35min).

Ferries

St-Malo to: Dinan (mid-April to late Sept; 2hr 45min); Dinard (April to early Nov; 10min); Jersey (2 daily; 1hr 10min); Poole (via Guernsey or Jersey; 1 daily late May to Sept; 4hr 30min); Portsmouth (1–2 daily, 8–11hr); Weymouth (via Guernsey or Jersey; 1 daily Jan to mid-Nov; 5hr 15min–7hr 45min).

Flights

Dinard to: London Stansted with Ryanair (Ⓦwww.ryanair.com; 5 weekly; 1hr 5min); Jersey by Aurigny Air Services (Ⓣ02.99.46.70.28; Ⓦwww.aurigny.com; 1–2 daily; 20min).

5

Finistère

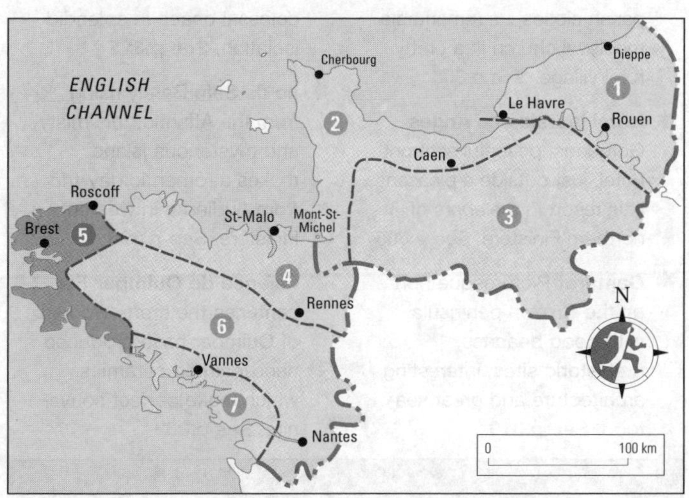

ENGLISH CHANNEL
Cherbourg
Dieppe
Le Havre
Rouen
Caen
Roscoff
Brest
St-Malo
Mont-St-Michel
Rennes
Vannes
Nantes
1
2
3
4
5
6
7
N
0
100 km

CHAPTER 5 Highlights

* **Île de Batz** Small, car-free island, a perfect family destination only a few hundred metres offshore from the attractive ferry port of Roscoff. See p.293
* **Guimiliau** One of the finest parish closes – a remarkable medieval church in a pretty rural village. See p.300
* **Hôtel la Baie des Anges** Gorgeous, peaceful seafront hotel, just outside a pleasant little resort in the *abers* of northern Finistère. See p.305
* **Camaret** Picturesque port on the Crozon peninsula, with good beaches, prehistoric sites, interesting architecture and great seafood. See p.319
* **Locronan** Jewel-like hilltop village that has hardly changed in five centuries. See p.321
* **Hôtel de la Baie des Tréspassés** Romantic land's-end hotel, facing its own colossal beach in splendid isolation. See p.325
* **Île de Sein** Barely rising from the Atlantic, this misty and mysterious island makes a romantic day-trip from Audierne in western Finistère. See p.325
* **Faïence de Quimper** For centuries the crafts workers of Quimper have produced hand-painted ceramics, which make perfect souvenirs. See p.333

△ Jetty at Roscoff

5

Finistère

Finistère has always been isolated from the French (and even Breton) mainstream: its name literally means "the end of the world". This remote rural landscape was the last refuge of the Druids from encroaching Christianity, and its mysterious forests and elaborate parish closes testify to its role as the province's spiritual heartland. Today, the port of

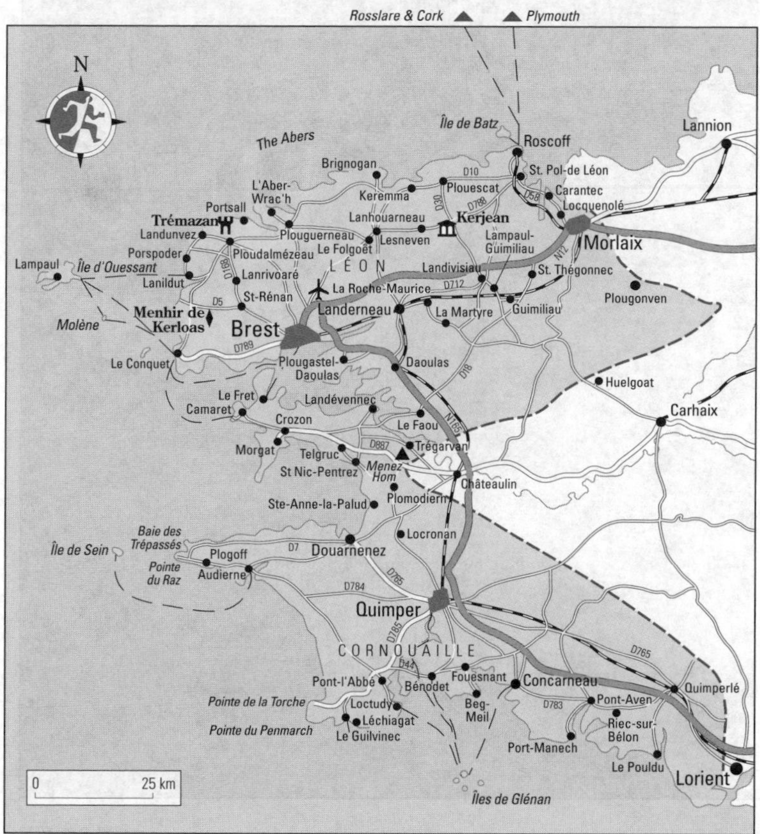

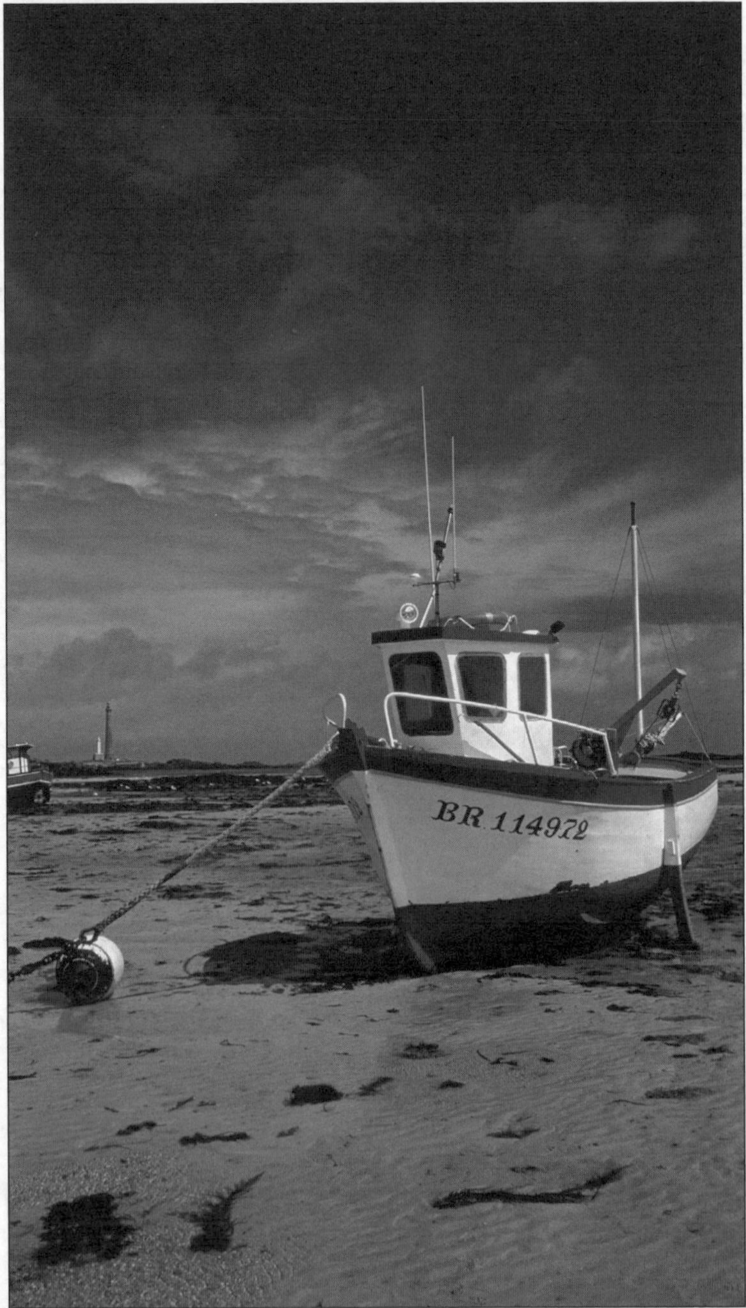

△ Boat in Finistère

Roscoff has reopened the old maritime links with England; high-speed TGV trains mean that Brest is just four hours from Paris; and the motorway makes a complete loop around the end of the peninsula. And yet Finistère remains only sporadically touched by modern industry, and agriculture and low-key tourism are the mainstays of the economy. Breton survives as a spoken language here more than anywhere else, and traditional costumes are still worn in reverence of culture not tourism at many a Breton festival, especially in the "Bigouden country" in the south.

Memories of the days when Brittany was "Petite Bretagne", as opposed to "Grande Bretagne" across the water, linger in the names of Finistère's two main areas. Both the northern peninsula – **Léon**, once Lyonesse – and its southern neighbour – **Cornouaille**, the same word as "Cornwall" – feature prominently in Arthurian legend. The ragged **coastline**, indented with a succession of estuaries each of which shelters its own tiny harbour, is the prime attraction. Rarely are conditions as bleak as you might expect from a land exposed to the full force of the Atlantic; heading west from **Roscoff**, your most likely point of arrival, there are possible stopping places all the way to **Le Conquet**, either along a beautifully wild stretch of coastline typified by a series of *abers* surrounded by quietly subdued resorts, or inland past equally sleepy villages notable for the outstanding church architecture of their parish closes. A notoriously treacherous stretch of ocean separates the mainland from **Ouessant** and **Molène**; and yet those two islands have the mildest winter climate anywhere in France.

In the south, Cornouaille boasts two classic resorts in **Bénodet** and **Loctudy**, either side of the Odet estuary, while if you'd rather stay in a genuine lived-in town, **Quimper** is just upriver – the liveliest place here and one of the most pleasant, and least-known, little cities in France. A short distance east, **Concarneau** is an atmospheric old fishing port turned tourist trap, while **Pont-Aven** was Gauguin's home before he made off to the South Seas, and still maintains its artistic traditions. There are surprises everywhere – take the perfectly preserved medieval village of **Locronan**, used as a film set for Roman Polanski's *Tess*, or the extraordinary world apart that is the tiny **Île de Sein**.

Finistère's most popular region for holidaymakers, the **Crozon Peninsula**, juts into the sea beneath the **Menez-Hom** mountain as a distinct entity between the two ancient realms. **Morgat** and **Camaret** here are both ideal for long and leisurely seaside stays, and all around there are opportunities for secluded camping.

Léon

The sequence of estuaries that score the coast in the north – the wildest and most dramatic in Brittany – are known both as *abers* (as in Welsh place names) and as *rias* (as in Spanish Galicia). In season, the vast beaches and dunes on the open Atlantic coast, for example around **Porspoder**, can be magnificent, while at any time you can stumble across tiny deserted coves as the twisting and narrowing estuaries reach inland. One of the choicest spots is at **Trémazan**, where the ruins of an ancient castle look out across a great expanse of sand, while the working fishing village of **Le Conquet** is perhaps the best holiday base: picturesque with a good beach, and offering a modest selection of hotels and restaurants, without being in any way over-developed. The one coastal destination you might prefer to avoid is the regional capital, and lone big city, of **Brest**, the base of the French Atlantic fleet.

Inland, the **parish closes** lie strung across the little villages southwest of **Morlaix**, each ornate church and its associated ensemble still perpetuating a fierce medieval rivalry. Also deserving a detour from the coast are the Renaissance **château of Kerjean** and the **Menhir de Kerloas**, the highest stone monolith still standing in Brittany.

Roscoff and around

ROSCOFF has long been a significant port – Mary Queen of Scots, for example, landed here in 1548 on her way to Paris to be engaged to the son of Henri II of France, and so too did Bonnie Prince Charlie in 1746, after his defeat at Culloden. The opening of its deep-water harbour in 1973 had especial significance in the general revitalization of the Breton economy. The town itself, however, has remained delightfully small and unspoiled. Almost all activity is confined to the pedestrianized medieval lanes around **rue Gambetta** and the **old port** – the rest of the roads are residential backstreets full of retirement homes and stern institutions. The preservation of its old character is helped by the fact that both the ferry port and *gare SNCF* are some way from the town centre.

Arrival and information

Boats from Plymouth, Cork and Rosslare dock at the Port de Bloscon, a couple of kilometres to the east (and just out of sight) of Roscoff. To get into the town, turn right from the terminal and follow the signs across a narrow promontory and down into the crescent of Roscoff's original natural harbour. In summer, a direct **bus** service to Morlaix and Quimper leaves from the ferry terminal (Tues, Wed, Fri & Sat 7.30am; Mon, Thurs & Sun 3.30pm; CAT; Ⓣ02.98.90.88.89). The **gare SNCF** lies a few hundred metres south of the town proper. From here, a restricted rail service (often replaced by buses) runs to Morlaix, with connections beyond. Most **local buses** also go from here, including a direct service to Brest run by Voyages Biham (Ⓣ02.98.44.46.73).

The helpful **tourist office** is at 46 rue Gambetta in town (July & Aug Mon–Sat 9am–12.30pm & 1.30–7pm, Sun 10am–12.30pm; Sept–June Mon–Sat 9am–noon & 2–6pm; Ⓣ02.98.61.12.13, Ⓦwww.roscoff-tourisme.com), next to a boulangerie and the **post office** at 19 rue Gambetta (Mon–Fri 9am–12.30pm & 1–5.30pm, Sat 9am–noon).

Bikes can be rented from *Camping de Perharidy* (see below).

Accommodation

For a small town, Roscoff is well equipped with **hotels**, which are accustomed to late-night arrivals from the ferries. Be warned, however, that most of them are relatively expensive and close for some or all of the winter. There's also a **hostel** on the Île de Batz (see p.293), and a two-star **campsite**, the municipal beachfront *Camping de Perharidy*, 2km west, just off the route de Santec (Ⓣ02.98.69.70.86; Ⓔcamping-perharidy@wanadoo.fr; closed mid-Oct to March).

Hôtel-Restaurant des Arcades 15 rue Amiral-Réveillère ⓣ02.98.69.70.45, ⓕ02.98.61.12.34. Sixteenth-century building with superb views from some of its modernized rooms and from the restaurant, which despite being slightly overrun by tourists, has economical menus at €9.90, with a particularly good €24.90 option. En-suite facilities cost around €14 extra. Closed Nov–Easter. ❷

Hôtel Armen Le Triton rue du Docteur Bagot ⓣ02.98.61.24.44, ⓦwww.hotel-letriton.com. Peaceful hotel in a residential neighbourhood a short walk from the town centre, with bright rooms on three floors. Surrounded by a pleasant garden and plenty of private parking space. Closed mid-Nov to mid-Feb. ❸

Hôtel-Restaurant le Bellevue rue Jeanne-d'Arc ⓣ02.98.61.23.38, ⓕ02.98.61.11.80. Seafront Logis de France, on the opposite side of the pleasure harbour to the town centre, and thus somewhat nearer the ferry terminal. It would be quieter were it not for the lively downstairs bar. Well-appointed, en-suite rooms, and fine views from the dining room, which has menus from €16. Closed mid-Nov to mid-March, except Christmas and New Year. ❸

Hôtel du Centre 5 rue Gambetta ⓣ02.98.61.24.25, ⓕ02.98.61.15.43. Family hotel above the café-bar *Chez Janie*, and entered via the main street but looking out on the port. Rooms with sea views are around €15 extra. Closed mid-Dec to mid-Feb. ❹

Hôtel les Chardons Bleus 4 rue Amiral-Réveillère ⓣ02.98.69.72.03, ⓕ02.98.61.27.86. Very friendly and helpful hotel in the heart of the old town, with a good restaurant (closed Thurs & Sun eve Sept–June) where menus start at €17. Closed mid-Feb to mid-March. ❹

Grand Hôtel Talabardon 27 place Lacaze-Duthiers ⓣ02.98.61.24.95, ⓦwww.bestwestern-talabardon.com. Imposing old stone building in the main square, facing the church on the inland side but with big sea-view balconies attached to several rooms. Seafood menus in the attractive dining room range from €25 to €45. Closed Nov–Feb. ❺

Hôtel le Gulf Stream 400 rue Marquise de Kergariou ⓣ02.98.69.73.19, ⓦwww.hotelroscoff.com. One of Roscoff's more expensive options, just south of the Institute of Oceanology, with a heated swimming pool and a gourmet restaurant serving such delights as roasted scampi and sweet-and-sour turbot. Closed mid-Oct to mid-March. ❺

Hôtel Regina 1 rue Ropartz-Morvan ⓣ02.98.61.23.55, ⓦwww.hotel-regina.fr. Very comfortable rooms, but relatively expensive considering the location, some distance from the sea next to the *gare SNCF*. Menus from €16 in the restaurant, and live jazz in the bar in what might otherwise be the quieter months. Closed Nov to late March. ❹

Hôtel aux Tamaris 49 rue É-Corbière ⓣ02.98.61.22.99, ⓦwww.hotel-aux-tamaris.com. Renovated, comfortably furnished rooms looking out towards the Île de Batz. Closed mid-Nov to March. ❹

The Town

The old **harbour** is very much the liveliest part of Roscoff. Two long stone jetties enclose the fishing port – the local economy is still heavily based on the sea – while pleasure boats bob in the bay behind. Tourists gather all through the day to watch the fishermen at work, and to join the low-key pleasure trips to the **Île de Batz**. The island looks almost walkable; a narrow pier stretches over 400m towards it before abruptly plunging into deep rocky waters. The Pointe de Bloscon and the white fisherman's chapel, the Chapelle Ste-Barbe, make a good vantage point, particularly when the tide is in. Below the headland are the *viviers*, where you can see trout, salmon, lobsters and crabs being reared for the pot.

In addition to the island ferries, detailed on p.294, the Compagnie Maritime Armein (ⓣ02.98.61.77.75) operate two-and-a-half-hour cruises from here around the **Bay of Morlaix** (July to mid-Sept Mon–Sat 2.30pm; €11).

Until the last couple of centuries, Roscoff made most of its money from piracy, like so many other ports along the Breton coast. Reminders of that wealth can be found along **rue Gambetta**, which becomes rue Amiral-Réveillère, both of which run parallel to the old harbour, 50m or so inland. Two of rue Gambetta's ornate grey-granite houses, including no. 25 ("the House of Mary Stuart"), have been claimed to be where Mary Queen of

Scots spent her first night after eighteen stormy days at sea – despite the fact that both were built after she landed. More recently, the town earned a more respectable living from the **onion** trade, which began in 1828, when Henri Ollivier chartered a barge and took the first Roscoff onions over to England. The trade flourished until the 1930s; older locals remember travelling as children with their fathers as far afield as Glasgow to sell their produce. The whole story of the "Johnnies" – that classic French image of men in black berets with strings of onions hanging over the handlebars of their bicycles – is told at **La Maison des Johnnies et de l'Oignon Rosé de Roscoff**, 48 rue Brizeux, near the *gare SNCF* (mid-June to mid-Sept daily except Tues 3–7pm; mid-Feb to mid-June & mid-Sept to Dec Sat & Sun 2–6pm; €4) by way of a not overly gripping display of nostalgic photos and animated exhibits. The town has recently instigated an **onion festival**, held annually on slightly varying dates at the end of August, with such amusements as onion cart-making contests, a vintage tractor parade and onion soup tasting.

Back down by the sea at the end of rue Amiral-Réveillère in place de l'Église, the sculpted ships and protruding stone cannons of the Renaissance belfry that tops the sixteenth-century town church, **Notre Dame de Croas Batz**, also recall the seafaring days. From the side, rows of bells can be seen hanging in galleries, one above the other, like a tall narrow wedding cake created by the young Walt Disney.

A short way past the church, on place Georges-Teissier, the **Charles Perez Aquarium** (closed for renovation at the time of writing; contact the tourist office for the latest information), has a comprehensive collection of marine fauna of the Channel. It's an interesting enough place, if a little disappointing for anyone expecting the exotic. Some way beyond the aquarium is the **Thalassotherapy Institute** of Rock Roum (Ⓣ08.25.00.20.99, Ⓦwww.thalasso-roscoff.com). Specializing in seawater cures, it opened in 1899 as the first such establishment in France, and is still thriving over a century later. A kilometre further on, you come to Roscoff's best **beach**, at Laber, surrounded by expensive hotels and apartments.

Alexis Gourvennec and Brittany Ferries

Few British holidaymakers sailing to France with **Brittany Ferries** will realize the significance of the company's original ideology. The ferry services from Roscoff to Plymouth and to Cork were started not simply to bring tourists, but also to revive the traditional trading links between the Celtic nations of Brittany, Ireland and southwest England – links which were suppressed for centuries as an act of French state policy after the union of Brittany with France in 1532.

Until the 1960s, there were no direct ferries crossing the Channel to Brittany, and, until Brittany Ferries started up, all the cross-Channel operators were British-owned. Brittany Ferries is the creation of Alexis Gourvennec, who in 1961, at 24, was the militant leader of a Breton farmers' cooperative. Frustrated by the lack of French government support, the farmers decided to start their own shipping line to find new markets for their produce – the immediate region of Roscoff and Morlaix being particularly noted for its artichokes and cauliflowers.

The company's financial success has allowed it to expand, running services from Britain to St-Malo, the Norman ports of Cherbourg and Caen, as well as to Spain. Above all, however, Brittany Ferries has been an important factor in a resurgence of Breton fortunes, with as much cultural as commercial significance.

See p.21 and p.24 for more details.

In the opposite direction from town, a short walk south along the coast from the ferry terminal, is the **Jardin Exotique** – tropical garden – at Rock Hievec (March & Nov daily 2–5pm; April, May & Oct daily 10.30am–12.30pm & 2–6pm; June–Sept daily 10am–7pm; €4.50). In this slightly surreal enclave, cactuses, palm trees and flowers of South America and the Pacific flourish in the mild Gulf-Stream climate.

Eating

The obvious places to **eat** in Roscoff are the dining rooms of the hotels themselves, but the town does hold a few specialist **restaurants** as well, plus a bunch of appealing crêperies around the old harbour. If you're arriving on an evening ferry out of season, it can be difficult to find a restaurant still serving any later than 9.15pm.

Crêperie de la Poste 12 rue Gambetta ⓣ02.98.69.72.81. Central crêperie, open from 11.30am until late, where an à la carte meal of sweet and savoury pancakes should work out inexpensive; more exotic seafood options cost up to €7.40. They also serve fish soup, mussels and other simple meals. Closed Wed Sept–June, or Tues July & Aug.

L'Écume des Jours quai d'Auxerre ⓣ02.98.61.22.83. Cosy restaurant in a grand old house facing the port, offering good-value set lunches for €11.20 on weekdays, plus dinner menus from €20, featuring such delights as braised oysters or scallops with local pink onions. Closed Dec & Jan and Tues & Wed in low season.

Le Temps de Vivre place de l'Église ⓣ02.98.61.27.28. Long-standing gourmet restaurant, with sea views, on the main church square – next to but separate from the *Hôtel Ibis* – serving rich French cuisine with a modern twist. Almost the only deviations from the chef's recommendations on menus ranging from €35 to €80 are to accommodate oyster *refuseniks*. Try the lamb, which is raised on milk, resulting in whiter meat than normal that melts in the mouth. Closed two weeks in both March & Oct.

The Île de Batz

The long, narrow **ÎLE DE BATZ** (pronounced "ba") forms a sort of mirror image of Roscoff across the water, separated from it by a sea channel that's barely 200m wide at low tide, but perhaps five times that when the tide is high. Appearances from the mainland are somewhat deceptive, however; the island's old town, home to a thousand or so farmers and fishermen, may fill much of its southern shoreline, but those parts of Batz that aren't visible from Roscoff are much wilder and more windswept. With no cars permitted, and some great expanses of sandy beach, it makes a wonderfully quiet retreat for families in particular, whether you're camping or staying in one of its two old-fashioned little hotels.

The island's first recorded inhabitant was a "laidly worm", a dragon that infested the place in the sixth century. Such dragons normally symbolize pre-Christian religions, in this case perhaps a Druidic serpent cult. Allegorical or not, when St Pol arrived to found a monastery he wrapped a Byzantine stole around the unfortunate creature's neck and cast it into the sea. These days, there are no dragons; there are hardly even any trees, just an awful lot of seaweed, which is collected and sold for fertilizer.

There's a nice small beach near where the ferry docks, along the edge of the harbour, though the sea withdraws so far at low tide that the entire port turns into an endless morass of slimy seaweed. You may well have spotted the island's best beach already from the boat: the white-sand **Grève Blanche** towards its eastern end, reached by turning right when you get to the town church. Turning left at the church leads to the 44-metre **lighthouse** that stands on the island's peak, all of 23m above sea level (second half of June & first half of Sept Thurs–Tues 2–5pm; July & Aug daily 1–5.30pm; €1.70).

Practicalities

Ferries from Roscoff arrive at the quayside of the old town. Three separate ferry companies make the crossing, for a return fare of €6.50. Compagnie Maritime Armein (Ⓣ02.98.61.77.75), Compagnie Finistèrienne or CFTM (Ⓣ02.98.61.78.87), and Armor Excursions (Ⓣ02.98.61.79.66) have ticket booths at the landward end of Roscoff's long pier. At low tide, the boats sail from the far end of the pier, a good five minutes' walk further on. In summer only, all of the companies work together and your ticket will be valid on any ferry. The crossing takes about ten minutes. Between late June and mid-September, the service is pretty much nonstop between 8am and 8pm daily; for the rest of the year, each company runs eight to ten trips daily between 8.30am and 7pm.

The nicer of the two **hotels** on the island is the *Grand Hôtel Morvan*, at the centre of the harbour (Ⓣ02.98.61.78.06; ❷; closed Dec–March), which serves good meals on its large seafront terraces. Closer to the ferry landing, the *Hôtel-Restaurant Roch Ar Mor* (Ⓣ02.98.61.78.28; ❷; closed Nov–March), makes a cheaper alternative, though a better bet for budget travellers would be the island's **hostel**, which is in a far more beautiful setting, right by **Grève Blanche,** the beach at the evocatively named *Creach ar Bolloc'h* (Ⓣ02.98.61.77.69; closed Nov–March; €11.45), which also runs sailing classes. A quirky little **crêperie-restaurant**, *Les Couleurs du Temps* (Ⓣ02.98.61.75.75), tucked away behind *Grand Hôtel Morvan*, offers good-value lunch menus, and prepares the weird Breton speciality *kig ha farz*, a kind of seafood stew topped by a crêpe.

St-Pol-de-Léon

The main road south from Roscoff passes by fields of the famous Breton artichokes before arriving after 6km at **ST-POL-DE-LÉON**. Only accessible with your own tranpsort but pleasantly sited amid rich gardens, this is not an exciting place but has two churches that merit a pause. The **cathedral**, in the main town square, was rebuilt towards the end of the thirteenth century along the lines of Coutances – a quiet classic of unified Norman architecture. The remains of St Pol are inside, alongside a large bell, rung over the heads of pilgrims during his *pardon* on March 12 in the unlikely hope of curing headaches and ear diseases.

Just downhill, the **Kreisker Chapel** is notable for its sharp-pointed soaring granite belfry, now coated in yellow moss. It was originally modelled on the Norman spire of St-Pierre at Caen, which was destroyed in the last war (see p.142); as an elegant improvement on its Norman counterpart, it was itself much copied, and similar "Kreisker" spires are dotted all over rural Brittany. The dramatic view to be seen if you climb this spire (daily 10–11.30am & 2–6pm; free), out across the **Bay of Morlaix**, should be enough to persuade you to follow the road along the shore.

If you're looking for **accommodation** in St-Pol, rooms at the *Hôtel de France*, 29 rue des Minimes (Ⓣ02.98.29.14.14, Ⓦwww.hoteldefrancebretagne.com; ❸), are slightly more comfortable than the cheaper *Hôtel-Restaurant le Passiflore*, near the station at 28 rue Pen-ar-Pont (Ⓣ02.98.69.00.52; ❷; closed Sun eve). Both are central, open all year and have reasonable restaurants.

Carantec

From St-Pol, if you take the foliage-covered lane down to join the D58, you can cross the pont de la Corde to reach the resort and peninsula of **CARANTEC**, studded with small coves and secluded beaches. The nicest of all the local beaches, the **plage du Kelenn**, is the first to the east of the slightly drab town itself. The **Île de Callot**, an enticing hour's walk from Carantec at low tide, is the scene of a *pardon* and blessing of the sea on the Sunday after August 15 – a rather dour occasion, as are most of the religious festivals around Finistère.

Practicalities

Buses serve Carantec from Morlaix, dropping you either at the church or by the beach. This stretch of coast comes alive in summer with a scattering of seasonal **campsites**, among them the excellent four-star *Les Mouettes* (Ⓣ 02.98.67.02.46, Ⓦ www.les-mouettes.com; closed mid-Sept to April), where you pay well over the usual odds for the benefit of having a supermarket, a swimming pool with an impressive water slide, a bar and a disco on site. For **rooms** in Carantec, the *Hôtel de Carentec*, 20 rue de Kelenn (Ⓣ 02.98.67.00.47, Ⓦ www.hoteldecarantec.com; ❽; closed Jan), is a very expensive, beachfront option, where some of the luxurious rooms have terraces with magnificent views of the sea.

Right on the waterfront in town, the twin **restaurants** *La Cambuse* and *Le Cabestan* (Ⓣ 02.98.67.01.87; closed Mon & Tues in low season) provide the focus of Carantec's nightlife, with the *Cabestan* having the edge on seafood, while the *Cambuse* concentrates on live music. Several snack bars with spacious open-air terraces also face the plage du Kelenn, including the *Restaurant Les Îles* (Ⓣ 02.98.67.05.24; lunch daily, dinner Fri & Sat only, closed Dec–Feb), which serves *moules frites* for around €10. For the finest seafood, the *Maison de l'Huître*, in a gorgeous and very clearly signposted waterfront spot east of the centre, sells prize **oysters** from the beds at Prat-Ar-Coum in western Finistère (July & Aug Mon–Sat 9.30am–1pm & 3–7pm, Sun 10am–noon; Sept–June Mon–Fri 10am–noon & 3–6pm, Sat 9.30am–12.30pm & 2.30–7pm, Sun 10am–noon; Ⓣ 02.98.78.30.68).

The Château de Taureau

A short way east of Carantec, the fortified **Château de Taureau**, off Pointe de Pen-al-Lann, guards the entrance to Morlaix Bay, 12km north of Morlaix itself. It was built after a succession of skirmishes that began in 1522 when Morlaix pirates raided and looted Bristol. Henry VIII's pride was hurt and, seeking revenge, he sent a sizeable fleet to storm Morlaix. The citizens were absent at a neighbouring festival when the English arrived; when they returned, they found the English drunk in their wine cellars. Once the Bretons had routed their enemies, they built the château to forestall further attacks from the sea. In the seventeenth century, the Château de Taureau was used as a prison; now it's a sailing school. Meanwhile, Morlaix adopted the motto which it keeps to this day: "If they bite you, bite them back."

The only way to get a close-up view of the château is from out on the water, and there are organized boat trips around the Bay of Morlaix from Roscoff (see p.291). The best place on the mainland from which to admire the castle is at the tip of the **Pointe de Pen-al-Lann**, 2km east of Carantec. Incidentally, a steep footpath from the car park here leads 300m down to one of the most delightful – and quiet – **beaches** in this region.

Towards Morlaix

The D73 runs on southeast from Carantec beside the sea, the estuary narrowing until at **Locquenolé** it is just the width of the River Morlaix. From then on it's a beautiful deep valley, with promenades and gardens along the stone-reinforced banks, and views across to isolated villages such as Dourduff on the other side.

Morlaix

The long-established transport junction of **MORLAIX**, 25km southeast of Roscoff where the Queffleuth and Jarlot rivers join to flow together into broad Morlaix Bay, now seems too far from the open sea to attract many long-stay visitors. Though many attractive buildings still survive from its medieval heyday, it's a strange-looking place, literally overshadowed by a massive nineteenth-century railway viaduct. During the "Golden Period" of the late Middle Ages, however, this was one of the great old Breton ports, thriving – in between wars – on trade with England. Its sober stone houses climbed up either side of a steep valley, originally protected by an eleventh-century castle and a circuit of walls. Little is left of either, but the old centre remains in part medieval – with its fair share of cobbled streets and half-timbered houses. Later, the town grew still more prosperous on piracy and the tobacco trade (both legal and illegal), and spread north, down the valley, towards the port.

Arrival and information

The **gare SNCF** is on rue Armand-Rousseau, high above the town at the western end of its railway viaduct. It was originally supposed to be linked to town by a funicular railway, but as this was never built you still have to reach it on foot, climbing the steep steps of the Venelle de la Roche. If you can't face the long trek up to the station to buy a ticket, you can make reservations at travel agencies down in the town proper.

All **buses** conveniently depart from place Cornic, right under the viaduct; long-distance routes include those south to Huelgoat and Carhaix (Effia Voyageurs; ⓣ02.98.93.06.98), and also Quimper (CAT; ⓣ02.98.72.01.41).

The **tourist office** in Morlaix is in a solitary but central one-storey building, almost under the viaduct in place des Otages (June–Sept Mon & Sat 10am–noon & 2–6pm, Tues–Fri 10am–12.30pm & 1.30–7pm, Sun 10.30am–12.30pm; Sept–June Tues–Sat 10am–noon & 2–6pm; ⓣ02.98.62.14.94). The **post office** is on rue de Brest (ⓣ02.98.88.23.03).

Accommodation

The **hotels** in Morlaix are dotted around the old town and tend to be fairly uninspiring, although there are a few decent budget places.

Hôtel de l'Europe 1 rue d'Aiguillon ⓣ02.98.62.11.99, ⓦwww.hotel-europe-com.fr. Slightly eccentric but very central old place, near the Jacobin convent. While the rooms are modern, well equipped and decorated in muted tones, the public spaces, furnished in a variety of styles, are more flamboyant. They offer one, much cheaper, single room, as well as sumptuous suites. The on-site brasserie has simple but good menus featuring a *plat du jour* from €11–14. ❹–❾

Hôtel de la Gare 25 place St-Martin ⓣ02.98.88.03.29, ⓕ02.98.63.97.80. Reasonable value en-suite rooms above a cosy bar with a small terrace, close to the *gare SNCF* at the top of the hill. ❸

Hôtel du Port 3 quai de Léon ⓣ02.98.88.07.54, ⓦwww.lhotelduport.com. Bright, modern option, overlooking the port from the left bank. All rooms are en suite with satellite TV, and most have views of the port. ❹

Hôtel le Roy d'Ys 8 place des Jacobins ⓣ02.98.63.30.55. Small central hotel, across the square from the town museum. The cheapest rooms do not have their own showers; either pay to use a shared one, or an extra €7.55 for an en-suite room. No restaurant, but a downstairs bar. Bikes can also be rented by guests. ❶

Hôtel-Restaurant le St-Mélaine 75–77 rue Ange-de-Guernisac ⓣ02.98.88.54.76. Family hotel, not easy to find, above place Cornic and all but under the viaduct. Inexpensive but dull. The restaurant has menus from €10. Closed Sat eve & Sun. ❶

The Town

Morlaix is dominated by its pink-granite **railway viaduct**, built high above the valley in the 1860s to carry trains en route between Paris and Brest. Despite all Allied attempts during World War II to destroy it with bombs, it still looms 60m above the central **place des Otages**, and as you enter the town today by road from the north your first view is of shiny yacht masts in the pleasure harbour paralleling its slender pillars. The first level of the viaduct is intermittently open to visitors, usually (but not always) from 11am until 7pm each day. There are few actual sights in town, but it's a great place to roam the length of the steep stairways that lead up from the places des Otages and Cornic, or walk up to the viaduct from the top of Venelle aux Prêtres, along an almost rural overgrown path lined with brambles.

On her way from Roscoff to Paris, Mary Queen of Scots passed through Morlaix in 1548, and stayed at the **Jacobin convent** which fronts place des Jacobins. She was at the time just five years old, an aspect which may have contributed to local interest in the spectacle. A contemporary account records that the crush to catch a glimpse of the infant was so great that the inner town's "gates were thrown off their hinges and the chains from all the bridges were broken down". The convent (entrance on rue des Vignes), along with a sixteenth-century half-timbered house, the Maison à Pondalez, on Grande Rue, just to the west of the convent, both house temporary exhibits of the collection of the **Musée de Morlaix**, a reasonably entertaining assortment of Roman wine jars, bits that have fallen off medieval churches, cannons and kitchen utensils, and a few modern paintings (April, May & Sept Wed–Sun 1.30–6pm; July & Aug daily 11am–6.30pm; Oct–March & June Wed–Sat 1.30–6pm; €4.10).

Coreff – real ale in Brittany

The year 1985 saw the inauguration of an unlikely new product in Morlaix – the first Breton **real ale**. Two young Frenchmen, Christian Blanchard and Jean-François Malgorn, set up their own brewery, with the ambition of emulating the beers they had enjoyed on visits to Wales.

You should be able to find the resultant brew, Coreff – logically enough, the name is an old Breton word meaning "beer" – both locally and throughout Brittany in those bars which take pride in all things Breton. In July and August, it's also possible to visit the brewery, the Brasserie des Deux-Rivières, 1 place de la Madeleine, for a tour and a sample (45-minute tours Mon–Fri 11am & 2pm; ⓣ02.98.63.41.92).

The beer itself is a sweet, rich brown ale – authentically "real" in that it isn't filtered or pasteurized – that can make a welcome change from the lagers on offer everywhere else.

The austere church of **St-Mathieu**, off rue de Paris a short walk southeast of the convent, contains a sombre and curious statue of the Madonna and Child, made in Cologne around 1400 AD. Mary's breast was apparently lopped off by a prudish former priest, to leave the babe suckling at nothing. The whole statue stands open down the middle, to reveal a separate figure of God the Father, clutching a crucifix; interior panels hold painted scenes from the life of the Virgin, including the Annunciation and the Assumption. In 1993, the figure of Christ was stolen, but the thief, who preferred to pray at home, repented in 1994 and returned it anonymously.

Duchess Anne of Brittany visited Morlaix in 1506, by which time she had become queen of France. She is reputed to have stayed at the **Maison de la Reine Anne**, not far west of St-Mathieu church at 33 rue du Mur (May & June Mon–Sat 11am–6pm; July & Aug Mon–Sat 11am–6.30pm; Sept Mon–Sat 11am–5pm; €1.60), which, although much restored, does indeed date from the sixteenth century. Its intricate external carvings, and the lantern roof and splendid Renaissance staircase inside, make it the most beautiful of the town's ancient houses, each of its storeys overhanging the square below by a few more centimetres.

Eating

The best area for **restaurants** in Morlaix is between St-Mélaine church and place des Jacobins, but there are plenty of other options tucked away on the backstreets.

Les Bains Douches 45 allée du Poan-Ben ⓣ02.98.63.83.83. Small bistro that doesn't quite live up to its unusual location – set in the former public baths, and reached via a little footbridge across a canal – but makes an attractive spot for a light €10 lunch. Closed Sat lunch & Sun eve.

Brocéliande 5 rue des Bouchers ⓣ02.98.88.73.78. Located in the southeast of town, beyond the place des Halles and St-Mathieu church, this place offers elegant evening-only dining in a *fin-de-siècle* atmosphere. Menus cost €15, €23 and €30. Closed Mon & Tues.

La Dolce Vita 3 rue Ange-de-Guernisac ⓣ02.98.63.37.67. Italian place at the foot of a pretty central alley, with pizzas mostly priced at €8–10, plus pasta, salads, and traditional Italian dishes such as *osso bucco*. Closed Mon, plus three weeks in Feb and two weeks in Oct.

La Marée Bleue 3 rampe St-Mélaine ⓣ02.98.63.24.21. Well-respected seafood restaurant, a minute's walk up from the tourist office. The €14 menu is a bit limited, but €27 ensures you a superb *assiette de fruits de mer*, and €36.50 buys a five-course feast. Closed Oct & Sun eve & Mon Sept–June.

Nightlife and drinking

Among Morlaix's **bars**, the best are the venerable half-timbered *Ty Coz*, 10 Venelle au Beurre, near place Allende, which has boisterous Bretons playing darts, and draught Coreff beer, and the lively and much more salubrious – or aseptic, depending on your perspective – *Tempo Piano Bar*, facing the port on quai de Tréguier, where there are occasional jazz and blues concerts.

The parish closes

A few kilometres west of Morlaix, bounded by the valleys of the Elorn and the Penzé rivers, lies an area remarkable for the wealth and distinction of its church architecture. This region holds the best-known examples of what the French call *enclos paroissiaux* – a phrase that translates into English as "**parish closes**", and describes a walled churchyard which in addition to the church itself incorporates a trinity of further elements: a cemetery, a calvary and an ossuary.

The **ossuaries** – which now tend to contain nothing more alarming than a few rows of postcards – were originally charnel houses, used to store the exhumed bones of less recent burials. They are the most striking features of the closes, making explicit a peculiarly Breton proximity and continuity between the living and the dead. Parishioners would go to pray, with the informality of making a family visit, in the ossuary chapels where the dead bones of their families were on display. The relationship may have originated with the builders of the megalithic passage graves, which were believed to serve as doorways between our world and the netherworld.

The **cemeteries** tend to be small, and in many cases have disappeared altogether, while the **calvaries** that complete the ensemble are tenuously based on the hill of Calvary. Each is therefore in theory surmounted by a Crucifixion, but the definition is loose enough to take in any cluster of religious statuary, not necessarily even limited to biblical scenes, standing on a single base.

That there are so many fine *enclos* in such a small area is thanks to a period of intense inter-village rivalry during the sixteenth and seventeenth centuries, when each parish competed to outdo the next in the complexity and ornament of its village church. It's no coincidence that most such Breton churches date from the two centuries to either side of the union with France in 1532 – Brittany's wealthiest period – and nothing is more telling of the decline in the province's fortunes than the contrast between the riches on show and the relative lack of prosperity of the present-day villages. An additional, more positive, layer is contributed, however, by the current revival of artisan traditions in the parishes. In several of the towns and villages, stonemasons are once more producing sculptures in granite.

A clearly signposted **route** leading past several of the most famous churches – St-Thégonnec, Guimiliau and Lampaul-Guimiliau – can be joined by leaving the N12 between Morlaix and Landivisiau at St-Thégonnec.

This is not an area to attempt to explore without your own vehicle.

St-Thégonnec

At the **ST-THÉGONNEC** *enclos*, just off the N12 10km southwest of Morlaix, the church **pulpit**, carved by two brothers in 1683, is the acknowledged masterpiece, albeit so swamped with detail – symbolic saints, sibyls and arcane figures – that it is almost too intricate to take in. The painted oak **entombment** in the crypt under the ossuary has more immediate effect. Complete with a stunning life-size figure of Mary Magdalene, it was sculpted by Jacques Laispagnol of Morlaix in 1702. The entire east wall of the church is a carved and painted altarpiece, with saints in niches and a hundred different scenes depicted. Although a severe fire in June 1998 resulted in extensive damage to the roof and certain of the side chapels, the principal treasures of the church were spared.

The upmarket *Auberge de St-Thégonnec*, 6 place de la Mairie (Ⓣ02.98.79.61.18, Ⓦwww.aubergesaintthegonnec.com; ❺; closed Mon lunch & Sat lunch in July & Aug; Sun, Mon lunch & Sat lunch Sept–June, plus all Jan), is a surprisingly smart **hotel** for such a small village. Its main building houses a superb restaurant, where menus start at €23.50 and rise to €44 for the gourmet option featuring scallops, crab, veal and the like, carefully prepared in original and delicious sauces. The *Restaurant du Commerce* at 1 rue de

Paris (☎02.98.79.61.07; closed Sat, Sun & Aug), very near the church, serves more basic, good-value meals from €10.50, while the *Crêperie Steredden*, nearby at 6 rue de la Gare (☎02.98.79.43.34; closed Mon, plus Tues Sept–June, & all Dec & Jan), is a friendly village crêperie that offers numerous speciality pancakes, with set menus costing around €10. Finally, in an almost absurdly pastoral riverside setting 2km west of St-Thégonnec, the *Moulin de Kerlaviou* (☎02.98.79.60.57; ❸) is a ravishing farmhouse **B&B**, offering two well-equipped en-suite rooms.

Guimiliau

The showpiece at the pretty flower-filled village of **GUIMILIAU**, 6km southwest of St-Thégonnec, is its **calvary**. This incredible ensemble holds over two hundred granite figures, depicting scenes from the life of Christ and rendered all the more dramatic by being covered with what has been called "secular lichen". A uniquely Breton illustration, just above the Last Supper, depicts the unfortunate Katell Gollet – a figure from local myth who stole consecrated wafers to give to her lover, who naturally turned out to be the Devil – being torn to shreds by demons.

Inside the church, years of patient restoration have turned the seventeenth-century organ, until recently a tangle of mangled wood, back into its original harmonious condition.

Lampaul-Guimiliau

The third of the major parish closes, **LAMPAUL-GUIMILIAU**, is a few kilometres further on. Here the painted oak **baptistry**, the dragons on the beams and the appropriately wicked faces of the robbers on the **calvary** are the key components. An unusual stoup depicts a couple of devils squirming as they're doused with holy water. The *Hostellerie des Enclos* (☎02.98.68.77.08; ❸; restaurant closed Sat lunch, Fri eve & Sun eve Nov–March), 300m beyond the church on the left, is a modern hotel with good rooms and a very reasonable restaurant.

Landivisiau

LANDIVISIAU, just south of the N12 20km west of Morlaix, makes a good alternative to Morlaix as a base from which to tour the nearby parish closes. There's not much to the town itself, but the **tourist office** at 12 av Foch (July & Aug Mon–Fri 9am–12.30pm & 2–6pm, Sat 10am–12.30pm & 2–6pm; Sept–June Mon–Fri 9am–noon & 2–5pm; ☎02.98.68.33.33, Ⓦwww.ot-paysdelandivisiau.com) provides details of recommended bike routes, and coach tours operate regularly from the main square. There's also a choice of cheap **hotels**, the best value of which are *Le Terminus*, 94 av Foch (☎02.98.68.02.00; ❷; restaurant closed Sat lunch, Fri eve & Sun eve), which serves excellent meals, and *Hotel de l'Avenue*, 16 av de Coatmeur (☎02.98.68.11.67, Ⓦwww.avenue-hotel-landivisiau.com; ❷; closed mid-Sept to mid-Oct). Halfway between Landivisiau and La Roche-Maurice is a lovely rural restaurant, *Moulin de Brézal* (☎02.98.20.46.57; weekends only), facing a little bridge that leads to the ruined 1533 chapel of Notre Dame de Bon Secours. All of its menus, priced from €15 upwards, include a scallop kebab. This beautiful riverside spot would also make an ideal setting for a picnic.

La Roche-Maurice

West of Landivisiau, the N12 races towards Brest, but the lesser D712 and the railway follow a far more pleasant route, along the banks of the pretty Elorn River. After about 12km – not far beyond the chapel of **Pont-Christ**, beside a broad waterfall – the village of **LA ROCHE-MAURICE** occupies a steep high bluff above a curve in the river.

Only the solemn ivy-covered keep now remains of the **castle** that has occupied this site since the eleventh century, and was once supposedly home to Katell Gollet. It was abandoned at the end of the seventeenth century, and its stones used to build the houses that now surround it. Visitors are free to climb the wooden stairway that's rather clumsily attached to the outside, but not to ascend any further inside the ruin itself.

Nearby stands another large **parish close**, notable mainly for its rendition of the death-figure **Ankou** (see p.281). This time he's carved above the holy-water stoup on the wall of the ossuary, facing the church, beneath the warning "I kill you all". The interior of the church is gorgeous, the nave divided in two by a lovely green and red rood screen, which shows the Twelve Apostles propped up by grotesque animals. Ringed by older carvings, the blue ceiling holds a celestial choir of angels. In summer, the ossuary houses local information and an exhibition on the history of the town.

La Roche-Maurice has no hotels, but the *Auberge du Vieux Château* (Ⓣ02.98.20.40.52; closed eve Mon–Fri), in the square immediately below the castle, serves excellent **food**, with menus starting at €12.50.

La Martyre

The oldest parish close of all, built in 1460, stands at the heart of **LA MARTYRE**, 7km south of La Roche-Maurice on the road to Sizun (see Chapter 6). This is the most attractive of all the local villages, with stones of its complete parish close seamlessly integrated into the walls of its main street. Ankou clutches a severed head above the stoup in the peculiarly lopsided entrance porch, watched over not only by a carved red-ochre Virgin, giving birth, but also a nestful of house martins. Inside, the church is damp and somewhat faded, but it does have an attractive gilt altar.

Landerneau

Back on the D712 from La Roche-Maurice, you soon reach **LANDERNEAU**, at the mouth of the Elorn estuary. This, too, was once a major port, but is now more of a tourist showpiece. The **pont de Rohan** in the middle of town is said to be, along with the Ponte Vecchio in Florence, the last inhabited bridge in Europe, and is also the site of the local **tourist office** (June & Sept Tues–Sat 9am–noon & 2–6pm; July & Aug Mon–Sat 9.15am–12.30pm & 1.30–7pm, Sun 10am–1pm; Oct–May Tues–Sat 9am–noon & 2–5pm; Ⓣ02.98.85.13.09, Ⓦwww.tourisme-landerneau-daoulas.fr).

Landerneau offers several **accommodation** possibilities. *Le Clos du Pontic*, south of the river at 3 rue du Pontic (Ⓣ02.98.21.50.91, Ⓦwww.clos-pontic.com; ❹; restaurant closed Mon lunch, Sat lunch & Sun eve Sept–June), and the cheaper *l'Amandier*, 53–55 rue de Brest (Ⓣ02.98.85.10.89; ❸; restaurant closed Sun eve & Mon), are comfortable old-style hotels with excellent restaurants.

Plougastel-Daoulas

West of Landerneau, the Elorn broadens dramatically as it enters the Rade de Brest. The city of Brest (see p.309) sprawls along its northern banks at this point, but the southern side holds one final site associated with the parish closes. The church in the village of **PLOUGASTEL-DAOULAS** was built in 1870, and is far from interesting, but just outside it stands a **calvary** that ranks among the finest in Brittany.

This extraordinarily elaborate affair was completed in 1604, to celebrate the passing of an outbreak of the plague – hence the bumps on the shaft of the main cross, designed to recall the sores on the bodies of the victims. Carvings on each of the four sides of the base depict scenes from the Life of Christ. Sadly, the rest of the village has not been restored so sensitively after the bombing of World War II. A weird shopping mall now overlooks the calvary, equipped with a giant Scrabble board for local senior citizens and a truly awful mural recounting the history of cinema.

Between the parish closes and the sea

The swathe of land north of the parish closes on your way to Finistère's rugged northern coastline holds relatively few tourist attractions, the notable exception being the Renaissance château of **Kerjean**. Also worth a stop is the village of **Le Folgoët**, whose pretty church compares favourably with those in the parish closes.

Kerjean

If not quite the "Versailles of Brittany", as it is promoted, but for this remote corner of France, **Kerjean** is a surprisingly classic **château** (April & May Wed–Mon 2–6pm; first half of June & second half of Sept Wed–Mon 2–6pm; July & Aug daily 10am–7pm; second half of June & first half of Sept Wed–Mon 10am–6pm; Oct Wed–Mon 2–5pm; Nov–March Wed & Sun 2–5pm; €4; ☎02.98.69.93.69). Despite being little more than 15km from Roscoff, it's not that easy to find – you need to be on the D30, running from Plouescat to Landivisiau, and to turn right shortly after St-Vougay. Roscoff–Brest buses stop at **Lanhouarneau**, 5km west of the château.

The moated Renaissance château, set in its own park, was built in the sixteenth century by the lords of Kerjean, with the express intention of overshadowing the mansion of their former feudal overlord, the Carman of Lanhouarneau, who, under some archaic quirk of fealty, made them take an egg, in a cart, each year and cook it for the Carman.

The building, today state property, is an odd jumble of the authentic, the restored and the imported. There is one original ceiling, one original floor and one original door; and the guide on the optional 45-minute tours (some of which are in English) has one original joke to match. Nevertheless it's an interesting place, and if you choose to wander around on your own there's a certain amusement to be derived from the bizarre placing of objects and the lack of explanations. In the scullery are two thirteenth-century choirstalls from St-Pol cathedral, each seat carved with the head of its occupant; a statue of St Sebastian "run through with arrows" has not an arrow in sight, and it is unclear quite what St Anthony is doing "with the little pig". More standard Breton furnishings are the cupboard-like panelled box-beds, which people used to climb inside to sleep, shut in tight for the night.

Kerjean is also used in summer for temporary exhibitions, and open-air theatrical performances have been scheduled in recent years for Friday nights in July and August. Call the château for details.

Lesneven and Le Folgoët

Continuing west from Kerjean inland, whether you are headed for southern Brittany or for Le Conquet and Ouessant island, it's worth making a stop at Le Folgoët. It's more easily accessible than Kerjean, though by bus you'll probably find yourself dropped a couple of kilometres out at the small town of **LESNEVEN**. The main features here are an **abbey**, on the main square, and some eccentric houses – slate-roofed and convex-panelled – in the narrow lanes. A visit to the **German war cemetery**, a short distance southeast of the centre, is a sobering experience.

Lesneven does not itself hold any great interest, though its ivy-coated **café** on the main square is an attractive place to break your journey, and the **hotel** *Le Week-End*, pont du Châtel (Ⓣ02.98.25.40.57; ❷; restaurant closed Mon lunch July & Aug, Sun eve & all day Mon Sept–June), is a Logis de France that provides good-value food and accommodation.

LE FOLGOËT is about half an hour's walk southwest of Lesneven. At first sight no more than a small village, with a well-kept and rather English-looking green, it owes both its **Notre Dame** church, and its name, which means "Fool's Wood", to a fourteenth-century simpleton called Solomon. After an unappreciated lifetime repeating the four Breton words for "O Lady Virgin Mary", he found fame in death by growing a white lily out of his mouth. The church was erected on the site of his favourite spring, and holds a *pardon* on September 8 or the preceding Sunday. (On the fourth Sunday of July there is also a *pardon* of St Christopher, which involves a blessing of cars that non-motorists may find verging on the blasphemous.) It's a lovely church colourfully garnished with orange moss and clinging verdure (a sign of the penetrating damp inside), and with a bumpy and stubbly approximation of a "Kreisker" spire. It has been restored bit by bit since the damage of the Revolution, and an unusual amount of statuary has been placed on the many low niches all around the outside.

The abers

The coast west of Roscoff has some of the most dramatic shoreline in Brittany, a jagged series of **abers** – narrow estuaries, neither as deep nor as steep-sided as the Norwegian fjords with which they are occasionally compared – in the midst of which are clustered small, isolated **resorts**, heavy on modern holiday homes but relatively short on hotels and other amenities. These resorts all have adequate beaches, but it's the coastal scenery that is the real attraction. It's a little on the bracing side, especially if you're making use of the numerous **campsites**, but in summer, at least, the temperatures are mild enough, and things get progressively more sheltered as you move towards Le Conquet and Brest. You can get as far as Plouescat and Brignogan by **bus,** as well as to Le Conquet from Brest, but to explore the region you'll really need your own transport.

Plouescat

PLOUESCAT is the first real resort to the west of Roscoff. It is not quite on the sea itself, but there are **campsites** nearby on each of three adjacent

Plouescat's red faces

The council of **Plouescat** attained notoriety in 1987, when its members decided they could no longer live with the embarrassing presence of an exceptionally phallic rock on one of the local beaches and dynamited it to smithereens in the dead of night. Local artists responded by creating several much more embarrassing substitutes, which you might care to look out for around the town's beaches

beaches, the nicest being *Poul Foën* (Ⓣ02.98.69.81.80; closed mid-Sept to mid-June). In the town, you'll find a high-roofed old wooden market hall for picnic provisions, and an unexpected, slightly surreal statue of a seahorse with a yin and yang symbol in its tail. Of the **hotels**, the best value is the little *Roc'h-Ar-Mor*, 18 rue Ar Mor, right on the beach at Porsmeur (Ⓣ02.98.69.63.01, Ⓔroch.ar.mor@wanadoo.fr; ❶; closed Oct–March). Roscoff to Brest **buses** stop at Plouescat before turning inland.

At the village of **Keremma**, inland from the sea on the way between Plouescat and Brignogan, there's another lovely little **campsite** (Ⓣ02.98.61.62.79; closed early Sept to late June), set along a green avenue lined with meadows of purple and yellow flowers.

Brignogan-Plage

BRIGNOGAN-PLAGE, on the next *aber*, has a small natural harbour, once the lair of wreckers, with beaches and weather-beaten rocks to either side, as well as its own menhir. The tide here recedes way out towards the mouth of the bay, leaving surreal clumps of seaweed-coated stone bulging up among the stranded boats. The **plage de Méného**, 2km west of town, is a gem of a beach.

There are two high-season **campsites** in the vicinity, both with two stars – the central municipal site at Keravézan, on the western side of the bay slightly north of Brignogan town centre, *Camping de la Côte des Legendes* (Ⓣ02.98.83.41.65, Ⓔcamping-cote-des-legendes@wanadoo.fr; closed Nov–March), which is 50m from the Centre Nautique, and the *Camping du Phare*, east of Brignogan (Ⓣ02.98.83.45.06 Ⓦwww.camping-du-phare.com; closed Oct–March) – while the **hotel** *Castel Regis* (Ⓣ02.98.83.40.22, Ⓦwww.castelregis.com; ❹; closed Oct–March) is a trifle expensive for what it is, but does have an outdoor swimming pool (in summer), a sauna, tennis courts and a beautiful location among the rocks right at the headland. *Ar Reder Mor*, at 35 av de Gaulle in the centre of Brignogan town (Ⓣ02.98.83.40.09, Ⓔarredermor@wanadoo.fr; ❷), is cheaper but fairly nondescript. For details of local opportunities to learn sailing and riding, contact the **tourist office** in Brignogan's main square (July & Aug Mon 10am–1pm & 4–7pm, Tues–Sat 9.30am–1pm & 4–7pm, Sun 10am–1pm; Sept–June Tues–Fri 10am–noon & 2–4.30pm, Sat 10am–noon; Ⓣ02.98.83.41.08, Ⓦwww.ot-brignogan-plage.fr).

Plouguerneau, Lilia and Grouannec

Moving west along the D10 you'll come to the inland village of **PLOUGUERNEAU**; with just over 5000 inhabitants it was the unlikely recipient in 1990 of the **Prix de l'Europe**, awarded each year by the Council of Europe to the most exemplary European community. Previous winners included Istanbul, Avignon and The Hague; Plouguerneau was chosen largely on the basis of its vigorous and successful twinning with the German town of Edingen-Neckerhausen, near Heidelberg, which has so far produced more than twenty Franco-German marriages.

With little to keep you in Plouguerneau, push on 5km northwest to the dramatic waterfront community of **LILIA,** a perfect setting for the **hotel** *Castel Ac'h* (Ⓣ02.98.37.16.16; ❹), which has an excellent seafood **restaurant** that serves what amounts to a Breton version of sushi. In summer, pleasure boats from here take a short cruise out to bob at the foot of the shaft of the **Vierge lighthouse** – at 78m it's said to be the tallest in Europe (boats operate Easter–Sept; standard cruise €14; restricted visits to the lighthouse itself are possible mid-June to mid-Sept, €2.50; for boat schedules call Vedettes des Abers Ⓣ02.98.04.74.94).

Plouguerneau is also near to an unexpected pleasure, the church of **Notre Dame de Grouannec**, a small but complete parish close ensemble about 4km further inland. It has been extensively restored, and looks all the better for it, with its fountain, ossuary, mini-cloister and profusion of gargoyles.

L'Aber-Wrac'h

The *aber* between Plouguerneau and the yachting port of **L'ABER-WRAC'H** has a stepping-stone crossing just upstream from the bridge at Lanillis, built in Gallo-Roman times, and its long cut stones still cross the three channels of water (access off the D28 signposted "Rascoll"), and continue past farm buildings to the right.

L'Aber-Wrac'h itself – which you may well also see referred to as "Landeda" – is a promising place to spend a little time. It's an attractive, modest-sized resort, within easy reach of a whole range of sandy beaches and a couple of worthwhile excursions. Beyond the tiny fishing port, which is home to a busy sailing school, the Baie des Anges stretches away towards the Atlantic, with the only sound the cry of seagulls feasting on the oyster beds. The coastal waters nearby are prime territory for **divers**; boat trips can be arranged through Abersub (Ⓣ02.98.04.81.22, Ⓦperso.wanadoo.fr/abersub).

At the start of the bay, a couple of hundred metres past the town's little strip of bars and restaurants, the irresistible *Hôtel la Baie des Anges*, 350 rte des Anges (Ⓣ02.98.04.90.04, Ⓦwww.baie-des-anges.com; ❺; closed Jan & Feb), commands stunning views out to sea from the start of its vast curve; part of the *Châteux & Hotels de France* organization, it's a peaceful and exceptionally comfortable place to **stay**, featuring a spacious bar with a small waterfront terrace – for the use of guests only. The municipal **campsite**, the three-star *Camping des Abers* (Ⓣ02.98.04.93.35, Ⓦwww.camping-des-abers.com; closed late Sept to April), nestles amid the dunes at the very tip of the headland.

The best **restaurant** in L'Aber-Wrac'h, *Le Brennig* (Ⓣ02.98.04.81.12; closed Tues & early Nov to Feb), is back at the other end of the main strip, and prepares fine menus from €23.50. However, you can be more sure of getting a table at the *Cap'tain* in the port proper (Ⓣ02.98.04.82.03; closed Mon in low season, plus all Feb), a busy but friendly crêperie that offers continuous service not only of crêpes but also any seafood speciality you care to name.

Clearly signposted 4km west of L'Aber-Wrac'h, on the right side of the next inlet along, L'Aber-Benoît, the **oyster beds** of **Prat-Ar-Coum** (Ⓣ02.98.04.00.12, Ⓦwww.prat-ar-coum.fr) are renowned for producing the best oysters in western Brittany. A quayside stall sells them year-round, and a small restaurant is open in July and August only.

Portsall

At the small harbour of **PORTSALL**, 5km along the coast from L'Aber-Benoît, the **Espace Amoco Cadiz** (July & Aug Tues–Sun 2.30–6.30pm; Sept–June Sat & Sun 2.30–6.30pm; free) commemorates a defining moment in local history: on March 17, 1978, the sinking of the *Amoco Cadiz* super-tanker resulted in an **oil spill** that devastated 350km of the Breton coastline, and threatened to ruin the local economy. Displays and films document not only the immense task of cleaning up the mess, but also the long legal battle to obtain compensation from the "multinational monster" responsible. The French government eventually obtained 1045 million francs in 1992, of which 100 million were passed on to local councils and communities. The ship's huge **anchor** now stands in the car park across from the hall, while the wreck itself, 1100 metres off shore, has become a popular dive site.

Trémazan and around

Once past Portsall, the coast becomes a glorious succession of dunes and open spaces, with long beaches stretching at low tide way out towards tiny islands. Each little inlet here seems to shelter a treasure of a beach, ideal for family swimming, while bracing walks lead through the heather-covered headlands that abut the open sea. One especially romantic spot comes just 5km beyond Portsall, where the crumbling walls of the *Sleeping Beauty*-style **castle** of **Trémazan** look down on a magnificent beach. The fleeing Tristan and Iseult are said to have made their first landing in Brittany here, and the cracked ivy-covered keep still stands proud, pierced by a large heart-shaped hole. The castle is not formally open to the public; it's totally overgrown, and to reach it you have to scramble your way through the brambles that fill its former moat. Once you're here, however, it's a real haven for a summer afternoon.

In the nearby nondescript village of **KERSAINT LANDUNVEZ**, the *Hostellerie du Castel* (☎02.98.48.63.35; ❸; restaurant closed Sun eve & Mon, hotel closed Oct–March except for advance reservations), makes an ideal overnight stop, with very comfortable and moderately priced en-suite rooms, and a good restaurant. If you are continuing west to Porspoder pause to look at the exquisite wooden seaside **chapel of St Samson** on the way.

Porspoder

PORSPODER is a pretty quiet resort, but does serve as a centre for the many campers who set themselves up on the dunes of the **Presqu'île St-Laurent** which lies opposite. It's an attractive place to be, looking out over the ocean, and relatively busy in season, but rather bleak in winter when many of the surrounding houses are unoccupied. There's a cheap **hotel**, the *Pen Ar Bed* (☎02.98.89.90.38; ❷; closed Oct–March), on the long seafront rue de l'Europe.

Le Conquet and around

LE CONQUET, the southernmost of the *abers* resorts, at the far western tip of Brittany and 24km beyond Brest, makes the best holiday base in the region. A wonderful place, scarcely developed, it is flanked by a long **beach** of clean white sand, protected from the winds by the narrow spit of the Kermorvan peninsula, and has ferry access to the islands of Ouessant and Molène. It is very much a working fishing village, the grey-stone houses leading down to the stone jetties of a cramped harbour, which occasionally floods, to the intense amusement of the locals, the waves washing over the cars left by tourists making the trip to Ouessant – so leave your car slightly inland while visiting the island.

The **coast** around Le Conquet is low-lying, not the rocky confrontation that one might expect, and Kermorvan, across the estuary, seems to glide into the sea – its shallow cliffs topped by a strip of turf. Apart from the lighthouse at the end, the peninsula is just grassland, bare of buildings and a lovely place to walk in the evening across the footbridge from Le Conquet.

A good walk 5km south of Le Conquet brings you to the lighthouse at **Pointe St-Mathieu**, looking out to the islands of Ouessant and Molène from its site among the ruins of the Benedictine **Abbaye de St-Mathieu**. A small exhibition (April & May Wed, Sat & Sun 2.30–6.30pm; June & Sept Wed–Mon 2.30–6.30pm; July & Aug Wed–Sat & Mon 10am–12.30pm & 2–7pm, Sun 2–7pm; Oct–March Wed & Sat 2.30–6.30pm; €1.50) explains the abbey's history, including the legend that it holds the skull of St Matthew, brought here from Ethiopia by local seafarers.

Practicalities

Buses from Brest drop you at various points in Le Conquet, with the one daily express service going all the way to where the boats depart for Ouessant. The *Relais du Vieux Port*, 1 quai Drellac'h (ⓣ02.98.89.15.91; ❷; closed Jan), offers a handful of inexpensive but attractive **rooms** right by the jetty in Le Conquet, and has a simple crêperie downstairs. Nearby, the larger *Pointe Ste-Barbe* (ⓣ02.98.89.00.26, ⓦwww.hotelpointesaintebarbe.com; ❷-❼; hotel closed mid-Nov to mid-Dec, restaurant closed Mon in low season) offers amazing sea views to guests in its more expensive rooms, and has a great restaurant, where menus start at €16. There's also a well-equipped two-star **campsite** over on the Kermorvan peninsula, *Le Théven* (ⓣ02.98.89.06.90; closed Oct–March). **Market** day in Le Conquet is Tuesday.

The *Hostellerie de la Pointe St-Mathieu*, housed in a thirteenth-century stone structure opposite the abbey entrance at Pointe St-Mathieu (ⓣ02.98.89.00.19, ⓦwww.pointe-saint-mathieu.com; ❹; closed Feb & Sun eve in low season), is a top-quality restaurant with menus from €25–68 featuring foie gras, *pot au feu* (a vegetable and beef stew). and blue lobster; the *hostellerie* also has a modern wing of tasteful ocean-view rooms, an indoor swimming pool and a sauna.

Ouessant and Molène

The island of **Ouessant** (Ushant in English) lies 30km northwest of Le Conquet. It was first described by the geographer Pytheas as early as 325 BC, under the name of Uxisama. Standing at the outermost end of a chain of smaller islands and half-submerged granite rocks, its lighthouse at Creac'h (said to be have the strongest beam in the world) is regarded as the entrance to the English Channel. Most of the archipelago is uninhabited, save perhaps for a few rabbits, but **Molène**, midway between Le Conquet and Ouessant, has a village and can also be visited.

Ouessant

The ride to **OUESSANT** is generally a tranquil affair, though the ferry has to pick its way from buoy to buoy, through a sea which is liable suddenly to

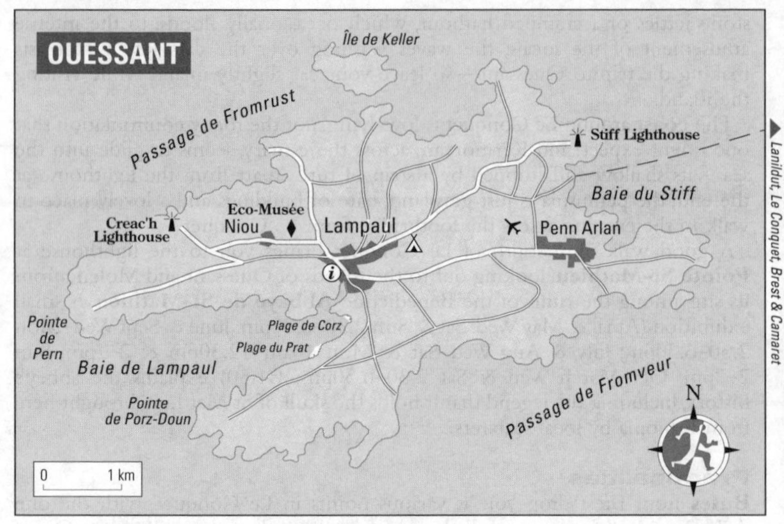

become choppy and dangerous to navigate. There have been many wrecks among the reefs, most famously the *Drummond Castle* which foundered as the finale to a concert celebrating the end of its voyage from Cape Town to England in June 1896. For all its storms, though, the climate is mild – Ouessant even records the highest mean temperatures in France in January and February.

You arrive on Ouessant at the modern **harbour** in the ominous-sounding Baie du Stiff. There are a scattering of houses here, and dotted about the island, but the only town (with the only hotels and restaurants) is 4km distant at **LAMPAUL**. Everybody from the boat heads here, either by the bus that meets each arriving ferry, by bike, or in a long walking procession that straggles along the one road. Bicycle rental (€10–14 per day; rental operators meet arriving ferries) is the most convenient option, as the island is really too big to explore on foot; it's worth going for a (more expensive) mountain bike as many of the tracks are of uneven terrain.

As well as its more mundane facilities, Lampaul has Ouessant's best **beaches** sprawled around its bay. There are few specific sights but the town **cemetery** is worth visiting, with its war memorial listing all the ships in which the townsfolk were lost, and its graves of unknown sailors washed ashore. A unique Ouessant tradition is also on show in the cemetery chapel – an array of wax *proëlla* crosses, which were used during the funerals of those islanders who never returned from the sea, to symbolize their absent remains.

At **NIOU**, 1km northwest, the Maison du Niou is actually two houses, which together form the **Éco-Musée d'Ouessant** (Easter–Sept Tues–Sun 10.30am–6.30pm; Oct–Easter Tues–Sun 1.30–5.30pm; €3.20, or €6.30 for combined admission with the Musée des Phares et Balises). One house contains a museum of island history, the other is a reconstruction of a traditional island house, complete with two massive "box-beds", one for the parents and the other for the children. Another kilometre west, the **Creac'h lighthouse** contains the **Musée des Phares et Balises** (same hours as the Éco-Musée; €4 or €6.30 for both museums), a small museum about lighthouses. It makes a

Getting to Ouessant and Molène

Both islands are served by at least one **ferry** each day from Le Conquet and Brest; however, it is not practicable to visit more than one in a single day. Ferries can be very crowded in summer, and it's well worth booking your **tickets** in advance if at all possible.

Penn Ar Bed (Ⓣ02.98.80.80.80, Ⓦwww.pennarbed.fr) sail to Ouessant and Molène all year, with one to six daily departures from **Le Conquet** (first sailing at 8am daily mid-July to August; Ouessant return €25.90, to Molène €22.80), and one to three daily from **Brest**, always including one at 8.30am, which is the only one that stops at Molène (Ouessant return €29; Molène return €26.80). They also depart from **Camaret** to Ouessant at 8.40am on Wednesday from early April until early September, and Monday to Saturday at 8.40am from early July until the end of August (return €26.80). Only on Fridays between mid-July and August is it possible to sail from Camaret to Molène, at 8.40am (return €22.80).

Finist'Mer (Ⓦwww.finist-mer.fr) operate high-speed ferries to Ouessant in summer only. From **Camaret**, they offer a daily departure from mid-June until early July, and again from late August until mid-September, at 8.45am, while from early July until late August the boat leaves daily at 9.25am (Ⓣ02.98.27.88.44; return €25.50). From **Le Conquet**, they offer two to five departures daily between April and September, with the first one being at 8.40am from early July until late August, and 9.30am otherwise (Ⓣ02.98.89.16.61; €24.50 return). Between early July and late August, they also sail to Ouessant from **Lanildut**, 25km northwest of Brest, with the first departure from Le Conquet calling there at 9.10am (Ⓣ08.00.50.03.88; €25.50 return).

In addition, you can **fly** to Ouessant with **Finist'Air** (Ⓣ02.98.84.64.87, Ⓦwww.finistair.fr). The fifteen-minute flights leave Brest's Guipavas airport daily at 8.30am and 4.45pm, with an adult one-way fare of €60.98 and groups of three or more adults costing €50.31 each.

good starting point from which to set out along the barren and exposed rocks of the north coast. Particularly in September and other times of migration, it's a remarkable spot for birdwatching, frequented by puffins, storm petrels and cormorants. The star-shaped formations of crumbling walls you can see were built so that the sheep – peculiarly tame here – could shelter from the strong winds.

Practicalities

General information on Ouessant is available from the **tourist office** in the main square in Lampaul (Mon–Sat 10am–noon & 1.30–5pm, Sun 10am–noon; Ⓣ02.98.48.85.83, Ⓦwww.ot-ouessant.fr). The town boasts a small **hostel**, *La Croix Rouge* (Ⓣ02.98.48.84.53, Ⓔajouessant@club-internet.fr), where a dorm bed plus breakfast costs €13.35. Also in Lampaul, the adjacent **hotels** *Océan* (Ⓣ02.98.48.80.03; ❸; closed mid-Nov to mid-Dec; currently closed for renovations, call to check reopening date), and *Fromveur* (Ⓣ02.98.48.81.30; ❸; closed Jan to early Feb & mid-Nov to mid-Dec) both offer reasonable renovated rooms; *Fromveur*'s restaurant specializes in traditional island cooking, which consists of attempting to render seaweed and mutton as palatable as possible. The *Roch Ar Mor*, just down the street (Ⓣ02.98.48.80.19, Ⓦperso.wanadoo.fr/rocharmor; ❹; closed Jan to mid-Feb & late Nov to mid-Dec), is a marginally more attractive alternative hotel. There is a small official **campsite**, the *Penn ar Bed* (Ⓣ02.98.48.84.65; closed Oct–March). You could, in fact, camp almost anywhere on the island, making arrangements with the nearest farmhouse (which may well let out rooms, too).

If you've just come for a day and don't fancy eating at the *Fromveur* or *Roch Ar Mor* **restaurants** (both offering menus at €20), it's a good idea to buy a picnic before you set out – the Lampaul shops have limited and rather pricey supplies.

Molène

MOLÈNE is quite well populated for a sparse strip of sand. The port itself is better protected than that of Ouessant, and so there are more fishermen based here. The island's inhabitants derive their income from seaweed collection and drying – and to an extent from crabbing and crayfish, which they gather on foot, canoe and even tractor at low tide. The tides are more than usually dramatic, halving or doubling the island's territory at a stroke and giving the island its name, which comes from the Breton for "the bald isle".

There are no real sights here and walking the rocks and the coast is the basic activity, though, as on Ouessant, the island **cemetery** is poignant and interesting. Illustrating small community life is the concentration of babies' graves from a typhoid epidemic in the last century; marked by silver crosses they are repainted each November 1.

Few visitors come for longer than an afternoon, but it's possible to stay in the **rooms** – very chilly in winter – at *Kastell An Doal* (Ⓣ02.98.07.39.11; ❸; closed Jan), one of the old buildings by the port. It's also possible to arrange to stay in a private house (for details, call the town hall on Ⓣ02.98.07.39.05).

Brest

Set in a magnificent natural harbour, known as the Rade de Brest, the city of **BREST** is doubly sheltered from the ocean storms by both the bulk of Léon to the north, and by the Crozon peninsula to the south. The Rade (or roadstead) is entered by the narrow deep-water channel of the Goulet de Brest, 5km long and 1.5km wide, with steep banks on both sides.

As one of the finest natural harbours in Europe, Brest has always played an important role in war and in trade whenever peace allowed. All the great names in French strategic planning – including Richelieu, Colbert, Vauban and Napoléon – have been instrumental in developing the port, which is today the base of the French Atlantic Fleet. Its dry dock can accommodate ships of up to 500,000 tonnes and, as a ship-repair centre, it ranks sixth in the world.

During World War II, Brest was relentlessly bombed to prevent the Germans from using it as a submarine base. When the Americans liberated it on September 18, 1944, after a six-week siege, they found the town devastated beyond recognition. In order for the city to resume normal life as soon as possible, rebuilding was rushed at the expense of restoration, and the architecture of the postwar town is raw and bleak. There have been attempts, as in Caen, to green the city, but despite the heaviest rainfall in France, the site has proved too windswept to respond fully to these efforts.

From across the bay, the city can look appealing but on closer inspection, it is a real effort of will to decide to stop longer than it takes to change buses or trains. The roads are racetracks; the suburbs, remorselessly industrial; and the last war comprehensively destroyed any historic interest that may once have

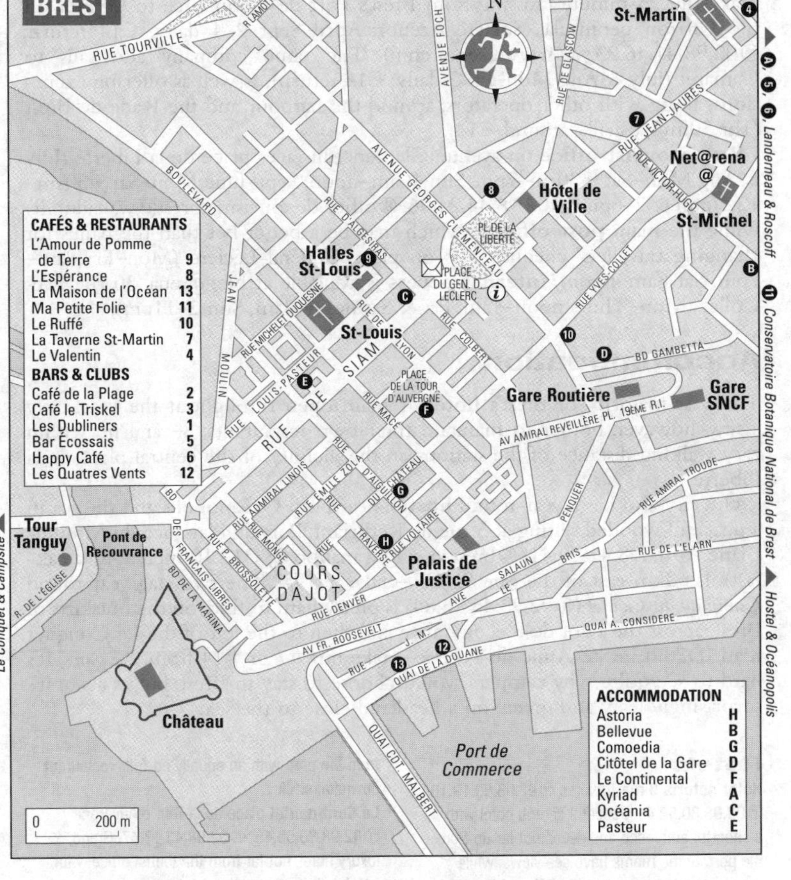

existed. The most rational reason for an outsider to visit would probably be for the **bagpipe festival**, held here for three days in August.

Arrival and information

The **gare SNCF** and **gare routière** (☎02.98.44.46.73) stand shoulder-to-shoulder in place du 19ème RI at the bottom of avenue Clemenceau. Though right at the end of the railway system, Brest is just four hours away from Paris by TGV (which follows the northern route, via Morlaix and Rennes; the journey via Quimper takes much longer). **Bus** services include those to Plouescat and Roscoff, the Crozon peninsula via Le Faou, and to Le Conquet.

Brest's **airport** (☎02.98.32.01.00), 9km northeast of the centre at Guipavas, is served by flights to Ouessant (see p.309). An **airport shuttle** bus runs from the *gare SNCF* and the tourist office (6–11 daily; 25min; ☎02.98.32.01.00). All the major international **car rental** chains, such as Avis, Hertz, National and Europcar, are represented at the airport.

As well as the sailings to Ouessant, detailed on p.309, in summer **boats** make the 25-minute crossing from Brest's Port de Commerce to Le Fret on the Crozon peninsula (Société Azenor; April–Sept 2–4 daily; €14 return; Ⓣ02.98.41.46.23, Ⓦwww.azenor.com). The same company also sails to Camaret (July & Aug Mon–Fri 2 daily; €14 return), as well as offering excursions, along with other operators, around the harbour and the Rade de Brest (1hr 30min; usually around €14).

Brest's **tourist office** on avenue Clemenceau faces place de la Liberté (July & Aug Mon–Sat 9.30am–7pm, Sun 10am–noon; Sept–June Mon–Sat 9.30am–12.30pm & 2–6pm; Ⓣ02.98.44.24.96, Ⓔoffice.de.tourisme.brest@wanadoo.fr) while the main **post office** – which may be a better bet than the banks for changing travellers' cheques – is on place Général-Leclerc (Mon–Fri 8am–7pm, Sat 8am–noon). **Internet access** is available at Net@rena, 30 rue Yves Collet (Mon–Thurs noon–1am, Fri & Sat noon–4am, Sun 2–11pm).

Accommodation

The vast majority of Brest's **hotels** remain open throughout the year; only a few, however, bother to maintain their own restaurants. Several lie within easy walking distance of the stations, in the vicinity of the central place de la Liberté.

The city also has a year-round **hostel**, near both Océanopolis and the sea in a peaceful wooded setting at 5 rue de Kerbriant, Port de Plaisance du Moulin-Blanc (Ⓣ02.98.41.90.41, Ⓔbrest.aj.cis@wanadoo.fr; €12.10 including breakfast). It's 3km east of the *gare SNCF* – take bus #7. The two-star, year-round *Camping du Goulet* (Ⓣ02.98.45.86.84) is pretty hard to find, on the outskirts of Brest, across the Pont de Recouvrance and then to the left of the Le Conquet road (D789) in Ste-Anne du Portzic – take bus #7 or #14 from the *gares*. It's hard to see quite why campers would choose to stay in Brest, but as a site it's surprisingly leafy and green, on a headland close to the sea.

Hotels

Hôtel Astoria 9 rue Traverse Ⓣ02.98.80.19.10, Ⓕ02.98.80.52.41. Peaceful central hotel with a cheerful ambience and decor, not far up from the port. Some rooms have sea views, while the cheapest only have a sink. Closed 3 weeks Dec–Jan. ❶

Hôtel Bellevue 53 rue Victor-Hugo Ⓣ02.98.80.51.78, Ⓦwww.hotelbellevue.fr. Six-storey sound-proofed building, equipped with a lift and bright, modern but not very fancy rooms. A short walk from the *gare SNCF* and well on the way to the lively St-Martin area, near the St-Michel church. Distant sea views. ❸

Citôtel de la Gare 4 bd Gambetta Ⓣ02.98.44.47.01, Ⓕ02.98.43.34.07. En-suite rooms opposite the stations; you can pay a little extra for an uninterrupted view of the Rade de Brest from the upper storeys. Internet access for guests. ❸

Hôtel Comoedia 21 rue d'Aguillon Ⓣ02.98.46.54.82. Simple but very cheap rooms – none of them en suite – in a quiet street just up from the port, with an equally no-frills restaurant downstairs. ❶

Le Continental place de la Tour d'Auvergne Ⓣ02.98.80.50.40, Ⓕ02.98.43.17.47. Grand, luxury hotel, not far from the tourist office, with helpful staff and spotlessly clean rooms, several of them with fine Art Deco features; rooms on the fourth floor have large balconies. ❼

Hôtel Kyriad 157 rue Jean-Jaurès Ⓣ02.98.43.58.58, Ⓦwww.kyriadbrest.com. Although the rooms are on the sterile and small side, this hotel enjoys a good location near the town's nightlife, has good buffet breakfasts (€7.50) and is close to a free public car park. ❹

Hôtel Océania 82 rue de Siam Ⓣ02.98.80.66.66, Ⓕ02.98.80.65.50. Good-quality upmarket hotel, offering large, attractively fitted rooms on the town's principal thoroughfare, plus a classy restaurant. ❹

Hôtel Pasteur 29 rue Louis-Pasteur Ⓣ02.98.46.08.73, Ⓕ02.98.43.46.80. Clean, good-value budget hotel, offering plain en-suite rooms above a bar near the St-Louis church. ❷

The Town

As a tourist centre, Brest has little to offer, and few relics of the past remain. The fifteenth-century **château** looks impressive on its headland, and offers a superb panorama of the city, but it's not especially interesting inside. Three of its towers house part of the collection of the **Musée National de la Marine**, including a German "pocket submarine" based in Brest during World War II (April to mid-Sept daily 10am–6.30pm; mid-Sept to March Wed–Mon 10am–noon & 2–6pm; €4.60). The same institution operates six other museums in France, including one at Port Louis near Lorient (see p.382).

The fourteenth-century **Tour Tanguy** on the opposite bank of the River Penfeld, with its conical slate roof, serves as the **Musée du Vieux Brest** (June–Sept daily 10am–noon & 2–7pm; Oct–May Wed & Thurs 2–5pm, Sat & Sun 2–6pm; free). Dioramas convey a vivid impression of just how attractive a city Brest used to be, before World War II.

The **Conservatoire Botanique National de Brest**, a short distance north of Océanopolis in the Parc du Vallon de Stang-Alar beyond the football stadium, claims to be second in Europe only to Kew Gardens (gardens: daily: July to mid-Sept 9am–8pm; mid-Sept to June 9am–6pm; free; greenhouses: July to mid-Sept Sun–Thurs 2–5.30pm; mid-Sept to June by guided tour only, Sun 4.30pm; €3; bus #3, #17, #25 or #27, stop "Palaren").

If all this fails to impress, you can always stroll through the area known as the **Cours Dajot**, which displays the docklands in all their glory. It holds schools of various naval disciplines, arsenals, the marine records office and the **Pont de Recouvrance**, the largest drawbridge in Europe.

Océanopolis

Brest's most up-to-the-minute attraction is **Océanopolis** (daily: April to early Sept 9am–6pm; early Sept to March Tues–Sat 10am–5pm, Sun 10am–6pm; €14.50; Ⓦwww.oceanopolis.com), a couple of kilometres east of the city centre beside the Port de Plaisance du Moulin-Blanc, and accessible on bus #7. Year on year, this futuristic complex seems to get larger and larger (not to mention more and more expensive), and currently consists of three distinct **aquariums**. Its original white dome, now known as the **Temperate Pavilion**, focuses on the Breton littoral and Finistère's fishing industry, with its half-million gallons of water holding all kinds of fish, seals, molluscs, seaweed and sea anemones. The emphasis is very much on the edible, with displays on the life-cycle of a scallop, for example, culminating in a detailed recipe.

To that has been added a **Tropical Pavilion**, with a tankful of ferocious-looking sharks plus a myriad of rainbow-hued smaller fish that populate a highly convincing coral reef; a **Polar Pavilion**, complete with polar bears and penguins; and a **3-D cinema**. Everything's very high-tech, and perhaps a little too earnest for some visitors' tastes, but it's quite possible to spend a whole entertaining day on site – especially if you take the assorted restaurants, snack bars and gift stores into consideration.

Eating and drinking

As well as a concentration of low-priced places in the immediate area of the stations, Brest also offers a wider assortment of **restaurants**. Rue Jean-Jaurès, which climbs up east from the place de la Liberté, holds plenty of bistros and bars, while just off to the north, place Guérin is the centre of the student-dominated *quartier* St-Martin.

L'Amour de Pomme de Terre 23 rue des Halles ☎02.98.43.48.51. The name says it all: this central restaurant, facing the market *halles*, specializes not merely in potatoes, but in one single kind of potato, the "samba". The most basic dish is simply a baked potato topped with cheese or sausage, but the eccentric owner has also invented all kinds of strange treatments and concoctions, typically costing around €20, and there are also some tasty Breton stews. Open daily until late.

L'Espérance 6 place de la Liberté ☎02.98.44.25.29. Busy, inexpensive conventional brasserie in the corner of the square opposite the Hôtel de Ville, with a wide range of imaginative menus, achieving a good balance of meat and fish dishes, that start at €13.80 midweek. Closed Sun eve & Mon, plus last two weeks in Aug.

La Maison de l'Océan 2 quai de la Douane ☎02.98.80.44.84. Blue-hued fish restaurant down by the port, open daily for lunch and dinner, and serving wonderful assortments of seafood menus from €14.50.

Ma Petite Folie plage du Moulin-Blanc ☎02.98.42.44.42. Converted fishing boat, moored in the pleasure port, which serves a wonderfully fishy €20 set menu and also offers a wide range of *à la carte* dishes and daily specials. Closed Sun & two weeks in mid-Aug.

Le Ruffé 1bis rue Yves-Collet ☎02.98.46.07.70. An attractive place between the *gare SNCF* and the tourist office, open late, that prides itself on good, traditional French seafood dishes, served on menus costing €17 and upwards. Closed Sun eve.

La Taverne St-Martin 92 rue Jean-Jaurès ☎02.98.80.48.17. Warm and friendly brasserie/restaurant, a few hundred metres up from the tourist office, behind a wooden half-timbered facade. Menus €13.50–18.30, plus lots of *à la carte* snacks. Steak tartare is the house speciality. Open daily 11am–midnight.

Le Valentin 16 rue Louis Blanc ☎02.98.33.20.00. Delicious, rich Southwestern cuisine – *fricassée*, *confit de canard*, and meaty stews – served by a charming husband-and-wife team near the Église St-Martin, with outstanding desserts and a great walnut brandy. Closed Wed & Sun.

Bars and nightlife

Brest is unusual by Breton standards in having plenty of lively **bars.** The basic choice lies between hanging out with the sailors and fishermen down by the port, with the business community around the place de la Liberté, or with the seriously trendy student population in the St-Martin quarter, high up on and around Jean-Jaurès. In July and August, Thursday night is party night, with a free open-air festival taking place along the quai de la Douane.

Café de la Plage 32 rue Massillon. Classic-looking open-fronted bar, on one corner of place Guérin. Heavy maroon decor and a transient population of citizens of all ages who share a common interest in talking at the tops of their voices. Closed Sun.

Café le Triskel 31 rue Massillon. Pub-style place with wooden tables, across the square from the *Plage*. Students and Breton activists come to drink and listen to the odd bit of music (literally).

Les Dubliners 28 rue Mathieu-Donnart. Lively Irish pub in the St-Martin district, about ten minutes' walk from St-Martin church. Open daily from mid-afternoon until late, with Irish dancing on Mondays and live music on Thursdays and Sundays.

Bar Écossais 241 rue Jean-Jaurès. An unlikely spectacle, way up at the top of the hill and positively festooned with Scottish memorabilia, which attracts an exuberant Celtic crowd. On November 11 each year (the anniversary of its opening), the owner hides a large Scottish shield in an unnamed pub somewhere in the city, and the regulars, dressed in full Highland costume and making passable attempts at reproducing the drone of the bagpipes by means of holding their noses and grunting, set off in a drunken stupor to try and find it.

Happy Café 193 rue Jean-Jaurès. Popular gay bar where the flashing lights bounce off corrugated iron walls and the clientele is as offbeat and adventurous as the decor.

Les Quatres Vents 18 quai de la Douane. Busy, friendly café-bar with a nautical-themed interior down by the port, which also sells simple snacks.

Around Brest

ST-RÉNAN, 15km northwest of Brest on the D5 has no real attractions but it's quite a pleasant small town, and there are two noteworthy **prehistoric sites** in the immediate area.

Lanrivoaré

Five kilometres northwest of St-Rénan is the **church** of **LANRIVOARÉ**, which has a tiny plot in its graveyard where, alongside eight round stones, the 7777 victims of a fifth-century massacre are supposed to lie buried. Legend records that the stones were transformed from loaves of bread by St Hervé – but they're in fact most likely to be "cursing-stones", which exist in several Irish chapels and were used for calling down disease or destruction on an enemy. The person invoking the curse, after a certain number of prayers, turned the stone round seven times.

The Menhir de Kerloas

To find the **Menhir de Kerloas** (also known as Kervéatous or Plouarzel), you need to walk or drive (there's no bus) about 5km west of St-Rénan on the *old* Plouarzel road, parallel to the more modern D5. The menhir stands in a small clearing hedged in by fields, and is the highest point for miles around in these flatlands. Although the tip was knocked off by lightning a little over 200 years ago (and was subsequently used as a cattle-trough), it is at 11m the tallest menhir still standing in western Europe. Newly married couples would rub their naked bodies against the **circular protuberances**, over a metre from the ground on either side, in the hope of begetting children.

Towards the Crozon peninsula

Heading south from Brest, cyclists and pedestrians can cut straight over to the Crozon peninsula by **ferry**. A regular service will shuttle you across the bay to Le Fret, or, on weekdays during July and August, to Camaret. The ferry doesn't, however, carry cars, so **drivers** have a longer and more circuitous route, crossing the Elorn River over the vast spans of the **Pont Albert-Louppe** (42m high and almost 1km long) and then skirting the estuaries of the **Plougastel peninsula**.

Plougastel-Daoulas, just across the bridge, is at the edge of the main parish closes region, see p.302.

Daoulas

Ten kilometres beyond Plougastel-Daoulas, the **abbey** at **DAOULAS** holds Brittany's only Romanesque cloister. It now stands beautiful and isolated at the edge of cool monastery gardens, since its surrounding buildings were destroyed during the Revolution. The abbey is a short walk above the town, and a welcome oasis on a hot summer's day. It doubles as a cultural centre for Finistère, staging ambitious historical exhibitions lasting for around six months at a time (daily: mid-May to June & Sept to mid-Nov 10am–6pm; July & Aug 11am–7pm; current information on ⓣ02.98.25.84.39 or ⓦwww.abbaye-daoulas.com; €6 for the abbey, gardens and exhibition).

Le Faou

From Daoulas, the motorway and railway cut down to Châteaulin and Quimper. For Crozon, you'll need to veer west at **LE FAOU**, a tiny medieval port which has retained some of its sixteenth-century gabled houses and is set on its own estuary. From beside the pretty little village **church** – whose porch contains some intriguing carved Apostles – a sheltered corniche follows the river to the sea, where there are sailing and windsurfing facilities.

Le Faou has two good and very similar Logis de France **hotels**, both with top-class restaurants – the *Relais de la Place* (Ⓣ02.98.81.91.19; ❷; closed Sat & all of Jan), and the *Hôtel de Beauvoir* (Ⓣ02.98.81.90.31, Ⓦwww.hotel-beauvoir.com; ❹; closed Mon & Tues lunch mid-June to mid-Oct, Mon lunch & Sun eve mid-Oct to mid-June). The one snag is that they're not in the most attractive part of town, near the river, but a few hundred metres south in the newer and much noisier main square place aux Foires.

The Crozon peninsula

Though the spectacular **Crozon peninsula**, thrusting out into the Atlantic between Léon and Cornouaille, is almost entirely given over to tourism, its wild beaches and craggy cliffs remain remarkably unspoiled, and it's hard to beat as a family destination. **Morgat** is a classic traditional resort, arrayed along a splendid curve of golden sand, while **Camaret** is more of a historic port with a sideline in superlative seafood restaurants. For an initial overview of the layout of this whole dramatic promontory, it pays to start by making the detour to climb up the **Menez-Hom** at its inland, eastern end.

The entire peninsula forms part of the **Parc Naturel Régional d'Armorique**, a haphazard area stretching from the forest of Huelgoat to the island of Ouessant that is, in principle at least, a protected natural landscape area. What this means in reality is hard to fathom. Doubtless there are firm

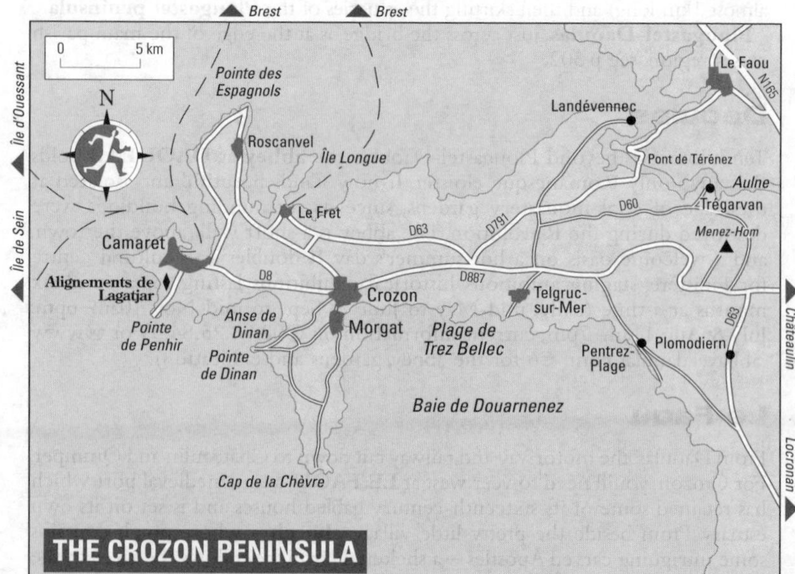

Ferries to the peninsula

Regular summer ferries run from the port du Commerce in **Brest** to **Le Fret** and **Camaret**. It's also possible to take a ferry direct from Le Fret or Camaret to **Océanopolis** for the day (Société Azénor; July & Aug departures from Le Fret Mon–Sat 9am, 10.30am & 1pm, Sun 10.30am, from Camaret daily 10am; April–June & Sept departures from Le Fret only, Tues–Fri 1pm; ⓣ02.98.41.46.23, ⓦwww.azenor.com; €26.50 return, including admission).

French bylaws against disturbing the wild flowers; however, for some reason these don't prevent nuclear submarines from lurking in the bay of Brest, nor low-flying helicopters from sporadically sweeping the skies above.

The **tourist office** for the whole peninsula is at Crozon (see p.318) and there are smaller tourist offices at Camaret and Morgat. **Public transport** around the peninsula is limited to routes between the main towns and tourist resorts: the Brest–Camaret bus stops at Crozon and Morgat, while the Quimper–Camaret bus stops at Locronan, St-Nic Pentrez, Telgruc-sur-mer and Crozon.

The Menez-Hom and around

At just 330m, the **Menez-Hom** is not really a mountain. But the summit stands sufficiently alone to command tremendous views across Crozon – a chaos of water, with lakes, rivers and bridges wherever you look, and usually a scattering of hang-gliders dangling in the sky. The exposed and windswept viewing table reveals it to be 300 miles (483km) from both London and Paris.

Landévennec

Nine kilometres west of Le Faou, by way of a beautiful shoreline road, the **Pont de Térénez** spans the Aulne – outlet for the Nantes–Brest canal – to the Crozon peninsula. Doubling back to the right as soon as you cross the bridge brings you after a further 5km to **LANDÉVENNEC**, where archeologists are uncovering the outline of what may be Brittany's oldest **abbey** (May, June & last 2 weeks of Sept daily except Sat 2–6pm; July to mid-Sept daily 10am–7pm; Oct–April Sun 2–6pm; €4). Nothing survives above ground of the original thatched hut, constructed in a forest clearing by St Gwennolé around 485 AD. After the abbey had been pillaged by raiding Normans in 913 AD, however, it was rebuilt in stone. Those foundations can now be seen, together with displays on monastic history and facsimile manuscripts.

There's a small but attractive **hotel** in the heart of Landévennec, *Le St-Patrick* (ⓣ02.98.27.70.83; ❷; closed mid-Oct to mid-March).

Trégarvan

Still inland from the peninsula, roughly 3km north of the Menez-Hom and unfortunately not on any bus routes, is the village of **TRÉGARVAN**. At a solitary crossroads outside town, where the Argol–Dinéault and Trégarvan–Menez-Hom roads meet, you'll find the **Musée de l'École Rurale** (mid-Feb to June daily except Sat 2–6pm; July & Aug daily 10.30am–7pm; Sept daily 2–6pm;

Oct & Nov daily except Sat 2–5pm; Dec to mid-Feb Mon–Fri 2–5pm; €4). Housed in what used to be the local secondary school, it's a fascinating glimpse of rural educational life in the last century. The school was closed down due to lack of numbers in 1974, then reopened a decade later as a re-creation of a Breton classroom circa 1920. At that time, all the kids would have spoken Breton at home – but they were forbidden to speak it here. The teacher gave a little wooden cow to the first child to utter a word in the mother tongue, and they could get rid of the *vache* only by squealing on the next offender. Breton was efficiently suppressed in the area and has only recently begun to be revived; for more on this see p.465.

St-Nic Pentrez and Telgruc-sur-mer

Beyond the Menez-Hom, a magnificent road sweeps down across the heather onto the Crozon peninsula. At the foot of the hill, to the south, **ST-NIC PENTREZ** has excellent beaches (at Pentrez Plage) – this is the sandy side of the peninsula – and several **campsites**, among them the three-star *Ker-Ys* on the main beach (ⓣ02.98.26.53.95, ⓦwww.ker-ys.com; closed Oct–Easter).

Further round towards Crozon, the village of **TELGRUC-SUR-MER** is poised well above the sea, leaving the gorgeous **Trez Bellec** beach below remarkably pristine for most of the year, though in high summer countless caravans seem to fill the meadows just behind it. A two-star **campsite**, the *Pen Bellec* (ⓣ02.98.27.31.87; closed mid-Sept to May), stands at the eastern end of the beach, while the four-star *Le Panoramic* (ⓣ02.98.27.78.41, ⓦwww.camping-panoramic.com; closed mid-Sept to May), perches a few hundred metres above its western end.

Some of the smaller towns inland hold **hotels**, such as the *Hôtel-Crêperie de Pors Morvan* (ⓣ02.98.81.53.23; ❸; closed Jan & Feb) at **Plomodiern**.

Western Crozon peninsula

The western part of the peninsula holds its largest towns and the lion's share of its tourist facilities, though nowhere is overrun and the atmosphere remains essentially peaceful. There's not much to stop for in **Crozon** and it makes much more sense to head straight on either to **Morgat** and **Camaret** if you're looking for hotels and restaurants; to the **Anse de Dinan** if you want a large empty beach; or to the **Pointe du Penhir** if you like bracing coastal walks. **Buses** serve Crozon, Morgat and Camaret, but for elsewhere you'll have to rely on other means of transportation.

Crozon

The first town on the peninsula proper, **CROZON**, is not much more than a one-way traffic system to distribute tourists among the various resorts though it does keep a market running most of the week. It also boasts the main **tourist office** for the peninsula, which keeps a constantly updated list of which hotels have rooms available; it's based in the *gare routière*, which also houses an SNCF ticket office (June & Sept Mon–Sat 9.15am–noon & 2–6pm; July & Aug Mon–Sat 9.15am–7pm, Sun 10am–1pm; Oct–March Mon–Sat 9.15am–noon & 2–5.30pm; ⓣ02.98.27.07.92, ⓦwww.menez-hom.com).

Morgat

MORGAT, just down the hill from Crozon, makes a more realistic and enticing base than its larger neighbour. It has a long and very sandy crescent beach, much loved by windsurfers, which ends beneath a pine slope, and a well-sheltered harbour that's filled with pleasure boats raced down from England and Ireland. The main attractions are **boat trips** around the various headlands, such as the Cap de la Chèvre (which is a good clifftop walk if you'd rather make your own way). The most popular is the 45-minute tour of the **Grottes** (daily May–Sept; ⓣ02.98.27.10.71 or ⓣ02.98.26.20.10; €8) – multicoloured caves in the cliffs, accessible only by sea but with steep "chimneys" up to the clifftops, from which in bygone days saints allegedly emerged to rescue the shipwrecked. Organized by two rival companies on the quay, the trips run every quarter of an hour in high season; they often leave full, however, so it's worth booking a few hours in advance.

Practicalities

Morgat's summer-only **tourist office** is in the resort's main square, place d'Ys (June & Sept Mon–Sat 10am–noon & 3–6pm; July & Aug Mon–Sat 10am–1pm & 3–7pm, Sun 4–6.30pm; ⓣ02.98.27.29.49, ⓦwww.crozon.com). **Bikes** and **kayaks** can be rented from Crapato Bicyclo, next to the tourist office on the boulevard de la Plage (mid-June to mid-Sept daily 9am–7pm; ⓣ06.88.71.72.22; bike €9 per day, kayak €19 per day).

When looking for a **hotel**, appealing options include the *Grand Hôtel de la Mer*, an imposing 1930s structure set at the eastern end of the beach (ⓣ02.98.27.02.09; ❸; closed mid-Oct to March), and the quieter *Julia*, 400m from the beach at 43 rue de Tréflez (ⓣ02.98.27.05.89; ❷; closed Nov–Feb). The fading cream-coloured *Hôtel de la Baie*, in the heart of town at 46 bd de la Plage (ⓣ02.98.27.07.51, ⓔhotel.de.la.baie@club-internet.fr; ❷), has no restaurant, but offers some very cheap rooms with shared bathrooms, more expensive en-suites, and a couple of family rooms capable of sleeping two adults and two children for around €60. With around nine hundred pitches available, **campers** are spoilt for choice: the best options are the three-star sites at *Plage de Goulien* (ⓣ02.98.26.23.16, ⓔcamping.delaplage.degoulien@presquile-crozon.com; closed mid-Sept to May) and *Les Pins*, towards the pointe de Dinan (ⓣ02.98.26.23.16, ⓔcamping.lespins@presquile-crozon.com; closed Nov–March).

A flowery stone cottage near the port at 24 quai du Kador holds *Les Échoppes* (ⓣ02.98.26.12.63; closed Oct–Easter), Morgat's best **restaurant**, which serves refined menus from €23, plus some original *à la carte* choices such as a plate of marinated raw fish for €16. Alongside it, the *Bar Kerguélen* puts on reggae and jungle nights on Fridays during July and August. The central *Restaurant Assiette et Marée*, across from the tourist office at 52 bd de la Plage (ⓣ02.98.26.23.18), has outdoor seating. As the name might suggest, its €39 menu features an *assiette de fruits de mer* and a *marmite de homard* (lobster stew).

Camaret

At **CAMARET** – another sheltered port, at the very tip of the peninsula – the most prominent building is the pink-orange **château de Vauban**, standing foursquare at the end of the long jetty that runs back parallel to the main town waterfront. Walled, moated, and accessible via a little gatehouse reached by means of a drawbridge, it was built in 1689 to guard the approaches to

Brest. These days it guards no more than a picturesque assortment of decaying half-submerged fishing boats, abandoned to rot beside the jetty. There are two **beaches** nearby – a small one to the north and another, larger and more attractive, in the low-lying (and rather marshy) Anse de Dinan to the south.

Camaret also boasts one moment of historical significance. It was here in 1801 that an American, Robert Fulton, tested his first **submarine**. The *Nautilus* was a stuffy, leaking, oar-powered wooden craft, whose five-man crew spent some time scuttling about beneath the waves in the hope of sinking a British frigate. Fulton was denied his glory, though, when the frigate chose to sail away, ignorant of the heavy-breathing peril that was so frantically seeking it out.

Practicalities

Camaret is not a large town, but in season it offers all the shops and supplies you could need, as well as some of the best **seafood** you'll find anywhere in Brittany. The local **tourist office** is at 15 quai Kléber in the port (July & Aug Mon–Sat 9am–7pm, Sun 10am–1pm; Sept–June Mon–Sat 9am–noon & 2–6pm; ⓣ02.98.27.93.60, ⓦwww.camaret-sur-mer.com).

A little walk away from the centre around the port towards the protective jetty, the quai du Styvel contains a row of excellent **hotels**. Both the *Vauban* (ⓣ02.98.27.91.36; ❷; closed Dec & Jan) and *Du Styvel* (ⓣ02.98.27.92.74; ❷; closed Jan) are exceptionally hospitable, with rooms that look right out across the bay, but only the *Styvel* has a restaurant, with a €14 menu offering *moules à la Ouessane*, and a €25 menu with crabs, oysters and salmon. At the more modern, upmarket *Thalassa* next door (ⓣ02.98.27.86.44; ❸–❻; closed Oct–March), which has a heated sea-water swimming pool and a Jacuzzi, paying a little extra will get you a room with a seaview balcony. There are also several **campsites** nearby, such as the four-star *Grand Large* (ⓣ02.98.27.91.41, ⓦwww.campinglegrandlarge.com; closed Jan–March) and the two-star municipal *Lannic* (ⓣ02.98.27.91.31; closed Oct–Easter).

Back along the quayside in the centre of town, *La Voilerie*, 7 quai Toudouze (ⓣ02.98.27.99.55; closed Wed & Sun eve in low season), is an excellent **fish restaurant**. There is a single menu at €25, based principally on fish and seafood, or you could choose an *assiette de fruits de mer* or an *à la carte* option such as pizza or steak.

In summer Penn Ar Bed (ⓣ02.98.80.80.80, ⓦwww.pennarbed.fr) operates an irregular **ferry** service from Camaret to the islands of Ouessant (€26.80 return) and Sein (€26.80 return), while Finist'Mer sails to Ouessant only (ⓣ02.98.27.88.44, ⓦwww.finist-mer.fr; €25.50 return). Société Azénor runs seasonal day-trips over to Océanopolis in Brest (July & Aug departures daily 10am; ⓣ02.98.41.46.23, ⓦwww.azenor.com; €26.50 return, including admission).

The Pointe du Penhir

At the **Pointe du Penhir**, 3km south of Camaret, footpaths lace around the various exposed and windy headlands, frequented mainly by binocular-toting twitchers eyeing up the guillemots and other sea birds that swoop on the **Tas de Pois** rock stacks, scattered out in the sea. Even crazier individuals abseil their way down similar rock stacks still attached to the mainland; here and there, a few paths pick their way down the sheer cliffs, but most peter out in the little natural amphitheatre that faces the Tas de Pois. A monument to the Breton Resistance stands nearby.

To one side of the road on the way out to the *pointe*, amid the brilliant purples and yellows of the heathland, are the megalithic **Alignements de Lagatjar**. Perhaps, though, you need to imagine that this heath is still blasted and empty, and that there's no "Dolmens" housing estate next to the stones, to appreciate this forlorn, unsignposted prehistoric ruin. The stones are little more than weather-beaten stumps, and it's hard to discern a pattern on the ground; the experts responsible for their restoration say there are four distinct lines rather than a circle.

The Pointe des Espagnols

Heading north from Camaret or Morgat brings you to the **Pointe des Espagnols**, where a viewing point signals the end of the peninsula. Brest is very close and very visible – without being any the more enticing. Around the cape are several forbidden military installations and abandoned wartime bunkers. You're not allowed to leave the road, and neither are you encouraged to turn the provided telescope towards the nuclear submarine base on the Île Longue.

Locronan

LOCRONAN, a short way from the sea on the minor road that leads down to Quimper from the Crozon peninsula, and enjoying long countryside views from its hilltop eminence, is a prime example of a Breton town that has remained frozen in its ancient form thanks to subsequent economic decline.

From 1469 through to the seventeenth century, Locronan was a hugely successful centre for woven linen, supplying sails to the French, English and Spanish navies. It was first rivalled by Vitré and Rennes, before suffering the "agony and ruin" of the nineteenth century so graphically described in its small **museum** (Feb–June & Sept Mon–Fri 10am–noon & 2–6pm; July & Aug Mon–Sat 10am–1pm & 2–7pm, Sun 2–7pm; €2), just off the main square. The consequence of that ruin has been that the rich medieval houses of the town centre have never been superseded or surrounded by modern development. Film directors love its authenticity, even if Roman Polanski, to film *Tess*, deemed it necessary to change all the porches, put new windows on the Renaissance houses, and bury the main square in mud to make it all look a bit more English.

Today Locronan is once more prosperous, with its main source of income from the sale of wooden statues carved by local artisans, pottery brought up from the Midi, and handbags and leather jackets of less specified provenance. Although this commercialization and the subsequent high prices make Locronan a bit of a tourist trap, this shouldn't put you off making at least a passing visit, for the town itself is genuinely remarkable, centred around the focal **Église St-Ronan**. Be sure to take the time to walk down the hill of the **rue Moal**, where the lovely little stone chapel of Notre Dame de Bonne Nouvelle holds some surprising modern stained glass, as well as a wooden statue of a depressed-looking Jesus, sitting alone cross-legged.

Each year on the second Sunday in July the town hosts a **pardon** at St-Ronan church; the procession, known as the *petit Tromenie*, expands to a week-long festival, the *grand Tromenie*, every sixth year (the next is in 2007). The processions follow a time-hallowed route said by some to be St Ronan's favourite Sunday walk, and by others, to be the outline of a long-vanished Benedictine abbey. It could even be a pre-Christian circuit of megalithic sites.

Practicalities

Simply to park on the outskirts of Locronan costs €3, though your ticket remains valid for a full year. Once in the centre, you'll find the **tourist office** next to the museum (same hours as the museum; ⓣ02.98.91.70.14, ⓦwww.locronan.org), which can provide lists of local B&Bs. The one **hotel**, *du Prieuré*, on the main approach street at the edge of town at 11 rue du Prieuré (ⓣ02.98.91.70.89, ⓦwww.hotel-le-prieure.com; ❹; closed mid-Nov to mid-March, plus Fri in low season), is normally fully booked well in advance. Though not particularly attractive in itself, it's lovely and quiet in the evenings when the day-trippers have gone, and offers well-equipped rooms, including some suitable for families. It also has a good restaurant with menus from €16.50 upwards. The municipal **campsite** (ⓣ02.98.91.87.76; closed Oct–May) is in a pleasant wooded position a few hundred metres down the hillside.

A handful of **crêperies** and snack bars are located in and around the main square, including the good-value *Crêperie Ty Coz* facing the church (ⓣ02.98.91.70.79; closed Nov–Easter), while the *Restaurant Au Coin de Feu*, across from the hotel, (ⓣ02.98.51.82.44; closed Sun, Mon & Tues), serves more substantial menus starting at €16, with views from its glassed-in terrace that reach all the way (just) to the sea.

Cornouaille

Once past Locronan, you enter the ancient kingdom of **Cornouaille**. Its capital, **Quimper**, is one of the most enticing cities in Brittany, with plenty to see and a vibrant atmosphere, while thriving resorts such as **Bénodet**, **Loctudy** and **Pont-Aven** (the last made famous by Gauguin) line the south coast. Roads radiate from Quimper in all directions, but the **western tip** of Finistère, if you follow the line of the Bay of Douarnenez, still feels isolated. With a few exceptions – most notably its "land's end" capes – it has kept out of the tourist mainstream.

The seaside village of **Ste-Anne-la-Palud**, north of **Douarnenez**, holds one of the best-known *pardons* in Brittany on the last Sunday in August.

Douarnenez

Sufficient quantities of tuna, sardines and assorted crustaceans are still landed at the port of **DOUARNENEZ**, in the superbly sheltered Baie du Douarnenez, south of the Crozon peninsula, to keep the largest fish canneries in Europe busy. However, the catch has been declining ever since 1923, when 800 fishing boats brought in 100 million sardines during the six-month season. Over the last twenty years or so, Douarnenez has therefore set out – at phenomenal expense, the subject of considerable local controversy – to redefine itself as a living museum of all matters maritime.

Since 1993, the area of **Port-Rhû**, on the west side of town, has officially been designated as the **Port-Musée**, with its entire waterfront taken up with fishing and other vessels gathered from throughout northern Europe. Its centrepiece, the **Musée du Bateau** (Boat Museum) in place de l'Enfer (April to mid-June & mid-Sept to Oct Tues–Sun 10am–12.30pm & 2–6pm; mid-June to mid-Sept daily 10am–7pm; €6.20) houses slightly smaller vessels than those found in the port, including a *moliceiro* from Portugal and coracles from Wales and Ireland, with exhaustive explanations on boat construction techniques and a strong emphasis on fishing.

The most appealing part of the Port-Musée, however, is back at the waterfront, where you can roam in and out of five of the boats moored in the port and peer into their oily metallic-smelling engine rooms and cramped sleeping quarters. This part of the visit operates to the same opening hours as the museum and is included in the ticket price.

Of the three separate harbour areas still in operation in Douarnenez, by far the most appealing is the rough-and-ready **port du Rosmeur**, on the east side, which is nominally the fishing port used by the smaller local craft. Its quayside – which is far from totally commercialized, but holds a reasonable number of cafés and restaurants – curves between a pristine wooded promontory to the right and the fish canneries to the left, which continue around the north of the headland. You can buy fresh fish at the waterfront, or go on a sea-fishing excursion yourself – or simply a tour of the bay – with Vedettes Rosmeur (ⓣ02.98.92.83.83; fishing trips €30, cruises of the bay €11). The various **beaches** around town look pretty enough, but the sea here is dangerous for swimming.

Practicalities

The **tourist office** in Douarnenez is at 2 rue du Dr-Mével (July & Aug Mon–Sat 10am–noon & 2–7pm, Sun 10am–12.30pm & 3–6pm; Sept–June Mon–Sat 10am–noon & 2–6pm; ⓣ02.98.92.13.35, ⓦwww.douarnenez-tourisme.com), a short walk up from the Port-Musée. Among good-value **hotels** are *Le Bretagne*, nearby at 23 rue Duguay-Trouin (ⓣ02.98.92.30.44, ⓦwww.le-bretagne.fr; ❷), above a restaurant serving reasonable Tex-Mex dishes for around €10, and the more upmarket *De France*, also nearby, on the main street at 4 rue Jean Jaurès (ⓣ02.98.92.00.02, ⓔhotel.de.france.dz@wanadoo.fr; ❸; closed Mon, Sat lunch & Sun eve), which has a good restaurant where menus start at €19. Close by on the bay, at Tréboul/Les Sables Blancs, there's a two-star **campsite**, *Croas Men* (ⓣ02.98.74.00.18, ⓦwww.croas-men.com; closed Oct–Easter). In addition to the hotel **restaurants**, *Le Bigorneau Amoureux*, 2 boulevard Richepin (ⓣ02.98.92.35.55; closed Tues), is a good seafood place which has a terrace overlooking the plage des Dames. Next to the Musée du Bateau on quai de Port-Rhû you'll find a **bar**, *Le Pourquoi Pas*, serving local beers and occasionally hosting live performances of Breton music.

Audierne and around

Though the exposed southwestern extremities of Brittany are not areas you'd normally associate with a classic summer sun-and-sand holiday, **AUDIERNE**,

25km west of Douarnenez on the Bay of Audierne, is something of an exception. An active fishing port, specializing in prawns and crayfish, it squeezes into the narrow inlet of the Goyen estuary, a short way back from the Atlantic. From out to sea, you'd hardly know there was a town here.

At the inland end of town, an **aquarium** called L'Aquashow (April–June & Sept daily 10am–7pm; July & Aug daily 10am–10pm; Oct–March school holidays only 2–5pm; €10.50) holds tankfuls of mostly local fish, captioned as ever with the stress on gastronomy – "the flesh is firm and much enjoyed", or "its flesh is really tasteful". You'll also learn that an octopus can squeeze through a hole as small as its eye, while under-14s can take the "La Tempête" thrill-ride. There's no great point watching the fifteen-minute, commentary-free film show of tropical fish in some unspecified South Seas location, but do make a point of sticking around for one of the regular shows in the open-air riverfront arena, in which captive cormorants and gulls, joined occasionally by their wild brethren, put on aerobatic displays in return for dead sprats. An on-site snack bar serves simple meals on a pleasant terrace, and there's plenty of open space for picnics just outside.

From the town centre, the road continues just over 1km to the long, curving and surprisingly sheltered **beach** of **Ste-Evette**, which has its own crop of hotels and grand homes. Its southern end, 1km further on and close to the open ocean, is the departure point for boats to the Île de Sein (see opposite).

Practicalities

Audierne's **tourist office** is on the main square in the heart of town, at 8 rue Victor-Hugo (July & Aug Mon–Sat 10am–7pm; Sept–June Mon–Sat 9am–noon & 2–6pm; ⓣ02.98.70.12.20, ⓦwww.audierne-tourisme.com). One of the few buildings on the seaward side of the road out, in a superb position facing the mouth of the estuary at the very start of Ste-Evette beach, is the **hotel** *Au Roi Gradlon*, 3 av Manu-Brusq (ⓣ02.98.70.04.51, ⓦwww.auroigradlon.com; ❸; closed mid-Dec to Jan). Its unusual design means that the street-level dining room – where the €18 menu offers changing daily specials – is in fact on the top storey, with several further floors, concealed from the road, dropping down below it to the beach. The same management is also responsible for running the significantly larger *L'Horizon*, slightly nearer the town proper at 41 rue J-J-Rousseau (ⓣ02.98.70.09.91; ❸; closed Oct–March), where rooms are a little cheaper, and identical menus are served. Alternative options nearby include the aptly named *Hôtel de la Plage*, a Logis de France facing the middle of the beach at 21 av Manu-Brusq (ⓣ02.98.70.01.07; ❸; hotel closed Oct–Easter, restaurant closed Oct to mid-June), where many of the more expensive sea-view rooms have balconies.

Plogoff

Many visitors take in Audierne en route to the Pointe du Raz, which is connected directly to Quimper by bus. Just short of the Pointe du Raz, signalled by fading graffiti on its walls and hoardings, is the tiny village of **PLOGOFF**, where ecologists, autonomists and local people fought riot police and paratroopers for six weeks in 1980, attempting to stop the opening move in a nuclear power station project. Although they lost the fight, abandonment of the project was part of François Mitterrand's manifesto for the 1980 presidential election – and he kept his promise.

The Pointe du Raz

The **Pointe du Raz** – the Land's End of both Finistère and France – is designated as a "Grand Site National", and makes a dramatic spectacle. You can walk out to the plummeting fissures of the *pointe*, filling and draining with a deafening surf-roar, along precarious paths with unrivalled views – shoes with grip are a good idea. That said, don't come in summer expecting to get the place to yourself; it attracts a million visitors every year, and at busy periods you'll have to walk a long way from the central welcome and **information** complex if you want to escape the crowds (April–June & Sept daily 10.30am–6pm; July & Aug daily 9.30am–7pm; ⓣ02.98.70.67.18, ⓦwww.pointeduraz.com). A couple of **cafés** sell adequate simple meals, but there's no accommodation or camping, and there's a €5 parking fee for cars, €3 for motorcycles.

The Baie des Trépassés

The **Baie des Trépassés** (Bay of the Dead), just north of the Pointe du Raz, gets its grim name from the shipwrecked bodies that were once washed up here, and is a possible site of the sunken city of Ys (see p.332). However, it's actually a very attractive spot; green meadows, too exposed to support trees, end abruptly on the low cliffs to either side, there's a huge expanse of flat sand (in fact little else at low tide), and out in the crashing waves surfers and windsurfers get thrashed to within an inch of their lives. Beyond them, you can usually make out the white-painted houses along the harbour on the Île de Sein, while the various uninhabited rocks in between hold a veritable forest of lighthouses.

In total, less than half a dozen scattered buildings intrude upon the emptiness. There are no facilities for casual visitors on the beach, but the parking lot just back from the dunes is usually filled with campervans from all over Europe, and there are also two **hotels**, both with tremendous views. Right in the middle is the pink *Hôtel de la Baie des Trépassés* (ⓣ02.98.70.61.34, ⓔhoteldelabaie@aol.com; ❷; closed mid-Nov to mid-Feb), which has menus of wonderfully fresh seafood from €19. The larger *Relais de la Pointe du Van*, run by the same management, is slightly higher up, to the right (ⓣ02.98.70.62.79, same email; ❸; closed Oct–March).

The Île de Sein

Of all the Breton islands, the tiny **Île de Sein**, just 8km off the end of the Pointe du Raz, has to be the most extraordinary. Nowhere does it rise more than six metres above the surrounding ocean, and for much of its 2.5-km length it's barely broader than the breakwater wall of bricks that serves as its central spine. Its very grip on existence seems so tenuous that it's hard to believe anyone could truly survive here. However, the island has in fact been inhabited since prehistoric times. Roman sources tell of a shrine served by nine virgin priestesses, and it was reputed to have been the very last refuge of the Druids in Brittany, who held out there long after the rest of the country was Christianized. It also became famous during World War II, when its entire male population, a total of 140 men, answered General de Gaulle's call to join him in exile in England. During his first muster of the Free French army, de Gaulle observed that Sein appeared to constitute a quarter of France. He subsequently awarded the island the Ordre de la Libération, and came here in 1960 to unveil a monument to its bravery. Over three hundred islanders continue to make their living from the sea, gathering rainwater and seaweed and fishing for scallops, lobster and crayfish.

According to a traditional saying, "Who sees Sein, sees his death", though that's more because it happens to rhyme in French ("*qui voit Sein, voit sa fin*") than because it holds any particular evil. Setting off to reach the island on a misty morning, however, feels as though you're sailing off the edge of the world; in fact, it's so notoriously inconspicuous that it was described by the French Admiral Tourville as the most dangerous reef in the world.

Depending on tide levels, island **boats** pull in at one or other of the two adjoining harbours that constitute Sein's one tightknit village. There are no cars on the island, its few streets being far too narrow for them to squeeze through, and even bicycles are not permitted. A little **beach** appears in front of the village at low tide, and there's also a **museum** of local history (June & Sept daily 10am–noon & 2–4pm; July & Aug daily 10am–noon & 2–6pm; €2.50), packed with black and white photos and press clippings, and displaying a long list of shipwrecks from 1476 onwards. The basic activity for visitors, however, is to take a bracing walk.

The **eastern tip** of the island, barely connected to the rest when high tides eat away at the slender natural causeway, was in days gone by laboriously cleared to create scores of tiny agricultural terraces. These have long been overgrown with sparse yellow broom and left to the rabbits, however, so if you fancy picking your way through the rock pools you'll have the place to yourself. Heading **west** from town, on the other hand, takes you past the Free French Monument and a couple of sandy little bays to the island's main **lighthouse**, the Phare de Goulenez.

Practicalities

The principal departure point for **boats** to Sein is Ste-Evette beach, just outside **Audierne** (see p.324); the crossing takes around an hour. Services are operated by Vedette-Biniou (daily: second half of June & first half of Sept 10am; early July 10am & 1.30pm; mid-July to Aug 10am, 1.30pm & 5pm; ⓣ02.98.70.21.15, ⓦwww.vedette-biniou.fr.st; €21.60 return), and Penn Ar Bed (daily: July & Aug 9am, 11.30am & 4.50pm; Sept–June 9.30am; ⓣ02.98.70.70.70, ⓦwww.pennarbed.fr; €22.50 return). On Sundays from late June to early September, Penn Ar Bed also run trips to Sein from **Brest** (departs 8am; 1hr 30min; €30 return) via **Camaret** (8.40am; 1hr; €26.80 return).

If you come for the day in high summer, you may well be asked to specify in advance the ferry on which you'll return to Audierne (Penn Ar Bed sail at 3.30pm & 6.15pm, Vedette-Biniou at 3.40pm & 6.30pm). This is not necessary if you are returning to Brest or Camaret since there is only one sailing, on Sundays departing Sein at 5pm. Great day out it may be, but nonetheless you may find yourself running out of things to do, so consider opting for a shorter trip and returning by the afternoon rather than the evening boat.

Sein is hardly bursting with facilities for tourists, but it does have two **hotels**. The *Trois Dauphins*, looking out over the beach from the middle of the port (ⓣ02.98.70.92.09; ❷, sea view ❸; closed Mon), offers cosy and attractive rooms, completely fashioned and furnished in wood. It doesn't have a restaurant, but the bar downstairs sells sandwiches. The *Hôtel-Restaurant d'Armen* (ⓣ02.98.70.90.77, ⓦwww.hotel.armen.free.fr; ❸) is the very last building you come to as you walk west out of town, which makes it the last restaurant in

Europe, and goes some way towards explaining why it refuses on principle to sell Coke, resisting Americanization by selling Breton apple juice instead. All its rooms face the sea, as there's ocean on both sides, while its restaurant has seating outside when weather permits.

Of the other **restaurants** in town, *Le Men Brial*, right by the picturesque little Men Brial lighthouse (☎02.98.70.90.87), makes a good lunch spot, offering crêpes, inexpensive menus, and *moules frites*, while *Chez Brigitte*, facing the beach (☎02.98.70.91.83; closed mid-Oct to March), is a fancier option, with seafood specialities ranging up to €53.

The Penmarch peninsula

At one time the **Penmarch peninsula** – the southwestern corner of Finistère, which stretches south of Audierne and southwest of Quimper – was one of the richest areas of Brittany. That was before it was plundered by the pirate La Fontenelle, who led three hundred ships in raids on the local peasantry from his base on the island of La Tristan in the Bay of Douarnenez, and also before the cod, staple of the fishing industry, stopped coming.

Now, in the local tourist literature, the region is known as the **Pays de Bigouden**, *bigouden* being the name of the traditional and very elaborate lace headgear that you may see still worn by the women in many of the villages around Pont l'Abbé. Often as much as a foot high, they are sometimes supported by half-tubes of cardboard; sometimes just very stiffly starched. The white of the *coiffes* swaying in the wind provides one of the memorable colours of the area, along with the red fields of poppies and verges of purple foxgloves.

Pont l'Abbé

PONT L'ABBÉ, the principal town of the peninsula, has a Bigouden museum, spread over three storeys of the keep of its fourteenth-century **château** (April–May Mon–Sat 10am–noon & 2–6pm; June–Sept daily 10am–12.30pm & 2–6.30pm; €2.50) – though you'd need to be quite inspired by the costumes to find it of great interest. More accessible pleasures lie in a stroll through the woods along the banks of its estuary. The *Hôtel de Bretagne*, in the main square at 24 place de la République (☎02.98.87.17.22; ❸; restaurant closed Sun eve & Mon in low season months), is the prettiest hotel in town, and has a fine restaurant. There are also several decent crêperies around, including the *Bigoudène* at 33 rue de Gaulle (☎02.98.87.20.41; closed Sun, plus Mon in low season months) and the *Quatres Saisons*, nearby at 2 rue Burdeau (☎02.98.87.06.05; closed Sun, plus Mon in low season months).

Le Guilvinec and around

West of Pont L'Abbé, the world **windsurfing** championships have frequently been held at **Pointe de la Torche**, and at any time there are likely to be aficionados of the sport twirling effortlessly about on the dangerous water. The coast only becomes swimmable, however, as you round the Pointe de Penmarch towards Loctudy.

The first village you come to, **LE GUILVINEC**, is a not especially attractive, but surprisingly busy, fishing port, sheltered in the mouth of a little river, that's home to the fourth largest fish auction (*criée*) in France. It's also playing a pioneering role in a government initiative to turn fishing into a tourist spectacle. To that end, the second storey of the long harbourfront buildings where the fish are landed and sold has been converted to become **Haliotika**, a sort of museum of the fishing industry that combines exhaustive displays on all aspects of the whole messy business with an open-air terrace offering ringside views as the fleet return each afternoon, from around 4pm. How much you pay for admission depends on whether you coincide with the early-evening fish auction (mid-March to Oct Mon–Fri 2.30–7pm, Sun 3–6.30pm; €4.80, or €6 including guided visit to the auction; ⓣ02.98.58.28.38). Le Guilvinec's other main attraction is its small but very pleasant **beach**, facing onto the open sea.

For a place to **stay**, the excellent *Hôtel du Port* at 53 av du Port in **LÉCHIAGAT**, on the far side of the estuary (ⓣ02.98.58.10.10, ⓔhotel-du-port@wanadoo.fr; ❷), is thoroughly recommended – especially for its fish suppers, which start at €19.50 with a tasty array of scallops, skate and all sorts of dessert, and culminate in a lobster feast for €48. Don't confuse the *Hôtel du Port* with the *Auberge du Port*, back in Le Guilvinec itself; if you do choose to stay in town, the very plain exterior of the *Hôtel du Centre* at 16 rue du Général-de-Gaulle conceals an attractive garden behind (ⓣ02.98.58.10.44; ❸; hotel closed mid-Oct to mid-March, restaurant closed Sun eve & Mon lunch in low season months). The restaurant here isn't bad, so long as you ignore the cheapest menu which is very run-of-the-mill and go for the €20 one instead.

Loctudy

LOCTUDY, across the mouth of the Odet from Bénodet, is well located for boat trips up and down the river and to the nearby islands, and also has its own attractive beaches, while at the same time being relatively uncommercial and laid-back. There are several **campsites** along its main beach, including the two-star *Kergall* (ⓣ02.98.87.45.93; closed Oct–Easter) and the three-star *Mouettes* (ⓣ02.98.87.43.51; closed Sept to mid-June), as well as some good-value **hotels**, such as the *Hotel de Bretagne*, 19 rue du Port (ⓣ02.98.87.40.21, ⓔhoteldebretagne@msn.com; ❸). In summer, **boats** belonging to Vedettes de l'Odet (ⓣ02.98.87.45.63, ⓦwww.vedettes-odet.com) sail from Loctudy up and around the Odet estuary, though not quite as far as Quimper (June to early July & first week of Sept, Wed 2pm; second week of July daily 2.30pm; last 2 weeks of July & all Aug daily 1.30pm; €21.50).

The Îles de Glénan

The **Îles de Glénan** are a string of islands 16km off the mainland, surrounded by a lagoon with surprisingly clear water and a few pleasant sandy beaches. However, apart from a couple of basic restaurants on the main island, **St-Nicholas**, there are neither the facilities nor enough to keep oneself occupied to warrant any more than a day-trip. Although in theory the trips depart daily during the summer, you need to check whether they're running on any particular day; services are cancelled in bad weather or simply if not enough people show up.

Vedettes de l'Odet (ⓣ02.98.87.45.63, ⓦwww.vedettes-odet.com) **sails** to the islands from Loctudy (June to early July & first week of Sept Thurs 2pm; early July to mid-July daily 2pm; last 2 weeks of July & all Aug daily 10am & 2pm; €25 return), Quimper (mid-July to late Aug daily 10.45am; €25 return), Bénodet (early April to early May & late Sept to Oct Wed & Thurs 1.30pm;

early May to mid-July & first 3 weeks of Sept daily 10am & 1.30pm; mid-July to Aug daily 9.30am, 10am, 11.30am & 1.30pm; €25 return) and from Concarneau (June to early July Thurs 2pm; first 2 weeks of July daily 11am; mid-July to Aug daily 11am & 2pm; €25 return). Ferries also run from Concarneau with Vedettes Glénn (☎02.98.97.10.31; mid-July to end Aug 2 daily 10am & 2.15pm; mid-June to early July and first 2 weeks of Sept 1–2 daily except Sat 10am & 2.15pm; €24 return).

Quimper

QUIMPER, capital of the ancient diocese, kingdom and later duchy of Cornouaille, is the oldest Breton city. According to the only source – legend – the first bishop of Quimper, St Corentin, came with the first Bretons across the channel to the place they named Little Britain some time between the fourth and seventh centuries. He lived by eating a regenerating and immortal fish all his life, and was made bishop by one King Gradlon, whose life he later saved when the sea-bed city of Ys was destroyed (see box, p.332).

Modern Quimper is very relaxed, though active enough to have the bars and atmosphere to make it worth going out café-crawling. Still "the charming little place" known to Flaubert, it takes at most half an hour to cross it on foot. The word *kemper* denotes the junction of the two rivers, the Steir and the Odet, around which are the cobbled streets (now mainly pedestrianized) of the medieval quarter, dominated by the cathedral towering nearby. As the Odet curves from east to southwest, it is crossed by numerous low flat bridges, bedecked with geraniums, and chrysanthemums in the autumn. You can stroll along the boulevards on both banks of the river, where several ultramodern edifices blend in an oddly harmonious way with their ancient – and attractive – surroundings. Overlooking all is tree-covered **Mont Frugy** (all of 87m above the river), which you can climb for good views over the city. There is no great pressure in Quimper to rush around monuments or museums, and the most enjoyable option may be to take a boat and drift down the Odet "the prettiest river in France" to the open sea at Bénodet.

Arrival, information and city transport

The **gare SNCF** and **gare routière** (☎02.98.90.88.89) are next to each other on avenue de la Gare, 1km east of the town centre. Both are connected to the centre by bus #6, and all city buses pass the tourist office, via either place de la Résistance or along rue du Parc on the other side of the river, depending on which direction you are going.

The **tourist office** organizes a complex schedule of **guided tours** of the city in season, and is housed in a small single-storey building on the south bank of the Odet at 7 rue de la Déesse, place de la Résistance (mid-March to June & last 2 weeks in Sept Mon–Sat 9.30am–12.30pm & 1.30–6.30pm; June & first two weeks of Sept Mon–Sat 9.30am–12.30pm & 1.30–6.30pm, Sun 10am–12.45pm; July & Aug Mon–Sat 9am–7pm, Sun 10am–12.45pm & 3–5.45pm; Oct to mid-March Mon–Sat 9.30am–12.30pm & 1.30–6pm; ☎02.98.53.04.05, Ⓦwww.quimper-tourisme.com).

Although Quimper is well connected with the rest of Brittany by both train and bus, if you want to use public transport to get to the coast anywhere in the immediate vicinity, the **bus** is your only option. The most useful local

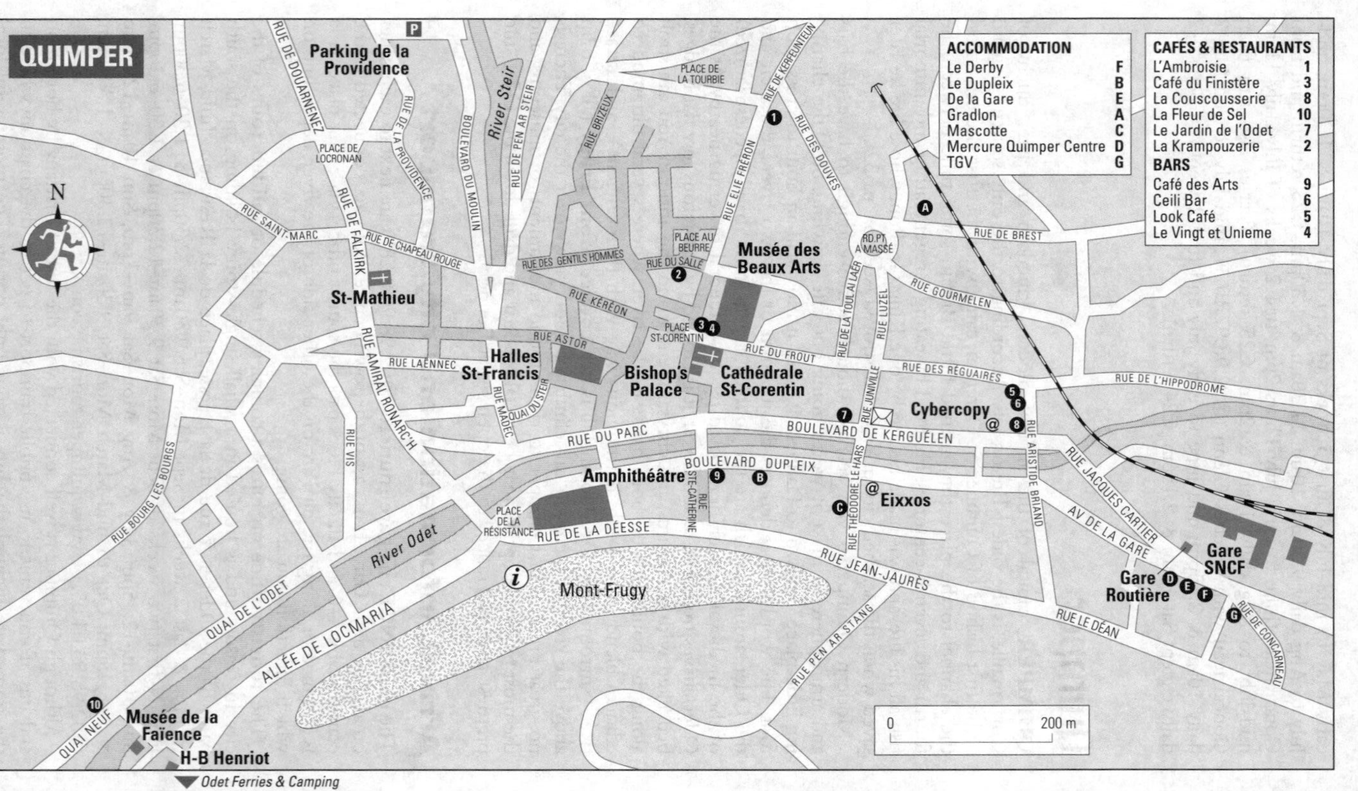
QUIMPER
ACCOMMODATION
Le Derby F
Le Dupleix B
De la Gare E
Gradlon A
Mascotte C
Mercure Quimper Centre D
TGV G
CAFÉS & RESTAURANTS
L'Ambroisie 1
Café du Finistère 3
La Couscousserie 8
La Fleur de Sel 10
Le Jardin de l'Odet 7
La Krampouzerie 2
BARS
Café des Arts 9
Ceili Bar 6
Look Café 5
Le Vingt et Unieme 4
Parking de la Providence
St-Mathieu
Halles St-Francis
Bishop's Palace
Cathédrale St-Corentin
Musée des Beaux Arts
Cybercopy
Eixxos
Amphithéâtre
Mont-Frugy
Gare Routière
Gare SNCF
Musée de la Faïence
H-B Henriot
River Steir
River Odet
RUE DE DOUARNENEZ
PLACE DE LOCRONAN
RUE DE LA PROVIDENCE
BOULEVARD DU MOULIN
RUE DE PEN AR STEIR
RUE BRIZEUX
PLACE DE LA TOURBIE
RUE DE KERFEUNTEUN
RUE ELIE FRERON
RUE DES DOUVES
RUE SAINT-MARC
RUE DE FALKIRK
RUE DE CHAPEAU ROUGE
RUE DES GENTILS HOMMES
PLACE AU BEURRE
RUE DU SALLÉ
RD.PT A.MASSÉ
RUE DE BREST
RUE GOURMELEN
RUE KÉRÉON
PLACE ST-CORENTIN
RUE ASTOR
RUE DU FROUT
RUE DE LA TOUL AL LAER
RUE LUZEL
RUE LAËNNEC
RUE AMIRAL RONARC'H
RUE MADEC
QUAI DU STEIR
RUE DES RÉGUAIRES
RUE DE L'HIPPODROME
RUE JUNIVILLE
RUE DU PARC
BOULEVARD DE KERGUÉLEN
RUE VIS
BOULEVARD DUPLEIX
RUE STE-CATHERINE
RUE THÉODORE LE HARS
RUE ARISTIDE BRIAND
RUE JACQUES CARTIER
AV DE LA GARE
RUE BOURG LES BOURGS
PLACE DE LA RÉSISTANCE
RUE DE LA DÉESSE
RUE JEAN-JAURÈS
RUE LE DÉAN
RUE DE CONCARNEAU
RUE PEN AR STANG
QUAI DE L'ODET
ALLÉE DE LOCMARIA
QUAI NEUF
0 200 m
N
Hostel & Camping
Odet Ferries & Camping

Boat trips from Quimper

Between June and September you can **sail** from Quimper down the Odet to Bénodet, which takes about 1hr 15min, on Vedettes de l'Odet (Bénodet ⓣ02.98.57.00.58, Quimper ⓣ02.98.52.98.41, ⓦwww.vedettes-odet.com; €21.50 return). Between one and three boats sail each day, with both the schedules and the departure point varying according to the tide; check with the tourist office (who also sell tickets). The same company also sails between Quimper and the **Îles de Glénan** (see p.328).

operator is the Compagnie Amoricaine de Transport, or CAT, 10 rue Jules Verne (ⓣ02.98.90.88.89), who run services to Bénodet, leaving from the *gare routière* or place de la Résistance; to Audierne and Pointe du Raz, from the *gare routière* or place de Locronan; and to Concarneau and Quimperlé, also from the *gare routière* or place de la Résistance.

Finding a **parking** space in the centre of Quimper can be difficult; it's often best to head for the 1000-place Parking de la Providence, a ten-minute walk north of the centre (free).

Accommodation

There are remarkably few **hotels** in the old streets in the centre of Quimper, though several can be found near the station. Rooms can be especially difficult to find in late July or early August, when reservations are advisable.

Quimper's refurbished **hostel**, which has a few private rooms as well as dorms, is 2km downstream (west) of town at 6 av des Oiseaux in Bois de Seminaire (ⓣ02.98.64.97.97, ⓔquimper@fuaj.org; €8.90; closed Oct–March), on bus route #1 (direction "Penhars", stop "Chaptal"). Guests have use of a kitchen, there's a quiet garden, and bikes are available for rent. You can **camp** either at the municipal campsite alongside (ⓣ02.98.55.61.09), which stays open year-round but is reserved for caravans in winter, or at the plusher four-star *Orangerie de Lanniron* site on the route de Bénodet (ⓣ02.98.90.62.02, ⓦwww.lanniron.com; closed mid-Sept to mid-May).

Hotels

Hôtel le Derby 13 av de la Gare ⓣ02.98.52.06.91, ⓕ02.98.53.39.04. Inexpensive, surprisingly quiet option above a corner bar facing the station. ❷

Hôtel le Dupleix 34 bd Dupleix ⓣ02.98.90.53.35, ⓦwww.hotel-dupleix.com. Modern concrete hotel, not very attractive from the outside but airy and bright within, in a good central location overlooking the Odet, with fine views across the river to the cathedral. The private garage is a major advantage in this part of town. ❺

Hôtel de la Gare 17 av de la Gare ⓣ02.98.90.00.81, ⓦwww.hoteldelagarequimper.com. Simple rooms, all with TV, shower and phone, arranged around a quiet patio and above a simple snack bar across from the station. Parking. ❸

Hôtel Gradlon 30 rue du Brest ⓣ02.98.95.04.39, ⓦwww.hotel-gradlon.com. Central but quiet (with a pleasant garden), and exceptionally friendly. The rooms are not cheap, but they're very nicely decorated. ❹

Hôtel Mascotte 6 rue Théodore Le Hars ⓣ02.98.53.37.37, ⓕ02.98.90.31.51. Large, spacious rooms and excellent buffet breakfasts at this comfortable and centrally located hotel. ❹

Hôtel Mercure Quimper Centre 21bis av de la Gare ⓣ02.98.90.31.71, ⓦwww.mercure-quimper.com. Smart chain hotel squeezed into a very ordinary building by the station, and offering three grades of room: *classique*, *élegance* and *club élegance*, the latter two distinguishing themselves by such luxuries as a/c and minibars. ❹

Hôtel TGV 4 rue de Concarneau ⓣ02.98.90.54.00, ⓦwww.hoteltgv.com. Yet another cheap option near the station, this time offering plain but clean rooms with shower and TV at bargain rates. ❷

The drowned city of Ys

Legend has it that **King Gradlon** built **Ys** in the Baie de Douarnenez, protected from the water by gates and locks to which only he and his daughter had keys. She sounds like a pleasant sort, giving pet sea-dragons to all the citizens to do their errands, but **St Corentin** saw decadence and suspected evil. He was proved right: at the urging of the Devil, the princess used her key to open the floodgates, the city was flooded, and Gradlon escaped only by obeying St Corentin and throwing his daughter into the sea. Back on dry land, and in need of a new capital, Gradlon founded Quimper. Ys remains on the sea floor – it will rise again when Paris ("*Par-Ys*", "equal to Ys") sinks – and, according to tradition, on feast days sailors can still hear church bells and hymns under the water.

The Town

The enormous **Cathédrale St-Corentin** is said to be the most complete Gothic cathedral in Brittany, though its neo-Gothic spires date from 1856, and several years of elbow grease have now turned it a sparkling white. When the nave was being added to the old chancel in the fifteenth century, the extension would either have hit existing buildings or the swampy edge of the (then) unchannelled river. The masons eventually found a solution and placed the nave at a slight angle – a peculiarity which, once noticed, makes it hard to concentrate on the other Gothic splendours within.

The exterior, however, gives no hint of the deviation, with King Gradlon now mounted in perfect symmetry between the spires – though whether he would have advised a river-bed nave is another question. Before the Revolution, each St Cecilia's Day a climber would ascend to give the king a drink, and there was a prize of 100 *écus* for whoever could catch the glass, thrown down afterwards. During the sixteenth century, 1500 refugees died of plague inside the building.

Alongside the cathedral, the quirky-looking **Bishop's Palace** nestles against one of the few remaining fragments of the old city walls. Inside you'll find a wonderful staircase, and the beautifully laid out **Musée Départemental Breton** (June–Sept daily 9am–6pm; Oct–May Tues–Sat 9am–noon & 2–5pm, Sun 2–5pm; €3.80). Its collections start with Bronze Age spear- and axe-heads and prehistoric golden jewellery, move rapidly through Roman and medieval statues, and culminate with a remarkable assortment of Breton oddments and *objets d'art*. The highlights are probably the sixteenth-century statues of polychromed wood, some of which stood originally in the cathedral, but upstairs you'll also find prized examples of regional costumes, furniture and ceramics.

Even more compelling is the **Musée des Beaux Arts**, alongside the Hôtel de Ville at 40 place St-Corentin (April–June, Sept & Oct Mon & Wed–Sun 10am–noon & 2–6pm; July & Aug daily 10am–7pm; Nov–March Mon & Wed–Sat 10am–noon & 2–6pm, Sun 2–6pm; €4). Refurbished to very classy effect, with new floors and suspended walkways, it focuses especially on an amazing assemblage of drawings by Max Jacob – who was born in Quimper – and his contemporaries. Jean-Julien Lemordant's vibrant murals of Breton scenes, commissioned in 1907 for Quimper's *Hôtel de l'Epée* (which closed in 1974) get a room to themselves, and there's also quite a selection of nineteenth- and twentieth-century paintings from the Pont-Aven school, though you'd hardly notice the only Gauguin, a goose he painted on the door of Marie Henry's inn in Pont-Aven itself.

The faïenceries of Quimper

Faïence – tin-glazed earthenware – was first popularized by the city of Faenza in Italy in the sixteenth century. Its production was subsequently taken up by Delft in Holland, Majolica in Spain – and in Quimper, from 1690 onwards. The whole story is told by the city's excellent pottery museum, the **Musée de la Faïence Jules Verlinque**, not far west of the tourist office, on the south bank of the Odet at 14 rue Jean-Baptiste-Bousquet (mid-April to mid-Oct Mon–Sat 10am–6pm; €4).

As well as revealing the minerals used to create different colours, such as copper (green), cobalt (blue) and antimony (yellow), the museum demonstrates that little has changed in the Breton pottery business since some unknown artisan hit on the idea of painting ceramic ware with naive "folk" designs. That was in around 1875, just as the coming of the railways brought the first influx of tourists in search of authentic souvenirs. Highlights of the collection include pieces commemorating such events as World War I, the first automobile accident, and the death of Zola, but there are also some fascinating specimens produced by fine artists in the 1920s. In the age before plastics, they handled commissions like designing bonnet ornaments for Citroën cars.

As you walk through the town, it is impossible to ignore *faïence* – you are invited to look and to buy on every corner. On weekdays, as well as on Saturdays in July and August, it's also possible to visit the major atelier **H-B Henriot**, which under American ownership continues to produce hand-painted pottery in the allée de Locmaria just behind the museum (July & Aug Mon–Sat 9.15–11.15am & 1.30–4.15pm; Sept–June Mon–Fri 9.15–11.15am & 2–4.15pm; ⓣ02.98.90.09.36, ⓦwww.hb-henriot.com; €3). H-B Henriot maintain a bright, modern **gift shop** alongside; the prices, even for the seconds, are similar to those on offer everywhere else, but the selection is superb (Mon–Sat 9.30am–7pm).

The heart of **old Quimper** lies in and to the west of place St-Corentin, in front of the cathedral. This is where you'll find the liveliest shops and cafés, housed in the old half-timbered buildings, such as the Breton Keltia-Musique record shop at 1 place au Beurre, and the Celtic shop, Ar Bed Keltiek, between the cathedral and the river at 2 rue du Roi-Gradlon. The old market hall was burned down in 1976, but the light and spacious new **Halles St-Francis**, rue Astor, built to replace it is quite a delight, not just for the food, but for the view past the upturned boat rafters through the roof to the cathedral's twin spires. It's open from Monday to Saturday, with an extra-large market spreading into the surrounding streets on Saturdays.

Eating

Although the pedestrian streets west of the cathedral are unexpectedly short on places to eat, there are quite a few **restaurants** further east on the north side of the river, en route to the *gare SNCF*. For crêperies, place au Beurre, a short walk northwest of the cathedral, is a good bet.

Restaurants

L'Ambroisie 49 rue Élie-Fréron ⓣ02.98.95.00.02. Upmarket French restaurant a short climb north from the cathedral, featuring lots of fine seafood (including tuna) and meat dishes on menus from €21. Closed Mon, plus Sun eve in winter.

Café du Finistère 34 place St-Corentin ⓣ02.98.95.01.48. The average brasserie-style food here comes in third place behind a great location, with plenty of tables on the square facing the cathedral, and the opportunity of ordering banana splits and other delicious cold desserts for €6–7.

La Couscousserie 1 bd de Kerguélen ⓣ02.98.95.46.50. Plush, enjoyable Middle Eastern restaurant by the river, serving couscous platters at €11–22, and *tajines* for around €15, in two Arabian Nights-themed rooms decked out with hookahs and the like. Closed Aug.

La Fleur de Sel 1 quai Neuf ⓣ02.98.55.04.71. Gourmet French cooking not far west of the town centre opposite the Musée de la Faïence on the north bank of the river, with menus ranging from €19 up to €33 that are strong on fish and seafood, but do also have some meat. Closed Sat & Sun.

Le Jardin de l'Odet 39 bd de Kerguélen ⓣ02.98.95.76.76. Lovely Art-Deco restaurant, facing the river close to the cathedral and with a nice garden too, which serves top-value menus at €19, €27 and €35, featuring imaginative dishes such as duck with figs along with the ubiquitous oysters. Closed Sun & Mon.

La Krampouzerie 9 rue du Sallé ⓣ02.98.95.13.08. One of the best of Quimper's many crêperies, with some outdoor seating on the place au Beurre. Most crêpes cost around €3, though you can get a wholewheat *galette* with smoked salmon and cream cheese for €5.80, or with Roscoff onions and seaweed for €3.50. Closed Sun, plus Mon in winter.

Drinking and entertainment

Quimper is a young and, by Breton standards, exuberant city, and there are enough **cafés and bars** dotted around the centre to keep you well entertained of an evening.

Quimper's **Festival de Cornouaille** started in 1923, and has gone from strength to strength since. This great jamboree of Breton music, costumes, theatre and dance is held in the week before the fourth Sunday in July, attracting guest performers from the other Celtic countries and a scattering of other, sometimes highly unusual, ethnic-cultural ensembles. The whole thing culminates in an incredible Sunday parade through the town. The official programme does not appear until July, but you can get provisional details in advance from the tourist office or at ⓦwww.festival-cornouaille.com. Accommodation is at a premium in Quimper during the festival.

Not so widely known are the **Semaines Musicales**, which follow in the first three weeks of August. The music is predominantly classical, and tends to favour French composers such as Berlioz, Debussy, Bizet and Poulenc. Founded in 1978, the event serves to bring the rather stuffy nineteenth-century theatre on boulevard Dupleix alive each year.

Bars

Café des Arts 4 rue Ste-Catherine ⓣ02.98.90.32.06. Young, sociable café on the south bank of the river, which holds debates on the first Friday of every month, where patrons are encouraged to speak out on subjects such as "Men and Women" or "War and Peace".

Ceili Bar 4 rue Aristide Briand. The place to go for all things Breton: beer, music – sometimes performed live on the cramped premises – and opinionated conversation.

Look Café 9 rue des Réguaires. Small bar decorated with plenty of tinsel, making the most of being Quimper's only gay and lesbian hangout.

Le Vingt et Unieme 36 place St-Corentin. Very central bar with contemporary decor, including stainless steel walls, and a loungy atmosphere enjoyed by a young, trendy crowd.

Listings

Banks Banque de France, 29 av de la Gare; Crédit Agricole, 33 rue St-Mathieu; Société Générale, 2 rue du Parc.

Bike rental Torch VTT, 58 rue de la Providence ⓣ02.98.53.84.41; Cycle Lennez, 13 rue Aristide Briand ⓣ02.98.90.14.81.

Bookshop For Breton books, try Ar Bed Keltiek, 2 rue du Roi-Gradlon (ⓦwww.arbedkeltiek.com).

CDs Keltia-Musique, 1 place au Beurre (ⓦwww.keltiamusique.com) stocks an enormous range of Breton CDs and DVDs.

Horse riding Centre Équestre UCPA, chemin de Toulven ⓣ02.98.54.84.02; Centre Équestre de Kerfeunteun et Magic Poney, Ferme de Leuriou, 61 chemin Penhoat ⓣ02.98.64.39.38.

Internet access Cybercopy, 3 bd de Kerguélen (Mon 1–7pm, Tues–Fri 9am–7pm, Sat 9am–3pm,

closed mid-July to mid-Aug); Eixxos, 10 bd de Kerguélen (Mon–Sat 1–10pm).
Laundry Lavoir de Kerfeunteun, 6 av de la France Libre.
Post office 37 bd de Kerguélen (Mon–Fri 8am–6.30pm, Sat 8am–noon).
Water park Aquarive, 159 bd de Creac'h Gwen ⓣ02.98.52.00.15.

Bénodet

Once out of its city channel, the Odet takes on the anarchic shape of most Breton inlets, spreading out to lake proportions then turning narrow corners between gorges. The resort of **BÉNODET** at the mouth of the river (reachable by boat from Quimper) has a long sheltered beach on the ocean side. The town is a little overdeveloped but the sands are undeniably good, especially for kids, for whom there's a lot laid on – including windsurfing and "beach club" crèches (Club Mickey is highly recommended). During its less busy periods, such as spring or autumn, Bénodet is one of the best spots for a family holiday in the whole of Brittany.

Across the rivermouth, the equally attractive town of **Ste-Marine** is served by regular pedestrian-only ferries. You can also drive here in a matter of minutes over the graceful **Pont de Cornouaille**, 1km upstream, which offers spectacular views of the estuary.

Practicalities

During the school holidays, three **buses** a day run each way between Quimper and Bénodet, dropping you in the town centre; in school time, services are more frequent, with up to eight buses daily. For details, contact CAT in Quimper (ⓣ02.98.90.88.89). You can also arrive at Bénodet by **boat** from Quimper, and sail west along the coast to Loctudy; these trips as well as fishing excursions are run by Vedettes de l'Odet (see p.331).

Bénodet's **tourist office** is at 51 av de la Mer (April to mid-June Mon–Sat 9.30am–noon & 1.30–6pm; mid-June to mid-Sept Mon–Sat 9am–7pm, Sun 10am–6pm; mid-Sept to March Mon–Sat 9.30am–noon & 2–5pm; ⓣ02.98.57.00.14, ⓦwww.benodet.fr). **Bicycles** can be rented from Cycletty, 5 av de la Mer (ⓣ02.98.57.12.49).

One of the nicest **hotels** in Bénodet is *Les Bains de Mer*, 11 rue du Kerguélen (ⓣ02.98.57.03.41, ⓦwww.lesbainsdemer.com; ❸; closed mid-Nov to Feb), which has comfortable rooms, is close to the port and beach, and has the added attraction of an outdoor heated swimming pool, while nearby *Ker Vennaïk*, 45 av de la Plage (ⓣ02.98.57.15.40; ❷; closed mid-Nov to March), is a reasonable, lower-priced alternative, where some rooms have balconies. Bénodet also has several large **campsites** including uniformly comfortable and well-equipped four-star ones such as *Camping du Port de Plaisance* (ⓣ02.98.57.02.38, ⓦwww.campingbenodet.fr; closed late Sept to March), which has a heated swimming pool; the enormous *Camping du Letty*, southeast of the village next to the plage du Letty, on rue du Canvez (ⓣ02.98.57.04.69, ⓦwww.campingduletty.com; closed early Sept to mid-June), and the *Camping de la Pointe St-Gilles* (ⓣ02.98.57.05.37, ⓦwww.camping-stgilles.fr; closed mid-Sept to April).

Recommended **restaurants** include *Le Spi*, the restaurant at the *Hôtel Gwell-Kaër*, 3 av de la Plage (ⓣ02.98.57.04.38; ❺; closed Jan) – which serves a fantastic €25 menu – and the restaurant at *Hôtel de Ste-Marine* at 19 rue Bac across the rivermouth (ⓣ02.98.56.34.79; ❺; closed Nov, plus Mon in low season), though in summer the *Ste-Marine* tends to be too full to feed non-guests.

Along the south coast

The final, rocky stretch of the Finistère coast that lies east of Bénodet, cut repeatedly by deep valleys, holds some of the region's most ruggedly attractive scenery. Every little indent and inlet seems to harbour its own gorgeous pocket **beach**, around which resorts such as **Fouesnant** have developed, becoming especially popular for family holidays, and there are also a couple of more substantial communities to attract day-trippers: the walled town of **Concarneau**, and the artists' haven of **Pont-Aven**. The inland town of **Quimperlé** and **Le Pouldu** on the coast are the final two stops of any note before you leave Finistère and enter Morbihan. Trains between Quimper and Lorient run well inland from the sea, meaning that only Quimperlé of the towns en route has a rail service, while Concarneau is the only one it's at all practicable to reach by bus.

Fouesnant and around

Not so much a town as a loose conglomeration of villages, **FOUESNANT**, 9km east of Bénodet, is coming to rival its neighbour as a prime destination for family holidays. While Fouesnant itself is renowned for its cider-makers, and holds a pretty little Romanesque church, most local tourist amenities are gathered in its sister community of **LA FORÊT-FOUESNANT**, 3km further east. Clustered along the waterfront at the foot of a hill so steep that caravans are banned from even approaching, it holds an assortment of attractive **hotels** such as the *Hôtel de l'Espérance*, place de l'Église (Ⓣ02.98.56.96.58, ❷; closed mid-Nov to March) and the pricier *Aux Cerisiers*, 3 rue des Cerisiers (Ⓣ02.98.56.97.24, Ⓦwww.auxcerisiers.com; ❸; closed mid-Dec to mid-Jan).

The small resort of **BEG-MEIL**, perched at the headland 3km south of Fouesnant but still under its overall aegis, barely survived the hurricane of 1987, with just a handful of trees to protect its vast expanse of dunes. However, as well as boasting the hotel *Thalamot*, just back from the seafront at 4–6 Le Chemin-Creux (Ⓣ02.98.94.97.38, Ⓦwww.hotel-thalamot.com; ❸; closed Oct–Easter), it makes an ideal spot for campers. Four-star **campsites** include *La Roche Percée* (Ⓣ02.98.94.94.15, Ⓦwww.campingbrittany.com; closed late Sept to early April), which has two pools and a waterslide, and the seafront *Kervastard* (Ⓣ02.98.94.91.52; closed mid-Sept to March). In July and August, a **ferry service**, on the *Vedette Jean-Yvonne* connects Beg-Meil with Concarneau across the bay (departs Beg-Meil Mon–Fri 11am, 2.15pm, 5pm & 6pm; Sat & Sun 2.30pm & 6pm; Ⓣ02.98.97.10.31; €12 return).

Concarneau

CONCARNEAU, on the far side of Fouesnant's Baie de la Forêt and 20km east of Bénodet, ranks as the third most important fishing port in France. Nonetheless, it does a reasonable job of passing itself off as a holiday resort. Its greatest asset is its **Ville Close**, the small and very well-fortified old city located a few metres offshore on an irregular rocky island in the bay.

Arrival and information

Concarneau's **tourist office** (May, June & Sept Mon–Sat 9am–12.30pm & 2–7pm, Sun 9.30am–12.30pm; July & Aug daily 9am–8pm; Oct–April Mon–Sat 9am–noon & 2–6.30pm; Ⓣ02.98.97.01.44, Ⓦwww.ville-concarneau.fr) is just outside the Ville Close on the quai d'Aiguillon, not far from the long-distance

bus stop; there's no rail service, but SNCF buses connect with Quimper and Rosporden. **Bikes** can be rented from Cycles Gloannec, 65 av Alain le Lay (ⓣ02.98.97.09.77).

In summer, Vedettes Glénn (ⓣ02.98.97.10.31) run **ferries** up the Odet to Quimper (Tues–Fri & Sun at 2.15pm from early July to end of August; Wed only at 2.15pm from mid-June to early July and first two weeks of Sept; €22 return); and out to the Îles de Glénan (see p.328). Vedettes de l'Odet also sail to the Îles de Glénan in high season (see p.331). Also in summer, *Vedette Jean-Yvonne* sails across the estuary to **Beg-Meil** (ⓣ02.98.97.10.31; July & Aug Mon–Fri 10.15am, 1.45pm, 4.30pm & 5.30pm, Sat & Sun 2pm & 5.30pm; €12 return).

Accommodation

The Ville Close is almost completely devoid of accommodation options and due to the steady flow of tourists they tend to be full for the majority of the time during the summer, which makes reserving in advance a good idea. The **hostel** (ⓣ02.98.97.03.47, ⓔconcarneau.aj.cis@wanadoo.fr; €10; open all year) is, for once, very near the city centre and enjoys magnificent ocean views; it's just around the tip of the headland on the quai de la Croix, with a good crêperie opposite and a nearby windsurfing shop. There are also some lovely **campsites** a little further on from the hostel, close to the Sables-Blancs beach; the spacious *Prés Verts* spreads through verdant fields at Kernous beach at the far western end of town (ⓣ02.98.97.09.74; closed late Sept to April).

Hôtel de France et d'Europe 9 av de la Gare ⓣ02.98.97.00.64, ⓦwww.hotel-france-europe.com. Bright, modernized and very central hotel near the main bus stop; has a small gym. ❸

Hôtel des Halles place de l'Hôtel de Ville ⓣ02.98.97.11.41, ⓦwww.hoteldeshalles.com. Spruce pastel-orange hotel near the fish market, across from the entrance to the Ville Close, offering well-equipped rooms at reasonable rates. ❸

Hôtel Kermoor plage les Sables-Blancs ⓣ02.98.97.02.96, ⓕ02.98.97.84.04. Lovely old-fashioned seafront hotel, nautically themed throughout, right on the beach 2km west round the headland from town. You pay a little extra for a full-on sea view. ❺

Hôtel-Restaurant les Océanides 3 & 10 rue du Lin ⓣ02.98.97.08.61, ⓦlesoceanides.free.fr. Good-value place a couple of streets up from the sea, above the fishing port, with a highly recommended and reasonably priced restaurant (see p.338). Some of the fancier rooms are in the nominally distinct *Petites Océanides* across the street. ❷

The Town

Although in the height of summer the **Ville Close** can get too crowded for comfort, it's otherwise a real delight. You reach it by crossing a narrow bridge and then passing through two successive gateways, marked by a little clock tower and a sundial. Like those of the *citadelle* at Le Palais on Belle-Île, the ramparts were completed by Vauban in the seventeenth century. The island itself, however, had been inhabited for at least a thousand years before that, and is first recorded as the site of a priory founded by King Gradlon of Quimper.

Concarneau boasts that it is a *ville fleurie*, and the flowers are most in evidence inside the walls, where climbing roses and clematis swarm all over the various gift shops, restaurants and crêperies. Walk the central pedestrianized street to the far end, and you can pass through a gateway to the shoreline to watch the fishing boats go by. In summer, however, the best views of all come from the promenade on top of the **ramparts** (daily 9am–8pm; mid-June to mid-Sept €0.80; mid-Sept to mid-June free).

The **Musée de la Pêche**, immediately inside the Ville Close (daily: July & Aug 9.30am–8pm; Sept–June 10am–noon & 2–6pm; €6), provides an insight into the traditional life Concarneau shared with so many other Breton ports. The four rooms around the central quadrangle illuminate the history and practice of four specific aspects of fishing. The whaling room contains model boats and a genuine open boat from the Azores; the tuna room shows boats dragging nets the size of central Paris; there is a herring room and a model of a sardine cannery – which this building once was. Also on show are oddities collected by fishermen in the past: the swords of swordfish and the saws of sawfish; a Japanese giant crab; photos of old lifeboatmen with fading beards; cases full of sardine and tuna cans; and a live aquarium, where the lobsters little realize they are in no immediate danger of being eaten. In addition, you can buy diagrams and models of ships, and even order a diorama of the stuffed fish of your choice.

Eating

For an atmospheric **meal** in Concarneau, your best bet is to choose from any of the restaurants along the main street that runs through the Ville Close, or explore the little lanes that lead off it. There are, however, plenty of cheaper places back in town.

The main **market** is held in front of the Ville Close on Friday, with a smaller one on Monday; the covered market *halles* on the far side of the square are open every morning, and hold plenty of snack stalls.

Le Bélem 2 rue Hélène Hascoët ⓣ02.98.97.02.78. Pretty little indoor restaurant, next to the market on the mainland, serving mussels for €8.50 and good seafood menus from €15.60. Closed Wed, plus Thurs eve & Sun eve in low season.

Chez Armande 15 av du Dr-Nicholas ⓣ02.98.97.00.76. Excellent seafood not far south of the market on the mainland, on menus starting at €18.90. Closed Wed, & Tues in winter.

Crêperie du Musée 10 rue Vauban ⓣ02.98.97.30.26. Good inexpensive crêpes, served in a family atmosphere, on the right just inside the walled city. Closed Thurs.

L'Escale 19 quai Carnot ⓣ02.98.97.03.31. Waterfront restaurant on the main road in town that's a favourite with local fishermen; lunch menus available for around €9. Closed Sun.

Hôtel-Restaurant les Océanides 3 & 10 rue du Lin ⓣ02.98.97.08.61. One of the better hotel restaurants, again specializing in seafood, with menus up to €25; the €17 option has scallops as a starter and the fish of the day as the main course.

Pont-Aven

PONT-AVEN, 14km east of Concarneau and just inland from the tip of the Aven estuary, is a small port packed with tourists and art galleries. This was where **Paul Gauguin** came to paint in the 1880s, before he left for Tahiti in search of a South Seas idyll. By all accounts Gauguin was a rude and arrogant man who lorded it over the local population (who were already well used to posing in "peasant attire" for visiting artists). As a painter and printmaker, however, he produced some of his finest work in Pont-Aven, and his influence was such that the **Pont-Aven School** of fellow artists developed here. He spent some years working closely with these – the best known of whom was Émile Bernard – and they in turn helped to revitalize his own approach.

For all the local hype, however, the town has no permanent collection of Gauguin's work. The **Musée Municipal** (daily: Feb–June & Sept–Dec 10am–12.30pm & 2–6.30pm; July & Aug 10am–7pm; €4), in the Mairie, holds changing exhibitions of the numerous members of the school, and other artists active in Brittany during the same period, but you can't count on paintings by the man himself.

Gauguin aside, Pont-Aven is pleasant in its own right, with countless galleries making it easy to while away an afternoon, and the small neat pleasure port boasting a watermill and the odd leaping salmon. Just upstream of the little granite bridge at the heart of town, the **promenade Xavier-Grall** crisscrosses the tiny river itself on landscaped walkways, offering glimpses of the backs of venerable mansions, dripping with red ivy, and a little "chaos" of rocks in the stream itself. A longer walk – allow an hour – leads into the **Bois d'Amour**, wooded gardens which have long provided inspiration to visiting painters – and a fair tally, too, of poets and musicians.

If you can't afford to take a souvenir canvas home with you, the town's other speciality is more affordable, and tastes better too. Pont-Aven is the home of two manufacturers of **galettes** – which here means "butter biscuits" rather than "pancakes" – and their products are on sale everywhere.

Practicalities

Pont-Aven's **tourist office**, 5 place de l'Hôtel de Ville (April–June & Sept Mon–Sat 9.30am–12.30pm & 2–7pm, Sun 10am–1pm; July & Aug Mon–Sat 9.30am–7.30pm, Sun 10am–1pm & 3–6.30pm; Oct–March Mon–Sat 10am–12.30pm & 2–6pm; ⓣ02.98.06.04.70, ⓦwww.pontaven.com), sells an excellent and inexpensive English-language guide booklet to the town, which includes route maps of local walks.

Once the day-trippers have gone home, Pont-Aven makes a tranquil place to spend a night. Much the best of the town's three relatively expensive **hotels** is the central *Hôtel des Ajoncs d'Or*, 1 place de l'Hôtel de Ville (ⓣ02.98.06.02.06; ❸; closed Jan, plus Mon & Sun eve in low season), where gourmet menus start at €16.50. The nicest of the local **campsites** is the four-star *Domaine de Kerlann* (ⓣ02.98.06.01.77; closed late Oct to mid-April), set in a large wooded park with a swimming pool, tennis courts and mini-golf.

Throughout the summer, Les Vedettes Aven-Bélon (ⓣ02.98.71.14.59) run **cruises** from the pleasure port down to the sea at Port-Manech. Some continue around to **Port-Bélon** near the mouth of the next estuary, where it's also possible to board the boats. The precise schedule is determined by the state of the tides (April–June & Sept 1 departure daily; July & Aug 1–2 departures daily; short cruises €10, long trips €13).

Bélon

From the unremarkable village of **RIEC-SUR-BÉLON**, 5km southeast of Pont-Aven, back roads snake down for another 4km to reach a dead end at the **port du Bélon**, on the delightfully sinuous estuary of the Bélon River. The coastal footpath that leads away from here along the thickly wooded shoreline is clearly signposted to offer optional loop trails of 3km, 6km and 8km.

Quimperlé

Another 14km east of Pont-Aven, the final town of any size in Finistère, **QUIMPERLÉ**, straddles a hill and two rivers, the Isole and the Elle, cut by a sequence of bridges. It's an atmospheric place, particularly in the medieval muddle of streets around **Ste-Croix church**. This was copied in plan from schema of the Church of the Holy Sepulchre in Jerusalem, brought back by Crusaders, and is notable for its original Romanesque apse. There is a Friday **market** on the square higher up on the hill.

Reasonable **rooms** can be had at *Le Brizeux*, 7 quai Brizeux (ⓣ02.98.96.19.25; ❷), and *Le Kervidanou*, in the village of Mellac 5km northwest (ⓣ02.98.39.18.00; ❸). The best **campsite** in the vicinity is the two-star, British-owned *Bois des Ecureuils* (ⓣ02.98.71.70.98, ⓦwww.bois-des-ecureuils.fr; closed mid-Sept to mid-May), 15km northeast in the verdant countryside at Guilligomarch, north of **Arzano**.

Le Pouldu

At the mouth of the River Laïta, which constitutes the eastern limit of Finistère, the community of **LE POULDU** was another of Paul Gauguin's favourite haunts. It is divided into two distinct sections. The tiny **port**, on one bank of the estuary – most of which has not even a road alongside, let alone any buildings – is shielded from the open sea by a curving spit of sand. The **beach**, more developed than in Gauguin's day but still very picturesque, is a couple of kilometres away, with the headland that separates the two indented with a succession of delightful little sandy coves.

For **rooms**, head to the appealingly weather-beaten white *Hôtel du Pouldu* (Ⓣ02.98.39.90.66; ❸; closed Oct–March), which stands next to the port. Le Pouldu would also make an ideal spot to **camp** for a few days; among sites near the beach is the *Vieux Four* (Ⓣ02.98.39.94.34; closed mid-Sept to Easter).

Travel details

Trains

Brest to: Landerneau (19 daily; 15min); Landivisiau (8 daily; 20min); Morlaix (16 daily; 35min); Paris-Montparnasse (7 TGVs daily; 4hr 20min); Quimper (4 daily; 1hr 15min), with a further 3 SNCF buses daily; Rennes (8 daily; 2hr 15min) .
Quimper to: Lorient (5 daily; 40min); Nantes (3 daily; 2hr 30min); Redon (6 daily; 1hr 40min); Vannes (8 daily; 1hr 10min).
Roscoff to: Morlaix (4 daily; 35min).

Buses

A good source for up-to-date bus timetables in Finistère is Ⓦ infotransports.cg29.fr.
Brest to: Brignogan (7 daily; 1hr); (Camaret (5 daily; 1hr 10min); Le Conquet (7 daily; 40min); Le Faou (7 daily; 30min); Quimper (5 daily; 1hr 15min); Roscoff (3 daily; 1hr 50min), via Plouescat, Lanhouarneau, Lesneven and St-Pol.
Concarneau to: Rosporden (6 daily; 20min).
Morlaix to: Carantec (7 daily; 20min); Carhaix (3 daily; 1hr 30min); Huelgoat (3 daily; 55min); Lannion (Mon–Sat 4 daily; 1hr); Plougasnou (4 daily; 30min); Quimper (1 daily; 1hr 50min); Roscoff (5 daily; 1hr); St-Jean-du-Doigt (4 daily; 25min).
Quimper to: Audierne (10 daily; 50min); Beg-Meil (8 daily; 50min); Bénodet (3–8 daily; 30min); Camaret (3 daily; 1hr 20min); Concarneau (7 daily; 30min); Crozon (3 daily; 1hr 10min); Douarnenez (10 daily; 40min); Fouesnant (8 daily; 30min); Locronan (3 daily; 20min); Plugaffan (7 daily; 20min); Pointe du Raz (5 daily; 1hr 30 min); Quimperlé (3 daily; 1hr 40min); Roscoff (1 daily; 2hr 30min); Telgruc (3 daily; 50min).
Roscoff to: Brest (3 daily; 2hr); Morlaix (5 daily; 1hr); Quimper (1 daily; 2hr 30min).

Ferries

Audierne to: the Île de Sein (June–Sept 1–3 daily; 1hr).
Beg-Meil to: Concarneau (July & Aug Mon–Fri 2–4 daily; 15min).
Brest to: Camaret (July & Aug 2 daily Mon–Fri); Île de Sein (June–Sept 1–3 daily; 1hr 30min); Le Fret (April–Sept 2–4 daily; 25min); Molène (1 daily; 2hr); Ouessant (1–3 daily; 2hr 30min).
Camaret to: Île de Sein (June–Sept 1–3 daily; 1hr); Brest (see p.312); Ouessant and Molène (April–Sept only; see p.309).
Concarneau to: Beg-Meil (July & Aug 2–4 daily; 15min).
Lanildut to: Ouessant (July & Aug 1 daily; 30min).
Le Conquet to: Molène (1–11 daily; 45min); Ouessant (1–11 daily; 30min).
Loctudy to: Îles de Glénan (see p.328).
Quimper to: Bénodet (June–Sept 1–3 daily; 1hr 15min); Îles de Glénan (see p.331).
Roscoff to: Île de Batz (very frequent; 15min).

Flights

Brest airport (Guipavas): to Ouessant, subject to good weather (2 daily; 15min).
Quimper airport (Plugaffan) to: Paris (2–4 daily; 1hr 10min).

6

Inland Brittany: The Nantes–Brest Canal

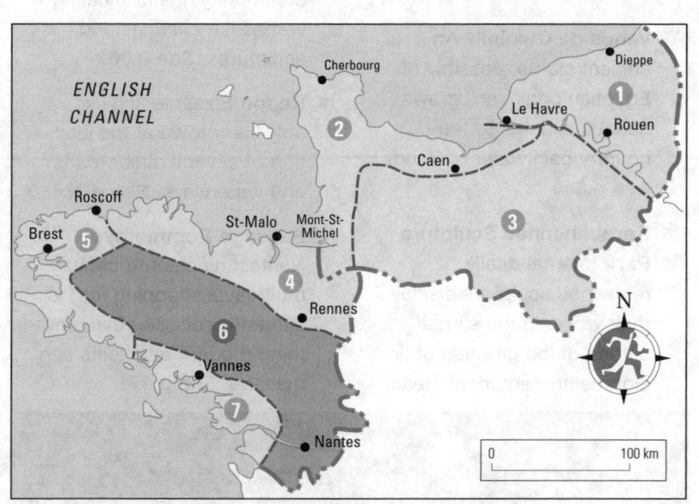

CHAPTER 6

Highlights

* **Huelgoat** A tangled ancient forest, concealing mysterious ruins and deep caverns, all but surrounds an archetypal Breton village. See p.350
* **Hôtel Beau Rivage** Welcoming little hotel in a stunning waterfront location beside the lac de Guerlédan. See p.352
* **Venus de Quinipily** An ancient statue, possibly of Egyptian origin, still draws curious pilgrims to the country backwater of Baud. See p.354
* **Kerguéhennec Sculpture Park** Internationally renowned sculptors display their works in the surreal setting of the grounds of an eighteenth-century château – and you can see them all for free. See p.356
* **Relais de Brocéliande** Delightful village hotel, serving meaty feasts, deep in the heart of the legend-shrouded Arthurian forest of Brocéliande. See p.359
* **Malestroit** The town square in this quiet medieval community has fascinating vernacular carvings and sculptures. See p.361
* **Redon** Sizeable and likeably lively town at the junction of several major roads and waterways. See p.364
* **Passage Pommeraye** Nantes' nineteenth-century multi-level shopping mall is altogether classier than anything modern architects can manage. See p.371

△ Malestroit sculpture

6

Inland Brittany: The Nantes–Brest Canal

The meandering chain of waterways known as the **Nantes–Brest canal**, which interweaves natural rivers with purpose-built stretches of canal, runs all the way from Finistère down to the Loire. En route it passes through medieval riverside towns, such as **Josselin** and **Malestroit**, which long predate its construction; commercial ports and junctions – **Pontivy**, most notably – that developed along its path during the nineteenth century; the old port of **Redon**, where the canal crosses the River Vilaine; and a succession of scenic splendours, including the string of lakes around the **Barrage de Guerlédan** dam near Mur-de-Bretagne. The canal ends at **Nantes**, a major French city with a few interesting things to see – an antique shopping mall among them – amid an awful lot of concrete and chaos.

The canal is ideal as a focus for exploring **inland Brittany**, perhaps cutting in to the towpaths along the more easily accessible stretches, and then heading out to the towns and sights around. Detours can be picked at will; among the least known and most enjoyable are the **sculpture park** at Kerguéhennec, near Josselin, and the village of **La Gacilly** near Malestroit.

According to legend, this area was supposedly covered in the distant past by one vast forest, the *Argoat*. Though vestiges of ancient woodland do remain in several areas, natural and human forces seem to be conspiring to destroy them. The **forest of Huelgoat**, which, with its boulder-strewn waterfalls, bubbling streams and grottoes, was the most dramatic natural landscape in Brittany, is still recovering from the devastating hurricane of 1987. **Paimpont** – the legendary forest of Brocéliande, said to have concealed the Holy Grail – survived that storm, only to be damaged by a succession of serious fires.

You cannot make the whole journey described in this chapter by keeping next to the canal. For much of the way there is no adjacent road, and even though the **towpath** is normally clear enough for walking, it's not really practicable to cycle along for any great distance. However, it's certainly worth following the canal in short sections, which you can do quite easily by car, better by bike, or best of all by renting a **boat**, **barge** or even a **houseboat** along the navigable stretches. Trains and buses are virtually nonexistent.

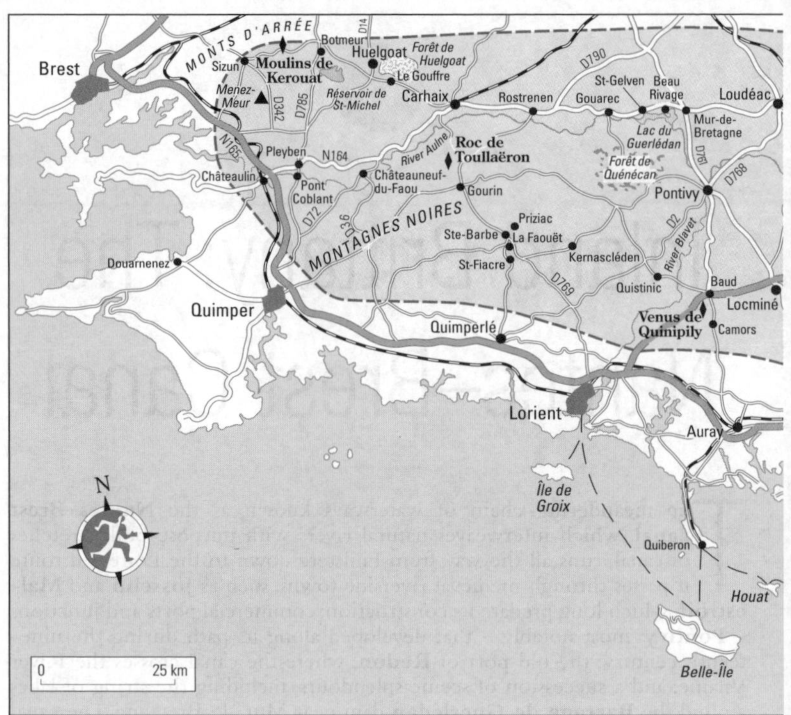

The canal in Finistère

The westernmost section of the canal, passing through Finistère, is now one of its least-used stretches. Those travellers who do set out to follow its course are far more likely to do so from the Crozon peninsula or the Menez-Hom – both covered in the previous chapter – than from Brest itself. However, as recently as the 1920s, steamers made their way across the Rade de Brest and down the River Aulne to Châteaulin. The contemporary *Black's Guide*

The canal

The idea of joining together the inland waterways of Brittany dates back to 1627 – though, as usual, nothing was done to implement the scheme until it was seen as a **military necessity**. That point came during the Napoleonic wars, when English fleets began to threaten the ships circumnavigating the Breton coast. To relieve the virtual blockade of Brest in 1810, Napoléon authorized the construction of a canal network to link it with both Nantes and Lorient.

In the event, economic disasters held up its completion, but by 1836 a navigable path was cut and the canal officially opened. It was not an immediate success. Having cost sixty million francs to construct, the first years of operation, up to 1850, raised a mere 70,000 francs in tariffs. It survived, however, helped by a navy experiment of transporting coal cross-country to its ports. By the end of the nineteenth century, the canal's business was booming: in the years between

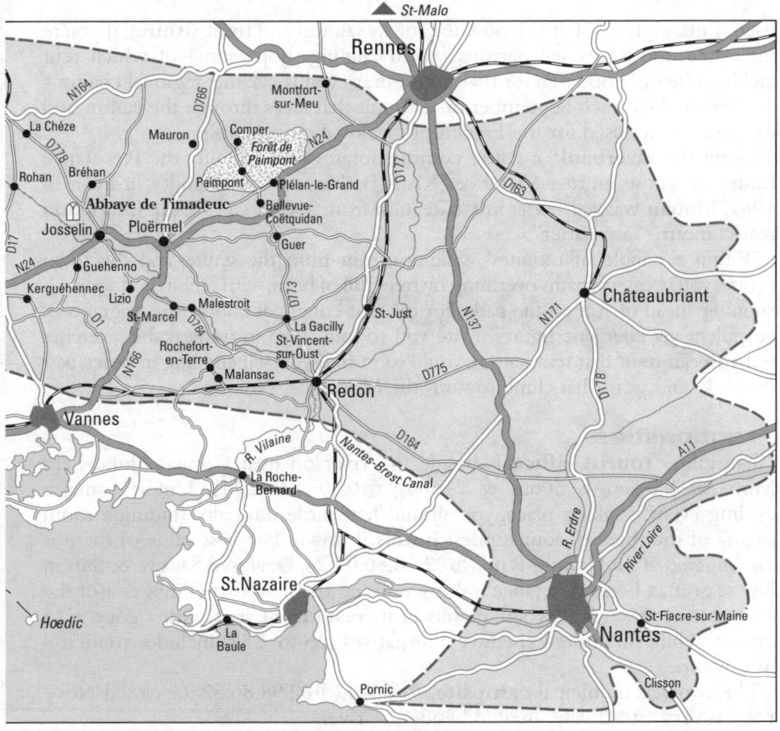

reckoned the six-hour journey "tedious [in a] boat often overcrowded with cattle" – a judgement that seems a little churlish now that such pleasures are no longer available.

Châteaulin and on to Carhaix

CHÂTEAULIN, the first real town on the canal route, amounts to little more than a brief, picturesque waterside strip, overlooked by the pretty little chapel of Notre Dame. It's a quiet place and the main reason to stay is the River Aulne

1890 and the outbreak of World War I, an annual average of 35,000 tonnes of cargo were carried. In addition to coal, the **cargoes** were mainly slate from the quarries near Châteaulin, and fertilizer, which helped to develop agricultural production inland.

After the war, motor transport and more effective roads brought swift **decline**. The canal had always been used primarily for short journeys at either end – from Brest to Carhaix and Pontivy to Nantes – and in 1928 the building of a dam at Lac Guerlédan cut it forever into two sections, with the stretch from Carhaix to Pontivy becoming navigable only by canoe. Plans for the dam were approved on the basis that either a hydraulic lift, or a side channel, would enable barges to bypass it – but neither was ever built. The last barge arrived at Châteaulin in 1945; today, the only industry that has much use for the canal is tourism.

itself. Enticingly rural, it is renowned for its salmon and trout **fishing**; if you're interested, most bars sell permits (as do angling shops, some of which rent tackle). The only other factor that might draw you is cycling: regional championships are held each September on a circuit that races through the centre, and on occasion it's used for the French professional championship.

Along the **riverbank**, a statue commemorates Jean Moulin, the Resistance leader of whose murder SS officer Klaus Barbie was found guilty in Lyon in 1987. Moulin was *sous-préfet* in Châteaulin from 1930 to 1933; the inscription reads "mourir sans parler".

Within a couple of minutes' walk upstream from the statue, and the town centre, you're on towpaths overhung by trees full of birds, with rabbits and squirrels running ahead of you on the path. For the first couple of kilometres, diagrams of corpulent yet energetic figures incite you to join them in unspeakable exercises – if you can resist that temptation, you'll soon find yourself ambling in peace past the locks and weirs that climb towards the Montagnes Noires.

Practicalities

Châteaulin's **tourist office** is beside the river on quai Cosmao (June–Sept Mon–Sat 9.30am–12.30pm & 2–6pm; ☎02.98.86.02.11). Unless a major cycling event is taking place, you should have little difficulty finding a room in any of the three or four modest **hotels** in town. The best value of them is *Le Chrismas* at 33 Grande-Rue (☎02.98.86.01.24; ❸; closed Sat eve & Sun in low season), a Logis de France a short walk up the road that climbs east of the town centre towards Pleyben; menus in its **restaurant** start with a good €13 option, while the more expensive alternatives (up to €32) include wonderful hot oysters.

The two-star municipal **campsite**, *Rodaven* (☎02.98.86.32.93; closed Nov–Feb), is very attractively situated beside the river.

Pont Coblant

If you set out to walk the canal from Châteaulin, the small village of **PONT COBLANT** may look just 10km distant on the map, but be warned: the meanders make it a hike of several hours (pick your side of the water, too, as there are no bridges between Châteaulin and Pont Coblant – if you stay on the north side, it's easier to take a short cut back by road if you're getting tired).

It's possible to rent **kayaks** and **canoes** in Pont Coblant (call ☎02.98.73.34.69). The village also has a tiny, six-room **hotel**, the *Auberge du Poisson Blanc* (☎02.98.73.34.76; ❸), and a two-star **campsite** (☎02.98.73.31.22; closed mid-Sept to mid-June).

Pleyben

PLEYBEN, 4km north of Pont Coblant, is renowned for its sixteenth-century **parish close** (see p.298). On its four sides the calvary traces the life of Jesus, combining great detail with an appealing naivety. The well-scrubbed church of St-Germain itself – twin-towered, with a huge ornate spire dwarfing its domed Renaissance neighbour – features an altarpiece that's blackened and buckled by age.

A summer-only **tourist office** (mid-June to mid-Sept Mon–Sat 10am–12.30pm & 2.30–6pm; ☎02.98.26.71.05; at other times, contact the Mairie ☎02.98.26.68.11) stands in the spacious and grandiose main square, the place de Gaulle, across from one of the village's few **restaurants**, *La Blanche Hermine* (☎02.98.26.61.29; closed Wed), which serves various à la carte Breton specialities from around €9 and up. The nearest hotel is in Pont Coblant (see opposite). On the N164 in between Châteaulin and Pleyben, the *Run Ar Puns* (☎02.98.86.27.95; closed Sun & Mon) is a lively **music club** and bar, housed in old farm buildings, serving a wide selection of beers and specializing in Breton music; rock bands from further afield also play here, but there are no concerts in summer.

Châteauneuf-du-Faou

CHÂTEAUNEUF-DU-FAOU, a little way south of the N164, 25km east of Châteaulin, is much the same sort of low-key destination as Châteaulin and Pleyben, sloping down to the tree-lined river. It's a little more developed, though, with a riverside **tourist complex**, the *Penn ar Pont* (☎02.98.81.81.25; closed mid-Nov to March), which boasts a swimming pool, *gîtes* and camping, as well as cycle and boat rental.

The **canal proper** separates off from the Aulne a few kilometres to the east at Pont Triffen, making its own way past Carhaix, and out of Finistère.

Carhaix and onwards

CARHAIX, a further 25km east, is a road junction that dates back to the Romans, with cafés and shops to replenish supplies, but not much else to recommend it. The most interesting building in town is the granite Renaissance **Maison de Sénéchal** on rue Brisieux, which houses the **tourist office** (July & Aug Mon–Sat 9am–12.30pm & 1.30–7pm, Sun 10am–1pm; Sept–June Mon–Sat 10am–noon & 2–6pm; ☎02.98.93.04.42, Ⓦwww.poher.com). The modern *Hôtel Noz Vad* at 12 bd de la République, near the church (☎02.98.99.12.12, Ⓦwww.nozvod.com; ❸), makes a comfortable if slightly pricey place to spend the night, as well as being the venue for live music concerts in the spring, and art, sculpture and photo exhibitions year-round. In mid-July each year, Carhaix hosts a 3-day **rock festival**, Les Vieilles Charrues.

Beyond Carhaix, the canal – as far as Pontivy – is navigable only by canoe. If that's not how you're travelling, it probably makes more sense to loop round to the south, through the **Montagnes Noires**, Le Faouët and Kernascléden, before rejoining the canal at the **Lac de Guerlédan**. Alternatively, to the north – assuming you resisted the detour from Morlaix – you could explore the **Forêt de Huelgoat** and the **Monts d'Arrée**. These routes are covered in the next two sections.

South through the Montagnes Noires

South of Châteauneuf, the **Montagnes Noires** delineate the southern borders of Finistère. Despite the name, they are really no more than escarpments, though bleak and imposing nonetheless in a harsh, exposed landscape at odds with the gentle canal path. Their highest point is the stark slate **Roc de Toullaëron**, on the road between Pont Triffen and Gourin. From its 318-metre peak, you can look west and north over kilometres of what seems like totally deserted countryside.

Le Faouët to Kernascléden

If you are driving, the D769 beyond Gourin offers access to the twin churches of St-Fiacre and Kernascléden, built simultaneously, according to legend, with the aid of an angelic bridge. En route is the secluded town of **LE FAOUËT**, served neither by buses nor trains, and distinguished mainly by its large old market hall. Above a floor of mud and straw, still used by local traders on market days on the first and third Wednesday of every month, rises an intricate latticework of ancient wood, propped on granite pillars and topped by a little clock tower.

Practicalities

Two similar and highly recommendable **hotels** in the immediate area of Le Faouët both offer good food. The *Croix d'Or*, opposite the old market in the heart of town at 9 place Bellanger (ⓣ02.97.23.07.33; ❸; closed mid-Dec to mid-Jan, plus Sun eve & Mon in low season), has an €25 menu that changes according to the season, but can feature the likes of snail ravioli and skate's wing with thyme. The *Cheval Blanc*, 5 rue Albert St-Jalmes (ⓣ02.97.34.61.15, ⓦwww.hotelrest-cheval-blanc.com; ❸) stands by a lake a few kilometres east in **PRIZIAC**, reached along the pleasant (but steep) D132. Le Faouët also has its own three-star riverside municipal **campsite**, the *Beg-er-Roch* (ⓣ02.97.23.15.11; closed Oct–Feb).

St-Fiacre

The church at **ST-FIACRE**, just over 2km south, is notable for its rood screen, brightly polychromed and carved as intricately as lace. The original purpose of a rood screen was to separate the chancel from the congregation – the decorations of this 1480 masterpiece go rather further than that. They depict scenes from the Old and New Testaments as well as a dramatic series on the wages of sin. Drunkenness is demonstrated by a man somehow vomiting a fox; theft, by a peasant stealing apples; and so on.

Ste-Barbe

The fifteenth-century chapel of **Ste-Barbe** perches on a rocky outcrop a couple of kilometres east of Le Faouët. Accessible only along a very poor road that crosses a bridge over the main D769, it commands views of the deep wooded ravine of the Ellé River. Visitors ring a large bell in the crude bell tower on the hilltop, before descending a steep stone staircase to the chapel itself.

Kernascléden

At the ornate and gargoyle-coated church at **KERNASCLÉDEN**, 15km southeast of Le Faouët along the D782, the focus turns from carving to frescoes. The themes, however, contemporary with St-Fiacre, are equally gruesome. On the damp-infested wall of a side chapel, horned devils stoke the fires beneath a vast cauldron filled with the souls of the damned, and you may be able to discern the outlines of a Dance of Death, a faded cousin to that at Kermaria (see p.268). The ceiling above the main altar holds better-preserved but less bloodthirsty scenes.

The Monts d'Arrée

A broad swathe of the more desolate regions of Finistère, stretching east from the Crozon peninsula right to the edge of Finistère, is designated as the **Parc Régional d'Armorique**. The park, in theory at least, is an area of conservation and of rural regeneration along traditional lines; in reality, lack of funding creates rather less impact. The **Monts d'Arrée**, however, which cut northeast across Finistère from the Aulne estuary, are something of a nature sanctuary; kestrels circle high above the bleak hilltops, sharing the skies with pipits, curlews and great black crows.

Over to the east, the ancient woods of the **Forêt de Huelgoat** can offer an atmospheric afternoon's walking, with the lakeside village of Huelgoat itself making an attractive base if you have the time to linger.

East across the Monts d'Arrée

The most obvious place to pick up information on the Parc d'Armorique is at **MENEZ-MEUR**, off the D342 near the Forêt de Cranou – just inland from the Brest–Quimper motorway. Menez is an official **animal reserve**, with wild boar and deer roaming free, and a museum of Breton horses (March, April, Oct & Nov Wed, Sun & hols 1.30–5.30pm; May, June & Sept daily 10am–6pm; July & Aug daily 10am–7pm; Dec–Feb Wed, Sun & hols 1–5pm; €3.20). Rangers at the reserve gate can provide a wealth of detail on the park and all its various activities (Ⓣ02.98.68.81.71, Ⓦwww.parc-naturel-armorique.fr).

Ten kilometres north, at **SIZUN**, a research station, **aquarium** and fishing exhibition sets out to increase public awareness of the significance of Brittany's rivers and inland waterways (June & Sept Mon–Fri 10am–noon & 2–5.30pm, Sun 2–5.30pm; July & Aug daily 10am–7pm; Oct–May Mon–Fri 10am–noon & 2–5.30pm, Sun 2–5.30pm during hols only; €4; Ⓣ02.98.68.86.33, Ⓦwww.maison-de-la-riviere.fr).

The Moulins de Kerouat

Another 3km east of Sizun, along the D764 to Commana, is the abandoned hamlet of **MOULINS DE KEROUAT** (*Milin-Kerroc'h* in Breton – and on the Michelin map), which has been restored as an **Eco-Musée** (Feb hols & Christmas hols Mon–Fri 10am–5pm; mid-March to May, Sept & Oct Mon–Fri 10am–6pm, Sun 2–6pm; June Mon–Fri 10am–6pm, Sat & Sun 2–6pm; July & Aug daily 11am–7pm; €4.50). Kerouat's last inhabitant died in 1967 and, like many a place in the Breton interior, it might have crumbled into indiscernible ruins. However, one of the hamlet's water mills has been restored to motion, and its houses repaired and refurnished as part of the museum. The largest belonged in the nineteenth century to the mayor of Commana, who also controlled the mills, and its furnishings are therefore those of a rich family.

Into the mountains

The highest point of the Monts d'Arrée is the **ridge** which curves from the **Réservoir de St-Michel** (also known as the Lac de Brennilis) to Menez Kaldor. It is visible as a stark silhouette from the underused but attractive and well-equipped **campsite** at **NESTAVEL-BRAS** on the eastern shore of the lake (Ⓣ02.98.99.66.57; closed mid-Sept to mid-June). From this deceptively tranquil vantage point, the army's antennae near **Roc Trévezel** to the north are obscured, as are those of the navy at Menez-Meur to the west. Right behind you, however, is the Brennilis nuclear power station. In a rare manifestation of separatist terrorism, Breton nationalists attacked this in 1975 with a rocket-launcher; it survived. In 1987, the British SAS conducted an astonishingly offensive exercise in this area, when they were invited by the French government to subdue a simulated Breton uprising, and in the process managed to run over a local inhabitant.

Perhaps appropriately, across the lake where the tree-lined fields around the villages end, is **Yeun Elez** – a hole to hell, according to legend. You can walk around the lake – gorse and brambles permitting; be very careful not to stray from the paths into the surrounding peat bogs. The ridge itself is followed most of the way by a road, but in places it still feels as if miles from any habitation.

In the village of **BOTMEUR**, a couple of kilometres northwest of Yeun Elez, you'll find an attractive and welcoming **B&B**, run by Mme Solliec, in a small cluster of converted country houses (Ⓣ02.98.99.63.02, Ⓔmsol@club-internet.fr; ❸).

The Forêt de Huelgoat

The **FORÊT DE HUELGOAT** spreads out to the north and east of the village of Huelgoat, the halfway point between Morlaix and Carhaix on the minor road D769, and is served by the three daily buses that connect the two towns. **HUELGOAT** itself was the ancestral home of the Kerouac family, as in Jack Kerouac of *On The Road* fame; it still makes quite a pleasant overnight stop, next to its own small **lake**.

While there may be doubt as to whether the *Argoat*, the great forest supposed to have stretched the length of prehistoric inland Brittany, ever existed, the antiquity of Huelgoat cannot be questioned. Until 1987, this was a staggering landscape of trees, giant boulders and waterfalls tangled together in primeval chaos. Just how fragile it really was, just how miraculous had been its long survival, was demonstrated by the **hurricane** of that October, which smashed it to smithereens in the space of fifteen minutes.

After several years of restoration, the forest has now returned to a fairly close approximation of its former glories. You might be a little puzzled by some of the hyperbolic descriptions that survive from the old days in the local tourist

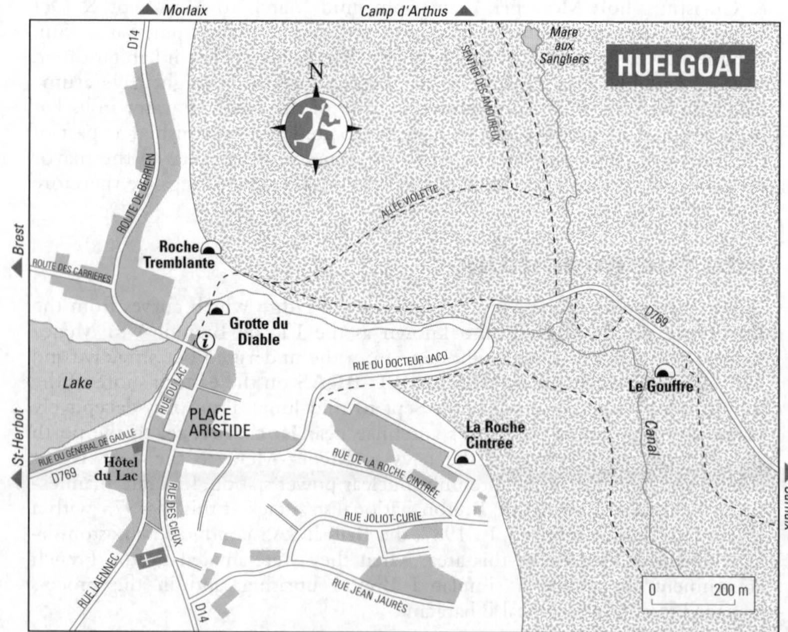

literature and other sources, but it is once again possible to walk for several kilometres along the various paths that lead into the depths of the woods, and in spring and autumn in particular Huelgoat merits a substantial detour.

The strange granite formations of Huelgoat have survived better than the trees, and a half-hour stroll in the area close to the village enables you to scramble over, among, and even under a number of inconceivably large specimens. At the **Grotte du Diable** ("Devil's Cave"), you can make a somewhat perilous descent, between the rocks, to a subterranean stream. The local story is that a Revolutionary soldier, fleeing from the *Chouans* (see p.431), hid in the cave, lighting a fire to keep warm; when his pursuers saw him by the red glow, brandishing a pitchfork to defend himself, they thought they'd found the Devil. In summer, a "teahouse" and crêperie (☎02.98.99.93.00) serves snacks to walkers, a few metres from the disappointingly stable **Roche Tremblante** ("trembling rock").

Further into the forest, not far from the waterfall known as the **Mare aux Sangliers**, the **Camp d'Arthus** has been identified as a Gallo-Roman *oppidum*, or hillfort, large enough to be a settlement for a whole community rather than just a military encampment. Until the hurricane, it was also the spitting image of Astérix the Gaul's fictional village. It's now barely recognizable, although the obliteration of the tree cover enabled archeologists to get a clearer view of its history.

Practicalities

Huelgoat's **tourist office**, in the old Maison du Moulin, alongside the outflow from the lake where the forest footpath begins (July & Aug Mon–Sat 10am–12.30pm; Sept–June Mon–Fri 10am–noon & 2–4.30pm; ☎02.98.99.72.32), supplies walking maps of the forest. One or two of the village's **hotels** were too hard hit by the post-hurricane decline in tourism to survive, but the *Hôtel du Lac*, beside the lake at 9 rue du Général-de-Gaulle (☎02.98.99.71.14; ❸; closed Mon & Jan), is still there, offering well-refurbished rooms and an inexpensive grill **restaurant**, serving chicken from €7, steaks from €11, and *moules frites* for €8.50. Also alongside the lake, on the road towards Brest, the two-star *Camping du Lac* (☎02.98.99.78.80; closed mid-Sept to mid-June) is complete with swimming pool. Five kilometres south of Huelgoat in the small village of **PLOUYÉ**, the *Ti Elise* (☎02.98.99.96.44) is a **bar** well known in these parts for its concerts of traditional Breton music.

Le Gouffre

A walk out from Huelgoat that avoids the heart of the forest takes you along the **canal** to the east. This stretch – not linked to any of the main Nantes–Brest waterways – was originally built to serve the old lead and silver mines, worked here from Roman times right up to this century. **LE GOUFFRE**, close by at the junction where the road out from Huelgoat joins the D769 between Morlaix and Carhaix, is worth the walk to admire its deep cave.

Back to the canal

Although between Carhaix and Pontivy the **Nantes–Brest canal** is limited to canoeists, it's worth some effort to follow on land, particularly for the scenery along the middle stretch from **Gouarec** to **Mur-de-Bretagne**. At the centre lies the artificial **Lac de Guerlédan**, backed to the south by the **Forêt de Quénécan**.

Approaching by road, the canal path is easiest joined at Gouarec, covered by the three daily buses between Carhaix and Loudéac. En route, you pass the rather subdued (and unmemorable) town of **ROSTRENEN**, whose old facades are given a little life at the Tuesday **market**.

Gouarec

At **GOUAREC**, the River Blavet and the canal meet in a confusing swirl of water that shoots off, edged by footpaths, in the most unlikely directions. The old houses of the town are barely disturbed by traffic or development, nor are there great numbers of tourists.

For a comfortable overnight stop, the *du Blavet* **hotel** (Ⓣ02.96.24.90.03, Ⓔlouis.le-loir@wanadoo.fr; ❷; restaurant closed Sun eve & Mon in low season) is in an ideal waterside position; its restaurant is principally aimed at gourmets prepared to spend a small fortune on a single bottle of wine to go with their €50 menus, although the cheapest menu (weekdays only; €14) is also of good quality. There's a well-positioned, British-run two-star **campsite**, the *Tost Aven* (Ⓣ02.96.24.85.42; closed Oct–Easter), next to the canal and away from the main road, which also rents bikes.

Lac de Guerlédan

For the 15km between Gouarec and Mur-de-Bretagne, the **N164** skirts the edge of the **Forêt de Quénécan**, within which is the series of artificial lakes created when the Barrage of Guerlédan was completed in 1928. It's a beautiful stretch of river, if a little overpopular with British camper-caravanners, but peaceful enough nonetheless.

Just off the road at the village of **ST-GELVEN**, the beautiful **Abbaye de Bon-Repos** nestles beside the water at the end of an avenue of ancient trees. Most of what now survives of this twelfth-century Cistercian abbey, largely destroyed during the French Revolution, are its former outbuildings, which until recently housed a lovely little hotel. The ruins of the abbey are open to visitors (March to mid-June & mid-Sept to Oct daily 2–6pm; mid-June to mid-Sept daily 11am–7pm; €3; Ⓣ02.96.24.82.20, Ⓦwww.bon-repos.com) and also play host to *son et lumière* spectacles in August (information on Ⓣ02.96.24.85.28, Ⓦwww.pierresdelegendes.fr.fm; €15), while its grounds are taken over by an **organic farmers' market** on Sundays from Easter to November. A little further down the lane, a tiny stone bridge crosses the canal, and the towpath squeezes alongside meadows that are popular with picnickers.

From just before **CAUREL**, the brief loop of the D111 leads to tiny sandy beaches – a bit too tiny in season. At the spot known justifiably as **Beau Rivage** stands the *Hôtel Beau Rivage* (Ⓣ02.96.28.52.15; ❸; closed Mon & Tues). It may not be at all prepossessing as a building, and the bedrooms though new and well equipped are carpeted all the way up the wall in the worst French tradition, but it commands magnificent views of the lake and serves great food, with dinner menus from €17 and even crêpes for breakfast. *L'Embarcadère* **restaurant** here (Ⓣ02.96.28.52.64) serves good meals on its own terrace, and also serves as the base for two glass-topped sightseeing boats, the *Duc de Guerlédan I* and *II*, that offer pleasure cruises (€8.20) as well as three-hour dinner trips (€28.80–54.50) on the Lac de Guerlédan to no very fixed schedule between March and October (Vedettes de Guerlédan Ⓣ02.96.28.52.64, Ⓦwww.guerledan.com). Beau Rivage is a very popular spot for **water-skiing** (Ⓣ02.96.26.02.18), and holds several **campsites** too, including the four-star

Nautic International (☎02.96.28.57.94; closed Oct to mid-May), complete with heated swimming pool and offering plenty of water sports, and the simpler, two-star *Les Pins* (☎02.96.28.52.22; closed Oct–March).

Mur-de-Bretagne and Loudéac

MUR-DE-BRETAGNE, set back from the eastern end of the lake, is a lively place with a wide and colourful pedestrianized zone around its church. It's the nearest town to the barrage – just 2km distant – and has a **campsite**, the *Rond-Point du Lac* (☎02.96.26.01.90; closed mid-Sept to mid-June), with facilities for windsurfing and horse-riding.

LOUDÉAC, useful for changing buses, is in itself unmemorable. Travelling on from Mur-de-Bretagne under your own steam, you'd do better to take the D767 instead and follow the River Blavet south.

The central canal

Beyond the barrage of Guerlédan, the historic town of **Pontivy** is the central junction of the Nantes–Brest canal, where the course of the canal breaks off once more from the Blavet and you can again take **barges** – all the way to the Loire. Until you get as far as **Josselin**, with its imposing waterfront ducal castle, none of the towns en route are all that enthralling, but there are some quirky rural attractions nearby, such as the enigmatic statue known as the Venus de Quinipily near **Baud**.

Pontivy and on to Bréhan

PONTIVY owes much of its appearance, and its size, to the canal. When the waterway opened, the small medieval centre was expanded, redesigned and given broad avenues to fit its new role. It was even renamed **Napoléonville** for a time, in honour of the instigator of its new prosperity, and still uses the name fairly interchangeably.

These days it is a bright market town, its twisting old streets contrasting with the stately riverside promenades. At the north end of the town, occupying a low eminence above the main through road, is the **Château de Rohan**, built by the lord of Josselin in the late fifteenth century (April–June & Sept daily 10am–noon & 2–6pm; July & Aug daily 10.30am–7pm; Oct, Nov, Feb & March Wed–Sun 2–6pm; €4). Used in summer for low-key cultural events and temporary exhibitions, the castle still belongs to the Josselin family, who are slowly restoring it. At the moment, one impressive facade, complete with deep moat and two forbidding towers, looks out over the river – behind that, the structure rather peters out.

Practicalities

Pontivy's *gare SNCF* is close to the River Blavet, roughly ten minutes' walk south of the helpful local **tourist office**, which is immediately below the castle in a cottage that was once a leprosy hospital at 61 rue du Général-de-Gaulle (Mon–Sat 10am–noon & 2–6pm; ☎02.97.25.04.10). If you're looking for a place to stop over, the town has several **hotels**, among them the smart but inexpensive *Porhoët*, very near the tourist office at 41 rue du Général-de-Gaulle (☎02.97.25.34.88, ⓔhotel-duporhoet@wanadoo.fr; ❸), which has a bar but no restaurant, and the central, opulent *Europe*, 12 rue

François-Mitterand (Ⓣ02.97.25.11.14, Ⓦwww.hotellerieurope.com; ④), where menus start at €15. In addition, the local **hostel**, 2km from the *gare SNCF* on the Île des Récollets (Ⓣ02.97.25.58.27; €9.30), has undergone a long-overdue renovation, and looks great; it also serves cheap meals.

Rohan

Immediately beyond Pontivy, the **course of the canal** veers north for a while, away from the Blavet. As it curves back, the stretch from St-Maudan to Rohan is wide and smooth-flowing, with picnic and play areas but without a road or towpath you can follow for any distance.

ROHAN looks prominent on the map, but it's little more than a strip of houses by the canalside. To the northeast, the attractive village of **La Chèze** has a tiny and private lake, with an equally diminutive one-star **campsite**, *La Rivière* (Ⓣ02.96.26.61.86; closed mid-Sept to mid-June). **La Trinité Porhoët**, 22km east of Rohan, also has a two-star **campsite**, *St-Yves* (Ⓣ02.97.93.92.00; closed mid-Sept to mid-June), on the long wooded slopes of the valley of the Ninian – otherwise scattered with stone farms and manor houses.

Southeast from Rohan, continuing along the canal towards Josselin, is the Cistercian **Abbaye de Timadeuc** (daily 9am–7pm, closed Sat & Sun 11am–12.30pm for Mass; free), founded as recently as 1841 and as picturesque a church as you'll find, with its front walls and main gate covered in flowers at the end of an avenue of old pines.

West from Pontivy: along the Blavet

If you choose to follow the **River Blavet** west from Pontivy towards Lorient – rather than the canal – take the time to go by the smaller roads along the valley itself. The Blavet connects the canal with the sea, and once linked Lorient to the other two great ports of Brittany, Brest and Nantes.

Quistinic

The D159 to **QUISTINIC** passes through lush green countryside, its hedgerows full of flowers, where by June there's already been one harvest and grass is growing up around the fresh haystacks. The ivy-clad church of **St-Mathurin** in Quistinic is the scene of a pardon (in the second week of May) that dates from Roman times. The devotion to the saint is strongly evident on the village's war memorial, too – his name is that of almost half the victims.

You can **camp** on the edge of Quistinic, near the river at the two-star *Île de Minazen* (Ⓣ02.97.39.70.99; closed mid-Sept to mid-June).

Baud: the Venus de Quinipily

The main reason to go on to **BAUD**, a major road junction just to the east of the river, is to see the **Venus de Quinipily**. Signposted off the Hennebont road, 2km out of town, the Venus is a crude statue that at first glance looks Egyptian. Once known as the "Iron Lady", it is of unknown but ancient origin. It stands on, or rather nestles its ample buttocks against, a high plinth above a kind of sarcophagus, commanding the valley in the gardens of what was once a château. Behind its stiff pose and dress, the statue has an odd informality, a half-smile on the otherwise impassive face. It used to be the object of "impure rites" and was at least twice thrown into the Blavet by Christian authorities, only to be fished out by locals eager to reindulge. It may itself have been in some way "improper" before it was recarved, perhaps literally "dressed", some time in the eighteenth century.

The **gardens** around the statue, despite being next to a dry and dusty quarry, are luxuriantly fertile. To visit, you pay a small fee to a woman at the gatehouse, who matter-of-factly maintains that "pagans" still come to worship here (Jan–April & Nov to mid-Dec Wed–Mon 11am–5pm; May–Oct daily 10am–7pm).

There are **rooms** to suit all price ranges at the *Relais de la Forêt* (Ⓣ02.97.51.01.77; ❷), opposite the town hall in Baud, and the similarly inexpensive *Auberge du Cheval Blanc*, a Logis de France nearby at 16 rue de Pontivy (Ⓣ02.97.51.00.85; ❷; closed Jan). Both of these hotels have **restaurants**, where menus start at around €13.

Camors and Locminé

CAMORS, just south of Baud, has a smart square-towered **church**, with a weathercock on top and a little megalith set in the wall. You can spend the night here at the *Hôtel-Restaurant Ar Brug*, at 14 rue Principale opposite the church (Ⓣ02.97.39.20.10; ❶), which has rather run-of-the-mill rooms, but also an excellent restaurant that doesn't scrimp on the portions. For campers, there's a two-star **campsite**, *du Petit Bois* (Ⓣ02.97.39.18.36; closed Sept–June), situated at one end of the series of forests that grow bleaker and harsher eastwards to become the Lanvaux Moors.

Heading east from Baud, to rejoin the canal at Josselin, you pass through **LOCMINÉ**, another one of those towns reduced to piping rock music in its lifeless streets on summer afternoons in a desperate attempt to draw visitors. It, too, has a reasonable little **hotel**, the *Hôtel-Restaurant de Bretagne*, 10 rue Max-Jacob (Ⓣ02.97.60.00.44; ❷; restaurant closed Sun), with a cheap good-value dining room.

Josselin and on to Ploërmel

The three Rapunzel towers of the **Château de Rohan** at **JOSSELIN**, embedded in a vast sheet of stone above the water, are the most impressive sight along the Nantes–Brest canal. However, they turn out on close inspection to be no more than a facade. The building behind was built in the last century, the bulk of the original castle having been demolished by Richelieu in 1629 in punishment for Henri de Rohan's leadership of the Huguenots. The Rohan family, still in possession, used to own a third of Brittany, though the present incumbent contents himself with the position of local mayor.

Tours of the oppressively formal apartments of the ducal residence are not very compelling, even if it does contain the table on which the Edict of Nantes was signed in 1598. But the duchess's collection of ancient **dolls**, around 600 in total, housed in the **Musée des Poupées**, behind the castle, is something special (château and doll museum April, May & Oct Sat, Sun & hols 2–6pm; June–mid-July & Sept daily 2–6pm; mid-July–Aug daily 10am–6pm; each €6.60, combined ticket €11.50). English-language tours of the castle start daily at 2.30pm in June and September, and daily at 11am and 2.30pm in July and August.

The **town** is full of medieval splendours, from the castle ramparts to the gargoyles of the basilica of **Notre Dame du Roncier**, as well as the half-timbered houses in between. The basilica was built on the spot where in the ninth century a peasant supposedly found a statue of the Virgin under a bramble bush. The statue was burned during the Revolution, but an important *pardon* is held each year on September 8. As ever, the religious procession and open-air services are solemn in the extreme, but there's a lot of other stuff going on to keep you entertained.

One of the most famous episodes of late chivalry, the **Battle of the Thirty**, took place nearby in 1351. Rivalry between the French garrison at Josselin and the English at Ploërmel led to a challenge being issued to settle differences in a combat of thirty unmounted knights from each side. The French won, killing the English leader Bemborough. The actual battle site, marked by a small monument, is now isolated between the two carriageways of the N24 from Josselin to Ploërmel.

Practicalities

Josselin's **tourist office** is in a superb old house on the place de la Congrégation, up in town next to the castle entrance (April–June & Sept Mon–Sat 10am–noon & 2–6pm; July & Aug daily 10am–6pm; Oct–March Mon–Fri 9.30am–noon & 2–5.30pm, Sat 10am–noon; ⓣ02.97.22.36.43, ⓦwww.paysdejosselin-tourisme.com).

A good place to **stay** is the lovely *Hôtel du Chateau*, a Logis de France facing the castle from across the river at 1 rue du Général-de-Gaulle (ⓣ02.97.22.20.11, ⓦwww.hotel-chateau.com; ❷–❹; closed Feb), where rooms with views of the château are slightly more expensive, but worth it. The nearest good **campsite** is the three-star *Bas de la Lande* (ⓣ02.97.22.22.20, ⓔcampingbasdelalande@wanadoo.fr; closed Nov–March), half an hour's walk from the castle, south of the river and west of town, where some simple chalets are also available for rental, by the week in summer. There's also the **Gîte d'étape de l'Écluse** nearby, right below the castle walls, where a dorm bed for the night costs €7.94, and you can also rent canoes or kayaks (ⓣ02.97.75.67.18 or ⓣ02.97.22.24.17; closed mid-Jan to Feb).

Guéhenno

At **GUÉHENNO**, 10km south of Josselin on the D123, you'll find one of the largest and best of the Breton **calvaries**. Built in 1550, the figures include the cock that crowed to expose Peter's denials, Mary Magdalene with the shroud, and a recumbent Christ in the crypt. Its appeal is enhanced by the naivety of its amateur restoration. After damage caused by Revolutionary soldiers in 1794 – who amused themselves by playing boules with the heads of the statues – all the sculptors approached for the work demanded exorbitant fees, so the parish priest and his assistant decided to undertake the task themselves.

Kerguéhennec Sculpture Park

Another unusual sculptural endeavour, this time contemporary, takes place at the **Domaine de Kerguéhennec**, signposted a short way off the D11 near St-Jean-Brévelay, 7km west of Guéhenno. This innovatory **sculpture park** (mid-Jan to mid-June & mid-Sept to mid-Dec Tues–Sun 10am–6pm; mid-June to mid-Sept Tues–Sun 10am–7pm; free; ⓣ02.97.60.44.44, ⓦwww.art-kerguehennec.com) is progressively building up a fascinating permanent international collection, under the auspices of the *département* of Morbihan.

Among the first pieces to be installed, back in 1986, was a massive railway sleeper painstakingly stripped down by Giuseppe Penone to reveal the young sapling within; since then the park has become an increasingly compelling stop. Its setting is the lawns, woods and lake of an early eighteenth-century château; studios and indoor workshops in the outbuildings are used by visiting artists.

Lizio

Nine kilometres in the opposite direction from Guéhenno, off the D151, the little village of **LIZIO** has also set itself up as a centre for arts and crafts, with ceramic and weaving workshops as its speciality. For most of the year, you might pass along its single curving street of stone cottages without seeing a sign of life; on the second Sunday in August, however, it's the scene of a **Festival Artisanal**, featuring street theatre (and pancakes). In addition, if you do take the trouble to stop, you may spot that one venerable old cottage, from the outside looking much like the rest, houses an **Insectarium** (April– Sept daily Mon 10am–noon & 1.30–6.30pm; Oct–March Sat & Sun 1.30–6pm; €5.50). Creepy-crawlies within include all sorts of hairy spiders, giant millipedes, huge iridescent butterflies, praying mantises that look like dead leaves, and stick insects in amazing colours. It's a little expensive for twenty minutes on the verge of nausea, but the kids will probably love it.

Various farmers in the nearby countryside, who welcome visitors, are working to re-create traditional skills such as beekeeping and cider-making, and one is even rearing wild boars for food. For details of them all, and an overview of long-lost agricultural techniques and implements, call in at the **Eco-Musée des Vieux Métiers**, 4km out of Lizio on the D174 towards Ploërmel (Feb, March & Oct daily 2–6pm; April–Sept daily 10am–noon & 2–7pm; €5).

Lizio has no hotels, but it does have a couple of restaurants. There's also a two-star municipal **campsite**, *Le Val Jouin* (Ⓣ02.97.74.92.67; closed mid-Oct to mid-June), as well as several **gîtes** in the immediate area (for information, call Ⓣ02.97.74.92.67).

Ploërmel

PLOËRMEL, whose English garrison was defeated by Josselin in the fourteenth-century Battle of the Thirty (see opposite), is still not quite a match for its rival. It's not on the canal, and neither is it any longer served by trains. Attractions are the artificial **Étang au Duc**, well stocked with fish, 2km to the north, and an interesting array of houses: James II is said to have spent a few days of his exile in one on rue Francs-Bourgeois, while the **Maison des Marmosets** on rue Beaumanoir has some elaborate carvings.

Ploërmel's **tourist office**, 5 rue du Val (mid-June to mid-Sept Mon–Sat 9.30am–7pm, Sun 9.30am–12.30pm; Ⓣ02.97.74.02.70, Ⓦwww.ploermel.com), holds a nice model of the town as it looked in 1500. A couple of good-value **hotels** – *St-Marc*, near the long-defunct railway station at 1 place de St-Marc (Ⓣ02.97.74.00.01; ❷), and the very fancy *Cobh*, behind a yellow facade at 10 rue des Forges (Ⓣ02.97.74.00.49, Ⓔle.cobh@wanadoo.fr; ❹), where menus start at €15 – make suitable bases for venturing further away from the canal, up into Paimpont forest.

The Forêt de Paimpont

A definite magic still lingers about the **FORÊT DE PAIMPONT**. Though now just forty square kilometres in extent, it seems to retain the secrets of a forest once much larger, and everywhere recalls legends of the vanished *Argoat*, the great primeval forest of Brittany. The one French claimant to an Arthurian past that carries any real conviction, it is just as frequently known by its Arthurian name of **Brocéliande**. Its central village, **Paimpont**, is much the nicest of the little settlements scattered in and around the woodlands, and has a great hotel.

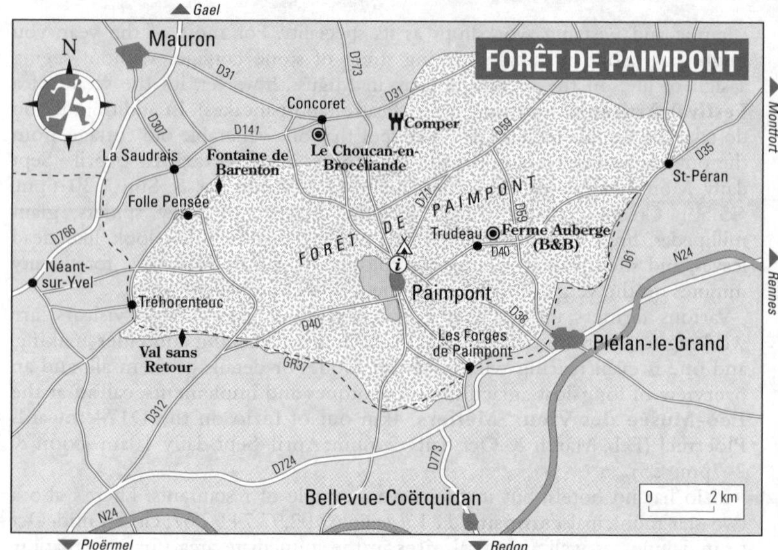

The Forest and its myths

Medieval Breton minstrels, like their Welsh counterparts, set the tales of King Arthur and the Holy Grail both in *Grande Bretagne* and here in *Petite Bretagne*. The particular significance of Brocéliande was as the forest where **Merlin** made his home; some say that he is still here, in "Merlin's stone", where he was imprisoned by the enchantress Viviane.

The stone is next to the **Fontaine de Barenton**, a lonely spot high in the woods that is far from easy to find. Turn off the main road into the forest from **Concoret** (a village notable for having once supposedly had the Devil as its rector) at La Saudrais, and you will come to the village of **Folle Pensée**. Go past the few farmhouses, rather than up the hill, and you arrive at a small car park. A footpath leads up to the right, running through pine and gorse. At a junction of forest tracks, continue straight ahead for about 200m, then veer left along an unobvious (and unmarked) path which leads into the woods, turning back to the north to the spring – walled in mossy stone in the roots of a mighty tree, and filled with the most delicious water imaginable.

Chrétien de Troyes sang of the fountain in the early Middle Ages:

You will see the spring which bubbles
Though its water is colder than marble.
It is shaded by the most beautiful tree
That Nature ever made,
For its foliage is evergreen
And a basin of iron hangs from it,
By a chain long enough
To reach the spring;
And beside the spring you will find
A slab of stone which you will recognize –
I cannot describe it
For I have never seen one like it.

Legend has it that, if after drinking, you splash water on to the stone slab, you instantly summon a mighty storm, together with roaring lions and a horseman in black armour. This story dates back at least to the fifth century and is recounted, somewhat sceptically, in Robert Wace's *Romance of the Rose*, written around 1160:

Hunters repair (to the fountain) in sultry weather; and drawing water with their horns, they sprinkle the stone for the purposes of having rain, which is then wont to fall, they say, throughout the forest around; but why I know not. There too fairies are to be seen (if the Bretons tell truth), and many other wonders happen. I went thither on purpose to see these marvels. I saw the forest and the land, and I sought for the marvels, but I found none. I went like a fool, and so I came back. I sought after folly, and found myself a fool for my pains.

The parish priest of Concoret and his congregation are reported nonetheless to have successfully ended a drought by this means in 1835, and a procession endorsed by the church went to the spring as recently as 1925.

Comper and the Val sans Retour

At Barenton, you are at the very spot where Merlin first set eyes on Viviane, although you are not at the Fountain of Eternal Youth, which is hidden somewhere nearby and accessible only to the pure in heart. The enchantress is supposed to have been born at the château at **COMPER**, at the northern edge of the forest near Concoret. Today it serves as the **Centre de l'Imaginaire Arthurien**, which means that each summer it's the venue of different exhibitions and entertainments on Arthurian themes; the centre also organizes tours of the actual forest. Unless you're sure the theme of this year's temporary exhibition will interest you, don't bother paying to go in – the permanent displays of pointlessly posed mannequins are boring in the extreme (April–June & Oct Thurs–Mon 10am–5.30pm; July–Sept Thurs–Tues 10am–7pm; €5; ⓣ02.97.22.79.96, ⓦwww.centre-arthurien.com).

Viviane's rival, Morgane le Fay, ruled over the **Val sans Retour** (Valley of No Return) on the western edge of the forest. The valley is situated just off the GR37 footpath from Tréhorenteuc to La Guette. Follow the path that leads out from the D141 south of Tréhorenteuc to a steep valley from which exits are barred by thickets of gorse and giant furze on the rocks above. At one point it skirts past an overgrown table of rock, the **Rocher des Faux Amants** ("Rock of the False Lovers") – from which the seductress Morgane was wont to entice unwary and faithless youths.

Paimpont village and other forest bases

PAIMPONT village is the most obvious and enjoyable base for exploring the forest. Consisting of little more than a single little street of stone cottages, it's right at the centre of the woods, backs onto a marshy lake whose shores are thick with wild mushrooms (*cèpes*), and has some excellent accommodation. At the **hotel** *Relais de Brocéliande* (ⓣ02.99.07.84.94, ⓦwww.le-relais-de-broceliande.fr; ❸), a real flower-bedecked delight that centres on a gorgeous carved and painted bar and fireplace, you can stuff yourself for €23.50 in the restaurant under the gaze of stuffed animal heads. The food is hearty in the extreme, with Breton dishes interspersed with the odd Alsacian offering, betraying the owner's origins.

Information on local walking opportunities – the best megalithic site in the vicinity is undoubtedly the **Site des Pierres Droites**, a stone circle not far to the south – can be picked up from the **tourist office** next to the lakeside abbey (Feb–June & Sept–Dec Tues–Sat 10am–noon & 2–5pm; July & Aug daily 10am–noon & 2–6pm; ⓣ02.99.07.84.23). There are a couple of **campsites** in the heart of the forest, including the two-star municipal one on the edge of the village (ⓣ02.97.07.89.16; closed Oct–April); a *Ferme Auberge* that doubles as both a B&B and a *gîte d'étape* in tiny **TRUDEAU** on the D40, 2km east (ⓣ02.99.07.81.40; dorm beds €8.80, B&B ❸), and a lovely **hostel** at Le Choucan-en-Brocéliande, a couple of kilometres out on the Concoret road (ⓣ02.97.22.76.75; dorm beds €7.70; closed Oct–May).

Alternative places in which to base yourself include **Plélan-le-Grand**, at the southern edge of the forest, **Mauron** at the north, and, further out to the east, **Montfort-sur-Meu**.

Plélan-le-Grand

The tiny village of **PLÉLAN-LE-GRAND**, 6km southeast of Paimpont, has a more interesting history than you might expect. In the ninth century it was the capital of one of Brittany's early kings, Solomon; its appeal presumably lay in its inaccessibility to Norse or other raiders. Later, in the sixteenth century, it was a part of the short-lived independent republic of Thélin, awarded to the local people after they had paid the ransom of their liegelord. And finally, after the Revolution, Plélan served as the headquarters of Puisaye, the Breton *Chouan* leader.

Despite this, Plélan today is not in any sense an attractive place to stay. It does, however, have an affordable **hotel** in the *Bruyères*, 10 rue de Brocéliande (ⓣ02.99.06.81.38; ❷; closed Wed lunch & Sun eve), with a restaurant offering satisfactory menus at €11 and up.

Bellevue, Guer and Mauron

If you continue south, after 10km you come to **BELLEVUE-COËTQUIDAN**, dominated by a large military camp; its hotels, full of the relatives of soldiers, aren't the most attractive resting places. Another 5km or so beyond is **GUER**, a gentle little town containing not much more than a rusty ideas box placed in the main square and a heated covered swimming pool. From here, the D776 rolls and tumbles through further woods until it reaches the canal at Malestroit.

At the **northern** edge of the forest, the nearest rooms are at **MAURON**. A rambling, charming country town, this has a reasonable **hotel**, the *Brambily*, in the town centre at 14 place Henri-Thebault (ⓣ02.97.22.61.67; ❷; closed Sun eve in low season). It also has a swimming pool, rather on the small side, but still more than welcome after a hot day in the forest.

Montfort-sur-Meu

If you've been seduced by the Paimpont forest, **MONTFORT-SUR-MEU**, east of the forest 25km short of Rennes, has an illuminating **Eco-Musée** at 2 rue de Château which serves to provide some background information (Tues–Fri 9am–noon & 2–6pm, Sat 10am–noon & 2–6pm, Sun 2–6pm; €3.50). Set in the one surviving tower of what in the fourteenth century was a complete walled town, it appears at first glance to consist of the usual small-town museum assortment – costumed dolls and the like. But don't be put off. Upstairs there is a detailed comparison between the forests of Paimpont and Trémelin, proving the shocking fact that the former is artificially planted (and therefore a poor candidate really to be Brocéliande). Of more tangible appeal, there's a remarkable display of the area's quarries – some of which can be seen from the top of the tower – and its stone, exhibited along with modern sculptures exploring texture or building techniques. The museum also runs workshops, where children are taught traditional crafts with materials such as cow dung, and where sculptors explain their work to casual visitors.

Montfort is on the railway, with a reasonable **hotel**, the *Relais de la Cane*, 2 rue de la Gare (Ⓣ02.99.09.00.07; ❷), close by the **gare SNCF**. Being only a few minutes away from Rennes by train, it is a possible point from which to set out if you're coming to Paimpont from the north.

Malestroit, Rochefort and La Gacilly

If you follow the course of the canal southwest from Josselin, as opposed to making the detour to the Forêt de Paimpont, the next significant town you come to is the small but appealing **Malestroit**. Beyond that, if you are not actually travelling on the canal, which at this stage is the **River Oust**, the D764 on the south bank, or the D147/149 on the north, will keep you parallel for much of its course towards Redon. Along the way there are two worthwhile detours: south of the canal to **Rochefort-en-Terre**, or north to **La Gacilly**.

Malestroit and around

Although not a lot happens in **MALESTROIT**, founded in 987 AD, the town is full of unexpected and enjoyable corners. As you come into the main square, the **place du Bouffay** in front of the church, the houses are covered with unlikely carvings – an anxious bagpipe-playing hare looks over its shoulder at a dragon's head on one beam, while an oblivious sow in a blue buckled belt threads her distaff on another. The church itself is decorated with drunkards and acrobats outside, torturing demons and erupting towers within; a placard outside explains the various allegories. The only ancient walls without adornment are the ruins of the **Chapelle de la Madeleine**, where one of the many temporary truces of the Hundred Years War was signed.

Beside the grey canal, the matching grey-slate tiles on the turreted rooftops bulge and dip, while on its central island overgrown houses stand next to the stern walls of an old mill.

Practicalities

If you arrive in Malestroit by barge – this being a good stretch to travel on the water – you'll moor very near the town centre. The helpful local **tourist office** stands at the edge of the main square at 17 place du Bouffay (July & Aug Mon–Sat 9am–7pm, Sun 10am–4pm; Sept–June Mon–Sat 9.30am–12.30pm & 2.30–6.30pm; Ⓣ02.97.75.14.57, Ⓦwww.malestroit.com); they can provide details of **boat rental**.

The nearby **gare routière** is served by buses from Vannes, while across the river there's a two-star **campsite**, *La Daufresne* (Ⓣ02.97.75.13.33; closed mid-Sept to mid-June), down below the bridge in the Impasse d'Abattoir next to the swimming pool, and a **gîte d'étape** up at the canal lock (M. Hallier; Ⓣ02.97.75.11.66; €8.50). The town also has an inexpensive **hotel**, *Le Cap Horn*, 1 Faubourg St-Michel (Ⓣ02.97.75.13.01; ❷), where the cheapest rooms come with shower, basin and a bidet so close to the bed that it doubles as a bedside table. For something to **eat**, the *Vieille Auberge* opposite the church at 9 place de Bouffay (Ⓣ02.97.75.20.35) serves simple, hearty meals.

The Musée de la Résistance Bretonne

Two kilometres west of Malestroit (and with no bus connection), the village of **ST-MARCEL** hosts the **Musée de la Résistance Bretonne** (mid-June to mid-Sept daily 10am–7pm; mid-Sept to mid-June Wed–Mon 10am–noon & 2–6pm; ⓣ02.97.75.16.90, ⓦwww.resistance-bretonne.com; €6.30). The museum stands on the site of a June 1944 battle in which the Breton *maquis*, joined by Free French forces parachuted in from England, successfully diverted the local German troops from the main Normandy invasion movements.

The museum's newest buildings house documents and artefacts highlighting the history of the Free French SAS. Its strongest feature, however, remains its presentation of the pressures that made so many French collaborate: the reconstructed street corner overwhelmed by the brooding presence of the occupiers; the big colourful propaganda posters offering work in Germany, announcing executions of *maquis*, equating resistance with aiding US and British big business; and, against these, the low-budget, shoddily printed Resistance pamphlets. All the labelling is in French, which non-speakers may find frustrating.

Rochefort-en-Terre and around

ROCHEFORT-EN-TERRE overlooks the River Arz from a high eminence 17km south of Malestroit. It may be a prettified and polished version of its neighbour, and something of a tourist trap with its little antique shops and expensive restaurants, but it ranks nonetheless among the most delightful villages in Brittany. Every available stone surface, from the window ledges to the picturesque wishing well, is permanently bedecked in flowers, to the extent that Rochefort has been banned since 1967 from taking part in regional and national contests for the town with the best floral decorations (*villes fleuries*).

The flowery tradition originated with the painter Alfred Klots, who was born in France to a wealthy American family in 1875, and who bought Rochefort's ruined **château** in 1907. Perched on the town's highest point, the castle is open for guided tours (April & May Sat & Sun 2–7pm; June & Sept daily 2–7pm; July & Aug daily 10am–7pm; €4), though not until you go through its dramatic gateway do you find out that in fact that gateway is all that survives of the original fifteenth-century structure. Instead, the castle as it stands today was cobbled together by Klots using assorted pieces from various other ruins in the vicinity. It contains his own relatively unremarkable paintings, along with those of his son, plus family memorabilia such as the "Cardinal Room", where a US cardinal once stayed and appears to have left his clothes and suitcase behind when he left. The highlights are Klots' former studio, a detached building with magnificent views over the surrounding hills and gorges, and garden terraces on all sides.

At the bottom end of town, the church of **Notre Dame de Tronchaye** holds a Black Virgin that was found hidden from Norman invaders in a hollow tree in the twelfth century, and is the object of a pilgrimage on the first Sunday after August 15. More interesting, though, is the **Lac Bleu**, just to the south, where the deep galleries of some ancient **slate quarries** are the home of blind butterflies and long-eared bats.

Practicalities

Rochefort's modern **tourist office**, in the central place des Halles (mid-June to mid-Sept Mon–Fri 10am–12.30pm & 2–6pm, Sat & Sun 2–6pm; mid-Sept to mid-June Mon–Fri 10am–12.30pm & 2–5.30pm; ⓣ02.97.43.33.57, ⓦwww.rochefort-en-terre.com), displays a list of rather expensive *chambres d'hôtes* in the neighbourhood, and operates the three-star municipal **campsite**, *Le Moulin Neuf*, in the chemin de Bogeais (☎02.97.43.37.52; closed mid-Sept to mid-May). The one **hotel** in town, *Le Pélican* (☎02.97.43.38.48; ❸; closed mid-Jan to mid-Feb, plus Mon & Sun eve), stands alongside the tourist office, and offers reasonable rooms and good food, with dinner menus starting at €12. *Les Ardoisières* in place St-Michel (☎02.97.43.41.28) is a **restaurant** with a very Celtic flavour, from its well-balanced menus featuring plenty of Breton specialities right down to its Guinness on tap.

At the village of **ST-VINCENT-SUR-OUST**, on the D764 halfway between Rochefort and Redon, a **hostel**, *Tŷ Kendalc'h* (☎02.99.91.28.55; closed Jan), serves as a centre for **Breton music and dance**, although accommodation is only available for groups.

The Parc de Préhistoire de Bretagne

Two kilometres southeast of Rochefort, outside the small community of **MALANSAC**, the very heavily publicized **Parc de Préhistoire de Bretagne** is a theme park aimed overwhelmingly at children (April to mid-Oct daily 10am–7pm; mid-Oct to mid-Nov Sun 1.30–6pm; €8). Separate landscaped areas contain dioramas of gigantic (if stationary) dinosaurs, and human beings at various stages in their evolution; the story ends shortly after a bunch of deformed but enthusiastic Neanderthals hit on the idea of erecting a few megaliths.

La Gacilly and around

Fourteen kilometres north of the canal, **LA GACILLY** makes a good base for walking trips in search of megaliths, sleepy villages and countryside. The town itself has prospered recently thanks to the creation of a beauty-products industry based on the abundantly proliferating flowers in the Aff valley. It's also a centre for many active craftsworkers; a walk down the old stone steps of the cobbled street that runs parallel to the main road between town centre and river is both a pleasure in itself and an opportunity to look in on their workshops. The only real disappointment is that the riverfront is not accessible to walkers, though you can enjoy views of it from a couple of restaurants; and rent boats to take out on it by the hour or day (☎02.99.72.41.11, Ⓦwww.bateaux-fluviaux-bretagne.com).

Practicalities

Up in the town centre, the *Hôtel de France*, 15 rue Montauban (☎02.99.08.11.15, Ⓦwww.hoteldefrancelagacilly.com; ❷; closed Sun eve), is an extremely hospitable logis, with quiet and comfortable **rooms** in what used to be the separate *Hôtel du Square*, reached through the long gardens at the back, and a good traditional restaurant serving menus from €15. The *patron* is happy to provide detailed information on local walks and attractions for his guests. Alternatively, the *chambre d'hôte* (☎02.99.70.07.40, Ⓔpfmorrier@aol.com; ❸) in the nearby sixteenth-century Manoir de Pommery in **Sixt-sur-Aff** provides ideal countryside accommodation.

The Megaliths of St-Just

Around 10km east of La Gacilly, in the vicinity of the village of **ST-JUST**, the small windswept **Cojoux** moor is rich in ancient megalithic remains. Only in the last couple of decades have they received any great public attention, as a programme of excavations has gradually uncovered all sorts of ancient tombs and sacred sites. During the summer, you should find posters in local villages giving the times of explanatory **walking tours** of the various sites, many of them led by the archeologists responsible for the digs; alternatively, call ⓣ02.99.72.61.02 for the current schedule. In any case, it's a rewarding area to ramble around yourself; the larger menhirs and so on are signposted along dirt tracks and footpaths, and you'll probably stumble upon a few lesser ones by chance.

Redon

Thirty-four kilometres east of Malestroit, at the junction of the rivers Oust and Vilaine, on the Nantes–Brest canal, linked by rail to Rennes, Vannes and Nantes, and at the intersection of six major roads, **REDON** is not a place it's easy to avoid. And you shouldn't try to, either. A wonderful mess of water and locks – the canal manages to cross the Vilaine at right angles in one of the more complex links – the town has history, charm and life. It's among the best stops along the whole course of the canal.

Arrival and information

The **gare SNCF** is in place de la Gare, five minutes' walk west of the tourist office. Regular trains leave from here to Nantes, Rennes, Vannes and Quimper.

Redon's friendly and helpful **tourist office** is in the place de la République, north across the railway tracks from the town centre (July & Aug Mon–Sat 9am–12.30pm & 1.30–6pm, Sun 10am–12.30pm & 3–5.30pm; Sept–June Mon–Sat 9am–noon & 2–6pm; ⓣ02.99.71.06.04, ⓦwww.tourisme-pays-redon.com); in summer they have an annexe in the port. There's a **post office** at 16 rue St-Michel, north of the centre (ⓣ02.99.71.67.93), and **Internet access** is available at E'scape Zone, across from the tourist office at 5 place de Bretagne (ⓣ02.99.72.43.10; daily noon–midnight; €3 per hr).

Bicycles can be rented from Chedaleux Nicolas, 44 rue Notre Dame (ⓣ02.99.72.19.95); and **barges** from Bretagne Croisières, 71 rue de Vannes (ⓣ02.99.71.08.05, ⓦwww.bretagnecroisieres.com), or Bretagne Plaisance, 12 quai Jean-Bart (ⓣ02.99.72.15.80, ⓦwww.bretagne-plaisance.fr).

Accommodation

Redon's **hotels** are mostly concentrated in the town and near the *gare SNCF* rather than in the port area, but it's a small enough place that it makes little difference where you stay. The off-white *Hôtel le France* looks down on the canal from 30 rue Duguesclin, at the corner with the quai de Brest (ⓣ02.99.71.06.11, ⓦhttp://perso.worldonline.fr/lefrance; ❶); its renovated

On Thursdays in July and August, Vedettes Jaunes (ⓣ02.97.45.02.81, ⓦwww.vedettesjaunes.com) run trips along the Vilaine from the Arzal dam – which is as close as they can get to the sea – upstream past La Roche-Bernard to Redon (2hr 30min). The departure from Arzal is at 9.30am and the return from Redon at 3.30pm. The return trip costs €22 and tickets can also be reserved at the tourist office.

rooms, all with en-suite bathrooms and TVs, offer a considerable degree of comfort for the price, but it lacks a restaurant. Across (or rather under) the railway tracks from the tourist office, the *Hôtel Asther*, 14 rue des Douves (☎02.99.71.10.91; ❷), has its own brasserie, *Le Théâtre* (closed Sat lunch & Sun), which serves couscous on Thursdays. A little nearer the station, the *Hôtel Chandouineau*, 1 rue Thiers (☎02.99.71.02.04; ❹; closed Sat & Sun eve), is an upmarket establishment with just seven bedrooms but mediocre service, where the restaurant serves gourmet menus from €21.

The Town

Redon was founded in 832 AD by St Conwoïon at the instigation of Nominoé, the first king of Brittany, and was a place of pilgrimage until the seventeenth century. Its Benedictine abbey is now the focus of the church of **St-Sauveur** – the rounded angles of the dumpy twelfth-century Romanesque lantern tower are unique in Brittany. All but obscured by later roofs and the high choir, the four-storey belfry is best seen from the adjacent cloisters. The later Gothic tower was entirely separated from the main building by a fire in 1780. Every Friday and Saturday from the end of June to the end of July, Redon puts on a large-scale *son et lumière* re-enactment of ten of the earliest years of its history, from 835 until 845 AD.

Under the chapel of Joan of Arc, the church crypt holds the tomb of Pierre l'Hospital, the judge who condemned **Gilles de Rais** to be hanged in 1440 for satanism and the most infamous orgies. Gilles had fought alongside Joan, burned for heresy, witchcraft and sorcery in 1431, and in both cases the court procedures were irregular to say the least. Legends of the atrocities of Gilles de Rais served as the source for tales of the monstrous wife-murderer Bluebeard.

Until World War I Redon was the seaport for Rennes. Its industrial docks – or what remains of them – are therefore on the Vilaine, while the canal, even in the very centre of town, is almost totally rural, its towpaths shaded avenues. Ship-owners' homes from the seventeenth and eighteenth centuries can be seen in the port area – walk via quai Jean Bart next to the *bassin* along the **Croix des Marins promenade**, returning along quai Duguay-Trouin beside the river, where you'll also find the *Attis*, a US boat that was used in the Normandy landings, and being no longer seaworthy is now moored here permanently. A rusted wrought-iron workbridge, equipped with a crane rolling on tracks, still crosses the river, but the main users of the port now are **cruise ships**, which come from 40km downstream at the Arzal dam.

Flowers abound throughout Redon, which achieves regular success in *villes fleuries* – in 1983, it won the national first prize. As late as October, swathes of chrysanthemums in autumn tints hang from balconies and the numerous iron bridges.

Eating, drinking and entertainment

La Bogue, in a flowery mansion in place du Parlement at 3 rue des États (☎02.99.71.12.95; closed Thurs & Sun eve), is a friendly and good-value **fish restaurant**. Menus start with a very simple €16 option that features "filet of mullet with beetroot aroma", and range up to a sumptuous feast for €39. Elsewhere, *L'Akène*, 10 rue de Jeu-de-Paume (☎02.99.71.25.15; closed Tues eve, plus Wed eve in winter), is a crêperie in an equally lovely old house in an alleyway close to the port. On Mondays a large **market** (at which you can buy superb crêpes) sprawls through most of town on both sides of the railway tracks. There are several **bars and pubs**: the *Loch Ness*, 12 rue Notre Dame (☎02.99.72.17.12), and the *O'Shannon Pub*, next to the canal at 62 Grande Rue (☎02.99.71.48.28), are both good places to go for a drink. Art exhibitions and occasionally **live music** can be found at *Les Art et Cie*, 44 rue Notre Dame (☎02.99.72.41.25), while the *Cubana Café* on avenue Jean Burel in St-Nicolas-de-Redon, on the other side of the Vilaine from the port (☎02.99.71.30.64), is a more ambitious establishment, with themed rooms, such as the "*Mille et une nuits*" incorporating real sand, where you can drink cocktails, eat tapas and take Latin dance classes on Saturdays. Redon also has a modern **theatre**, Le Canal (☎02.99.71.09.50), near the main square, where the season runs from October to June.

Châteaubriant

Sixty kilometres east of Redon, and the same distance north of Nantes, the fortified town of **CHÂTEAUBRIANT** guards the border of Brittany and Anjou. While it's not a place to go out of your way to see, and the flat surrounding countryside holds precious little of interest, a couple of hours spent wandering in and around its venerable **Château** makes a welcome interruption in a day spent travelling.

The castle walls still encircle the crest of a knoll just east of the town proper, although only the entrance keep (*donjon d'entrée*) remains of the original tenth-century structure. Visitors can simply stroll through that mighty gateway to find a disparate assembly of buildings of different eras, in similarly assorted states of repair, interspersed with peaceful lawns and formal gardens. The most complete edifice is a self-contained Renaissance château, built from 1521 onwards, and equipped with a sort of secular cloisters. To see some of the apartments inside, join one of the regular **guided tours** (mid-June to mid-Sept Wed–Mon 11am, 2.30pm & 4.30pm; mid-Sept to mid-June Sat & Sun 3pm; €3).

Châteaubriant's **tourist office** is in the centre of the old town, just north of the church, at 21 rue du Couéré (Mon 2–6pm, Tues–Fri 9.30am–12.30pm & 2–6pm, Sat 9.30am–12.30pm; ☎02.40.28.20.90). Close to the tourist office, the *Hôtel du Pont St-Jean*, 5 rue Denieul et Gastineau (☎02.40.28.04.54; ❶) has inexpensive **rooms**, while nearby the *Le Poêlon d'Or*, 30 rue du 11-Novembre (☎02.40.81.43.33; closed Sun eve & Mon, plus 2 wks in Feb and first 3 weeks of Aug), is an excellent little homely restaurant where menus start at €15.50.

Nantes

Despite having for centuries been the capital of Brittany, **NANTES** is no longer officially part of the province: it was transferred to the Pays de la Loire in 1962 when the modern administrative regions were established. Nonetheless, such bureaucracy is not taken too seriously in a city whose history is so intimately bound up with Breton fortunes, and whose inhabitants still consider it to be an integral part of the province. A considerable medieval centre, it later achieved great wealth from colonial expeditions, and by the end of the eighteenth century had become the principal port of France. Huge fortunes were made on the "ebony" (slave) trade, which brought in as much as 200 percent profit per ship. It's estimated that 500,000 Africans were carried to the Americas in vessels based in Nantes. However, the abolition of slavery coincided with an increased use of domestic French sugar beet as opposed to Caribbean sugar cane, the port began to silt up as it declined in significance, and heavy industry and wine production became more important.

Thanks to the tower blocks that mask the Loire and the motorways that tear past the city, Nantes is no longer especially attractive on first acquaintance. Although it's not a place to make a great priority on your travels, if you have the time and energy it has plenty worth seeing – especially the **Château des Ducs** and the **Beaux Arts** museum – while the River Erdre, the vineyards of the Loire and the remarkable Italianate town of **Clisson** all lie within reach.

Arrival and information

The **gare SNCF** (☎08.92.35.35.35), a little way east of the château, is served by fast trains between Paris and Brittany – a dozen TGVs daily reach Paris in as little as two hours – as well as being the terminus for the local line westwards to St-Nazaire, La Baule and Croisic. The station has two exits; for most facilities (tramway, buses, hotels) use *Accès Nord*.

There are two main **bus** stations. The one just south of the centre on allée Baco, near place Ricordeau ("Nantes Baco"), is used by buses heading south and southwest, to Pornic for example, as well as being the place where Eurolines

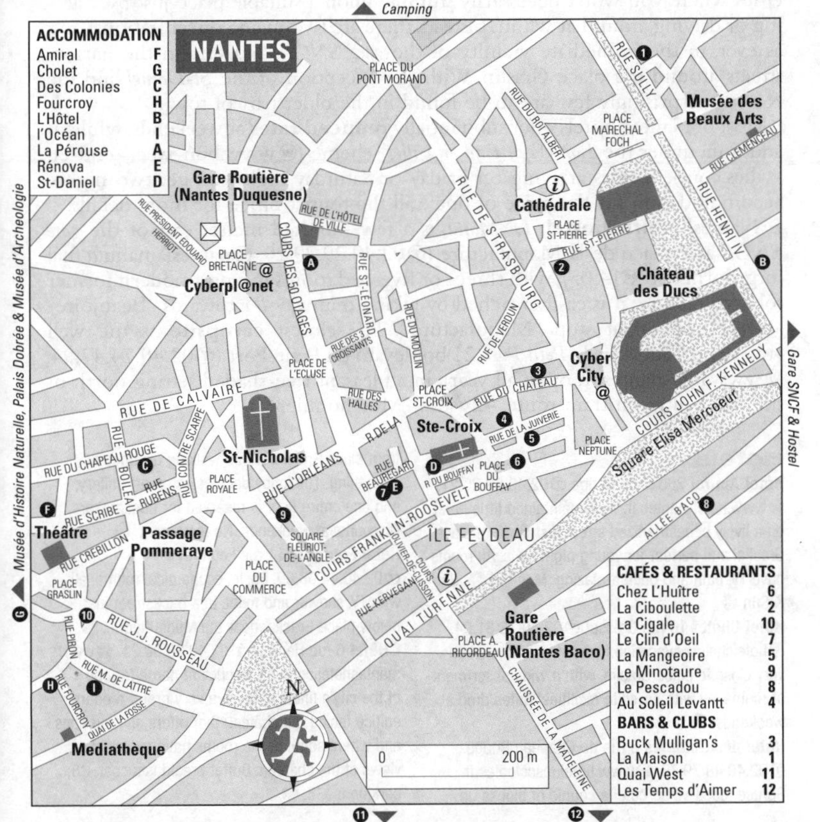

buses (Ⓣ02.51.72.02.03) to London and other European destinations arrive and depart. The one where the cours des 50-Ôtages meets rue de l'Hôtel de Ville ("Nantes Duquesne") serves routes that stay north of the river. Modern rubber-wheeled **trams** run along the old riverfront, past the *gare SNCF* and the two bus stations. Flat-fare tickets, at €1.20, are valid for one hour, rather than just a single journey, though one-day tickets are also available for €3.30. There are ticket distributors at every tram station; tickets cannot be brought on board.

Nantes' **tourist office** is strategically located between the medieval city and the nineteenth-century town at 3 cours Olivier-de-Clisson (Thurs 10.30am–6pm, Fri–Wed 10am–6pm; Ⓣ02.40.20.60.00, Ⓦwww.nantes-tourisme.com) and provides guides to local and region-wide hotels and restaurants, as well as running various guided tours of the city. They also sell the **Carte Nantes Découvertes**, available in 24-hour (€14), 48-hour (€24) and 72-hour (€30) versions, which grants unrestricted use of local transport, including river cruises, and free admission to a wide range of museums. A subsidiary information office is located next to the cathedral at 2 place St-Pierre (Tues, Wed & Fri–Sun 10am–1pm & 2–6pm, Thurs 10.30am–1pm & 2–6pm).

Accommodation

Although it has plenty of **hotels** to suit all budgets, Nantes is one of those cities where you won't necessarily stumble upon a suitable place just by walking or driving around at whim. Instead, there are two main concentrations; one, as ever, in the immediate vicinity of the *gare SNCF*, and one in the narrow streets around the place Graslin. With the exception of the *St-Daniel* and the *Renova*, surprisingly few are to be found in the older part of town.

Most of Nantes' hotels offer substantially **reduced rates** at weekends, while in addition, under the *Bon Week End en Villes* scheme (Ⓦwww.bon-week-end-en-villes.com), visitors arriving on Friday or Saturday night can get two nights' accommodation for the price of one; call the tourist office for more details.

Nantes' **youth hostel**, *Le Manu*, is a few hundred metres east of the *gare SNCF* at 2 place de la Manufacture (Ⓣ02.40.29.29.20, Ⓔnanteslamanu@fuaj.org; dorm bed €14.05), with three- or five-bed rooms in a postmodern former tobacco factory; it is easily reached by taking tramway #1 towards "Beaujoire" and getting off at stop "Manufacture". The closest **campsite** is the well-managed, four-star *du Petit Port*, 21 boulevard du Petit-Port (Ⓣ02.40.74.47.94, Ⓦwww.nge-nantes.fr; open all year), in a pleasant tree-shaded setting north of the city centre on tram route #2 (stop "Morrhonnière").

Hotels

Hôtel Amiral 26bis rue Scribe Ⓣ02.40.69.20.21, Ⓦwww.hotel-nantes.fr. Well-maintained little hotel on a lively pedestrianized street just north of place Graslin, and perfect for young night owls. All rooms have TV, bath and double-glazing. Mon–Fri ❹, Sat & Sun ❸

Hôtel Cholet 10 rue Gresset Ⓣ02.40.73.31.04, Ⓔhotelcholet@wanadoo.fr. Quiet, friendly option very close to place Graslin, with a wide assortment of rooms, all with en-suite facilities. Rates drop at weekends. ❸

Hôtel des Colonies 5 rue du Chapeau Rouge Ⓣ02.40.48.79.76, Ⓦwww.hoteldescolonies.fr. Spruce, good-value hotel a couple of blocks up from place Graslin, within walking distance of everything. The lobby doubles as an art gallery, and one entire floor is reserved for nonsmokers. Discounts at weekends. No restaurant. ❸

Hôtel Fourcroy 11 rue Fourcroy Ⓣ02.40.44.68.00. Basic, economical rooms, all with TV, shower and toilet, in a backstreet just below place Graslin, near the Médiathèque. ❷

L'Hôtel 6 rue Henri IV Ⓣ02.40.29.30.31, Ⓦwww.nanteshotel.com. An insouciant name for one of the city's finest options, a very grand modern edifice facing the château that offers all mod cons and where some of the rooms have excellent views of the château. Buffet breakfasts cost €8; parking is €6. ❹

Hôtel l'Océan 11 rue Maréchal-de-Lattre-de-Tassigny ⓣ02.40.69.73.51, ⓦwww.hotel-nantes.com. A pleasant hotel, with helpful management, just below place Graslin near the Médiathèque. All rooms have TV, while a private bedroom costs only €2 extra. Parking space is available around the back. No restaurant. Closed last two weeks of Dec. ❷

Hôtel La Pérouse 3 allée Duquesne ⓣ02.40.89.75.00, ⓦwww.hotel-laperouse.fr. Superb contemporary building ingeniously integrated with the older architecture that surrounds it – right down to its leaning north-facing side. The interior is decorated with 1930s furniture, stucco walls and ultramodern touches such as high-tech TVs and wireless Internet access in the rooms. An original, comfortable and friendly place to stay, with excellent breakfasts to boot. ❼

Hôtel Rénova 11 rue Beauregard ⓣ02.40.47.57.03, ⓕ02.51.82.06.39. Basic central rooms; far from fancy, but the price is great, even for en-suite facilities. ❶

Hôtel St-Daniel 4 rue du Bouffay ⓣ02.40.47.41.25. These simple but pleasant and well-lit rooms, on a cobbled street just off the place du Bouffay in the very heart of the old city, are much in demand in summer. Paying €3 extra secures a TV and en-suite toilet. ❶

The City

The **Loire**, the original source of Nantes' riches, has progressively disappeared from the centre. As recently as the 1930s, the river crossed the city in seven separate channels, but German labour as part of reparations for World War I filled in five of them. What are still called "islands" in the centre are now surrounded and isolated not by water, but by hectic dual carriageways. These thoroughfares are not easy to cross, but they do at least mean that Nantes is separated into a series of readily discernible districts, each of which can be experienced on its own terms.

The main distinction lies between the older **medieval city**, concentrated around the cathedral and with the château prominent in its southeast corner, and the elegant **nineteenth-century town** to the west, across the cours de 50 Ôtages (whose name – "50 hostages" – commemorates a bloody incident during the Nazi occupation in World War II). In a sense, that division has an additional political significance, for Nantes is not solely Breton. As trade along the Loire made the French influence on the city ever more significant, from the end of the eighteenth century onwards this newer area earned the nickname of "little Paris".

Place Royale, at the heart of the nineteenth-century town, was first laid out in the 1790s; damaged by bombing in 1943, it has now been restored. **Place**

River cruises from Nantes

One of Nantes' most popular tourist attractions is to take a **river cruise**, either along the relatively short stretch of the **Loire**, close to the city, that's currently navigable for cruise ships, or up the **Erdre**, which is lined by a fine selection of châteaux, as far as the point where it's joined by the last section of the **Nantes–Brest canal**. Most trips on the Loire depart from quai Malakoff on the **Bassin St-Felix**, a short distance southwest of the *gare SNCF*, although some leave from the same place as the Erdre cruises – the **gare fluviale**, on quai de la Motte-Rouge a little way north of central Nantes. Boats operate between April and November, on weekends only in low season but with much greater frequency in midsummer. Typically, the choice is between a simple cruise (1hr 45min) costing around €9, and setting off at about 3pm, or a three-hour trip on a floating restaurant for lunch (noon) or dinner (8pm), for something in the region of €50–60. The tourist office in town is bursting with brochures and leaflets from rival companies, the best known of which is Bateaux Nantais (ⓣ02.40.14.51.14, ⓦwww.bateaux-nantais.fr), who also operate similar trips southwards along the **Sèvre**.

△ Passage Pommeraye

Graslin, 200m to the west, with its **theatre**, dates from the same period; the theatre's Corinthian portico contrasts with the 1895 Art Nouveau of *La Cigale*, opposite, embellished with mosaics and mirrors and still a popular brasserie (see p.373).

A spectacular nineteenth-century multi-level indoor shopping centre, the **Passage Pommeraye**, drops down three flights of stairs towards the river on nearby rue Crebillon. The attention to detail lavished upon it by its architects is on a scale undreamed of in modern malls; each of the gas lamps that light the central area is held by an individually crafted marble cherub. Although the building itself remains impressive, business is not exactly booming, and the presence of the odd shop selling candles or ethnic jewellery only adds to its run-down feel.

Many of the streets in the two principal regions of the city have been semi-pedestrianized, and they abound in pavement cafés, brasseries and shops. Just south of them both is the elongated **Île Feydeau**, a typical victim of the modern "development" of Nantes. Its eighteenth-century houses, seen at their best in rue Kervegan, retain some of their Baroque charm – but the road is bisected by busy cours Olivier-de-Clisson and the traffic jams of today.

The Château des Ducs

Though no longer on the waterfront, and subjected to a certain amount of damage over the centuries, the **Château des Ducs** still preserves the form in which it was built by two of the last rulers of independent Brittany, François II and his daughter Duchess Anne, born here in 1477. The list of famous people who have been guests or prisoners, defenders or belligerents, of the castle is impressive. It includes Gilles de Rais (Bluebeard), publicly executed in 1440; Machiavelli (author of *The Prince*), a member of a Florentine delegation in 1498; the firebrand Scottish preacher John Knox as a galley slave in 1547–49; and Bonnie Prince Charlie preparing for Culloden in 1745. The most significant act in the castle, from the point of view of European history, was the signing of the **Edict of Nantes** in 1598 by Henri IV (who is said to have exclaimed, on first sight of the castle, "God's teeth, these dukes of Brittany were no small beer"). The edict ended the Wars of Religion by granting a certain degree of toleration to the Protestants, but had far more crucial consequences when it was revoked by Louis XIV in 1685. To their credit, the people of Nantes took no part in the subsequent general massacres of the Huguenots.

The stout ramparts of the château remain pretty much intact, and most of the encircling moat is filled with water, surrounded by well-tended lawns that make a popular spot for lunchtime picnics. Within the walls stand a rather incongruous potpourri of buildings added in differing styles over the years. At the time of writing the entire château complex – the courtyard, ramparts interior and exterior – were in the process of a major facelift, which meant that no visits were being conducted. Plans to re-open the whole site - which should include an impressive museum - in the autumn of 2006, with the courtyard only reopening at least a year earlier. For the latest information on these proposed schedule, call ⓣ02.51.17.49.00.

The cathedral

In 1800 the Spaniards' Tower (the castle's arsenal) exploded, shattering the stained glass of the fifteenth-century **Cathédrale de St-Pierre-et-St-Paul** over 200m away. This was just one of many disasters that have befallen the church. It was used as a barn during the Revolution, bombed during World War II, and damaged by a fire in 1972. Now finally reopened – though still subject to ongoing restoration work – the building is made to seem especially light and soaring by its clean white stone. It contains the tomb of François II, the last duke of Brittany, and his wife, Margaret, the parents of Duchess Anne – with somewhat grating symbols of Power, Strength and Justice for him and Fidelity, Prudence and Temperance for her. This imposing monument is illuminated by a superb modern stained-glass window devoted to Breton and Nantais saints.

The Mur des Cheminées

Five centuries of Nantais history can be seen written in stone, brick and mortar on the **Mur des Cheminées**, just off the place du Bouffay in the centre of the old city, where bomb damage during the war left exposed the huge wall of a venerable and much-reconstructed town house. Successive layers of masonry show the development of the building since it was erected in 1453; a fascinating if rather faded diagram of this living cross-section illustrates exactly which pieces belong to which era.

The Museums

The **Musée des Beaux Arts**, east of the cathedral at 10 rue Clemenceau, has a respectable collection of paintings displayed in excellent modern galleries, and plays host to a very high standard of temporary exhibitions (Mon, Wed & Fri–Sun 10am–6pm, Thurs 10am–8pm; €3.10, free Thurs 6–8pm & first Sun of every month). Not all its Renaissance and contemporary works are on display at any one time, but you should be able to take in canvases ranging from a gorgeous *David Triumphant* by Delaunay and Léon Comerre's disturbing *Le Déluge*, a writhing orgy of drowning flesh, to Chagall's *Le Cheval Rouge* and one of Monet's *Nymphéas*.

Rue Voltaire runs west of the place Graslin, leading to the **Musée d'Histoire Naturelle** at no. 12 (Wed–Mon 10am–6pm; €3.10). This holds an eccentric assortment of oddities, including tatty stuffed specimens of virtually every bird and animal imaginable, plus rhinoceros toenails, a coelecanth, a giant fossil spider, an aepyornis egg, Neanderthal skulls, and an Egyptian mummy. A small vivarium shelters living snakes and reptiles, including two enormous pythons, an anaconda, and a black crocodile. There's even a complete tanned human skin, taken in 1793 from the body of a soldier whose dying wish was to be made into a drum. That proved unsuccessful – he wasn't resonant enough – so he ended up here.

Also on rue Voltaire, at no. 18, you'll find the **Palais Dobrée** (Tues–Fri 1.30–5.30pm, Sat & Sun 2.30–5.30pm; €3, free on Sun), an eccentric "Old Irish" style mansion house that was formerly home to Thomas Dobrée (1810–95). Oddments he accumulated include sundry swords and helmets, and fragments of statues, but pride of place goes to a little reliquary of beaten gold that contains Duchess Anne's heart in a box. Jean V, duke of Brittany, died in 1442 in an older manor house that now stands in the same grounds, while nearby an ugly new building serves as the **Musée d'Archéologie** (same hours & ticket) which holds a quite nicely displayed but ultimately rather meagre collection of Greek, Egyptian and Etruscan artefacts.

The **Musée Jules-Vernes**, further northwest of the centre at 3 rue de l'Hermitage (Mon & Wed–Sat 10am–noon & 2–6pm, Sun 2–6pm; €1.50) commemorates the birthplace of the first serious writer of science fiction.

If you have time to kill, take the tram or walk to the **Médiathèque** at 24 quai de la Fosse, where you'll find a modern library with bookshops and facilities to watch any of an eclectic selection of videos (Mon, Tues, Thurs & Fri noon–7pm, Wed 10am–7pm, Sat 10am–6pm). From there, you can walk along quai de la Fosse to the point where the two remaining branches of the Loire meet up, with a good view of the port.

Eating

Unlike hotels, **restaurants** fill the winding lanes of the old city in abundance. It shouldn't take you long to find somewhere once you start wandering the pedestrian streets in the centre. Nantes is a big enough city to have all sorts of ethnic alternatives as well, with lots of North African, Italian, Chinese, Vietnamese and Indian places – especially in the rue de la Juiverie – in addition to those listed here.

Chez L'Huître 5 rue des Petites-Écuries ⓣ02.51.82.02.02. Much as the name suggests, this lovely little restaurant specializes in oysters of all sizes and provenance, priced from €5.50–12 per half-dozen. You can also get smoked fish, fish soup and other simple dishes. Open until late nightly, closed Sun lunch.

La Ciboulette 9 rue St-Pierre ⓣ02.40.47.88.71. Simple neighbourhood French restaurant, tucked away on a side street very close to the cathedral, and serving imaginative dinner menus at €17.80 and €24.30. Closed Wed, Sat lunch & Sun eve.

La Cigale 4 place Graslin ⓣ02.51.84.94.94. Famous late-nineteenth-century brasserie, offering fine meals in opulent surroundings, with seating either at tiled terrace tables or in a more formal indoor dining room. Fish is a speciality, with seafood platters from €28.90 up to €84.90. The €11.90 and €22.90 menus are served until midnight in keeping with the tradition of providing post-performance refreshments for patrons of the theatre opposite.

Le Clin d'Oeil 15 rue Beauregard ⓣ02.40.47.72.37. Characterful and cheap little local restaurant in the heart of the old city, serving reliable French favourites plus quirky daily specials. Lunch from €9 plus eclectic menus at €11.90 (without dessert) and €15.80 (with dessert), where you can have humus as a starter, *confit de canard* as a main course, and apple crumble for dessert. Closed Sun.

La Mangeoire 16 rue des Petites-Écuries ⓣ02.40.48.70.83. Very good country food. The €9.30 lunch menu in particular is a real bargain, there's a solid €15 dinner menu, and the *Chef* for €26 is a delight, featuring a decadent *millefeuillle* of foie gras followed by a tasty scallop bisque. Closed Sun & Mon.

Le Minotaure 5 square Fleuriot-de-l'Angle ⓣ02.40.20.35.20. Bright, brisk brasserie a short walk west of the cours des 50 Ôtages and just east of place Royale. Its slogan, "enter and you'll be astonished", may overstate things a little, but it still has something for everyone: steak for €13.50, a good fishy and meaty menu for €15.25, and plenty of lighter options. Open daily from noon until after midnight, with outdoor seating on the pedestrianized square.

Le Pescadou 8 allée Baco ⓣ02.40.35.29.50. Despite being somewhat off the beaten track, near the *gare routière*, this is Nantes' most fashionable venue for fresh fish, with menus from €19.50. Closed Mon eve, Sat lunch & Sun.

Au Soleil Levant 12 rue de la Juiverie ⓣ02.40.35.68.65. One of several Asian options along a little pedestrian street, with seating both indoors and out, this Japanese restaurant serves good-quality sushi, sashimi, *maki* rolls and noodles in all sorts of combinations, with full dinners €15–20, and lunch menus as cheap as €9 for brochettes and €11 for raw fish. Closed Mon lunch.

Drinking and nightlife

By regional standards, Nantes by night is very lively indeed. Most of the action takes place in the alleyways of the medieval city, where students pack the **bars** until the small hours, though more mature visitors may prefer the fancier but less atmospheric cafés around the place Graslin to the west.

Buck Mulligan's 12 rue du Château ⓣ02.40.20.02.72. Irish-themed bar with genuine Irish owners and a dingy, dungeon-like setting, tucked away close to the château. Organizes plenty of events, from quiz nights to live music.

La Maison 4 rue Lebrun ⓣ02.40.37.04.12. Small bar-cum-bistro in a very secluded location just off rue Sully near the place Maréchal Foch, which features regular live music and attracts a youthful throng. Until 2am daily.

Quai west 3 quai François-Mitterand ⓣ02.40.47.68.45, ⓦwww.quaiwest.fr. Large and quite garish nightclub on the south bank of the Loire, roughly opposite the Médiathèque and specializing in contemporary dance music. Fri & Sat 11.30pm–6.30am.

Les Temps d'Aimer 14 rue Alexandre-Fourny ⓣ02.40.89.48.60, ⓦhttp://tdasys.free.fr. Nantes' premier gay club, just south of the centre on the Île de Nantes, puts on a wide programme of events and shows. Nightly midnight–7am.

Listings

Banks and exchange Banque de France, 14 rue La Fayette ⓣ02.40.12.53.53 (Mon–Fri 8.45am–12.30pm); Change Graslin, 17 rue Jean-Jacques Rousseau ⓣ02.40.69.24.64 (Mon–Fri 9am–noon & 2–6pm, Sat 10am–noon & 2–5pm).

Bicycle rental NGE, 18 rue Scribe ⓣ02.51.84.94.51 – bike hire available at the following NGE-run car parks: Graslin, Commerce, Bretagne, Cité des Congrés and Gare nord; as well as *Camping du Petit Port* (see p.368).

Book, CD and video shops FNAC in the Palais de la Bourse on place du Commerce ⓣ02.51.72.47.24; Virgin, centre commercial Beaulieu, 7 rue du Dr-Zamenhoff ⓣ02.40.35.98.60.

Car rental Avis ⓣ08.20.61.16.75; Budget ⓣ02.40.20.25.70; Europcar ⓣ02.40.89.40.88; Hertz ⓣ02.40.35.78.00.

Cinemas Le Cinématograph, 12bis rue des Carmélites ⓣ02.40.47.94.80 (shows arty and foreign films); Gaumont, 12 place du Commerce ⓣ08.92.69.66.96; Le Katorza, 3 rue Corneille ⓣ08.92.68.06.66; UGC Apollo, 20–21 rue Racine ⓣ08.36.68.71.14.

Laundry Laverie de la Madelaine, 11 chaussée de la Madelaine ⓣ02.40.47.10.17 (Mon–Sat 9am–8pm); Le Lavoire d'Aujourd'Hui, 3 rue du Bouffay (Mon–Sat 10am–8pm).

Internet access Cyber City, 14 rue de Strasbourg ⓣ02.40.89.57.92 (daily 10–1am; €3 per hr); Cyberpl@net, 18 rue de l'Arche Sèche ⓣ02.51.82.47.97 (Mon–Sat 10–2am, Sun 2–10pm; €3 per hr).

Post Office The main post office is on place de Bretagne ⓣ02.40.12.60.60 (Mon–Fri 8.30am–6.45pm, Sat 8.30am–12.30pm), and includes a postal museum.

Swimming pools Les Dervallières, rue des Dahlias ⓣ02.40.40.57.74; Jules Verne, rue de la Haluchère ⓣ02.51.89.16.20; Petit-Port, bd de Petit-Port ⓣ02.51.84.94.51.

Around Nantes

Immediately **upstream from Nantes** you are into the Loire wine-growing country that produces the two classic dry white wines, Gros-Plant and Muscadet. Any **vineyard** should be happy to give you a *dégustation*. Most operate on a very small scale; the largest, however, the **Chasseloir vineyard** (ⓣ02.40.54.81.15, ⓔcontact@chereau-carre.fr) at **ST-FIACRE-SUR-MAINE**, is perhaps the most interesting. This occupies the grounds of a former château, with fifty acres of vines – some a century old. The vineyard sells mostly within the catering trade, but anyone is welcome to visit their cellars, which are decorated with painted Rabelaisian carvings and candelabras made from vine roots. Like so many of the vineyards in this region, the grapes are now picked and pressed by machines – the old tradition of employing seasonal migrant labour on the harvest is a thing of the past.

Clisson

To the south, at the point where the Sèvre meets the Maine, and the crossroads of the three ancient duchies of Brittany, Anjou and Poitou, is the town of **CLISSON**. This was remodelled by two French architects in the last century into a close approximation of an Italian hill town. The fact that they already had the raw material of a ruined fortress (April–Sept Wed–Mon 9am–noon & 2–6pm; Oct–March Wed–Sun 9am–noon & 2–6pm; €2.20), a covered market hall and a magnificent situation makes it a sight not to be missed. The best **place to stay** is the *Hôtel de la Gare*, on place de la Gare (Ⓣ02.40.36.16.55; ❷).

Travel details

Trains

No railway line cuts across central Brittany; however, certain towns mentioned in this chapter can be reached by train.

Carhaix to: Guingamp (4 daily; 1hr).

Châteaulin to: Brest (7 daily; 1hr); Quimper (7 daily; 20min).

Loudéac to: St-Brieuc (5 daily; 1hr); Vannes (2 daily; 1hr 20min).

Nantes to: Paris (12 TGVs daily; 2hr 5min); Rennes (6 daily; 1hr 40min); Quimper (2 daily; 2hr 40min).

Pontivy to: St-Brieuc (3 daily; 1hr 15min); Vannes (2 daily; 55min).

Redon to: Nantes (8 daily; 50min); Quimper (6 daily; 1hr 50min); Rennes (13 daily; 40min); Vannes (11 daily; 30min).

Buses

Carhaix to: Châteaulin (1 daily; 1hr 10min); Loudéac (3 daily; 1hr 30min); Morlaix (3 daily; 1hr 30min), via Huelgoat (30min).

Châteaulin to: Châteauneuf-du-Faou (2 daily; 30min); Pleyben (2 daily; 15min).

Nantes to: Pornic (7 daily; 1hr 10min); St-Nazaire (2 daily; 40min), Rennes (5 daily; 1hr), Vannes (1 daily; 2hr 40min).

Pontivy to: Rennes (4 daily; 2hr) via Josselin (30min) and Ploërmel (45min).

Vannes to: Elven (3 daily; 25min); Loudéac (2 daily; 1hr 25min); Malestroit (3 daily; 45min); Ploërmel (3 daily; 1hr); Pontivy (8 daily; 1hr 20min).

7

The South Coast

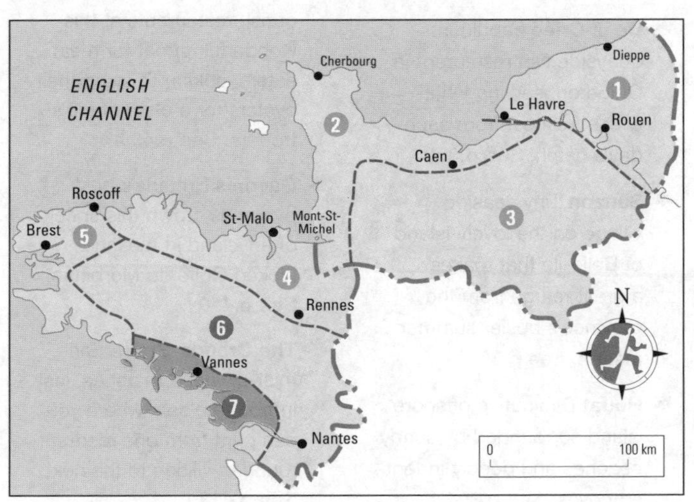

CHAPTER 7 Highlights

* **The Inter-Celtic Festival** The world's largest pan-Celtic jamboree, held every August, turns otherwise sleepy Lorient into Brittany's liveliest town. See p.382

* **De la Criée** Fabulous quayside fish restaurant in Quiberon, serving whatever's freshest from each day's catch. See p.388

* **Sauzon** Tiny seaside village on the lovely island of Belle-Île that makes a great refuge from the province's busier summer resorts. See p.391

* **Houat** Diminutive offshore island surrounded by sandy beaches and deeply indented coves. See p.394

* **The megaliths of Carnac** Said to be the oldest inhabited spot on earth, Carnac is still surrounded by relics of its ancient past. See p.397

* **Le Gavroche** Take a break from Brittany's multitude of fish restaurants at this wonderful retreat for meat-eaters looking to swap their oysters for a plate of pig's trotters. See p.406

* **Gavrinis** Brittany's best pyramids crown this speck of an island in the land-locked Golfe du Morbihan. See p.410

* **The Grande-Brière** Eerie, mist-swathed marshes, just in from the sea, where you can punt from one reed-surrounded village to the next. See p.413

△ Gavrinis stones

7

The South Coast

Brittany's **southern coast** takes in several of the province's most famous sites, and also offers its warmest swimming. Not surprisingly, therefore, it's very popular with tourists. Around the **Gulf of Morbihan**, and especially to the south at **La Baule**, you can be hard pushed to find a room in summer – or to escape the crowds.

The whole coast is a succession of wonders, of both natural and human creation. If you have any interest in prehistory, or even if you just enjoy ruins, then the concentration of **megaliths** around the **Morbihan** should prove irresistible. **Carnac**, the most important site, may well be Europe's oldest settlement; the sun has risen more than two million times over its extraordinary and intriguing alignments of menhirs. **Locmariaquer**, too, has a gigantic ancient stone, which some theories hold to be the key to a prehistoric astronomical observatory, while the most beautifully positioned of all is the great tumulus on **Gavrinis**, one of the fifty or so islets scattered around the Morbihan's inland sea.

As for more hedonistic pastimes, in theory the best of the south's **beaches** are at La Baule. This, however, is also the one resort in Brittany to be conspicuously affected and overpriced, and almost entirely lacks the character of the rest of the region. Excellent, lower-key alternatives can be found all along the south coast: close by La Baule at **Le Croisic** and **Piriac-sur-mer**; at the megalith centres of Carnac and Locmariaquer; at **Quiberon**; and out on the **islands** of **Groix** and **Belle-Île**. The largest Breton island, Belle-Île is a perfect microcosm of the province – a beautiful place with grand countryside and a couple of lively towns.

The south coast is also host to Brittany's most compelling **festival**, the ten-day **Inter-Celtic** gathering at **Lorient** in August. The same month sees a **jazz festival** at the main Morbihan town, **Vannes**, the location of some of the region's best restaurants.

Lorient and its estuary

LORIENT, the fourth largest city in Brittany, is an immense natural harbour, sheltered from the ocean by the **Île de Groix** and strategically located at the junction of the rivers Scorff, Ter and Blavet. Though still the second most important fishing port in France, it's now far more functional than exciting. Once, however, it was a key base for French colonialism, founded in the mid-seventeenth century (in what its charter called a "vague, vain, and useless place")

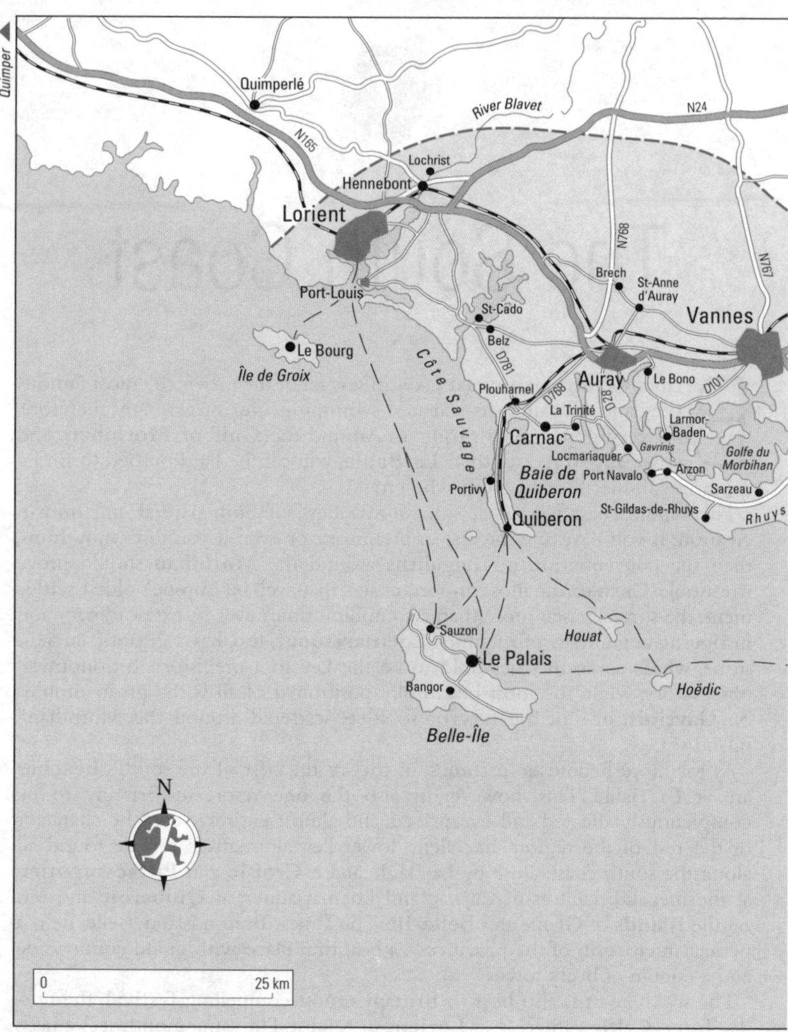

for trading operations by the **Compagnie des Indes**, the French equivalent of the Dutch and English East India Companies. The port's name was originally *L'Orient* ("The East"), and came from a mighty trading vessel, the *Soleil d'Orient*, which was the first ship to be built in its nascent dockyards

Little remains in the town itself to suggest the plundered wealth that used to arrive here. During the last war, Lorient was a major target for the Allies; the Germans held out until May 1945, by which time the city was almost completely destroyed. The only substantial traces to survive were the U-boat pens, which were subsequently greatly expanded by the French to hold their nuclear submarines. As a result, Lorient is somewhat reminiscent of Le Havre, in that it had to be entirely reconstructed as rapidly as possible. Here, however,

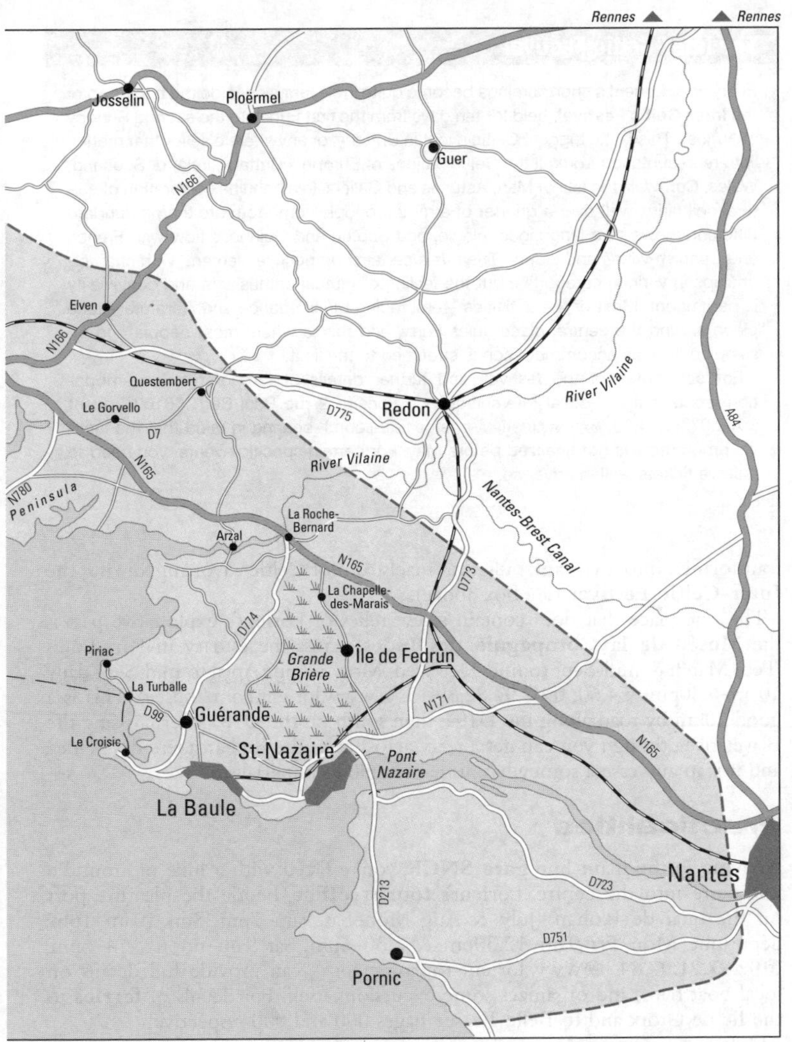

virtually nothing of interest was created; the church of **Notre Dame de Victoire** is typical of the drab concrete facades everywhere you look. Most of the waterfront is taken up by off-limits naval bases, and the one splash of colour is the little pleasure port that serves to separate the old town from the new – not that there's any very discernible difference between the two. If you imagine things might be a little more interesting or lively if you head to the **fishing port**, a couple of kilometres south of the centre, you're much mistaken. All in all, considering the many joys elsewhere in Brittany, it would be mad to suggest Lorient as a holiday destination. For most of the year, the only reason you might feel it worthwhile to pause here is to take the boat trip out to the Île de Groix (see p.383). Briefly each August, however, Lorient is

The Inter-Celtic Festival

Every year, Lorient's shortcomings become quite irrelevant alongside the backdrop of the **Inter-Celtic Festival**, held for ten days from the first Friday to the second Sunday in August. This is the biggest Celtic event in Brittany, or anywhere else for that matter, with representation from all the Celtic nations of Europe – Brittany, Ireland, Scotland, Wales, Cornwall, the Isle of Man, Asturias and Galicia. In a genuine celebration of cultural solidarity, well over a quarter of a million people come to more than a hundred different shows, five languages mingle, and Scotch and Guinness flow with French and Spanish wines and ciders. There is a certain competitive element, with championships in various categories, but the feeling of mutual enthusiasm and conviviality is paramount. Most of the activities – embracing music, dance and literature – take place around the central place Jules-Ferry, and this is where most people end up sleeping, too, as accommodation is stretched to the limit.

For **schedules** of the festival, and further details of temporary accommodation, contact the Festival Interceltique de Lorient, 2 rue Paul-Bert, 56100 Lorient (ⓣ02.97.21.24.29, ⓦwww.festival-interceltique.com), bearing in mind that the festival programme is not finalized before May. For certain specific events, you need to reserve tickets well in advance.

transformed into a vibrant, pulsating maelstrom of Celtic cavorting, during the **Inter-Celtic Festival** (see box above).

The one place that does contain a few relics of Lorient's exploitative past is the **Musée de la Compagnie des Indes**, across the estuary in Port Louis (Feb–March & mid-Sept to mid-Dec Wed–Mon 2–6pm; April to mid-Sept daily 10am–6.30pm; €4.60; ⓣ02.97.82.19.13; ⓦwww.lorient.com/musee). This is a good 20km by road along the D194, then south on the D781 after crossing the Blavet river, though you can get a ferry across from the Embarcadère des Rades, and it is in any case a somewhat dismal temple to imperialism.

Practicalities

Arriving in the main-line **gare SNCF**, you're faced with a hike of around a kilometre into the centre. Lorient's **tourist office**, beside the pleasure port on the quai de Rohan (July & Aug Mon–Sat 9am–7pm, Sun 10am–1pm; Sept–June Mon–Fri 9am–12.30pm & 1.30–6pm, Sat 9am–noon & 4–6pm; ⓣ02.97.21.07.84, ⓦwww.lorient-tourisme.com), can provide full details on local boat trips, and organizes some excursions itself. For details of **ferries** to the Île de Groix and to Belle-Île, see pages 000 and 000 respectively.

Unless you arrive during the festival, when prices tend to be considerably higher, there's a huge choice of **hotels**. Among reasonable, fairly central options are two on rue Lazare-Carnot as it curves away south of the tourist office. All the rooms in the *Victor Hugo Hôtel* at no. 36 (ⓣ02.97.21.16.24; ❷) have TV and there is also Internet access – which, without wishing to labour the point, is something to be thankful for in Lorient – while the *Hôtel d'Arvor*, further west at no. 104 (ⓣ02.97.21.07.55; ❶), is cheaper but more spartan.

If you're desperate to find somewhere at festival time, there are a few more hotels along avenue de la Perrière, the main thoroughfare in the fishing port, including the basic but inexpensive *Hôtel-Restaurant Gabriel* at no. 45 (ⓣ02.97.37.60.76; ❷; restaurant closed Sun Oct–June), where reasonable menus cost from around €10. There's also an appealing (if noisy) **hostel** (ⓣ02.97.37.11.65, ⓔlorient@fuaj.org; €9.30), next to the River Ter at 41 rue

Victor-Schoelcher, 3km out on bus line C from the *gare SNCF*, which has space for **camping** as well in summer.

Le Pic, just south of the *gare SNCF* at 2 boulevard Maréchal-Franchet-d'Esperey (ⓣ02.97.21.18.29; closed Sat lunch & Sun) is an imaginative little **restaurant**, with varied menus from €14.50. More central alternatives include *Yesterday's*, 1 cours de la Bôve (ⓣ02.97.84.85.07), a brasserie near the town hall that serves an excellent €16 menu, and *Le Café Leffe* (ⓣ02.97.21.21.30; closed Jan), in the same building as the tourist office, facing the port, which is particularly strong on seafood. One of the most congenial **bars** is the *Galway Inn*, near the train station at 18 rue Belgique, while plenty more can be found around place Aristide-Briand.

The Île de Groix

The steep-sided, eight-kilometre-long rock of the **Île de Groix**, which shields Lorient ten kilometres out to sea from the mouth of the Blavet estuary, is a sort of little sister to the better-known island of Belle-Île (see p.388). With its own crop of lovely beaches, and its own throngs of summer visitors – not to mention a similar abundance of exclusive holiday homes – it's in no way inferior to its larger neighbour, however, and taking a day-trip out from Lorient is well worth the effort.

Groix flourished during the seventeenth and eighteenth centuries in tandem with Lorient, and was even the target of invasions by both the English (in 1663) and the Dutch (in 1774). Subsequently, after the island's first proper port was constructed in 1792, it went on to become a major centre for catching and canning tuna. That industry has long since gone into decline, however, and Groix now makes its living from summer tourism, with beach-lovers joined both by birdwatchers in search of migratory species, and by geologists, who come to study its peculiar rock formations.

The boat from Lorient docks at **PORT-TUDY**, where a former tuna cannery houses the **Eco-Musée**, chronicling the island's history since the Bronze Age (April, Oct & Nov Tues–Sun 10am–12.30pm & 2–5pm; May, June & Sept daily 10am–12.30pm & 2–5pm; July & Aug daily 10am–12.30pm & 3–7pm; Dec–March Wed, Sat & Sun 10am–12.30pm & 2–5pm; €4.20). While the more general displays are interesting enough, the museum's real strong point is in its depiction of the patterns and traditions of individual life. Countless personal and family sagas are covered in exhaustive detail upstairs, from birth and the acquisition of language (which meant Breton at least until World War I), through school, apprenticeship, and marriage, all the way to death.

About 500m uphill from the port is the largest of the island's 27 villages, **LE BOURG** (also known as Loctudy, or even, simply, Groix). Although it's attractive enough, with a tuna-fish weathervane topping its little church, its appeal soon palls, and a more obvious way to spend a day on Groix is to tour its dramatic coastline. The easiest and cheapest way to do this is to rent a **bicycle** from one of several outlets at the port, costing around €11 per day. Crossing the island north to south takes barely ten minutes by bike; east to west requires more like an hour, especially as it can be hard to spot which coastal paths will prove negotiable, and which merely peter out into the sand.

At their tallest, at the **Pointe du Grognon** in the northwest, the **cliffs** of Groix rise fifty metres out of the sea; that may not sound all that high, but only Belle-Île in Brittany surpasses it. Much of the western tip serves as a bird sanctuary; the southeastern corner, by contrast, close to the **Pointe des Chats** and its little lighthouse, is renowned for its unusual green-tinged mineral deposits.

The best **beaches** are also at the eastern end of the island. Locals claim that the **Plage des Grandes Sables**, jutting out into the sea, is the only convex beach in Europe. Palpable nonsense that may be, but it is a beautiful little unsheltered strip of sand that offers calm swimming (supervised by lifeguards in summer), with pleasure boats bobbing at anchor just off shore. The next group of beaches to the south are even better, a succession of little sandy coves tucked between the rocks known collectively as **Les Sables Rouges**.

Practicalities

It takes 45 minutes to reach the Île de Groix by **boat** from the south quay of Lorient's new port (Société Morbihannaise de Navigation; ⓣ08.20.05.60.00, or, from outside France, ⓣ02.97.35.02.00, ⓦwww.smn-navigation.fr). There are between four and nine sailings daily all year, with the first daily departure from Lorient at 7.30am in July and August, and usually 8am otherwise. In summer, adults pay €22.99 return, under-25s pay €13.87, and over-60s €15.72. Small cars and bikes can be taken on almost all sailings, for €105.34 and €13.10 return respectively.

Groix's **tourist office** is the first building you come to on the quayside at **Port-Tudy** (April–June & Sept daily 9am–12.30pm & 2–6pm; July & Aug daily 9am–6pm; Oct–March Mon–Fri 9am–noon & 2–5pm, Sat 9am–noon; ⓣ02.97.86.53.08). The most informative **website** is ⓦwww.ile-de-groix.info. Three **hotels** stand nearby: the pink pastel *de l'Escale* (ⓣ02.97.86.80.04; ❸), which has rather characterless but perfectly adequate guest rooms inside and café seating outside; the slightly fancier *Ty Mad* (ⓣ02.97.86.80.19; ❸; closed Nov–Easter), set back behind an attractive lawn, which serves good seafood meals in the open air; and the *de la Jetée* (ⓣ02.97.86.80.82, ⓔlaurence.tonnerre@freesbee.fr; ❸; closed Jan to mid-Feb), at the far right end of the port, which holds the nicest rooms of the lot. The **restaurant** here, *Le Pub de la Jetée* (ⓣ02.97.86.59.42; closed Nov to mid-March), is the best for seafood-lovers, where the simple menu is dominated by oysters of various shapes; half a dozen can be had for around €7.

Up the hill in **Le Bourg**, the **hotel-restaurant** *de la Marine*, 7 rue Générale-de-Gaulle (ⓣ02.97.86.80.05, ⓦwww.hoteldelamarine.com; ❸; closed Jan to mid-Feb, plus Sun eve & Mon in low season), is a large, well-furnished house that offers comfortable rooms and serves delicious fish dinners in its front garden, including burbot brochettes and fish couscous on menus starting at €15, while the *Moulin d'Or*, 8 rue St-Jean (ⓣ02.97.86.82.16; ❶), is a much more basic alternative in terms of both accommodation and food.

A few hundred metres east of town, close to the sea en route towards the small beach at the Pointe de la Croix, the **Fort du Méné** holds a simple but beautifully sited summer-only **hostel** (ⓣ02.97.86.81.38; €7.70 or €11 including breakfast; closed mid-Oct to March), with a **campsite** alongside (ⓣ02.97.86.81.13; closed Oct–May). The nicest campsite on the island, however, is further on – the lovely three-star *Les Sables Rouges* (ⓣ02.97.86.81.32; closed mid-Sept to May), above the beaches at the southeast corner.

Hennebont

A few kilometres upstream from Lorient, at the point where the River Blavet first starts to widen into the estuary, stands the old walled town of **HENNEBONT**. The fortifications, and especially the main gate, the Porte Broerec'h, are imposing, and walking around the top of the ramparts there are wide views of the river below. What you see of the old city within, however, is entirely residential – an assortment of washing-lines, budgies and garden sheds. All its public buildings were destroyed by wartime bombing, and now not even a bar (or rented room) is to be found in the former centre.

The one time Hennebont comes alive is at the **Thursday market**, held below the ramparts and through the squares by the church. It's one of the largest in the region, with a heady mix of good fresh food, crêpes and delicacies from around the world, alongside livestock, flowers, carpets and clothes. On other days, the only places where you'll find any activity are along the **place Maréchal-Foch** (in front of the basilica) and the **quai du Pont-Neuf** beside the river.

Practicalities

Hennebont's **gare SNCF** is roughly 1km from the centre, on the west bank of the Blavet. Cross the river to reach the **tourist office**, at 9 place Maréchal-Foch (mid-June to mid-Sept Mon–Sat 9am–7pm, Sun 10am–12.30pm; mid-Sept to mid-June Mon–Sat 9am–12.30pm & 2–6pm; ⓣ02.97.36.24.52). If you decide to **stay** – and few people do – the renovated *Hôtel-Restaurant du Centre*, 44 rue du Maréchal-Joffre (ⓣ02.97.36.21.44; ❶) is good value, and as near the town centre as its name implies. The seafood-dominated menus in its restaurant (closed Sun eve & Mon) are uniformly superb, starting at €14.50 and with a €24.50 *Menu du Terroir* featuring hot oysters. The town's two-star **campsite**, *Camping Municipal de St-Caradec* (ⓣ02.97.36.21.73; closed mid-Sept to mid-June), has a prime site on the riverbank opposite the fortifications.

Lochrist

At **LOCHRIST**, just north of Hennebont, the great chimneys of the town's **ironworks** still stand, smokeless and silent, looking down on the Blavet. Strikes and demonstrations failed to prevent the foundry's closure in 1966, and the only work since then has been to convert it into the **Musée Forges d'Hennebont** (June Mon–Fri 10am–noon & 2–6pm, Sat & Sun 2–6pm; July & Aug Mon–Fri 10am–6.30pm, Sat & Sun 2–6.30pm; Sept–May Mon–Fri 10am–noon & 2–6pm, Sun 2–6pm; €4.50), which documents its hundred-year history from the workers' point of view. Some of the men made redundant contributed their memories and tools; for others turning their workplace into a museum was adding insult to injury. It is in fact excellent, both in content and presentation – though in view of the joyful pictures of successful strikes in the 1930s, its very existence seems a sad defeat.

St-Cado

Fifteen kilometres southeast of Hennebont, or 12km east of Port-Louis, a large bridge spans the broad estuary of the **Etel** River. A short detour north of the village of **BELZ** on the eastern shore brings you to the delightful islet of **ST-CADO**, a round speck on the water dotted with perhaps twenty white-painted houses.

From the mainland, you walk across a spindly little bridge to reach the island itself. Its main feature is a **twelfth-century chapel** that stands on the site of a Romanesque predecessor built by St Cado around the sixth century. Cado, who was a prince of "Glamorgant", returned in due course to his native Wales and was martyred, but Welsh pilgrims still make their way to this pretty little spot. As Cado is a patron saint of the deaf, it's said that hearing problems can be cured by lying on his stone "bed" inside the chapel. A little fountain behind the chapel only emerges from the sea at low tide.

There's nowhere to stay on St-Cado, nor are there any restaurants; just a couple of **bars** facing it from the quayside on the mainland, such as *Les Asturies*, 10 rue de la Jetée. Between May and September it's possible to rent **boats** by the hour, day or week from St-Cado Plaisance (☎02.97.55.46.57).

The Quiberon peninsula

The **Presqu'île de Quiberon** is as close to being an island as any peninsula could conceivably be; the long causeway of sand that links it to the mainland narrows to as little as 50m in places. In the past this was always a strategic military location. The English held the peninsula for eight bloody days in 1746; *Chouans* (see p.431) and royalists landed here in 1795 in the hope of destroying the Revolution, only to be sealed in and slaughtered; and the defoliation that threatens the dunes today is in part the result of German fortifications constructed during the last war. The peninsula is now packed with tourists during the summer. They come not so much to visit the towns, which, other than **Quiberon** itself, are generally featureless, but to use them as a base for trips out to **Belle-Île** or around the contrasting coastline.

The coast here has two quite distinct characters. The **Côte Sauvage**, facing the Atlantic to the west, is a bleak rocky heathland, lashed by heavy seas. It is the scene of innumerable drownings – the official tourist brochure contains a chilling description of just why it is absolutely impossible for *un imprudent* to swim back to land having once strayed beyond a certain distance. The sheltered eastern side, however, the **Baie de Quiberon**, contains safe sandy beaches, as well as one of the innumerable Thalassotherapy Institutes that line the Breton coast.

The route onto the peninsula

As the D768 curves around the bay outside **PLOUHARNEL**, on its way to the start of the peninsula, you can't fail to notice a reconstructed **Spanish galleon**, standing in something less than 8cm of water. This is an obsessive shell museum and shop, with dioramas – created entirely from shells – of eighteenth-century street scenes in Venice and in China, of Donald Duck and his friends, Sioux Indians and flamenco dancers (Easter–Sept daily 10am–noon & 2–5pm; €3.70). Across the road and the train line, there's a rather uninspiring **waxwork museum** (April–Sept daily 10am–noon & 2–5.30pm; €5), which focuses on the *Chouan* rebellion of 1795.

PORTIVY, tucked into the only real shelter along the Côte Sauvage just beyond the slender neck of the *presqu'île*, is a popular rendezvous for **surfers** and **windsurfers**. There is a charming **hotel**, *La Taverne*, facing the port (☎02.97.30.91.61; ❸), with good sea views from most rooms, and also a **campsite** just outside Portivy, the two-star *Camping de Port Blanc* on the route du Port Blanc (☎02.97.30.91.30; closed mid-Sept to mid-June). Other two-star sites nearby include the *Camping Municipal de Penthièvre* (☎02.97.52.33.86; closed Oct–March) and the *Camping Municipal de Kerhostin* (☎02.97.30.95.25; closed early Sept to April).

Quiberon

Much of the peninsula has become built up over the years, but it still holds only one true town, **QUIBERON**, at its southern tip. Its most active area,

Port-Maria, is home to the **gare maritime** for the islands of Belle-Île, Houat and Hoëdic (see p.389), and also holds a fishing harbour that was once famous for its sardines. Stretching away to the east is a long curve of fine sandy beach, lined for several hundred yards with bars, cafés and restaurants. At its centre is a busy little park and miniature golf course, but few of the streets further back hold anything of great interest. The exception is the little hill that leads down to the port from the *gare SNCF*, where browsing around is rewarded with some surprisingly good clothes and antique shops.

Port-Haliguen, the other port, is on the eastern coast. Today, it's an active marina, with a little commercial fishing. Boats from the islands occasionally shelter here, and use it for embarkation in rough weather. Captain Alfred Dreyfus disembarked here on his return from Devil's Island in 1899.

Arrival and information

In July and August, the special Tire Bouchon train links Quiberon's **gare SNCF**, which is a short way above the town proper, with Auray. (The name, which means "corkscrew", refers to the bottleneck at the mouth of the peninsula rather than any circuitousness in the route.) Bus #1 (TIM; ⓣ02.97.24.26.20) runs right to the *gare maritime* from Vannes, via Auray and Carnac.

The **tourist office** is at 14 rue de Verdun (July & Aug Mon–Sat 9am–1.30pm & 2–7pm, Sun 10am–1pm & 2–5pm; Sept–June Mon–Sat 9.30am–12.30pm & 2–6pm; ⓣ02.97.50.07.84, ⓦwww.quiberon.com), downhill and left from the *gare SNCF*, while the **post office** is on rue Gambetta (Mon–Fri 9am–12.30pm & 2–5pm, Sat 9am–noon; ⓣ02.97.50.11.92), where you can also access the **Internet**.

Bicycles can be rented from Cycl'omar, 47 place Hoche (ⓣ02.97.50.26.00), while **horse-riding** can be arranged with the Centre Équestre l'Éperon, 38 rue Jean-Pierre-Callock, in Kerné (ⓣ02.97.50.28.32).

Accommodation

For the greater part of the year, it's hard to get a **room** in Quiberon. In July and August, the whole peninsula is packed, while in winter it gets very quiet indeed, with virtually all its facilities closed down. The nicest area in which to stay is along the seafront in **Port-Maria**, where several good hotel-restaurants face the Belle-Île ferry terminal.

The local **hostel**, the spartan *Filets Bleus*, inland at 45 rue du Roc'h-Priol (ⓣ02.97.50.15.54; €7.70; closed Oct–March), 1.5km southeast of the *gare SNCF*, also provides space for camping. **Campsites** along the sheltered east coast near Quiberon town include the three-star *Do-Mi-Si-La-Mi*, St-Julien Plage (ⓣ02.97.50.22.52, ⓦwww.domisilami.com; closed Nov–March), and the four-star *du Conguel*, boulevard de la Teignouse (ⓣ02.97.50.19.11, ⓦwww.campingdeconguel.com; closed Nov–March), which has a large pool with elaborate water slides. The Côte Sauvage has only one site, the *Camping Municipal* in the village of **Kerné**, 2km northwest of central Quiberon (ⓣ02.97.50.05.07; open July & Aug only).

Hôtel-Restaurant Bellevue rue de Tiviec ⓣ02.97.50.16.28, ⓦwww.bellevuequiberon.com. Relatively quiet Logis de France, set slightly back from the sea near the Casino 500m east of the port, with its own pool and a restaurant where menus cost €20 and up. Closed Oct–March. ❺

Hôtel-Restaurant au Bon Accueil 6 quai de Houat ⓣ02.97.50.07.92, ⓕ02.97.50.28.62. Seafront hotel that's Port-Maria's best option for budget travellers. The rooms are basic but inexpensive, and there's a particularly good restaurant downstairs (see p.388). Closed mid-Nov to mid-Dec. ❷

Hôtel de la Mer 8 quai de Houat ⓣ02.97.50.09.05, ⓦwww.hoteldelamer.com. Blue-trimmed hotel with a lift at the western end of Port-Maria's seafront strip, offering an adequate standard of comfort and sea views from some rooms, but rather poor en-suite bathrooms. The heated swimming pool is open only during summer. Good menus in the *Turbotin* restaurant downstairs range from a €16 option via the €22 *Houat* up to the six-course €25 *Belle-Île*. Closed mid-Nov to mid-Feb & Thurs. ❹

Le Neptune 4 quai de Houat ⓣ02.97.50.09.62, ⓕ02.97.50.41.44. Very close to *Au Bon Accueil* in Port-Maria, and significantly more luxurious; if you're happy to pay that bit extra, it's the best value around. All the rooms have either sea or garden views – some with private balconies – and there are the usual seafood menus available ranging from €17 to €29. Closed Jan & Mon in low season. ❹

L'Océan 7 quai de l'Océan ⓣ02.97.50.07.58, ⓕ02.97.50.27.81. Attractive little hotel in the port, with multicoloured pastel shutters. It seems to have given up the unequal struggle to keep a restaurant going, but still has reasonably priced rooms. Closed Oct–March. ❷

Eating and drinking

Once again, the most appealing area in which to go browsing the menus looking for a good **meal** is along the waterfront in Port-Maria, with its line of seafood restaurants competing to attract the ferry passengers. Hotel owners are very insistent on persuading guests to pay for half-board – and at the *Bon Accueil*, for example, that's no great hardship – but there are plenty of alternatives to choose from if you do manage to escape their clutches. To stock up on provisions, try the morning **markets** at Kerhostin, at the neck of the peninsula 5km north of Quiberon on Wednesday, at St-Pierre-Quiberon, just south of Kerhostin on Thursday, and in Quiberon itself on Saturday. The most promising **bar** is *Le Nelson*, a short way back from the beach at 20 place Hoch (ⓣ02.97.50.31.37; closed Sun in low season), where, along with the usual beers plus a wide selection of rums, you can also use the Internet.

Hôtel-Restaurant au Bon Accueil 6 quai de Houat ⓣ02.97.50.07.92. Friendly dining room with something of the atmosphere and decor of a village bar, serving good fish soup and seafood specialities such as *cassolette de la mer* on menus that start at €15. Closed Wed in low season.

La Chaumine 36 place de Manémeur ⓣ02.97.50.17.67. Manémeur is technically a separate village to Quiberon, though it's not too far to walk around the headland west of the port. Set close to the menhir in the main square, this lovely little fish restaurant serves menus from €13 to €45, with an €22.50 option featuring salmon braised in champagne. Closed Sun eve & Mon, plus Nov to mid-Dec & 3 weeks in March.

Le Corsaire 24 quai de Belle-Île ⓣ02.97.50.42.69. Large waterfront restaurant, facing the ferry terminal and serving fine seafood spreads on a sprawling terrace for €12.70 and upwards.

De la Criée 11 quai de l'Océan ⓣ02.97.30.53.09. Truly superb local fish restaurant, serving changing fish specialities every day, fresh from the morning's catch; make your choice from the baskets arrayed along the front. The sole menu, at €16, includes ling and sea bass, for example, and fish smoked on the premises, while €17 buys a great seafood couscous. Closed Sun eve & Mon in low season, plus Jan.

Belle-Île

The island of **Belle-Île**, 15km offshore, due south of Quiberon, mirrors Brittany in its make-up. On the landward side it is rich and fertile, interrupted by deep estuaries with tiny ports; facing the ocean, along its own Côte Sauvage, sparse heather-covered cliffs trail rocky crags out into the sea.

With the island measuring 17km east to west and up to 10km north to south, some kind of transport is essential to appreciate these contrasts, even if you just come for a day-trip. This presents no great problem: bicycles are available in

Getting to Belle-Île

Throughout the year, the Société Morbihannaise de Navigation (ⓣ08.20.05.60.00, or, if you're calling from outside France, ⓣ02.97.35.02.00, ⓦwww.smn-navigation.fr) sends at least five **ferries** daily – and up to thirteen in high summer – from **Port-Maria**, at the southernmost tip of the Quiberon peninsula, to **Le Palais** on Belle-Île. In July and August, the first departure each day is usually at 8am, and the crossing normally takes 45 minutes, though the high-speed vessel *Locmaria 56* makes three to seven crossings daily between May and August in just 20 minutes. In summer, the standard adult return fare is €22.99, rising to €25.45 for the high-speed trip; under-25s pay €13.87 or €15.39; and over-60s €15.72 or €17.35. Small cars can be taken on the slower crossings for €105.34 return, while bikes cost €13.10 return. Despite the high number of sailings, it is a good idea to reserve in advance on the website if travelling at peak times such as Easter and high summer.

Between Easter and mid-September, the same company sends two boats daily direct to **Sauzon** from **Port-Maria**, which takes either 30 minutes, or, for occasional trips in July and August, 20 minutes. The same passenger fares apply, with no supplement for the high-speed crossings; no cars or bikes can be carried. From mid-July until the end of August, the *Locmaria 56* also makes one daily return trip to **Sauzon** from **Lorient**, departing at 8.20am from Lorient's *gare maritime* and taking 1 hour to get there. Adults pay €26.64 return, under-25s €18.64, and under-13s €13.32; there are no reductions for over-60s, and no vehicles can be taken.

During the summer, Compagnie des Îles (ⓣ02.40.23.34.10 or ⓣ08.25.16.91.30, ⓦwww.compagniedesiles.com) sails direct to **Le Palais** from **La Turballe**, between Piriac and Guérande on the coast not far north of La Baule. The crossing takes 1 hour 45 minutes (April to mid-July & first ten days of Sept – sporadic sailings; mid-July to Aug daily, departing 8.15am; adults €32 return, under-15s €21.50).

Navix (ⓣ02.97.46.60.00, ⓦwww.navix.fr) also operate day-trips to the island. From **Vannes** and **Port-Navalo**, these run roughly thrice weekly in April, daily in May, June to mid-July and the first two weeks in September, and twice daily from mid-July to August; from **La Trinité**, they run twice daily in July and August only. Adults pay €29 return, under-15s €19.

profusion at the island port of **Le Palais**, and if you're happy to pay for the privilege, you can also take a small car over on the ferries.

The island once belonged to the monks of Redon, and later to the ambitious Nicholas Fouquet, Louis XIV's minister, whose hubris in buying it in 1658 contributed to his downfall at the hands of the Three Musketeers three years later. It was subsequently captured by the English in 1752, who swapped it for Menorca in 1761 in an unrepeatable bargain deal. Along the way Belle-Île has seen a fair number of distinguished exiles. The citadel prison at Le Palais closed only in 1961, having numbered among its inmates an astonishing succession of state enemies and revolutionary heroes – including the son of Toussaint L'Ouverture of Haiti, Ben Bella of Algeria, and even, for a brief period after 1848, Karl Marx. Less involuntarily, such celebrated figures as the painters Monet and Matisse, the writers Flaubert and Proust, and the actress Sarah Bernhardt all spent time on the island.

Le Palais

As you dock at the pleasant little harbour town of **LE PALAIS**, the abrupt star-shaped fortifications of the **Citadelle** are the first thing you see, towering above the port. Once you've explored the few little streets of the town proper,

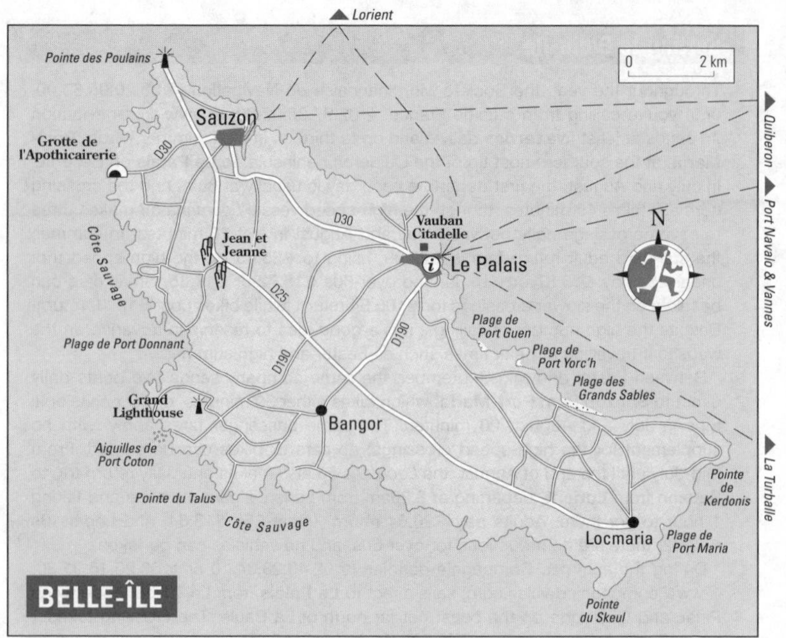

it's well worth crossing the small lock and climbing up to have a closer look at the Citadelle. Now the very picture of tranquillity, the fortress is surrounded by lawns, flowers and ornate topiary. Constructed along stylish and ordered lines by the great builder Vauban early in the eighteenth century, it is startling in size – filled with doorways leading to mysterious cellars and underground passages, endless sequences of rooms and dungeons and deserted cells. Though largely empty, the structure is quite sound, and fitted out with sturdy new floors.

An informative **museum** (daily: April–June, Sept & Oct 9.30am–6pm; July & Aug 9am–7pm; Nov–March 9.30am–noon & 2–5pm; €6.10) documents the island's history, including its involvement in Dumas' tales of *The Three Musketeers* (which feature an account of the death of Porthos on the island). Displays cover Vauban himself, and also the 78 Acadian families who settled here in 1765 after the defeat of French Canada – part of the mass migration that was also responsible for populating Louisiana, in what's now the southern US, with "Cajuns". There's disappointingly little explanation of perhaps the prison's most enigmatic inmates, however: the Le Voisin family of poisoners, incarcerated here in perpetual silence in 1682.

Practicalities

The **tourist office** for the whole island is alongside the *gare maritime* in Le Palais, on the left side of the harbour (July & Aug Mon–Sat 8.45am–7.30pm, Sun 8.45am–1pm; Sept–June Mon–Sat 9am–12.30pm & 2–6pm; ⓣ02.97.31.81.93, ⓦwww.belle-ile.com). Several waterfront outlets rent out **bicycles** at around €11 per day, including Cyclotour (ⓣ02.97.31.80.68) and Roue Libre (ⓣ02.97.31.49.81); Didier Banet (ⓣ02.97.31.84.74) rents **mopeds** as well, while Vélo Fun (ⓣ02.97.31.57.48) also offers boogie-boards.

Cars, costing in the region of €70 per day, can be rented from Locatourisle (Ⓣ02.97.31.83.56) or Belle-Île Tourisme (Ⓣ02.97.31.81.88) both of wich are also located in Le Parais. Finally, Belle-Île also has its own **bus** system, operated by Taol Mor (Ⓣ02.97.31.32.32), centred in Le Palais and offering around eight daily connections in summer to each of Sauzon, Bangor and Locmaria.

Accommodation in Le Palais includes the simple quayside *Frégate*, above a nice little bar on quai de l'Acadie (Ⓣ02.97.31.54.16; ❶; closed mid-Nov to March) and a couple of more expensive options that flank it to either side: the *Hôtel-Restaurant de Bretagne* (Ⓣ02.97.31.80.14, Ⓦwww.hotel-de-bretagne.fr; ❹), and the *Atlantique* (Ⓣ02.97.31.80.11, Ⓦwww.hotel-atlantique.com; ❹). Both the latter have excellent sea-view **restaurants**, but the *Grand Café* at the *Atlantique* just takes the edge, with a great value €15 menu that offers salmon or mackerel in a beetroot coulis or duck terrine followed by steamed or grilled fish or grilled meat. A little way back, but still enjoying sea views, the *Hôtel Vauban*, 1 rue des Remparts (Ⓣ02.97.31.45.42, Ⓦwww.hotelvauban.com; ❹; closed mid-Oct to mid-Feb), is a Logis de France that makes a good alternative.

There are also three **campsites** in the immediate vicinity of the town, including the three-star *Camping de l'Océan* (Ⓣ02.97.31.83.86, Ⓦwww.camping-ocean-belle-ile.com; closed mid-Oct to March), and a **hostel** (Ⓣ02.97.31.81.33, Ⓔbelle-ile@fuaj.org; €9.30; closed Oct), which despite holding almost a hundred beds is always wildly oversubscribed; it's located a short way out of town along the clifftops from the Citadelle, at Haute-Boulogne.

Sauzon

SAUZON, Belle-Île's second town, is also located on the island's sheltered north coast. A beautiful little village, it's arrayed along one side of the mouth of a slender estuary, 6km west of Le Palais (and a 20min ride on bus #1). There's next to nothing to see here, but if you're staying any length of time, and you've got your own transport, it's a lovely spot in which to base yourself.

In a magnificent setting, next to its eponymous little lighthouse on the headland at the very tip of the estuary, the *Phare* is a good, inexpensive thirteen-room **hotel** (Ⓣ02.97.31.60.36; ❸; closed Oct–March), which insists that guests eat its delicious fish dinners. There's also a very fancy, comfortable **B&B** slightly uphill nearby, *La Touline* (Ⓣ02.97.31.69.69, Ⓦwww.hostellerielatouline.com; ❻; closed mid-Nov to mid-March). In addition, Sauzon can offer two two-star **campsites**, *Pen Prad* (Ⓣ02.97.31.64.82, Ⓔmariedesauzon@wanadoo.fr; closed Oct–March) and *La Source* (Ⓣ02.97.31.60.95, Ⓦwww.belleile-lasource.com; closed Oct–March).

Around the island

Assuming that you have a car or bicycle, the ideal way to explore the island is to cross to its southern side and then walk at least part of the coastal footpath that runs on bare soil for the full length of the Côte Sauvage. Head first for the village of **BANGOR**, 6km south of Le Palais (a 30min ride on bus #2), where you're confronted by an incongruous row of huge and very expensive hotels. President Mitterrand, once a regular guest, came for a farewell visit shortly before his death to the *Castel Clara* (Ⓣ02.97.31.84.21, Ⓦwww.castel-clara.com; ❾; closed mid-Nov to mid-Feb).

Another 2km west of Bangor, the **Grand Lighthouse**, which dates from 1835, commands sweeping views of the entire coastline. Even if you don't have

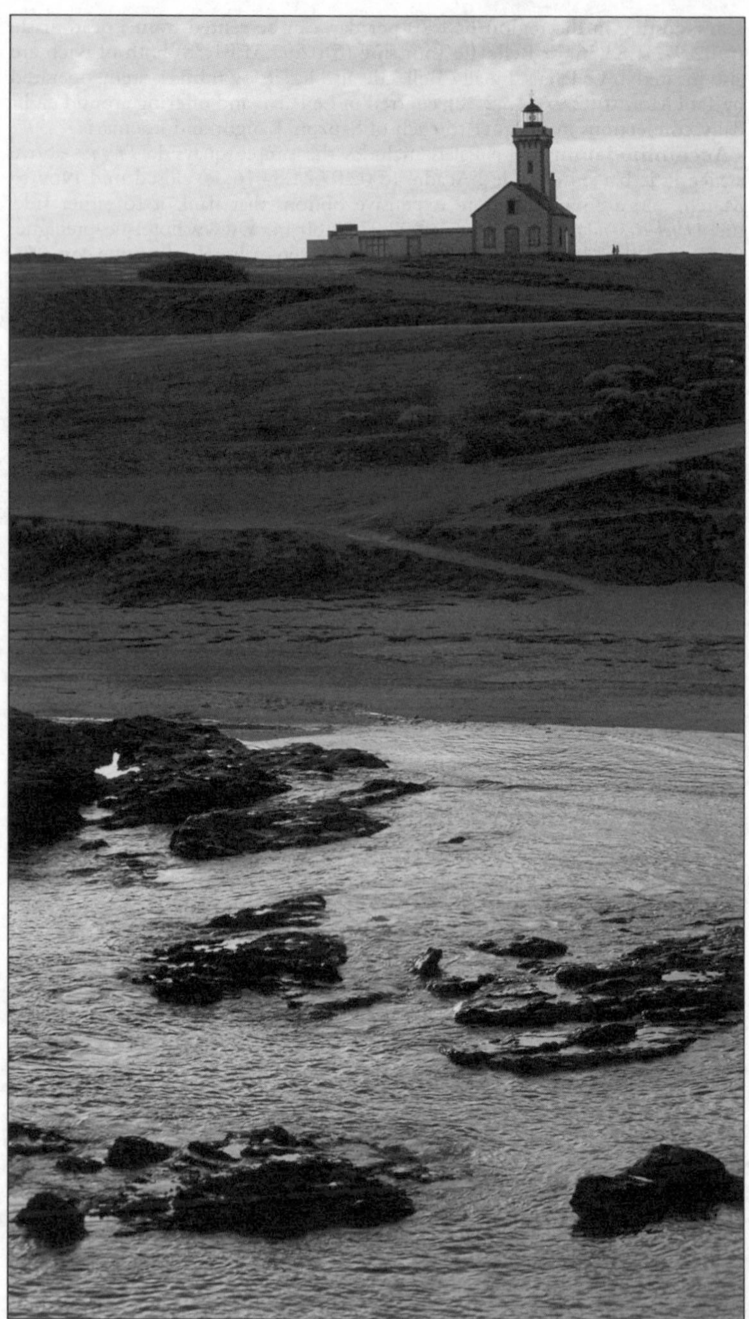

△ Poulains lighthouse, Belle-Île

the energy to climb its 256 steps (open at irregular hours depending on the presence of the lighthouse keeper, but usually July & Aug 2–6pm; free), you'll be able to see the **Aiguilles de Port-Coton** rock formation just offshore to the south, where a savage sea foams in the pinnacles of rock, and the pretty beach of **Port-Donnant** a kilometre to the west – an easy stroll from the lighthouse, but unfortunately bathing, despite appearances, is dangerous.

You can get to the beach by road, but the only way to follow the coastline any further north is on foot, by means of the footpath that clings to the clifftops. Five kilometres along – a walk of something over an hour – the path meets up with another road just short of the **Grotte de l'Apothicairerie**. This precarious oceanfront cave is so called because it used to be filled with the nests of cormorants, arranged like the jars on a pharmacist's shelves.

The **D30 inland** from the cave leads along a miniature tree-lined valley sheltered from the Atlantic winds. If you take the **D25** back towards Le Palais you pass the two **menhirs**, Jean and Jeanne, said to be lovers petrified as punishment for wanting to meet before their marriage. Another (larger) menhir used to lie near these two – it was broken up to help construct the road that separates them.

The **Pointe des Poulains**, at the northwestern tip of the island where the Côte Sauvage comes to an end, is an exposed little headland that holds a picturesque little lighthouse-cum-cottage and is all but separated from the rest of the island at high tide. The road comes to an end just short of the slender sandy spit that leads to the point, alongside the country estate where actress and world celebrity **Sarah Bernhardt** used to spend her summers.

Houat and Hoëdic

Houat and **Hoëdic**, two smaller and much quieter islands to the east of Belle-Île, can also be reached by ferries from Quiberon and elsewhere. Most visitors come to the islands on day-trips, to seek out their magnificent – and usually all but empty – golden **beaches**, but both do offer facilities for extended stays if you can't tear yourself away.

Getting to Houat and Hoëdic

Ferries to **Houat** and **Hoëdic** from **Quiberon-Port-Maria** are operated by the Société Morbihannaise de Navigation (ⓣ08.20.05.60.00, or, from outside France, ⓣ02.97.35.02.00, ⓦwww.smn-navigation.fr). They run between one and six sailings daily all year, with the first departure from Quiberon at 9am in July and August, and usually 9.15am otherwise. In summer, adults pay €22.99 return, under-25s pay €13.87, and over-60s €15.72. Bikes cost €13.10 return extra, and cars cannot be taken. The crossing to Houat takes 40 minutes, to Hoëdic another 25 minutes.

In addition, Compagnie des Îles (ⓦwww.compagniedesiles.com) run day-trips to Houat only from **Vannes** (ⓣ08.25.16.41.00), **Locmariaquer** (ⓣ08.25.16.41.30) and **Port Navalo** (ⓣ08.25.16.41.20), daily in July and August (adults €25 return, under-15s €16 return). Boats depart from Vannes at either 10am (first three weeks in July and the last week in August) or 8.15am (late July to late August), from Locmariaquer at 10.45am and Port Navalo at 11.15am.

Finally, Navix (ⓣ02.97.46.60.00, ⓦwww.navix.fr) run day-trips to Houat only on most days in July and August, leaving **La Trinité** at 8am. Adults pay €25 return, under-15s €16.

The Île de Houat

The island of **Houat**, which in Breton means "duck", measures 5km from east to west, and much less than half that north to south. It's an idyllic spot, populated largely by rabbits and lizards, with hardly a tree to its name. Most of what marginally higher ground it has to offer consists of open heathland, with its thin covering of turf petering out at the head of pink granite cliffs which look down on long sandy beaches and lovely little coves.

Boats draw in at **Port St-Gildas**, a not especially picturesque little harbour just below the island's one "town", the flowery village of **HOUAT**. A private house to the right of the road up into the village rents out poor-quality **bicycles** at around €12.50 per day (☎02.97.30.66.64), but the island is small enough for walking to be a pleasure, and it's not in any case legal to cycle along the coastal footpaths. The finest **beaches** lie to the east and south, in the shape of the sheltered **Tréac'h er Gourèd** that runs the full length of the eastern shoreline, and the **Tréac'h Salus** nearby.

During the 1980s, the islanders tried to boost their economy by raising lobsters in tanks in a large shed-like building known as the *écloserie*, 1km southwest of Houat. That experiment never proved profitable, so the structure has since 1994 served instead as the **Eclosarium** (Easter–Sept daily 10am–6pm; €3.50), a museum dedicated almost exclusively to the microscopic marine world of **phytoplankton**, the organisms responsible for producing eighty percent of the oxygen on earth. It's more interesting than it might sound, with a healthy dose of local history thrown in. Fetid-looking vials demonstrate how algae is now being cultivated locally, for use in the manufacture of products such as shower gel, sun cream, moisturizer and even pasta – if you're tempted, the gift shop sells them at discounted prices.

Practicalities

Two small **hotels** offer Houat's most comfortable accommodation. At the edge of town, overlooking the harbour, the *Hôtel-Restaurant des Îles* (☎02.97.30.68.02; ❹; closed Dec & Jan) offers tasteful sea-view rooms and serves good food both indoors and out on its terrace; it's a great spot for lunch, with the main set menu costing €15.20. Alternatively, *L'Ezenn*, on the main road above the Tréac'h er Gouréd beach (☎02.97.30.69.73; ❷), has excellent modernized rooms but no restaurant. Strictly speaking, **camping** is illegal, but in summer scores of visitors set up their tents along the slender ridge that divides the two beaches south of town. For more **information** about the island and its facilities, call the Mairie (☎02.97.30.68.04).

The Île de Hoëdic

At a mere 2.5km end to end, Hoëdic – in Breton the "duckling" to Houat's "duck" – is that much tinier still. It's such a sleepy place, the story goes, that during the eighteenth century the rector of Hoëdic lost not only his sense of time but also his calendar, and ended up reducing Lent from forty days down to a more manageable three.

The island's sole settlement – **HOËDIC**, naturally – stands right in the centre, a short walk up from the ferry landing at **Port-Argol**. Other than the appealing nineteenth-century church of St-Goustan, the only activity is to walk off in search of **beaches**. Once again the best are to the south and east; take care how far you stroll out at low tide, as some patches become isolated offshore sandbanks when the sea comes in.

Hoëdic boasts just one **hotel**, *Les Cardinaux* (ⓣ02.97.52.37.27, ⓔlescardinaux@aol.com; ❸; closed Sun eve & Mon in winter), which offers extensive sea views and insists on half-board. There's also a large, well-equipped municipal **campsite** (ⓣ02.97.52.48.88; closed Sept–June), between the harbour and the village, plus a dozen or so **gîtes**, rented year-round by the week through the Mairie (ⓣ02.97.52.48.88).

Carnac

CARNAC is the most important prehistoric site in Europe – in fact this spot is thought to have been continuously inhabited longer than anywhere else in the world. Its **alignments** of two thousand or so menhirs stretch over 4km, with great burial tumuli dotted amid them. In use since at least 5700 BC, the site long predates Knossos, the Pyramids, Stonehenge and the great Egyptian temples of the same name at Karnak.

The town of Carnac is split into two distinct halves – the popular seaside resort of Carnac-Plage and, further inland, Carnac-Ville near the alignments. It's an amalgam that can verge on the ridiculous, with rows of shops named Supermarché des Druides and the like; but, for all that, Carnac is a relaxed and attractive place, and any commercialization doesn't intrude on the megaliths themselves. Fortunately, the ancient builders had the foresight to construct their monuments well back from the sea.

Arrival and information

Buses to Auray, Quiberon and Vannes stop near the tourist office on avenue des Druides, and on rue St-Cornély in Carnac-Ville. The nearest **train** station to Carnac is at Plouharnel, 4km northwest, from which the Tire Bouchon rail link with Auray and Quiberon runs in July and August. In addition, a motorized **Petit Train** chugs around a circuit between the town, the beach, the Maison des Mégalithes visitor centre, La Trinité, and various alignments in summer (April–Sept every 30min, roughly 10am–6pm; €5.50).

The main **tourist office** is slightly back from the main beach at 74 avenue des Druides in Carnac-Plage (July & Aug Mon & Sat 9am–7pm, Tues–Fri 9am–1pm & 2–7pm, Sun 3–7pm; Sept–June Mon–Sat 9am–noon & 2–6pm; ⓣ02.97.52.13.52, ⓦwww.ot-carnac.fr). An annexe in the place de l'Église in town is open between April and September (Mon–Sat 10am–1pm & 2–6pm, Sun 10am–12.30pm). Both provide fully comprehensive maps and details. You can access the **Internet** at *Le Baobab*, 3 allée du Parc (ⓣ02.97.52.29.96), a cybercafé in Carnac-Plage.

Bicycles are available for rent from several of the town's campsites (see p.397), or from Le Randonneur, 20 avenue des Druides, Carnac-Plage (ⓣ02.97.52.02.55), or Lorcy, 6 rue de Courdiec, Carnac-Ville (ⓣ02.97.52.09.73). The *Grande Métairie* campsite (see p.397) also arranges tours on **horseback**.

Accommodation

Hotels in Carnac are at a premium in July and August, when you can expect higher prices and intense pressure to take half-board (*demipension*). Carnac-Ville is marginally cheaper than Carnac-Plage, although the distinction is

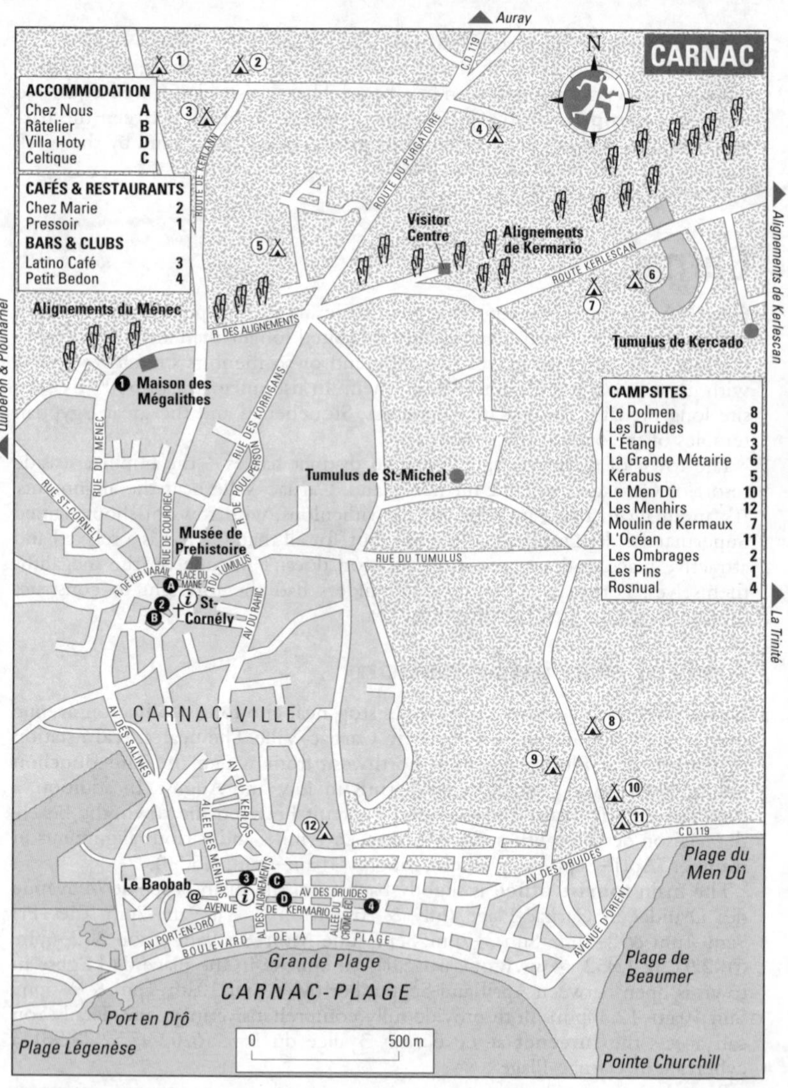

blurred where the two merge. In **Carnac-Ville**, *Hôtel Chez Nous*, 5 place de la Chapelle (ⓣ02.97.52.07.28; ❷; closed mid-Nov to March), is central and convenient, with spacious rooms at very reasonable prices and a nice garden, but no restaurant; the old stone, ivy-clad *Hôtel le Râtelier*, 4 chemin de Douët (ⓣ02.97.52.05.04, ⓦwww.le-ratelier.com; ❸; restaurant closed Tues & Wed Oct–March), has slightly fancier rooms and top-quality food on menus that start from €17. In **Carnac-Plage**, the *Villa Hoty*, 15 avenue de Kermario (ⓣ02.97.52.11.12; ❷; closed Nov–Easter), is the best value, with clean, cosy little rooms in a traditional prewar seaside house, while the *Hôtel Celtique*, 82 avenue des Druides (Ⓣ02.97.52.14.15, Ⓦwww.hotel-celtique.com; ④) has a heated swimming pool and another great restaurant.

As befits such a family-oriented place, there are around twenty **campsites** in and around Carnac. Among the best are the two-star *Men Dû* (Ⓣ02.97.52.04.23, Ⓦwww.camping-mendu.fr; closed Oct–Easter), near the sea, inland from the plage du Men Dû; the central three-star *Dolmen* (Ⓣ02.97.52.12.35; closed mid-Sept to April), immediately north of Carnac-Plage but still an easy walk from the sea; and the more expensive four-star *Grande Métairie* (Ⓣ02.97.52.24.01, Ⓦwww.lagrandemetairie.com; closed mid-Sept to March), near the Kercado tumulus, which offers tennis, horse-riding and a swimming pool.

The alignments

All sorts of conjectures have been advanced about the **Carnac megaliths**. One of the oldest stories was that they were Roman soldiers turned to stone as they pursued Pope Cornély; among the most recent is the alleged belief of US soldiers in the last war that they were German antitank obstructions. The general consensus today is that they had a religious significance connected with their use as some sort of astronomical observatory. Professor Thom, whose popular theories have made him the best-known writer on the alignments, sees them – and most of the megaliths of the Morbihan – as part of a unified system for recording such phenomena as the extreme points of the lunar and solar cycles. According to this hypothesis, the Carnac stones provided a grid system – a kind of neolithic graph paper – for plotting heavenly movements, and hence to determine the siting of other stones (see the further account, together with map, in Contexts, pp.421–424).

However, it's hard to see real consistency in the size or shape of the stones, or enough regularity in the lines to pinpoint their direction. Local tradition has it that new stones were added to the lines, illuminated by fire, each June. An annual ceremony in which willing participants set up one stone does sound more plausible than a vast programme of slave labour to erect them all at once. In any case, the physical aspect and orientation of the stones may have been subsidiary to their metaphysical significance; it's possible no practical purpose or precise pattern was involved, and their importance was entirely symbolic.

The way you see them today cannot be said to be authentic. Having been used for generations as a source of ready-quarried stone, they were later also surreptitiously removed by farmers attempting to prevent the influx of

Seeing the stones

Thanks to increasing numbers of visitors (and despite vehement local opposition), the principal alignments are currently fenced off. The long-term plan is to allow the area to revegetate at a natural pace, but there's no predicting how long that process will take, and even when it's complete the chances are that access will still be restricted. Currently you are allowed to walk freely around the best-preserved sites from October to March; from April to September access is on guided tours only (€3). For more information on guided tours, and to buy books and maps of the site, the **Maison des Mégalithes** across the road from the Alignements de Menec (daily: May–Aug 9am–7pm; Sept–April 10am–5.15pm; Ⓣ02.97.52.89.99) is the official visitor centre. Despite the restrictions on access, it must be said that the alignments, though fenced off, can be seen perfectly well by walking along the network of paths that weave among them. Indeed, from this (or almost any) distance they tend to look like no more than stumps in the heather.

academics and tourists damaging precious crops. Not only is it impossible to say how many of the stones have disappeared, but those that remain are not necessarily in their original positions – small holes filled with pink concrete at the base of the stones denote those that have been restored or re-erected.

The **menhirs** range in size from mere stumps to five-metre-high blocks; some stand alone, others in circles known as **cromlechs**, or in approximate lines. In addition there are **dolmens**, groups of standing stones roofed with further stones laid across the top, which are generally assumed to be burial chambers. And there are tumuli – most notably the **Tumulus de St-Michel**, near the town centre, a vast artificial mound containing rudimentary graves. You can scramble through subterranean passages and tunnels beneath the mound to view little stone cairns and piles of charred bones; the tunnels are, however, again not authentic, being the recent creation of archeologists.

Taken all together, the stones make up three distinct major alignments, running roughly in the same northeast–southwest direction, but each with a slightly separate orientation. These are the **Alignements de Ménec**, "the place of stones" or "place of remembrance", with 1169 stones in eleven rows; the **Alignements de Kermario**, "the place of the dead", with 1029 menhirs in ten rows; and the **Alignements de Kerlescan**, "the place of burning", with 555 menhirs in thirteen lines. All three are sited parallel to the sea alongside the Route des Alignements and Route de Kerlescan, 1km or so to the north of Carnac-Ville.

The Museum of Prehistory

Carnac's **Musée de Préhistoire** (mid-June to mid-Sept Mon, Tues & Thurs–Sun 10am–12.30pm & 1.30–7pm, Wed 1.30–7pm; mid-Sept to mid-June Mon, Tues & Thurs–Sun 10am–12.30pm & 1.30–6pm, Wed 1.30–6pm; €5) is located at 10 place de la Chapelle, Carnac-Ville. It's a disappointingly dry museum of archeology that's likely to leave anyone whose command of French is less than perfect almost completely in the dark as to what all the fuss is about. It traces the history of the area from earliest times, starting with 450,000-year-old chipping tools and leading by way of the Neanderthals to the megalith-builders and beyond. As well as authentic physical relics, such as the original "twisted dolmen" of Luffang, with a carving of an octopus-like divinity guaranteed to chill the blood of any devotee of H. P. Lovecraft, there are reproductions and casts of the carvings at Locmariaquer, a scale model of the Alignements de Ménec, and diagrams of how the stones may have been moved into place. The captions are exclusively written in an impenetrable academic French, and the exhibits alone tend to be too mundane to hold the interest for long.

The town and the beaches

Carnac itself, divided between the original **Carnac-Ville** and the seaside resort of **Carnac-Plage**, is extremely popular and crowded, swarming with holidaymakers in July and August. For most of these, the alignments are only a sideshow. But, as a holiday centre, Carnac has its special charm, especially in late spring and early autumn, when it is less crowded – and cheaper. The town and seafront remain well wooded, and the tree-lined avenues and gardens are a delight – the climate is mild enough for the Mediterranean mimosa and evergreen oak to grow alongside the native stone pine and cypress.

Near the Museum of Prehistory (see above), in the centre of Carnac-Ville, the **church of St-Cornély** was built in the seventeenth century in honour of the patron saint of horned animals. Archeological discoveries suggest that the custom of bringing diseased cattle to Carnac to be cured, still honoured at least in theory at the saint's *pardon* on the second Sunday in September, dates back as far as the Romans. The Romans also had heated seawater baths here; today the **Thalassotherapy Centre** is an ultramodern building where, among other things, they treat *maladies de civilisation*.

Carnac's five **beaches** extend for nearly 3km in total, with the largest of them – logically enough, the Grande Plage – running for the full length of the built-up area known as Carnac-Plage. For much of the way it's hidden from view by the slightly raised line of dunes that separates it from the boulevard de la Plage, which is in turn very low-key; the parallel avenue des Druides, a couple of blocks inland, is much busier, with shops and restaurants.

Further west, nearer the yacht club, the small **plage Légenèse** is reputed to be the beach on which the ill-fated *Chouan* royalists landed in 1795. The two most attractive beaches, usually counted together as one of the five, are **plages Men Dû** and **Beaumer**, which lie to the east towards La Trinité beyond Pointe Churchill.

Eating and drinking

Most of the **restaurants** worth recommending in Carnac are in the hotels, as described on p.396, but *Chez Marie*, facing St-Cornély church at 3 place de l'Église (Ⓣ02.97.52.07.93; closed Nov–Easter), and the *Pressoir* by the Ménec *alignements* (Ⓣ02.97.52.01.86; closed mid-Sept to Easter) are worthwhile crêperies. There's a **market** in Carnac-Ville on Wednesday and Sunday mornings; in the surrounding area, Locmariaquer holds them on Tuesday and Saturday, La Trinité on Tuesday and Friday, and Auray on Monday. Avenue des Druides has a few **bars**, such as the *Latino Café* at no. 62 (Ⓣ02.97.52.22.38), with its palm trees, leopard-skin furnishings and Latin music, and the *Petit Bedon* at no.108 (Ⓣ02.97.52.11.62), which starts off the evening playing predominantly rock, but has covered most musical styles by the time it closes at 4am.

La Trinité

An alternative base to Carnac proper is **LA TRINITÉ**, three or four kilometres along the coast to the east, around the sweep of Beaumer bay. The town itself is uninteresting – a modern and very upmarket yacht harbour without a proper beach – but has achieved fame as the former home of yachtsman Eric Tabarley, twice winner of the single-handed transatlantic race in 1964 (*Pen Duick I*) and 1976 (*Pen Duick VI*), who was lost at sea off Wales in 1998, and as the birthplace of Jean-Marie Le Pen, founder of France's ultra-right National Front.

La Trinité does at least hold some high-quality **hotel-restaurants**, among them the *Ostrea*, facing the port at 34 cours des Quais (Ⓣ02.97.55.73.23, Ⓦwww.hotel-ostrea.com; ❹; closed Dec to mid-Feb, plus Sun eve & Mon in low season), where you dine on a sea-view terrace, and a crop of four-star **campsites** nearby, including the attractive *Camping La Baie* on the plage de Kervillen (Ⓣ02.97.55.73.42, Ⓦwww.camping-la-baie.com; closed mid-Sept to mid-May).

Locmariaquer

LOCMARIAQUER, easily accessible from Auray or Carnac, stands right at the mouth of the Gulf of Morbihan – its cape separated by only a few hundred metres from the tip of the Rhuys peninsula. On the ocean side, it has a long sandy beach, popular not only with swimmers but also with beachcombers and shellfish-scavengers; on the Gulf side, it has a small tidal port. Like Carnac, however, the main reason to go out of your way to visit Locmariaquer is for its fine crop of megaliths.

Menhirs and dolmens

The **Grand Menhir Brise** at Locmariaquer (daily: May–Sept 10am–7pm; Sept–April 10am–12.30pm & 2–5.15pm; €4.60) is supposed to have been the crucial central point of the megalithic observatory of the Morbihan (see Contexts, pp.421–424). Before being floored by an earthquake in 1722, it was by far the largest known menhir – 20m high and at 347 tonnes weighing more than a jumbo jet. It now lies on the ground in four pieces (a possible fifth is missing). Archeologists have established that the stone itself was quarried at Kerdaniel, 4km north, and estimate that the job of moving it required a workforce of between two thousand and four thousand people.

Alongside the Grand Menhir, and covered by the same ticket, the **Table des Marchand** is a dolmen that was once exposed but has now been reburied for its protection under a tumulus. You can, however, go inside, along a narrow passage, and stand beneath its huge roof. Carvings overhead seem to depict ploughing, which may well have been a recent innovation at the time they were made. It has recently been discovered that this roof is part of the same stone as that on the tumulus at Gavrinis and on another local dolmen – the carvings match like a jigsaw. That constitutes a fresh puzzle for the archeologists, as it appears to imply that the builders did not revere the stones in themselves, as most theories had previously assumed. In addition, the stone at the end of the central chamber was originally erected as a stand-alone menhir, so the "table" must have been built around an earlier monument.

The rest of the megaliths of Locmariaquer are open at all times – and open to the weather as well, so watch out for muddy and waterlogged underground passages, and be sure to take a torch if you want to explore them thoroughly. The most interesting are the **Dolmen des Pierres Plates**, at the end of the town beach, with what looks like an octopus divinity deep in its long chamber, and the **Dolmen de Mané-Rethual**, a long covered tunnel leading to a burial chamber capped with a huge rock, reached along a narrow footpath that starts behind the phone boxes next to the Mairie/tourist office. At a third dolmen, the **Mané-Lud**, a horse's skull was found on top of each stone during excavations.

Practicalities

There are a couple of reasonable small **hotels** in Locmariaquer, both with good restaurants. *L'Escale* (ⓣ02.97.57.32.51; ❸; closed mid-Sept to mid-April)

Boats from Locmariaquer

Boat trips set out from Locmariaquer in all directions, for which rival companies sell tickets both in the town centre and at the port further down towards the narrow straits, with precise departure points depending on the level of the tides. Two main operators, Vedettes l'Aiglon (ⓣ02.97.57.39.15) and Vedettes Angélus (ⓣ02.97.57.30.29 ⓦwww.vedettes-angelus.com), run gulf tours, as detailed on p.409. In summer, Vedettes l'Aiglon also regularly make the three-kilometre crossing to Port Navalo on the Rhuys peninsula (see p.412), carrying bikes but not cars, while Compagnie des Îles (ⓣ08.25.16.41.30, ⓦwww.compagniedesiles.com) run day-trips to the Île de Houat (see p.394).

is right on the waterfront at 2 place Dariorigum, so you get a great view from its terrace, while the *Lautram* is set slightly back from the sea, facing the church on place de l'Église (Ⓣ02.97.57.31.32; ❷; closed Oct–March). The food at the *Lautram* is superb, but the cheaper rooms are pretty minimal.

Campsites include the excellent two-star *Ferme Fleurie* (Ⓣ02.97.57.34.06; closed Jan), 1km towards Kerinis, and the two-star, summer-only *Lann Brick* (Ⓣ02.97.57.32.79; closed mid-Sept to May), 1.5km further on, nearer the beach.

Auray and around

Though some people find **AURAY**, with its over-restored ancient quarter, slightly dull, it's a lot less crowded than Vannes, much cheaper than Quiberon town, and usefully placed for exploring Carnac, the Quiberon peninsula and the Gulf of Morbihan.

The natural centre of the town these days is the **place de la République**, with its eighteenth-century Hôtel de Ville. In a neighbouring square, linked to the place de la République by rue du Lait, is the seventeenth-century **church of St-Gildas**, with its fine Renaissance porch. A **covered market** adjoins the Hôtel de Ville, while on Mondays an open-air market fills the surrounding streets with colour – and stops all traffic for a considerable radius.

However, Auray's showpiece is undoubtedly the ancient quarter of **St-Goustan** down by the river, with its delightful, albeit restored, fifteenth- and sixteenth-century houses. This bend in the River Loch, an early defended site, made a natural setting for a town – and, with its easy access to the gulf, it soon became one of the busiest ports of Brittany. Today, as you look at it from the Promenade du Loch on the opposite bank, with the diminutive seventeenth-century stone bridge still spanning the river, it is not difficult to imagine it in its heyday. In 1776, Benjamin Franklin landed here on his way to seek the help of Louis XVI in the American War of Independence; Auray is also said to have been the last place Julius Caesar reached in his conquest of Gaul.

Practicalities

Auray's **gare SNCF** is twenty minutes' walk from the centre; alternatively buses run from the station through the centre of Auray and on to La Trinité, Carnac and the *gare SNCF* at Quiberon. The **tourist office** is up in town at 20 rue du Lait, very near the Hôtel de Ville on place de la République (July & Aug Mon–Sat 9am–7pm, Sun 9am–noon; Sept–June Mon–Sat 9am–noon & 2–6pm; Ⓣ02.97.24.09.75, Ⓦwww.auray-tourisme.com). A small annexe is maintained in July and August at the *gare SNCF*.

The most appealing place to **stay** in Auray would be right by the port in the St-Goustan quarter, but in the absence of waterfront hotels the best options are the new *Hôtel Le Marin*, just round the corner from the quayside at 1 place du Rolland (Ⓣ02.97.24.14.58; ❹; closed Jan to mid-Feb), which offers smart, well-equipped rooms above a brasserie, and the similarly pleasant *Hôtel Le Branhoc*, 300m short of the sea on the road down at 5 route du Bono (Ⓣ02.97.56.41.55, Ⓔle.branhoc@wanadoo.fr; ❸; closed mid-Nov to Jan), which has a reasonable restaurant. Up in town, *Hôtel Le Cadoudal*, 9 place Notre-Dame (Ⓣ02.97.24.14.65; ❷), is a cheaper, more basic alternative.

North of Auray

A short way north of Auray's train station – and thus quite a long way out from the town, on the B768 towards Baud – the imposing and evocative **Abbaye de Chartreuse** (April, July & Aug Wed–Mon 2.30–4.30pm; free) houses a David d'Angers mausoleum of black and white marble, commemorating the failed *Chouan* landing at Quiberon in 1795 (see p.386). For Bretons, the event was something more than an attempt at a royalist restoration, with strong undertones of a struggle for independence. Another gloomy piece of counter-Revolutionary history is recalled by the nearby **Champ des Martyrs**, where 350 of the *Chouans* were executed. It's located on the right of the D120, going out of town.

Two kilometres further along the D120, towards Brech, you come to the **Eco-Musée St-Degan** (April–June & Sept daily 2–5.30pm; July & Aug daily 10am–7pm; Oct–March school holidays only, daily 2–5.30pm; €4), a group of reconstructed farm buildings representing local peasant life at the beginning of the twentieth century. It's a bit determinedly rustic and charming, but at least it does attempt to escape the glass cases and wax models of most folk museums.

In **BRECH** itself there's a fine parish **church**, with a weather-beaten and faded calvary in its yard; a nice **café**, *des Bretons*; and a **gîte d'étape** – not a very eventful place to stay, perhaps, but a peaceful one.

Ste-Anne d'Auray

If you're in the area of Auray around July 26, you should head for **STE-ANNE D'AURAY**, which holds one of the largest of the Breton *pardons* on that day. Some 25,000 pilgrims gather for the occasion to hear Mass in the church, mount the *scala sancta* on their knees and buy trinkets and snacks from the street stalls.

The origin of this **pardon**, typical of many, was the discovery in 1623 of a statue of St Anne (the mother of Mary) by a local peasant, one Nicolazic. He claimed that the saint directed him to the spot where the statue had been buried for over nine hundred years and instructed him to build a church. Twenty years later, on his deathbed, Nicolazic was still being interrogated by the ecclesiastical authorities as to the truth of his story, but the church had been constructed and had already become a place of pilgrimage. Nicolazic was an illiterate peasant who spoke no French; it is a testimony to his obduracy that his claims were eventually accepted against the opposition of sceptical clergy and nobility. The continuing campaign for his canonization is polarized along similar lines today. Nicolazic's supporters see him as a representative of the downtrodden classes, and as a symbol of Breton independence; the wealthy Church establishment, on the other hand, continues to oppose him.

As a major centre for pilgrimage – Pope John Paul II visited as recently as September 1996 – Ste-Anne was chosen as the site for the vast **Monument aux Morts** erected by public subscription as a memorial to the 250,000 Breton dead of the Great War. One in fourteen of the population died, the highest proportion of losses of any region involved. The monument, a crypt topped by a dome with a granite altar, is surrounded by a wall that must be 200m long, covered with inscriptions to the dead; and yet even that huge and sombre wall does not contain room to list them all by name, often just cataloguing the horrific death tallies of tiny and obscure villages.

A short distance north on the D102 is a **National Necropolis**, holding dead from all wars since 1870.

Practicalities

Ste-Anne is a sad and solemn place. The town, away from the spacious promenades for the pilgrims, is small, low and drab; not really a place for a long stay, although there is no particular shortage of **hotels**. Among the best value in the centre are the *Moderne*, 8 rue de Vannes (Ⓣ02.97.57.66.55; ❷; closed mid-Dec to mid-Jan), and the *Croix Blanche*, nearby at 25 rue de Vannes (Ⓣ02.97.57.64.44; ❷; closed Jan, plus Sun eve & Mon in low season), both of which have good restaurants.

Vannes

Thanks to its position at the head of the Golfe du Morbihan, **VANNES**, 20km east of Auray, is southern Brittany's major tourist town. Modern Vannes is such a large and thriving community that the small size of the old walled town at its core, **Vieux Vannes**, may well come as a surprise. Its focal point, the old gateway of the **Porte St-Vincent**, commands a busy little square at the northern end of the long canalized port that provides access to the gulf itself. Once inside the ramparts, the old centre of chaotic streets – crammed around the cathedral, and enclosed by gardens and a tiny stream – is largely pedestrianized, in refreshing contrast to the somewhat insane road system beyond.

It was from Vannes that the great Breton warrior hero Nominoë (see p.426) set out to unify Brittany at the start of the ninth century; he defeated the Franks resoundingly, and pushed the borders past Nantes and Rennes to where they were to remain up until the French Revolution nearly a millennium later. Here too, the Breton *États* assembled in 1532 to ratify the Act of Union with France, in the building known as La Cohue; and here, also, 22 of the royalists captured at Quiberon (see p.386) were executed in the Jardins de la Garrène in 1795. Parisian soldiers fired the shots because local regiments refused.

Arrival and information

Vannes' **gare SNCF** is 25 minutes' walk north of the town centre. Buses to Auray, Carnac, Quiberon, Plöermel, Malestroit and other destinations leave from the **gare routière** opposite (CTM; Ⓣ02.97.01.22.01). **Parking** can be a problem unless you head straight for the west side of the port, south of town.

The **tourist office**, which has a well-restored seventeenth-century frontage, is close to the waterfront, near place Gambetta at 1 rue Thiers (July & Aug Mon–Sat 9am–7pm, Sun 10am–6pm; Sept–June Mon–Sat 9.30am–12.30pm & 2–6pm; Ⓣ02.97.47.24.34, Ⓦwww.tourisme-vannes.com). Staff can advise on availability at local hotels, though they charge €1 to make an actual booking for you; they also have details of an extensive summer programme of **walking tours** around the town.

Boats around the gulf are operated from the **gare maritime**, a little way south of the centre on the parc du Golfe, by Navix (Ⓣ02.97.46.60.00 or Ⓣ08.25.16.21.00, Ⓦwww.navix.fr) and Compagnie des Îles (Ⓣ08.25.16.41.00, Ⓦwww.compagniedesiles.com), among others (see p.409). Pick up all the latest brochures and schedules in the tourist office.

Accommodation

In peak season Vannes can become quite claustrophobic, but it still offers a more extensive choice of **hotels** than anywhere else around the Golfe du Morbihan,

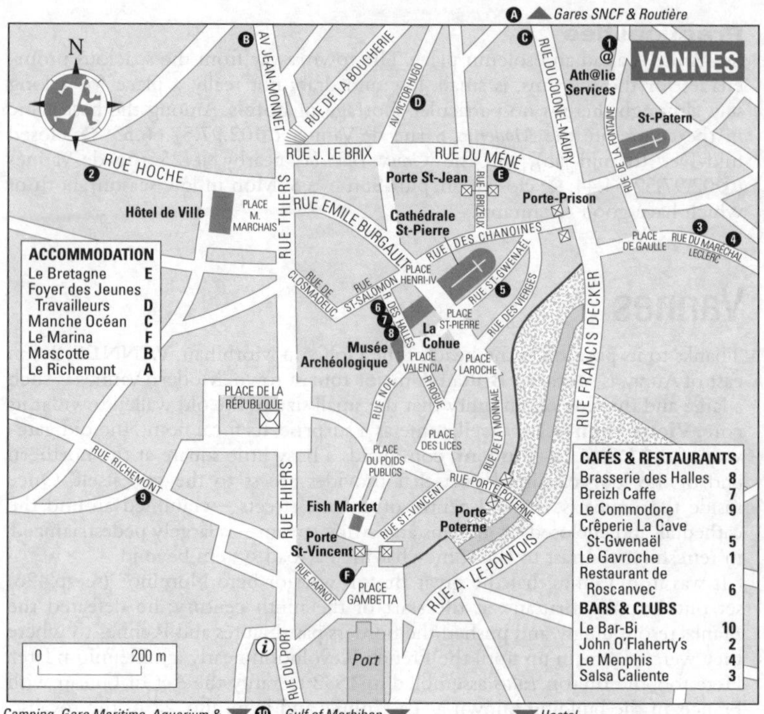

though most, unfortunately, are well away from the centre. By far the nicest place to stay, if you can get a room, is **place Gambetta** overlooking the port. This is the one part of Vannes that stays busy well into the evening throughout the year, and the traffic noise is not too bad. Vannes also has two **hostels**. One, the *Foyers des Jeunes Travailleurs*, is at 14 avenue Victor Hugo (Ⓣ02.97.54.33.13; ❶), a short way north of the town walls, and charges €15 for a basic single room without en-suite facilities in July and August only (and even then you should note that availability is limited); the other, the *Centre International de Séjour*, is 4km southeast of the town centre in Séné (Ⓣ02.97.66.94.25; dorm bed €10.50; closed July & Aug; Ⓔsene@wanadoo.fr), on bus route #4 from place de la République. The nearest **campsite** is the three-star *Camping Conleau* at the far end of avenue du Maréchal-Juin, beyond the Aquarium, and alongside the gulf (Ⓣ02.97.63.13.88; closed Oct–March).

Hôtel le Bretagne 36 rue du Méné Ⓣ02.97.47.20.2. Reasonable hotel situated just outside the walls, around the corner from the Porte-Prison. The rooms aren't fancy, but all have showers or bath plus TV. ❷

Hôtel Manche Océan 31 rue du Col Maury Ⓣ02.97.47.26.46, Ⓦwww.manche-ocean.com. Ordinary but perfectly acceptable modern rooms between the station and the walled town, used mainly by tour groups. Small-scale buffet breakfasts for €8. ❹

Hôtel le Marina 4 place Gambetta Ⓣ02.97.47.00.10, Ⓕ02.97.47.00.34. Fifteen pleasantly refurbished rooms – and a downstairs bar – right in the thick of things by the port, with sea views and bright sun in the morning. En-suite facilities cost €4 extra. ❷

Hôtel Mascotte av Jean-Monnet Ⓣ02.97.47.59.60, Ⓕ02.97.47.07.54. Functional upscale hotel a short walk northwest of the walled town, with 65 soundproofed, en-suite and air-conditioned rooms and an adequate restaurant. ❻

Hôtel le Richemont 26 place de la Gare ⓣ02.97.47.17.24, ⓦwww.hotel-richemont-vannes.com. Bright, recently renovated and soundproofed rooms in a friendly hotel opposite the *gare SNCF* where the management is a good source of local information. ❷

The Town

The new town centre of Vannes is **place de la République**; the administrative headquarters were shifted outside the medieval city during the nineteenth-century craze for urbanization. The grandest of the public buildings here, guarded by a pair of sleek and dignified bronze lions, is the **Hôtel de Ville** at the top of rue Thiers.

By day, however, the cobbled streets of the old city, especially in the area around the cathedral, are the chief source of pleasure, as well as being where most of Vannes' busy commercial life takes place. With their skew-windowed and half-timbered houses – most overhanging and witch-hatted, some tumbling down, some newly propped-up and painted – they amply repay time spent wandering. **Place Henri-IV** in particular, with its charming fifteenth - and sixteenth-century gabled houses, is stunning, as are the views from it down the narrow side streets. Here and there, it's possible to climb up onto the **ramparts** to admire the views, though much of the way you have to trace the circuit around the outside instead, from the far side of what used to be the city moat, which now consists of neat and colourful flowerbeds. Near the **Porte Poterne**, the "back gate", an old slate-roofed wash house survives.

La Cohue, which fills a block between rue des Halles and place St-Pierre, and takes its name from a word meaning "bustling crowd", currently houses the **Musée des Beaux Arts** (daily: July–Sept 10am–6pm; Oct–June 1.30–6pm; €4), having served at various times over the past 750 years as High Court and assembly room, prison, Revolutionary tribunal, theatre and marketplace. Upstairs it houses a dull collection of paintings and engravings, heavy on worthy Breton artists such as J.-F. Boucher and Jean Frélaut, while the main gallery downstairs is the venue for different temporary exhibitions.

The **Cathédrale St-Pierre** is a rather forbidding place, with its stern main altar almost imprisoned by four solemn grey pillars. The light, purple through the new stained glass, spears in to illuminate the finger of the Blessed Pierre Rogue, who was guillotined in the main square on March 3, 1796. Opposite this desiccated digit is the black-lidded sarcophagus that marks the current site of the tomb of the fifteenth-century Spanish Dominican preacher St Vincent Ferrier (which has meandered around the cathedral for centuries). For a small fee, you can in summer examine the assorted **treasure** in the chapterhouse, which includes a twelfth-century wedding chest, brightly decorated with enigmatic scenes of romantic chivalry.

Housed in the sombre fifteenth-century Château Gaillard on rue Noé, the **Musée Archéologique** is said to have one of the world's finest collections of prehistoric artefacts (July–Sept daily 10am–6pm; currently closed in low season for building and restoration work; €3). But, much like the displays at Carnac, it's all pretty lifeless – some elegant stone axes, more recent Oceanic exhibits by way of context, but nothing very illuminating. Further collections of fossils, shells and stuffed birds, equally traditional in their display, are on show around the corner in the **Hôtel de Roscannec** at 19 rue des Halles (same hours as museum).

There's a bit more life about the city's excellent **fish market**, held in the covered hall on place de la Poissonnerie every morning between Tuesday and Saturday. A general market spreads slightly higher up on the streets towards the cathedral on Wednesday and Saturday.

The Parc du Golfe

Vannes' **parc du Golfe**, about 2 km south of place Gambetta along the west (right) bank of the port, features a modern **aquarium** (daily: April, May & June 10am–12.30pm & 2–7pm; July & Aug 9am–7.30pm; Sept, Oct, Feb & March 10am–12.30pm & 2–6.30pm; €8.50; ⓣ02.97.40.67.40, ⓦwww.aquariumdevannes.com), that claims to have the best collection of tropical fish in Europe. Certainly it holds some pretty extraordinary specimens, including four-eyed fish from Venezuela that can see simultaneously above and below the surface of the water, and are also divided into four sexes for good measure; cave fish from Mexico that by contrast have no eyes at all; and *arowana* from Guyana, which jump two metres out of the water to catch birds. A Nile crocodile found in the Paris sewers in 1984 shares its tank with a group of piranhas, while elsewhere there's a huge tank of black- and white-tipped sharks. Most species are identified with their French and Latin names, not necessarily their English ones. It will take you roughly ten minutes to walk to the aquarium from place Gambetta. Alternatively, **free shuttle buses** do the trip every fifteen minutes or so between 10am and 7pm from Monday to Saturday in July and August.

Eating, drinking and entertainment

Dining out in old Vannes can be an expensive, but generally very positive, experience, whether you eat in the intimate little restaurants along the rue des Halles, or down by the port. Other, cheaper restaurants can be found in the St-Patern quarter, the area outside the walls in the northeast, extending from the Porte-Prison towards the *gare SNCF*, with rue de la Fontaine containing an assortment of simple Chinese and North African places along with a few more formal restaurants.

Brasserie des Halles 9 rue des Halles ⓣ02.97.54.08.34. Inexpensive brasserie which manages to squeeze a few tables out onto the pavement. For €8.70 you can get a bowl of mussels, for €16.50 a seafood *choucroute*, and there's a wide range of mainly fishy dishes at similar prices. Closed Sat lunch & Sun eve.

Breizh Caffe 13 rue des Halles ⓣ02.97.54.37.41. One of the less pricey options on this attractive cobbled street, with a strong emphasis on Breton dishes and ingredients. Weekday lunches from €11.60, traditional evening menus from €18. Closed Sun & Mon lunch in low season.

Le Commodore 3 rue Pasteur ⓣ02.97.46.42.62. Unassuming marine-themed local restaurant, tucked away around the back of the post office, which offers plenty of fishy treats on menus that start at €8.50 at lunchtime and go up to €18.50 in the evening. Closed Mon lunch, Sat lunch & Sun.

Crêperie La Cave St-Gwenaël 23 rue St-Gwenaël ⓣ02.97.47.47.94. Atmospheric, good-value crêperie in the cellar of a lovely old house, facing the cathedral. Closed Sun & Mon, plus all Jan.

Le Gavroche 17 rue de la Fontaine Pasteur ⓣ02.97.54.03.54. A true godsend for meat-lovers in a region dominated by fish restaurants. Here you can feast on truly excellent meat-packed menus starting at a mere €13, where the steaks are cooked to perfection and original starters such as pig's trotters – along with the complementary glass of potent home-made rum – will put hairs on your chest. Closed Sun, Mon & Wed eve.

Restaurant de Roscanvec 17 rue des Halles ⓣ02.97.47.15.96. Absolutely superb formal gourmet restaurant, in a lovely half-timbered house in the heart of the old town, with dining on two levels and also outdoors. Lunch at €17 is a bargain, while even the cheapest dinner menu, at €23.50, features unusual dishes such as *carbonara d'huîtres*, beautifully prepared and presented. Menus go all the way up to €74 for a lobster special. Closed Sun in summer, Sun eve & all Mon Sept–June.

Nightlife

The St-Patern quarter offers the highest single concentration of **bars** in the town centre, especially on or not far from place de Gaulle or next to the

St-Patern church, though most of them are low-key affairs. At the end of July and the start of August, the open-air concerts of the **Vannes Jazz Festival** take place in the Théâtre de Verdure.

Le Bar-Bi Parc de Golfe. The closest discotheque to the town centre is recommended only to the very open-minded: the type of people who enjoy (or at least are not offended by) dancing, scantily-clad, on bars and other such vantage points. House music predominates and men must have a date to enter.

John O'Flaherty's 22 rue Hoche ⓣ02.97.42.40.11. A leading venue for live music, this popular Irish pub just west of place de la République has traditional Irish music on Fridays. Closed Sun.

Le Menphis 33 rue du Maréchal Leclerc. Just east of place de Gaulle, this is a no-nonsense gay bar where meeting people is very much the priority. Closed Mon Oct–April.

Salsa Caliente 27 rue du Maréchal Leclerc ⓣ02.97.47.04.53. Latino bar decorated with all things Cuban, a few doors down from the *Menphis*, where you can listen to the occasional live band and drink *mojitos* and other cocktails made, of course, with Cuban rum.

Listings

Banks Banque de France, 55 Victor Hugo ⓣ02.97.54.43.34; Crédit Lyonnais, 14 place M. Marchais ⓣ02.97.01.21.80; Société Générale 25 rue Thiers ⓣ02.97.01.57.00.

Bicycle rental Cycles Le Mellec, place de la Madeleine, 51 rue Jean Gougaud ⓣ02.97.63.00.24.

Car rental Some of the main companies have offices at the *gare SNCF*, including: Avis ⓣ02.97.47.54.54; Budget ⓣ02.97.54.25.22; and Europcar ⓣ02.97.69.05.05.

Cinemas Eden, 7 rue Pasteur ⓣ02.97.63.31.62; La Garenne, 12bis rue A. Le Pontois ⓣ08.36.68.06.66.

Internet access Ath@lie Services, 33 rue de la Fontaine (Mon–Sat 9.30am–12.30pm & 2–8.45pm; ⓣ02.97.47.59.02; €3 per hr).

Pharmacie 19 rue Thiers ⓣ02.97.47.20.57 (Mon–Sat 8.45am–12.15pm & 2–7pm).

Post office 25 place de la République 56000 ⓣ02.97.68.30.20 (Mon–Wed & Fri 8.30am–6.30pm, Thurs 8.30am–1.15pm & 2.30–6.30pm; Sat 8.30am–12.15pm).

Swimming pools Piscine Municipal, rue Winston Churchill ⓣ02.97.62.69.00; Piscine Municipal VANOCÉA, 20 rue Émile Jourdan ⓣ02.97.62.68.00.

East of Vannes

Though Gavrinis and the Morbihan islands are the most exciting excursions from Vannes, various sights inland, **east of the city**, can fill a day's round-trip. Vannes' **traffic system** will do its damnedest to prevent you leaving the city in any direction, however, so you can't be too choosy about where you end up. Public transport is, as ever, not a viable alternative.

The Château de Largoët

If you follow the **N166** 10km towards **Elven**, and then turn off to the left about 4km short, you come to the ruins of the **Château de Largoët**, perched on an eminence in the small forest (mid-March to May & last week in Oct Sat & Sun 2–6.30pm; June & Sept Wed–Mon 10.30am–12.10pm & 2.20–6.30pm; July & Aug daily: same hours; €4). It's still guarded by its old gatehouse, carved all over with granite bunnies.

The castle consists mainly of two stark towers, inside which the wooden flooring has long since rotted away to leave the shafts open to the sky. The *donjon* proper is topped by a finger-like watchtower, one of the highest in the country at over 45m, where from 1474 until 1476 the Breton Duke François imprisoned the future English king, Henry VII. At that time simply Henry Tudor, Duke of Richmond – a title traditionally awarded to royal bastards or English nobility with Breton connections – he had fled to Brittany after the

Battle of Tewkesbury, in which Lancastrian ambitions in the Wars of the Roses were defeated. François welcomed Henry as a guest, then realized his value and held him for ransom.

Le Gorvello and Questembert

There's little point going to Elven itself, though if you've always wondered where René Descartes grew up you can find the answer en route at the manor house of Kerleau. More rewarding is to head south to the beautiful village of **LE GORVELLO**, at a crossroads with the D7 10km south of the château. Bedecked with potted geraniums and huge azaleas, it has at its centre a perfect roadside cross.

Beyond Le Gorvello, the D7 leads on into **QUESTEMBERT**, where the low-roofed wooden market hall from 1675 makes a classy cycle park. Purely as a **hotel**, the ivy-coated *Hôtel Le Bretagne* at 13 rue St-Michel (ⓣ02.97.26.11.12, ⓦwww.paineaulebretagne.com; ❼–❾; closed Jan, plus Mon, Tues lunch & Wed lunch) is very appealing, with lavish fittings to merit its sky-high room rates. As a **restaurant**, it's a strange place. Chef Georges Paineau is regarded, not least by himself, as one of the finest chefs in France, and prepares unarguably sumptuous menus for €39, €79 and €115, doing wonderful things with foie gras, sole and truffles. However, the air of formality in the oak-panelled and often all-but-empty dining room can be very intimidating – which is especially ludicrous because M Paineau also fancies himself as a painter, and his truly dreadful pop-art acrylics adorn every spare centimetre of wall space.

Continue east or north from Questembert, and you come to the **Nantes–Brest canal** at Malestroit (see p.361) or Redon (see p.364).

The Golfe du Morbihan

By popular tradition, the **Golfe du Morbihan** ("little sea" in Breton) holds 365 scattered islands – one for every day of the year. For centuries, though, the waters have been rising, and the figure now is more like one per week. Of these, some thirty are owned by film stars and the like, while two – the **Île aux Moines** and **Île d'Arz** – have regular ferry services and permanent populations, and end up extremely crowded in summer. The rest are the best, and a **boat tour** around them, or at least a trip out to **Gavrinis**, near the mouth of the gulf, and a short ferry-trip from the port of **Larmor-Baden**, ranks among the most compelling attractions in southern Brittany.

As the boats thread their way through the baffling muddle of channels, you swiftly lose track of which is island and which is mainland; and everywhere there are megalithic ruins, stone circles disappearing beneath the water and solitary menhirs on small hillocks. At the time when they were built, the sea level is thought to have been around 5m lower than it is today, and the islands may have been mounds amid the marshlands. Flaubert evocatively described Celtic mercenaries far off in Carthage pining for the Morbihan – "*Les Celtes regrettaient trois pierres brutes, sous un ciel plouvieux, dans un golfe remplie d'îlots*" – not that the Celts actually set up the stones in the first place.

Le Bono and Larmor-Baden

Making your own way to Larmor-Baden, the departure point for trips to Gavrinis, the best route is along the main road down the Auray estuary, the

Gulf tours

In season, dozens of boats leave for **gulf tours** each day from Vannes, Port Navalo, La Trinité, Locmariaquer, Auray, Le Bono and Larmor-Baden. These are among the options:

Compagnie des Îles (Ⓦwww.compagniedesiles.com) run gulf tours (€13.50–26.50) from **Vannes** (Ⓣ08.25.16.41.00), with departures at 9.15am, 10.30am, 2pm and 5pm daily between April and September, supplemented by additional cruises at 11.15am and 4pm daily in July and August. They also operate a more limited programme of gulf cruises from **Port Navalo** (Ⓣ08.25.16.41.20; April–June Sun at 2.15pm; July & Aug daily at 10am, 11am, 2.15pm, 3pm & 4.15pm; €13.50–26.50); **Locmariaquer** (Ⓣ08.25.16.41.30; April–Sept daily at 10.45am, 2pm & 4.15pm; €12–26.50); and Port Haliguen in **Quiberon** (Ⓣ08.25.16.41.40; April–June departures normally Mon only at 2pm; July & Aug daily at 9am & 2pm; €21.50–24.50). The price of each cruise generally depends on the number of stops you make, with possibilities of getting off at Île aux Moines and Île d'Arz.

Izenah Croisières (Ⓣ02.97.57.23.24 or 02.97.26.31.45, Ⓦwww.izenah-croisieres.com) run gulf tours in summer (April–Sept daily 3pm, €16; July & Aug additionally at 11am & 5pm; €12) and a year-round ferry service, with departures every half-hour, to the Île aux Moines (July & Aug Mon–Sat 7am–10pm, Sun 8am–10pm; Sept–June Mon–Sat 7am–7.30pm, Sun 8am–8pm; €3.50 return), from **Port Blanc** at **Baden**.

Navix (Ⓣ02.97.46.60.00 or Ⓣ08.25.16.21.00, Ⓦwww.navix.fr), who are based in **Vannes**, run up to six deluxe half-day (€19) and full-day (€26.50) tours around the gulf every day between April and September, most of which offer the option of stopping off on the Île aux Moines and/or the Île d'Arz; you can have lunch or dinner on the Île d'Arz for an all-inclusive price of €43. From April until the end of August the first boat sails each day at 8.45am (10am in Sept). Much the same programme of tours, at the same prices, also departs from **Port Navalo**, with the first boat at 9.45am daily in July & Aug, 10.15am from April to June and in September. There's a slightly smaller selection from **Locmariaquer**, from where the first boat sails at 10am daily between April and September, with prices ranging from €12 up to €26.50. In July and August, Navix also operates daily from either **Auray** (departures at 9am & 2.15pm) or **Le Bono** (departures at 9.15am & 2.30pm), as well as **La Trinité** (daily 8.45am & 1.45pm), with cruises costing from €19 up to €26.50. Between April and September, they also go to **Belle-Île** (see p.388; €29 return) from **Vannes** and **Port Navalo**, and **Houat** (see p.394; €25) from **La Trinité**.

Vedettes Angelus (Ⓣ02.97.57.30.29, Ⓦwww.vedettes-angelus.com) also run up to five gulf tours of varying lengths daily from **Locmariaquer**, between Easter and late September, with their first departure at 10am. Prices range from €11 up to €23.

D17. This crosses the River Bono on a high bridge; visible way below it to the left is a beautiful iron bridge. A side turning before the river leads across that bridge into **LE BONO**, a harbour village that looks almost ludicrously idyllic seen from one of the *vedettes* out in the gulf. Quaint **rooms** with balconies and views of the river are available at *Le Forban*, 1 rue du Générale-de-Gaulle (Ⓣ02.97.57.88.65, Ⓦwww.hotelleforban.fr; 3; closed Jan, plus Sun eve & Mon

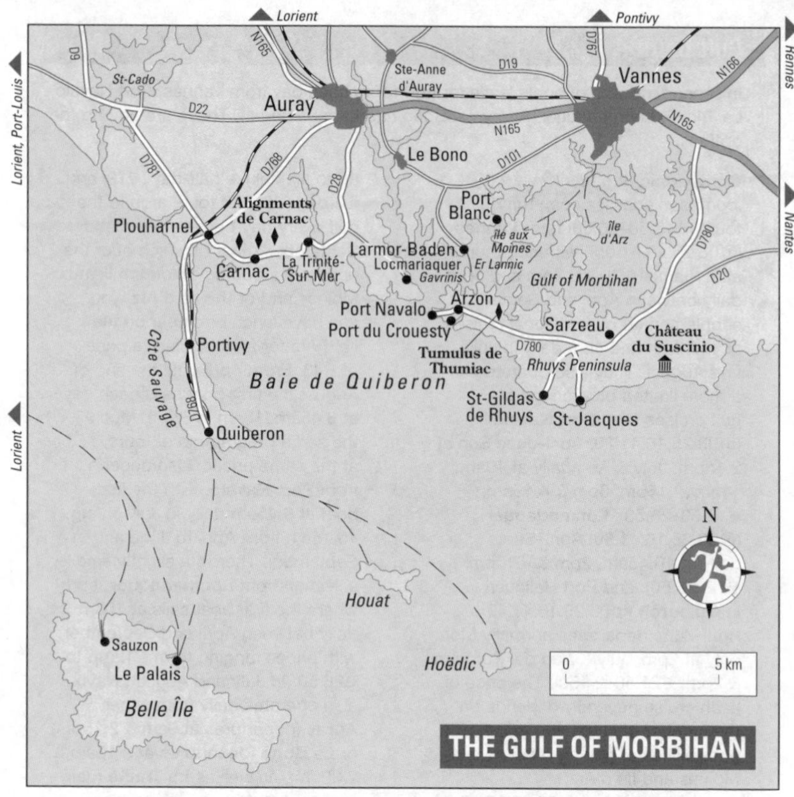

Oct–March), which has a good **restaurant**, again with a terrace overlooking the river. Elsewhere, the *Vieux-Pont*, 23 rue Pasteur (ⓣ02.97.57.87.71; closed Mon in low season) sells decent crêpes and pizzas.

LARMOR-BADEN itself is a subdued little town lying at the bottom of a long slope of fields of dazzling sunflowers. The port looks out on the tangle of islands in the Gulf of Morbihan, which at this point is so narrow that Arzon on the Rhuys peninsula (see p.412) appears to be on just another nearby island. It is not an inspiring place to stay – neither a resort nor a town – but there's a three-star beachfront **campsite**, *Les Algues* (ⓣ02.97.65.55.47; closed mid-Sept to mid-June), and a fair number of **hotels** including the *Auberge du Parc Fétan*, 17 rue de Berder (ⓣ02.97.57.04.38, ⓦwww.hotel-parcfetan.com; ❸).

Gavrinis

The reason to visit the island of **Gavrinis** is its **megalithic site**. The most impressive and remarkable in Brittany, it would be memorable just for its location. But it really is extraordinary as a structure, standing comparison with Newgrange in Ireland and – in shape as well as size and age – with the earliest pyramids of Egypt.

It is essentially a **tumulus**, an earth mound covering a stone cairn and "passage grave". However, in 1981 half of the mound was peeled back and, using the original stones around the entrance as a basis, the side of the cairn that faces the water was reconstructed to make a facade resembling a step-pyramid. Inside, every stone of the passageway and chamber is covered in carvings, with a restricted "alphabet" of fingerprint whorls, axe-heads and other conventional signs, including the spirals familiar in Ireland but seen only here in Brittany. The long-held view of archeologists that the stones had been brought at least the few kilometres from Locmariaquer received dramatic confirmation in 1984, when the roof was shown to be made from the self-same piece of carved stone as covers the Table des Marchand there (see p.400).

Another mystery, however, has consistently eluded explanation: the purpose of the three holes leading to a recessed niche in one of the walls of the chamber. Some medieval monks were buried in the mound, but the cairn itself seems never to have been a grave.

Erosion since the site was opened has so rapidly damaged the tumulus that it may well soon be barred to visitors altogether; it is no longer possible to climb on the mound itself, and conceivably a replica will be built.

From Gavrinis, you can look across to the half-submerged stone circle on the tiny island of **Er Lanic**, which rests on its skirt of mud like an abandoned hovercraft. It has been identified as a major centre for the manufacture of ceremonial axes, using stone brought from Port Navalo.

Practicalities

Gavrinis can be visited between April and November only, and is reached by a fifteen-minute **ferry** ride from Larmor-Baden. Tides permitting, the ferry service operates at half-hourly intervals during the opening hours of the monument, with the last departure from Larmor-Baden each day being an hour and a half before it closes. The cost of the trips includes both ferry ride and a guided tour of the cairn (April, June & Sept daily 9.30am–12.30pm & 1.30–6.30pm; May Mon–Fri 1.30–6.30pm, Sat & Sun 9.30am–12.30pm & 1.30–6.30pm; July & Aug daily 9.30am–12.30pm & 1.30–7pm; Oct & Nov Wed–Mon 1.30–5pm; ⓣ02.97.57.19.38; €10). Most gulf cruises sail close enough to the island to give a view of the cairn, but do not land.

Southern Morbihan: the Rhuys peninsula

Though the tip of the **Presqu'île de Rhuys** is just a few hundred metres across the mouth of the Gulf of Morbihan from Locmariaquer, it somehow seems to mark a distinctly southwards shift in climate. The Côte Sauvage is lost and in its wake appear pomegranates, fig trees, camellias, even vineyards (Rhuys produces the only truly Breton wine), along with cultivated oysters down below in the mud.

Unfortunately, due to fierce currents in the gulf, it's very unsafe for swimming all the way along the north side of the peninsula. The **ocean beaches**, however, make much more promising destinations if you're hoping to sunbathe or play in the water. They break out intermittently to either side of **St-Gildas-de-Rhuys**, amid the glittering gold- and silver-coloured rocks. For details on the whole peninsula, call in at the **information centre** (Feb–June, Sept & Oct Mon–Sat 9.15am–12.15pm & 2–6pm, Sun 2–5.30pm; July & Aug daily 9am–7pm; Nov–Jan Mon–Sat

9.15am–12.15pm & 2–6pm; ⓣ02.97.26.45.26, ⓦwww.rhuys.com), just off the main D780 as you come into **Sarzeau**.

Four daily **buses** run to Sarzeau, St-Gildas, Arzon and Port Navalo from Vannes' place de la Gare (CTM; ⓣ02.97.01.22.10).

Sarzeau and the Château de Suscinio

The D780 runs through the heart of the Rhuys peninsula, with no sea views to speak of. As it starts an extravagant curve to the south of the central town of **SARZEAU**, a short detour to the left, south along the D198, will bring you to the impressive fourteenth-century **Château de Suscinio**. This completely moated castle, once a hunting lodge of the dukes of Brittany, is set in marshland at the edge of a tiny village, and contains a sagging but vivid mosaic floor. You can take a precarious stroll around its high ramparts (April–Sept daily 10am–7pm; Oct–March Thurs–Tues 10am–noon & 2–6pm; €5), and you can also visit on summer evenings, when it opens for musical or theatrical performances.

The nicest place to stay in Sarzeau itself is the *Hôtel Le Connétable*, 3 place Richemont (ⓣ02.97.41.85.48, ⓦhttp://perso.wanadoo.fr/hotelfermine; ❸), which has a decent restaurant, while 6km south in **St-Jacques**, at the beautifully positioned little *Hôtel du Port*, (ⓣ02.97.41.93.51; ❹), all nine rooms have balconies that look out across the port to the Atlantic.

St-Gildas-de-Rhuys

At **ST-GILDAS-DE-RHUYS**, 6km southwest of Sarzeau, Pierre Abelard, the theologian/lover of Héloïse, was abbot for a period from 1126, having been exiled from Paris. "I live in a wild country where every day brings new perils", he wrote to Héloïse, eventually fleeing after his brother monks – hedonists unimpressed by his stern scholasticism – attempted to poison him.

Alongside the beaches around the village are a handful of **campsites**, among them the luxurious four-star *du Menhir* (ⓣ02.97.45.22.88; closed Sept–May), but there's no hotel.

Arzon and Port Navalo

If you're spending any length of time on the peninsula, the most appealing area is at its far western end, around the village of **ARZON**. Immediately before the centre, however, the **Port du Crouesty** is a desperately unattractive modern marina, dominated by the hideous crab-like *Hôtel Miramar* (ⓣ02.97.53.49.00, ⓦwww.miramarcrouesty.com; ❾; closed mid-Nov to Dec), where the cheapest single room costs well over €200.

On first glance, **PORT NAVALO** at the very tip has little more character, but there's a cute beach tucked into the headland. For details of the **gulf cruises** that depart from here, see p.409.

The two-star **campsite** *de Bilouris*, on the pointe de Kerners immediately north of Arzon (ⓣ02.97.53.70.55, ⓦwww.campingdebilouris.com; closed Nov to mid-March), is well poised for the less crowded beaches east of St-Gildas.

The Tumulus de Thumiac

Not far from the end of the peninsula, clearly visible to the north of the main road, the **Tumulus de Thumiac** is also known as the Butte de César, or "Caesar's Mount". From its summit, Julius Caesar is supposed to have watched the sea battle in which the Romans defeated the Veneti (see p.425) – the only naval victory they ever won away from the Mediterranean and out on the ocean. In fact, excavations in the nineteenth century revealed a 5000-year-old burial, complete with 32 stone axes and a pearl necklace.

Today, it's easy enough to walk to the top of the tumulus, but there's nothing to see apart from the view over the gulf. A short way north, the ivy-covered twelfth-century **Moulin du Pen Castel** is no longer run as a restaurant, but still makes an attractive spot for a picnic.

La Roche-Bernard

The southern shoreline of the Rhuys Peninsula segues imperceptibly into the northern bank of the estuary of the Vilaine, which flows into the sea roughly thirty kilometres southeast of Vannes. When the Vikings first settled this region, their longboats used the river to access the heart of Brittany. Approaches to the Vilaine were guarded by the fortified settlement of **LA ROCHE-BERNARD** on the south bank, where the harbour continued to serve as what the French call the *avant-port* for Redon and Rennes into the twentieth century. Thanks to a massive dam near **ARZAL**, 5km downstream, sea-going vessels can no longer enter the Vilaine, but La Roche-Bernard remains a pretty little village that's well worth the detour down from the mighty suspension bridge that now carries the N165 *autoroute* across the Vilaine gorge towards Nantes.

Most of the village stands atop the rocky headland that gave it its name, and fine medieval buildings cluster around the lovely little central square, among them a flower-bedecked **hotel-restaurant**, *Auberge des Deux Magots*, 1–2 place du Bouffay (ⓣ02.99.90.60.75; ❸; closed last two weeks in June & Oct, plus Mon & Tues lunch). The harbour lies a short walk below, and holds a couple of small waterfront **bars**.

In season, irregularly scheduled 90-minute-long **river trips** set off to explore the broad estuary waters as far downstream as the dam, offering close-up views of the densely wooded slopes along the north bank (Les Vedettes Jaunes; July & Aug three times each afternoon, April–June & Sept by reservation only; €8.50; ⓣ02.97.45.02.81, ⓦwww.vedettesjaunes.com).

The Grande-Brière

South of the **River Vilaine**, at La Roche-Bernard, you leave the Morbihan – and technically you leave Brittany as well, entering the *département* of Loire Atlantique. The roads veer firmly east and south – to Nantes and La Baule respectively. Inland between them, as you approach the wide Loire estuary, are the otherworldly marshes of the **Grande-Brière**.

These 20,000 acres of peat bog have for centuries been deemed to be the common property of all who live in them. The scattered population, the *Brièroise*, continue to make their living by fishing for eels in the streams, gathering reeds, and – on the nine days permitted each year – cutting the peat. The few villages are known as *îles*, being hard granite outcrops in the boggy wastes. Most of them consist of a circular road around the inside of a ring of thatched cottages, slightly raised above the waters onto which they back. For easy access to the watery flatlands, filled with lilies and irises and browsed by Shetland ponies, each village is encircled by its own canal, or *curée*. The houses themselves typically consist of two rooms and a stable, with a door on the north side and windows on the south. A few crops are grown in the adjacent ring of fields, which always remain above high water.

Though this can be a captivating region for unhurried exploration, if you're simply passing through, the waterways are not very visible from the road unless you pause on one of the occasional humpback bridges. Instead, the widely touted attraction is **renting a punt**, known as a *chaland* or a *blain*. This activity seems to be promoted with the unstated intention of getting you lost for a few hours with your pole tangled in the rushes. Operators include La Chassée Neuve (Ⓣ02.40.01.24.64), based 6km northeast of La Baule at **ST-ANDRÉ-DES-EAUX**.

Much of the Grande-Brière has been designated as a **bird sanctuary**, with waterfowl the obvious main beneficiaries. The main **tourist office** for the region is on the northern fringes of the marshes, at 38 rue de la Brière in the village of **LA-CHAPELLE-DES-MARAIS** (June–Sept daily 10am–12.30pm & 2.30–6.30pm; Oct–May Mon–Fri 10am–12.30pm & 2–6pm, Sat 10am–12.30pm & 2–5.30pm; Ⓣ02.40.66.85.01), but the headquarters of the sanctuary itself is in the most authentic surviving village, the **ÎLE DE FEDRUN** (same hours; Ⓣ02.40.91.68.68, Ⓦwww.parc-naturel-briere.fr). Filled with traditional dwellings, the village also has a small, pricey **hotel**, the *Auberge du Parc* (Ⓣ02.40.88.53.01, Ⓦwww.auberge-du-parc.com; ❺; closed Jan & Feb), where dinner menus start at €35.

The coast at the mouth of the Loire

There is something very surreal about emerging from the Brière to the coast at **La Baule**. For this is by far Brittany's most upmarket pocket – an imposing, moneyed landscape where the dunes are bonded together no longer with scrub and pines but with massive apartment blocks and luxury hotels. **St-Nazaire**, guarding the mouth of the Loire itself, is a rundown industrial port. However, in the vicinity of La Baule, **Guérande** is a superb medieval walled town, while **Piriac-sur-mer**, and to a lesser extent **Le Croisic**, are less frenetic alternatives to the giant resort.

Guérande

On the southwestern edge of the marshes of the Grande-Brière, just before you come to the sea, stands the gorgeous walled town of **GUÉRANDE**, which no visitor to the region should miss. Guérande gave its name to this peninsula, and derived its fortune from controlling the saltpans that form a chequerboard across the surrounding inlets. This "white country" is composed of bizarre-looking *oeillets*, each 70 to 80 square metres in extent, in which sea-water, since Roman times, has been collected and evaporated.

Guérande today, a tiny little place, is still entirely enclosed by its stout fifteenth-century **ramparts**. Although you can't walk along them, a spacious promenade leads right the way around the outside, passing four fortified gateways; for half its length, the broad old moat remains filled with water. Historically, the main entrance was the **Porte St-Michel** on the east side of town, the upper three floors of which now hold a small **museum** of local history (daily: April–Sept 10am–12.30pm & 2.30–7pm; Oct 10am–noon & 2–6pm; €3.50).

Within the walls, pedestrians throng the narrow cobbled streets during high season; the main souvenir on sale is locally produced salt, but abundant shops sell the usual trinkets from all over the world, and there are also lots of restaurants and crêperies. So long as the crowds aren't too oppressive, it makes a great day out, with the old houses bright with windowboxes. On Wednesdays and Saturdays, there's a market in full swing in the centre, next to the **church of St-Aubin**. Another, smaller church stands just to the south; this is **Notre Dame La Blanche**, where the second Treaty of Guérande was signed in 1381.

Practicalities

Guérande's **tourist office** is just outside the Porte St-Michel at 1 place du Marché au Bois (June & Sept Mon–Sat 9.30am–12.30pm & 1.30–6pm, Sun 10am–1pm & 3–5pm; July & Aug Mon–Sat 9.30am–7pm, Sun 10am–1pm & 3–5pm; Oct–May Mon–Sat 9.30am–12.30pm & 1.30–6pm; ⓣ02.40.24.96.71, ⓦwww.ot.guerande.fr).

Near St-Aubin church, but tucked out of sight behind the market, the pretty *Roc-Maria*, 1 rue du Vieux Marché aux Grains (ⓣ02.40.24.90.51, ⓦwww.hotelcreperierocmaria.com; ❸; closed Mon in low season), is a lovely little village **hotel** that offers cosy rooms above a crêperie in a fifteenth-century town house. Opposite the porte Vannetoise and the most impressive stretch of ramparts, to the north, the *Hôtel Les Voyageurs*, 1 place du 8 Mai (ⓣ02.40.24.90.13, ⓦwww.hotel-des-voyageurs-44.com; ❸; closed Sun eve & Mon), is a logis serving reasonable menus from €12. A short way further around the walls, near the tourist office, the *Remparts*, 14–15 boulevard du Nord (ⓣ02.40.24.90.69; ❸; closed mid-Nov to Jan; restaurant closed Sun eve & Mon Sept–July), offers less appealing rooms but better food.

Of the many **restaurants** in the centre, the *Vieux Logis*, set within the walled garden of a grand old house facing the main church doors at 1 place de la Psalette (ⓣ02.40.62.09.73), has something to suit every palette, with traditional menus from €20 at dinner, plus a separate crêperie/pizzeria.

Piriac-sur-mer

If you prefer your seaside resorts quiet and peaceful, head west from Guérande to **PIRIAC-SUR-MER**, 13km distant, instead of continuing to La Baule. Although the adjacent headland offers some fine sandy beaches within a couple of minutes' walk from the centre, the pleasant little village itself turns its back on the Atlantic, preferring to face the protective jetty that curls back into the little bay to shield its small fishing fleet.

Piriac's twisting narrow lanes see enough tourists in summer to keep half a dozen crêperies in business, of which the nicest is the *St-Michel* (ⓣ02.40.15.50.15), whose courtyard tables take up most of the place de la Chope, between the old granite church and the beach.

There are also a handful of **hotels**, including *Hôtel-Restaurant de la Poste*, in a large house at 26 rue de la Plage (ⓣ02.40.23.50.90; ❸; closed Nov–March, restaurant closed Mon in low season), a few streets in from the sea. The shady four-star *Parc du Guibel* (ⓣ02.40.23.52.67, ⓦwww.parcduguibel.com; closed Oct–March), further on towards Mesquer, is among the best of several local **campsites**.

La Baule

LA BAULE is certainly a place apart from its rival Breton resorts, almost any of which can seem appealingly rustic and shambolic by comparison. Sited on the long stretch of dunes that link the former island of Le Croisic to the mainland, it owes its existence to a violent storm in 1779 that engulfed the old town of Escoublac in silt from the Loire, and thereby created a wonderful crescent of sandy beach that's sometimes claimed to be the largest in Europe. That has survived, albeit now lined for several kilometres with a Riviera-style spread of palm-tree-fronted hotels and residences.

Neither La Baule's permanence nor its affluence seems in any doubt these days. This is a resort that very firmly imagines itself in the south of France: around the crab-shaped bay, bronzed nymphettes and medallion men stride across the sands against a backdrop of cruising lifeguards, horse-dung removers and fantastically priced cocktails. It can be fun if you feel like a break from the more subdued Breton attractions – and the beach is undeniably impressive. It's not a place to imagine you're going to enjoy strolling around in search of hidden charms, however; the backstreets have an oddly rural feel, but hold nothing of any interest.

Practicalities

La Baule has two **gares SNCF**, the barely used La-Baule-les-Pins, and the main La-Baule-Escoublac on place Rhin-et-Danube, where the TGVs from Paris arrive. The **gare routière** is at 4 place de la Victoire (Ⓣ02.40.11.53.00).

Full details on staying in La Baule can be had from the **tourist office**, away from the seafront in a new postmodern office at 8 place de la Victoire (July & Aug daily 9.30am–7.30pm; Sept–June Mon & Wed–Sat 9.15am–12.30pm & 2–6pm, Tues 10.15am–12.30pm & 2–6pm; Sun 10am–1pm; Ⓣ02.40.24.34.44, Ⓦwww.labaule.tm.fr).

Few of the **hotels** are cheap, particularly in high season, and in low season more than half are closed. Low-priced options near the main *gare SNCF* include the comfortable *Marini*, 22 avenue Clemenceau (Ⓣ02.40.60.23.29, Ⓦwww.lemarinihotel.com; ❸), which has a lift and a swimming pool, while the *Mascotte*, 26 avenue Marie-Louise (Ⓣ02.40.60.26.55, Ⓦwww.la-mascotte.fr; ❹; closed Jan), is a quieter and classier option less than 100m back from the beach. The finest of the many local **campsites**, 2km from the sea, is the four-star *La Roseraie*, 20 avenue Sohier (Ⓣ02.40.60.46.66, Ⓦwww.laroseraie.com; closed Oct–March).

Right in the centre, set back less than 50m from the sea and not far from the tourist office, the *Lutetia* at 13 avenue des Evens (Ⓣ02.40.60.25.81; ❺; closed Jan), is home to the *Rossini* **restaurant** (closed Sun eve, Mon & Tues lunch), which offers magnificent fish cookery on menus that start at €20.

Le Croisic

The small port of **LE CROISIC**, sheltering from the ocean around the corner of the headland, is probably a more sensible (and to many perceptions, more attractive) place to stay than La Baule.

These days, Le Croisic is basically a pleasure port, but fishing boats do still sail from its harbour, near the very slender mouth of the bay, and there's a modern **fish market** near the long Tréhic jetty, where you can go to see the day's catch auctioned. Incidentally, the hills on either side of the harbour, Mont Lénigo and Mont Esprit, are not natural; they are formed from the ballast left by the ships of the salt trade.

Practicalities

If you are staying in Le Croisic, choose between the **hotels** *Les Nids*, 15 rue Pasteur (Ⓣ02.40.23.00.63, Ⓦwww.hotellesnids.com; ❸; closed Oct–March), which has its own small indoor swimming pool, or the purple and white *Estacade*, near the end of the port at 4 quai de Lénigo (Ⓣ02.40.23.03.77, Ⓦwww.estacade.com; ❹), where the €14.50 menu includes *soupe de poissons* and fish of the day.

Close by, all around the rocky sea coast known as the **Grande Côte**, are a whole range of **campsites**. Just outside Le Croisic itself is the *Océan* (Ⓣ02.40.23.07.69, Ⓦwww.camping-ocean.com; closed Oct–March), while Batz, another former island, holds the *Govelle* (Ⓣ02.40.23.91.63; closed mid-Sept to mid-June).

For equally good beaches, you could alternatively go east from La Baule to **PORNICHET** or to the tiny **ST-MARC**, where in 1953 Jacques Tati filmed *Monsieur Hulot's Holiday*.

St-Nazaire

The best sandy coves in the region, bizarrely enough, are to be found on the outskirts of **ST-NAZAIRE**: just off to the west, a kilometre out of town, they are linked by wooded paths and almost deserted. But the city itself is gloomy, distinguishable from afar by the black silhouettes of its mighty cranes and the soaring arch of the Loire bridge. Bombed to extinction in the last war, its shipyards, in more or less continuous operation since they built Julius Caesar's fleet, are closing all around it.

The one reason you might want to stay in St-Nazaire is the relative ease of finding an inexpensive **hotel** – so elusive in this area in summer. Modern, well-equipped options include the *Touraine*, 4 avenue de la République (Ⓣ02.40.22.47.56, Ⓔhoteltouraine@free.fr; ❶), and the smarter, more expensive *Korali*, opposite the station on place de la Gare (Ⓣ02.40.01.89.89, Ⓦwww.hotelkorali.fr; ❸).

South of the Loire

From St-Nazaire you can cross the mouth of the Loire via an inspired piece of engineering, the **Pont St-Nazaire**. This is a great elongated S-curve of a suspension bridge, its lines only visible at an acute angle at either end. A hefty toll is demanded for the privilege of driving across its three-kilometre length, but bikes go for free.

From this high viewpoint (up to 131m), you can see that the **Loire** is a definite climatic dividing line (a point regularly confirmed by French television weather bulletins). To the north of the river, the houses have steep grey-slate roofs against the storms; to the south, in the Pays de Retz, the roofs are flat and red-tiled. Nonetheless, the vast deposits of Loire silt have affected both banks of the huge estuary – they buried the ancient town of Montoise on the southern side just as they did Escoublac to the north.

As you continue **south** along the coast, Brittany begins to slip away. Dolmens stand above the ocean, and the rocky coast is interspersed with bathing beaches, but the climate, the architecture, the countryside and, most obvious of all, the vineyards make it clear that this is the start of the south.

Pornic

The **Pays de Retz** coast is developed for most of its length – an almost unbroken line of holiday flats, Pepsi, *frites* and crêpes stands. **PORNIC** is the nicest of the resorts, with a functional fishing port and one of "Bluebeard" Gilles de Rais' many castles. It is a small place: you can walk beyond the harbour and along the cliffs to a tiny beach where the rock walls glitter from phosphorescent sea water.

The **hotels** in town are not cheap, though they are better value than those of La Baule. The nicest in the near vicinity has to be the seafront *Hôtel les Sablons*, at 13 rue des Sablons in Ste-Marie-sur-mer (☎02.40.82.09.14; ❹; restaurant closed from Sun eve until Tues lunch mid-Sept to mid-June), which serves good menus from €17.

Inland towards Nantes

As you head away from the coast, towards the metropolis of Nantes, the countryside is once more marshy, although richer than that of the Brière, with some scenic lakes and waterways. The largest of the lakes, the **Grand-Lieu**, contains two drowned villages, Murin and Langon. Along the Loire **estuary** itself, the towns are depressed and depressing, their traditional industries struck hard by unemployment. For **Nantes** itself, see p.366.

Travel details

Trains

Auray to: Plouharnel (July & Aug 12 daily; 20min); Quiberon (July & Aug 12 daily; 40min); SNCF buses to both Carnac (8 daily; 45min) and La Trinité (8 daily; 25min).
Le Croisic to: La Baule (10 daily; 15min); Nantes (10 daily; 1hr 10min); Paris (4 daily TGVs; 3hr 15min); St-Nazaire (10 daily; 30min).
Pornic to: Nantes (2 daily; 1hr), with connections to Paris.
Vannes to: Auray (13 daily; 15min); Lorient (13 daily; 40min), with connections to Quimper (13 daily; 1hr 40min).

Buses

Auray to: Carnac (9 daily; 30min); Quiberon (10 daily; 1hr); Vannes (8 daily; 30min). Services operated by Transports Le Bayon (☎02.97.24.26.20).
Lorient to: Pontivy (2 daily; 1hr 40min).
Vannes Cariane Atlantique (☎02.97.47.29.64) run to Auray (8 daily; 30min); Carnac (7 daily; 1hr 20min); La Roche-Bernard (3 daily; 1hr); Quiberon (7 daily; 2hr). CTM (☎02.97.01.22.10) run from the place de la Gare to: Arzon (4 daily; 50min); Pontivy (9 daily; 1hr 10min); and Ploërmel (3 daily; 1hr 10min) via Elven (20min) and Malestroit (50min).

Ferries

Groix For details of ferries to Groix (from Lorient), see p.384.
Lorient Shuttle service to Port-Louis (6.30am–8pm, every 30min; ☎02.97.21.28.29).
Belle-Île For details of ferries to Belle-Île from Quiberon, Lorient, La Turballe, Vannes, La Trinité, and Port-Navalo, see p.389.
Gulf of Morbihan For details of gulf tours and trips to the islands, from Vannes, Locmariaquer, Auray, Quiberon, Port-Navalo, La Trinité and Le Bono, see p.409 or contact Navix (☎02.97.46.60.00 or ☎08.25.16.21.00, ⓦwww.navix.fr) or Compagnie des Îles (☎08.25.16.41.00, ⓦwww.compagniedesiles.com).
Houat and Hoëdic For details of ferries to Houat and Hoëdic from Quiberon, La Trinité, Le Croisic and La Turballe, see p.393.

Contexts

Contexts

History

Although Brittany and Normandy have belonged to the French state for over 450 years, they have been distinct entities throughout recorded history and their traditions and interests remain separate.

Brittany, for most of the five millennia during which its past can be traced, drew its cultural links and influences not inland, from the rest of France, but from the Atlantic seaboard. Isolated both by the difficulty of its marsh and moorland terrain, and its sheer distance from the heartland of Europe, it was nonetheless at the centre of a sophisticated prehistoric culture that was intimately connected with those of Britain and Ireland. It is populated today by descendants of the Celtic immigrants who arrived from Britain and Ireland at around the time that the Romans were leaving Gaul. The "golden age" of Brittany came in the fifteenth century, when it was ruled as an independent duchy, but it was eventually absorbed into France after centuries of military and dynastic struggles with the English.

The economic decline of the province in recent centuries is attributed by Breton nationalists wholly to the union with France. Other factors, inevitably, were also at play, but it's certainly true to say that the rulers of France often ignored or oppressed their westernmost region, and even now the current revival of Brittany's fortunes is largely due to the conscious attempt to revive the old pan-Celtic trading routes.

Normandy has no equivalent prehistoric remains, and only very briefly did it possess the identity of an independent nation. Its founders were Scandinavian, the Vikings who raided along the Seine in the ninth century. These Northmen gave the region its name, and were the warriors who brought it military glory in the great Norman age of the eleventh century, when William conquered England and his nobles controlled swaths of land as far afield as Sicily and the Near East. They were also responsible for the cathedrals, castles and monasteries that still stand as the most enduring monuments of Normandy's past.

The Normans blended into the general mass of the population, both in France and in England, and Normandy itself was formally surrendered to Louis IX by Henry III of England in 1259. After the fluctuations of the Hundred Years War, the province was firmly integrated into France, and all but disappears from history until the Allied invasion of 1944. Supposedly, a handful of Normans still regard Queen Elizabeth II as the true duchess of Normandy – which is one of the many titles she still bears. The majority of contemporary Normans, however, put their faith in the industrial and agricultural resources of the province, and take pride in their individualism and conservatism.

The megaliths of Brittany

Megalithic sites can be found all around the Mediterranean, most notably in Malta and Sardinia, and along the Atlantic seaboard from Spain to Scandinavia. Among the most significant are Newgrange in Ireland, Stonehenge in England, and the Ring of Brodgar in the Orkneys. However, the megalith-building culture did not necessarily originate in the Mediterranean and spread out to the "barbarian" outposts of Europe. In fact, the tumuli, alignments and single standing stones of Brittany are of pre-eminent importance. The very

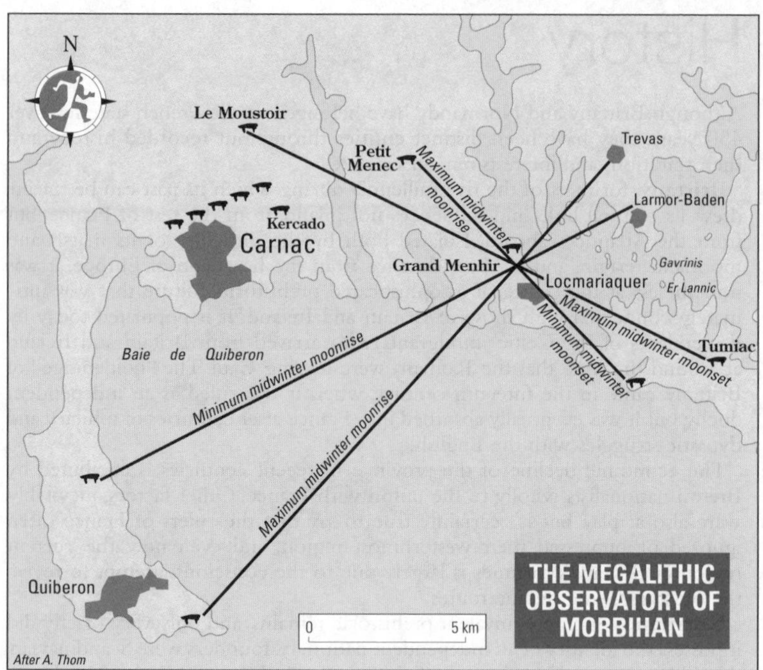

words used for the megaliths today are Breton: menhir (long stone), dolmen (flat stone), cromlech (stone circle).

Archeological evidence suggests that late Stone Age settlements had been established at various points along the Breton coast by around 6000 BC. Soon afterwards, the culture responsible either evolved to become the megalith builders, or was displaced by megalith-building newcomers. Dated at 5700 BC, the tumulus of Kercado at **Carnac**, in southern Brittany, appears to be the earliest stone construction in Europe, predating the palace of Knossos on Crete and even the Egyptian pyramids.

Each megalithic centre seems to have had its own distinct styles and traditions. Brittany has relatively few stone circles, and a greater proportion of free-standing stones; fewer burials, and more evidence of ritual fires; different styles of carving; and, uniquely, the sheer complexity of the Carnac alignments, which may be an astronomical observatory. (The fact that so many megalithic remains are now found on bleak seaside heathland sites may just be because these were the most likely to survive; for example those at Rétiers and Fougères do not fit the stereotype.)

Little is known of the **people** who erected the megaliths. Only rarely have skeletons been found in the graves, but those few that have been unearthed seem to indicate a short, dark, hairy race with a life expectancy of no more than the mid-30s. There's no firm evidence to support the legends that speak of shambling subhuman giants who served as their slaves, assisting Merlin, for example, in bringing the slabs of Stonehenge from Wales, and building the Giant's Causeway on the coast of Antrim in Northern Ireland. What is certain is that the civilization was long-lasting;

the earliest and the latest constructions at Carnac are over five thousand years apart.

As for the actual **purpose of the stones**, there are numerous theories and few definite conclusions. Flaubert commented: "those who like mythology see them as the Pillars of Hercules; those who like natural history see here a symbol of the Python ... lovers of astronomy see a zodiac". In the eighteenth century, for example, enthusiasts managed to see snakes in everything, and declared the megalithic sites to be remnants of some Druidic serpent cult; in fact the stones were already ancient before the Druids appeared. Countless writers have advanced fanciful speculations that range from "Lost Atlantis" through water divining, mysterious psychic energies and extraterrestrial assistance.

These days, the most fashionable **theories** – with the general public at least – see the megaliths as part of a vast system of **astronomical measurement**, record-keeping, and prediction. Precise measurements of sites all over Europe suggest that they share a standard measure of length, the "megalithic yard" – equivalent to 83 modern centimetres. In Brittany, the argument goes, the now fallen Grand Menhir of Locmariaquer was erected, using this prehistoric calibration, as a "universal lunar foresight". Its alignments with eight other sites are said to correspond to the eight extreme points of the rising and setting of the moon during its 18.61-year cycle. The Golfe de Morbihan made an ideal location for such a marking stone – set on a lagoon surrounded by low peninsulas, the menhir was visible from all directions. Once the need for the Grand Menhir was decided upon, it would then have taken hundreds of years of careful observation of the moon to fix precise positions for all the relevant sites. It is thought that this was done by lighting fires on the top of high poles at trial points on the crucial nights every nine years. The alignments of Carnac are thus explained as the graph paper, as it were, on which the lunar movements were plotted.

This "megalithic observatory" explanation, researched in great detail by Professor Thom – despite being hindered by occasional "encounters with irate peasants" – and most clearly expounded in his *Megalithic Remains in Britain and Brittany* (1978), is certainly appealing. However, **rival experts** have come up with damning counterevidence. To quote from Aubrey Burl's authoritative *Megalithic Brittany* (1985): "of the eight proposed backsights, three do not exist, and of the five others the Carnac mound at Tumiac is not accurately placed, the Goulvarch menhir, the stone at Kerran, the Carnac mound of Le Moustoir with its menhir, and the passage grave of Petit-Mont, are too dissimilar in architecture and date to be convincing purpose-built Neolithic viewing-stations." Controversy rages as to whether the Grand Menhir ever stood or, if it did, whether it fell or was broken up before the eight supposedly associated sites came into being. In addition, scientists are accused of ignoring the fact that the sea level in southern Brittany 6600 years ago was 10m lower than it is today.

In any case, the stones at Carnac have been so greatly eroded that perhaps it is little more than wishful thinking to imagine that their original size, shape and orientation can be accurately determined. They have been knocked down and pulled out by farmers seeking to cultivate the land; they have been quarried for use in making roads; they have been removed by landowners angry at the trespass of tourists and scientists; nineteenth-century pseudo-scientists have tampered with them, re-erecting some and shifting others; and what may have gone on in much earlier periods is anyone's guess.

An alternative approach, more popular with conventional archeologists, places much greater emphasis on sociological factors. This argues that the stones date from the great period of transition when humankind was changing from a predatory role to a productive one, and that they can only have been put in place by the coordinated efforts of a large and stable **community**. It's possible that the megaliths were erected by Neolithic settlers, who generation by generation advanced across Europe from the east bringing advances in agriculture. As they came into conflict with existing Stone Age groups, they may have set up menhirs as territorial markers. The ability to construct large monuments – which probably required the acquisition of a large agricultural surplus – would also have demonstrated that the group in question was "favoured" by the gods, and thus of "pure" or "noble" lineage.

An experiment in 1979 demonstrated that 260 people, using rollers, were required to set up a 32,000-kilogram stone, together with a large number of auxiliaries to provide food and shelter. The united physical exertion created a festival-type atmosphere, and the participants described the event as a "bonding" experience. Those who originally and perhaps unwillingly dragged the Carnac stones into place might feel that to be a trifle sentimental. Even so, it does make some sense to imagine the act of setting up a menhir as serving a valuable social purpose, both as an achievement in its own right and as a celebration of some other event. The annual or occasional setting-up of a new stone is easier to envisage than the vast effort required to erect them all at once – in which case the social significance of constructing these lines, mounds and circles could have been of greater importance than any physical characteristics of the arrangements themselves.

For all the pervasive legends, the megaliths cannot be attributed to the Celts. Even so, theological parallels have been drawn between ancient and modern **Breton beliefs**. It is argued that there is a uniquely Breton attitude to death, dating back thousands of years, in which the living are in everyday communication with the dead. The phenomenon of the "parish close" (described on p.298) is said to mirror the design of the ancient passage graves, with the Christian ossuary serving the same function as the buried passageways of the old tombs – a link between the place of the dead and the place of the living.

True or false, the popular significance of the prehistoric sites was something about which later Christian authorities were somewhat ambivalent. They felt it necessary to place crosses on the top of many menhirs, or even to destroy them altogether. There are reports of the "Indecent Stone" at Reguiny being "cut down and made harmless" in 1825, and of steps being taken to stop naked couples sliding down the Grand Menhir on May Day as a fertility rite, or rubbing against the "protuberances" of the Kerloas menhir.

Celts and Romans

While Brittany in particular prospered during the **Bronze Age**, and was a major manufacturer of bronze axes that were distributed throughout Atlantic Europe, its peoples were left behind by the technological advances of the **Iron Age**, and became increasingly peripheral from around 700 BC onwards. The economy turned instead towards supplying raw materials to the more developed cultures of Germany and southern France, and it is as traders in **tin and copper** that both the Bretons and the Normans make their first appearance in recorded history. Small trading ports emerged all along the Atlantic coast, and the routes went up the rivers Loire and Seine. The tin itself was mined in both

Brittany and Cornwall, and the Seine became important as the "Tin Road", the most direct means for the metals to be transported towards the heart of Europe. Iron Age forts, traces of one of which remain in the forest of Huelgoat, show evidence of large-scale, stable communities even far inland.

That was why the **Romans**' top priority, when they came to Gaul centuries later, was to secure control of the Seine valley and tie the province firmly into the network of empire. Brittany, less accessible to the invading armies, was able to put up a more spirited resistance, although sadly there was no such last-ditch rebel stronghold as Astérix's fictional village. The **Breton Gauls**, descendants of a first influx of Celts, were divided into five major tribes, each of which controlled an area roughly corresponding to the modern *départements*.

The most powerful of these tribes were the **Veneti**, based in the Morbihan with what is now Vannes as their capital. The decisive sea battle in which they were defeated in 56 BC took place around the Golfe de Morbihan, and was the only major naval battle the Romans ever won outside the Mediterranean. Ocean-going expeditions beyond the Pillars of Hercules were not among the Romans' strong points – hence their predilection for roads and foot-slogging – but on this occasion their galleys, built somewhere near St-Nazaire, had far superior mobility to the leather-sailed ships of the Veneti. The cost of defeat for the tribes was severe; those who were not killed were sold into slavery, and their children mutilated. Julius Caesar was there to see the battle; he went no further than Auray, but the whole Breton peninsula was swiftly conquered, and incorporated with much of Normandy into the province of Armorica.

Roman Armorica experienced five hundred years of peace, though without the benefit of any great prosperity. While the Roman-built roads were the first efficient means of land communication, they served mainly to channel wealth away towards the centre of their empire. Walled cities were founded, such as Rennes, Vannes, Rouen and Caen, but little was done to change, let alone improve, the lives of the native population. During the fourth century, a couple of Bretons, Magnence and Maximus, managed to become emperors of Rome, but by then pirate incursions had made fortifications essential along the coast.

Christianization and the Franks

What civilizing effect the Romans had had disappeared in any case during the **barbarian invasions** as the Empire disintegrated at the start of the fifth century. The one thread of continuity was provided by the **Christian** Church. The first Christians had already arrived in Normandy during Roman rule, and the bishopric at Rouen had been established by St Mellon as early as 300 AD. They were followed in the fifth and sixth centuries by waves of Celtic immigrants crossing from Britain to Brittany. Traditional history considered these to be "Dark Ages" of terror and chaos throughout Europe, with the immigrants as no more than panic-stricken refugees. However, recent evidence of stable diplomatic and trading contact across the Channel suggests that there was a much more ordered process of movement and interchange.

The vigorous Welsh and Irish missionaries named their new lands **Little Britain**, and their Christianity supplanted the old Celtic and Roman gods. That process is remembered in myth in terms of the confrontation of elemental forces – the Devil grappling with the Archangel Michael from

Dol to Mont-St-Michel, St Pol driving out the "laidley worm" from the Île de Batz – which surely symbolize the forcible expulsion of paganism. Often the changes were little more than superficial: crosses were erected on top of menhirs, mystical springs and wells became the sites of churches, Christian processions such as *pardons* traced circuits of megalithic sites, and ancient tales of magic and witchcraft were retold as stories of Jesus and the saints. The names of innumerable Celtic religious leaders – Malo, Brieuc, Pol – have survived in place names, even if the Church has never officially recognized them as saints.

Cultural links with Britain and Ireland meant that Brittany played an important role in many of the **Arthurian legends**. Breton minstrels, like their Welsh counterparts, did much to popularize the tales in the Middle Ages. None of the local sites that claim to be Arthur's Camelot carries much conviction, although Tristan who loved Iseult came from Brittany (the lovers may have hidden at Trémazan castle in Finistère), as did King Ban and his son Lancelot. Sir Galahad found the Holy Grail somewhere in Brocéliande Forest, said also to be the home of such diverse residents as Merlin, Morgane le Fay, and the Fisher King.

Such legends reflect the fact that, for all this time, central Brittany was an almost impenetrable wilderness. The region as a whole was split into two separate petty monarchies, **Dumnonia** in the north and **Cornubia** (the basis of Cornouaille) in the south. Charlemagne amalgamated the two by force under **Frankish control** in 799, after they had consistently failed to pay tribute. When the Frankish Empire began to fall apart, their appointee as governor, **Nominoë**, seized the opportunity to become the first ruler of an independent Brittany, by defeating the Frankish leader Charles the Bald in the Battle of Redon (near modern La Bataille) in 845. Breton history has come to see him as a prototype independent leader.

Without Celtic immigration on anything like the same scale, it took longer for **Normandy** to become fully Christianized. It was only when it too came under the control of Charlemagne's **Merovingian** dynasty that the newly founded monasteries of Jumièges and St-Wandrille became pre-eminent.

As the authority of the Franks weakened over the succeeding centuries, there were repeated **Viking** raids along the Seine, while similar raids on the Breton coast drove many monks into exile across the Channel. Major Viking incursions took place in the second half of the ninth century, interspersed with attempts to conquer England. The Vikings came more often and for longer, until in 911 King Charles the Simple acknowledged the inevitable and granted their leader **Rollo** formal title to the **Duchy of Normandy**. A few years later, in 932 AD, the Breton prince known as Alain Barbetorte returned from England to re-establish control over Brittany, and many of its monasteries were subsequently rebuilt in the new Romanesque style.

The Normans

In the eleventh century **the Normans** became one of the most significant forces in Europe. Not only did the dukes of Normandy invade and conquer England, but Norman mercenaries and adventurers fought to gain lands for themselves wherever they found the opportunity. They insinuated themselves into the wars of Italy, individually acquiring control of Aversa, Apulia and

Calabria, as well as most of Sicily, their greatest prize. They took part in the Church's wars, too, fighting in campaigns in Greece against Byzantium, and in the First Crusade – which in 1098 saw the Norman leader Bohemond take Antioch.

In their adopted French homeland, the pagan Scandinavians acquired the culture, language and religion of their new subjects so rapidly that spoken Norse died out in Rouen by the time of Rollo's grandson, Duke Richard I. Yet they were still seen as a race apart – and not a very pleasant one at that. One authority describes them as without exception physically repellent, cruel and unscrupulous.

Duke William's **invasion of England** is portrayed by the Bayeux Tapestry as a just struggle: the result solely of William's conviction that he was the rightful heir to Edward the Confessor, a succession acknowledged under oath by Harold. Be that as it may, the sheer speed of what proved to be such a permanent conquest indicates the extent of Norman power at the time. Having crossed the Channel to defeat the usurper Harold in September 1066, the Conqueror was crowned king in Westminster Abbey on Christmas Day, and by the next Easter was secure enough to be able to return to Normandy. The **Battle of Hastings** was a decisive moment in the balance of Europe. Almost paradoxically, the Norsemen from France finally freed England from the threat of invasion from Scandinavia, which had persisted for centuries. English attention was thus reorientated towards the mainland of Europe – a shift that was to have a major impact on history.

The Norman capacity for **organization** was primarily responsible not just for these military triumphs, but also for the consolidation of power and wealth that followed. The Domesday Book, which catalogued the riches of England, was paralleled by a similar undertaking in Sicily, the *Catalogus Baronum*. William's son Henry introduced trial by jury in the king's Courts – justice that had to be paid for. Henry II established the Exchequer to collect royal revenue.

Intellectually, too, the Normans were dominant; the Abbey of Bec-Hellouin, for example, was a renowned centre of learning, inspired first by Lanfranc and then by the theologian Anselm, each of whom moved on to become archbishop of Canterbury. And **architecturally**, the wealth and technical expertise of the Normans made possible the construction of such lasting monuments as the cathedrals of Bayeux, Coutances and Durham, and the monasteries of Mont-St-Michel, Jumièges and Caen.

The twelfth-century "**Anglo-Normans**" who invaded Ireland were recognizably descended from the army of the Conqueror, and Norman French remained the legal and administrative language of England until 1400. Elsewhere the mark of the conquerors was less distinct. The Norman kings of Sicily did not style themselves Normans, and ruled over a cosmopolitan society dependent largely on the skills of Moslem craftsmen. Their architecture barely resembles what is thought of today as "Norman", and the Norman bloodline soon vanished into the general population of Sicily.

However, for the duchy and the kingdom on either side of the Channel, the shared rulers made close connections inevitable. The Norman lords in England required luxury items to be imported. Flemish weavers were encouraged to settle in London and East Anglia, and gradually the centre of affluence and importance shifted away from Normandy. By the time Henry II, great-grandson of William the Conqueror, inherited the throne, England was a major power and the seeds of the Hundred Years War had been sown. Fifteen years later Château Gaillard on the Seine was taken by **Philippe Auguste**, and Normandy for the first time became part of France.

The Hundred Years War

While Normandy was at the height of its power, **Bretons** lived in constant fear of invasion by their belligerent neighbours. Although their own leaders had managed to prevent a parallel Viking takeover of Brittany, it was at the price of numerous **warlords** setting up their own private strongholds. Their emergence seriously weakened the authority of Nominoë's successors, and the resultant anarchy devastated the Breton economy. Frequent power bids by the Norman English and the kings of France – now referred to as **The Hundred Years War** – hardly helped the situation.

Bertrand du Guesclin, born in 1321 in the unprepossessing town of Broons, south of Dinan, ranks among the outstanding military geniuses of the Middle Ages. After an ignominious start, when his father disowned him because of his ugliness, he developed his novel approach to war as an outlaw chief in the heart of Brittany. With little truck for chivalric conventions, he simplified the chaotic feudal map, and in a bewildering succession of French and Spanish campaigns earned the command of the French army. Eschewing prearranged battles in favour of ambush and general guerrilla tactics, he taught the French to fight dirty – in medieval terms. Nobles were forced to dismount and fight on foot, while the fact that his soldiers were paid ensured that they did not alienate the peasantry by plundering. This formidable man was also responsible for the development of the use of gunpowder, combined with new assault techniques capable of devastating the strongest fortresses.

The net result of du Guesclin's strategies was that by 1377 the English had been driven almost completely out of France. Virtually every town and castle in Brittany and Normandy seems to have some du Guesclin connection; not only did he live, besiege or fight almost everywhere, but after his death in 1380 parts of his body were buried in no fewer than four different cities. Yet, despite all his myriad intrigues and battles, Brittany benefited very little from his activities.

The Hundred Years War resurfaced after du Guesclin's death, with much of the fighting taking place in Normandy. Henry V of England recaptured the province step by step, until by 1420 he was in a position to demand recognition of his claim to the French throne. Eight years later, the French were defending their last significant stronghold, Orléans on the Loire. It was here that the extraordinary figure of **Joan of Arc** appeared on the scene and relieved the siege of the city. Through moral inspiration as much as military leadership, she ensured that the mass of ordinary, miserable peasants, not to mention the demoralized soldiers of the French army, made the enemy occupation untenable. Within two astonishing years, the Dauphin had been crowned, to become King Charles VII of France. Joan herself was captured by the Burgundian allies of the occupiers, tried by a French bishop and an English commander, and burned at the stake as a witch in Rouen – for a full account, see p.108. Nonetheless, in 1449, Charles VII was able to make a triumphal entry into the regional capital. Within twelve months this latest 32-year English occupation of Normandy was at an end.

The Duchy of Brittany

Breton involvement in the opening stages of the second phase of the Hundred Years War was minimal. Between 1399 and 1442, **Duc Jean V** took a neutral stance, allowing the economy of the province to prosper. Fishing, shipbuilding and sail manufacture developed, accompanied by a flowering of the arts. It was during this period that the Kreisker chapel and the church of Folgoët were built.

Although involvement in the Anglo-French conflict was inevitable, Jean's heirs for a time continued to rule over a successful and **independent duchy**. Arthur III, duke in the mid-fifteenth century, had fought alongside Joan of Arc, but he used his connections with the French army to protect Breton autonomy. His successor, however, Duc François II, was less astute. Brittany, the last large region of present-day France to resist agglomeration, was a very desirable prize for King Louis XI. To resist encroachment, François needed allies beyond France; and in looking for those allies he antagonized and alarmed the French. A pretext was eventually found for the royal army to invade Brittany, where the Breton army was defeated at the battle of St-Aubin-du-Cormier in 1488. Duc François was forced to concede to the French king the right to determine his own daughter's marriage, and died of shame (so the story goes) within a few weeks.

François's heiress, **Duchess Anne**, was to be the last ruler of an independent Brittany. Having once been engaged to the Prince of Wales, she then married Maximilian of Austria by proxy in December 1490, in the hope of a strong alliance against the French. Charles VIII of France (who was himself in theory married to Maximilian's daughter) demanded adherence to the treaty of 1488, captured Nantes, advanced north and west and proposed to Anne.

By and large the population preferred a royal wedding to death by starvation or massacre, and it duly took place on September 16, 1491. Anne bemoaned "Must I thus be so unfortunate and friendless as to have to enter into marriage with a man who has so ill-treated me?" – and then, to the amazement of all, the couple actually fell in love with each other. Despite the marriage, the duchy remained independent, but Anne was contractually obliged to marry Charles's successor should he die before they produced an heir. When Charles duly bumped his head and died in 1498, his successor, Louis XII, divorced his wife and married Anne. This time Anne's position was considerably stronger, and in the contract she laid down certain conditions that were to be a source of Breton pride and frustration for many centuries. The three main clauses stipulated that no taxes could be imposed without the consent of the Breton *États*; conscripts were only to fight for the defence of Brittany; and Bretons could only be tried in their own courts. When Anne died, Bretons mourned – all records show that she was a genuinely loved leader.

In 1514, the still independent duchy passed to Anne's daughter Claude, whom the future François I of France married with every intention of incorporating Brittany into his kingdom. This he did, and the permanent **union of Brittany and France** was endorsed by the Breton *États* at Vannes in 1532. In theory, the act confirmed Anne's stipulations that all the rights and privileges of Brittany would be observed and safeguarded as inviolable. However, it was rarely honoured, and its subsequent violation by successive French kings and governments has been the source of conflict ever since.

The ancien régime

As the French Crown gradually consolidated its power and began to centralize its economy, the ports of the two western provinces developed, serving the

colonial interests of the state. As early as 1364, sailors from **Dieppe** had established the settlement of Petit Dieppe in what is now Sierra Leone. **Le Havre** was founded in 1517 to be France's premier Atlantic port and, between intermittent attacks and takeovers by the English, became a centre for the coffee and cotton markets. Sailors from Granville, Dieppe and Cherbourg set up colonies in Brazil, Canada, Florida and Louisiana.

In Brittany, **St-Malo** and **Lorient** were the two top trading ports, with the latter benefiting every time the English decided to harass Channel ports and shipping. **Jacques Cartier** of St-Malo sailed up the St Lawrence River and added Canada to the possessions of France. Nantes too was an important base for trade with the Americas, India and the Middle East, with **slaves** one of the most profitable "commodities". Though the business of exploitation and battles with rival foreign ships was motivated by private profit, the net result was very much to the advantage of the state.

Thanks to its early contacts with England, and the cosmopolitan nature of its Channel ports, Normandy became one of the main **Protestant** centres of France, with Caen and its university having very active Huguenot populations. The region was therefore in the front line when the **Wars of Religion** flared up in 1561–63, and again in 1574–76. When the Edict of Nantes, with its privileges and immunities for Protestants, was revoked, large-scale Huguenot emigration took place, seriously damaging the local textile industry.

Brittany on the other hand had a minimal Protestant presence, and the Wars of Religion were only significant as a cover for a brief attempt to win back independence. Breton linen manufacture had taken advantage of the lack of French tolls and customs dues, and only declined much later, when England, post-Industrial Revolution, was flooding the market with mass-produced textiles.

Although the power of the French kings increased over the centuries, practical considerations meant that outlying regions were not always completely under royal control. The rural nobles were persistently lawless, and intermittent **peasant revolts** took place, such as that of the dispossessed *nu-pieds* in 1639. In 1675 came the most serious rebellion against the Crown, when Louis XIV's finance minister put a tax on tobacco, pewter and all legal documents to raise money for the war with Holland. This "Stamped Paper" revolt, which started with riots in Nantes, Rennes and Guingamp, soon spread to the country, with the peasants making demands very similar in their content to those of the revolutionaries over a hundred years later. The aristocracy took great delight in brutally crushing the uprising, pillaging several towns and stringing up insurgents and bystanders from every tree.

The reign of **Louis XIV** saw numerous infringements of Breton liberties, including the uprooting of vines throughout the province on the royal grounds that the people were all drunkards. If the Bretons could not get revenge they could at least be entertained by court scandals. In 1650 Louis's Superintendent of Finance, **Nicolas Fouquet**, bought the entire island of Belle-Île and fortified it as his own private kingdom. The alarmed king had to send D'Artagnan and the three musketeers to arrest him before his ambitions went any further.

While taxes on Brittany increased in the early eighteenth century, Normandy found new prosperity from the proximity of Paris for its edible produce. Lacemaking too became a major regional industry, and several abbeys that had been closed during the Wars of Religion were now revitalized. However, by 1763 France had lost Canada and given up all pretensions to India. The ports declined and trade fell off as England became the workshop of the world.

Revolution

At first, the people of both Brittany and Normandy welcomed the **French Revolution**. Breton representatives at the États Généraux in Paris seized the opportunity to air all Brittany's grievances, and the "Club Breton" they formed was the basis of the **Jacobins**. Caen, meanwhile, became the centre of the bourgeois **Girondist** faction. In August 1789 it was a Breton *député* who proposed the abolition of privileges. However, under the Convention it became clear that the price to be paid for the elimination of the *ancien régime* was further reductions in local autonomy and the suppression of the Breton language.

Neither province was sympathetic to the execution of the king – 30,000 people took to the streets in Rouen to express their opposition. The Girondins came out worst in the factional infighting at the Convention, having opposed the abolition of the monarchy and supported the disastrous war in the Netherlands. Some Girondist deputies managed to flee the edict of June 2, 1793 which ordered their arrest, but the army they organized to march on Paris was defeated at Pacy-sur-Eure. The final major Norman contribution to Revolutionary history was provided on that same day by **Charlotte Corday** of Caen, when she stabbed Jean-Paul Marat in his bath.

The concerted attack on religion and the clergy was not happily received, particularly in Brittany where the Church was closely bound up with the region's independent identity. An attempt to conscript an army of 300,000 Bretons was deeply resented as an infringement of the Act of Union. The popular image of the Revolution in Brittany was now further damaged by the brief **Reign of Terror** in 1793 of Carrier, the Convention's representative in Nantes. Under the slogan "all the rich, all the merchants are counter-revolutionaries", he killed perhaps 13,000 people in three months, by such methods as throwing prisoners into the Loire tied together in pairs. This was done without Tribunal sanction or approval, and Carrier was himself guillotined before the end of the year.

All this made Brittany an inevitable focal point for the Royalist **counter-revolution** known as the *Chouannerie*, which also had adherents in a few outlying areas of Normandy. A vast invasion force of exiled and foreign nobility, backed by the English, was supposed to sweep through France, rallying all dissenters to the royalist flag. In the event only 8000 landed at Quiberon in 1795, and they were not even capable of escaping from the self-imposed trap of the peninsula. Instead, they devastated what little they could before being brutally massacred. Much local support was motivated by the age-old desire to win back independence, but Breton *Chouans* ("screech owls") fighting elsewhere ended up being tarred with the same aristocratic brush and then abandoned to years of quixotic and doomed guerrilla warfare.

A rebel army continued to fight sporadically in the Cotentin and the Bocage until 1800, while in Brittany another **royalist revolt** in 1799 was easily crushed. In 1804, Cadoudal, "the last *Chouan*", was captured and executed in Paris, where he had gone to kidnap Napoléon – having refused the emperor's offer of a generalship if he surrendered. The rebel movement lingered on until 1832, when the Duchess of Berry failed to engage anyone's interest in the restoration of the *ancien régime*.

The nineteenth century

Normandy at the beginning of the nineteenth century remained a wealthy region despite the crippling of its ports by the blockade imposed by the European coalition against Napoléon. Proportionally, five times as many of its people were eligible, as property owners, to vote as in the impoverished mountain areas of the south, while its agriculture accounted for eleven percent of France's produce on six percent of its land. Only industry remained relatively unadvanced.

When protectionist tariffs were removed from grain in 1828, and Normandy was forced to compete with other producers, widespread **rural arson and tax riots** ensued. But, when the revolution of 1848 offered the prospect of socialism, the deeply conservative Catholic peasantry showed little enthusiasm for change. Even the re-emergence of a rural textile industry in the 1840s, relying on outworkers brutally exploited by the capitalists of Rouen, added no radical impetus.

The advent of the **railways** and the patronage of the imperial court encouraged the development of Normandy's resorts, while along the Seine watermills provided the power for major spinning centres at Louviers, Évreux and Elbeuf. Serious decline did not come until the 1880s, when **rural depopulation** was brought on by emigration combined with a low birth rate – and a high death rate in which excessive drinking played a part.

Nineteenth-century Brittany was no longer an official entity, save as five *départements* of France. The railways were of negative benefit, submitting the province to competition from more heavily industrialized regions, while the Nantes–Brest canal did not achieve the expected success, and **emigration** increased from here too. Culturally, the century witnessed a revival of Breton language, customs and folklore, but the initiative came from intellectuals rather than from the mainly illiterate masses.

Around the turn of the **twentieth century** both provinces experienced a surge of artistic creativity, with painters such as Gauguin in Pont-Aven and Monet in Giverny, and such writers as Marcel Proust in Normandy and Pierre Loti in Brittany.

As everywhere in Europe, this idyll was shattered by the **Great War**. Although far from the actual front, both Brittany and Normandy were dramatically affected. Brittany, for its size, suffered the heaviest death toll of anywhere in the world. The vast memorial at Ste-Anne-d'Auray is testimony to the extent of the loss, while a parallel spiritual grief can be seen in the dramatic growth in Normandy of the cult of the recently dead Thérèse of Lisieux. Symbols of a changing world are embodied in the two leading aristocratic families of the regions; the heir to the Rohans of Josselin was killed on the Somme, while Prince Louis de Broglie became the first physicist to question the solidity of matter.

World War II and the Battle of Normandy

That the **beaches of Normandy** were chosen as the site of the Allied invasion of Europe in June 1944 was by no means inevitable. Far from the major disputed areas and communication routes of Europe, Normandy had seen almost no military activity since the Hundred Years War. But in that blazing summer six armies and millions of men fought bloody battles across the placid Norman countryside. A whole swath of the province was laid in ruins before Hitler's defensive line was broken and the road to Paris cleared.

France, under **Marshal Pétain**, had surrendered to the Germans in 1940. A year later, the fascist armies turned east to invade the Soviet Union, America and Britain declaring full support for the Soviets but resisting Stalin's demand for a second front. In 1942 the two western powers promised a landing in northern France, but all that ensued was an abortive commando raid on Dieppe. By the time the second front materialized, the tide of the war had already been turned at Stalingrad.

The Germans had meanwhile fortified the whole northwest seaboard of Europe. Their **Atlantic Wall** was constructed from spring 1942 onwards by the Todt organization, previously responsible for building the German *autobahn* network. It used thirteen million cubic metres of concrete, and 1.2 million tons of steel.

From the Allied point of view, any invasion site had to be within range of air support from Britain, which meant anywhere from Rotterdam to St-Malo. Nonetheless, the Nazis expected the attack to come at the Channel's narrowest point, across the Straits of Dover. The **D-Day invasion** of June 6, 1944, was presaged by months of intensive aerial bombardment across Europe, without concentrating too obviously on the chosen landing sites. In the event, the Nazis vastly overestimated Allied resources – two weeks after D-Day Rommel still thought the Normandy landings might be no more than a preliminary diversion to a larger-scale assault around Calais. After all, as a British photographic survey of the whole Norman coast – even prewar holiday snaps had been requisitioned – had conclusively established, none of the Norman channel ports was susceptible to easy capture.

As a result, the landings used amphibious craft to storm the beaches of Normandy rather than its ports. On Utah Beach, the Atlantic Wall lasted for little more than five minutes; on Gold, Juno and Sword beaches, it was overrun in about an hour; and even on Omaha, where the sea turned red with blood, it took less than a day for the Allies to storm through.

Albert Speer summed up the failure of the wall by saying: "A fortnight after the first landings by the enemy, this costly effort was brought to nothing by an idea of simple genius . . . the invasion forces brought their own harbours with them". These **"Mulberry" harbours**, as described on p.152, proved the key to the Allied victory.

The basic plan was for the British and Commonwealth forces under Montgomery to strike for Caen, the pivot around which the Americans (whose General Eisenhower was in overall command) were to swing following their own landings further west. Not everything went smoothly. There are appalling stories of armoured cars full of men plunging straight to the bottom of the sea as they rolled off landing craft unable to get near enough to the shore. Many of the early objectives took much longer to capture than was originally envisaged – the British took weeks rather than hours to reach Caen, while American hopes of a rapid seizure of the deep-water port at Cherbourg were thwarted. Most notorious of all, the opportunity to capture the bulk of the German army, which was all but surrounded in the "Falaise pocket", was lost.

On D-Day itself, almost five thousand of the 150,000 soldiers who landed on D-Day were killed. In all, between June 6 and August 22 1944, a total of 124,400 US soldiers and 82,300 from the UK and Canada lost their lives.

Military historians say that man for man the German army was the more effective fighting force; but with their sheer weight of resources the Allies achieved a fairly rapid victory. Crucially, the concentration of German air power on the eastern front meant that there was never a significant German air presence over Normandy. Parachutists, reconnaissance flights and air support for ground troops were all able to operate virtually unimpeded, as too were the bombing raids on Norman towns and on every bridge across the Seine west of Paris. Furthermore, the muddled enemy command, in which generals at the front were obliged to follow broad directives from Berlin, caused an American general to comment, "one's imagination boggled at what the German army might have done to us without Hitler working so effectively for our side".

Within a few days of D-Day, the leader of the Free French, **General de Gaulle** was able to return to France, making an emotional first speech at Bayeux (see p.159), while a seasick Winston Churchill sailed up to Deauville in a destroyer and "took a plug at the Hun". At the end of July, General Patton's Third Army broke out across Brittany from Avranches with the aid of 30,000 **French Resistance** fighters, and on August 25 Allied divisions entered Paris, where the German garrison had already been routed by the Resistance. In the east the Red Army were sweeping back the Axis powers.

Though the war in Europe still had several bloody months to run – Hitler made a desperate last attempt to smash the western front during the Ardennes offensive of December 1944 – the road to Berlin was finally opening up.

Postwar: the Breton resurgence

The war left most of **Normandy** in ruins: while it remained relatively prosperous in terms of its produce, decades of reconstruction were required. The development of private transport also meant that Normandy became ever more filled with the second homes of the rich. This has often been resented – the movie actor Jean Gabin, for example, was literally besieged in his new country house by hundreds of peasants insisting that he had "too much land", and was obliged to sell some of it off.

Meanwhile, there was very little happening in **postwar Brittany** save ever-increasing migration from the countryside to the main towns, and from there, often, out of the province altogether. By the 1950s some 300,000 Bretons lived in Paris, industry was almost exclusively limited to the Loire estuary, and agriculture was dogged by archaic marketing and distribution.

However, since the late 1960s Brittany has experienced considerable economic regeneration, due in part to the initiatives of **Alexis Gourvennec**. He first came to prominence at the age of 24, in 1961, when he led a group of fellow farmers into Morlaix to occupy the government's regional offices in an effective (if violent) protest at exploitation by middlemen. The act set the pace for his lifetime's concern – to obtain the best possible price for Breton agricultural produce. To this end he lobbied Paris for a deep-water port at Roscoff, and once that was built his farmers' cooperative set up Brittany Ferries to carry Breton artichokes and cabbages to English markets. The company was an explicit move to re-establish the old trading links of the Atlantic seaboard, independent of Paris and central French authority.

Brittany Ferries has prospered, thanks to the British and Irish entry to the EC upon which Gourvennec had gambled. And it has proved that Brittany's future economic fortunes may well be more closely linked to its old Celtic connections than to the French state. Yet, despite Gourvennec's enthusiasm for his Celtic cousins, there have been several instances of ugly **protectionism** – attacking British lorries importing meat, violently breaking up strikes in Brittany, and forcibly preventing Townsend Thorensen from starting a rival ferry service to St-Malo.

In 1973 a semi-decentralized **regional administration** was set up to provide an intermediate level between the *départements* and the State. Normandy, being rich, became two regions – *Basse*, with its capital in Caen, and *Haute*, centred on Rouen – while Brittany was a single entity, but lost the Loire-Atlantique *département*, which included what was traditionally its principal city, **Nantes**. The new boundaries had no impact on people's perception of the provinces, though they did start to have some practical consequence when the Socialist government increased regional powers in 1981.

Fishing and **agriculture** remain the mainstays of the Breton economy, though the former has never benefited from an equivalent to Gourvennec. Both arenas have been subject to increasingly bitter intra-European disputes. The economic survival of Breton fishermen in particular has been seriously threatened by a flood of cheap imports from the factory-fishing trawlers of the former Soviet Union. In February 1994, the streets of Rennes were turned into a battlefield when five thousand fishermen rioted during a visit by Prime Minister Édouard Balladur, and a stray flare set light to the roof of the ancient Breton Parliament, which was so badly damaged that it only reopened in 2000. The following month, the GATT talks on world trade were briefly derailed by a French blockade on fish flown in from the US; American threats to retaliate by banning imports of Camembert and other French cheeses soon forced a climb-down.

Thirty percent of fish caught by British vessels are exported to Europe through French ports, and there have been repeated instances of the blockading of various Channel ports, with hypermarkets being ransacked and Scottish fish landed at Roscoff destroyed by angry mobs. In response to a threat by trawlermen wishing to fish for scallops and spider crabs to blockade the Channel Islands, the French government reduced the tax burden on self-employed fishermen, and set minimum prices for cod, haddock, coley and monkfish. The summer of 2000 saw further disputes, focusing on the cost of diesel oil to fishermen; following the usual disruption to cross-Channel ferries. the French government once again caved in and cut the relevant taxes.

Despite the loss of its traditional industrial centres on the Loire estuary, including the shipbuilding town of St-Nazaire, Brittany has nonetheless managed to expand its industrial base, with the advent of a Citroën plant at Rennes being one high-profile example. The development of the ultra-fast Paris–Brest TGV rail link in particular, inaugurated in 1989, has made a considerable difference. The simultaneous boom in Ireland has even led to talk of Brittany as being a "Celtic tiger". Growth in Normandy has been less spectacular, but after a recession during the the 1990s the region has entered the twenty-first century with something of a resurgence, spearheaded by the high-tech facilities of Caen.

Politically, Bretons have consistently provided an above-average proportion of the conservative vote, with the most traditional, rural, areas being the most conservative of all. Perhaps for that reason the **separatist movement**, as a positive celebration of the Breton nation rather than a reactionary throwback, has never been all that powerful. In 1932 a bomb in Rennes destroyed the monument to Franco-Breton unity, and since 1966 the Front de Libération de Bretagne has intermittently attacked such targets as the nuclear power station in the Monts d'Arrée, and the Hall of Mirrors at the palace of Versailles in 1978.

They were joined in 2000 by the shadowy **Breton Liberation Army** (ARB), which carried out a succession of bombings including attacks on the town hall in La Baule and a post office in Rennes. The campaign culminated with an explosion that killed an employee at a *McDonald's* restaurant outside Dinan. Seven activists received heavy prison sentences in 2004 for their involvement in the ARB campaign, though none was specifically found guilty of the Dinan outrage. Arguably, the *McDonald's* bombing was an extreme manifestation of a nationwide surge of resentment that depicted McDonald's as epitomizing multinational incursion into France. Although even government ministers expressed sympathy with such views, the official response to the perceived threat to French identity and traditions mitigated against Breton aspirations. President Jacques Chirac refused to ratify the European Charter on Regional and Minority Languages, which would require France to alter its constitution to recognize the rights of Breton speakers,

Meanwhile, the emphasis for most Breton activists these days is on cultural pride rather than militancy. The idea is to establish a clear and vital sense of national identity – to create, as one leader put it, "the spiritual basis for a new political thrust". Although overall use of the Breton language may be declining, great stress has been placed on its historical and artistic significance.

Perhaps the biggest ongoing story in recent years has been the catastrophic succession of **oil spills** along the coastline. Ever since the foundering of the *Torrey Canyon* off Ouessant in March 1967 (see p.309), and the devastation when the *Amoco Cadiz* sank off northern Finistère in 1978, Bretons have come to dread the coming of the *marées noires* or "black tides". Another major disaster came at the end of 1999, when the Maltese super-tanker *Erika* sank off southern Brittany, releasing around 23,000 tonnes of pollutants into the Atlantic ocean. The subsequent mopping-up operation was thrown into jeopardy by reports that its cargo consisted of cancer-causing toxic waste from refineries rather than ordinary fuel oil, as its owners claimed. While the clean-up of physical traces of the wreck was ultimately deemed a success, its economic impact far outweighed any potential compensation, and included an estimated fifteen percent drop in tourism during 2000.

Another headline-hitting controversy has centred on Cogema's UP3 nuclear reprocessing plant at **Cap de la Hague**, near Cherbourg in Normandy. The state-owned facility "reprocesses" spent nuclear fuel from power stations all over the world, and in doing so discharges 230 million litres of nuclear waste each year into the Atlantic. Analysis of the ocean floor in the vicinity has shown it to be so contaminated that legally the stones on the sea bed should themselves be classified as controlled nuclear waste. Researchers from the environmental group **Greenpeace** have labelled the La Hague plant as being "the single largest source of radioactive contamination in the European Union", and also "the single largest source of aerial radioactivity in the world". Campaigners have focused in particular on the demonstrable contamination of the beach at the Plage des Moulinets, nearby, where a waste pipe from the plant is exposed at low tide, and also on the independently verified high incidence of leukemia in the local population. The French authorities continue to stonewall on the issue, proud of the fact that 75 percent of the country's electricity is produced by nuclear power stations.

How **tourism** to northern France will be affected by the 2004 decision of P&O Ferries to abandon five cross-Channel ferry routes remains to be seen. Certainly there's no sign that visitor numbers are dropping; as the Channel Tunnel finally comes into its own, it's said that sixty percent of rural homes sold in Normandy are now bought by British purchasers, while Brittany has experienced a similar influx. 2004 also witnessed poignant ceremonies to commemorate the sixtieth anniversary of the D-Day landings, which were attended by German and Russian leaders as well as representatives of the invading Allies. A further reminder of the strong links between France and the US, strained by differences over the war in Iraq, came with the nomination of John Kerry as the Democratic candidate for the US presidency. Kerry's maternal grandmother lived in St-Briac, Brittany – his cousin, Brice Lalonde, is a former environment minister who himself stood for the French presidency – and Kerry spent many of his childhood summers there.

Books

Where separate editions exist in the UK and US, publishers are detailed below with the British publisher first, followed by the American publisher. Where books are published in one country only, this follows the publisher's name. O/p signifies an out-of-print, but still recommended, book. University Press has been abbreviated to UP. Titles marked ★ are especially recommended.

Prehistory and megaliths

Aubrey Burl *Megalithic Brittany* (Thames & Hudson, o/p). Detailed guide to the prehistoric sites of Brittany, area by area. Very precise on how to find each site, and what you see when you get there, but little historical or theoretical overview. It is not intended as a practical guidebook for anything other than ancient stones.

★ **John Michell** *Megalithomania* (Thames & Hudson; Cornell UP). General popularizing work about megaliths everywhere, with a lot of entertaining descriptions of how modern visitors have reacted to them.

Mark Patton *Statements in Stone* (Routledge). Sober, scientific account of Brittany's megalithic heritage, reappraised in the light of recent archeological discoveries.

A. Thom and A. S. Thom *Megalithic Remains in Britain and Brittany* (OUP, UK, o/p). A scientific rather than anecdotal account of the Thoms' extensive analysis. The mathematics and astronomy can be a bit overpowering without necessarily convincing you of anything.

★ **Uderzo and Goscinny** *Astérix the Gaul* (Hodder). Breton history mixed together in a magic cauldron.

History and politics

John Ardagh *France Today* (Penguin). Detailed journalistic survey of modern France, with an interesting and relevant section on "Brittany's revival".

Alfred Cobban *A History of Modern France* (Penguin, three vols). Very complete political history from Louis XIV to de Gaulle.

Patrick Galliou and Michael Jones *The Bretons* (Basil Blackwell). Accessible and illuminating hardback account of Breton history from the megaliths, through the Romans, as far as the union with France.

David C. Douglas *The Norman Achievement 1050–1100* (Fontana, o/p; University of California Press, o/p). Comprehensive and readable assessment of the Norman conquerors.

Jonathan Fenby *On The Brink* (Warner Books; Arcade). Entertaining overview of French politics and culture at the end of the twentieth century.

★ **Frank McLynn** *1066: The Year of The Three Battles* (Pimlico; UK). Myth-busting exploration of what really happened in 1066, which reveals how close the Norman invasion came to failure.

Barbara Tuchman *Distant Mirror* (Papermac; Ballantine). A history of the fourteenth century as experienced by a French nobleman. Makes sense of the human complexities of the Hundred Years War.

★ **Mark Twain** *Joan of Arc* (Ignatius; US). Little-known fictionalized biography of Joan by America's greatest nineteenth -century writer; quite extraordinarily hagiographic considering his normal scorn for religion.

Ian W. Walker *Harold: The Last Anglo-Saxon King* (Sutton UK). This first full-length biography puts flesh on the bones of the man whom William defeated at the Battle of Hastings.

Marina Warner *Joan of Arc* (Vintage). Stimulating examination of the symbolism and mythology of the Maid of Orléans.

Theodore Zeldin *France 1845–1945* (OUP). Five thematic volumes on French history.

The Normandy landings

Stephen Ambrose *D-Day* (Pocket Books; Touchstone). 600-page extravaganza by the doyen of American historians, chronicling the minutiae of the Normandy landings.

Paul Fussell *The Boys' Crusade: American GIs in Europe – Chaos and Fear in World War Two* (Modern Library Chronicles; Weidenfeld). This short reflection on the lives of the young American soldiers who took part in the D-Day campaign is heavily coloured by Fussell's own wartime experiences, which makes for a fascinating polemic.

★ **Max Hastings** *Overlord* (Papermac; Simon & Schuster). Detailed history of D-Day and its aftermath. Balanced and objective; Hastings distances himself thoroughly from propaganda and myth-making.

Donald Horne *The Great Museum: the Re-presentation of History* (Pluto; Westview). A stimulating analysis of how history is presented to the tourist. Particularly interesting for its treatment of the D-Day landing sites.

John Keegan *Six Armies in Normandy* (Pimlico; Penguin). A fascinating military history, which combines the personal and the public to original effect. Each of the participating armies in the Battle of Normandy is followed during the most crucial phase of its involvement; some of the lesser details of the conflict are missed, but the overall sweep is compelling.

Anthony Kemp *D-Day; The Normandy Landings and the Liberation of Europe* (Thames & Hudson; Abrams). Full-colour pocketbook guide to the D-Day story, with a wealth of fascinating information. Published to mark the fiftieth anniversary of the invasion.

★ **Studs Terkel** *The Good War* (Ballantine; New Press). Excellent collection of interviews with participants of every rank and nation, including civilians, in World War II.

Art and architecture

Henry Adams *Mont-St-Michel and Chartres* (Princeton UP; US). Extraordinary, idiosyncratic account of the two medieval masterpieces, attempting through prayer, song and sheer imagination to understand the society and the people that created them. A tribute to Norman wisdom.

John Ardagh *Writers' France* (Hamish Hamilton, o/p). Entertaining anecdotes about most of the writers mentioned in this book, with colour photos.

Christina Björk *Linnea in Monet's Garden* (Raben & Sjogern; Farrar, Straus & Giroux). A Swedish book for children, which tells the story of a young girl achieving her unlikely lifetime's dream of visiting Monet's home in Giverny. A well-illustrated introduction to the Impressionists.

Sophie Bowness and others *The Dieppe Connection* (Herbert Press; New Amsterdam Books). Companion volume to a fascinating exhibition in Brighton, exploring Dieppe's nineteenth-century role as a meeting place for artists. Colour reproductions of Dieppe scenes by Turner, Whistler, Gauguin and Renoir, among others.

★ **Claire Joyes** *Monet at Giverny* (Matthews Millar Dunbar). Large-format account of Monet's years at Giverny, combining biography with good reproductions of the famous waterlilies.

Brittany in fiction

Honoré de Balzac *The Chouans* (Penguin). A hectic and crazily romantic story of the royalist *Chouan* rebellion shortly after the Revolution, set mainly in Fougères.

Alexandre Dumas *The Three Musketeers* (OUP; Penguin). Brilliant swashbuckling romance with peripheral Breton scenes on Belle-Île and elsewhere.

Victor Hugo *Ninety-Three* (Carroll & Graf, US). Rather more restrained, but still compelling, *Chouan* novel.

Jack Kerouac *Satori in Paris* (Harper Collins; Grove) . . . and in Brittany. Inconsequential anecdotes.

Pierre Loti *Pêcheur d'Islande* (Livre de Poche). Much-acclaimed novel (on which the film was based) which focuses on the whaling fleets that sailed from Paimpol. Not available in translation.

Normandy in fiction

Julian Barnes *Flaubert's Parrot* (Picador; Random House). A light-weight novel which rambles around the life of Flaubert, with much of the action taking place in Rouen and along the Seine.

Peter Benson *Odo's Hanging* (Sceptre, UK). Delicate but dramatic fictionalized account of the human stories behind the creation of the Bayeux Tapestry.

Gustave Flaubert *Bouvard and Pécuchet* (Viking, US). Two petits-bourgeois retire to a village between Caen and Falaise and attempt to practise every science of the time. Very funny or dead boring, according to taste.

★ **Gustave Flaubert** *Madame Bovary* (Wordsworth; Bantam Books). "The first modern novel", by the Rouennais writer. Drawn from a real-life story from Ry – see p.119 – it contains little that is specifically Norman, however.

Marcel Proust *In Remembrance of Things Past* (Penguin; Random House). Dense, dreamily disturbing autobiographical trilogy, evocative of almost everything except the places in Normandy and Brittany to which his memories take him back.

★ **Julian Rathbone** *The Last English King* (Abacus; St Martin's Press). Lyrical and extremely readable fictionalized version of the Norman Conquest, as told by King Harold's one surviving bodyguard. The Normans themselves are depicted as heartless villains.

Jean-Paul Sartre *Nausea* (Penguin, UK; Norton, US). Sartre's relentlessly gloomy description of just how unpleasant it was to drag out one's existence in Le Havre (or "Bouville") in the 1930s.

★ **Henry Treece** *Hounds of the King* (Bodley Head, UK, o/p) and *Man with a Sword* (OUP, UK). Classic children's fiction that provides a vivid picture of the Normans and their world.

Breton myth and folk tales

Pierre-Jakez Hélias *The Horse of Pride* (Yale UP). A deeply reactionary and sentimental account of a Breton childhood in the Bigouden district of the early twentieth century, which has sold over two million copies in France.

★ **Professor Anatole Le Braz** *Celtic Legends of the Beyond: A Celtic Book of the Dead* (Llanerch Enterprises, Lampeter, Wales; Red Wheel). The definitive French text on Breton myths centred on Ankou and the prescience of death, now available in translation.

F. M. Luzel *Celtic Folk-Tales from Armorica* (Llanerch, see above). A collection of timeless Breton fairy stories, in English, and complete with commentaries.

W.Y. Evans Wentz *The Fairy Faith in Celtic Countries* (Citadel Press; Carol Publishing). Bizarre survey of similarities and differences in folk beliefs and religion between Celtic nations, with extensive details about Brittany.

Breton music

Breton music, which draws richly in its themes, style and instrumentation on the common Celtic heritage of the Atlantic seaboard, has remained for centuries a unifying and inspiring part of the culture of the province. It has survived the union with France and the general attempt by the French state to suppress indigenous art and language.

However, attempting to pin even an approximate date on the origins of traditional Breton music is a haphazard business. No literature survives in the native tongue from any period prior to the fifteenth century, although we do know that wandering Breton minstrels, known as *conteurs*, had enjoyed great popularity abroad long before this. Many of the songs they wrote were translated into French, being otherwise unintelligible to audiences outside Brittany, but unfortunately both versions have vanished with time. Only a number of Norse and English translations, probably dating from the twelfth century, escaped destruction. These works tell of romances won and lost, acrimonious relationships between fathers and their sons, and the testing of potential lovers.

The historical record of Breton music really begins with the publication of **Barzaz-Breiz**, a major collection of traditional songs and poems, in 1839. It was compiled by a nobleman, Hersart de la Villemarqué, from his discussions with fishermen, farmers and oyster-and-pancake women, and in view of the scarcity of other literature in the native language has come to be acknowledged as a treasure of Breton folk culture. Though serious doubts have frequently been raised as to its authenticity – many sceptics believe Villemarqué doctored those parts of the material he found distasteful, and even composed portions of it himself – it is unquestionably a work of linguistic brilliance and great beauty, and its appearance triggered the serious study of popular Breton culture. Following in La Villemarqué's footsteps, the far more scrupulous folklorist **Francois-Marie Luzel** (1821–95) published four large volumes of ballads and songs, and three volumes of folk tales, between 1868 and 1890.

In the 20th century, especially since World War II, Brittany's traditional music and folk culture has been a major vehicle for the expression of Breton national identity. Countless Breton music and dance clubs were formed all over Brittany and beyond (notably Paris). In order to bequeath this rich and unique culture to future generations, huge effort was put into collecting and recording Breton music and songs, and **Dastum**, a central library of Breton music, song and folklore, was established. Like its Irish and Scottish counterparts, Breton music remains popular with all ages.

Styles and instrumentation

According to the harper Alan Stivell, "Breton music is a Celtic music… While other Europeans favour a diatonic scale, Celtic musics have a tendency to go back to a pentatonic scale". Produced for example by playing just the black keys on a keyboard, the pentatonic scale has five tones to the octave. Its widespread use is what gives not only traditional Breton music, but also Gregorian chant, and traditional Scottish, Irish and Chinese music, their distinctively melancholy, minor-key sound.

Perhaps the most quintessentially Breton of all instruments is the **bombarde**, a double-reed descendant of the medieval shawm. While it looks like a shortened version of the oboe, its tone is more vigorous and bracing; depending on your mood, it can sound like either a hypnotic trance-inducing paean to the gods, or a sackful of weasels being yanked through a mincer. Traditionally, the *bombarde* is played either solo or as part of a duet or *couple*, alongside a **biniou** or bagpipe. Brittany boasts two principal kinds of bagpipe: the **biniou braz** or "big bagpipe" is the Scottish bagpipe with three drones, while the **biniou koz** or "old bagpipe" is much smaller, has a single drone, and its piercing sound is an octave higher. In a *couple*, the *bombarde* can be played in unison with the *biniou* or in a call-and-response alternation known as *kan ha diskan*, in which the opening and closing phrases overlap. Other than the drone(s) of the *biniou*, there are no harmonies.

Pipe-bands or **bagadou** are very popular, and pipe-band competitions attract large crowds. Although the precise size and make-up of each band tends to vary, they consist as a rule of around twenty-five musicians: eight *binious (braz)*, ten *bombardes,* and seven drums, of which four are snare drums, two tenor drums, and one a bass drum. The repertoire of most *bagadou* includes both traditional and composed material, and the most accomplished are renowned for their innovation and range. Thus **Bagad Men ha Tan** have collaborated with Senegalese percussionists, while **Bagad Kemper** have expanded to include a brass section, and have recorded with traditional vocalists, jazz musicians and rock groups.

While the *biniou* and *bombarde* were traditionally played outdoors, the **telenn** or **Breton harp** began life in the Middle Ages as an indoor, courtly instrument. Its use had dwindled almost to the point of extinction before the Breton cultural resurgence of the nineteenth and twentieth centuries led to its revival. Although Jord Cochevelou achieved local fame as both a maker of, and a composer for, the Breton harp, it was his son **Alan Stivell** who brought it to worldwide fame, with his milestone 1972 recording *Renaissance of the Celtic Harp*. Several other Breton harpers are worth looking out for, such as the group **An Triskell**, which features the virtuoso brothers Pol and Herve Queffeleant; **Dominig Bouchaud**; **Kristen Nogues**; and **Myrzhin**, who has played with Afro-Celt Sound System among others.

Instruments more familiar to outsiders include the **violin**, which is descended from the medieval rebec (*rebed* in Breton). Until a century ago, this was very common in Brittany, but it only returned to prominence with the folk revival of the 1960s, and the increasing influence of Irish bands. The best known Breton practitioners are **Jacky Molard**, **Christian Lemaitre** and **Fanch Landreau**. The **guitar** too has become ubiquitous, whether played solo or as part of larger groups; **Dan Ar Braz**, **Soig Siberil** and **Jacques Pellen** are equally renowned in both roles. In addition, the **accordion** has enjoyed a certain popularity ever since it was brought back to Brittany by soldiers returning from the trenches of the First World War; **Yann-Fanch Perroches** is the best-known modern practitioner.

Until the 1960s, Breton **songs** were normally sung unaccompanied, often by solo performers. Performances and recordings of either unaccompanied, or minimally accompanied, singing remain common. Traditional songs fall into several distinct categories, including **gwerziou**, sombre or serious ballads; **soniou**, lighter songs about love, for instance, or drinking; and sacred songs, known as **kanticou**. This latter style is particularly deeply rooted and beautiful, and has been enhanced by the twentieth-century development of combining **church organ** with *bombarde* to produce haunting renditions of religious music. At the same time, a number of Breton **singer-songwriters** are producing original material of high quality. Pre-eminent among them is **Gilles Servat**, who sings in both Breton and French, and mixes his own protest songs and modern chansons with long-established Breton pieces.

Traditional dance music

Each of the many different rhythms in **Breton dance tunes** tends to be associated with different dance steps, and to originate from a distinct region of Brittany. The most common form of dance music has long been that performed by **sonneurs de couple**, a pair of musicians playing *bombarde* and *biniou*. While following the same melody line, with a drone from the *biniou*, they pursue a steadily accelerating tempo, each taking turns in call and response. The second player chimes in with the last three or so notes of the first player, and then vice versa, each musician overlapping and covering as the other pauses for breath.

The purely vocal counterpart to this is known as **kan ha diskan**. Once again intended as dance music, this is performed by a pair of "call-and-response" singers. In its basic form, the two unaccompanied singers – the *kaner* and the *diskaner* – alternate phrases, joining each other at the end of each phrase. As there were no amplifiers in the past, singers used a high-pitched nasal tone to ensure that their voices would carry. They might also give dancers the odd break by performing a *gwerz*, or ballad, again unaccompanied.

Over the last thirty years, such traditional accompaniments have been increasingly supplanted by four- or five-piece **folk groups**, who add fiddle and accordion, and sometimes electric bass and drums, to the *bombarde*, and less often the *biniou*. As the tunes are reinterpreted, the *gwerz* singers are giving way to folk-style singer-songwriters, with guitar backing. Purists might regret the changes, but they have probably ensured the survival of *festou-noz*, with the enthusiastic participation of musicians and dancers of all ages.

Festou-noz

The liveliest setting in which to hear traditional Breton music is a *Fest-Noz* or "Night Feast", a night of serious dancing (and drinking). A *Fest-Noz* was originally an outdoor music-and-dance event, and thus especially suited to the summer months. Nowadays, however, *festou-noz* take place all year round, usually in large halls but also in barns in more rural areas. Once the evening gets underway, people dance in great circles, often in their hundreds, hour after hour, sometimes lively and leaping, sometimes slow and graceful with their little fingers intertwined. Joining in is an exhilarating experience – it's easy to learn, just copy what everyone else does.

Festou-noz have nurtured successive generations of Breton musicians, and served as a springboard for bands such as **Strobinell**, with their line-up of

Festou-noz are well publicized locally with posters and leaflets, and you can also find up-to-the minute listings online at ⓦwww.bretagnenet.com.

bombarde, biniou, violin, flute and guitar, who eventually move on to join the festival and concert circuit. Over the years, an electrified *fest-noz* sound has also developed, complete with drum kit, as epitomized by bands like **Bleizi Ruz** (Red Wolves) and **Sonerien Du** (Black Musicians). The most musically innovative band of all, **Gwerz**, started out by making several CDs of traditional songs and instrumentals, using *bombarde, biniou*, clarinet, violin and guitars.

Contemporary Breton Music

Breton music has come a long way since Alan Stivell led one of the first folk-rock bands in Europe, in the late 1960s. Stivell played harp and bagpipes alongside Dan Ar Braz on electric and acoustic guitar, performing a repertoire that drew on wider Celtic traditions. Both artists still perform and record separately in the folk-rock idiom.

Thirty years on, groups such as Gwerz and latterly **Skolvan** have added subtle jazz and Eastern European touches to their interpretations of Breton music, while Gwerz's singer **Erik Marchand** has been even bolder, performing *gwerziou* with a Romanian gypsy band and playing with Sardinian and Gallego musicians. Marchand is emblematic of a recent, steady flow of innovative cross-cultural music from Breton musicians, due in no small part to the fact that more Bretons live in Paris – one of the great hubs of world music – than in any city in Brittany. Notable collaborations include those of **Kerhun** with Moroccan Gnawa musicians, and the Breton/Algerian confluences to be found in the music of Cheb Mami, Thalweg, Mugar, Idir and Tayfa.

An exhilarating creativity pervades current Breton "roots" music. **Manau** and **Denez Prigent** have mixed techno and club sounds with traditional airs and ballads, while Prigent has also presented very contemporary messages within the ancient tradition of *gwerziou*. His work with Lisa Gerrard (for the movie soundtrack *Black Hawk Down*) and Nabil Khalidi has produced thrilling new blends and textures. Similarly, **Bagad Kemper** have performed and recorded with the South African Zulu rock group Johnny Clegg & Savuka, as well as splicing together jazz horns including saxophone, guitarists and a singer with a full pipe band. Meanwhile **Didier Squiban's** *Breton Piano Trilogy* displays classically polished solo piano jazz variations on traditional Breton themes.

Breton singing too is exploring new territory, from the dramatic Brechtian cabaret delivery of **Marthe Vassallo's** *gwerziou*, with their stark and lurid accordion accompaniment, to the bluesy, surreal, satirical, darkly poetic songs of **Bernez Tangi** and **Denez Abernot**.

Websites

General information on Breton music can be found online at ⓦwww.breizh.net and ⓦwww.dastum.com. For anyone who doesn't live in France, the Internet is the best source of Breton music CDs. Good websites include those of the Ar Bed Keltiek music and book shop at ⓦwww.arbedkeltiek.com; ⓦwww.amazon.fr; ⓦwww.amazon.co.uk; ⓦwww.fnac.com; and ⓦwww.cdroots.com.

By Paul Matheson, drawing on an original piece by Raymond Travers.

Recommended Discography

As a place to start, the sampler album *Fest Vraz*, a 35-track compilation of most types of Breton music, is highly recommended.

Bombarde and biniou

Youenn Le Bihan *(bombarde)* and **Patrick Molard** *(biniou koz) Er Bolom Koh.*

Patrick Molard *(biniou braz) Deliou.*

Bagadou (Pipe-bands)

Bagad Bleimor *Sonerezh Geltiek.*
Bagad Kemper *Hep Diskrog*; *Azeliz Iza.*

Bagad Men Ha Tan & Doudou N'Diaye Rose *Dakar.*

Telenn

Dominig Bouchaud *L'Ancre d'Argent.*
Alan Stivell *Renaissance of the Celtic Harp*; *Trema'n Inis*; *E Langonned.*

Triskell *Rowan Tree.*

Violin

Christian Lemaitre, Jacky Molard, Fanch Landreau et al. *Archétype.*

Jacky Molard, Patrick Molard & Jacques Pellen *Triptyque.*

Live Music and Festivals

Visitors to Brittany get the chance to enjoy Breton music at several annual festivals. The most famous of these is the Lorient festival inter-Celtique. Others include Quimper's Festival de Cornouaille (mid–late July), Rennes's Tombées de la Nuit (early July), and the intimate Printemps de Châteauneuf-du-Faou (Easter Sunday).

In addition, most Breton towns and villages have cafés and pubs that offer live music. Try:

Brest *Café de la Plage, Café le Triskel and the Bar Écossais.*

Douarnenez *Le Pourquois Pas.*

Gouarec (near Gourin) *Bar de Daoulas.*

Lorient *Galway Inn.*

Plouyé *Ti Elise.*

Plouhinec (near Lorient) *Café de la Barre.*

Quimper *Ceili Bar.*

Quimperlé *OK Pub.*

Redon *Le Chant de l'Alouette* (music shop).

Rennes *Barantic.*

Guitar

Dan Ar Braz *Xavier Grall chanté par Dan Ar Braz.*
Jacques Pelenn *Les Tombées de la Nuit.*
Soig Siberil *Gwenojenn.*

Church music

Anne Auffret, Jean Baron & Michel Ghesquiere *Sacred Music from Brittany.*
Anne Auffret, Daniel Le Feon & Loik Le Griguer *Pardoniou.*
Yann-Fanch Kemener & Anne Auffret *Roue Gralon/Ni ho Salud!*

Vocal

Annie Ebrel *Tre ho ti ha ma hini.*
Yann-Fanch Kemener & Didier Squiban *Enez Eusa.*
Erik Marchand & Thierry Robin *Songs of Central Brittany.*
Denez Prigent *Live Holl a-gevret!*
Marthe Vassallo & Philippe Ollivier (aka "Bugel Koar") *Ar Solier.*

Dance music

Various *Kan ha Diskan.*
Various *Voix de Bretagne.*

Festou-noz

Bleizi Ruz *En Concert.*
Gwerz *Live.*
Pennou Skoulm *Fest-noz.*
Sonerien Du *Steir.*

Singer-songwriters

Louis Capart *Patience; Rives Gauches de Bretagne et d'Ailleurs.*
Gilles Servat *Les Albums de la Jeunesse.*
Triskell/Gilles Servat *L'Albatros Fou.*

Contemporary Breton Sounds

Denez Abernot *Tri Miz Noz.*
Bernez Tangi *Eured an Diaoul.*
Cheb Mami *Meli Meli.*
Idir *Deux Rives, un Rêve.*
Kerhun et les Gnawa *Lila-Noz.*
Erik Marchand *Kan.*
Erik Marchand et le Taraf de
Caransebes *Dor; Sag an tan ell.*
Mugar *Kabily-touseg.*
Denez Prigent *Live Holl a-gevret!*
Skolvan *Chenchet'n eus an amzer.*
Storlok *Stok ha Stok.*
Tayfa *Assif.*
Thalweg *Berbero Celtic.*

Language

Language

Language

Although **Breton** (see box on p.465) is still a living language, every encounter you have with the local people in both Brittany and Normandy will almost certainly be conducted in **French**. Thanks to the number of words and structures it shares with English, French can seem deceptively familiar, but it's not a particularly easy language to pick up. The bare essentials, however, are not difficult to master, and can make all the difference. Even just saying "Bonjour Madame" or "Bonjour Monsieur" when you go into a shop, and then pointing, will usually get you a smile and helpful service. People working in hotels, restaurants, and tourist offices almost always speak some English, and tend to use it even if you're trying in French – be grateful, not insulted.

Phrasebooks and courses

Rough Guide French Phrasebook (Rough Guides). Mini-dictionary-style phrasebook with both English–French and French–English sections, along with cultural tips for tricky situations and a menu reader.
Mini French Dictionary (Harrap/Prentice Hall). French–English and English–French, plus a brief grammar and pronunciation guide.
Breakthrough French (Pan; book and two cassettes). Excellent teach-yourself course.
French and English Slang Dictionary (Harrap/Prentice Hall). **Dictionary of Modern Colloquial French** (Routledge). Both volumes are a bit large to carry, but they are the key to all you ever wanted to understand about the French vernacular.
Verbaid (Verbaid, Hawk House, Heath Lane, Farnham, Surrey GU9 0PR). CD-size laminated paper "verb wheel" giving you the tense endings for the regular verbs.
À Vous La France; France Extra; Franc-Parler (BBC Publications /EMC Publishing; each consists of a book and two cassettes). BBC courses, running from beginners' level to fairly advanced. Ⓦwww.bbc.co.uk/education /languages/french has a number of online courses ranging from beginner level to more advanced.

Pronunciation

One easy rule to remember is that **consonants** at the ends of words are usually silent. *Pas plus tard* (not later) is thus pronounced "pa-plu-tarr". But when the following word begins with a vowel, you run the two together: *pas après* (not after) becomes "pazaprey".

Vowels are the hardest sounds to get right. Roughly:

a as in h**a**t
e as in g**e**t
é between g**e**t and g**a**te
è between g**e**t and g**u**t
eu like the **u** in h**u**rt
i as in mach**i**ne
o as in h**o**t
o, au as in **o**ver
ou as in f**oo**d
u as in a pursed-lip version of **u**se

More awkward are the **combinations in/im, en/em, an/am, on/om, un/um** at the ends of words, or followed by consonants other than **n** or **m**. Again, roughly:

in/im like the **an** in **an**xious
an/am, en/em like the **on** in D**on**caster when said with a nasal accent
on/om like the **on** in D**on**caster said by someone with a heavy cold
un/um like the **u** in **u**nderstand

Consonants are much as in English, except that: *ch* is always "sh", *c* is "s", *h* is silent, *th* is the same as "t", *ll* is mostly like the "y" in yes, *w* is "v", and *r* is growled (or rolled).

Basic words and phrases

French nouns are divided into masculine and feminine. This causes difficulties with adjectives, whose endings have to change to suit the gender of the nouns they qualify. If you know some grammar, you will know what to do. If not, stick to the masculine form, which is the simplest – it's what we have done here.

today	**aujourd'hui**
yesterday	**hier**
tomorrow	**demain**
in the morning	**le matin**
in the afternoon	**l'après-midi**
in the evening	**le soir**
now	**maintenant**
later	**plus tard**
at one o'clock	**à une heure**
at three o'clock	**à trois heures**
at ten-thirty	**à dix heures et demie**
at midday	**à midi**
man	**un homme**
woman	**une femme**
here	**ici**
there	**là**
this one	**ceci**
that one	**celà**
open	**ouvert**
closed	**fermé**
big	**grand**
small	**petit**
more	**plus**
less	**moins**
a little	**un peu**
a lot	**beaucoup**
cheap	**bon marché**
expensive	**cher**
good	**bon**
bad	**mauvais**
hot	**chaud**
cold	**froid**
with	**avec**
without	**sans**

Numbers

1	**un**
2	**deux**
3	**trois**
4	**quatre**
5	**cinq**
6	**six**
7	**sept**
8	**huit**
9	**neuf**
10	**dix**
11	**onze**
12	**douze**
13	**treize**
14	**quatorze**
15	**quinze**
16	**seize**

17	**dix-sept**	80	**quatre-vingts**
18	**dix-huit**	90	**quatre-vingt-dix**
19	**dix-neuf**	95	**quatre-vingt-quinze**
20	**vingt**	100	**cent**
21	**vingt-et-un**	101	**cent-et-un**
22	**vingt-deux**	200	**deux cents**
30	**trente**	300	**trois cents**
40	**quarante**	500	**cinq cents**
50	**cinquante**	1000	**mille**
60	**soixante**	2000	**deux milles**
70	**soixante-dix**	5000	**cinq milles**
75	**soixante-quinze**	1,000,000	**un million**

Days and dates

January	**janvier**	Monday	**lundi**
February	**février**	Tuesday	**mardi**
March	**mars**	Wednesday	**mercredi**
April	**avril**	Thursday	**jeudi**
May	**mai**	Friday	**vendredi**
June	**juin**	Saturday	**samedi**
July	**juillet**	August 1	**le premier août**
August	**août**	March 2	**le deux mars**
September	**septembre**	July 14	**le quatorze juillet**
October	**octobre**	November 23	**le vingt-trois novembre**
November	**novembre**	2004	**deux mille quatre**
December	**décembre**		
Sunday	**dimanche**		

Talking to people

When addressing people a simple *bonjour* is not enough; you should always use *Monsieur* for a man, *Madame* for a woman, *Mademoiselle* for a young woman or girl. This isn't as formal as it seems, and it has its uses when you've forgotten someone's name or want to attract someone's attention.

Excuse me	**Pardon**	…American	**…américain[e]**
Do you speak English?	**Parlez-vous anglais?**	…Australian	**…australien[ne]**
How do you say it in French?	**Comment ça se dit en français?**	…Canadian	**…canadien[ne]**
What's your name?	**Comment vous appelez-vous?**	…a New Zealander	**…néo-zélandais[e]**
My name is…	**Je m'appelle…**	yes	**oui**
I'm…	**Je suis…**	no	**non**
…English	**…anglais[e]**	I understand	**Je comprends**
…Irish	**…irlandais[e]**	I don't understand	**Je ne comprends pas**
…Scottish	**…écossais[e]**	Can you speak slower?	**S'il vous plaît, parlez moins vite?**
…Welsh	**…gallois[e]**	OK/agreed	**d'accord**
		please	**s'il vous plaît**

thank you	**merci**
hello	**bonjour**
goodbye	**au revoir**
good morning /afternoon	**bonjour**
good evening	**bonsoir**
good night	**bonne nuit**
How are you?	**Comment allez-vous?/Ça va?**
Fine, thanks	**Très bien, merci**
I don't know	**Je ne sais pas**
Let's go	**Allons-y**
See you tomorrow	**À demain**
See you soon	**À bientôt**
Sorry	**Pardon/Je m'excuse**
Leave me alone (aggressive)	**Fichez-moi la paix!**
Please help me	**Aidez-moi, s'il vous plaît**

Finding the way

bus	**autobus/bus/car**
bus station	**gare routière**
bus stop	**arrêt**
car	**voiture**
train/taxi/ferry	**train/taxi/ferry**
boat	**bâteau**
plane	**avion**
shuttle	**navette**
train station	**gare (SNCF)**
platform	**quai**
What time does it leave?	**Il part à quelle heure?**
What time does it arrive?	**Il arrive à quelle heure?**
a ticket to...	**un billet pour...**
single ticket	**aller simple**
return ticket	**aller retour**
validate your ticket	**compostez votre billet**
valid for	**valable pour**
ticket office	**vente de billets**
how many kilometres?	**combien de kilomètres?**
how many hours?	**combien d'heures?**
hitchhiking	**autostop**
on foot	**à pied**
Where are you going?	**Vous allez où?**
I'm going to...	**Je vais à ...**
I want to get off at...	**Je voudrais descendre à ...**
the road to...	**la route pour...**
near	**près/pas loin**
far	**loin**
left	**à gauche**
right	**à droite**
straight on	**tout droit**
on the other side of	**à l'autre côté de**
on the corner of	**à l'angle de**
next to	**à côté de**
behind	**derrière**
in front of	**devant**
before	**avant**
after	**après**
under	**sous**
to cross	**traverser**
bridge	**pont**
upper town	**ville haute/haute ville**
lower town	**ville basse/basse ville**
old town	**vieille ville**

Questions and requests

The simplest way of asking a question is to start with *s'il vous plaît* (please), then name the thing you want in an interrogative tone of voice. For example:

Where is there a bakery?	**S'il vous plaît, la boulangerie?**
Which way is it to Caen?	**S'il vous plaît, la route pour Caen?**

Similarly with requests:

Can we have a room for two?	**S'il vous plaît, une chambre pour deux?**

Can I have a kilo of oranges?	**S'il vous plaît, un kilo d'oranges?**
Question words	
where?	**où?**
how?	**comment?**
how many/how much?	**combien?**
when?	**quand?**
why?	**pourquoi?**
at what time?	**à quelle heure?**
what is/which is?	**quel est?**

Accommodation

a room for one/ two persons	**une chambre pour une/deux personne(s)**
a double bed	**un lit double**
a room with a shower	**une chambre avec douche**
a room with a bath	**une chambre avec salle de bain**
for one/two/ three nights	**pour une/deux/trois nuits**
Can I see it?	**Je peux la voir?**
a room on the courtyard	**une chambre sur la cour**
a room over the street	**une chambre sur la rue**
first floor	**premier étage**
second floor	**deuxième étage**
with a view	**avec vue**
key	**clef**
to iron	**repasser**
do laundry	**faire la lessive**
sheets	**draps**
blankets	**couvertures**
quiet	**calme**
noisy	**bruyant**
hot water	**eau chaude**
cold water	**eau froide**
Is breakfast included?	**Est-ce que le petit déjeuner est compris?**
I would like breakfast	**Je voudrais prendre le petit déjeuner**
I don't want breakfast	**Je ne veux pas de petit déjeuner**
bed and breakfast	**chambre d'hôte**
Can we camp here?	**On peut camper ici?**
campsite	**un camping/terrain de camping**
tent	**une tente**
tent space	**un emplacement**
hostel	**foyer**
youth hostel	**auberge de jeunesse**

Cars

car	**voiture**
garage	**garage**
service	**service**
to park the car	**garer la voiture**
car park/parking lot	**un parking**
free parking	**parking gratuit**
paid parking	**parking payant**
no parking	**défense de stationner /stationnement interdit**
petrol/gas (unleaded)	**essence (sans plomb)**
petrol/gas station	**poste d'essence**
diesel fuel	**gasoil**
petrol/gas can	**bidon**
fill the tank	**faire le plein**
oil	**huile**
air line	**ligne à air**
inflate the tyres	**gonfler les pneus**
battery	**batterie**
the battery is dead	**la batterie est morte**
plugs	**bougies**
to break down	**tomber en panne**
insurance	**assurance**
green card	**carte verte**
traffic lights	**feux**
red light	**feu rouge**
green light	**feu vert**
slow down	**ralentir**
give way	**cédez le passage**
give way to pedestrians	**priorité aux piétons**

Cycling

to adjust	**raxler**	loose	**déserré**
ball bearing	**le roulement à billes**	to lower	**baisser**
battery	**la pile**	mudguard	**le garde-boue**
bent	**tordu**	pannier	**le pannier**
bicycle	**le vélo**	pedal	**le pédale**
bottom bracket	**le logement du pédalier**	pump	**la pompe**
brake cable	**le cable**	puncture	**la crevaison**
brakes	**les freins**	rack	**le porte-bagages**
broken	**cassé**	to raise	**remonter**
bulb	**l'ampoule**	to repair	**réparer**
chain	**la chaîne**	saddle	**la selle**
cotter pin	**la clavette**	to screw	**visser/serrer**
to deflate	**dégonfler**	spanner	**la clef (mécanique)**
dérailleur	**le dérailleur**	spoke	**le rayon**
frame	**le cadre**	to straighten	**rédresser**
gears	**les vitesses**	stuck	**coincé**
grease	**la graisse**	tight	**serré**
handlebars	**le guidon**	toe clips	**les cale-pieds**
to inflate	**gonfler**	tyre	**le pneu**
inner tube	**la chambre à air**	wheel	**la roue**

Health matters

doctor	**médecin**	stomach ache	**mal à l'estomac**
I don't feel well	**Je ne me sens pas bien**	period	**règles**
medicines	**médicaments**	pain	**douleur**
prescription	**ordonnance**	it hurts	**ça fait mal**
I feel sick	**Je suis malade**	chemist	**pharmacie**
I have a headache	**J'ai mal à la tête**	hospital	**hôpital**

Other needs

bakery	**boulangerie**	tobacconist	**tabac**
food shop	**alimentation**	stamps	**timbres**
delicatessen	**charcuterie, traiteur**	bank	**banque**
cake shop	**patisserie**	money	**argent**
cheese shop	**fromagerie**	toilets	**toilettes**
supermarket	**supermarché**	police	**police**
to eat	**manger**	telephone	**téléphone**
to drink	**boire**	cinema	**cinéma**
tasting, eg wine tasting	**dégustation**	theatre	**théâtre**
camping gas	**camping gaz**	to reserve/book	**réserver**

Food and dishes

Basic terms

l'addition	bill/check
beurre	butter
bio or biologique	organic
bouteille	bottle
chauffé	heated
couteau	knife
cru	raw
cuillère	spoon
cuit	cooked
emballé	wrapped
à emporter	takeaway
formule	lunchtime set menu
fourchette	fork
fumé	smoked
huile	oil
lait	milk
moutarde	mustard
œuf	egg
offert	free
pain	bread
pimenté	spicy
plat	main course
poivre	pepper
salé	salted/savoury
sel	salt
sucre	sugar
sucré	sweet
table	table
verre	glass
vinaigre	vinegar

Snacks

un sandwich/ une baguette	a sandwich
au jambon	with ham
au fromage	with cheese
au saucisson	with sausage
à l'ail	with garlic
au poivre	with pepper
au pâté (de campagne)	with pâté (country style)
croque-monsieur	grilled cheese and ham sandwich
croque-madame	grilled cheese and bacon, sausage, chicken or egg sandwich
pain bagnat	bread roll with egg, olives, salad, tuna, anchovies and olive oil
panini	toasted Italian sandwich
tartine	buttered bread or open sandwich
œufs	eggs
au plat	fried
à la coque	boiled
durs	hard-boiled
brouillés	scrambled
omelette	omelette
nature	plain
aux fines herbes	with herbs
au fromage	with cheese

Pasta (pâtes), pancakes (crêpes) and flans (tartes)

nouilles	noodles
pâtes fraîches	fresh pasta
raviolis	pasta parcels of meat or chard – a Provençal, not Italian invention

crêpe au sucre/ aux œufs	pancake with sugar/eggs
galette	buckwheat pancake
socca	thin chickpea flour pancake
panisse	thick chickpea flour pancake
pissaladière	tart of fried onions with anchovies and black olives
tarte flambée	thin pizza-like pastry topped with onion, cream and bacon or other combinations

Soups *(soupes)*

baudroie	fish soup with vegetables, garlic and herbs
bisque	shellfish soup
bouillabaisse	soup with five fish
bouillon	broth or stock
bourride	thick fish soup
consommé	clear soup
garbure	potato, cabbage and meat soup
pistou	parmesan, basil and garlic paste added to soup
potée auvergnate	cabbage and meat soup
potage	thick vegetable soup
rouille	red pepper, garlic and saffron mayonnaise served with fish soup
soupe à l'oignon	onion soup with rich cheese topping
velouté	thick soup, usually fish or poultry

Starters *(hors d'œuvres)*

assiette anglaise	plate of cold meats
assiette composée	mixed salad plate, usually cold meat and vegetables
crudités	raw vegetables with dressings
escargots	snails
hors d'œuvres	combination of the above plus smoked or marinated fish

Fish *(poisson)*, seafood *(fruits de mer)* and shellfish *(crustaces or coquillages)*

amandes	clams
aiglefin	small haddock or fresh cod
anchois	anchovies
anguilles	eels
barbue	brill
bar	bass
baudroie	monkfish or anglerfish
bigorneau	periwinkle
brème	bream
bulot	whelk
cabillaud	cod
calmar	squid
carrelet	plaice
claire	type of oyster
colin	hake
congre	conger eel
coques	cockles
coquilles St-Jacques	scallops
crabe	crab
crevettes grises	shrimp
crevettes roses	prawns
daurade	sea bream
écrevisses	crayfish
éperlan	smelt or whitebait
favou(ille)	tiny crab

flétan	halibut
friture	assorted fried fish
gambas	king prawns
hareng	herring
homard	lobster
huîtres	oysters
julienne	ling
langouste	spiny lobster
langoustines	saltwater crayfish (scampi)
lieu	pollock
limande	lemon sole
lotte	burbot
lotte de mer	monkfish
louvine, loubine	similar to sea bass
loup de mer	sea bass
maquereau	mackerel
merlan	whiting
moules (marinières)	mussels (with shallots in white wine sauce)
oursin	sea urchin
palourdes	clams
poissons de roche	fish from shoreline rocks
praires	small clams
raie	skate
rouget	red mullet
saumon	salmon
sole	sole
St Pierre	John Dory
thon	tuna
tourteau	crab
truite	trout
turbot	turbot
violet	sea squirt

Fish dishes and terms

aïoli	garlic mayonnaise served with salt cod and other fish
anchoïade	anchovy paste or sauce
arête	fish bone
assiette de fruits de mer	seafood platter
assiette de pêcheur	assorted fish
beignet	fritter
darne	fillet or steak
la douzaine	a dozen
frit	fried
friture	deep-fried small fish
fumé	smoked
fumet	fish stock
gigot de mer	large fish baked whole
grillé	grilled
hollandaise	butter and vinegar sauce
à la meunière	in a butter, lemon and parsley sauce
mousse/mousseline	mousse
pané	breaded
poutargue	mullet roe paste
raïto	red wine, olive, caper, garlic and shallot sauce
quenelles	light dumplings
thermidor	lobster grilled in its shell with cream sauce

Meat (*viande*) and poultry (*volaille*)

agneau (de pré-salé)	lamb (grazed on salt marshes)
andouille /andouillette	tripe sausage
bavette	French cut of beef equivalent to flank
bifteck	steak
bœuf	beef
boudin blanc	sausage of white meats
boudin noir	black pudding
caille	quail
canard	duck
caneton	duckling
contrefilet	sirloin roast
coquelet	cockerel

dinde/dindon	turkey
entrecôte	rib steak
faux filet	sirloin steak
foie	liver
foie gras	(duck/goose) liver
gibier	game
gigot (d'agneau)	leg (of lamb)
grenouilles (cuisses de)	frogs (legs)
grillade	grilled meat
hâchis	chopped meat, mince or hamburger
langue	tongue
lapin/lapereau	rabbit/young rabbit
lard/lardons	bacon/diced bacon
lièvre	hare
merguez	spicy, red sausage
mouton	mutton
museau de veau	calf's muzzle
oie	goose
onglet	French cut of beef steak that makes a prime steak
os	bone
poitrine	breast
porc	pork
poulet	chicken
poussin	baby chicken
ris	sweetbreads
rognons	kidneys
rognons blancs	testicles
sanglier	wild boar
steak	steak
tête de veau	calf's head (in jelly)
tournedos	thick slices of fillet
tripes	tripe
tripoux	mutton tripe
veau	veal
venaison	venison
volailles	poultry

Meat and poultry dishes and terms

aïado	roast shoulder of lamb stuffed with garlic and other ingredients
aile	wing
au feu de bois	cooked over wood fire
au four	baked
baeckoffe	Alsatian hotpot of pork, mutton and beef baked with potato layers
blanquette, daube, navarin, ragoût, estouffade, hochepôt	types of stew
blanquette de veau	veal in cream and mushroom sauce
bœuf bourguignon	beef stew with Burgundy, onions and mushrooms
canard à l'orange	roast duck with an orange and wine sauce
canard pâté de périgourdin foie gras	roast duck with prunes and truffles
carré	best end of neck, chop or cutlet
cassoulet	casserole of beans, sausages and duck /goose
choucroute	pickled cabbage with peppercorns, sausages, bacon and salami
civet	game stew
confit	meat preserve
côte	chop, cutlet or rib
cou	neck
coq au vin	chicken slow-cooked with wine, onions and mushrooms
cuisse	thigh or leg
épaule	shoulder
en croûte	in pastry
farci	stuffed
grillade	grilled meat
garni	with vegetables
gésier	gizzard
grillé	grilled
hâchis	chopped meat or mince hamburger
magret de canard	duck breast

LANGUAGE | Food and dishes

marmite	casserole
médaillon	round piece
mijoté	stewed
pavé	thick slice
pieds et paques	mutton or pork tripe and trotters
poêlé	pan-fried
poulet de Bresse	chicken from Bresse – the best
râble	saddle
rôti	roast
sauté	lightly fried in butter
steak au poivre (vert/rouge)	steak in a black (green/red) peppercorn sauce
steak tartare	raw chopped beef, topped with a raw egg yolk
tagine	North African casserole
tournedos	beef fillet with foie gras rossini and truffles
viennoise	fried in egg and breadcrumbs

Terms for steaks

bleu	almost raw
saignant	rare
à point	medium rare
bien cuit	well done
très bien cuit	very well done
brochette	kebab

Garnishes and sauces

américaine	white wine, cognac and tomato
arlésienne au porto	with tomatoes, onions, aubergines, potatoes and rice in port
auvergnat	with cabbage, sausage and bacon
béarnaise	sauce of egg yolks, white wine, shallots and vinegar
beurre blanc	sauce of white wine and shallots, with butter
bonne femme	with mushroom, bacon, potato and onions
bordelaise	in a red wine, shallot and bone-marrow sauce
boulangère	baked with potatoes and onions
bourgeoise	with carrots, onions, bacon, celery and braised lettuce
chasseur	white wine, mushrooms and shallots
châtelaine	with artichoke hearts and chestnut purée
diable	strong mustard seasoning
forestière	with bacon and mushroom
fricassée	rich, creamy sauce
mornay	cheese sauce
pays d'auge	cream and cider
périgourdine	with foie gras and possibly truffles
piquante	gherkins or capers, vinegar and shallots
provençale	tomatoes, garlic, olive oil and herbs
savoyarde	with gruyère cheese
véronique	grapes, wine and cream

Vegetables (*légumes*), herbs (*herbes*) and spices (*épices*)

ail garlic
algue seaweed
anis aniseed
artichaut artichoke
asperge asparagus
avocat avocado
basilic basil
betterave beetroot
blette/bette Swiss chard
cannelle cinnamon
capre caper
cardon cardoon, a beet related to artichoke
carotte carrot
céleri celery
champignons, cèpes, ceps, girolles, chanterelles, pleurotes mushrooms
chou (rouge) (red) cabbage
choufleur cauliflower
concombre cucumber
cornichon gherkin
echalotes shallots
endive chicory
épinard spinach
estragon tarragon
fenouil fennel
férigoule thyme (in Provençal)
fèves broad beans
flageolets flageolet beans
gingembre ginger
haricots haricot beans
verts string beans
rouges kidney beans
beurres butter beans
laurier bay leaf
lentilles lentils
maïs maize (corn)
menthe mint
moutarde mustard
oignon onion
panais parsnip
pélandron type of string bean
pâte pasta or pastry
persil parsley
petits pois peas
piment rouge/vert red/green chilli pepper
pois chiche chick peas
pois mange-tout snow peas
pignons pine nuts
poireau leek
poivron (vert, rouge) sweet pepper (green, red)
pommes de terre potatoes
primeurs spring vegetables
radis radish
riz rice
safran saffron
salade verte green salad
sarrasin buckwheat
tomate tomato
truffes truffles

Vegetable dishes and terms

alicot puréed potato with cheese
allumettes very thin chips
à l'anglaise boiled
beignet fritter
duxelles fried mushrooms and shallots with cream
farci stuffed
feuille leaf
fines herbes mixture of tarragon, parsley and chives
gratiné browned with cheese or butter
à la grecque cooked in oil and lemon
jardinière with mixed diced vegetables
mousseline mashed potato with cream and eggs

à la parisienne	sautéed potatoes, with white wine and shallot sauce	**râpée**	grated or shredded
parmentier	with potatoes	**sauté**	lightly fried in butter
petits farcis	stuffed tomatoes, aubergines, courgettes and peppers	**à la vapeur**	steamed
		en verdure	garnished with green vegetables

Fruit (*fruit*) and nuts (*noix*)

abricot	apricot	**mangue**	mango
acajou	cashew nut	**marron**	chestnut
amande	almond	**melon**	melon
ananas	pineapple	**mirabelle**	small yellow plum
banane	banana	**myrtille**	bilberry
brugnon, nectarine	nectarine	**noisette**	hazelnut
cacahouète	peanut	**noix**	walnuts; nuts
cassis	blackcurrant	**orange**	orange
cérise	cherry	**pamplemousse**	grapefruit
citron	lemon	**pastèque**	watermelon
citron vert	lime	**pêche**	peach
datte	date	**pistache**	pistachio
figue	fig	**poire**	pear
fraise (de bois)	strawberry (wild)	**pomme**	apple
framboise	raspberry	**prune**	plum
fruit de la passion	passion fruit	**pruneau**	prune
grenade	pomegranate	**raisin**	grape
groseille	redcurrant	**reine-claude**	greengage

Fruit dishes and terms

agrumes	citrus fruits	**fougasse**	bread flavoured with orange-flower water or almonds (can be savoury)
beignet	fritter	**frappé**	iced
compôte	stewed fruit		
coulis	sauce of puréed fruit		
crème de marrons	chestnut purée		
flambé	set aflame in alcohol		

Desserts (*desserts or entremets*) and pastries (*pâtisserie*)

bombe	moulded ice-cream dessert	**chichi**	doughnut shaped in a stick
brioche	sweet, high yeast breakfast roll loaf	**clafoutis**	heavy custard and fruit tart
calisson	almond sweet	**crème Chantilly**	vanilla-flavoured and sweetened whipped cream
charlotte	custard and fruit in lining of almond fingers	**crème fraîche**	sour cream

crème pâtissière	thick, eggy pastry filling
crêpe suzette	thin pancake with orange juice and liqueur
fromage blanc	cream cheese
gaufre	waffle
glace	ice cream
Île flottante/ œufs à la neige	whipped egg-white floating on custard
macaron	macaroon
madeleine	small sponge cake
marrons Mont Blanc	chestnut purée and cream on a rum-soaked sponge cake
mousse au chocolat	chocolate mousse
omelette norvégienne	baked alaska
palmier	caramelized puff pastry
parfait	frozen mousse, sometimes ice cream
petit-suisse	a smooth mixture of cream and curds
petits fours	bite-sized cakes/pastries
poires belle hélène	pears and ice cream in chocolate sauce
tarte tatin	upside-down apple tart
tarte tropezienne	sponge cake filled with custard cream topped with nuts
tiramisu	mascarpone cheese, chocolate and cream
yaourt/yogourt	yoghurt

Glossary

abbaye	abbey
aber	estuary
accueil	reception
arrêt d'autobus	bus stop
Assemblée Nationale	the French parliament
auberge de jeunesse	(AJ) youth hostel
autobus	city bus
autoroute	motorway/freeway
banque	bank
bassin	harbour basin
Beaux-arts	fine arts school (and often museum)
bibliothèque	library
bistro	small restaurant or bar
bois	wood
boulangerie	baker
brasserie	café/restaurant
bureau de change	money exchange
calvaire	("calvary") a cluster of religious statues standing on a single base, usually topped by a Crucifixion, as found in many Breton churchyards.
car	coach, bus
cave	(wine) cellar
centre ville	town centre
chambre d'hôte	B&B
charcuterie	delicatessen
chasse, chasse gardée	hunting grounds beware
château	castle or mansion
cimetière	cemetery
citadelle	fortified city
cloître	cloister
confiserie	sweet shop
consigne	left luggage
couvent	monastery
crêperie	pancake restaurant
dégustation	tasting
département	administrative division, equivalent to an English county
dolmen	megalithic stone "table"
donjon	castle keep
église	church
enclos	group of church buildings

Breton

Breton is one of the Celtic family of languages, strongly linked with both Welsh and Gaelic even if it's not mutually comprehensible. It has an especially strong oral tradition ranging from medieval minstrels to modern singers and musicians.

Current estimates put the number of people who understand spoken Breton at between 400,000 and 800,000. However, only perhaps a third of those actually speak the language with any fluency or frequency. You're very unlikely to find it spoken as a first, day-to-day language; the only conceivable possibilities are among the very old, or in exceptionally remote parts of Finistère. For centuries it was efficiently suppressed by the state; its use was forbidden for official and legal purposes, and even Breton-speaking parents would seek to enhance their children's prospects by bringing them up to speak French. Although Breton is now taught in some schools once again, and there is even a Breton regional bank, learning the language is not really a viable prospect for visitors who do not already have a good grounding in another Celtic language.

However, as you travel through the province it's interesting to note the roots of Breton **place names**, many of which have a simple meaning in the language. The list of Breton words below includes some of the most common, as well as a few everyday words and greetings.

Breton vocabulary

aber estuary
avel wind
bihan little
bran hill
braz big
Breizh Brittany
creach height
cromlech stone circle
dol/taol table
dour water
du black
enez island
gavre goat
goat/coat/koat forest
goaz stream
gwenn white
hen old
heol sun
hir long
kastell castle
kenavo goodbye
ker town, village
koz old
lan church, holy place
lann heath
lech flat stone
loc isolated, holy place
mad good
men stone
menez mountain
mario dead
menhir long stone
meur big
mor sea
nevez new
parc field
penn end, head
plou parish
pors port, farmyard
roch stone
ster river
stivel fountain, spring
ti house
traez sand, beach
trugarez thank you
trou valley
wrach witch
ya yes

enclos paroissial ("parish close") a walled churchyard that incorporates a church, a cemetery, a calvary and an ossuary.

entrée entrance
fermeture closing time/period
forêt forest
formule lunchtime set menu
fouilles archeological excavations

foyer	residential hostel for young workers or students
gare routière	bus station
gare	SNCF train station
gîte d'étape	countryside hostel
grotte	cave
halles	covered market
HLM	publicly subsidized housing
hôpital	hospital
hôtel	hotel – but also used for an aristocratic town house or mansion
Hôtel de Ville	town hall
île	island
jours fériés	public holidays
mairie	town hall
maison	literally a house – can also be an office or base of an organization
marché	market
menhir	single megalithic stone
office du tourisme (OT)	tourist office
ouverture	opening time/period
pâtisserie	pastry shop
pharmacie	chemist
place	square
plage	beach
plat du jour	daily special
porte	gate
poste	post office
presqu'île	peninsula
privé	private
PTT	post office
quartier	quarter of a town
Relais Routier	truck-stop restaurant
rez-de-chaussée	ground floor (uk), first floor (us)
RN route nationale	(main road)
salon de thé	tearoom
SI	tourist office (see syndicat d'initiative below)
SNCF	French railways
syndicat d'initiative (SI)	tourist office
tabac	bar or shop selling stamps, cigarettes, etc
tour	tower
traiteur	delicatessen
Vauban	seventeenth-century military architect
zone bleue	parking zone
zone piétonnière	pedestrian zone

Rough Guides

advertiser

...music & reference

Africa & Middle East
Cape Town
Egypt
The Gambia
Jordan
Kenya
Marrakesh DIRECTIONS
Morocco
South Africa, Lesotho & Swaziland
Syria
Tanzania
Tunisia
West Africa
Zanzibar
Zimbabwe

Travel Theme guides
First-Time Around the World
First-Time Asia
First-Time Europe
First-Time Latin America
Skiing & Snowboarding in North America
Travel Online
Travel Health
Walks in London & SE England
Women Travel

Restaurant guides
French Hotels & Restaurants
London
New York
San Francisco

Maps
Algarve
Amsterdam
Andalucia & Costa del Sol
Argentina
Athens
Australia
Baja California
Barcelona
Berlin
Boston
Brittany
Brussels
Chicago
Crete
Croatia
Cuba
Cyprus
Czech Republic
Dominican Republic
Dubai & UAE
Dublin
Egypt
Florence & Siena
Frankfurt
Greece
Guatemala & Belize
Iceland
Ireland
Kenya
Lisbon
London
Los Angeles
Madrid
Mexico
Miami & Key West
Morocco
New York City
New Zealand
Northern Spain
Paris
Peru
Portugal
Prague
Rome
San Francisco
Sicily
South Africa
South India
Sri Lanka
Tenerife
Thailand
Toronto
Trinidad & Tobago
Tuscany
Venice
Washington DC
Yucatán Peninsula

Dictionary Phrasebooks
Czech
Dutch
Egyptian Arabic
EuropeanLanguages (Czech, French, German, Greek, Italian, Portuguese, Spanish)
French
German
Greek
Hindi & Urdu
Hungarian
Indonesian
Italian
Japanese
Mandarin Chinese
Mexican Spanish
Polish
Portuguese
Russian
Spanish
Swahili
Thai
Turkish
Vietnamese

Music Guides
The Beatles
Bob Dylan
Cult Pop
Classical Music
Country Music
Elvis
Hip Hop
House
Irish Music
Jazz
Music USA
Opera
Reggae
Rock
Techno
World Music (2 vols)

History Guides
China
Egypt
England
France
India
Islam
Italy
Spain
USA

Reference Guides
Books for Teenagers
Children's Books, 0–5
Children's Books, 5–11
Cult Fiction
Cult Football
Cult Movies
Cult TV
Ethical Shopping
Formula 1
The iPod, iTunes & Music Online
The Internet
Internet Radio
James Bond
Kids' Movies
Lord of the Rings
Muhammed Ali
Man Utd
Personal Computers
Pregnancy & Birth
Shakespeare
Superheroes
Unexplained Phenomena
The Universe
Videogaming
Weather
Website Directory

Also! More than 120 Rough Guide music CDs are available from all good book and record stores. Listen in at www.worldmusic.net

NOTES

NOTES

NOTES